T0361262

Extended reporting frameworks that encompass intellectual capital have been demonstrated to return the investment made in them many times over. They also evince corporate social, environmental and good corporate governance. An efficient response by companies seeking an optimal market result would be to increase the disclosure and transparency of intellectual capital. Readers of this book will better understand this and discover how to add value in a way that benefits all stakeholders.

Richard Petty, Professor and Executive Director International, Macquarie Graduate School of Management, Macquarie University, Australia.

Routledge Companions are marvelous assemblies of scholarship in specialized fields. I welcome intellectual capital now featuring in this series. Intellectual capital is highly interdisciplinary. This book contains a smörgåsbord of coverage, addressing cross-cutting intellectual capital issues by topic (business model mapping, customer performance measurement, digital communication, disclosure, firm performance, integrated reporting, investors, value creation), by geography (Australia, China, Japan, New Zealand, Russia, Sweden, US) and by sector (banking, healthcare, universities). Some of the earliest writers feature as authors (who the editors call "grandfathers" of intellectual capital), as do some of the most prolific intellectual capital scholars, together with some active intellectual capital practitioners. The thirty chapters represent a mix of theory and practice, including case studies. This text will quickly become one of the leading resources for intellectual capital researchers.

Niamh Brennan, Michael MacCormac Professor of Management, University College Dublin, Ireland.

The Routledge Companion to Intellectual Capital is a wide-ranging book that shows how, over time, intellectual capital concepts and analyses have extended their reach. Starting from the platform of the firm's external disclosure, intellectual capital in the form of human, organizational and relational capital has extended its reach to many other types of settings. The book testifies that the notion of intellectual capital is vibrant and offers perspectives about and to organizations and societies to manage and disclose valued capitals and resources. *The Routledge Companion* is a valuable step for anyone who wishes to participate in dialogues about intellectual capital theoretically and practically.

Jan Mouritsen, Professor, Copenhagen Business School, Denmark.

THE ROUTLEDGE COMPANION TO INTELLECTUAL CAPITAL

The Routledge Companion to Intellectual Capital offers a wide-ranging overview of an important field that has seen a diverse range of research developments in recent years. Edited by leading scholars and with contributions from top academics and practitioners from around the world, this volume will provide not just comprehensive theoretical analysis but also evaluate practice through case studies.

Uniquely combining theoretical and practice perspectives, this cutting-edge Companion addresses the role of IC inside and between organizations and institutions and how these contribute to the IC of nations, regions and clusters.

The Routledge Companion to Intellectual Capital will be of interest to scholars who want to understand IC from a variety of perspectives, as well as students who are seeking an authoritative and comprehensive source on IC and knowledge management.

James Guthrie is Professor of Accounting at Macquarie University, Australia. He has published 182 articles in both international and national refereed and professional journals, and over 42 chapters in books.

John Dumay is Associate Professor in Accounting at Macquarie University, Australia. He is currently the Associate Editor of the *Journal of Intellectual Capital* and the Editor of the *Electronic Journal of Knowledge Management*.

Federica Ricceri is Associate Professor of Accounting at the University of Padua, Italy. She has published numerous articles in international refereed journals. She is the author of *Intellectual Capital and Knowledge Management: Strategic Management of Knowledge Resources*.

Christian Nielsen is Professor and Head of the Business Model Design Centre (BMDC) at Aalborg University, Denmark. He is the founding Editor of the *Journal of Business Models* and his research has led to published works in leading international scholarly journals.

ROUTLEDGE COMPANIONS IN BUSINESS, MANAGEMENT AND ACCOUNTING

Routledge Companions in Business, Management and Accounting are prestige reference works providing an overview of a whole subject area or sub-discipline. These books survey the state of the discipline including emerging and cutting edge areas. Providing a comprehensive, up to date, definitive work of reference, Routledge Companions can be cited as an authoritative source on the subject.

A key aspect of these Routledge Companions is their international scope and relevance. Edited by an array of highly regarded scholars, these volumes also benefit from teams of contributors which reflect an international range of perspectives.

Individually, Routledge Companions in Business, Management and Accounting provide an impactful one-stop-shop resource for each theme covered. Collectively, they represent a comprehensive learning and research resource for researchers, postgraduate students and practitioners.

Published titles in this series include:

THE ROUTLEDGE COMPANION TO INTELLECTUAL CAPITAL

*Edited by James Guthrie, John Dumay,
Federica Ricceri and Christian Nielsen*

Routledge
Taylor & Francis Group

LONDON AND NEW YORK

First published 2018
by Routledge
2 Park Square, Milton Park, Abingdon, Oxon OX14 4RN

and by Routledge
711 Third Avenue, New York, NY 10017

Routledge is an imprint of the Taylor & Francis Group, an informa business

First issued in paperback 2021

British Library Cataloguing-in-Publication Data
A catalogue record for this book is available from the British Library

Library of Congress Cataloging-in-Publication Data
Names: Guthrie, James, 1952- editor.
Title: The Routledge companion to intellectual capital / [edited by] James
    Guthrie, [and three others].
Description: Abingdon, Oxon ; New York, NY : Routledge, 2018. | Includes
    bibliographical references and index.
Identifiers: LCCN 2017019702 (print) | LCCN 2017035267 (ebook) | ISBN
    9781315393100 (eBook) | ISBN 9781138228214 (hardback : alk. paper)
Subjects: LCSH: Intellectual capital.
Classification: LCC HD53 (ebook) | LCC HD53 .R6874 2018 (print) | DDC
    658.4/038—dc23
LC record available at https://lccn.loc.gov/2017019702

ISBN: 978-1-138-22821-4 (hbk)
ISBN: 978-1-03-209624-7 (pbk)
ISBN: 978-1-315-39310-0 (ebk)

Typeset in Times New Roman
by Swales & Willis Ltd, Exeter, Devon, UK

CONTENTS

FIGURES

TABLES

CONTRIBUTORS

Mary Adams is the founder of Smarter-Companies, a strategy consulting firm specializing in next generation measurement and management tools. Her company's network includes consulting firms on five continents. She is the co-author of *Intangible Capital: Putting Knowledge to Work in the 21st Century Organization* and active in the integrated reporting movement. Previously, she spent 14 years as the founder of Trek Consulting and 14 years as a high-risk lender in the US and Latin America at Citicorp and Sanwa Business Credit. She received a BA Political Science from Rice University and a Master of International Management from the Thunderbird School (now part of Arizona State), both USA.

Tatiana Andreeva, PhD, is a Lecturer in Management and Organizational Behaviour in the Maynooth University School of Business, National University of Ireland Maynooth. Her current research addresses the challenges of managing knowledge in organizations, with particular regard to the micro-foundations of knowledge processes and peculiarities of the contexts in which they evolve. Her ongoing research with Tatiana Garanina on the intellectual capital elements and knowledge management practices in Russian companies received the Emerald/Baltic Management Development Association Borderless Management Research Fund research award.

Diogenis Baboukardos is a Lecturer in Accounting at Essex Business in the United Kingdom. He received his PhD in 2016 for the thesis *Essays on the Market Valuation Implications of Mandatory Corporate Reporting* at Jönköping International Business School, Jönköping University, Sweden.

Cristiana Bernardi was awarded a PhD in Accounting from Roma Tre University, Italy in May 2015 and is a Lecturer in Accounting at The Open University Business School, UK. Her main research interests are in the area of financial reporting, including the use of narrative disclosures, integrated reporting, and corporate social responsibility reporting.

Manfred Bornemann earned his PhD at Karl Franzens University, Austria in 1996 and is a consultant with experience of some 250 projects on intellectual capital. He focuses on qualitative research and has contributed to intellectual capital management and reporting in research institutions and, during the last decade, in industrial environments as well as governmental institutions in the EU, Germany, and Austria. He has trained more than 400 consultants to apply "Wissensbilanz – Made in Germany". He has been an invited lecturer at 15 international institutions of higher education and universities and is author of three books and more than 50 articles about intellectual capital, organizational learning and development, quality management, and strategic management.

Peter Beusch, PhD, Lic, MSc, is Assistant Professor at the School of Business, Economics, and Law at Gothenburg University, Sweden and also holds a part-time position at Trondheim Business School, Norway. His teaching and research areas cover management accounting and control, actor-based performance management, the intersection of management accounting and sustainability, and integrated reporting and accounting education connected to sustainability.

Bino Catasús is a Professor of Accounting and Auditing at Stockholm University, Sweden. His research spans a broad set of issues such as corporate governance, management control, and intellectual capital. His work on intellectual capital springs from an interest in how knowledge of, and in, the organization is being used and represented. Bino's research often builds on critical reflection of practice.

Maria Serena Chiucchi is a Professor of Accounting at the Università Politecnica delle Marche, Ancona, Italy. Her main research interests are in management accounting, performance measurement, and intellectual capital accounting. She is a member of national and international research groups on intellectual capital and management accounting. She is a member of the editorial boards and advisory boards of several national and international journals.

Suresh Cuganesan is Professor of Organizational Control and Performance at the University of Sydney Business School, Australia. His research interests span strategy execution, organizational design, and performance measurement. He is particularly interested in how organizations balance competing goals and manage tensions in the pursuit of value. Prior to his academic career, Suresh worked in institutional banking and management consulting.

Henrik Dane-Nielsen, BSc in Electronic Engineering, MSc in Medical Engineering, MBA, BA in Sinology, has worked in academic fields within the humanities, social sciences, and natural sciences. His current research, situated in economic sociology, applies an emergentist perspective, originating in the fields of biology and neurology, to the study of the value of knowledge and intellectual capital in organizations and temporary organizational settings, such as development projects. This emergent-entity perspective applies hierarchical structures at sub-organism levels and social levels to the understanding of corporate value creation at organizational and market levels.

Paola Demartini is Professor in Accounting at Roma Tre University, Italy. She is Executive Editor of the review *Small Business/Piccola Impresa* and Head of the Corporate Governance Lab at Roma Tre University. Her research interests include corporate financial communication, managerial accounting, and intellectual-based management.

Charl de Villiers is Professor of Accounting at the Graduate School of Management, The University of Auckland, New Zealand, where his research and teaching interests include integrated reporting, sustainability accounting, and management accounting. He is also an Adjunct

Professor at the University of Pretoria and the University of the Western Cape, both South Africa, as well as a research fellow at the Centre for Sustainability Management at Leuphana University Lüneburg, Germany. Charl has more than 250 research-based publications and presentations, including over 60 articles in refereed journals. He publishes in both the qualitative and the quantitative research traditions and has published, among other journals, in *Accounting, Organisations and Society*, and *Journal of Management.*

John Dumay is Associate Professor of Accounting at Macquarie University, Australia. Originally a consultant, he joined academia after completing his PhD in 2008. His thesis won the European Fund for Management Development and Emerald Journals Outstanding Doctoral Research Award for Knowledge Management. John researches intellectual capital, knowledge management, non-financial reporting, methodologies, and academic writing. He has written more than 60 peer-reviewed articles and is highly cited in Scopus and Google Scholar. He is the Associate Editor of the *Journal of Intellectual Capital* and *Meditari Accountancy Research,* Editor of the *eJournal of Knowledge Management,* on the Editorial Board of Advice of the highly regarded *Accounting, Auditing and Accountability Journal, Journal of Knowledge Management* and several other leading accounting and management journals.

Leif Edvinsson is a Professor and pioneer in the theory and practice of intellectual capital. The world's first director of intellectual capital in 1991, he led the prototyping in 1996 of the the Skandia Future Centre as a laboratory for organizational design. In 1998, he was awarded the UK Brain Trust's "Brain of the Year". Leif is an associate member of The Club of Rome and cofounder and founding chairman of The New Club of Paris. In 2015 he was appointed to the advisory board of the Japan Innovation Network and in 2016 to the advisory board of the Norway Open Innovation Forum.

Tatiana Garanina, PhD (Econ.), is an Associate Professor in the Department of Finance and Accounting at the Graduate School of Management, St Petersburg University (GSOM SPbU), Russia. Her teaching and research interests include intellectual capital evaluation, financial statement analysis, and value-based management. With her co-author, she received an Emerald "Highly Commended Paper" Award in 2013 and "Citations of Excellence" Awards in 2016. Tatiana is also Academic Director of EMBA Programs at GSOM SPbU.

Marco Giuliani is Associate Professor of Accounting at the Università Politecnica delle Marche, Ancona, Italy. His main research interests are in financial accounting, auditing, and intellectual capital accounting. He is a member of national and international research groups on intellectual capital and company valuation and of a number of editorial boards and advisory boards of several national and international journals.

James Guthrie is a Professor of Accounting at Macquarie University, Australia. His research and teaching interests include public sector accounting, auditing, accountability and management, social and environmental reporting and auditing, management of knowledge and intellectual capital, and the measurement of intangibles. He also consults on public and private sector management, management of knowledge, intellectual capital, budget performance, and annual reporting strategies. He has published widely in international journals and books and is the editor of *Accounting, Auditing, and Accountability Journal*, as well as sitting on numerous editorial boards.

John Holland has been a member of staff at Glasgow University in Scotland since 1979. He is a Professor in the accounting and finance group in the Adam Smith Business School. He has published and researched in the areas of intangibles in financial firms (banks, fund managers, analysts, etc.) and financial markets (for capital, and for information). He has also published on corporate disclosure concerning the role of intangibles in company business models, their role in value creation, and their valuation by financial markets and by financial firms.

Pei-Chi Kelly Hsiao is a PhD student and casual academic staff member at the University of Auckland, New Zealand. Kelly holds an MMS in Accounting and GradCert in Economics from the University of Waikato, New Zealand. Her research interest is broadly in the area of corporate reporting and investment decision making, with a particular focus on integrated reporting.

Henri Inkinen is a post-doctoral researcher in Knowledge Management and Intellectual Capital at the School of Business and Management at the Lappeenranta University of Technology, Finland. His current research interests are in the areas of knowledge management practices, intellectual capital, firm performance, innovation management, business model innovations, and strategic human resource management. His research has been published or accepted in, among others, *Journal of Knowledge Management*, *Journal of Intellectual Capital*, and *Accounting, Auditing, & Accountability Journal*.

Ulf Johanson is Professor Emeritus at Karolinska Institutet, Sweden. His research interest is in understanding the role of intangibles (e.g. health, working environment, competence) in public as well as private organizations' value creation. He has investigated and suggested different analytical frameworks as well as normative management models as complements to more traditional management control tools. Some concepts that have been addressed are human resource costing and accounting, balanced scorecards, intellectual capital, health statements, and performance management. He has collaborated in research with colleagues from Sweden, as well as from many European countries, Japan, Australia, and the US.

Kristina Jonäll, PhD, is a Senior Lecturer at the School of Business at the School of Business, Economics and Law at Gothenburg University, Sweden. She received her PhD in 2009 for the thesis *Bilden av det Goda Företaget – text och siffror i VD-brev (Image of the Good Company – Text and Numbers in CEO letters)*. She is part of the research programme "Accounting for Sustainability – Communication through Integrated Reporting".

Aino Kianto, DSc (Econ. & Bus. Adm.), is Professor of Knowledge Management and the Academic Director of the Master's Programme on Knowledge Management and Leadership at the School of Business and Management at Lappeenranta University of Technology, Finland. Her teaching and research focus is on knowledge management, intellectual capital, creativity, innovation, and organizational renewal. She has authored or co-authored more than 100 academic articles, papers, books, and book chapters on these topics and received several related acknowledgements and rewards. She is the initiator and leader of the international research project "Intellectual Capital and Value Creation" that examines intellectual capital and knowledge management practices and their impact on organizational performance in Finland, Russia, China, Italy, Spain, and Serbia.

Chitoshi Koga is Professor at the School of Business Management, Tokaigakuen University and Professor Emeritus, Kobe University, Japan. He is also President of Japan Intellectual

Asset-Based Management Association and a member of the board for a number of Japanese academic organizations. Among his research interests are intellectual capital management, measurement, and reporting. He has various publications in several academic books and journals in English and Japanese, including several joint papers in the *Journal of Intellectual Capital*.

Joanna Krasodomska is an Associate Professor in the Department of Financial Accounting at the Cracow University of Economics, Poland. Her main fields of research include integrated reporting, non-financial disclosures, and worldwide accounting diversity. She has participated in research grants contracted by the Polish Ministry of Science and Higher Education and National Science Centre. She is a member of the European Accounting Association, International Association for Accounting Education and Research, and <IR> Academic Research Support Group, which operates under the auspices of the International Integrated Reporting Council.

Antonio Lerro is a Lecturer in Innovation Management at the University of Basilicata, Italy. His research interests are focused around knowledge and intellectual capital management supporting innovation and value creation dynamics, both at firm and territory level.

Morten Lund, PhD, is Assistant Professor at Aalborg University, Denmark and Director of the Business Model Design Centre. He holds a PhD in Business Models from the Technical Faculty at Aalborg University. He is dedicated to strengthening industry–university collaborations through a series of business model research programmes, creating value for industry, and valuable data for research. Besides his theoretical and methodological expertise, Morten has solid practical experience as a consultant, manager, and business owner. This experience includes building businesses from scratch, turnarounds, and M&A activities.

Stefano Marasca is a Professor of Accounting at the Università Politecnica delle Marche, Ancona, Italy. His main research interests are in management accounting, strategic control, and intellectual capital accounting. He is a member of national and international research groups on intellectual capital and management accounting. He is a member of the editorial boards and of the advisory boards of several national and international journals.

Maurizio Massaro, PhD, has been an Assistant Professor at Udine University, Italy, since 2008. Before joining academia, he worked in the field of knowledge management and intellectual capital as a consultant for several multinational companies. Maurizio is an international member of the Most Admired Knowledge Enterprise (MAKE) Award assessment committee for Iran. He has been visiting Professor at Florida Gulf Coast University, US, 2010–13 and Leicester University, UK, 2013–14. He enjoys research partnerships with universities in the US, continental Europe, UK, and Australia.

Jan Michalak is as an Adjunct (Assistant Professor) at Łódź University (Poland), Faculty of Management, Department of Accounting. He is a researcher, educator, and consultant, with more than 15 years' experience. His research interests are focused on performance measurement and management in both the private and public sectors, business models, intellectual capital, and disclosure quality. He is the author of more than 50 articles and author or co-author of six books, mainly on performance measurement, business models, and intellectual capital. He has managed and participated in several EU financed research projects investigating, for example, communities' performance and SMEs' business model ratings.

Elizabeth (Lissa) Monk is a Senior Lecturer at the University of Dundee School of Business, Scotland. Elizabeth's academic work focuses on the transition between education and the workplace, and particularly on the employable skills needed to move between these two worlds. More recently she has extended this area of research into transitions within work, looking at the development of leadership skills in managers, and, more generally, at the increasing importance of employee health and wellbeing.

Marco Montemari, PhD, is a Research Fellow at the Università Politecnica delle Marche, Italy. His research interests concern management accounting, business models, and intellectual capital. Other relevant interests concern balanced scorecard and performance measurement systems in general, with regard to their design and implementation process, and their ability to map and measure the value creation process.

Vijaya Murthy, PhD, is an active researcher in the management accounting field, specifically in relation to the use of non-financial information by managers for management controls. She has published in leading accounting journals including *Accounting, Auditing & Accountability Journal, Australasian Accounting Business and Finance Journal, Accounting Research Journal, Journal of Business Ethics*, and *Information Systems Frontiers*, amongst others. Vijaya has won the Emerald Literari Award twice for her papers on intellectual capital published in the *Journal of Human Resource Costing and Accounting* and has contributed chapters to several accounting books.

Christian Nielsen, PhD, is Professor at Aalborg University, Denmark and Høgskolen i Innlandet, Norway, and a director of the Business Model Design Centre (BMDC). Since the establishment of this highly multidisciplinary research centre in 2011, over 200 companies, ranging from local start-ups and SMEs to multinationals with a global presence, have seen the value of collaborating with BMDC. The contributions of this research have led to published works in leading international scholarly journals. This reflects Christian's broad international research network, which spans Europe, the US, Australia, and Asia. Christian has recently completed an executive board education to sharpen his ability to improve the performance of companies.

Axel Nilsson holds an MSc from the School of Business, Economics, and Law at Gothenburg University, Sweden. He is currently working as an accounting professional in the tourism industry.

Federica Ricceri is Associate Professor of Accounting at the University of Padova, Italy. Her research and teaching interests include intellectual capital, corporate social responsibility, strategic performance management, and voluntary disclosure. She has published several articles in international and national refereed and professional journals (including *Critical Perspectives on Accounting, The British Accounting Review, Journal of Knowledge Management*, and *Journal of Intellectual Capital*) and chapters in national and international books. She is currently a member of the Editorial Advisory Board of *Accounting, Auditing and Accountability Journal* and Associate Editor for Europe of the *Journal of Intellectual Capital*. She is also a member of the editorial board of *Meditari Accountancy Research Journal* and of the Overseas Outstanding Advisory Board of the Japanese Intellectual Capital Association.

Gunnar Rimmel is a Professor and Chair in Accounting at Henley Business School, University of Reading, UK. He previously worked in Sweden as a Professor in Accounting at Jönköping International Business School and Gothenburg Research Institute at the University of

Gothenburg, Sweden. He received his PhD in 2003 for the thesis *Human Resource Disclosures* from the School of Business at the School of Business, Economics, and Law at Gothenburg University, Sweden. His research and teaching interests include accounting communication, human resource accounting, international financial accounting, and social and environmental reporting, specifically integrated reporting. In recent years, his research programme "Accounting for Sustainability – Communication through Integrated Reporting" has been externally funded by the Handelsbanken research foundations. He has also received grants from the NASDAQ OMX Nordic Foundation.

Paavo Ritala is a Professor of Strategy and Innovation at the School of Business and Management at Lappeenranta University of Technology, Finland. His research has been published in, for example, *Journal of Product Innovation Management, Industrial and Corporate Change, Industrial Marketing Management, British Journal of Management,* and *Technovation*.

Hannu Ritvanen has a long and extensive career in ICT. His main focus has been in bridging the gap between business and ICT, advising companies on knowledge-based systems, business intelligence, and enterprise architecture. He has written a book on managing with information (knowledge) within healthcare and contributed chapters to *Business Intelligence Competence Center*. He was for five years (2005–09) voted one of the most influential ICT experts in Finland. Hannu is also a gemologist FGA (at the Gemological Association of Great Britain) and has been an entrepreneur. Hannu's current research interest is in understanding intellectual capital-related uncertainties and risks, themes of which he is currently finalizing in his doctoral thesis.

Jim Rooney is a Senior Lecturer at the University of Sydney Business School, Australia. His research interests include corporate governance, risk management, management control, supply chain sustainability, and intellectual capital. His doctoral thesis examined the dynamics of management control change in outsourcing relationships. Jim has also been a Research Fellow at the Weatherhead Centre for International Relations at Harvard University, USA and the Sustainability Transparency Accountability Research Lab at Sydney University, working with senior academics at Harvard, Stanford, and Sydney Universities. Prior to his full-time appointment at the University of Sydney, Jim had 25 years' business experience in general management, service operations, accounting, and consulting roles with leading organizations such as Cap Gemini, Ernst & Young, KPMG, IBM, GE Money, Citibank, Abbey National, Westpac, and NAB.

Göran Roos is a member of the Economic Development Board of South Australia, the advisory board for Investment Attraction South Australia, METS Ignited Australia Limited's Innovation Advisory Council (MIAC), and an Invited Chair of the CSIRO Manufacturing Business Unit Advisory Committee, and a strategic Adviser to Defence SA and the Defence SA Advisory Board. He is an Adjunct Professor at the Entrepreneurship, Commercialisation and Innovation Centre, University of Adelaide and the University of Technology Sydney Business School, both in Australia, and Adjunct Associate Professor in the College of Business, Nanyang Business School, Nanyang Technological University, Singapore. Göran is a fellow of the Australian Academy of Technological Sciences and Engineering and of the Royal Swedish Academy of Engineering Sciences.

Robin Roslender holds the Chair in Accounting and Finance at the University of Dundee School of Business, Scotland. In addition to academic attainments in sociology he has a professional accounting qualification. A leading interdisciplinary accounting scholar, he recently sole-edited *The Routledge Companion to Critical Accounting*. A consistent focus of his work is the application of social and sociological theory perspectives within accounting studies. Formerly editor of the *Journal of Human Resource Costing and Accounting*, Professor Roslender is currently an associate editor of *Accounting Forum* and was recently appointed an editor of the *Journal of Business Models*. Professor Roslender has contributed extensively to the accounting for people literature during the past 25 years, in addition to the intellectual capital literature.

Grant Samkin is a Professor in the Department of Accounting at the University of Waikato, New Zealand, and a Professor in the Department of Financial Accounting at the University of South Africa. His research interests include narrative or non-financial reporting (including corporate social responsibility, sustainability, and intellectual capital issues), education, and accounting history. His recent work involves the development of a reporting and evaluation framework that can be used as an assessment tool and reporting guide by organizations with operations impacting on biodiversity.

Giovanni Schiuma is a Professor in Knowledge and Innovation Management at the University of Basilicata, Italy. Recently he has been Professor of Arts Based Management and Director of the Innovation Insights Hub at University of the Arts London, UK. As an international academic, he is widely recognized as one of the world's leading experts in the arts in business and strategic knowledge management. He serves as chief editor of the journal *Knowledge Management Research and Practice* and as co-editor-in-chief of the international journal *Measuring Business Excellence*. Giovanni chairs the International Forum on Knowledge Assets Dynamics.

Annika Schneider is a doctoral student in the Department of Accounting at the University of Waikato, New Zealand. Her PhD topic deals with the development of a biodiversity reporting framework for the New Zealand local government sector. Her research interests include non-financial accounting and reporting, intellectual capital, accounting for biodiversity, corporate social responsibility, and sustainability. Her work has been published in *Accounting, Auditing & Accountability Journal*, *Journal of Intellectual Capital* and *Meditari Accountancy Research*.

Sarah Jane Smith (previously known as Sarah Jane Thomson) is a Reader in Accounting at the University of Stirling, Scotland. Her PhD studies, funded by a prestigious Carnegie scholarship, examined the role of leasing in UK corporate financing decisions, its accounting treatment, and its market impact. Her thesis received the Leaseurope award for the best thesis on leasing across Europe in 2003. Intellectual capital reporting and disclosure have dominated her research interests in recent years and she has published a number of academic journal articles in this area.

Jesper Sort is a research assistant at the Business Model Design Centre at Aalborg University, Denmark. His research focuses on business models, value creation, business angels, investment processes, and university–industry collaboration. His work has led to initiatives in the Danish investment community and upgrading local government knowledge regarding the investment process between business angels and entrepreneurs. His current work involves understanding entrepreneurs and improving SMEs in developing their businesses in order for them to become future growth companies, as well as investigating how the university–industry aspect has an important influence on the development process.

Karl-Erik Sveiby is often described as one of the "founding fathers" of knowledge management, having developed several seminal concepts for both knowledge management and intellectual capital. Based on his 20 years of managerial experience in a major global corporation and a Swedish co-owned publishing company, he has also co-developed business simulations where participants learn by doing while applying theory to practice. Karl-Erik's current research interest is in leadership, sustainability, and innovation, where he applies a knowledge perspective to fulfil his mission to help make organizations better for people.

Dariusz Trzmielak is an Associate Professor at the Management Faculty, University of Lodz, Poland. He is also a member of the management board in the Polish Business and Innovation Centre Association. He was a member of the Lodz Region Operational Program Committee between 2007 and 2013. From 2003 to 2007, he was the director of the Innovation Centre, American–Polish Offset Program University of Texas, at the University of Lodz. He studied at Middlesex University Business School, London; Warwick Business School, UK; Justus–Liebig University in Giessen, Germany; the Technological Educational Institution of Messolonghi, Greece; and the Institute of Innovation Creativity and Capital at the University of Texas in Austin, USA.

Emidia Vagnoni is a Professor of Management Accounting at the University of Ferrara, Italy, and Director of the University Research Centre in Health Economics and Management. Her research and teaching interests include public sector accounting and management, intellectual capital, social and environmental reporting, performance measurement, and sustainability management. Emidia has been a visiting academic at Australian, Swedish, and English universities, and more recently she has been appointed Adjunct Professor at the University of Tehran, Iran. Her research activity has benefited from a number of grants from the EU, the Ministry of Health, the Regional Health Authority, and other funders, and she has published more than 100 articles and book chapters.

Mika Vanhala is a post-doctoral researcher in knowledge management and leadership at the School of Business and Management, Lappeenranta University of Technology, Finland. His primary research interests are the relationship between HRM practices, organizational trust, and organizational performance, as well as intellectual capital and knowledge management in value creation. His research has been published in, for example, *Personnel Review*, *Management Decision*, and *Journal of Managerial Psychology*.

Jun Yao is currently a Senior Assistant Professor at the School of Commerce, Meiji University, Japan. She gained her Master's Degree and PhD from Kobe University, Japan. She is also one of the advisory board members of the Japan Intellectual Capital Management Association and a research fellow at PwC Aarata Institute, Japan. She has extensive interests in the area of accounting and management control, including intellectual capital management, risk management, and corporate governance. She has several papers published in academic journals. She won the Academic Award of Japan Institute of Certified Public Accountants in 2014.

1

THE PAST, PRESENT, AND FUTURE FOR INTELLECTUAL CAPITAL RESEARCH

An overview

John Dumay, James Guthrie, Federica Ricceri,
and Christian Nielsen

Introduction

When we started this project three years ago, we started with the aim "to provide an overview of Intellectual Capital (IC) in practice and beyond. It will focus on the role of IC in organizations and between organizations, institutions and beyond". The *Routledge Companions* are similar to what some publishers call 'handbooks', being prestige reference works providing an overview of a whole subject area or sub-discipline, which survey the state of the discipline including emerging and cutting edge areas. The *Routledge Companions* produce a comprehensive, up to date, definitive reference that are usually cited as an authoritative source on the subject. Our goal in undertaking this project is to provide a collection of essays that address cross-cutting IC issues. We believe we have achieved our aims and our collected works should be of interest to people who want to understand IC from a variety of perspectives with a view that readers may or may not have background knowledge, as well as students who are learning to work with a particular aspect of IC and the management of knowledge. The material in this *Routledge Companion* relates not only to theory, but also to practice and case studies.

We are proud that this book features leading academic, policy, and practitioner articles examining the latest developments in the field of IC. The contents are organized thematically into sections that reflect the five stages of IC research developments (Dumay *et al.*, 2017). We believe no one stage is more important than another – the themes and stages provide a useful framework with which to present the 30 chapters, written by a variety of authors and covering a wide range of subject areas.

Frontiers of research, practice, and knowledge

Intellectual capital, intangible assets, and even intangible liabilities. These terms are most likely familiar to readers of this book. It is probable that what attracts you to this collection is that the chapters herein offer state-of-the-art thinking about IC practice and research. We believe we will not let down readers familiar with these terms as we provide new understandings into how established and new authors from research and practice outline their insights, critique, and ways forward for creating value for all organizations. Additionally, the chapters in this book also offer readers who are relatively new to the IC and intangible assets field access to contemporary research that allows them to quickly position themselves and take the journey that we have taken with many others.

To ensure we capture the progress being made in contemporary IC research, we include chapters by the seminal IC authors, or as Leif Edvinsson likes to call some of them, the 'grandfathers' of IC. Thus, we include chapters by James Guthrie, Robin Roslender, Leif Edvinsson, John Holland, Ulf Johanson, Henrik Dane-Nielsen, Karl-Erik Sveiby, Aino Kianto, and Göran Roos. A virtual who's who of the early days of IC research and many of whom have their roots in practice. In adding to contemporary IC practice, we also have the pleasure of including active IC practitioners such as Mary Adams (US), and Manfred Bornemann (Austria and Germany). Similarly, we also include some of the young(er) 'guns', who have since the mid 2000s been blazing a new trail, such as John Dumay, Jim Rooney, Grant Samkin, Gunnar Rimmel, Maria Serena Chiucchi, Emidia Vagnoni, Suresh Cuganesan, Christian Nielsen, Marco Giuliani, and Tatiana Garanina. Then there is the new blood in the likes of Henri Hussinksi, Paavo Ritala, and Marco Montemari. Thus, the authors of chapters in this book are inclusive of many of the best that have served IC research and practice well, along with those who will serve it well into the next generations of IC research.

Arguably, IC is having a resurgence because a new reporting framework, Integrated Reporting (<IR>), makes use of IC as part of its six capitals framework (International Integrated Reporting Council (IIRC), 2013). As Dumay (2016, p. 175) outlines:

> [w]hen you take away the physical capitals of financial, manufactured, and natural capital, the remaining three intangible capitals broadly align with IC's three capitals: human capital with human capital; social and relational capital with relational capital; and IC with structural capital.

The latter fact that IC in <IR> equates to structural capital in the traditional tripartite model of IC as human, relational, and structural capital (Petty and Guthrie, 2000), is an important point of departure for future IC and intangible assets research because, as noted, the terms are often used interchangeably (Eccles and Krzus, 2010), and in different contexts. For example, in European and North American business parlance, the term 'intangible assets' is used more often than 'intellectual capital' (Cuozzo *et al.*, 2017). So, while we see an initial resurgence in IC, we need to be clear about what it is as several authors discuss it in their chapters.

Another issue we need to be explicit about is that of 'value' or 'value creation', two terms frequently used without being adequately defined (see Bowman and Ambrosini, 1998). The meaning of value creation has evolved from Thomas Stewart's (1997, p. x) initial definition of IC whereby value creation is associated with the ability for IC to 'create wealth', more in line with Bowman and Ambrosini's (1998, p. 1) construct of "value capture" than 'value creation'. In contemporary IC research, Dumay (2016, p. 169) critically redefines "value in four ways: monetary, utility, social, and sustainable value", which is more in keeping with the contemporary emphasis on third stage performative IC (Guthrie *et al.*, 2012) and the fourth stage ecosystem approach (Dumay and Garanina, 2013). Several chapters in this book use this contemporary conceptualization of value creation, and Chapter 2 goes beyond and discusses the worth, rather than the value of IC (Dumay *et al.*, 2017).

What something is worth differs from its value, whether it be tangible or intangible. As a result, Dumay *et al.* (2017) outline the need for the fifth stage of IC research, to reframe the general research question of "What is IC worth to investors, customers, society and the environment?" to "Is managing IC a worthwhile endeavour?" Arguably, asking the latter question removes boundaries so that all manners of worth are included and recognizes that IC is a substantial part of what impacts everyone on a daily basis. There are still researchers who hold the view that IC and intangible assets are purely for creating wealth for investors and shareholders (Lev and Gu, 2016), while there is an opposite worldview that defines value creation as more encompassing and involving more stakeholders. Therefore, there is arguably a need to reconcile "the worth of IC to different people in different contexts and respecting that there will always be differences and that one view should not always prevail" (Dumay *et al.*, 2017, p. xx).

Introduction to IC as per the chapters

In this section we will describe how we frame IC for the purpose of presenting the chapters in this book. For those unfamiliar with the different stages of IC research, we recommend that you begin reading some of the seminal articles that will help you understand the evolution of IC. These would include works such as Petty and Guthrie (2000) for first and second stage research, Guthrie *et al.* (2012) for third stage research, and Dumay and Garanina (2013) for third and fouth stage research. Finally Dumay *et al.* (2017) in this book, for the first time, introduce the fifth stage of IC research (see Figure 1.1). Additionally, the latter chapter gives a comprehensive chronological outline of the path IC research has taken since the early 1990s, which is key to understanding how IC has emerged from an interesting idea, to a more comprehensive field of research and practice. As such, we lead with this chapter to introduce a comprehensive view of IC, especially for readers unfamiliar with IC research, to allow them to quickly grasp what IC is, why IC is important, and its trajectory to the time we took on this project. Consequently, we then work backwards from fifth to first stage chapters, noting a dominance of chapters addressing third stage practice-based IC research.

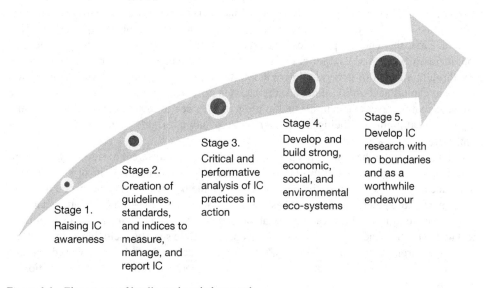

Figure 1.1 Five stages of intellectual capital research

Fifth stage chapters

In the first chapter of this section Dumay, Guthrie, and Rooney (2017) examine the path that critical IC research has followed from its conception until today and reflect on the possible future path for critical IC research. From the foundation of the four previously identified stages of research, the authors thus build a fifth, critical, research path for IC. In this fifth stage of IC research, IC researchers need to move beyond the boundaries of traditional, rather narrow, IC definitions, and instead of asking what IC is worth to various stakeholders, investors, customers, society, and the environment, instead ask whether managing IC is a worthwhile endeavour at all? Focusing on this big question helps recognize that IC is a substantial part of what impacts us on a day-to-day basis. In developing the fifth stage of research, there needs to be more research that focuses specifically on understanding how IC (or the various elements) helps improve value beyond organizational boundaries and, furthermore, that going beyond organizational boundaries also requires IC researchers to broaden their idea of IC.

The authors observe that the terms intangibles and IC are used synonymously, yet the term intangible assets is much broader than those assets that create an accounting financial value because it includes everything that is not tangible and put to use to 'create value'. The authors argue that in all forms value creation somehow relies on interaction with tangible assets. Dumay *et al*. (2017) then explore the key strengths of the <IR> approach, which includes financial, physical, and natural capital in its value creation model (IIRC, 2013), something that many IC researchers are only just coming to apply. They argue that it is time to take down the boundaries to IC research and work towards reconciling the worth of IC to different people in different contexts, respecting that there will always be differences and that one view should not always prevail.

Similarly, Roslender and Monk (2017), in the chapter "Accounting for people", go beyond recognized IC boundaries and address the consequences of progressing the challenge of accounting for people, a project that long predates the recognition of the significance of IC as an element within, but one which had largely become captured in past decades. Realizing the naivety of identifying a single aspect of the IC field as being the most significant, this chapter is founded on the premise of 'taking people into account', and links to fifth stage IC research by asking what IC is worth to various stakeholders, recognizing the importance of devoting further resources to the continued exploration of the IC field. First, this chapter provides an overview of the history of accounting for people, from its identification as a major challenge to the accountancy profession almost a century ago, through a series of general approaches to the task, and concluding with a discussion of human capital accounting. Second, the chapter provides a number of insights on three pathways that IC researchers interested in progressing accounting for people might pursue: employee health and wellbeing; a broader range of human rights issues; and the role for human capital self-accounting.

The authors argue that taking people into account has two different meanings. First, from an accounting perspective, it brings to mind the search for some means to incorporate people within accounts, most obviously by putting people on the balance sheet. The second meaning is of a much more practical nature, at least to anyone with an interest in people and what they bring to the workplace. This meaning for taking people into account translates into a commitment to demonstrate the scale and scope of what people gift to society, including as employees. This chapter argues that human capital is, by definition, the source of IC, as a consequence of which it demands to be taken into account more than ever, to ensure that its contribution to society is the most it can be, at all times and in all spaces.

Fourth stage chapters

Leif Edvinsson (2017) a founding father of IC in his chapter "Seven dimensions to address for intellectual capital and intangible assets navigation" provides an overview of the emerging global approaches to revealing the hidden value of both nations and enterprises, to the benefit of future generations, by identifying seven steps to address IC and intangible assets navigation. He argues that IC is about visibility, understanding, flow, networking of brain capacity, the velocity of the transformation of intangible human capital into more sustainability drivers of structural capital. The chapter contributes to the fourth stage of IC research. It is a paradigm in search of the drivers of value creation and reports to various stakeholders. In advanced economies, 75 per cent of GDP is related to IC. This chapter discusses the ELSS-Model that groups more than 60 countries over 15 years and covers the four traditional major pillars of national IC – human capital, relational capital, structural organizational capital, and renewal capital or innovation capital. It may also be refined to incorporate social capital and environmental capital dimensions.

Schiuma and Lerro (2017) in their chapter state that IC is playing a fundamental role in the development dynamics of regional economies. This chapter argues that there are two main issues. The first issue concerns the difficulty of identifying and measuring IC within regional systems. Despite the wide acknowledgement of IC as a key driver, there is still a lack of a coherent and shared framework for identifying, managing, assessing, and reporting IC at the regional level. Although there is quality and available data on different aspects of regional development, the second issue is that there is a lack of homogeneous and significant data about the use of IC. Their chapter contributes to the fourth stage of IC research, with its contribution in the way it addresses two issues. First, it analyses the role of IC and related components for regional development dynamics. Second, concerning territorial strategic resources, it presents the Knoware Tree, a framework to identify and classify territorial IC and the Knoware Dashboard, a framework driving the design of potential indicators and metrics to assess territorial IC.

Next the focus changes to IC and the public sector with Samkin and Schneider (2017) as their chapter reviews and critiques IC research undertaken in New Zealand. The identified research is positioned within the four stages of IC literature in order to answer the question: what has been the focus of IC research in a New Zealand context to date? The answer is that, despite New Zealand being heralded as a leader in public sector management following the reforms of the 1980s and 1990s, the extent and depth of research into how IC can be useful to the public sector to create public value is surprisingly limited. The majority of papers adopt a content analysis method using a disclosure index to determine the level of IC reporting in the annual reports of a sample set of organizations.

The authors state that the majority of the research identified has not moved beyond stage two IC research, which is concerned with guidelines and IC frameworks. In order to extend the frontiers of IC research beyond 'what is' into stage three research investigating IC in practice from a critical and performative perspective, and stage four research influenced by critical social and environmental accounting, a number of future research avenues are explored within the New Zealand public sector. Given a general acceptance of IC, understanding how the public sector views IC will become increasingly important. Additionally, how the public sector can leverage its IC in order to create value by providing better and more effective services provides several fruitful avenues of research.

The focus on the public sector continues with Vagnoni (2017) in her chapter "Intellectual capital in the context of healthcare organizations: Does it matter?" in which she states that healthcare organizations differ from others because of their fundamental mission to guarantee health protection to citizens and, therefore, their management process is driven by different criteria. Her point is that while many studies examine IC and management, regarding healthcare organizations IC is still a 'black box'. Costs and financial results are identified, but how IC interacts to share knowledge and create innovation and value, is not known or monitored. Despite efforts to mobilize knowledge and innovation to legitimize healthcare organizations' strategic role in society, the literature has devoted surprisingly limited attention to these IC dimensions. The chapter aims to fill this gap.

Vagnoni (2017) explores the literature and several examples to highlight that healthcare organizations are complex and IC has a particular role to play in their strategic management. In identifying IC variables, their relationships, and how to mobilize them, the chapter identifies the potential for IC to contribute to achieving financial goals as well as clinical outcomes and administration, thus contributing to the fourth stage of IC research. She states that medical journals have widely studied the IC framework and its operationalization in different dimensions, as well as criticizing the lack of methods and approaches to using IC for management and strategy effectively. Clinicians have emphasized the role of knowledge and IC for healthcare management, while directors of healthcare organizations are under pressure to manage budget constraints.

In conclusion, she argues that IC accounting scholars can play a vital role in bridging the gap and contributing to management and accounting practice change in the healthcare organizations. Thus, studies related to the use of IC frameworks for managerial purposes at all levels of the organization can contribute to practice and to closing the gap between administrative and healthcare roles, creating greater trust among health professionals in accounting technologies.

Third stage chapters

In the chapters that we classify as third stage research articles we have also identified two distinct themes. The first theme is based on chapters that examine IC in practice from an internal perspective. These chapters mainly present case studies of how IC is used by management and highlight how IC is needed not just in commercial organizations, but how it is applicable to public and not-for-profit organizations. The second distinct theme incorporates chapters that explore various frameworks

Practice-based chapters

Holland (2017) in "Rethinking models of banks and financial institutions using empirical research and ideas about intellectual capital" discusses the concept that traditional finance theory provides ways of developing theoretical models of financial firms, but is restricted to economic processes. Many of the economic problems faced by financial firms post-2000 have been located in their knowledge and social contexts, and thus this cannot be adequately explained by existing normative theory. This chapter, therefore, extends the analytical framework for banks and financial institutions through empirical research and theoretical ideas about IC and social factors relating to financial firms and their financial intermediation processes.

Holland (2017) argues that developments in financial firm research have occurred outside of the traditional finance theory (TFT) paradigm but have not made the same progress as IC research in recent years. This chapter broadly reflects the three stages of IC research in accounting outlined by Guthrie *et al.* (2012). The first stage reveals research to improve awareness of the role of IC in banks and financial institutions. The second stage illustrates research to develop guidelines and theoretical views of IC in banks and financial institutions. The first and second stages reflect attempts to formulate and legitimize the field of IC research in financial firms as an area of multi-disciplinary and multi-focused research like IC accounting research.

The chapter illustrates how ideas from field work and empirical narrative and alternative theory narrative can be 'connected to' TFT. The combined set of ideas acts as a "new theory frame for financial firms" (2017, p. xx). It reveals ways of critical thinking about financial firms and developing connections between the broader social science and management literature and TFT. This creates ways to critically evaluate the roles of banks and financial institutions in the economy and society, develop a critical examination of IC in financial firm practice, and critically appraise the role of TFT in explaining financial firms.

In another chapter that deals with financial institutions, Murthy and Guthrie (2017) in their chapter "Mobilizing intellectual capital in practice: A story of an Australian financial institution" examines how IC was mobilized in a large organization. Taking a narrative research approach and applying a theory of consequences to the case study organization, they find that when managers mobilized IC resources expecting certain intended consequences, there were also unintended consequences since elements of IC interacted, entangled, and acted with each other. The narrative sheds light on how the implementation of IC moved from a managerial perspective towards an ecosystem perspective as a deeper meaning relating to the effect of non-financial resources was uncovered.

Narratives have a plot, a beginning, a middle, and an end. Hence, the events gathered from the documents and interviews were not just temporal; they had a sequence where one event leads to another. The three stories of the financial institution's back office brought out unintended consequences from the mobilization of IC. Story one was a 'tragedy' where different meanings of customer needs were constructed that contradicted each other as to the amount of financial investment that could be made from the various IC resources. The tragedy transformed into a 'satire' in story two when managers struggled to mobilize the elements of IC within budgetary constraints. In the story, three managers promoted operations that did not require significant financial resources, and they were thereby able to transform the story into a 'romance'. These narratives illustrate how the implementation of IC moved from a managerial perspective towards an ecosystem perspective as it was discovered that there is a deeper meaning hidden within the confusion and ambiguity in the effect of non-financial IC resources.

The chapter by Michalak, Krasodomska, Rimmel, Sort, and Trzmielak (2017) examines IC in public universities. They state that universities are knowledge intensive organizations that cooperate with business and other stakeholders to commercialize research results. Their chapter contributes to the third stage of IC research because it draws attention to the influence of new public management on IC management and the ways in which IC acts as a source of universities' competitive advantage. Their chapter presents the main sources of this benefit, as well as describing the way university IC is linked to its market value. It discusses the knowledge commercialization process, which generates IC in a university and the ways in which university–industry collaboration enhances the value of IC.

Ritvanen and Sveiby's (2017) chapter contributes to the emergent stream of IC-as-practice, proposing that IC is seen as a 'lens' to guide, select activities, and assess effects and consequences of managerial action in its broadest sense. They argue that an IC-as-practice perspective is concerned with how managers deal with the fact that action is irreversible and may have unexpected outcomes. It does not shy away from issues of power and ethics. If the full implications of IC-as-practice are accepted, IC scholars must do more than analyse IC-statements or manipulate large databases. It signals a commitment to sociological theories of practice and close-up methods, such as ethnographic methods and action research.

They illustrate their proposition with the case of a large manufacturing company where management is facing strategic decision making in the face of uncertainty.

The chapter by Rooney and Dumay (2017) explores behavioural influences on innovation practice and its association with IC. In particular, it examines the performative interactions between IC and innovation and the conditions associated with innovation success and failure. The stated aim is to provide insights into the factors promoting as well as inhibiting innovation, and this is achieved by focusing on narratives, rather than numbers. Based on the literature linking IC and innovation practice, the authors examine their associations across a continuum including radical, evolutionary, and incremental innovation. From the discussions, it is demonstrated that the relationships between IC and innovation are substantively more nuanced than the IC-innovation grand theory suggests. The chapter concludes that different types of IC are more effective for various categories of innovation, and can also be mitigating factors in developing innovations, going some way to explaining the mixed empirical results of prior IC-innovation studies.

This chapter contributes to the third stage of IC research, and the findings have several implications for IC and innovation practice, research, and policy decision making. First, for practitioners, there is an imperative to resist the temptation to apply quantitative frameworks based on grand IC theories without critical review of the nuanced relationship between IC type and innovation categories. Given that innovation is, to a considerable extent, driven by strategy, there is a need for clarity on the desired strategic outcomes. Second, for researchers, there is a need to consider the influences on innovation failure as well as success. As for practitioners, this requires a more critical and nuanced understanding of the various relationships between IC type and the continuum of innovation categories not usually examined in 'grand theories' of IC. Finally, for policy decision makers, there is a need to critically analyse past preferences for 'one size fits all' innovation policies. All forms of innovation have a role in achieving national and global economic goals.

Massaro and Dumay's (2017) chapter explores IC disclosure (ICD) in digital communication channels. The chapter fits into the third stage of IC because it explores a mode whereby investors communicate with each other, specifically focusing on Internet Stock Message Boards. This study is novel since its focus on ICD assumes an investor perspective and investigates if and how much investors discuss IC. Additionally, the research looks at involuntary disclosure because we investigate what investors say about the company, rather than what a company says about itself. The research finds that investors use new media to acquire, discuss, and share information about companies and they discuss different IC elements according to the sector of the company. Additionally, topics discussed by investors do not match previous frameworks used in ICD research. Finally, messages containing ICD more likely disclose investor's sentiment (e.g. hold, buy, or sell), showing that IC matters to investors to justify their opinion about a company's future. Thus this chapter represents one of the new and emerging ICD studies that breaks away from analysing traditional ICD mediums such as an annual report.

Cuganesan's (2017) chapter studies the application of IC elements in the not-for-profit (NFP) sector and argues that despite being an important sector of the economy, it is often overlooked. Increasingly, NFPs have to acquire and maintain commercial revenue sources through the provision of earned income activities in order to ensure their financial sustainability. While customer performance measurement practices offer significant potential for NFPs, little is known about how these practices operate in this setting. Furthermore, characteristics of the NFP context mean that findings from the for-profit sector are not necessarily transferable to private sector organizations. Hence, this study sets out to examine: (a) how NFP orientation influences customer performance measurement practices comprising the measurement of value provided to customers as well as value extracted from customers; and (b) the effects of these customer performance measurement practices on non-financial performance and financial sustainability.

Based on the study's findings, this chapter concludes that measurement of value provided to customers contributes to the enhanced delivery of earned income activities to customers and the achievement of a social mission. Through this effect, the measurement of value provided to customers also has indirect benefits for the financial sustainability of NFPs. Also, the study provides insights into the nature of the benefits obtained from customer performance measurement practices in the NFP context. These appear to be operational in terms of enhancing individual customer relationships, rather than in terms of pricing or being portfolio related. Overall, this chapter adds to the knowledge of customer performance measurement practices and how these operate in NFP settings.

Moving from large companies to small to medium enterprises (SMEs), Yao and Koga (2017) in the chapter "Sustained competitive advantage and strategic intellectual capital management: Evidence from Japanese high performance small to medium sized enterprises" argue that IC is important as a source of competitive advantage in SMEs. They observe that there has been limited research into IC management in Japanese SMEs. This chapter explores how IC contributes to sustained competitive advantage through strategic management in Japanese SMEs by analysing five companies over ten years.

The chapter reveals that IC can deliver competitive advantage in the long run; only by combining with overall competitive strategy does it facilitate sustained long-term competitive advantage. The research has both practical and policy implications. It can help managers to review strategy formation and improve IC management and reporting for investors and other stakeholders to evaluate IC, and policy makers to provide more proper support for SMEs.

Framework chapters

This subsection presents the chapters that explore the second distinctive theme associated with frameworks. Johanson's (2017) thoughtful chapter "Towards an integrated intellectual capital management framework" outlines and argues that a deeper understanding of how IC management is performed is needed. Work health and work environment have many similarities with other IC elements and are often connected to each other. Linear causalities could be hard to find, but mutual dependence is evident, for example between health and exploitable competence. Therefore, it is also argued that because of the ageing population there is a need to improve understanding of how work environment and work health affect sustainability on the individual, organizational, and societal level.

The Montemari and Chiucchi (2017) chapter argues that although several frameworks for measuring and reporting IC have been developed, their actual use in practice is still limited. In particular, IC measurement frameworks have been criticized for their limited ability to capture the relationships between IC and value creation, and to show the impact of IC on company performance. The business model concept has been identified as a platform within which to refocus the IC debate. This chapter explores how the business model can support IC measurement and how the transition from the business model to measurement can be executed. This chapter contributes to the third stage of IC research, outlining a single, in-depth case study, conducted using an interventionist approach. The analysis finds that using the business model clarifies which IC elements are of utmost importance and what role they play in the company's value creation process.

Smith (2017) explores the important issue of IC disclosure: what benefits, what costs, is it voluntary? It explores the costs, benefits, restrictions, and alternative perspectives to IC disclosure through a synthesis of evidence obtained from a direct survey investigation of, and follow-up interviews with, 93 finance directors in UK listed companies. The findings show that benefits, costs, and restrictions are unequally associated with disclosure across the spectrum of IC information and that IC disclosure decisions are increasingly complex. This explains why IC components observed to be disclosed are not necessarily those that are the most critical in the value creation process.

Under contemporary international financial reporting regulations, many IC elements are not recognized in the financial statements, and various incentives are suggested in relation to the voluntary disclosure of IC. These include increased transparency to capital markets, establishing trustworthiness with stakeholders, and providing a valuable marketing tool. However, what creates value is potentially highly sensitive, and disclosing value creation-related information could be a serious burden. Therefore, IC management and IC disclosure are mutually dependent activities in the value creation process, with the disclosure in itself having the potential to create or destroy value; in theory, voluntary disclosure will occur if benefits exceed costs. However, due to bounded rationality, not all potential benefits and costs might be considered. Benefits and costs are unlikely to remain constant over time, and it is unclear if the IC disclosure decision is the product of a static or a dynamic trade-off, or indeed subject to periodic review. Further, disclosure cannot be said to be voluntary if private disclosure agreements or other restrictions/regulations are in place to safeguard highly sensitive information from the public domain.

Bornemann's (2017) stated purpose is to report on the situation of the discipline and experiences of IC reporting over the last 15 years in Germany. A national initiative plays a vital role in the process of reporting IC by the Federal Ministry of Economic Affairs which published the method of Wissensbilanz (IC Reporting and Management) Made in Germany: a management and reporting instrument for strategic organizational development that has been implemented and tested in Mittelstand companies since 2004. He concludes that with more than 100,000 downloads of the guideline for IC reporting, it is well received by enterprises and management education programs.

Demartini and Bernardi's (2017) chapter "A management control system for environmental and social initiatives: An intellectual capital approach" examines a company operating in the global aerospace and defence industry, which has designed a management control system focused on IC measurement to assess, manage, and monitor environmental and social initiatives. The tool is intended to meet the stringent criteria required for inclusion in the Dow Jones Sustainability Index. The study is an action research project, in which data were gathered from in-depth interviews with managers, as well as from group discussions.

The research illustrates how to link IC and environmental and social initiatives. To the best of our knowledge, no research has addressed this topic to date. Their chapter contributes to the third stage of IC research by investigating IC in practice from a critical and performative perspective.

Chiucchi, Giuliani, and Marasca (2017) argue that despite a plethora of IC concepts and reporting frameworks, none has been widely accepted. IC reporting has been criticized as more preached than practised, suggesting an urgent need to reflect on what are the levers and the barriers that can influence the successful implementation of IC reporting. This chapter examines IC reporting implementation from a longitudinal perspective, thus contributing to the third stage of IC research. It finds that the levers and barriers identified in the literature vary in space and time and that these include ambiguity of aims or indicators and the existence of grand theories. Also, corporate social responsibility reporting may hinder the effective implementation of IC reporting. Project leaders and sponsors, as well as external partners, have an active role in determining the fate of an IC project.

In Rimmel, Baboukardos, and Jonäll (2017) "Revival of the fittest? Intellectual capital in Swedish companies", the authors examine the amount of IC disclosure in the annual reports of the top 30 Swedish companies and compare it to Skandia's IC disclosure 20 years ago. The authors aim to discover the level of IC disclosure in the annual reports and if IR has led to a revival of IC reporting?

The study reveals that the level of Skandia's IC disclosure 20 years ago is on average above the level of IC items contained in current corporate reports by Swedish companies. Additonally, the study finds that IC disclosures in IR companies do differ from companies that do not report according to IR and rely on traditional annual reports. Overall, the results indicate that there are differences in IC reporting between companies that applied IR and traditional annual report companies, which is consistent with the aim of IR declared by the IIRC.

Adams (2017) analyses the emergence of <IR> practices in the US. The IR movement can be seen in the third stage of development of IC thinking: from raising awareness to theory building and frameworks, and now to IC in practice. While the <IR> movement is still in its infancy across the world and even less common in the US, there are already some compelling examples of <IR> practice in the US. This chapter examines the key characteristics of ten publicly available US integrated reports to get a sense of this emerging practice. Findings show that, if the reference to the IIRC Framework is a requirement for being considered an integrated report, then practice in the US is limited to just two US-based companies in her sample. However, if a broader definition of <IR> is adopted as providing information about the full set of capitals and how they relate to value creation, then a complete list of ten companies qualify here. Overall, the analysis shows that the practice of <IR> is still in an emergent form. Each of the analysed companies is taking steps in its way to tell its stories to shareholders and stakeholders in a more integrated way.

Beusch and Nilsson's (2017) stated purpose is to provide a longitudinal analysis of the 'what and how' of disclosure of capital in annual accounts of major Swedish companies in relation to the IIRC's six capitals concept. In doing so, the chapter explores the level of the stage of <IR> research and practice in Sweden and discusses the achievements of a possible shift from a 'financial capital market system' to an 'inclusive capital market system'. For this purpose, the annual reports for the years 2011 and 2015 of 20 of the largest companies listed on the OMXS 30 large cap list in Sweden are examined. Content analysis is performed on the reports, applying a scoring system with 25 items, derived from the IIRC's Integrated Reporting Framework (IIRC, 2013) and previous studies.

Findings illustrate increases in human, intellectual, and social and relationship capitals, whereas natural capital shows a small decrease between the years. Overall, there are no fundamental changes during the four-year period covered in this study regarding multiple capital reporting: a majority of companies score slightly higher in 2015 compared to 2011, attributable entirely to increases of disclosure within non-financial and non-material/intangible capital (former IC classification). This study indicates that there is a long way to go until one can speak about a real shift from a 'financial capital market system' to an 'inclusive capital market system'.

It is argued that a solution that would make IC reporting matter (more) attractive to the investment community is to emphasize the interconnectedness between parts of the narrative sections according to the logic of contemporary business model understandings. This chapter identifies a series of potential inconsistencies due to a mismatch between business reporting orientation and the general stakeholder orientation in the business community. It concludes that propositions of aligning management commentary with business models may lead to challenges for both companies and external interested parties, and that regulation should be concerned with creating guidance on how to structure management commentary and strengthen such narrative statements through appropriate performance measures.

Second stage chapters

Roos (2017) sets out to recap the contributions to the field of IC he has made with colleagues over the last 20 years, and as such he summarizes the ten key works in this respect. The chapter is structured according to the author's personal assessment of the importance of the given contribution. In the author's personal view, his most influential contribution is found in the development of the IC-Navigator, which sought to address the lack of tools to assist companies in adopting a resource-based view of the firm. The side-effect of this tool was that it complemented business model innovation as well as the management of IC in general. Also highlighted as an important work is the contribution to identifying and using performance measures to the field of IC in the form of the Conjoint Value Hierarchy (CVH) measurement system.

He states that this has since spread into related fields also encapsulating complex objects with difficult or multi-dimensional attributes of value that must be captured. However, the author argues that none of the above two contributions nor the contributions to the field of corporate governance (reporting and disclosure) would have been possible without the contributions to the taxonomy of the field that addresses confusions as to what stocks and flows of resources exist as well as dealing with the confusion around the distinction between intangibles and IC. It is clear from the work that is presently ongoing on the meso-economic scale that the IC lens is useful and able to contribute to insights around value creation on multiple scales.

Dane-Nielsen and Nielsen (2017) in their chapter argue that IC is the platform of any business model and its value creation, and that without IC no value creation can take place at all and thereby contribute to answering Dumay *et al.*'s (2017) fifth stage of IC research question, namely 'is managing IC a worthwhile endeavour?'. The answer is yes, because IC is the basis of all wealth creation. Through the notions of 'emergentist' sociological theory, this chapter offers a theoretically grounded lens for analysing and understanding business models. The authors argue that business model descriptions should focus on describing the connections between the different activities being performed in the company. Current perceptions of relationships and linkages in the business model literature often only reflect tangible transactions and relationships, and this is found to be problematic. Regardless of what an organization does, it is not possible to perform functions and activities without the appropriate IC to make use of machinery, apply financial capital, perform processes, create management actions, and so on. An organization's value drivers are always their IC.

The chapter introduces five examples of distinct business model configurations to illustrate that the value drivers of business models are IC entities at different levels of the organization. Individuals have relevant knowledge and work with other staff members in functional departments. An organization is made up of a number of interacting functional groups and departments, which together form the whole organization. Organizations, suppliers, and buyers act in a market, and the price and volume of products are ultimately determined by so-called market forces. The chapter contributes to a number of relevant action points for future studies that should be undertaken in order to further our understanding of IC in action, potentially in combination with business models. For example, the relationship between business models and different levels of organization.

In Lund and Nielsen (2017) "Making intellectual capital matter to the investment community", the authors discuss trends and dilemmas in reporting and disclosing IC in the light of two decades of attempts at creating guidelines and regulation for such corporate strategy narratives. They argue that to make IC reporting matter (more) to the investment community, the interconnectedness of parts of the narrative sections according to the logic of contemporary business model understandings should be emphasized. A series of potential inconsistencies that are the result of a mismatch between business reporting orientation and general stakeholder orientation in the business community are highlighted. The chapter concludes that propositions of aligning management commentary with business models may lead to challenges for both companies and external stakeholders, and that regulation should be concerned with creating guidance on how to structure management commentary and strengthen such narrative statements through relevant performance measures.

Hussinksi, Ritala, Vanhala, and Kianto (2017) in the chapter "Intellectual capital profiles and financial performance of the firm" argue that existing research demonstrates that IC is positively related to organizational outcomes. However, little is known about whether and how distinct configurations or profiles of different IC dimensions influence the real bottom line – the financial performance of firms. This chapter extends the traditional tripartite IC division into human/structural/relational capital with a finer-grained categorization and suggests three additional dimensions: renewal capital, entrepreneurial capital, and trust capital. In addition, it is suggested that relational capital could be divided into internal relational capital and external relational capital dimensions. We examine the types of configurations of these seven types of IC dimensions among groups of firms and look at how companies with different IC profiles vary in terms of their financial performance.

Continuing on the issue of performance, Kianto, Garanina, and Andreeva (2017) deliver an interesting chapter "Does intellectual capital matter for organizational performance in emerging markets? Evidence from Chinese and Russian contexts". The chapter uses a series of studies demonstrating the importance of IC for efficiency and value creation and that differences of cultural, economic, or institutional context pose a range of challenges for the management of IC. As most current studies have been conducted in developed countries, the significance of IC in emerging economies remains unclear, particularly as there are no comparative analyses of IC management in such contexts. This chapter's comparison of how IC impacts the performance of companies in China and Russia is of particular interest here because, while these emerging economies both prioritize innovation and are increasingly integrated into the global economy, their traditional management approaches differ significantly from those in developed countries. Based on survey data collected from 139 Chinese and 86 Russian companies, the chapter outlines the performance impact of the human, structural, and relational components of IC.

The finding that IC impacts performance in different ways in Russia and China shows that although emerging economies are sometimes grouped together, they should not be. The likelihood of fundamental institutional differences among emerging economies means that they should be examined individually rather than simplistically grouped together, with a view to identifying their idiosyncratic characteristics.

Stage one chapters

The De Villiers and Hsiao (2017) chapter discusses the relationship between IC and <IR>. <IR> is a reporting format that aims at communicating the interactions between financial and non-financial information in IR in the form of six distinct capitals. <IR> places considerable emphasis on articulating the future value creation story of the reporting entity with reference to the organization's strategy, business plan, and the six capitals: financial, manufactured, intellectual, human, social and relationship, and natural capital. Anyone with an interest in IC will immediately recognize its close relationship with <IR>. IC's 'structural capital' resembles <IR>'s 'intellectual capital', 'human capital' remains 'human capital', and IC's 'relational capital' maps to <IR>'s 'social and relationship capital'. Initially, this chapter provides details on the origins and developments of <IR>, and the connections between IR and IC and discusses prior literature.

The <IR> movement involves a number of important players at various levels in society and the capital markets. Early evidence suggests that <IR> is being implemented and adopted at a more rapid rate than previous reporting initiatives. As such, and given the similarities between several of the characteristics and components between IC and <IR>, it is worth researching IR and considering the implications for the IC movement. In addition, both the IR and the <IR> movement are argued to emphasize value creation and the business case for reporting. Therefore, any headway made by the <IR> movement in promoting IR can only benefit IC disclosure. Proponents of IC should consider ways to collaborate with the <IR> movement, as well as the means to leverage off the activities of the IIRC. The chapter concludes by pointing to research opportunities at the intersection between <IR> and IC.

In his chapter, Catasús (2017) asks the question: in which ways do numbers matter? This question is central to the discussion of the relevance of IC indicators. He argues that technologies such as accounting can move between practices and become important. Characteristics such as being trustworthy, fair, and moveable, make the measurements emanating from an accounting system into a technology *für alles*. It is thus not surprising that the practice as well as the study of accounting has become a more central activity in society in general, but in the IC discourse in particular. This, in turn, may lead to a focus on the measurements, accounts, reports, and KPIs for a plethora of aspects of the organization, begging the question: do we need all these numbers? To address this question the chapter is centred on the requirement of the relevance of indicators, and the idea that relevance is an issue related to whom the indicators are for, why we are measuring, and what is the ambition associated with IC indicators. The chapter also critically discusses the possible aims and use that can be made of IC indicators.

An important lesson from this chapter is that although we live in an age where measurements are omnipresent and where the measurement paradox drives measurement activities, we cannot expect all measurements to achieve what we want. Instead, we ought to approach a subset of measurement as IC indicators and use them as a means to mobilize interest about IC and reflect and learn about the ways IC affects practice because the conundrum of organizing will never be resolved – it is an eternal mystery.

Conclusion

To conclude this introductory chapter, we would like to leave on a note of curiosity and inspiration. We hope that from the insights gained from this *Routledge Companion* you will be inquisitive, and we encourage you to go out and pursue new research studies that will enrich companies and society. We also hope that eventually you will bring back new thoughts and ideas to further develop the field of IC in the future.

As was noted in this chapter, the five stages of IC research that organize the contributions of this *Routledge Companion* illustrate the trajectory that IC research has taken over the past 20 years. Throughout the development of a research field, it is necessary to have all stages of research in play for the construction of new knowledge and insights gained in the other stages, and therefore the stages presented here are interconnected rather than sequential.

The chapters presented in this *Routledge Companion* capture at a point of time our understanding of the field of IC. While the decade from 1997–2007 primarily saw the development of stages 1 and 2 research, it is evident that the ten years of research from 2007 to 2017, have moved from the ostensive stages 1 and 2 research and towards conducting performative analyses of IC practices in action (Mourtisen, 2006). This *Routledge Companion* has a majority of contributions representing the third stage of IC research. While the reporting agenda of the IC community has been focused on the <IR> initiative, the performative trend in IC has produced meaningful connections to fields such as innovation, entrepreneurship, and management.

If Dumay *et al.* (2017), are correct, there will be more research in stages 4 and 5 in the coming years. This will fill out several significant research gaps that will strengthen the IC agenda in relation to policy debates, as well as its overall societal impact. Asking whether managing IC, as is done in the depicted fifth stage of IC research, is a worthwhile endeavour, raises significant concerns about the 'return on investment' of the time and effort spent by companies, public organizations, and nations. If IC has any relevance for the performance of organizations, industries, and nations, there will surely be moves to capture, build, and manage it. And the question is whether this will be for the good of IC. As a community of practice and research, we need to be at the forefront of understanding these questions.

Arguably, the IC research agenda has not yet reached maturity levels capable of significantly affecting policy and regulation debates. Stage 4 research, which is specifically aimed at developing and building strong economic, social, and environmental ecosystems, brings with it a call for contemplating the good for society to the IC agenda. In addition to affecting policy and environmental debates, this ecosystem notion poses some interesting thoughts for further research on an organizational level too. From an organizational perspective, the idea of viewing oneself as a part of a collaborative ecosystem poses potential research to look into how IC can be practised in network-based business model settings. This would entail going beyond the understanding of the focal firm and contemplating effects further upstream and downstream in the value chain.

The current focus on stage 3 research and calls for research in stages 4 and 5 by no means indicates that stages 1 and 2 research are, or are going to be, obsolete. Because the outputs related to these three stages will alter our knowledge in the field, raising IC awareness in relation to IC with no boundaries, IC in an ecosystem context, and IC in reporting frameworks will be a continuous exercise. And because IC reporting is not a standalone communication vehicle, as it was to a large extent in the early 2000s, relationships with other concepts will be ever more important to review and address. Forthcoming research should aim to strengthen these ties and provide insights into the conditions under which IC can and cannot stand alone as measurement and reporting activities. Further, the creation of guidelines, standards, and indices to measure, manage, and report IC will need to be revisited to identify the effects of new regulation and new business models.

References

Adams, M. (2017), "Emerging integrated reporting practices in the United States", in Guthrie, J., Dumay, J., Ricceri, F., and Nielsen, C. (Eds), *The Routledge Companion to Intellectual Capital*, Routledge, London, p. 365–379.

Beusch, P. and Nilsson, A. (2017), "Capital reporting in Sweden: Insights about inclusiveness and integrativeness", in Guthrie, J., Dumay, J., Ricceri, F., and Nielsen, C. (Eds), *The Routledge Companion to Intellectual Capital*, Routledge, London, p. 380–395.

Bornemann, M. (2017), "Wissensbilanz made in Germany: Twelve years of experience confirm a powerful instrument", in Guthrie, J., Dumay, J., Ricceri, F., and Nielsen, C. (Eds), *The Routledge Companion to Intellectual Capital*, Routledge, London, p. 302–315.

Bowman, C. and Ambrosini, V. (1998), "Value creation versus value capture: Towards a coherent definition of value in strategy – an exploratory study", *British Journal of Management*, Vol. 11, No. 1, pp. 1–15.

Catasús B. (2017), "The relevance of IC indicators", in Guthrie, J., Dumay, J., Ricceri, F., and Nielsen, C. (Eds), *The Routledge Companion to Intellectual Capital*, Routledge, London, pp. 492–504.

Chiucchi, M. S., Giuliani, M., and Marasca, S. (2017), "Levers and barriers to the adoption of intellectual capital measurements: A field study", in Guthrie, J., Dumay, J., Ricceri, F., and Nielsen, C. (Eds), *The Routledge Companion to Intellectual Capital*, Routledge, London, pp. 332–346.

Cuganesan, S. (2017), "Enabling relational capital through customer performance measurement practices: A study of not-for-profit organizations", in Guthrie, J., Dumay, J., Ricceri, F., and Nielsen, C. (Eds), *The Routledge Companion to Intellectual Capital*, Routledge, London, pp. 211–235.

Cuozzo, B., Dumay, J., Palmaccio, M., and Lombardi, R. (2017), "Intellectual capital disclosure: A structured literature review", *Journal of Intellectual Capital*, Vol. 18 No. 1, pp. 9–28.

Dane-Nielsen H. and Nielsen, C. (2017), "Value creation in business models is based in intellectual capital: And only intellectual capital!", in Guthrie, J., Dumay, J., Ricceri, F., and Nielsen, C. (Eds), *The Routledge Companion to Intellectual Capital*, Routledge, London, pp. 418–434.

Demartini, P. and Bernardi, C. (2017), "A management control system for environmental and social initiatives: An intellectual capital approach", in Guthrie, J., Dumay, J., Ricceri, F., and Nielsen, C. (Eds), *The Routledge Companion to Intellectual Capital*, Routledge, London, p. 316–331.

De Villiers, C. and Hsiao, K. (2017), "Integrated reporting and the connections between integrated reporting and intellectual capital", in Guthrie, J., Dumay, J., Ricceri, F., and Nielsen, C. (Eds), *The Routledge Companion to Intellectual Capital*, Routledge, London, pp. 483–491.

Dumay, J. (2016), "A critical reflection on the future of intellectual capital: From reporting to disclosure", *Journal of Intellectual Capital*, Vol. 17, No. 1, pp. 168–184.

Dumay, J. and Garanina, T. (2013), "Intellectual capital research: A critical examination of the third stage", *Journal of Intellectual Capital*, Vol. 14, No. 1, pp. 10–25.

Dumay, J., Guthrie, J., and Rooney, J. (2017), "The critical path of intellectual capital", in Guthrie, J., Dumay, J., Ricceri, F., and Nielsen, C. (Eds), *The Routledge Companion to Intellectual Capital*, Routledge, London, pp. 21–39.

Eccles, R. G. and Krzus, M. P. (2010), *One Report: Integrated Reporting for a Sustainable Strategy*, John Wiley & Sons, Inc., Hoboken, New Jersey.

Edvinsson, L. (2017), "Seven dimensions to address for intellectual capital and intangible assets navigation", in Guthrie, J., Dumay, J., Ricceri, F., and Nielsen, C. (Eds), *The Routledge Companion to Intellectual Capital*, Routledge, London, pp. 56–66.

Guthrie, J., Ricceri, F., and Dumay, J. (2012), "Reflections and projections: A decade of intellectual capital accounting research", *The British Accounting Review*, Vol. 44, No. 2, pp. 68–92.

Holland, J. (2017), "Rethinking models of banks and financial institutions using empirical research and ideas about intellectual capital", in Guthrie, J., Dumay, J., Ricceri, F., and Nielsen, C. (Eds), *The Routledge Companion to Intellectual Capital*, Routledge, London, pp. 113–129.

Hussinksi, H., Ritala, P., Vanhala, M., and Kianto, A. (2017), "Intellectual capital profiles and financial performance of the firm", in Guthrie, J., Dumay, J., Ricceri, F., and Nielsen, C. (Eds), *The Routledge Companion to Intellectual Capital*, Routledge, London, pp. 450–462.

International Integrated Reporting Council (IIRC). (2013), *The International <IR> Framework*, International Integrated Reporting Council, London.

Johanson, U. (2017), "Towards an integrated intellectual capital management framework", in Guthrie, J., Dumay, J., Ricceri, F., and Nielsen, C. (Eds), *The Routledge Companion to Intellectual Capital*, Routledge, London, p. 252–265.

Kianto, A., Garanina, T., and Andreeva, T. (2017), "Does intellectual capital matter for organizational performance in emerging markets? Evidence from Chinese and Russian contexts", in Guthrie, J., Dumay, J., Ricceri, F., and Nielsen, C. (Eds), *The Routledge Companion to Intellectual Capital*, Routledge, London, p. 463–479.

Lev, B. and Gu, F. (2016), *The End of Accounting and the Path Forward for Investors and Managers*, John Wiley & Sons, Inc., Hoboken, New Jersey

Lund, M. and Nielsen, C. (2017), "Making intellectual capital matter to the investment community", in Guthrie, J., Dumay, J., Ricceri, F., and Nielsen, C. (Eds), *The Routledge Companion to Intellectual Capital*, Routledge, London, p. 435–449.

Massaro, M. and Dumay, J. (2017), "Intellectual capital disclosure in digital communication", in Guthrie, J., Dumay, J., Ricceri, F., and Nielsen, C. (Eds), *The Routledge Companion to Intellectual Capital*, Routledge, London, pp. 196–210.

Michalak, J., Krasodomska, J., Rimmel, G., Sort, J., and Trzmielak, D. (2017), "Intellectual capital management in public universities", in Guthrie, J., Dumay, J., Ricceri, F., and Nielsen, C. (Eds), *The Routledge Companion to Intellectual Capital*, Routledge, London, pp. 149–167.

Montemari, M. and Chiucchi, M. S. (2017), "Enabling intellectual capital measurement through business model mapping: The Nexus case", in Guthrie, J., Dumay, J., Ricceri, F., and Nielsen, C. (Eds), *The Routledge Companion to Intellectual Capital*, Routledge, London, pp. 266–283.

Mouritsen, J. (2006), "Problematizing intellectual capital research: Ostensive versus performative IC", *Accounting, Auditing & Accountability Journal*, Vol. 19, No. 6, pp. 820–41.

Murthy, V. and Guthrie, J. (2017), "Mobilizing intellectual capital in practice: A story of an Australian financial institution", in Guthrie, J., Dumay, J., Ricceri, F., and Nielsen, C. (Eds), *The Routledge Companion to Intellectual Capital*, Routledge, London, pp. 130–148.

Petty, R. and Guthrie, J. (2000), "Intellectual capital literature review: Measurement, reporting and management", *Journal of Intellectual Capital*, Vol. 1, No. 2, pp. 155–76.

Rimmel G., Baboukardos, D., and Jonäll, K. (2017), Revival of the fittest? Intellectual capital in Swedish companies", in Guthrie, J., Dumay, J., Ricceri, F., and Nielsen, C. (Eds), *The Routledge Companion to Intellectual Capital*, Routledge, London, pp. 347–364.

Ritvanen, H. and Sveiby, K. E. (2017), "Intellectual capital: A (re)turn to practice", in Guthrie, J., Dumay, J., Ricceri, F., and Nielsen, C. (Eds), *The Routledge Companion to Intellectual Capital*, Routledge, London, pp. 168–184.

Rooney J. and Dumay, J. (2017), "Intellectual capital and innovation", in Guthrie, J., Dumay, J., Ricceri, F., and Nielsen, C. (Eds), *The Routledge Companion to Intellectual Capital*, Routledge, London, pp. 185–195.

Roos, G. (2017), "Key contributions to the intellectual captial field of study", in Guthrie, J., Dumay, J., Ricceri, F., and Nielsen, C. (Eds), *The Routledge Companion to Intellectual Capital*, Routledge, London, pp. 399–417.

Roslender, R. and Monk, L. (2017), "Accounting for people", in Guthrie, J., Dumay, J., Ricceri, F., and Nielsen, C. (Eds), *The Routledge Companion to Intellectual Capital*, Routledge, London, pp. 40–56.

Samkin, G. and Schneider, A. (2017), "Past, present, and future: Intellectual capital and the New Zealand public sector", in Guthrie, J., Dumay, J., Ricceri, F., and Nielsen, C. (Eds), *The Routledge Companion to Intellectual Capital*, Routledge, London, pp. 76–98.

Schiuma, G. and Lerro, A. (2017), "Understanding and exploiting intellectual capital grounding regional development: Framework and metrics", in Guthrie, J., Dumay, J., Ricceri, F., and Nielsen, C. (Eds), *The Routledge Companion to Intellectual Capital*, Routledge, London, pp. 67–75.

Smith, S. J. (2017), "Intellectual capital disclosure: What benefits, what costs, is it voluntary?", in Guthrie, J., Dumay, J., Ricceri, F., and Nielsen, C. (Eds), *The Routledge Companion to Intellectual Capital*, Routledge, London, pp. 284–301.

Stewart, T. A. (1997), *Intellectual Capital: The New Wealth of Organisations*, Doubleday-Currency, London.

Vagnoni, E. (2017), "Intellectual capital in the context of healthcare organizations: Does it matter?", in Guthrie, J., Dumay, J., Ricceri, F., and Nielsen, C. (Eds), *The Routledge Companion to Intellectual Capital*, Routledge, London, pp. 99–109.

Yao, J. and Koga, C. (2017), "Sustained competitive advantage and strategic intellectual capital management: Evidence from Japanese high performance small to medium sized enterprises", in Guthrie, J., Dumay, J., Ricceri, F., and Nielsen, C. (Eds), *The Routledge Companion to Intellectual Capital*, Routledge, London, pp. 236–251.

PART I

Stage 5

Critical IC

2

THE CRITICAL PATH OF INTELLECTUAL CAPITAL

John Dumay, James Guthrie, and Jim Rooney

Introduction

This chapter examines the path that critical intellectual capital (IC) research has followed from its early days before and just after the new millennium, to where it stands in contemporary times. Understanding the path critical IC research is taking is essential because IC researchers need to know where others have travelled before embarking or reflecting on their own journey. Contemporary IC research has four stages. The first stage is raising awareness. The second stage is theory building and frameworks (Petty and Guthrie, 2000). The third stage is investigating IC in practice from a critical and performative perspective (Guthrie *et al.*, 2012, p. 69). A fourth stage is an ecosystem approach as outlined by Dumay and Garanina, 2013. These stages are the foundation of the critical path of IC.

IC is an interesting concept, but along with its espoused benefits, the concepts behind IC need to be questioned so that IC research and practice can progress (Dumay, 2012). This chapter shows how critical IC research continues to develop. First, it considers IC as a general concept, asking the question: what is intellectual capital? Defining IC is important because, like any common term, we need to know the context in which it is used. As Pike *et al.* (2006, p. 233) outline, a major obstacle when talking about IC is that there is no single agreed definition, and thus the first section explores three different, and useful, IC definitions.

Second, the chapter outlines the early critical paths found in the work of Sveiby (2007) and two special issues of the *Journal of Intellectual Capital* (*JIC*) by Chatzkel (2004) and O'Donnell *et al.* (2006a). Sveiby (2007), was especially critical of measuring intangibles and using them for management control and public relations purposes. Sveiby's criticisum is echoed in Chatzkel's (2004) argument that IC was at a crossroads of relevance and IC research needed to be critical to help make IC work, as it was in danger of fading away into insignificance.

Third, the chapter outlines the critical and performative practice turn in IC research. The original turning point is arguably an article by Jan Mouritsen (2006), which introduces a different way of thinking about IC based on the work of Latour (1986), using the dichotomy of ostensive versus performative IC. Later, a special issue of the journal *Critical Perspectives on Accounting* critically examined IC measurement (Mouritsen and Roslender, 2009).

Understanding the purpose of measuring IC is important because otherwise it might be used counterproductively. As Gowthorpe (2009, p. 830) aptly outlines "it is more likely the case that IC metrics will be interpreted in some quarters as offering new and exciting ways to bully people". From a different perspective, Dumay (2009a, p. 206) examines how IC is measured in contrast to the 'accountingization' of IC, leading to a more productive way of understanding IC.

Additionally, this section outlines how the outcomes of critical management studies, being insight, critique and transformative redefinition, are a useful way of examining IC from a critical perspective. Based on the work of Alvesson and Deetz (2000), Dumay (2008a) justifies a critical analysis of IC in action because IC development parallels critical theory, that is, it is in response to changing social conditions in "science, industrialization and communication/information technologies" (Alvesson and Deetz, 2000, p. 14). Similarly, IC came into prominence because of structural economic changes as knowledge, communication, and the importance of intangibles changed the way organizations operate (Meritum Project, 2002).

The chapter then examines what Guthrie *et al.* (2012) brand third stage IC research. Inspired by Mouritsen's (2006) ostensive versus performative IC theorization, Guthrie *et al.* (2012, p. 69) outline how IC "research is emerging based on a critical and performative analysis of IC practices in action". The Guthrie *et al.* (2012) article is important because its conclusion, which opens the opportunity for more research examining IC practices, has largely come to fruition. For example, a special issue of the *JIC* examining the IC third stage followed shortly after their article was published (Dumay, 2013), as did many other articles based on third stage IC research, making Guthrie *et al.* (2012) the most highly cited IC article since 2012.

A fourth section emanates from another important outcome of the IC third stage special issue, that is Dumay and Garanina's (2013) critical examination of the emergent third stage research. Their conclusion (p. 21) outlines the prospect of a fourth stage of IC research, which:

> [s]hifts the focus of IC within a firm to a longitudinal focus of how IC is utilized to navigate the knowledge created by countries, cities and communities and advocates how knowledge can be widely developed thus switching from a managerial to an eco-system focus.

The fourth stage has its roots in critical social and environmental accounting (Gray, 2006), and despite being not a theoretically new concept, has inspired an alternate form of IC research.

To conclude, the dominance of the managerial approach to IC is discussed, along with an examination of the possibilty that the wealth creation, rather than value creation, mantra is having a resurgence (International Integrated Reporting Council (IIRC), 2013; Lev and Gu, 2016) and that after losing its momentum a decade ago (Dumay, 2016), IC reporting may be once more attracting attention. However, this resurgence may be short lived if the focus is only on investors and managers – it is no longer responsible for companies to put profits before people and the environment. Therefore, more research is needed to understand how IC helps develop value beyond organizational boundaries.

Going beyond organizational boundaries also requires IC researchers to broaden their approach to IC because it is currently too narrow and disjointed. Currently, the term 'intellectual capital' is not in regular use in business and the term 'intangible assets' is more common (Cuozzo *et al.*, 2017). Additionally, current IC research mainly ignores the US and focuses on European academic journals, demonstrating the narrowness of IC as a research field. Broadening IC research will raise awarness and expand the potential of IC research.

What is IC?

Defining IC is important because, like any common term, we need to know the context in which we use it. As Pike *et al.* (2006, p. 233) outline, a major obstacle when talking about IC is that there is no single agreed definition. However, in this book (Guthrie *et al.*, 2017), most authors would refer to at least three common elements being human, structural, and relational capital, which has its origins in the Skandia Navigator model proposed by Leif Edvinsson in the early 1990s (Skandia, 1994). While the three IC elements help us classify different types of IC, it is by no means a definition.

Usually, when defining a term like 'intellectual capital', is it best to break it into separate components and then join the definitions together. As a noun, intellectual means a person having a high degree of intellect, while as an adjective, it relates to the intellect of a person or within an object. As for capital, when used as an adjective it relates to the principal assets used in business to create wealth. Thus, when putting these terms together, IC is the sum of the principal intellectual assets within a business used to create wealth. Hence, it is not surprising that people use the term IC synonymously with the terms intangible assets, intellectual assets, and intangibles (Eccles and Krzus, 2010).

The above definition is closely related to one of the original IC definitions by Thomas Stewart, a *Forbes Magazine* journalist in the 1990s, who wrote one of the first seminal books about IC (Stewart, 1997, p. x): "the sum of everything everybody in a company knows that gives it a competitive edge . . . Intellectual Capital is intellectual material, knowledge, experience, intellectual property, information . . . that can be put to use to create wealth".

However, Dumay (2016) replaces the word 'wealth' with the word 'value' for two reasons. First, most IC researchers, practitioners, and authors refer to 'value creation', rather than 'wealth creation' (Mouritsen *et al.*, 2001a). Second, in today's society, organizations can no longer just focus on creating wealth because they must also concentrate on creating useful products and services, while at the same time contributing to society and not destroying the environment. These are what Dumay (2016) refers to as utility, and social and environmental value in conjunction with economic value.

The focus on economic value has also led to another IC definition based on the difference between the market and book values of a company. The advantage of this definition is that it provides a simple means of putting a monetary value on IC. However, it does not break down IC into its components and is subject to change on a regular basis, and thus is an unreliable measure (Dumay, 2012).

Additionally, Pike *et al.* (2006, p. 233) offer a third IC definition being "a holistic management methodology". Here, IC is part of a management philosophy that places IC within the boundary of the entire company. Pike *et al.* (2006) base their definition on the resource-based-view (RBV) of the firm, which recognizes the interaction of a combination of resources as being core to the development of competitive advantage and economic value (Barney, 1991). However, the RBV creates as many questions as it does answers because there is causal ambiguity relating to the difficulty in identifying the correct resources to accumulate and the inability to control them (e.g. human resources) (Dierickx and Cool, 1989, p. 1509). Therefore, a holistic management approach, which is uncritical of IC, may not offer a complete definition of IC because the philosophy does not expand beyond the boundaries of the firm.

IC and its early critical path

As evidenced above, IC has different definitions because people have different philosophical ideas about IC and its purpose. In the early days of IC, the writings of Stewart (1991),

Edvinsson and Malone (1997), and Roos *et al.* (1997) helped to "render invisible visible by creating a discourse that all could engage in" (Petty and Guthrie, 2000, p. 156). This 'first stage' of IC research was firmly established by the turn of the millennium and the second stage emerged to establish IC's legitimacy and to promote its further development (Petty and Guthrie, 2000). However, rendering the invisible visible in the second stage proved to be problematic because people also then wanted to ascribe a dollar value to IC. But how can you measure something that does not exist?

Sveiby's criticisms

One of the first people to become critical of measuring IC or intangibles was Karl-Erik Sveiby, who set up a webpage in 2004 warning of the potential problems associated with measuring IC and continued to update the webpage for several years (Sveiby, 2010). Sveiby had three critical messages based upon what he called the "fundamental dilemma" of measuring intangibles "because it is not possible to measure social phenomena with anything close to scientific accuracy". First, he warned against the use of IC measures for management control purposes – as most employees react negatively to being measured, people would attempt to game the new system for their benefit. Similarly, Gowthorpe (2009) outlines that measuring IC may end up being just another interesting way to bully people rather than a way to understand and create value.

Additionally, using imprecise intangible measures could lead to producing unintended results. Kerr (1995, p. 7) argues that the behaviour rewarded is often the undesired behaviour, while the desired behaviour is not. Sveiby (2010) uses the example of Royal Dutch Shell, the managers of which in the late 1990s were rewarded for increasing the oil reserves under the company's control – unsurprisingly the reserves increased. However, in 2004, Shell was embarrassed to disclose that the managers were systemically overstating the reserves and had to adjust down previously disclosed reserves by 23 per cent. Shell fired the managers, but Sveiby (2010) lays the blame not just on the managers but also on the reward system (see also, Kerr, 1995).

Second, Sveiby (2010) warns against using IC reporting as a public relations exercise. For example, Swedish insurance company Skandia was famous for publishing the world's first external IC statement and was not shy about publicising its value creation story in subsequent IC supplements (Skandia, 1994, 1995, 1996, 1998). However, can a company always rely on its IC? As Sveiby (2010) observes, "those who bought Skandia shares based on their IC supplements back then were looking at losses amounting to 90% in 2002" as sales and profits fell sharply (Dumay, 2012). However, when Dumay (2016, pp. 170–171) interviewed Skandia's former chief IC architect, Leif Edvinsson, in 2012, a discussion ensued about the reasons for Skandia's demise, where Edvinsson disclosed:

> So there was a lot of financial muscle and market muscle and a lot of old customer value in it, and millions of customer relationships, which you could leverage if you renewed the organisation rather than doing the opposite saying "OK let's start to harvest!" They didn't actually say that but behaved that way. So they looked at the balance sheet and saw that "Wow, we can sell off!" … then they stripped the organisation of its velocity.

Thus, while Skandia made use of public relations to develop its business in the 1990s, it was switching to harvesting cash from the business and the subsequent lack of focus on IC led to its eventual demise. The executive managers did such a good job of harvesting cash that it eventually led to criminal fraud investigations[1] and the then CEO, Lars-Eric Petersson, was convicted of fraud and sentenced to two years jail for giving 156 million kronor ($21.4 million) in bonuses to company executives without board approval.[2]

Third, Sveiby (2010) advocates that IC should be used solely to help companies and their people learn. He argues that measuring intangibles and IC helps companies become more efficient by uncovering costs and giving them the opportunity to explore other value creation activities. However, Sveiby (2010) does admit that there is a fine line between management control and learning and advocates producing bottom-up, self-directed, open, and comparable metrics that are used to reward groups, rather than individual employees.

Critical accounting scholarship

While Sveiby was criticizing IC from a measurement perspective, a substantive critique of IC was also emerging from articles published by critical scholars in the *Accounting, Auditing and Accountability Journal* (*AAAJ*) in 2001 as well as the *JIC* in two special issues in 2004 by Marr and Chatzkel (2004) and 2006 by O'Donnell *et al.* (2006a). Each of these special issues is discussed next.

Sunrise in the knowledge economy: managing, measuring, and reporting IC

The first critical special issue was published in *AAAJ* in 2001 (Vol. 14 Issue 1). In the opening to the special issue, Guthrie *et al.* (2001, p. 365) outline "that critical and social accounting academics have a vital role to play in making visible a number of important social issues that stem from understanding better the value of IC within both organisations and the wider social fabric".

The prominent critical article in the special issue is by Roslender and Fincham (2001, p. 383), who examine the debate about IC accounting for reporting and managerial purposes versus IC providing its own accounts, "rather than remaining imprisoned within accounts devised by others". Their criticism of accounting includes discussion of whether the purpose of financial accounting is to provide a historical view of accounting transactions, rather than using financial accounting to explain how market values are derived (Roslender and Fincham, 2001, pp. 387–390). In its place Roslender and Fincham (2001, p. 393) argue that we should be more concerned with how IC "might account for itself" through IC reporting.

While Roslender and Fincham (2001) examine reporting as a solution, other authors also investigate the then newfound interest in IC reporting as it was emerging from the perspective of early adopter Skandia (Mouritsen *et al.*, 2001b), from Ireland (Brennan, 2001), and reporting in general (Van Der Meer-Kooistra and Zijlstra, 2001). While these authors critically examine IC reporting, most do not sway from recommending that IC reporting should complement financial accounting and help to develop "the building blocks of an IC reporting model" (Van Der Meer-Kooistra and Zijlstra, 2001, p. 456).

Other critical articles investigate the accounting treatment of goodwill and intangible assets (Stolowy and Jeny-Cazavan, 2001), the value of IC in the police force (Collier, 2001), and IC from a financial institution and corporate governance perspective (Holland, 2001). As evidenced by these and the previously discusssed articles, the special issue offers an early insight into IC just after it became a hot topic, and helped to stimulate further critical IC research by opening up research questions based on the realm of IC, the spread of IC measurement, organizational fit, the role of information and communications technology, and the costs and benefits of IC. The latter costs and benefits proved an instrumental question as they are at the heart of the debate about IC theory (Dumay, 2012), and are a major topic in the first *JIC* critical IC special issue edited by Chatzkel (2004).

IC at a crossroads: becoming critical of IC

The first *JIC* special issue, "IC at the crossroads: Theory and research" examines research after the importance of IC had already been established (Petty and Guthrie's (2000) first stage). The special issue examines IC measurement (Andriessen, 2004; Grasenick and Low, 2004; Pike and Roos, 2004), theory (Mouritsen, 2004; O'Donnell, 2004) and research methods (Guthrie *et al.*, 2004; Marr *et al.*, 2004), and its application to e-commerce (Bakhru, 2004). Thus, these papers began to critically examine *how* IC is measured, theorized, researched, and applied, rather than just providing normative arguments about *why* IC is important.

The last article in the special issue by Jay Chatzkel (2004) outlines how IC was at a cross-roads of relevance because IC was transitioning to its next stage. Chatzkel (2004) also argues that IC needed to transform into a working discipline, rather than a theoretical one, that was useful to organizations for achieving strategic outcomes. Furthermore, Chatzkel (2004, p. 337) outlines how IC needed to move forward as a discipline, otherwise "the notion of intellectual capital and all it stands for will be seen as merely one more set of very interesting ideas that is continuingly elusive to grasp and use". Thus, IC was a stage where it needed to break free from being a management fad or fashion, and become an established management tool (Serenko and Bontis, 2013, p. 477).

Becoming critical on IC

The Chatzkel (2004) article then helped inspire the second special issue by O'Donnell *et al.* (2006a) entitled "Becoming critical on intellectual capital". As O'Donnell *et al.* (2006a, p. 5) outline, "IC is at a 'crossroads'; one of these roads takes a critical stance and the purpose of both the CMS stream and this special issue is to initiate some exploratory discourse on IC from this perspective". The special issue emanates from papers presented during the IC Stream at the 4th International Critical Management Studies Conference at Cambridge University, UK, in July 2005. Most importantly, this *JIC* special issue sought understanding of how "IC could make a difference for the better" (O'Donnell *et al.*, 2006a).

To frame the special issue, O'Donnell *et al.* (2006a, p. 6) introduces a critical manage-ment studies perspective, which "addresses a wide range of issues that extend from diversity to globalization, from labour process to philosophy, from technology to sexuality and gen-der". The special issue is a collection of articles from differing perspectives critiquing IC based on philosophy (Chaharbaghi and Cripps, 2006; Spender, 2006), innovation (Voepel *et al.*, 2006), research (Abeysekera, 2006), language (Andriessen, 2006; Jørgensen, 2006), and labour (O'Donnell *et al.*, 2006b). To conclude the special issue, O'Donnell *et al.* (2006a, p. 6) ascertains that the articles "present a provocative range of perspectives that need to be taken into account as we move across through our threshold and onto the next stage of intellectual capital".

On reviewing the articles presented, it is evident that they do present a provocative per-spective on IC. For example, the Chaharbaghi and Cripps (2006) article, "Intellectual capital: Direction, not blind faith" challenges the very foundations of the first stage of IC. They argue that IC is not reducible to a number that indicates increases or decreases in an organiza-tion's IC. Rather, IC is fluid and indicators represent the direction "imagination, creativity and learning" is taking (Chaharbaghi and Cripps, 2006, p. 29). In support, Victor Newman, whose commentary at the end of the article outlines how two ideas presented in Thomas Stewart's seminal book *Intellectual Capital* (Stewart, 1997) – that IC can be managed similarly to physical assets and investing in knowledge helps create monetary wealth – are unproven assumptions (Chaharbaghi and Cripps, 2006, p. 42). In support, Dumay (2012) later argues that these assumptions are akin to unsubstantiated IC grand theories, which are barriers to implementing IC practices, rather than enablers of IC practice. Thus, the O'Donnell *et al.* (2006a) special issue came at a time where the foundations of IC were on shaky ground and outlined that a more critical path to IC was needed for it to progress beyond being just an interesting idea based on unproven assumptions.

The critical and performative practice turn

The next stage of IC thinking is now commonly known as the third stage, testing IC's ideology and assumptions (Guthrie *et al.*, 2012) and taking what Guthrie and Dumay (2015, p. 260) call the "practice turn". The original turning point is arguably an article by Mouritsen (2006), which introduces a different way of thinking about IC based on the work of Latour (1986), using the dichotomy of ostensive versus performative IC, or as Mouritsen labels it, IC1 and IC2 (Table 2.1). Put simply, ostensive relates to the IC 'big picture', attempting to make a predictable link to creating value. In contrast, performative is how IC works in organizations and society where knowledge transforms and is valuable because it accomplishes something.

The distinction between IC helping create value or being valued is an important philosophical difference. It questions whether managing IC makes an organization worth more,

Table 2.1 Themes in IC research

Theme	IC1 – Ostensive	IC2 – Performative
The IC proposition. Questions about how IC works in an organizational or social context	IC is related predictably to knowledge and value objects and objectives in a pre-set model	IC is part of a configuration of knowledge management and actively mobilized to condition effects
	IC, knowledge, and strategy are linked through causal mapping and related to effects of IC on value creation	IC is mobilized idiosyncratically in attempts to make a knowledge-based organization perform towards endogenously defined values
IC concepts. Questions about how IC elements are to be understood and analysed	IC consists of human, organizational and customer capital each of which has functional qualities and are thus value generating assets not visible in the firm's balance sheet. IC has descriptive qualities and measurement is essence	IC is a representation of knowledge resources the transformative qualities of which emerge in application. IC has classification qualities and measurement is convention
Value of IC. Questions about how IC is related to value creation	Risk and return Predictive information Market-to-book	Strategic values User values Ability to accomplish something

Source: Adapted from Mouritsen (2006, p. 824)

as Stewart and Losee (1994) and Skandia (1995) claimed in the 1990s. Thus, the third stage focused on whether IC could make a difference, rather than just make companies and their shareholders wealthier.

Critical IC

The view that measuring and accounting for IC, and that IC should be included on the balance sheet and thus needed managing to benefit financial capital, was well entrenched by 2005 (Fincham *et al.*, 2005). Thus, the time was ripe for a more critical examination of IC because the class that gives intellect "to intellectual capital – labour – finds itself subordinate to capital" (Fincham *et al.*, 2005, p. 351). This view led to another special issue on IC, this time in the journal *Critical Perspectives on Accounting (CPA)* in 2009 (Mouritsen and Roslender, 2009).

What emerges from this special issue is a continuing concern about the ethics of IC as a management technology. As Mouritsen and Roslender (2009, p. 802) outline, the concern raises two questions: 'does the measurement of knowledge (resources) produce effects; and is the concern to inscribe the person in the intellectual capital statement an act of appropriation which raises ethical concerns?' The papers in this *CPA* special issue challenge the accounting foundations of IC by examining calculation (Mårtensson, 2009), numbering (McPhail, 2009), reporting (Nielsen and Madsen, 2009), quantification (Gowthorpe, 2009), and measuring people (Roslender and Stevenson, 2009).

To conclude the special issue, Mouritsen and Roslender (2009, p. 803) outline how researchers and managers still struggle with accounting for IC to the point that scholars are "unquestioning" of IC, and muse that IC accounting has become part of the mainstream. Mouritsen and Roslender (2009, p. 803) argue that the papers in the special issue demonstrate how it is beneficial to take a more critical perspective towards IC to ensure it is useful for the betterment of society, and not just to take advantage of people for the sake of creating monetary wealth.

IC measurement: a critical approach

While Mouritsen and Roslender were developing their CPA special issue, a then Australian PhD student, John Dumay, was writing his thesis (Dumay, 2008a) based on IC in action and partly inspired by Mouritsen's (2006) ostensive versus performative IC agenda. In the thesis, Dumay included four published articles, which examine "How is IC?" rather than "What is IC?" (Dumay and Tull, 2007; Dumay, 2008b, 2009a, 2009b). Of the four articles in the thesis, arguably an important paper is "Intellectual capital measurement: A critical approach" (Dumay, 2009a), which is the most cited of the articles.[3]

Dumay (2009a) is important because it introduces complexity theory into IC research to help reduce the causal ambiguity problem (Dierickx and Cool, 1989) surrounding IC's ability to accomplish something. In considering how IC can be measured, Dumay (2009a) applies complexity theory because it deals with understanding systems exhibiting non-linear relationships between the elements of the system and is characterized by the observation that small changes to one or two parameters have significant, emerging, and unexpected effects on the system as a whole (Snowden and Boone, 2007). In his research Dumay (2009a) views organizations as complex systems. and by applying complexity theory-based research methods he develops different insights into IC, which may not be discovered using the then contemporary IC measurement and research frameworks. As Dumay (2009a) highlights, using both numbers and narratives shows how researchers can make sense of the complex interactions between

IC elements	IC components	Value dimension			
		Positive customer experience	Creates value for the company	Beating the competition	Creates value for the customer
Relational capital	Positive customer experience	X	***	***	***
	Creates value for the company	***	X	***	***
	I can see the customer	***	*	*	**
	Sharing knowledge externally	**	**	**	***
	Requires a knowledge worker	**	**	**	**
	Beating the competition	***	***	X	**
	Creates value for customer	***	***	**	X
	Requires a process worker	*	**	*	*
	Technology helping customers	***	***	***	***
Structural capital	Product focussed	**	**	**	***
	Innovative products	**	**	**	***
	Performance is product based	*	*	**	**
	Easy to use technology	**	**	**	**
	People helping customers	***	***	**	***
	Effective lines of communication	***	***	**	**
	Technology supports customers	***	**	**	***
	Technology supports processes	**	**	**	**
Human capital	The work is engaging	**	***	**	**
	Trained and competent staff	**	**	**	**
	Learning from others	**	**	**	**
	Long term career	***	**	**	**
	Set in their ways	*	*	*	*
	An attractive place to work	**	**	**	**
	The new generation	*	*	*	*
	Looking to retire	*	*	*	*

Figure 2.1   Value dimensions and inter-actions with IC components

Source: Adapted from Dumay (2009a, p. 202)

IC resources contributing to value creation and thus reduce the causal ambiguity of intangible resources (Dierickx and Cool, 1989, pp. 1508–1509).

To do so, Dumay (2009a) presents visual maps of IC interactions showing how different elements of IC interact to create value. In Figure 2.1, the dark squares indicate a strong relationship between an IC element (rows) and a value dimension (columns). In this case, he shows how structural and relational capital is needed more than human capital to create value, which goes against the common belief that human capital is the most important. Identifying what IC elements create value in specific cases allows for more effective IC management because the analysis diminishes the ambiguity surrounding value creation.

While the Dumay (2009a) article is important because it addresses the causal ambiguity problem, he also uses a critical management framework to analyse IC research based on the work of Alvesson and Deetz (2000).

Critical management studies as an analytical framework

A notable analytical feature in the Dumay (2009a) articles is inspired by the writing of Alvesson and Deetz (2000) in their book *Doing Critical Management Research*. The analysis is not original to the above article and first appeared in the conclusion section of Dumay (2008b) and later in his thesis of the same year (Dumay, 2008a). Dumay (2008a) justifies a critical analysis of IC in action because IC development parallels critical theory. Alvesson and Deetz (2000, p. 14) outline how critical theory is a response to changing social conditions in "science, industrialization and communication/information technologies". Similarly, IC came into prominence because of structural economic changes as knowledge, communication, and the importance of intangibles changed the way organizations now operate (Meritum Project, 2002). However, while most IC researchers promote the positive impacts of IC, the changes can also have negative impacts (e.g. Caddy, 2000; Leitner and O'Donnell, 2007).

Utilizing critique to examine IC transcends finding fault with IC by developing insights that identify and challenge the manner in which IC theory translates into practice. Examining contemporary theoretical IC frameworks is important because early academic research concentrated on establishing definitions, measures, and a proliferation of IC frameworks (e.g. Chatzkel, 2004; Sveiby, 2007; Guthrie *et al.*, 2012). Additionally, at that time, IC suffered from a lack of practice as evidenced by the relatively few organizations that systematically disclose their IC (e.g. Brennan, 2001; April *et al.*, 2003; Bontis, 2003; Ordóñez de Pablos, 2003; Guthrie *et al.*, 2006; Unerman *et al.*, 2007), which arguably continues to date (Dumay, 2016). Thus, a framework is needed to analyse what IC is (insight), to critique its application, and to offer new ways forward (transformative redefinition).

According to Alvesson and Deetz (2000, p. 17), the task of 'insight' is to demonstrate "our commitment to the hermeneutic, interpretive and ethnographic goals of local understandings closely connected to and appreciative of the lives of real people in real situations". So, insight from a critical IC perspective involves trying to understand the impact of IC practices on both the people and their organizations. Thus, the question is not 'What is intellectual capital?' but 'How is intellectual capital?' (O'Donnell *et al.*, 2006a, p. 7).

The objective of critique "is to counteract the dominance of taken-for-granted goals, ideas, ideologies, and discourses which put their imprints on management and organization phenomena" (Alvesson and Deetz, 2000, p. 18). Arguably, a critique of IC is important because of the development of contemporary IC terminology and ideas from traditional management thinking. The most prominent relates to the term 'intellectual capital', which leads to a misunderstanding of the nature of IC. For example, the word capital implies that knowledge is a form of material wealth to be managed like physical assets and that investing in these assets leads to the creation and possession of knowledge, resulting in more wealth, both of which are empirically unproven (Newman as quoted in Chaharbaghi and Cripps, 2006, p. 42). Thus, it is necessary to critique existing IC theories to understand whether they apply or are barriers to implementing in practice (Dumay, 2012).

The last task of this critical perspective "is the development of critical, managerially relevant knowledge and practical understandings that enable change and provide skills for new ways of operating" (Alvesson and Deetz, 2000, p. 19). This task is important for managing an organization's IC because of the inherent contradictions in IC's espoused benefits and the reality of organizational practices (Dumay, 2012). For example, as Mouritsen (2006, pp. 835–836) points out, organizations are more likely to invest in human capital when they are 'in the black' and to reduce the number of employees when they are 'in the red'. Reducing employees in lean times contradicts the espoused benefits of human capital, which advocates the need to invest in employees because investing in human capital is beneficial for long-term wealth generation. These and other contradictions will continue to evolve from ongoing IC research and are opportunities to develop IC research into future management practices (see Alvesson and Deetz, 2000, p. 20).

Introducing third stage IC research

An important turning point in IC research is the Guthrie *et al*. (2012) article reviewing a decade of IC accounting research, introducing the third stage of IC research. The analysis in this article uses Mouritsen's (2006) ostensive versus performative IC theorization to outline how "research is emerging based on a critical and performative analysis of IC practices in action" (Guthrie *et al*., 2012, p. 69). Their conclusion, based on finding that much of the past research into IC was commentary and normative policy rather than empirical papers, opens the opportunity for more research examining IC practices. As Guthrie *et al*. (2012, p. 79) emphasize:

> We must challenge the status quo, employ innovative methodologies, experiment with the novel and take risks. We encourage you to watch the ICA space in the next decade for more critical field studies which will provide empirical studies of IC in action and help develop broader theoretical research.

Since the Guthrie *et al*. (2012) article was published, it has inspired many IC researchers to follow the critical and performative path. Thus the article is the most influential IC article published since 2012. For example, the article is heavily cited[4] and was a winner of a prestigious Emerald Citations of Excellence Award[5] in 2015. While the call for performative research became prominent after the paper's publication, there is still a strong interest in ostensive IC research that examines IC's causal effect on organizational performance (e.g. Joshi *et al*., 2013). However, evidence of how important the critical perspective is to IC researchers is the large number of articles and growing number of citations that critical IC research is now receiving (e.g. Dumay, 2012; Dumay and Garanina, 2013; Edvinsson, 2013; Iazzolino and Laise, 2013). Additionally, the IC third stage was the topic of another special issue of the *JIC* (Vol. 14 Issue 1), in the following year (Dumay, 2013).

This *JIC* special issue called for case studies and/or reflections of how organizations have implemented IC in practice and what they learned from it and encouraged articles from academics and practitioners who have got their 'hands dirty' by working in or with organizations that have mobilized IC in practice. In response, the *JIC* special issue published articles critically examining innovation (Yu and Humphreys, 2013), IC in action (Giuliani, 2013), SMEs (Henry, 2013), sustainability (Wasiluk, 2013), and education (Oliver, 2013), but most importantly, included two articles that use an interventionist approach to IC research (Chiucchi, 2013; Demartini and Paoloni, 2013). The latter two articles are important because they demonstrate how academic researchers can develop critical insights into IC practice by working alongside managers to solve real-life problems, rather than just observe practices. Using interventionist research also helps bridge the gap between academia and practice because it allows for the testing of IC theory, and makes a practical and academic contribution (Jönsson and Lukka, 2007; Dumay, 2010; Dumay and Baard, 2017). In essence, these articles demonstrate how academics got their 'hands dirty' working with organizations implementing IC practices.

This *JIC* special issue also contains two commentary articles by Dumay (2013) and Edvinsson (2013), which openly question the future of IC. Most notably, Edvinsson (2013, p. 163) reflects on 21 years of IC research and laments, "We need to go beyond IC reporting. We are on the edge of something, but what?" In answering "What?", Edvinsson (2013) advocates expanding the boundaries of IC to include nations and society in general and to think of IC as more of a "strategic ecosystem for sustainable value creation". In the same special issue, the conclusion to Dumay and Garanina's (2013, p. 21) literature review of third stage research identifies the fourth stage of IC research, which:

> [s]hifts the focus of IC within a firm to a longitudinal focus of how IC is utilized to navigate the knowledge created by countries, cities and communities and advocates how knowledge can be widely developed thus switching from a managerial to an eco-system focus.[6]

Thus, one way forward for IC is to remove the boundaries that lock IC into an inward looking managerial and organizational focus (see also, Gowthorpe, 2009). Therefore, another critical approach based on the impact of IC on the wider ecosystem has evolved and is discussed next.

Fourth stage IC research: an ecosystem approach

While the idea of an IC research fourth stage first appears in Dumay and Garanina (2013, p. 21), its roots are in social and environmental accounting inspired by Gray's (2006) article "Social, environmental and sustainability reporting and organisational value creation?: Whose value? Whose creation?" In the article, referred to by Gray (2006, p. 793) as an 'essay', he challenges the role of social, environmental, and sustainability accounting and reporting, asking whether it should contribute to shareholder value and critiques the term value from a financial accounting perspective. Gray (2006, pp. 804–805) refers to three different approaches: managerialist, triple-bottom-line, and an ecological and ecojustice approach. Looking at the IC third stage, arguably it equates to a managerialist perspective because it is company-based and voluntary whereby IC is selectively managed, and it is assumed there is no conflict between economic value creation and the society in which the organization operates. As such the managerialist approach looks inward at the chosen practices of the organization and only considers how the society and environment impact the organization, rather than how the organization impacts society and the environment.

Arguably, the fourth stage ecosystem approach is not new to IC research and has its theoretical foundations in the work of Ahmed Bounfour. According to Chatzkel (2004, p. 339), it is Bonfour who in the late 1990s identified the transaction perspective as "the dominant perspective of capitalism" with efficiency being "the main driver for appraising individual and corporate actions". In contrast, Bonfour argued that we need to provide a community perspective beyond organizational boundaries (see also, Gowthorpe, 2009).SS

How the fourth stage develops will be interesting because researchers are already using it to inspire their research and publish articles using the ecosystem approach. For example, Dameri and Ricciardi (2015) use the approach to study "Smart city intellectual capital". Similarly, Secundo *et al.* (2016) use the IC fourth stage approach in developing an integrated IC framework for managing universities. Their article blends the IC fourth stage with a collective intelligence approach towards understanding how universities can achieve their third mission, which represents how universities "have moved from focusing exclusively on their traditional twin missions of teaching and research, towards a more active role for economic and cultural growth" (p. 298). Thus, fourth stage research is looking beyond the organization as to how IC benefits the wider ecosystem of society and the environment.

Is critical IC research running out of steam?

To conclude this chapter, it is worth reflecting on whether IC research is running out of steam. The evidence from a critical perspective is that IC research is healthy and making continuous insights into its use as a different way of looking at organizations and society beyond financial value (wealth) creation. The fourth stage, with its roots in critical social and environmental accounting, is the next, and potentially promising, area of critical IC research.

Additionally, there is a continuing discourse questioning the managerial approach to IC in an attempt to distance IC from a narrow to a broader focus. For example, Dumay (2016) has all but declared the death of IC reporting, which was at the heart of early academic and practitioner attempts to make IC relevant to organizations and their stakeholders, that is, aimed at shareholders and potential investors. However, the mantra that IC and intangibles are most important from an investor perspective lives on in continuing attempts to develop first and second stage research and practice agendas based on reporting (IIRC, 2013; Lev and Gu, 2016), showing how many researchers continue to be concerned with wealth creation, and not value creation (Dumay, 2016).

From an IC perspective, there is a potential resurgence in IC reporting because of the inclusion of IC, along with social and human capital, as part of the six capitals framework in the integrated reporting (<IR>) guidelines (IIRC, 2013). However, the <IR> guidelines have been suffering the same problem as IC in that there is a lower than expected take-up of <IR> than its supporters would like (Dumay, 2016), which has prompted a preliminary review of <IR> to understand the quality of <IR> adoption to date by examining issues such as interpreting the framework, costs, benefits, enablers and barriers to adoption, and the effectiveness of existing guidance and other tools.[7] Such a review may be helpful in further advancing how IC is integrated into corporate business models, and there is a role for critical IC researchers to play in developing inputs into the <IR> debate.

However, there is also a role for critical IC researchers to play in moving beyond the wealth creation myth because once again, another framework has emerged advocating how accounting is broken and offering a new way forward. The latest intangibles and thus IC reporting proposal comes from the US, where Lev and Gu (2016) propose a new report called the *Strategic Resources & Consequences Report* based on the resource-based theory of the firm. The report looks strikingly similar to IC reports and includes both numeric and narrative information (Mouritsen *et al.*, 2001a). However, the report is specifically targeted at investors and managers, and Lev and Gu (2016), rather than including social and environmental concerns, are somewhat dismissive of these essential elements of fourth stage IC. For example,

Lev and Gu (2016, pp. 1722–1723) outline "Even major environmental disasters, like the Exxon Valdez spill (March 1989), were, in retrospect, just a hiccup in the relentless growth path of the company". Unfortunately, there is a continuing discourse that considers intangibles as solely relevant for wealth creation and not for the benefit of society and the environment, or more disturbingly, despite society and the environment. Thus, there is a need for critical IC researchers to investigate the claims made by Lev and Gu (2016), and even take a stand against such biased rhetoric that puts profits before people.

While the above presents evidence that critical IC research is not running out of steam, the evidence also helps build an argument that IC research is becoming too narrow and disjointed. Notably, the Lev and Gu (2016) book is squarely targeted at a North American audience and this highlights the narrowness of research and thinking about intangible assets from an accounting perspective. However, from a European perspective, Cuozzo *et al.*'s (2017) recent review of IC disclosure studies reveals that the majority of IC disclosure research does not include the US, and the journals publishing IC disclosure studies are exclusively European journals.

IC research is also disjointed, because the term IC has different meanings in different contexts, especially in the US, where it is more synonymous with intellectual property (structural capital), rather than the combination of human, structural, and relational capital (Cuozzo *et al.*, 2017). Eccles and Krzus (2010, p. 84) note "intangible assets generally has no accepted meaning and is used interchangeably with the terms intellectual assets, IC, and intangibles. We will treat them as one, using the term intangible assets for the sake of simplicity". This quote reinforces that IC is ambiguous in different contexts.

As Cuozzo *et al.* (2017) outline, the term intangible assets is more common than IC in business parlance, while a narrow group of academics appear to be stuck on the term intellectual capital. The path forward for critical IC researchers is one that not only questions IC but also questions its foundations. Critical IC researchers need to recognize that IC means something different in different social, economic, and political contexts and there is a need to reflect on what and where we are researching. Doing so will help recharge the energy in the critical IC research agenda.

Fifth stage IC research: research without boundaries?

IC research is now almost 30 years old. However, it needs constant recharging if it is to remain relevant. In particular, by sticking to the narrow term intellectual capital based on a European conceptualization of IC, it will no doubt produce narrow research constrained to a narrow audience (Cuozzo *et al.*, 2017). As outlined above, the research most people reading this book will be familiar with refers to IC as human, structural, and relational capital. Unfortunately, while the definition helps to categorize IC and help people understand what IC is, it also constrains our thinking. A good example is the concept of value creation, which traditionally is based on a shareholder or customer (utility) perspective (Bourguignon, 2005). As exemplified in fourth stage IC research, the value concept is extended to include social and environmental value (see, Dumay, 2016, pp. 169–171). However, extending IC to include two additional values also constrains thinking. In the fifth stage of IC research, IC researchers need to remove these boundaries, and the question they ask needs changing from 'what is IC worth to investors, customers, society and the environment?' to 'is managing IC a worthwhile endeavour?' Asking the latter question removes the boundaries from IC research to include all manner of worth and recognizes that IC is a substantial part of what impacts everyone on a day-to-day basis.

One of the main challenges faced is that because of different views on IC value, different forms of IC value have different worths to different people and we, as IC researchers, have yet to reconcile this point (see, Boltanski and Thévenot, 2006). As identified earlier, the recent book by Lev and Gu (2016) clearly shows that worth to many people is primarily focused on building a strong capital market and that identifying the intangible assets that create value is the only shareholder interest. They base their argument on the belief that if managers disclose more information about the key intangibles that create economic value, a major driver of economic growth, benefits 'trickle down' to all of society (Lev and Gu, 2016). The argument is similar to the theory espoused by Aghion and Bolton (1997, p. 151) whereby "it is widely believed that the accumulation of wealth by the rich is good for the poor since some of the increased wealth of the rich trickles down to the poor". However, many IC researchers do not believe in the trickle-down theory and cannot reconcile that wealth creation is a paramount worth, especially when it relegates some members of society to poverty, and places weath creation ahead of social and environmental concerns. But without creating economic value, society cannot function either. So where is the balance? Or is there a balance?

In part, the current critical perspective on IC research may be partly to blame because it critiques the current thinking and has not done enough to expand IC boundaries. For example, Dumay (2009a) critiques the 'accountingization' of IC, rather than looking at the benefits of the approach that might provide valuable insights into how IC can be better measured economically, which in turn can help create economic value. While the European concept of IC research does not substantially focus on economic value, it appears that in North America they have taken the opposite approach and this helps explain why US researchers concentrate on investigating the accounting term intangible assets rather than IC (Eccles and Krzus, 2010, p. 84). In a society where wealth creation is considered paramount, this approach is consistent with the concept of worth.

Our observation is that these terms are generally used synonymously, yet the term intangible assets is much broader than those assets that create economic value and includes everything that is not tangible that is put to use to create value. However, we must also not forget that all forms of value creation always rely on tangible assets. For example, one of the key strengths of the <IR> approach is including financial, physical, and natural capital into its value creation model (IIRC, 2013), something that many IC researchers are only just coming to internalize. Therefore, it is time to take the boundaries off IC research and work towards reconciling the worth of IC to different people in different contexts and respecting that there will always be differences and that one view should not always prevail.

Notes

1 Chairman quits amid Skandia probe. *The Evening Standard*, 1 December 2003, p. 32.
2 Court sentences Skandia ex-CEO to jail for fraud. *The Wall Street Journal Asia*, 26 May 2006, p. 6.
3 As at 18 December 2016, the article had received 190 citations according to Google Scholar https://scholar.google.com.au/citations?user=zKFxle4AAAAJ&hl=en.
4 As at 26 December 2016, the article had 226 Google Scholar citations, see https://scholar.google.com.au/citations?view_op=view_citation&hl=en&user=zKFxle4AAAAJ&citation_for_view=zKFxle4AAAAJ:MXK_kJrjxJIC.
5 See www.emeraldgrouppublishing.com/authors/literati/citations/awards.htm?id=2015, accessed 26 December 2016. The selection process made by Emerald Journal's editorial experts is based initially on the citations being given to papers published in a previous year (in this case 2012). However, the judging panel also takes into account the content of the papers themselves in terms of novelty, interdisciplinary interest, and relevancy in today's world. While high academic and research standards are a prerequisite, these selections are ultimately peer-reviewed, but they are also a reflection of the high quality of work published in 2012.

6 Dumay, J. and Garanina, T. (2013), "Intellectual capital research: A critical examination of the third stage", *Journal of Intellectual Capital*, Vol. 14 No. 1, pp. 10–25 is also a 2016 winner of a prestigious Emerald Citations of Excellence Award. See www.emeraldgrouppublishing.com/authors/literati/citations/awards.htm?id=2016, accessed 27 December 2016.

7 See www.linkedin.com/groups/7019864/7019864-6217239579909455876, accessed 28 December 2016.

References

Abeysekera, I. (2006), "The project of intellectual capital disclosure: Researching the research", *Journal of Intellectual Capital*, Vol. 7, No. 1, pp. 61–77.

Aghion, P. and Bolton, P. (1997), "A theory of trickle-down growth and development", *The Review of Economic Studies*, Vol. 64, No. 2, pp. 151–172.

Alvesson, M. and Deetz, S. (2000), *Doing Critical Management Research*, Sage, London.

Andriessen, D. (2004), "IC valuation and measurement: Classifying the state of the art", *Journal of Intellectual Capital*, Vol. 5, No. 2, pp. 230–242.

Andriessen, D. (2006), "On the metaphorical nature of intellectual capital: A textual analysis", *Journal of Intellectual Capital*, Vol. 7, No. 1, pp. 93–110.

April, K. A., Bosma, P. and Deglon, D. A. (2003), "IC measurement and reporting: Establishing a practice in SA mining", *Journal of Intellectual Capital*, Vol. 4, No. 2, pp. 165–180.

Bakhru, A. (2004), "Managerial knowledge to organisational capability: New e-commerce businesses", *Journal of Intellectual Capital*, Vol. 5, No. 2, pp. 326–336.

Barney, J. B. (1991), "Firm resources and sustained competitive advantage", *Journal of Management*, Vol. 17, No. 1, pp. 99–120.

Boltanski, L. and Thévenot, L. (2006), *On Justification: Economies of Worth*, Princeton University Press, Princeton, NJ.

Bontis, N. (2003), "Intellectual capital disclosures in Canadian corporations", *Journal of Human Resource Costing and Accounting*, Vol. 7, No. 1, pp. 9–20.

Bourguignon, A. (2005), "Management accounting and value creation: The profit and loss of reification", *Critical Perspectives on Accounting*, Vol. 16, No. 4, pp. 353–389.

Brennan, N. (2001), "Reporting intellectual capital in annual reports: Evidence from Ireland", *Accounting, Auditing & Accountability Journal*, Vol. 14, No. 4, pp. 423–436.

Caddy, I. (2000), "Intellectual capital: Recognizing both assets and liabilities", *Journal of Intellectual Capital*, Vol. 1, No. 2, pp. 129–146.

Chaharbaghi, K. and Cripps, S. (2006), "Intellectual capital: Direction, not blind faith", *Journal of Intellectual Capital*, Vol. 7, No. 1, pp. 29–42.

Chatzkel, J. (2004), "Moving through the crossroads", *Journal of Intellectual Capital*, Vol. 5, No. 2, pp. 337–339.

Chiucchi, M. S. (2013), "Intellectual capital accounting in action: Enhancing learning through interventionist research", *Journal of Intellectual Capital*, Vol. 14, No. 1, pp. 48–68.

Collier, P. M. (2001), "Valuing intellectual capacity in the police", *Accounting, Auditing & Accountability Journal*, Vol. 14, No. 4, pp. 437–455.

Cuozzo, B., Dumay, J., Palmaccio, M. and Lombardi, R. (2017), "Intellectual capital disclosure: A structured literature review", *Journal of Intellectual Capital*, Vol. 18, No. 1, pp. 2–8.

Dameri, R. P. and Ricciardi, F. (2015), "Smart city intellectual capital:An emerging view of territorial systems innovation management", *Journal of Intellectual Capital*, Vol. 16, No. 4, pp. 860–887.

Demartini, P. and Paoloni, P. (2013), "Implementing an intellectual capital framework in practice", *Journal of Intellectual Capital*, Vol. 14, No. 1, pp. 69–83.

Dierickx, I. and Cool, K. (1989), "Asset stock accumulation and sustainability of competitive advantage", *Management Science*, Vol. 35, No. 12, pp. 1504–1511.

Dumay, J. (2008a), "Intellectual capital in action: Australian Studies", University of Sydney, Sydney.

Dumay, J. (2008b), "Narrative disclosure of intellectual capital: A structurational analysis", *Management Research News*, Vol. 31, No. 7, pp. 518–537.

Dumay, J. (2009a), "Intellectual capital measurement: A critical approach", *Journal of Intellectual Capital*, Vol. 10, No. 2, pp. 190–210.

Dumay, J. (2009b), "Reflective discourse about intellectual capital: Research and practice", *Journal of Intellectual Capital*, Vol. 10, No. 4, pp. 489–503.

Dumay, J. (2010), "A critical reflective discourse of an interventionist research project", *Qualitative Research in Accounting and Management*, Vol. 7, No. 1, pp. 46–70.

Dumay, J. (2012), "Grand theories as barriers to using IC concepts", *Journal of Intellectual Capital*, Vol. 13, No. 1, pp. 4–15.

Dumay, J. (2013), "The third stage of IC: Towards a new IC future and beyond", *Journal of Intellectual Capital*, Vol. 14, No. 1, pp. 5–9.

Dumay, J. (2016), "A critical reflection on the future of intellectual capital: From reporting to disclosure", *Journal of Intellectual Capital*, Vol. 17, No. 1, pp. 168–184.

Dumay, J. and Baard, V. (2017), "An introduction to interventionist research in accounting", in Hoque, Z., Parker, L. D., Covaleski, M. and Haynes, K. (Eds), *The Routledge Companion to Qualitative Accounting Research Methods*, Routledge, Taylor and Francis, Oxfordshire, UK.

Dumay, J. and Garanina, T. (2013), "Intellectual capital research: A critical examination of the third stage", *Journal of Intellectual Capital*, Vol. 14, No. 1, pp. 10–25.

Dumay, J. and Tull, J. (2007), "Intellectual capital disclosure and price sensitive Australian stock exchange announcements", *Journal of Intellectual Capital*, Vol. 8, No. 2, pp. 236–255.

Eccles, R. and Krzus, M. (2010), *One Report: Integrated Reporting for a Sustainable Strategy*, Wiley & Sons, Hoboken, NJ.

Edvinsson, L. (2013), "IC 21: Reflections from 21 years of IC practice and theory", *Journal of Intellectual Capital*, Vol. 14, No. 1, pp. 163–172.

Edvinsson, L. and Malone, M. S. (1997), *Intellectual Capital: Realising Your Company's True Value by Finding its Hidden Brainpower*, Harper Business, New York.

Fincham, R., Mouritsen, J. and Roslender, R. (2005), "Special issue on intellectual capital: Call for papers", *Critical Perspectives on Accounting*, Vol. 16, No. 3, pp. 351–352.

Giuliani, M. (2013), "Not all sunshine and roses: Discovering intellectual liabilities 'in action'", *Journal of Intellectual Capital*, Vol. 14, No. 1, pp. 127–144.

Gowthorpe, C. (2009), "Wider still and wider? A critical discussion of intellectual capital recognition, measurement and control in a boundary theoretical context", *Critical Perspectives on Accounting*, Vol. 20, No. 7, pp. 823–834.

Grasenick, K. and Low, J. (2004), "Shaken, not stirred: Defining and connecting indicators for the measurement and valuation of intangibles", *Journal of Intellectual Capital*, Vol. 5, No. 2, pp. 268–281.

Gray, R. (2006), "Social, environmental and sustainability reporting and organisational value creation? Whose value? Whose creation?", *Accounting, Auditing & Accountability Journal*, Vol. 19, No. 6, pp. 793–819.

Guthrie, J. and Dumay, J. (2015), "New frontiers in the use of intellectual capital in the public sector", *Journal of Intellectual Capital*, Vol. 16, No. 2, pp. 258–266.

Guthrie, J., Dumay, J., Ricceri, F., and Nielsen, C. (Eds), (2017), *The Routledge Companion to Intellectual Capital*, Routledge, London.

Guthrie, J., Petty, R. and Johanson, U. (2001), "Sunrise in the knowledge economy: Managing, measuring and reporting intellectual capital", *Accounting, Auditing & Accountability Journal*, Vol. 14, No. 4, pp. 365–384.

Guthrie, J., Petty, R. and Ricceri, F. (2006), "The voluntary reporting of intellectual capital: Comparing evidence from Hong Kong and Australia", *Journal of Intellectual Capital*, Vol. 7, No. 2, pp. 254–271.

Guthrie, J., Petty, R., Yongvanich, K. and Ricceri, F. (2004), "Using content analysis as a research method to inquire into intellectual capital reporting", *Journal of Intellectual Capital*, Vol. 5, No. 2, pp. 282–293.

Guthrie, J., Ricceri, F. and Dumay, J. (2012), "Reflections and projections: A decade of intellectual capital accounting research", *The British Accounting Review*, Vol. 44 No. 2, pp. 68–92.

Henry, L. (2013), "Intellectual capital in a recession: Evidence from UK SMEs", *Journal of Intellectual Capital*, Vol. 14, No. 1, pp. 84–101.

Holland, J. (2001), "Financial institutions, intangibles and corporate governance", *Accounting, Auditing & Accountability Journal*, Vol. 14, No. 4, pp. 497–529.

Iazzolino, G. and Laise, D. (2013), "Value Added Intellectual Coefficient (VAIC): A methodological and critical review", *Journal of Intellectual Capital*, Vol. 14, No. 4, pp. 547–63.

International Integrated Reporting Council (IIRC) (2013), *The International <IR> Framework*, International Integrated Reporting Council London.

Jönsson, S. and Lukka, K. (2007), "There and back again: Doing interventionist research in management accounting", in Chapman, C. S., Hopwood, A. G. and Shields, M. S. (Eds), *Handbook of Management Accounting Research*, Elsevier, Oxford, pp. 373–397.

Jørgensen, K. M. (2006), "Conceptualising intellectual capital as language game and power", *Journal of Intellectual Capital*, Vol. 7, No. 1, pp. 78–92.

Joshi, M., Cahill, D., Sidhu, J. and Kansal, M. (2013), "Intellectual capital and financial performance: An evaluation of the Australian financial sector", *Journal of Intellectual Capital*, Vol. 14, No. 2, pp. 264–285.

Kerr, S. (1995), "On the folly of rewarding A, while hoping for B", *Academy of Management Executive*, Vol. 9, No. 1, pp. 7–14.

Latour, B. (1986), "The powers of association", in Law, J. (Ed), *Power, Action and Belief: A New Sociology of Knowledge?*, Routledge & Kegan Paul, London, pp. 264–280.

Leitner, K.-H. and O'Donnell, D. (2007), "Conceptualizing IC management in R&D organizations: Future scenarios from the complexity theory perspective", in Chaminade, C. and Catasús, B. (Eds), *Intellectual Capital Revisited –Paradoxes in the Knowledge Organization*, Edward Elgar, Cheltenham, UK & Northampton MA, USA, pp. 80–101.

Lev, B. and Gu, F. (2016), *The End of Accounting and the Path Forward for Investors and Managers*, John Wiley & Sons, Inc., Hoboken, NJ.

Marr, B. and Chatzkel, J. (2004), "Intellectual capital at the crossroads: Managing, measuring, and reporting of IC", *Journal of Intellectual Capital*, Vol. 5, No. 2, pp. 224–229.

Marr, B., Schiuma, G. and Neely, A. (2004), "The dynamics of value creation: Mapping your intellectual performance drivers", *Journal of Intellectual Capital*, Vol. 5, No. 2, pp. 312–325.

Mårtensson, M. (2009), "Recounting counting and accounting: From political arithmetic to measuring intangibles and back", *Critical Perspectives on Accounting*, Vol. 20, No. 7, pp. 835–846.

McPhail, K. (2009), "Where is the ethical knowledge in the knowledge economy? Power and potential in the emergence of ethical knowledge as a component of intellectual capital", *Critical Perspectives on Accounting*, Vol. 20, No. 7, pp. 804–22.

Meritum Project (2002), *Guidelines for Managing and Reporting on Intangibles (Intellectual Capital Report)*, European Commission, Madrid.

Mouritsen, J. (2004), "Measuring and intervening: How do we theorise intellectual capital management", *Journal of Intellectual Capital*, Vol. 5, No. 2, pp. 257–267.

Mouritsen, J. (2006), "Problematising intellectual capital research: Ostensive versus performative IC", *Accounting, Auditing & Accountability Journal*, Vol. 19, No. 6, pp. 820–841.

Mouritsen, J. and Roslender, R. (2009), "Critical intellectual capital", *Critical Perspectives on Accounting*, Vol. 20, No. 7, pp. 801–803.

Mouritsen, J., Larsen, H. T. and Bukh, P. N. (2001a), "Intellectual capital and the 'capable firm': Narrating, visualising and numbering for managing knowledge", *Accounting, Organizations and Society*, Vol. 26, No. 7, pp. 735–762.

Mouritsen, J., Larsen, H. T. and Bukh, P. N. (2001b), "Valuing the future: Intellectual capital supplements at Skandia", *Accounting, Auditing & Accountability Journal*, Vol. 14, No. 4, pp. 399–422.

Nielsen, C. and Madsen, M. T. (2009), "Discourses of transparency in the intellectual capital reporting debate: Moving from generic reporting models to management defined information", *Critical Perspectives on Accounting*, Vol. 20, No. 7, pp. 847–854.

O'Donnell, D. (2004), "Theory and method on intellectual capital creation: Addressing communicative action through relative methodics", *Journal of Intellectual Capital*, Vol. 5, No. 2, pp. 294–311.

O'Donnell, D., Henriksen, L. B. and Voelpel, S. C. (2006a), "Guest editorial: Becoming critical on intellectual capital", *Journal of Intellectual Capital*, Vol. 7, No. 1, pp. 5–11.

O'Donnell, D., Tracey, M., Henriksen, L. B., Bontis, N., Cleary, P., Kennedy, T. and O'Regan, P. (2006b), "On the 'essential condition' of intellectual capital: Labour!", *Journal of Intellectual Capital*, Vol. 7, No. 1, pp. 111–128.

Oliver, G. R. (2013), "A micro intellectual capital knowledge flow model: A critical account of IC inside the classroom", *Journal of Intellectual Capital*, Vol. 14, No. 1, pp. 145–162.

Ordóñez de Pablos, P. (2003), "Intellectual capital reporting in Spain: A comparative view", *Journal of Intellectual Capital*, Vol. 4, No. 1, pp. 61–81.

Petty, R. and Guthrie, J. (2000), "Intellectual capital literature review: Measurement, reporting and management", *Journal of Intellectual Capital*, Vol. 1, No. 2, pp. 155–176.

Pike, S. and Roos, G. (2004), "Mathematics and modern business management", *Journal of Intellectual Capital*, Vol. 5, No. 2, pp. 243–256.

Pike, S., Boldt-Christmas, L. and Roos, G. (2006), "Intellectual capital: Origin and evolution", *International Journal of Learning and Intellectual Capital*, Vol. 3, No. 3, pp. 233–248.

Roos, J., Roos, G., Dragonetti, N. C. and Edvinsson, L. (1997), *Intellectual Capital: Navigating in the New Business Landscape*, Macmillan, Basingstoke, UK.

Roslender, R. and Fincham, R. (2001), "Thinking critically about intellectual capital accounting", *Accounting, Auditing & Accountability Journal*, Vol. 14, No. 4, pp. 383–399.

Roslender, R. and Stevenson, J. (2009), "Accounting for people: A real step forward or more a case of wishing and hoping?", *Critical Perspectives on Accounting*, Vol. 20, No. 7, pp. 855–869.

Secundo, G., Dumay, J., Schiuma, G. and Passiante, G. (2016), "Managing intellectual capital through a collective intelligence approach: An integrated framework for universities", *Journal of Intellectual Capital*, Vol. 17, No. 2, pp. 298–319.

Serenko, A. and Bontis, N. (2013), "Investigating the current state and impact of the intellectual capital academic discipline", *Journal of Intellectual Capital*, Vol. 14, pp. 476–500.

Skandia (1994), *Visualising Intellectual Capital at Skandia: Supplement to Skandia's 1994 Annual Report*, Skandia Insurance Company Ltd, Stockholm.

Skandia (1995), *Intellectual Capital: Value-Creating Processes: Supplement to Skandia's 1995 Annual Report*, Skandia Insurance Company Ltd, Stockholm.

Skandia (1996), *Power of Innovation: Intellectual Capital Supplement to Skandia's 1996 Interim Report*, Skandia Insurance Company Ltd, Stockholm.

Skandia (1998), *Human Capital in Transformation: Intellectual Capital Prototype Report, Skandia 1998*, Skandia Insurance Company Ltd, Stockholm.

Snowden, D. J. and Boone, M. E. (2007), "A leader's framework for decision making", *Harvard Business Review*, Vol. 85, No. 11, pp. 68–76.

Spender, J. C. (2006), "Method, philosophy and empirics in KM and IC", *Journal of Intellectual Capital*, Vol. 7, No. 1, pp. 12–28.

Stewart, T. A. (1991), "Brainpower", *Fortune*, Vol. 123, No. 11, pp. 44–50.

Stewart, T. A. (1997), *Intellectual Capital: The New Wealth of Organisations*, Doubleday-Currency, London.

Stewart, T. A. and Losee, S. (1994), "Your company's most valuable asset: Intellectual capital", *Fortune*, Vol. 130, No. 7, pp. 68–73.

Stolowy, H. and Jeny-Cazavan, A. (2001), "International accounting disharmony: The case of intangibles", *Accounting, Auditing & Accountability Journal*, Vol. 14, No. 4, pp. 477–497.

Sveiby, K. E. (2007), "Methods for measuring intangible assets", available at: www.sveiby.com/portals/0/articles/IntangibleMethods.htm (accessed 15 May 2007).

Sveiby, K. E. (2010), "Methods for measuring intangible assets", available at: www.sveiby.com/portals/0/articles/IntangibleMethods.htm (accessed 22 August 2010).

Unerman, J., Guthrie, J. and Striukova, L. (2007), *UK Reporting of Intellectual Capital*, ICAEW, University of London.

Van der Meer-Kooistra, J. and Zijlstra, S. M. (2001), "Reporting on intellectual capital", *Accounting, Auditing & Accountability Journal*, Vol. 14, No. 4, pp. 456–476.

Voepel, S., Leibold, M., Eckhoff, R. and Davenport, T. (2006), "The tyranny of the Balanced Scorecard in the innovation economy", *Journal of Intellectual Capital*, Vol. 7, No. 1, pp. 43–60.

Wasiluk, K. L. (2013), "Beyond eco-efficiency: Understanding CS through the IC practice lens", *Journal of Intellectual Capital*, Vol. 14, No. 1, pp. 102–126.

Yu, A. and Humphreys, P. (2013), "From measuring to learning? Probing the evolutionary path of IC research and practice", *Journal of Intellectual Capital*, Vol. 14, No. 1, pp. 26–47.

3

ACCOUNTING FOR PEOPLE

Robin Roslender and Lissa Monk

The emergence of intellectual capital (IC) as an exciting new field for study in the mid-1990s has resulted in a growing range of insights, many of which are documented in the various contributions to this collection. Among these are included a number that have had the consequence of progressing the challenge of accounting for people, a project that long predates the recognition of the significance of IC but which had largely become becalmed by that time. All too conscious of the naivety of identifying a single aspect of the IC field as being the most significant, this chapter is founded on the premise that in its contribution to 'taking people into account', we can readily recognize the importance of devoting further resources to the continued exploration of the IC field. And when doing so, it is desirable to ensure that people, from whom all IC emanates, are accorded the attention they clearly merit.

The first part of this chapter provides an overview of the history of accounting for people, from its identification as a major challenge to the accountancy profession almost a century ago, through a series of generic approaches to the task, and concluding with a discussion of human capital accounting envisaged as combining numbers and narratives to visualize the growth of an enterprise's stock of employee attributes. The second part of the chapter provides a number of insights on three pathways that IC researchers interested in progressing accounting for people might pursue: employee health and wellbeing; a broader range of human rights issues; and the role for human capital self-accounting.

So why would we wish to account for people?

As on previous occasions, the point of departure is evident in the assertion of Paton (1922, pp. 487–488), one of accounting's earliest theorists, that:

> In the business enterprise, a well-organized and loyal personnel may be a more important "asset" than a stock of merchandise ... At the present, there seems to be no way of measuring such factors in terms of the dollar; hence they cannot be recognized as specific economic assets. But let us, accordingly, admit the serious limitation of the conventional balance sheet as a statement of financial condition.

Paton believed that employees must be recognized as being as important to the pursuit of profit within the enterprise as its various other assets, not least stocks of raw materials and finished goods. In so doing, Paton would seem to have eschewed the popular notion that although labour had long been recognized as one of the three factors of production, it was now important to ensure it was not regarded as having an equivalent status to that presently accorded to either land or capital. Accounting for labour within the profit and loss (now income) statement, which was how the accountancy profession had traditionally taken people into account, in effect ensured a diminution of labour's importance. Labour was not to be viewed as an asset, to be cared for, even enhanced in some cases, but as a cost, an expense to be minimized in the pursuit of greater profitability. The cheaper the cost of labour, the more attractive an enterprise was represented to be for those who sought a return on their willingness to commit their financial capital through investment. Even at the time that Paton was writing there was a recognition that, in some instances, it might be possible to expel sections of labour from the enterprise, replacing it with machinery or physical capital as it was designated within the evolving accounting and finance literature. Physical capital is readily accommodated within the balance sheet.

It was clear to Paton that if accountants were to take employees into account in the guise of assets then, as the above quotation indicates, some means had to be found to 'put people on the balance sheet'. As a result, the critical role played by labour would be acknowledged. Almost a century later, most accounting practitioners would still identify the challenge of accounting for people in this way, reflecting both how many of them had become familiar with the issue in the course of their own training and how assets are normally taken into account. Whether they actually view employees as assets rather than costs is a different issue, however.

From theory to practice

It was some time before accounting scholars got round to seeking to enact Paton's suggestion. The first robust contribution to this exercise is identified with Hermanson some 40 years later, in the form of human asset accounting. Hermanson chose the topic as his doctoral work, producing a relatively short dissertation in 1963 (see also, Hermanson, 1964). The observation that he engaged with the issue of employees not being owned by enterprises, (i.e. not being slaves), suggests that some within the academy had already begun to think through the challenge. Hermanson's solution to the problem, identifying employees as operational assets as opposed to owned assets, still remains a useful response to those who might raise the slave issue in seminars and at conferences. This was the easy part of the challenge, however. What Hermanson quickly recognized was that if you want to put human assets on the balance sheet alongside other assets, then you need to identify their financial value. As with a whole range of intangible assets before them, and the much greater number of constituents of IC in the 21st century, this remains a major problem.

The general difficulty with valuing intangible assets is that such valuations attract the blanket criticism of being subjective in nature. The reason for this is that unlike tangible assets, many intangible assets are not initially purchased and therefore have no historical cost that might be identified via a transaction. When an enterprise purchases a piece of machinery, it can be incorporated into the balance sheet at its purchase price, its balance sheet value being reduced over time by means of the application of systematic depreciation charges. However, since the 1960s, there has been a reasonable degree of variation from this process. In some cases, it is accepted that certain assets actually appreciate in value after purchase, with land and buildings the most well-known examples. Their enhanced values are reported within the balance sheet accompanied by revaluation reserves designed to ensure that any increase in the value of an enterprise due to asset appreciation is not removed from the enterprise in the form of liquid assets. Only when the enterprise is sold is it possible to realize these enhancements in financial value. The price at which the enterprise is purchased then translates to being the new historical cost in the balance sheet of the purchaser.

For generations, it has been commonplace for acquiring enterprises to overpay when purchasing the assets (and liabilities) of another enterprise. This is understood to be the purchase of goodwill, arguably the quintessential intangible asset. Goodwill encompasses a whole range of different assets, including a workforce viewed as a collective asset that is recognized to gift a stock of attributes to an enterprise in excess, and often far in excess, of the cost of their contractual labour. Until relatively recently, convention was that an enterprise wrote off any purchased goodwill against its reserves, in pursuit of the prudence concept, leaving only acquired tangible assets on the balance sheet, to be depreciated over time. Nowadays the accounting treatment of goodwill is more enlightened, with provision for its systematic impairment or even its continued presence on the balance sheet at its purchase price. What is not permitted is any enhancement of financial value, even though in many enterprises the value of goodwill is recognized to appreciate over time. This state of affairs is arguably best understood in the context of brands, which for the past 30 years have been discussed as a critical standalone element of goodwill (and IC). During this time, the great majority of successful brands has appreciated in value but financial reporting regulations do not allow this to be reported on the balance sheet, even accompanied by the creation of a brand revaluation reserve. However, once a brand is sold, the acquiring enterprise can include it in its balance sheet at its new purchase price. What is particularly fascinating about this process is that for the past 30 years a growing number of brand consultancies have been able to determine financial valuations for brands, informing would be buyers (and sellers) on an on-going basis. Unfortunately, the global accountancy profession's subjectivity argument continues to prevail.

Understanding the value of the workforce as an element of goodwill was a situation in which Hermanson found himself. In any enterprise, such value is built up over time, as a consequence of which it might not readily be attributed to the individual workers currently employed in the enterprise. This before the issue of how different individuals might place a financial value on individual employees at different times as a result of inevitable personal preferences. And besides, there were no obvious signs of any objective valuations, since employees are not slaves! Hermanson's response to this situation was fundamentally academic in nature – to explore relevant financial valuation methodologies, which exercise accounted for the greater part of his dissertation. He identifies two that he regarded as being especially compelling: the unpurchased goodwill method and the adjusted present value method, although he must have recognized that it was extremely unlikely that either would be widely embraced in practice.

Hermanson was not the only person to advocate the development of some form of human asset accounting approach. The phrase 'putting people on the balance sheet' was coined in 1967 in a *Harvard Business Review* article by Hekemian and Jones, who seemed less concerned about the problem of identifying a subjective valuation methodology in order to do so, embracing something akin to an opportunity cost approach. Likert (1967) entitled one of the chapters of his text *The Human Organization* 'Human asset accounting', in which he identified a number of employee attributes that needed to be considered in any such exercise, and concluded with the confident assertion that accounting practitioners would be able to find a way to translate these attributes into robust financial numbers (for the balance sheet?). Thereafter the term 'human asset accounting' largely disappeared from the field, to be replaced by 'human resource accounting'. While the name change occurred, a continuing feature of the literature that accumulated over the next decade or so, after which the field went into steep decline, was focused around the pursuit of a silver bullet financial valuation methodology that would permit the incorporation of people on the balance sheet.

How about we try a different approach?

The term human resource accounting was coined by Brummet *et al.* (1968) in a seminal paper published in the *Accounting Review*. Flamholtz was to become the dominant presence within the accounting for people field quite soon thereafter, shifting the emphasis from one of identifying financial valuations for balance sheet purposes, although he did some of this in the early days in relation to service rewards (Flamholtz, 1971), to providing accounting information to managers for internal decision-making purposes. As a consequence, accounting for people was to be more usefully understood as a managerial accounting focus rather than a financial reporting focus. There is no dispute that Flamholtz viewed employees as assets but believed that the best way to take people into account was by means of a focus on the costs of human resource utilization. Putting people on the balance sheet held little attraction for Flamholtz.

Although Flamholtz commended a cost focus for his human resource accounting approach, he firmly rejected the conventional cost reduction emphases of such a perspective. His was a more nuanced position, one of drawing management's attention to the outlays they made on employees with the objective of promoting a greater level of efficiency in respect of the utilization of valuable human resources. Flamholtz was not interested in reducing labour costs by reducing the size of the workforce or the levels of its remuneration. Instead he sought to enable management to identify how it might better utilize its human resources, resources that he regarded as being crucial to successful enterprise performance. In a powerful articulation of his underlying philosophy published in 1974, Flamholtz identified three objectives of human resource accounting. The key objective was that of persuading management to "think people" at all times. It is possible to recognize Flamholtz as being one of the earliest advocates of what was later to be understood as strategic human resource management, as a development in human resource management, itself the successor to the long-established personnel management function.

For the greater part of the 1970s, human resource accounting and Flamholtz's perspective on it was a highly fashionable research field within accounting. It was also regarded as an aspect of behavioural accounting, itself similarly fashionable and in retrospect an important precursor to the emergence of organizational accounting as this was popularized in the early days of the journal *Accounting, Organizations and Society* (see Flamholtz, 1976). Despite a considerable emphasis on technical issues, including a continuing fascination with identifying a credible (financial) valuation model, by the beginning of the 1980s, human resource accounting was something of a spent force. A failure to contribute much in the way of a practical approach to accounting for people would seem to be the basic explanation of its passing. While 'putting people on the balance sheet' had an enduring popular appeal, it had made little or no progress in 20 years, with Flamholtz's enlightened managerialism probably being too radical for the vast majority of a profession that equated the management of labour costs with their reduction. Equally, there were other more important challenges in which to engage at this time, not least the perceived need to identify a conceptual framework for financial reporting (FASB, 1976) and the continuing presence of inflation within many advanced economies (Whittington, 1983).

The underlying thinking of Flamholtz's human resource accounting approach was embraced by a group of academics at Stockholm Business School's Personnel Economics Institute founded in 1988. As its name indicates, this was an interdisciplinary initiative that worked at the interface between several disciplines, including both accounting and finance. Human resource costing and accounting was identified as a potential successor to human resource accounting by two of the senior figures in the Institute, Gröjer and Johanson, most influentially in a 1991 pamphlet published by the Swedish Joint Industrial Safety Council. As with human resource accounting the balance sheet nexus was eschewed, human resource costing and accounting being promoted as a managerial development (Gröjer and Johanson, 1998). However, given Sweden's traditional social democratic inclinations it was inevitable that this was a largely progressive managerialism that took as axiomatic the need to ensure that any accounting for people be of benefit to all stakeholders. Johanson and Backlund (2006) provide evidence of Swedish enterprises promoting greater employee visibility within an expanded profit and loss statement. Human resource costing and accounting also identified utility analysis as a potentially insightful way of providing information on the outcomes of human resource investments, thereby complementing an accounting emphasis with one more akin to finance. The Personnel Economics Institute established the *Journal of Human Resource Costing and Accounting* in 1996, thereby providing an outlet for researchers who continued to be attracted to the idea of accounting for people, and within a few years the IC field.

Also strongly influenced by Flamholtz, Roslender and Dyson (1992) identified human worth accounting as a possible refinement of human resource accounting. Like Flamholtz, they were committed to the idea of taking employees into account as a managerial accounting development, with *worth* as the central focus. While accounting for the worth of employees was clearly an anathema to those who would seek to put people on the balance sheet, Roslender and Dyson took the view that recent developments with managerial accounting that had emerged in response to Kaplan's relevance critique (Kaplan, 1983, 1984; Johnson and Kaplan, 1987), meant that such a subjective notion as (employee) worth was no longer as forbidding as previously. It was now necessary to understand what attributes management valued in a workforce and which translated into their worth. Unfortunately, despite a number of interesting insights into what in principle was a radical approach to the challenge of accounting for people, Roslender and Dyson (1992) found themselves unable to fully escape the pursuit of some form of financial valuation perspective, albeit not for conventional balance sheet purposes.

Enter human capital

The identification of human capital as one of the three key components of IC, now recognized as an increasingly important foundation for competitive advantage, came as no surprise to anyone interested in accounting for people. Edvinsson (1997) strongly implies that human capital is in truth the more important component in his human capital/structural capital distinction, while Roslender and Fincham (2001) advance this view in a very explicit way, identifying human capital as primary intellectual capital and the origin of secondary intellectual capital, by which they mean many, although not all, of IC's various constituents. Human capital's (in the guise of employees') 'promotion' to the status of the key asset of any enterprise was the initial advance that the emergence of the IC field in the middle 1990s gifted anyone who retained a fascination with the challenge that had presented itself to Paton close to three quarters of a century earlier and that had consumed a significant extent of research effort during the 1970s. In this regard, it is not too surprising that among the influential contributions to the early growth of the IC literature we find a paper by Gröjer and Johanson (1998) in which they call for a renewal of research effort designed to take people into account.

The term human capital was by no means novel, however. In parallel with Hermanson's forays into human asset accounting, a number of labour economists had embraced the term (Schultz, 1961; Becker, 1964), drawing attention to many of the same attributes that the newly emergent IC literature focused on 30 years later. In the interim the human capital emphasis within labour economics had resulted in the accumulation of a sizeable literature that, perhaps inevitably, was quickly discovered by some IC writers. Fortunately, however, this literature did not have the consequence of smothering the embryonic IC field that quickly expanded in a number of directions in the next few years.

The introduction of IC into the accounting literature occurred at a time when the managerial accounting sub-discipline was beginning to demonstrate its new credentials as a source of relevant information for managers, following a decade of rapid, and at times iconoclastic, change. In the previous section the point has been made that Flamholtz, Gröjer and Johanson, and Roslender and Dyson were more attracted to the development of a managerial accounting perspective on accounting for people. For the most part, however, they remained locked into the traditional cost and value calculus that had characterized accounting for many decades. By the closing years of the 20th century some radical new thinking had begun to impact on accounting to management, which promised to make accounting for IC, including for human capital, more feasible.

Even before Kaplan (1983, 1984) began to question the relevance of contemporary management accounting theory and practice in the mid-1980s, a number of management accounting academics had identified the contribution of some new management accounting metrics. An interesting example of this is Simmonds' work on strategic management accounting in which he advocated a more outward-looking (strategic) approach to providing information to management in increasingly competitive markets (Simmonds 1981, 1982, 1986). Simmonds suggested the need to explore how it might be possible to collect information on competitors that managers might use to enhance and leverage their own competitiveness. From the outset, he questioned the wisdom of restricting such exercises to the development of accurate numbers, preferring to argue the case for more ballpark insights. This was something of a heresy to generations of accounting practitioners who had prided themselves on their calculative precision rather than their commercial acumen. Even more contentious was the observation that management accountants might make use of the numbers that were more normally associated with other management functions, including marketing management, Simmonds playfully warning that there was a danger that the latter function might soon pursue some reverse borrowing in their pursuit of greater influence in the enterprise. Several years later Bromwich and Bhimani made a strong case for the development of an even more progressive strategic management accounting oeuvre, premised on a perceived need to remove managerial accounting from the factory floor and refocused on the markets, products, and customers (Bromwich and Bhimani, 1989, 1994; see also Bromwich, 1990). By this time the idea of accounting for quality, time, product commonality, bottlenecks, value chains, and so on, using the most appropriate metrics available, was widely accepted.

Within the context of a rapidly evolving new management accounting discipline, termed accounting for strategic positioning by Roslender (1995), the balanced scorecard was quickly recognized as a complementary new direction to pursue (Kaplan and Norton, 1992, 1993; Maisel, 1992). What this new reporting framework permitted was the presentation of a set of key performance indicators that reflected an enterprise's chosen critical success factors, internally in the first instance but in principle externally also. Performance was to be considered in a balanced way (i.e. more comprehensively or inclusively), by complementing traditional accounting (and finance) numbers with those more relevant to reporting on customer interactions, internal resource consumption, future preparedness, and human capital issues. Beyond the suggestion of a generic four perspective scorecard architecture to be populated by relevant numbers, there were no normative prescriptions, the opposite of the stock-in-trade of the global financial reporting profession.

The various accomplishments of the new management accounting were not lost on Edvinsson, sometime self-proclaimed father of the IC field. In his seminal *Long Range Planning* paper, Edvinsson (1997) identifies the Skandia Navigator as the means of reporting the growth of an enterprise's key IC constituents on a periodic basis, using customized metrics selected to ensure the most favourable account of performance was presented. Such a scoreboard was deemed by Edvinsson to be a superior approach to any facile attempt to somehow determine IC values, perhaps derived using his own Skandia Value Scheme that is also discussed in the paper. Alternative scoreboards soon followed, most notably the Intangible Assets Monitor (Sveiby, 1997), the Eriksson Cockpit Communicator (Lovingsson *et al.*, 2000), and the Value Chain Scoreboard (Lev, 2001) (see also Starovic and Marr, 2003).

Human capital accounting

The basic lesson for accounting for people provided by the emergence of the new management accounting in general, and the balanced scorecard in particular, was that a human capital account should set out the key information on the stock of human capital (attributes) available to an enterprise, ideally emphasizing its continued growth. Such an account might be understood as an expanded human capital (people) perspective as in an IC scoreboard such as the Navigator or Intangible Assets Monitor. Equally, the HR Scorecard identified by Becker *et al.* (2001) or the Human Capital Scorecard developed by Fitz-enz (2000) would qualify as human capital accounts. Both would seem to affirm Simmonds' warning 20 years earlier in relation to the need to develop a strategic management accounting approach – that other professions are capable of incursions into accountancy's traditional jurisdiction.

To the purist, and irrespective of their merits and utility to managers, such innovations are not accountings. Underpinning such a stance is the belief that (true) accounting manifests itself in the traditions of financial accounting and reporting, in which the balance sheet and profit and loss account are of paramount importance. This explains why the enduring popular understanding of accounting for people equates it with 'putting people on the balance sheet', making use of reliable 'objective' financial valuations. The observation that the latter exercise has long been recognized by academics to be impossible actually provides ammunition to those more conservative elements of the accountancy profession who consider employees, among a number of admittedly valuable assets, do not belong on the balance sheet irrespective of Paton's assertion. Their place is within the profit and loss account, as costs, the magnitude of which necessarily impacts on levels of profitability. Given the objective of profit maximization, whether in small private enterprises or agency-managed large corporations, the role of the accountancy profession is to facilitate the processes necessary to deliver continued, and ideally increased, levels of profitability. In the last analysis, it is management who insist on labour cost reductions. A critical merit of Flamholtz's human resource accounting approach is that he signposted the way to (employee) cost management, almost 20 years before Kaplan recognized the fullest significance of the activity-based cost approach (Cooper and Kaplan, 1991) but ultimately lacked the tools to finish the job.

A human capital account identifies the key insights on how the enterprise has grown its stocks of human capital within a specified period. At base, this will reflect the many attributes that a workforce gifts to the enterprise, including their education and training, experience and expertise, a range of desirable qualities including capacity for teamwork, initiative and inge-nuity, together with their health and wellbeing. In addition, there are many factual attributes such as age and gender profile, longevity of service, retention levels, and so on, all of which are again well understood by human resource professionals. Those with responsibility for the production of such an account are challenged to identify the most important attributes that need to be disclosed, the enterprise's critical success factors, together with the most powerful metrics for that purpose in order to communicate the enterprise's commercial health going forward. As with the second generation balanced scorecard (Kaplan and Norton, 1996), there is merit in incorporating a set of human capital growth targets that are revisited on a continuing basis. Equally, the inherently dynamic nature of human capital means that careful considera-tion needs to be given to how the bundle of attributes incorporated within the account evolves over time. While there is an imperative to tell the most persuasive human capital story, it is also important that such stories exhibit a continuity over time.

From even this brief description of what a human capital account might look like, a couple of affinities with a conventional balance sheet can be identified. First, the objective is the same: to present a visualization of the position of the enterprise at a particular time, thereby communicating its commercial health as compared with the same at some earlier time, together with an indication of the future prospects of the enterprise, an attribute of the balance sheet that is too often overlooked. Second, and equally important: the requirement to provide largely the same set of information over time, thereby offering the means to identify the enterprise's improving position and reinforcing perceptions of commercial health. The differences are probably more significant, however. The initial difference is the truism that a human capital account is a highly focused account in contrast to a balance sheet, which in respect of assets alone is invariably much more wide ranging. Unlike a balance sheet, a human capital account is not composed of financial balances, principally valuations, and indeed may exclude such valuations on the grounds that in the case of employees these do not offer a useful way of representing the worth of a workforce (cf. Roslender and Dyson, 1992). The purposeful decou-pling of the worth from financial value circumvents concerns about admitting subjectivity into the balance sheet. Because worth is at base a subjective notion, albeit in the case of a workforce subject to a measure of verification within the operations of the market, the use of frameworks that do not have any pretensions of objectivity is a commensurate practice. One consequence of this is that comparing human capital accounts between enterprises becomes a difficult exercise to pursue, an observation that applies equally to any scoreboard approach to accounting. Financial reporting has traditionally identified such comparability as a major strength of stock-in-trade, and perhaps understandably views departures from it with some concern, if not trepidation.

In principle, there is no reason why an enterprise might not incorporate a human capital account within its annual report package, although it needs to be acknowledged that suggest-ing even more content be included within this document invariably provokes the knee jerk 'information overload' response from many within the accountancy profession. Nowadays annual reports commonly run to three figures in terms of the number of pages. In many cases, however, a growing part of the document takes the form of pictures that are designed to rein-force some of the key messages the enterprise is seeking to communicate to its stakeholders. At the very least there seems to be a strong case for providing enterprise human capital account information on enterprises' websites. This would have the benefit of permitting a fuller treat-ment of the issues, a feature that stakeholders with a particular interest in human capital and its promotion within the enterprise would appreciate.

It would be wrong at this point to move on to a number of further considerations in relation to the challenge of accounting for people without offering some observations on the contribution that narrative approaches to IC reporting could make to this task. In 1997 the Danish government initiated a project on IC that would identify the Intellectual Capital Statement as an alternative approach to IC reporting that was more reliant on narrative than numbers, as in the case of scoreboards or the financial indexes (e.g. Mouritsen, 1998; Mouritsen *et al.*, 2001a, 2001b). The first phase of the Danish Guideline Project resulted in the identification of a set of guidelines for IC reporting that was heavily informed by knowledge management thinking (DATI, 2001). The second phase was more extensive and involved working with 100 companies to refine these guidelines into "The New Guidelines" (Mouritsen *et al.*, 2003). While the Intellectual Capital Statement incorporated a scoreboard in its fourth section, the knowledge narrative, management challenges, and initiatives sections were predominantly narrative in nature, as well as being strongly reflexive in emphasis. Management was encouraged to carefully consider how it might best use its scarce IC resources, including human capital, to maximize the value created for and delivered to customers, as well as captured for shareholders (see also the Meritum Report (2002) for an alternative narrative-based approach to IC reporting).

While the Danish Guideline Project and the Intellectual Capital Statement have recently been documented to have been only moderately successful (Nielsen *et al.*, 2016, 2017), the benefits of adopting a narrative focus within human capital accounting remain very evident. Merely exchanging financial valuations for softer metrics, as in the case of scoreboard approaches, does not provide the panacea that those seeking to take people into account had sought for several decades. By combining numbers with narratives and other visualization, and as many of the examples from the Danish Guideline demonstrated, it becomes possible to produce a more nuanced story of human capital growth. This is not too surprising if one explores much of the content of 21st-century financial reports. Words are commonly used to explain and amplify the accounting numbers in the attempt to convince stakeholders of the soundness of particular discussions and/or their accounting representation. In this light, what is good for the mainstream is also good for those with more radical agendas. On the other hand, human capital accounting is likely to precipitate a considerable extent of complementary narrative, provoking further concerns about information overload.

Having provided an overview of the development of accounting for people to date, the second part of the chapter identifies and discusses three important pathways that researchers interested in developing human capital accounting could consider pursuing. These pathways are: health and wellbeing as human capital; the social accounting interface; and accounting by people.

Health and wellbeing as human capital

The list of generic human capital attributes identified earlier, the growth of which might be incorporated into a human capital account via a combination of numbers and narrative, included health and wellbeing. While all of the other attributes identified will be fairly familiar to readers, albeit sometimes in different guises, health and wellbeing is a rather novel attribute. Its inclusion might initially seem contentious, although nowadays its exclusion from the human capital accounting space is probably even more contentious. A moment's reflection demonstrates that any compromise of an employee's health and wellbeing threatens to reduce his or her capacity to contribute to the value creation, delivery, and capture processes now recognized to provide the rationale for all enterprise activities. Or put more simply: if an employee is unwell in some way, they are unable to perform at their best in the workplace.

While it would be disingenuous to suggest that all ill-health is caused by working, there is now considerable evidence to demonstrate that many employees are unwell because of their work. Traditionally musculo-skeletal problems were understood to be the cause of many lost working days. As both employees and employers have come to understand, a preventative approach to working activities, as an element of a broader health and safety culture, has resulted in many fewer days lost to musculo-skeletal problems in the workforce. For the past generation, however, evidence regarding sickness absence, such as that provided annually by the UK Chartered Institute of Personnel and Development in their absence management surveys, demonstrates that mental illness is now the most pressing work health challenge faced by enterprises and is reflected in an escalating charge to be set against both local profitability and national financial resources. Again, there is no suggestion that all mental ill-health is consequent on workplace factors, or that contemporary lifestyle choices do not contribute significantly to sickness absence statistics. Nevertheless, the continued growth of long-term sickness absence among non-manual employees, those whose role in the knowledge society is otherwise trumpeted as being so crucial, would seem to be a worrying process that demands to be taken into account in some way, in tandem with the modern day presenteeism and leavism phenomena that have the consequence of disguising the extent of the actual problem to some degree.

Twenty-first century work seems to impact on many people's health, despite the observation that these causal factors are well known. Concerns about staffing levels are a major consideration. The downsizing and rightsizing initiatives of the 1980s, subsequently reinforced by the generic business process re-engineering philosophy in the following decade (e.g. Hammer and Champy, 1993; Champy, 1995), have left many employees with workloads that they struggle to fulfil on a daily basis, resulting in increased unpaid overtime, fatigue and worry. In parallel a seeming obsession with continual organizational change has the same consequence for many employees. While change and the pace of change are now recognized to be a necessary feature of the enterprise by most employees, the problem seems to be that there is often too much change evident and for no clear reason, both of which have the effect of placing further pressure on employees. The observation that change management thinking consistently emphasizes the necessity for a continuing dialogue with those who experience its effects, at every level within the organization, coupled with extensive involvement and participation in such initiatives, is belied by practice in many instances, promoting even greater uncertainty and confusion that reinforces distress and dismay. As if this was not enough, many managers are regarded by their subordinates as engaging in bullying and kindred behaviours that regularly go unchallenged by their own superiors. A growth in employee on employee bullying is both a symptom and a cause of greater levels of workplace dissatisfaction, and at the extreme, fear, which simply exacerbates the negative responses that for many employees result in stress-related sickness absence.

In the present era, an enterprise that manifests these well-understood processes has a greater likelihood of experiencing high levels of sickness absence due to the incidence of mental ill-health, now recognized as a prominent challenge to work health. Such an enterprise would seem not to merit the designation of a 'healthy organization', one that despite its seeming 'unaccounting' resonances in fact takes us squarely back to the accounting space. The balance sheet is usually recognized as an indicator of the financial health of an enterprise, although certainly not the sole indicator. A balance sheet that communicates an upward trend in financial health is therefore likely to also convey the likelihood of future success for the enterprise. Conversely, any reversal in such a trend seems likely to promote caution among those who seek a sustained return of their willingness to invest their resources in the enterprise.

As an enterprise's most valuable asset, an unhealthy workforce would be recognized as a cause for concern. Given that such information is only rarely disclosed to anyone outside of the enterprise, it is possible for management to ignore these concerns and focus their attention on what must be disclosed, although they do so at their peril. Conversely, however, the lure of reporting a highly positive story about a healthy organization is powerful and holds out the same beneficial consequences as more conventional financial disclosures. It would involve selecting a set of insightful indicators and then combining these with a narrative that explains how the enterprise accomplishes being a healthy organization. In the light of what has already been outlined, the ability to be able to report a downward trend in long-term sickness absences due to stress and stress-related conditions would seem crucial, possibly by category of employee or length of employment. Some indication of what are regarded as successful attempts to promote high levels of employee engagement would also seem to be beneficial, together with complementary interventions such as the promotion of healthy eating, the pursuit of exercise, aromatherapy or yoga sessions, substance abuse initiatives, smoking cessation, and so on, many of which are already embraced by enterprises (see, Roslender *et al.*, 2010, chapter 4). It is only feasible to tell the story of the healthy organization if such an organization exists. Those enterprises in a position to make favourable disclosures of this sort can only enhance their credibility if they are also prepared to undergo an assurance process.

An attempt to develop this particular approach to human capital accounting was evident in Sweden a decade ago in the form of the health statement. Sweden had the unfortunate distinction of being in the vanguard of an excessive sickness absence phenomenon around the millennium, albeit in some part as a consequence of its relatively relaxed social security provisions (Johanson *et al.*, 2007). This was more pronounced in the state sector, which is where experimentation with health statements was focused (e.g. Mouritsen and Johanson, 2005; Almqvist *et al.*, 2007; Holmgren Caicedo and Martensson, 2010). Once sickness absence levels began to (appear to) reduce significantly, interest in health statements tailed off, although in fairness many initiatives had proved unsuccessful despite their good intentions. The desirability of revisiting such initiatives in the face of continued high levels of sickness absence, wherever these may be evident, is surely self-evident.

The social accounting interface

Despite what many readers might regard as a radical departure from mainstream accounting and reporting, accounting for health and wellbeing, as envisaged above, like human capital accounting in general, remains fairly conventional. What is being suggested is that employees, understood to be the most valuable asset within the enterprise, are accounted for using a combination of numbers and narratives incorporated into a scoreboard framework that largely eschews the traditional cost and value calculus evident throughout the history of financial accounting theory and practice. In the last analysis, however, the resulting information might be recognized as being designed principally to meet the needs of shareholders, senior managers, and the analyst community. This group might extend to include employees themselves, although as with previous attempts to deliver such insights it is unlikely that the vehicles for doing so will vary much from more established practices.

It is easy to overlook the observation that some early attempts at accounting for people had more in common with social accounting than either financial accounting or managerial accounting. Accounting to society, viewed as a complement to financial and managerial accounting, was conceived of as an attempt to provide the broader society with information that those who sought to fashion such accounts believed it had an interest in. Some of the early iconic attempts to account to society in this way were the work of groups and organizations such as Social Audit Ltd or Counter Information Services, who were far removed from the accounting mainstream, and were often politically motivated (Gray *et al.*, 1987). At base, these alternative accounts aimed to inform society about issues that enterprises excluded from their financial statements, often in a vivid way but equally in the measured way that was necessary to command attention. Over time this genre of radical social accounting evolved into corporate social reporting, arguably losing much of its cutting edge in the process, making it less threatening to enterprises that sought to extend their accounting information set in this way. Providing information on employees and employment issues through such mechanisms offered a third way of accounting for people, a programme that Flamholtz flirted with in the second edition of his seminal overview of the field (Flamholtz, 1985). By this time, however, accounting for people had largely disappeared from the research agenda, while corporate social reporting was beginning to become more oriented to environmental concerns, in place of an arguably more radical ecological emphasis (Gray *et al.*, 2017). The subsequent history of corporate social reporting has seen it become ever more palatable to the accounting mainstream, to such an extent that some formulations of Integrated Reporting barely countenance the idea that there is any real distinction between corporate reporting and corporate social reporting (Flower, 2015).

A return to a more radical social accounting model promises to facilitate the broadening of the accounting for people focus. Implicit in the story of the healthy organization identified above is the assumption that there is a positive story to tell, essentially of employees working within enterprises that do not compromise their health and wellbeing, and ideally adding to it in some discernible way. It would seem reasonable to observe that presently many enterprises are not in a position to provide positive accounts of this sort, as a result of which a strong imperative exists to engage in improvement projects and to do so in a transparent way. In so doing, enterprises may begin to incorporate a measure of critical accounting thinking into both their disclosure practices and the activities that they seek to represent (Roslender and Dillard, 2003). In this regard, critical accounting is understood to entail the attempt to document the conditions and the consequences of the many practices that enterprises and their management pursue in a reflexive way that is ultimately designed to produce social betterment. In other words, informing society about how the enterprise is striving for the creation of a better world, a project that is self-evidently more radical than the vast part of the corporate social reporting tradition.

One extension of accounting for people in this direction overlaps with recent interest in accounting for human rights. The concept of human rights embraces a wide range of attributes that attach to people as human beings rather than as employees. Over time these rights have become more apparent as society has sought to reflect upon how human beings impact upon each other as well as upon the environment. The Global Reporting Initiative's *G4: Sustainability Reporting Guidelines* identifies a range of generic categories of human rights upon which enterprises are encouraged to report (GRI, 2013). These include: non-discrimination, child labour, security, and respect for the rights of indigenous people. An extended account for people project should focus on what enterprises are doing to protect and promote human rights, and to report this to the broader society. It is of equal importance that enterprises acknowledge how their activities impact negatively on human rights, and their plans to reduce that impact over time. Although it might initially seem to be something of a trivialization of the pursuit of greater levels of human rights, the development of a scoreboard approach to crucial issues such as safety, security, equality, and so on, complete with improvement targets, certainly merits a second look (see, Roslender *et al.*, 2015 for a fuller discussion).

Accounting by people

The latter reference to scoreboard approaches to human rights disclosure also returns us to the role that narratives should play in the continued development of accounting for people. The case for the use of narratives in IC reporting was convincingly advanced in the many outputs from the Danish Guideline Project and its complementary literature (which are discussed elsewhere in this collection). Despite its modest success, the appeal of a combination of narratives and numbers remains undiminished. Narratives also exist as a major challenge to many within the global financial reporting community, as a consequence of which it is important not to lose sight of the many difficulties that its many enthusiastic advocates face in increasing their role in the coming years (Roslender and Nielsen, 2016).

In Roslender and Fincham (2001) the case was made for a further development of narratives, again heavily informed by a critical accounting perspective (see also, Roslender and Fincham, 2004). Despite their promise, Roslender and Fincham observe that the narratives envisaged within the Intellectual Capital Statement and the Intellectual Capital Reporting framework identified in parallel in the 2002 Meritum Report, remain management's narratives in the same way that both scoreboards and more conventional financial statements are the work of the accounting and finance function. As such, they are fundamentally inconsistent with the identification of human capital as primary IC, even if this designation is expanded to include the greater part of management itself. However well-meaning they may be claimed to be, management's narratives about human capital and its growth still have the effect of imprisoning people within other people's accounts, ensuring their continued control within the enterprise. In order to develop a radical, emancipatory narrative that can promote the position of employees within the enterprise, they must be able to devise and disseminate their own narratives, which must be independent of the control of their jailers. Roslender and Fincham (2001, 2004) commend the practice of self-accounting as the means to ensure that narratives can serve the interests of employees.

Self-narratives would entail employees talking about how they experience the many aspects of their employments and how the various attributes they gift to the enterprise are utilized. Roslender and Fincham advance a fundamentally positive view of self-accounting, although they should not be interpreted as being completely wide-eyed idealists about how most people experience work. Self-accounting's intellectual roots in the traditions of Marxist theory necessitate that it entails an exercise in self-reflection. In the course of thinking about and fabricating their individual self-accounts, employees are simultaneously challenged to consider how they might improve the situation so as to achieve personal growth whenever possible. The counterargument that this is something to be resisted at every turn by those charged with managing the enterprise is something of a truism, but the very idea of a critical accounting for people, as a modernist project, takes it as axiomatic that widespread social betterment remains a realistic prospect in the years and decades to come (Roslender *et al.*, 2015). So while it is desirable to remain fully sceptical about the rhetorical emphases of the assertion that 'our people are our greatest asset', many enterprises are becoming aware of the necessity of successfully participating in the increasingly competitive 'war for talent'.

Health and wellbeing self-accounts suggest themselves as being particularly interesting. Individuals would be able to take the opportunity to document their journeys to improved health and wellbeing, possibly placing particular emphasis on the importance of engaging in sporting activities, whether in isolation or on a team basis. The benefits of greater participation in sport are now widely publicized by the medical profession, but being able to access the experiences of one's own fellow employees on the one hand, or one's friendship group on the other, as well as the broader society via the various communications technologies and social media, promises a wealth of concrete lessons that might be emulated. Similarly, stories about tackling substance abuse, smoking cessation, reducing alcohol intake, healthier cooking as well as healthier eating, or beginning to pursue yoga classes, pilates, aromatherapy or similar initiatives, have the capacity to encourage anyone to embrace activities that are understood to counter negative pressures within the workplace. Insights on the utility of the vast array of legal pharmaceuticals can be derived from similar sources, together with lessons on how it has been possible to reduce dependency on the same. While it was previously emphasized that 21st-century work would appear to have developed the capacity to increase levels of long-term sickness absence, it would be wrong to believe that it is possible to eradicate such effects from the workplace. As a consequence, many of the above activities might be better understood to constitute valuable means of mitigating threats to health and wellbeing, both in the workplace and beyond (see Roslender *et al.*, 2006 for a fuller discussion).

To conclude

Taking people into account has two different meanings, reflecting the fundamentally interdisciplinary nature of the challenge it encompasses. From an accounting perspective, it brings to mind the search for some means to incorporate people within accounts, most obviously by putting people on the balance sheet. By implication this will be accomplished via the mechanism of determining reliable financial valuations for employees, perhaps individually or more likely in aggregate. As we have indicated earlier, this option has been rejected by the majority of accounting academics who have had an interest in accounting for people for close to half a century. It would be difficult to identify many financial accounting and reporting researchers who would readily admit to being interested in identifying financial valuations for employees in this way nowadays. Unfortunately, this appears not to be a position shared by their practitioner counterparts, who in large part remain disinterested in any such adventures. As a consequence, the various alternatives informed by over 20 years of research on IC reporting continue to be largely undiscovered.

The second meaning is of a much more commonsense nature, at least to anyone with a genuine interest in people and what they bring to the workplace. This meaning of taking people into account translates into a commitment to demonstrate the scale and scope of what people gift to society, including as employees. Flamholtz recognized this in his imperative to 'think people', a decade or so prior to the 'our people are our greatest asset' axiom of the emergent human resource management function. Leaving aside the debate as to whether the latter assertion has really had much more than a rhetorical purchase, for us 'people thinking', as the underlying objective of accounting for people, merits as much attention as it did when Paton drew the accountancy profession's attention to the importance of employees to the business enterprise. As we observed at the outset, human capital is, by definition, the source of all IC, as a consequence of which it demands to be taken into account more than ever, to ensure that its contribution to society is the most it can be, at all times and in all spaces. And to answer the question posed at the beginning of the chapter: 'why account for people?' Quite simply because people matter, arguably now more than ever.

Further reading

Absence Management Survey, published annually by the Chartered Institute of Personnel and Development.
Roslender, R. (2009), "So tell me again … just why would you want to account for people?", *Journal of Human Resource Costing and Accounting*, Vol. 13, No. 2, pp. 143–153.

Roslender, R. (2011), "Accounting for human resources revisited: Insights from the intellectual capital field", in Abdel-Kader, M. G. (ed.), *Review of Management Accounting Research*, Palgrave-Macmillan, Basingstoke, UK.

Special issue of *Critical Perspectives on Accounting* on "Accounting for human rights" (2011), Vol. 22, No. 8.

Special issue of *Accounting, Auditing & Accountability Journal* on "Accounting for human rights" (2016), Vol. 29, No. 4.

References

Almqvist, R., Backlund, A., Sjoblom, A., and Rimmel, G. (2007), "Management control of health: The Swedish example", in Johanson, U., Ahonen, G., and Roslender, R. (Eds) *Work Health and Management Control*, Thomson-Fakta, Stockholm, pp. 291–318.

Becker, B. E., Huselid, M. A., and Ulrich, D. (2001), *The HR Scorecard: Linking People, Strategy and Performance*, Harvard Business School Press, Boston, MA.

Becker, G. S. (1964), *Human Capital: A Theoretical and Empirical Analysis with Special Reference to Education*, University of Chicago Press, Chicago, IL.

Bromwich, M. (1990), "The case for strategic management accounting: The role of accounting information in competitive markets", *Accounting, Organizations and Society*, Vol. 15, No. 1, pp. 27–46.

Bromwich, M. and Bhimani, A. (1989), *Management Accounting: Evolution not Revolution*, Chartered Institute of Management Accountants, London.

Bromwich, M. and Bhimani, A. (1994), *Management Accounting: Pathways to Progress*, Chartered Institute of Management Accountants, London.

Brummet, R. L., Flamholtz, E. G., and Pyle, W. C. (1968), "Human resource measurement: A challenge for accountants", *The Accounting Review*, Vol. 43, No. 2, pp. 217–224.

Champy, J. A. (1995), *Reengineering Management*, Harper Business Books, New York.

Cooper, R. and Kaplan, R. S. (1991), "Profit priorities from activity-based costing", *Harvard Business Review*, Vol. 69, No. 3, pp. 130–135.

DATI (2001), *A Guideline for Intellectual Capital Statements*, Danish Agency for Trade and Industry, Copenhagen.

Edvinsson, L. (1997), "Developing intellectual capital at Skandia", *Long Range Planning*, Vol. 30, No. 3, pp. 266–273.

FASB (1976), *The Conceptual Framework for Financial Accounting and Reporting: Elements of Financial Statements and their Measurement*, Financial Accounting Standards Board, Stamford, CT.

Fitz-enz, J. (2000), *The ROI of Human Capital: Measuring the Economic Value of Employee Performance*, Amacom, New York.

Flamholtz, E. G. (1971), "A model for human resource valuation: A stochastic process with service rewards", *Accounting Review*, Vol. 46, No. 2, pp. 253–267.

Flamholtz, E. G. (1974), "Human resource accounting: A review of theory and research", *Journal of Management Studies*, Vol. 11, No. 1, pp. 44–61.

Flamholtz, E. G. (1976), "The impact of human resource valuation on management decisions: A laboratory experiment", *Accounting, Organizations and Society*, Vol. 1, Nos 2/3, pp. 153–165.

Flamholtz, E. G. (1985), *Human Resource Accounting: Advances in Concepts, Methods and Applications*, Jossey-Bass Publishers, San Francisco, CA.

Flower, J. (2015), "The International Integrated Reporting Council: A story of failure", *Critical Perspectives on Accounting*, Vol. 27, pp. 1–17.

Gray, R. H., Adams, C., and Owen, D. (2017), "Social and environmental accounting", in Roslender, R. (ed.), *Routledge Companion to Critical Accounting*, Routledge, London.

Gray, R. H., Owen, D. and Maunders, K. (1987), *Corporate Social Reporting: Accounting and Accountability*, Prentice-Hall Inc., Hemel Hempstead, UK.

GRI (2013), *G4: Sustainability Reporting Guidelines*, Global Reporting Initiative, Amsterdam.

Gröjer, J.-E. and Johanson, U. (1991), *Human Resource Costing and Accounting*, Swedish Joint Industrial Safety Committee, Stockholm.

Gröjer, J.-E. and Johanson, U. (1998), "Current development in human resource costing and accounting: Reality present, researchers absent?", *Accounting, Auditing & Accountability Journal*, Vol. 11, No. 4, pp. 495–506.

Hammer, M. and Champy, J. A. (1993), *Reengineering the Corporation: A Manifesto for Business Revolution*, Harper Business Books, New York.

Hekemian, J. S. and Jones, C. (1967), "Put people on your balance sheet", *Harvard Business Review*, Vol. 43, No. 2, pp. 105–113.

Hermanson, R. H. (1963), *A Method for Recording all Assets and the Resulting Accounting and Economic Implications*, PhD dissertation, Michigan State University, Michigan.

Hermanson, R. H. (1964), *Accounting for Human Assets*, Graduate School of Business, Michigan State University, Michigan.

Holmgren Caicedo, M. and Martensson, M. (2010), "Extensions and intensions of management control: The inclusion of health", *Critical Perspectives on Accounting*, Vol. 21, No. 8, pp. 655–668.

Johanson, U. and Backlund, A. (2006), "Can health be subject to management control?", in Arnertz, B. and Ekman, R. (Eds), *Stress in Health and Disease*, Wiley VCH, Weinheim, Germany.

Johanson, U., Ahonen, G., and Roslender, R. (2007), "What the book is about and not about", in Johanson U., Ahonen G., and Roslender R. (Eds), *Work Health and Management Control*, Thomson-Fakta, Stockholm.

Johnson, H. T. and Kaplan, R. S. (1987), *Relevance Lost: The Rise and Fall of Management Accounting*, Harvard Business School Press, Boston, MA.

Kaplan, R. S. (1983), "Measuring manufacturing performance: A new challenge to management accounting research", *Accounting Review*, Vol. 5, No. 4, pp. 686–705.

Kaplan, R. S. (1984), "The evolution of management accounting", *Accounting Review*, Vol. 59, No. 3, pp. 390–418.

Kaplan, R. S. and Norton, D. P. (1992), "The balanced scorecard: Measures that drive performance", *Harvard Business Review*, Vol. 70, No. 1, pp. 58–63.

Kaplan, R. S. and Norton, D. P. (1993), "Putting the balanced scorecard to work", *Harvard Business Review*, Vol. 71, No. 5, pp. 134–147.

Kaplan, R. S. and Norton, D. P. (1996), *The Balanced Scorecard: Translating Strategy into Action*, Harvard Business School Press, Boston, MA.

Lev, B. (2001), *Intangibles: Measurement, Management and Reporting*, Brooking Institution Press, Washington, DC.

Likert, R. M. (1967), *The Human Organization*, McGraw-Hill, New York.

Lovingsson, F., Dell'Orto, S., and Baladi, P. (2000), "Navigating with new managerial tools", *Journal of Intellectual Capital*, Vol. 1, No. 2, pp. 147–154.

Maisel, L. S. (1992), "Performance measurement: The balanced scorecard approach", *Journal of Cost Management*, Fall, pp. 47–52.

Meritum (2002), *Proyecto Meritum: Guidelines for Managing and Reporting on Intangibles*, Autonomous University of Madrid, Madrid.

Mouritsen, J. (1998), "Driving economic growth: Economic value added vs. intellectual capital", *Management Accounting Research*, Vol. 9, No. 4, pp. 461–482.

Mouritsen, J. and Johanson, U. (2005), "Managing the person: Human resource costing and accounting, intellectual capital and health statements", in Jonsson, S. and Mouritsen, J. (Eds), *Accounting in Scandinavia – The Northern Lights*, Liber Press/Copenhagen Business School Press, Copenhagen.

Mouritsen, J., Bukh, P. N., Flagstad, K., Thorjornsen, S., Johansen, M. R., Kotnis, S., Larsen, H. T., Nielsen, C., Kjaergaard, I., Krag, L., Jeppesen, G., Haisler, J., and Stakemann, B. (2003), *Intellectual Capital Statements – The New Guideline*, Danish Ministry of Science, Technology and Innovation, Copenhagen.

Mouritsen, J., Larsen, H. T. and Bukh, P. N. (2001a), "Intellectual capital and the 'capable firm': Narrating, visualising and numbering for management knowledge", *Accounting, Organizations and Society*, Vol. 26, Nos 7/8, pp. 735–762.

Mouritsen, J., Larsen, H. T., and Bukh, P. N. (2001b), "Valuing the future: Intellectual capital supplements at Skandia", *Accounting, Auditing & Accountability Journal*, Vol. 14, No. 4, pp. 399–422.

Nielsen, C., Roslender, R., and Schaper, S. (2016), "Continuities in the use of the intellectual statement approach: Elements of an institutional theory analysis", *Accounting Forum*, Vol. 40, No. 1, pp. 16–28.

Nielsen, C., Roslender, R., and Schaper, S. (2017), "Explaining the demise of the intellectual capital statement in Denmark", *Accounting, Auditing & Accountability Journal*, Vol. 30, No. 1, pp. 38–64.

Paton, W. (1922), *Accounting Theory*, Ronald Press, New York.

Roslender, R. (1995), "Accounting for strategic positioning: Responding to the crisis in management accounting", *British Journal of Management*, Vol. 6, No. 1, pp. 45–57.

Roslender, R. and Dillard, J. F. (2003), "Reflections on the interdisciplinary perspectives on accounting project", *Critical Perspectives on Accounting*, Vol. 14, No. 3, pp. 325–352.

Roslender, R. and Dyson, J. R. (1992), "Accounting for the worth of employees: A new look at an old problem", *British Accounting Review*, Vol. 24, No. 4, pp. 311–329

Roslender, R. and Fincham, R. (2001), "Thinking critically about intellectual capital", *Accounting, Auditing & Accountability Journal*, Vol. 4, No. 4, pp. 383–399.

Roslender R. and Fincham, R. (2004), "Intellectual capital: Who counts, controls", *Accounting and the Public Interest*, Vol. 4, pp. 1–19.

Roslender, R. and Nielsen, C. (2016), *Lessons for Progressing Narrative Reporting: Learning from the Experience of Disseminating the Danish Intellectual Capital Statement Approach*, Mimeo, University of Dundee, Dundee, UK.

Roslender, R., Kahn, H., and Stevenson, J. (2010), *Recognising Workforce Health as a Key Organisational Asset: A Study of Current Thinking and Practice*, Institute of Chartered Accountants of Scotland, Edinburgh, UK.

Roslender, R., Marks, A., and Stevenson, J. (2015), "Damned if you do, damned if you don't: Conflicting perspectives on the virtues of accounting for people", *Critical Perspectives on Accounting*, Vol. 27, pp. 43–55.

Roslender, R., Stevenson, J., and Kahn, H. (2006), "Employee wellness as intellectual capital: An accounting perspective", *Journal of Human Resource Costing and Accounting*, Vol. 10, No. 1, pp. 48–64.

Schultz, T. W. (1961), "Investments in human capital", *American Economic Review*, Vol. 52, No. 1, pp. 1–17.

Simmonds, K. (1981), "Strategic management accounting", *Management Accounting (UK)*, Vol. 59, No. 4, pp. 26–29.

Simmonds, K. (1982), "Strategic management accounting for pricing: a case example", *Accounting and Business Research*, Vol. 42, pp. 206–214.

Simmonds, K. (1986), "The accounting assessment of competitive position", *European Journal of Marketing*, Vol. 20, pp. 16–31.

Starovic, D. and Marr, B. (2003), *Understanding Corporate Value: Managing and Reporting Intellectual Capital*, Chartered Institute of Management Accountants, London.

Sveiby, K. E. (1997), "The intangible assets monitor", *Journal of Human Resource Costing and Accounting*, Vol. 2, No. 1, pp. 73–97.

Whittington, G. (1983), *Inflation Accounting: An Introduction to the Debate*, Cambridge University Press, Cambridge, UK.

PART II

Stage 4

IC ecosystems

4

SEVEN DIMENSIONS TO ADDRESS FOR INTELLECTUAL CAPITAL AND INTANGIBLE ASSETS NAVIGATION

Leif Edvinsson

Introduction and IC quizzics

This chapter discusses the different states of intellectual capital (IC) research, especially the fifth stage with its focus on macro aspects of IC. The purpose is to increase awareness of these different approaches in order to reveal the hidden value of both nations and enterprises, to the benefit of future generations. It asks: What is the fundamental question of the emerging volume of intangibles as a reality check of perception and authencity? What are we aiming for? What is the critical purpose? What is the unit of analysis? How do we agree upon the mapping before we proceed to the next step of navigation?

These questions are important because the traditional models of value and value creating seem to be distorted on several levels. Perhaps there is a fundamental lack of understanding and appreciation of the value of intangibles? In which case, a much more refined multidimensional value navigation approach is needed!

In the early 1980s, Japan launched the concept of Softnomics, (i.e. Soft Economics). At this time, debate was centred around value mapping and was a struggle between Japan's Ministry of Industry and Ministry of Finance. Today we have an enormous global power struggle on the impact of balance sheet issues and debt leveraging strategies behind the debt crises. One starting point for more navigation intelligence may be to address where sustainable value is emerging and in what way. In other words, we need to go beyond the perspectives of the financial capital balance sheet, on many levels.

National IC mapping

A growing insight among several groups of experts, such as the OECD, IBRD, and IMF, as well as among the younger generations, expressed on social media, is a strong concern that traditonal GDP mapping is not enough for societal navigation. Together with this observation is also the causal dimension: how to get relevant macro level data of national IC based on the micro level data of enterprises. The first prototype of a National Intellectual Capital (NIC) map

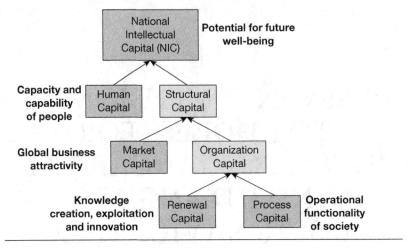

ELSS methodology and data base:
48 statistical indicators, 12 in each category, 59 countries

Figure 4.1 ELSS model for NIC

Source: www.bimac.fi

was presented in Sweden in 1997 by the National Agency for Investment, followed soon after by Israel and its Ministry of Finance, and the Ministry of Economics in Poland. Prior to this, Japan had been experimenting at the end of the 1980s with Softnomics, under the leadership of the Ministry of Finance. A special Softnomics Centre was created in Tokyo as a platform for knowledge creation.

In advanced economies, 75 per cent of GDP is related to IC. Today one of the pioneering maps of NIC has been developed through prototyping work that maps national intangibles in Taiwan and Finland, under the leadership of the New Club of Paris.[1] More than 60 countries over a time period of 15 years have developed a scientifically verified model called the ELSS-model (see Figure 4.1), covering the four traditional major pillars of NIC – HC as human capital, RC as relational capital, OC as structural organizational capital, and renewal capital as innovation capital. The model could also be refined to include social capital and environmental capital dimensions.

The work on NIC mapping is of global importance, both in terms of policy and governance. The New Club of Paris is at the forefront of this work, setting the knowledge agenda for nations.[2] The first global database is now available for NIC, based on the work undertaken in Taiwan and Finland. It highlights the value aspects of intangibles on a national level based on some 48 indicators, for more than 45 countries, during a period of more than 15 years. Reports, books, and booklets are emerging.[3]

Enterprise map

The work on intangibles began decades ago, with the global financial group Skandia, based in Sweden, among the first, presenting its first public annual IC report as a prototype in 1993. It has since been followed by many other organizations, seeking to present a supplementary report to the financial annual report that encompasses key drivers for the enterprise's value creation. These reports are a kind of navigational, forward-looking annual report of tomorrow.

This prototyping work was followed by growing testing, research, and educational work on a global scale. One of the most systemic approaches was initiated by the Bundes Ministerium in Germany, based on a systems dynamics approach developed by Jay Forrester at MIT, and subsequently followed by Japan and the Ministry of Economy, Trade and Industry (METI). The work in Japan has been labelled intellectual assets, and has had significant impact. For more than ten years, an annual Intellectual Assets week has been organized in a collaboration between METI, the Nikkei stock exchange, and Waseda University. Another early pioneering nation in relation to the reporting of intangibles is Denmark, with strong research support from the Copenhagen Business School and Ministry of Economics.

Germany's Ministry of Wirtschaft has pioneered work on intangibles at a national level, known as Wissenbilanz.[4] Growing development work has emerged based on system dynamics modelling from MIT, and spreading in Europe.[5] Special free software has been offered as well as on-line assessment.[6] And further IC and knowledge management pioneering work is in progress in Austria.[7]

This work has spread from German speaking nations to a number of applications in Europe,[8] as well as in Asia,[9] and South America through the Brazilian Development Bank, BNDES, with an investment portfolio based on the IC paradigm and reporting.[10]

The World Intellectual Capital Initiative (WICI) is a private/public sector collaboration aimed at improving capital allocation through better corporate reporting information, with three major objectives:

1   To develop a voluntary global framework for measuring and reporting corporate performance to shareholders and other stakeholders. Throughout the world, different terms such as opportunities, risks, strategies, plans, intellectual assets/capital, intangibles, or value drivers are often used to describe several of the concepts within corporate performance.
2   To develop guidelines for measuring and reporting on industry-specific key performance indicators.
3   To facilitate the development of XBRL taxonomies for this content.

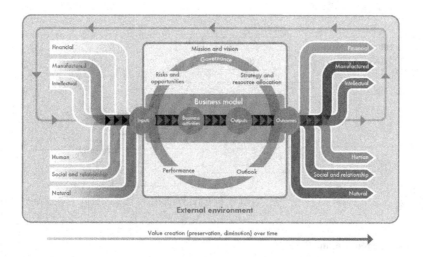

Figure 4.2   The International Integrated Reporting Council's approach to value creation
Source: www.theiirc.org

In Japan there has also been prototyping on integrated reporting (IR) initiatives, with the International Integrated Reporting Council in collaboration with METI and business.[11] The framework for IR is described in Figure 4.2.

Guidelines for financial analyst reporting on intangibles have been introduced by the European Federation of Financial Analysts Societies (EFFAS), set up in 1962 and now with some 15,000 financial analysts members from around 28 national chapters.[12] Within EFFAS there is a special group formed in 2008 on disclosure of intangibles, addressing ten principles for effective commuication of IC.[13]

Intangible assets modelling

The various approaches on a global scale for metrics of intangibles have different labels/taxonomy. There is a growing consensus that intangibles should be supplementary, sometimes also labelled complementary assets, based on research by among others Baruch Lev,

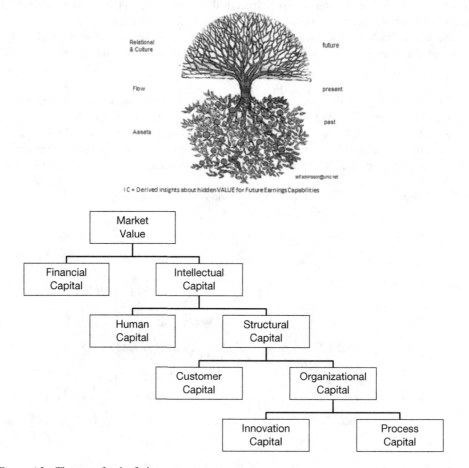

Figure 4.3   The roots for the fruits

Source: Edvinsson, L. (1997), *Accounting for Minds*, Skandia, Sweden

David Teece, Ahmed Bounfour, and James Guthrie, as well as practice prototyping by many others, including Göran Roos. However, a critical perspective may consider the assets as a residual, while the IC mapping and navigating is looking for the drivers of value creation. In a simplistic taxonomy, it can be thought of as 'the roots for the fruits'. Therefore I developed the visualizing model in 1992 (see Figure 4.3), inspired from Japan cultural perspectives of knowledge.

Perhaps even more essential is to look for the impact dimensions, as intelligence for forward navigation. The deeper meaning of IC is derived from insights of head value.

One of the efforts to move this modelling into practice emerged from the succesful work in Germany and Austria, and scaled up by the European Commission, with project leadership by the Fraunhofer Institute IPK, Berlin. The focus was on unlocking potential hidden value and communicating it properly.[14] Based on this work, a special communication approach emerged called CADIC, Cross Organizational Assessment and Development of Intellectual Capital.[15] In support of the Lisbon 2010 goals, both InCaS and CADIC aim to generate a practical model that addresses Europe's need to become a competitive and dynamic knowledge economy (see Figure 4.4).

It is a holistic model in search of the drivers of value creation and reporting to various stakeholders. It became valuable for credit analyses in the German banking sector. It also resulted in prototyping such as the Zukunftfähigkeit Index (i.e. an index of future earnings capabilites). This work on intangibles has also resulted in the introduction of International Accounting Standard IAS 38.[16]

Recently, in September 2016, *The WICI Intangibles Reporting Framework* was released, stemming from work that started in 2007 at the OECD. Initially a lot of prototyping and research work was done in Japan, by Professor Hanado and T. Sumita at METI. Now it incorporates Australia, Europe, Japan, and the US.[17] The report is supplemented by METI initiatives, such as the annual intangible assets week in Tokyo, a cross fertilaization between academics and practice that is an IC exchange.

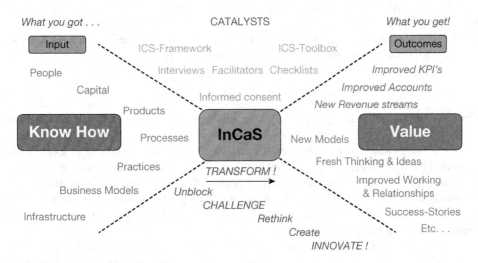

Figure 4.4   IC statement for Europe

Source: www.incas-europe.org

IC leadership mapping in progress

Traditional cost-based accounting is based on a paradigm of input–output, whereas IC leadership is more based on a paradigm of input–impact. The metrics of impact are among others based on opportunity-cost thinking: 'what if not?'

On a macro dimension we have been shifting over time towards a digitalized service economy, also highlighted by service research and innovation.[18] Examples of these include Skype, Spotify, and the gamification enterprise Mojang, with its game Minecraft, which started in Sweden but was purchased after only five years by Microsoft in 2014 for USD2.5 billion, with only 15 employees and millions of users.

Another dimension of IC leadership, which we prototyped in Skandia, is identifying the metrics of values. Initially researched and prototyped at Santa Clara University, California by the late Professor Brian Hall, a values system of 122 value attributes was identified and described and later refined into web-based models for leadership practice.[19] The challenge is to perceive, understand, and grasp the cross-cultural values space of intelligence in today's globalized world, with more or less integrated local multicultures.[20]

Clearly we need to re-paradigm away from the more than 500-year-old tradition of the cost-accounting paradigm. A start is to look for the three dimensions of value navigating, described in the book *Corporate Longitude* by Edvinsson in 2002. This was also prototyped into the Skandia Future Center that started in 1996 and has been followed by a number of such spaces in Europe with different labels, and 500 such Future Centers in Japan. The latest is a quest to develop the Wise Place, for innovation acceleration, under the leadership of the Japan Innovation Network and Professor Noburo Konno.

Holistic process of reframing

Mapping far beyond traditional cost accounting is critical for societal bridging. Work is already in progress on this among communities like Living Bridges Planet[21] and its community process of reframing through impact journey dialogues. In the future we may see impact navigators instead of financial controllers, whose job is not simply to take care of expenses but to have an impact on value creation over time. One such IC and IA knowledge exploration is taking place in a search for the new economics, such as the Evonomics Institute.[22]

Societal renewal and innovation

One observation about many societies is the growing population of the elderly, also refererred to as the silver economy. According to the European Commission, the silver economy brings new market opportunities arising from public and consumer expenditure related to the rights, needs, and demands of the growing population aged over 50. A project is in progress, with an expected report in February 2017, to consider the potential of this demographic.[23] While these senior citizens are mostly regarded as a burden to society, from an IC perspective they may, in fact, be the opposite, a silver potential, for whom we need to renew the societal framework.

One distinction of societal innovation is as a systemic change in the interplay of the state and civil society. It is a relative of social innovation, but differs by considering the state as an important co-creator in achieving sustainable systemic change (Lehtola and Ståhle, 2014). There are different societal innovation types to address, which can be viewed from different perspectives. See, for example, the following process approaches:[24]

- as a lumification process, or signal process in need of renewal and sustainabililty naviga-tion based on a perception of societal intelligence from knowledge navigators;
- as a new societal rulemaking process for a joint co-creative reframing, such as COP21 in Paris December 2015, or as civil rights innovations, like in Denmark with its ministerial prototyping Mind-Lab, or as in Malaysia's pioneering urban design with its super multi-media corridor and related specific e-law making, or the new business hybrid form in the US called L3C–Low–Profit Limited Liability company, or the Social Benefit Company in Australia;
- as a peace innovation process by triggering conflict resolution among citizens, by innova-tive harmonizing of citizens' relational interactions, such as the Aalto Camp for Societal Innovation in Finland;
- as a digital dialogue process across borders, generations, and cultures, such as Living Bridges Planet, that will initiate both local social innovation processes as well as create reframing collective perspectives.

For these value processes that are important for society's well-being, navigation as well as enterprising the mapping and metrics, needs to be both refined and more innovative (e.g. neuro science flow data on, for example, mirroring neurons).

Conclusion on intellectual capital 21: the next century in IC

IC is about visibility, understanding, flow, networking of brain capacity, velocity of transfor-mation of intangible human capital into more sustainable drivers of structural capital.

Its evolution is descibed in Edvinsson (2013). Like in the old economy, metrics have rele-vance and importance. Now it is even more essential to integrate the new metrics of intangibles into a new IC ruler for measuring, beyond the rough metrics like inches or expense-driven traditional accounting. Unfortunately insight and application of IC accounting still seem to be little known in the accounting and management profession. Consequently, there remains a distortion in the understanding of value creation in the knowledge economy as well as volatil-ity on stock exchanges. It raises the question: What is the measurement of the velocity of your innovative synapse making?

Notes

1 www.bimac.fi.
2 www.new-club-of-paris.org.
3 See, for example, www.NIC40.org and also recently a number of books and a 12 series booklets on National IC, www.springer.com/economics/growth/book/978-1-4614-5989-7.
4 www.akwissensbilanz.org.
5 www.incas-europe.org.
6 www.wissensbilanz-schnelltest.de.
7 http://ickm2016.org as well as www.km-a.net.
8 www.cadic-europe.org.
9 By among others www.wici-global.com.
10 www.bndes.gov.br/wps/portal/site/home/quem-somos/responsabilidade-social-e-ambiental/o-que-fazemos/relacionamento-clientes/analise-socioambiental/mae-capital-social-ambiental/.
11 http://integratedreporting.org/resource/international-ir-framework/.
12 www.effas.net.
13 http://effas.net/pdf/setter/EFFAS-CIC.pdf.
14 www.incas-europe.org.

15 www.cadic-europe.org/.
16 www.iasplus.com/en/standards/ias/ias38.
17 www.wici-global.com.
18 www.thesrii.org.
19 See, among others, www.culturengine.no and www.valuesonline.net.
20 A number of organizational practice approaches to IC are described in the 2014 book by Particia Ordonez des Pablos, www.routledge.com/books/details/9780415737821.
21 www.facebook.com/ImpactJourneyNews/.
22 http://evonomics.com.
23 See www.smartsilvereconomy.eu/home.
24 OISPG Yearbook 2016 – Open Innovation and Service Policy Group.

References

Edvinsson, L. (2002), *Corporate Longitude*, Bookhouse, Stockholm and Pearson, London.

Edvinsson, L. (2013), "IC 21: Reflections from 21 years of IC practice and theory", *Journal of Intellectual Capital*, Vol. 14, No. 1, pp. 163–172.

Lehtola, V. and Ståhle, P. (2014), "Societal innovation at the interface of the state and civil society", *The European Journal of Social Science Research*, Vol. 27, No. 2, pp. 152–174.

5

UNDERSTANDING AND EXPLOITING INTELLECTUAL CAPITAL GROUNDING REGIONAL DEVELOPMENT

Framework and metrics

Giovanni Schiuma and Antonio Lerro

Introduction

Academic and policy debate have widely recognized that knowledge-based factors, recently grouped according to the notion of intellectual capital (IC), increasingly play a fundamental role in territorial development dynamics (Boschma, 2004; Budd and Hirmis, 2004; Huggins and Izushi, 2007; Lerro and Schiuma, 2009; Pike *et al.*, 2006; Secundo *et al.*, 2016).

This acknowledgement is mainly linked to the recognition that territorial development is no longer based only on "hard" productivity, but on softer dimensions (Asheim, 1999; Dakhli and De Clercq, 2004; Kitson *et al.*, 2004; Maskell *et al.*, 1998; Morgan, 2004; Palma Lima and Ribeiro Carpinetti, 2012; Valkokari *et al.*, 2012). However, despite this acknowledgement, theory and practice highlight there remains a lack of clear, coherent, and shared frameworks for identifying, managing, assessing, and reporting IC (Dumay, 2009), particularly at regional level.

Two main issues emerge as relevant for academic and policy debate (Vieira *et al.*, 2011). First, the objective difficulty of identifying and measuring IC within regions. Second, although the quality and availability of data on different aspects of regional development has improved, there is still a lack of homogeneous and significant data about the endowment and use of IC. There is a need to define and collect data about knowledge sources that might explain why there are large differences in regional development patterns.

The aim of this chapter is to address these gaps. First, it briefly analyses the role of IC and its related components for regional development dynamics. Then, according to a knowledge-based interpretation of territorial strategic resources, the Knoware Tree as a framework for identifying and classifying territorial IC, and the Knoware Dashboard as a framework for driving the design of potential indicators and metrics to assess territorial IC, are presented. Finally, a set of key indicators for identifying and assessing IC that may support regional development paths is elaborated. We conclude the contribution by discussing directions of future research.

Knowledge and regional development: background

The first systematic attempts to study the relationship between knowledge and regional development were made by economic historians who wanted to understand why some territories managed to become richer while others continued to be poor (Abramovitz, 1986, 1994; Gerschenkron, 1962). The works of Gerschenkron and Abramovitz focused mainly on evidence from Europe and the US. However, from the 1970s onwards, several studies about the relevance of knowledge for development patterns emerged. Since the beginning of the 1970s, the most advanced economies in the world have been undergoing structural changes, turning them from industrialized economies based on labour, tangible capital, and material resources into economies based more and more on the creation, diffusion, and exploitation of new knowledge (Bell, 1973; Handy, 1989; Mandel, 2000). According to this perspective, different scholars have highlighted the emergence of a so-called knowledge-based economy (D'Aveni, 1995; Hitt *et al.*, 1998). Specifically, the concept of the knowledge-based economy indicates a new phase of development in which technology, scientific knowledge, and human resources represent the key strategic factors for growth and it is possible to identify a strong link between learning processes, innovation processes, competitiveness, and economic development. At the same time, the climate of crisis in manufacturing in most European countries, as well as in relation to traditional policies to support economic development, have determined a new interest in the local dimension of economic development. In turn, the emergence of a knowledge-based economy and a focus on models of development that are locally based has determined meaningful change in the way resources and capabilities to activate and enhance value creation are approached. Accordingly, in recent decades, various theoretical and practical contributions have argued that territorial development paths are supported by and linked to the ownership and use of assets, resources, and capabilities related – directly or indirectly – to the notion of knowledge (Secundo *et al.*, 2016).

Analysing specifically the local systems literature as well as territorial and regional development and competitiveness streams, it seems that there are a range of terms and concepts, frequently used interchangeably, with amgibuous definitions, that refer to territorial systems' resources and their role in activating dynamics of growth (Lerro and Schiuma, 2011; Moulaert and Sekia, 2003). There have been many convergent and/or competitive schools of thought, such as the Italian industrial district school (Albino and Schiuma, 2003; Becattini, 1987; Schiuma, 2000), the French stream of innovative milieux (Camagni, 2002; Ratti, 1992), and the learning region stream (Cooke, 1998; Morgan and Neuwelaer, 1998). Other scholars have highlighted, although not in a consistent way, the relevance of quality and skills to the labour force, the extent, depth, and orientation of social networks and institutional forms, the range and quality of cultural facilities and assets, the presence of an innovative and creative class, and the scale and quality of public infrastructure (Lerro and Schiuma, 2008). More recently, the strategic management research stream – concepts such as the resource-based view, dynamic capabilities, competence-based view, knowledge-based view, and economic and regional sciences streams – has considered these issues (Morgan, 2004; Pinch *et al.*, 2003). For example, Maskell *et al.* (1998) argues that the only economic production factors not subjected to 'ubiquification' are localized, sticky knowledge, including collective tacit, as well as disembodied codified, knowledge (Asheim, 1999). Storper's notion of "untraded interdependencies", such as flows of tacit knowledge, technological spillovers, networks of trust and cooperation, and local systems of norms and conventions, is also regarded as central to understanding the economic performance and competitive advantage of a territorial system (Storper, 1995). Carlsson and Jacobsson (1997) have underlined that the competitiveness of a region depends not only on the presence of a critical mass of qualified organizations within its boundaries but also on its capacity to coordinate the actions of these organizations.

However, the observation that 'soft' factors interact in the process of economic development might also be taken as supporting the view that a broader, more systematic approach that takes such interactions into account is required. This led to the development in the late 1990s of a new systemic conceptualization of the study of territories' capacity to generate and profit from knowledge, otherwise known as IC. Traditionally, IC has been analysed through three components: human capital, structural capital, and social and relational capital (Lerro and Schiuma, 2008, 2009). The first comprises essentially the know-how characterizing the different actors operating within the territorial system (Dakhli and De Clercq, 2004). Structural capital includes all those tangible and intangible assets relevant for the development, acquisition, management, and diffusion of knowledge (Lerro and Carlucci, 2007). Social and relational capital incorporates infrastructure related to relationship systems among stakeholders, local culture, history, attitudes, norms, values, behaviours, image, and other cultural dimensions characterizing territorial systems (Iyer *et al.*, 2005; Kitson *et al.*, 2004; Tura and Harmaakorpi, 2005).

Modelling IC: the Knoware Tree and the Knowledge Dashboard

The evaluation models of intangible resources proposed in the management literature are significant in that they are applied with the aim to identify and evaluate the resources that really define the knowledge domains of a territorial system.

However, most of the proposed models present two main limitations: they adopt a taxonomy based on a resource-based approach, rather than on a knowledge-based view, and generally disregard tangible resources as possible relevant knowledge resources. In order to take into account the knowledge-based nature of territorial resources, we propose the Knoware Tree. Starting from the recognition of the knowledge nature of the strategic territorial resources, the Knoware Tree, as a descriptive model, proposes a taxonomy of IC components building and representing the knowledge assets of the territorial systems.

In fact, the Knoware Tree is proposed as a framework for the assessment of IC components at the basis of value definition and value creation dynamics of a territorial system. The concept of Knoware – characterizing its definition – denotes all those resources that are made of, and/or embody knowledge, resulting from individual or collective cognitive activities. It stresses that a knowledge asset is a strategic resource characterized by the nature of knowledge, which can present in different forms, being tangible or intangible, alternative, tacit or codified, diverse and/ or related to its ability to satisfy specific wants and needs. The Knoware Tree is based on the recognition that, for any territorial system, it is possible to distinguish two main components: its actors, both internal and external, and its structural components, that is, all those elements that form the basis of its processes. Starting from this assumption, it defines two main categories of knowledge assets: those related to the stakeholders of a territorial system, named Stakeholder Knoware, and those related to the tangible and intangible infrastructures of a territorial system, named Structural Knoware. These two categories can be further divided into other sub-categories, specifically: Wetware and Netware for Stakeholder Knoware, and Hardware and Software for Structural Knoware. This taxonomy shares the basic hypotheses of other frameworks for the identification and evaluation of knowledge assets, which mainly adopt three categories of intangible resources: human resources, structural or organizational resources, and relational resources (Edvinsson and Malone, 1997; Roos *et al.*, 1997; Sveiby, 1997). However, it interprets them as knowledge assets that can be tangible or intangible as well as codified or tacit in nature.

The Wetware perspective, originally introduced by Romer (2003), denotes all knowledge related to the human resources of a territorial system. It gathers all that knowledge that forms the basis, and influences the behaviour and competencies, of human resources. The Netware perspective represents the set of knowledge assets that form the relationships characterizing a territorial system. This category of capital has been described in the strategic management literature in different ways, such as relational capital, customer capital, and social capital. It can be either internal to the local context, for example, the stakeholders networking dynamics taking place within a territorial system, or external representing all the possible ties linking a territorial system to its external economic, production, and socio-cognitive environment. The Hardware perspective includes all those assets relevant for the development, acquisition, management, and diffusion of knowledge, but tangible in nature as well as all the components linked to structural features of the territorial system. This category involves two main sub-categories, that is, physical and technological infrastructures. Finally, the Software perspective denotes the "soft externalities" (Kitson *et al.*, 2004) affecting the economic growth and wealth creation of a territorial system. It comprises attitudes, norms, values, behaviours, and other cultural dimensions of a territorial system and involves mainly aspects related to social resources, which affects the territorial output through changing the manner in which human resources use their cognitive abilities to innovate and develop enterprise, to leverage the tangible and financial resources, as well as to develop relational resources.

In order to deliver policy and managerial actions based on the exploitation of knowledge assets, policy-makers and managers need frameworks to identify, analyse, classify, and measure the knowledge assets of a territorial system. The Knoware Tree, as a descriptive framework, can support the identification and understanding of the IC of a territorial system both for interpretative as well as normative purposes. It represents a lens through which to analyse and interpret the key success resources and sources of local growth.

However, in order to make it operative, that is, to use it as a performance management tool, it needs to be populated with a set of measures that build an informative base to design, communicate, implement, and review policies and actions aimed at developing and managing territorial IC. This means that the Knoware Tree has to be integrated with a measurement system, that is, a systemic body of metrics to perform a qualitative and quantitative evaluation. For this reason, the Knoware Tree is complemented with the Knoware Dashboard (Figure 5.1). This latter adopts the four knowledge asset categories identified by the Knoware Tree and, consistent with the approach of performance measurement systems, defines four balanced measurement perspectives: Wetware, Netware, Hardware, and Software. Each perspective has to be populated with measures for evaluating the knowledge assets characterizing a specific local context. Regarding the definition of metrics, it is important to stress that knowledge assets are idiosyncratic and specific to their organizational context. This means that the definition of measures has to be mainly a context-related process. It has to take into account the properties of the context in which the evaluation is carried out as well as the strategic intent of the policy-makers and managers. The adoption of a high number of indicators could reduce users' managerial focus and hence the effectiveness of strategy (Marr and Schiuma, 2001).

Identifying indicators of knowledge-based factors at a regional level

Populating the Knoware Dashboard with a set of metrics acting as evaluation proxies allows researchers to measure the knowledge assets driving regional development dynamics. Single indicators provide relevant and useful management information in order to understand and

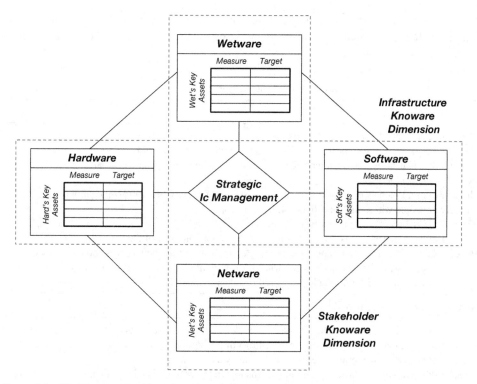

Figure 5.1   The Knoware Dashboard: the knowledge asset perspectives for identifying and assessing knowledge assets within regional systems

take action to manage specific and isolated performance issues. However, in order to get a holistic view of a phenomenon, we need measures that can offer an integrated picture of the investigated object.

Through the combination of single measures by an appropriate algorithm, it could be possible to define aggregate *indices*. The definition of such *indices* is particularly important for the assessment of local knowledge assets, since it can provide not only richer information about the knowledge assets ownership of a regional system, but also a 'thermometer' and a 'benchmarking' instrument for the definition, management, and review of territorial development strategies as well as for performing statistical analysis.

In recent years, various scholars (Lerro and Schiuma, 2008; Pasher and Shachar, 2005) and a number of institutions (e.g. the Council of Competitiveness, the European Union, the OECD, the United Nations, and the World Economic Forum) have focused on the identification and assessment of knowledge assets at a territorial level by adopting different measurement indicators and proxies. Some examples of these attempts are the EU Regional Yearbook, the EU Scoreboard, the EU Report on Science & Technology Indicators, the EU Sustainable Development Indicators, the Global Competitiveness Report, the Regional Intellectual Capital Index, and so on.

However, despite these different attempts to provide an informative basis for the identification and assessment of knowledge assets, characterizing geographic areas both at a meso- and meta-level, there is still a lack of consensus about the measures to be adopted for identifying and assessing the knowledge assets of a territorial system, and specifically, regional assets. Even if indicators and metrics need to be context specific, a set of standard indicators that can be used for identifying and assessing the ownership and use of knowledge assets needs to be identified.

Table 5.1 Measuring knowledge assets of a regional system

Wetware (Human Capital):

Number of graduates/100 people 25 years old
Number of Science and Engineering graduates/100 people 20–29 years old
Number of graduates employed after three years from the degree/100 people graduates
PC users/100 people
Number of professionals employed in public and private R&D activities/100 people employed
Number of people with basic educational skills/100 people
Number of PhD/number of graduates
Number of university students involved in a mobility program/number of the university students
Proxies about competence of public officials and Public Administration managers and employees
Number of professional managers leading firms of the region/number of firms of the regions
Number of participants in life-long learning/100 people aged 25–64

Netware (Relational Capital):

Number of firms associated in industry associations/total number of the firms of the region
Number of agreements among universities and firms of the regions
Number of agreements among universities and industry associations
Number of university stages activated within firms/total number of university students
Number of agreements among schools and firms of the region
Number of agreements among schools and industry associations

Hardware (Structural Capital):

Number of universities in the region
Number of research centres in the region
Number of technological districts in the region
Proxies about scientific production of the researchers of the universities of the region
Proxies about scientific production of the researchers of the research centres of the region
Internet access in schools
Proxies about patenting
Proxies about availability and use of e-governments services and tools.

Software (Social Capital):

Number of conflicting labour–employer relationships
Number of associations/100 people
Proxies about civic activities, trust and tolerance
Proxies about civil and political rights
Rate of irregular work
Crime rate
Gender pay gap
Proxies about citizens' confidence in EU institutions
Voter turnout in local elections
Voter turnout in national and EU parliamentary elections
Proxies about quality of governance: reputation, corruption, law and order, independence of courts, property rights, business friendly regulation.

This is a particularly important issue, since the definition of a list of standard measures can benefit both the assessment of the knowledge assets of a territorial system, and the benchmarking evaluation and definition of an information platform to integrate the different knowledge assets' measurement initiatives. Based on the discussion in the preceding section and on a review of previous sources (Castellacci and Archibugi, 2008; Chaminade and Vang, 2008; Fagerberg and Srholec, 2008), Table 5.1 presents an overview of the knowledge assets that we would expect to be used in supporting regional development dynamics, along with examples of possible empirical indicators.

Final remarks

This chapter has briefly analysed the role of the knowledge-based factors for regional development dynamics. According to a knowledge-based interpretation about territorial strategic resources, it has presented the Knoware Tree as a framework for identifying and classifying territorial knowledge-based factors and the Knoware Dashboard as a framework driving the design of potential indicators and metrics to assess territorial knowledge-based factors. Finally, a set of potential key indicators for identifying and assessing the knowledge-based factors that potentially support regional development paths has been elaborated.

We recognize some limitations of this study that need to be highlighted and call for further research on the identification and the assessment of the knowledge assets within territorial system. Unfortunately, there is a lack of data collected with the specific aim of capturing information about the knowledge assets characterizing regional systems. However, the national institutes of statistics and various institutions at a macro-level do gather a great amount of data which, if screened, can be used to assess knowledge dimensions. For this reason, it is critical to review and refine more and more the definition of a set of appropriate and standard indicators about knowledge assets at a territorial level. On the basis of an analysis of the theory and practitioner literature, we have identified a list of significant potential indicators that is not comprehensive, but represents a meaningful starting point for more rigorous analysis. Of course, further and different indicators about knowledge assets can be elaborated and defined, specifically in terms of building indicators on the base of primary sources. Finally, we call for further empirical investigation into the role and relevance of territorial knowledge assets for value creation within specific territorial systems in order to analyse differences and similarities in their development paths, as well as to refine the policy tools that can be used to identify and manage particular territorial resources.

References

Abramovitz, M. (1986), "Catching up, forging ahead, and falling behind", *Journal of Economic History*, Vol. 46, pp. 406–419.

Abramovitz, M. (1994), "The origins of the post-war catch-up and convergence boom", in Fagerberg, J., Verspagen, B., and von Tunzelman, N. (Eds), *The Dynamics of Technology, Trade and Growth*, Edward Elgar, Aldershot, UK.

Albino, V. and Schiuma, G. (2003), "New forms of knowledge creation and diffusion in the industrial district of Matera-Bari", in Belussi, F., Gottardi, G. and Rullani, E. (Eds), *The Net Evolution of Local Systems – Knowledge Creation, Collective Learning and Variety of Institutional Arrangements*, Kluwer, Dordrecht, The Netherlands.

Asheim, B. T. (1999), "Interactive learning and localised knowledge in globalising learning economies", *GeoJournal*, Vol. 49, No. 4, pp. 345–352.

Becattini, G. (1987), *Mercato e Forze Locali: Il Distretto Industriale*, Il Mulino, Bologna.

Bell, D. (1973), *The Coming of Post-industrial Society*, Basic Books, New York.

Boschma, R. A. (2004), "Competitiveness of regions from an evolutionary perspective", *Regional Studies*, Vol. 38, No. 9, 991–999.

Budd, L. and Hirmis, A. (2004), "Conceptual framework for regional competitiveness", *Regional Studies*, Vol. 38, No. 9, pp. 1015–1028.

Camagni, R. (2002), "On the concept of territorial competitiveness: Sound or misleading?", *Urban Studies*, Vol. 39, pp. 2395–2411.

Carlsson, B. and Jacobsson, S. (1997), "Diversity creation and technological systems: A technology policy perspective", in Endquist, C. (Ed.), *Systems of Innovation: Technologies, Institutions and Organizations*. Frances Pinter, London/Washington.

Castellacci, F. and Archibugi, D. (2008), "The technology clubs: The distribution of the knowledge across nations", *Research Policy*, Vol. 37, pp. 1659–1673.

Chaminade, C. and Vang, J. (2008), "Globalisation of knowledge production and regional innovation policy: Supporting specialized hubs in the Bangalore software industry". *Research Policy*, Vol. 37, pp. 1684–1696.

Cooke, P. (1998), "Introduction", in Braczyk, H. J., Cooke, P., and Heidenreich, M. (Eds), *Regional Innovation Systems*, UCL Press, London.

D'Aveni, R. (1995), "Coping with hypercompetition: Utilizing the new 7S's framework", *Academy of Management Executive*, Vol. 9, pp. 45–60.

Dakhli, M. and De Clercq, D. (2004), "Human capital, social capital, and innovation: A multi-country study", *Entrepreneurship & Regional Development*, Vol. 16, pp. 107–128.

Dumay, J. C. (2009), "Intellectual capital measurement: A critical approach", *Journal of Intellectual Capital*, Vol. 10, No. 2, pp. 190 – 210.

Edvinsson, L. and Malone, M. S. (1997), *Intellectual Capital: The Proven Way to Establish Your Company's Real Value by Measuring its Hidden Values*, Piatkus, London.

Fagerberg, J. and Srholec, M. (2008), "National innovation systems, capabilities and economic development", *Research Policy*, Vol. 37, pp. 1417–1435.

Gerschenkron, A. (1962), *Economic Backwardness in Historical Perspective*, The Belknap Press, Cambridge, MA.

Handy, C. B. (1989), *The Age of Unreason*, Harvard Business Review Press, Cambridge, MA.

Hitt, M. A., Gimeno, J., and Hoskinsson, R. E. (1998), "Current and future research methods in strategic management", *Organizational Research Methods*, Vol. 1, pp. 6–44.

Huggins, R. and Izushi, H. (2007), *Competing for Knowledge, Creating, Connecting, and Growing*, Routledge, London and New York.

Iyer, S., Kitson, M., and Toh, B. (2005), "Social capital, economic growth and regional development" *Regional Studies*, Vol. 39, No. 8, pp. 1015–1040.

Kitson, M., Martin, R., and Tyler, P. (2004), "Regional competitiveness: An elusive yet key concept?", *Regional Studies*, Vol. 38, No. 9, pp. 991–999.

Lerro, A. and Carlucci, D. (2007), "Intellectual capital and regions: Origins, theoretical foundations and implications for decision-makers", *International Journal of Learning and Intellectual Capital*, Vol. 4, pp. 357–376.

Lerro, A. and Schiuma, G. (2008), "Knowledge-based capital in building regional innovation capacity", *Journal of Knowledge Management*, Vol. 12, pp. 21–36.

Lerro, A. and Schiuma, G. (2009), "Knowledge-based dynamics of regional development: The case of Basilicata region", *Journal of Knowledge Management*, Vol. 13, pp. 287–300.

Lerro A. and Schiuma G. (2011), "Editorial knowledge-based dynamics of local development: A position paper", *International Journal of Knowledge-Based Development*, Vol. 2, No. 1, pp. 1–15.

Mandel, M. J. (2000), *The Coming Internet Depression*, Basic Books, New York.

Marr, B. and Schiuma, G. (2001), "Measuring and managing intellectual capital and knowledge assets in new economy organisations", in Bourne, M. (Eds), *Handbook of Performance Measurement*, Gee, London.

Maskell, P., Eskelinien, H., Hannibalsson, I., Malberg, A., and Vatne, E. (1998), *Competitiveness, Localized Learning and Regional Development*, Routledge, London, New York.

Morgan, K. (2004), "The exaggerated death of geography: Learning, proximity and territorial innovation systems", *Journal of Economic Geography*, Vol. 4, pp. 3–22.

Morgan, K. and Neuwelaer, C. (Eds), (1998), *Regional Innovation Strategies: The Challenge for Less Favoured Regions*, Jessica Kingsley, London.

Moulaert, F. and Sekia, F. (2003), "Territorial innovation models: A critical survey". *Regional Studies*, Vol. 37, No. 3, pp. 289–302.

Palma Lima, R. H. and Ribeiro Carpinetti, L. C. (2012), "Analysis of the interplay between knowledge and performance management in industrial clusters", *Knowledge Management Research & Practice*, Vol. 10, No. 4, pp. 368–379.

Pasher, E. and Shachar, S. (2005), "The intellectual capital of the State of Israel" in Bounfour, A. & Edvinsson, L. (Eds), *Intellectual Capital for Communities*, Elsevier Butterworth-Heinemann, Boston, MA.

Pike, A., Rodriguez-Pose, A., and Tomaney, J. (2006), *Local and Regional Development*, Regional Studies Association, Routledge, London.

Pinch, S., Henry, N., Jenkins, M., and Tallman, S. (2003), "From 'industrial districts' to 'knowledge clusters': A model of knowledge dissemination and competition in industrial agglomerations", *Journal of Economic Geography*, Vol. 3, pp. 373–388.

Ratti, R. (1992), *Innovation Technologique et Développement Régional*, Meta-Editions, Lausanne, Switzerland.

Romer, P. (2003), The soft revolution: Achieving growth by managing intangibles" in Hand, J. and Lev, B. (Eds), *Intangible Assets*, Oxford University Press, Oxford, UK.

Roos, J., Roos, G., Dragonetti, N. C., and Edvinsson, L. (1997), *Intellectual Capital: Navigating the New Business Landscape*, Macmillan, London.

Schiuma, G. (2000), "Dinamiche Cognitive nei Distretti Industriali in Evoluzione". *Economia e Politica Industriale*, Vol. 27, No. 106, pp. 105–138.

Secundo, G., Dumay, J. C., Schiuma, G., and Passiante, G. (2016), "Managing intellectual capital through a collective intelligence approach", *Journal of Intellectual Capital*, Vol. 17, No. 2, pp. 298–319.

Storper, M. (1995), "Competitiveness policy options: The technology-regions connection", *Growth and Change*, Spring, pp. 285–308.

Sveiby, K. E. (1997), "The Intangible Asset Monitor", *Journal of Human Resource Costing & Accounting*, Vol. 2, No. 1, pp. 73–97.

Tura, T. and Harmaakorpi, V. (2005), "Social capital in building regional innovative capability", *Regional Studies*, Vol. 39, No. 8, pp. 1111–1125.

Valkokari, K., Paasi J., and Rantala, T. (2012), "Managing knowledge within networked innovation", *Knowledge Management Research & Practice*, Vol. 10, No. 1, pp. 27–40.

Vieira, E., Neira, I., and Vazquez, E. (2011), "Productivity and innovation economy: Comparative analysis of European NUTS II 1995–2004", *Regional Studies*, Vol. 45, No. 9, pp. 1269–1286.

6

PAST, PRESENT, AND FUTURE

Intellectual capital and the New Zealand public sector

Grant Samkin and Annika Schneider

Introduction

Organizations seek to capture the value of knowledge and harness its value-creating potential through accounting for intellectual capital (IC). The IC movement emerged in the late 1980s when a group of forward-thinking practitioners began to seek alternatives to the traditional transactions-based financial accounting model. They sought methods of accounting that adequately accounted for the value drivers of the 'new' economy where the key value driver was knowledge (Guthrie and Petty, 2000; Dumay, 2014). By accounting for IC, organizations seek to capture the value of knowledge and harness its value-creating potential.

Since the 1990s, IC as a research discipline has grown and the proliferation of journals and papers covering the topic suggests that the current research literature on IC is well developed. For example, studies have examined IC reporting in private sector organizations in both developed and developing countries: Australia (Guthrie and Petty, 2000); Canada (Bontis, 2003); China (Yi and Davey, 2010; Liao *et al.*, 2013); India (Kamath, 2007, 2008; Vishnu and Gupta, 2014); Italy (Bozzolan *et al.*, 2003); Malaysia (Goh and Lim, 2004); New Zealand (Whiting and Miller, 2008); Spain (Ordóñez de Pablos, 2003; Oliveras *et al.*, 2008); Sri Lanka (Abeysekera and Guthrie, 2005); South Africa (April *et al.*, 2003; Firer and Stainbank, 2003), and the United Kingdom (Shareef and Davey, 2006).

A number of studies have also focused on the public sector. The level of IC research in the public sector is, however, limited when compared to that which has been undertaken in private sector settings. However, the public sector research that has been carried out has focused on a variety of organizational types (Dumay *et al.*, 2015) including: cultural and heritage organizations (Donato, 2008); digital or smart cities (Dameri *et al.*, 2014; Dameri and Ricciardi, 2015); government departments (Dumay and Guthrie, 2007); hospitals (Habersam and Piber, 2003); local governments (Sciulli *et al.*, 2002; Cinca *et al.* 2003; Schneider and Samkin, 2008a, 2008b; Farneti and Guthrie, 2009); territorial and regional development (Schiuma and Lerro, 2017); police departments (Collier, 2001); regional clusters (Pöyhönen and Smedlund, 2004); research organizations (Leitner and Warden, 2004); schools (Kelly, 2004); third sector (Fletcher *et al.*, 2003; Cuganesan, 2017); and universities (Sánchez and Elena, 2006; Cañibano and Sánchez, 2009; Sánchez *et al.*, 2009; Villasalero, 2014).

The purpose of this chapter is to review and critique the IC research that has been undertaken in New Zealand and, in particular, review the extent of public sector IC research. The research is then positioned within the four stages of IC research (Dumay *et al.*, 2017). First stage IC research was concerned with raising awareness. The second stage comprised theory building and IC frameworks. The third stage investigates IC in practice from a critical and performative perspective (see Guthrie *et al.*, 2012; Dumay, 2013, 2014). Influenced by critical research in social and environmental accounting, the fourth stage of IC research sets out to "broaden the scope of IC research beyond the managerialist approach of third stage research" (Dumay *et al.*, 2017). Academics need to be familiar with the four stages of IC research in order to position their work to achieve the most impact and avoid merely replicating past studies that do not present significant new findings (Dumay, 2016; Dumay *et al.*, 2017).

The four stages of IC research

Four stages of IC research emerged as the field developed. The progression of these four stages is illustrated in Figure 6.1. The larger spacing between stages two and three represents the divide that researchers need to cross in order to progress the field beyond 'what is IC' type research.

The first stage of research prior to the mid 1990s was predominantly practitioner-led, and focused on raising awareness of the importance of IC and, in particular, how it could be used to create and manage sustainable competitive advantage (Petty and Guthrie, 2000). As Dumay (2013) explains, the creation of standards and guidelines to make the invisible visible, became the foundation for IC development.

Organizational knowledge was considered to be central to competitive advantage. Second stage IC research, therefore, focused on financial performance and value creation with particular emphasis on gathering evidence to support IC as a legitimate field of enquiry. These efforts focused on the development of a taxonomy, as well as the creation of guidelines, standards, and

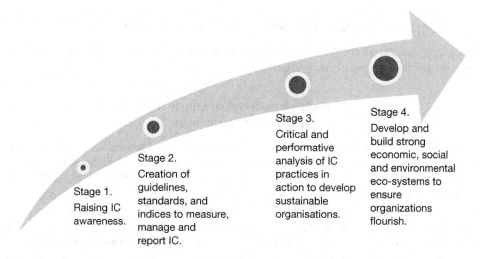

Figure 6.1   Four states of intellectual capital research

frameworks for measuring, managing, and reporting IC. Research also focused on how these normative frameworks could be used to understand the impact of IC on financial performance and value creation (Guthrie *et al.*, 2012; Dumay, 2013).

The first and second stages contributed to the codification of a common understanding of what IC is and why it is important in a 'top down' approach. From several alternative classifications that appear in the literature, three main IC components and related elements have emerged. While the terminology may differ between authors "they basically refer to: *human competencies*, the knowledge embedded in people; *structural capital*, knowledge embedded in the organisation and its systems; and *relational capital*, the knowledge embedded in customers and other relationships external to the organisation" (Guthrie *et al.*, 2012, p. 70, italics in original).[1]

By the early 2000s there was tacit recognition from several leading academics that IC research had failed to live up to its potential. In order for the field to progress further, IC research needed to move beyond the relatively well-developed stage one and stage two research, to a third stage. The third stage of IC research surpassed merely looking at 'what is' to critically examine IC practices in action. It promotes a practical, performative IC approach rather than a theoretical, ostensive one (Dumay, 2009; Guthrie *et al.*, 2012; Dumay and Garanina, 2013; Guthrie and Dumay, 2015). This 'bottom up' research stage focuses on and emphasizes how IC can be used and managed within an organization (Guthrie *et al.*, 2012). This perspective uses the evaluation methods detailed and refined in stage one and two research as tools that enable managers to create and sustain value. A broader definition of value is recognized that incorporates not only monetary value but considers the utility and importance of products and services (Dumay and Garanina, 2013).

While third stage research focuses on building strong organizations, Dumay (2013) explains that fourth stage research further extends this notion into developing IC ecosystems. These are strong social, environmental, and economic ecosystems where the healthy organizations built by incorporating stage three ideas can flourish (Dumay, 2013). Fourth stage research, while still in its infancy, complements rather than opposes third stage research, in order to progress "beyond the crossroads to a new IC-based future" (Dumay, 2013, p. 8).

Contextualizing New Zealand IC research

This section details and critiques the IC research undertaken in a New Zealand context to date. These studies are then positioned within the four stages of IC research.

IC research undertaken jointly with New Zealand academics

A literature search identified a small and narrowly focused body of research undertaken in New Zealand by selected academics (see, for example, Shareef and Davey, 2006; Davey *et al.*, 2009; Yi and Davey, 2010; Yi *et al.*, 2011a, 2011b, 2015; Liao *et al.*, 2013; Wang *et al.*, 2016). This research has been undertaken jointly with other authors and has tended to focus on an international rather than a New Zealand context. These ten studies are summarized in Appendix A.

The jurisdictions covered in these studies are limited. Of the ten studies, six make use of Chinese data (one study compares Indian and Chinese data), two use Australian data, and the remaining two use data from England and North America. The primary source of data in all ten studies was annual reports of a single reporting period (Clarke *et al.*, 2011 being an exception). Other than Yi *et al.* (2011a) who set out to construct an integrated theoretical framework that could be used to explain and predict voluntary IC disclosure practices by firms, the majority of the studies in Appendix A employ a content analysis methodology using a disclosure index to measure the level of IC disclosure of selected organizations. Clarke *et al.* (2011) and Whiting and Woodcock (2011) also employed statistical analysis.

IC research using New Zealand data

A literature search identified 12 articles that explored IC in a New Zealand context using data from New Zealand. These are summarized in Appendix B. These 12 articles can be split into 2 groups. The first group comprises nine papers that make use of data from the private sector, while the second group consists of three papers that use public sector data. Of the nine papers making use of New Zealand data, the majority used data derived from annual reports. Content analysis using a disclosure index was the primary data collection method. The remaining papers used data collected from a questionnaire survey and interviews.

The second group of three articles that used public sector data represents the entire body of IC research into this sector that has been undertaken in New Zealand to date. These three public sector studies used content analysis combined with a disclosure index as the method of data collection.

Critique of New Zealand IC research

Overall, the majority of New Zealand IC research is largely similar (exceptions are Gibb, 2007; Steenkamp and Northcott, 2007; Yi *et al.*, 2011a; Whiting *et al.*, 2017). The majority of the research reports the results of disclosure studies using content analysis. These disclosure indices are based on an early model reported by Guthrie and Petty (2000) and adapted or modified to fit a particular industry (Shareef and Davey, 2006; Davey *et al.*, 2009). External capital was the most frequently disclosed category, with further findings showing, rather unsurprisingly, large organizations tend to disclose more than smaller ones.

As a consequence of the methods used in the papers, their limitations are also similar. The sample sizes are relatively small and only one year's data is examined, which means that the results may not reflect the true extent of IC disclosures in a New Zealand context. Furthermore, the lack of longitudinal research results in a failure in providing any insight into IC disclosure trends. While comparative studies do hold some potential, limiting them to annual report disclosures ensures that the only findings of note may be that companies in one particular jurisdiction have more extensive or higher quality IC disclosures than companies in another jurisdiction. The results of these types of studies may be of little use to organizations wishing to harness the value-creating potential of IC. Despite these limitations, Goebel (2015) suggests that disclosure studies can be useful when used in meta-analysis.

Despite the differences in the IC frameworks used for the analysis, conclusions can be drawn across the results as long as most of the widely used IC items are included in the prior IC research frameworks (Goebel, 2015). Nevertheless, in regards to the generation of more disclosure studies, and drawing on Dumay and Cai (2014, p. 274), it is reasonable to conclude that unless something momentous occurs that requires changes to levels of IC disclosures in those jurisdictions, "what further knowledge might be gained from providing more research and articles from these countries" other than to "prove that companies are unwilling to publicly disclose IC to their stakeholders" (Dumay and Cai, 2014, p. 282; see also Dumay, 2016).

When the New Zealand IC capital research detailed in Appendix A and Appendix B is examined within the framework of the four stages of IC research (Guthrie *et al.*, 2012;

Dumay, 2013, 2014; Dumay *et al.*, 2017) the positioning of the studies is clear. The majority of New Zealand IC research considered in this chapter can be positioned as stage two IC research. With the exception of Gibb (2007), the research detailed in Appendix A and Appendix B demonstrates a failure of New Zealand academics to engage critically with the literature and move beyond capturing simply 'what is IC' into third and fourth stage research.

This position is supported by Dumay and Cai (2014, 2015) in their review and critique of the current status of IC research using content analysis (CA) of annual reports as a research method. Dumay and Cai (2014, 2015) argue that the uncritical use of CA as a research method means that the impact of this work is waning (see also Dumay, 2016). In fact, Dumay and Cai (2014, p. 265) go so far as to suggest that "CA-based ICD [IC disclosure] studies may no longer be relevant". Dumay and Cai (2014, 2015) provide a number of reasons for this including: using the method to drive the research question rather than the question driving the method; a lack of understanding and application of CA; the failure to use CA in an innovative way; and studies by research students from their own country, co-authored by supervisors, that make little effort to compare or contrast similar studies or propose models or frameworks that explain IC mechanisms or drivers (Yi *et al.*, 2011a; Wang *et al.*, 2016, are exceptions).

The future direction and outlook for IC research in the New Zealand public sector

The public sector differs from the private sector in that it tends to have multiple non-financial objectives. By making more intensive use of human resources and knowledge, the public sector produces a final product that is usually an intangible service (Cinca *et al.*, 2003). It relies on the generation and utilization of capabilities and knowledge to deliver public services (Cuganesan *et al.*, 2012). While profit-seeking is not a primary motivation, the public sector is a major contributor to GDP in most economies (Dumay *et al.*, 2015).

Like many jurisdictions, the New Zealand public sector underwent significant reform during the 1980s and 1990s. These reforms have been extensively covered in the literature (see for example, Lawrence *et al.*, 1994; Boston *et al.*, 1996, 1999; Boston and Pallot, 1997; Bale and Dale, 1998; Boston, 1998; Pallot, 1998; Guthrie *et al.*, 1999; Hay, 2001; Jones *et al.*, 2001) and have been described as one of the most comprehensive and far-reaching programs of public management reform ever undertaken (Boston, 2000). These reforms, which impacted all areas of the public sector, were consistent with the ideas, principles, and doctrines of new public management (Hood, 1991). The reforms drew on the "theoretical support of economics including principle choice theory and new institutional economics combined with managerialism" (Newberry, 2001, p. 259). In reviewing the New Zealand public sector reforms, Boston (2000) goes so far as to suggest that the comprehensive and far-reaching reforms "constitute one of best examples of systemic change anywhere in the world" (p. 25). They included:

- a systematic program of corporatization, privatization and commercialization;
- the devolution of human resource management responsibilities from the State Services Commission to the chief executives of individual departments and Crown agencies;
- the introduction of new financial management systems, including accrual accounting, an output-based system of appropriations, capital charges and a distinction (for the purposes of resourcing, monitoring and accountability) between the Crown's 'ownership' and 'purchase' interests;

- the institution of major structural changes, such as the transfer of many service delivery functions to separate, non-departmental agencies;
- the introduction of an extensive network of 'contractualist' devices to govern the relationship between 'principals' and 'agents' within the public sector, as well as between public and private organizations; and
- the development of a comprehensive system of strategic management under which ministers specify their strategic objectives over the medium term and use these to set departmental priorities.

(Boston, 2000, pp. 30–31)

These broad financial management reforms were aimed at increasing the efficiency, effectiveness, and accountability of central and local government. Private sector management models that included the setting of targets, contracting out of services, competition, and performance measurement were introduced and adopted (Kong, 2008). The rationale behind the reforms was to provide the public sector organizations with greater freedom to deliver programs and services to the public at reduced costs. Although profit was not the primary focus of the reforms, providing value for money services, or what Farneti and Dumay (2014, p. 377) describe as "delivery of public value", was emphasized.

In their comprehensive review of IC reporting literature, Guthrie *et al.* (2012) expressed surprise at the lack of emphasis on IC research in the public and not-for-profit sectors. Although the IC public sector research conducted to date has covered a number of organizational settings, the depth of IC research in this sector remains limited. The public sector comprises complex knowledge-intensive organizational forms financed largely from the public purse. As such, they are subject to various levels of public scrutiny, particularly when an organization fails to provide value for money services.

Knowledge and intangible value are a major source of competitive advantage for public entities, of which inputs in the form of human resources and knowledge, outputs in the form of public services, and performance measures in terms of value for money, are predominantly intangible (Ramírez, 2010). One possible answer to a measure of public value comes from incorporating IC management as an approach to increasing value in the public sector (Dragonetti and Roos, 1998; Ramírez, 2010). Traditionally, value is used in the context of financial or monetary wealth (Dane-Nielsen and Nielsen, 2017). Dumay (2016) expands the definition of value to include not only wealth, but utility, social, and environmental value. These are described as the creation of useful products and services, contributing to societal aims, and conserving the environment. This is especially applicable in the public sector, where outcomes and results are not measured purely in monetary terms. Thus if public value is dependent on the maximization of the three IC components, a number of questions arise according to Guthrie and Russo (2014, p. 4). How is public value conceptualized and practised? How is public value identified, managed, measured, and reported? How, when, and why should public agencies use public value performance measurement and management systems to enhance organizational performance? Can public sector organizations strengthen public accountability and create conditions that allow citizens, elected officials, and public managers to align and pursue a vision of public value creation?

Given a general acceptance that IC is a major value and growth creator, understanding how the public sector views IC and public value will become increasingly important. A general search on the websites of a number of New Zealand public sector organizations[2] that are likely to consider IC as an important asset revealed how these organizations view IC. Other than the website of the Controller and Auditor General of New Zealand, which returned two findings, and New Zealand Post, which returned one discrete finding, the search term 'intellectual capital' was not highlighted in any of the documents made available to stakeholders on the online platforms associated with those organizations. A similar search conducted using the term 'public value' as a substitute for IC also yielded limited results. One example from the New Zealand Government (2008, p. 88) acknowledged the existence of public value within the public sector as follows:

> The review team also explored the concept of public value originally proposed by Harvard Professor Mark Moore, which has permeated the thinking around performance of the State. Public value reflects, in broad terms, the kind of "good government" goals and expectations that are usually established in most Commonwealth countries. In particular the public value concept lies behind much of the UK work on consumer voice and choice.

However, despite the term public value being mentioned in 2008, a targeted search of a selection of New Zealand public sector organizational websites suggests it is not yet in widespread use within documents available in the public domain.

That these organizations did not acknowledge the importance of IC or public value on a platform easily accessible by all interested stakeholders is interesting. While these organizations may recognize that IC plays a role in the provision of services and the generation of public value, drawing on the work of Mouritsen *et al.* (2004, 2005) on the development of knowledge management and IC statements in Danish public sector organizations, one could conclude that these New Zealand organizations have failed to create IC or public value policy statements that are of interest or relevance to stakeholders.

In spite of the apparent lack of acknowledgement on the part of the New Zealand public sector of the importance of IC, there are a number of advantages associated with undertaking IC research in this area. The first is the number of individual organizational settings that could form the focus of research. These include, but are not limited to, the health sector, law enforcement including police and prison services, military, individual government departments such as the Ministry of Business, Innovation and Employment, Crown Research Institutes, state-owned enterprises, and local government. Second, the limited body of in-depth research into particular organizational forms to date means there is still ample opportunity for research in this area, especially given the evidence that new methods of measuring and accounting for value are required (Cuganesan and Lacey, 2011). Third, the way in which IC information is produced, audited, disseminated, and consumed has changed vastly, so that significant amounts of information are also now being produced by those outside the reporting entity (Dumay and Guthrie, 2017). Research into this 'involuntary disclosure' communicated by stakeholders and stakeseekers promises to contribute not only to the practice of IC but also to the wider social and environmental good (Dumay and Guthrie, 2017) in both the public and private sectors.

Thus, the public sector is likely to be a fruitful area for IC research moving forward due to both the number of individual organizations that occupy this space, as well as the number of different organizational settings. In practice, this means that in the context of a small developed country such as New Zealand, it is feasible to include all of the organizations in a particular study (see, for example, Schneider and Samkin, 2008a, 2008b) rather than relying on the annual reports of a limited number of organizations that may not be representative of the population as a whole. A number of areas likely to provide useful avenues of research are detailed below. This is not meant to be a comprehensive exposition of all the potential areas of study, but rather a suggestion of future research areas or research interest and the stages of IC research that it covers. This includes the knowledge sector and state-owned entities. 'Big data' and the role it could play in local government and health sector research is then explicated.

Knowledge sector

Public sector IC research focusing on the knowledge sector, particularly public universities, has been undertaken in a number of areas or jurisdictions including Denmark (Hellström and Husted, 2004), New Zealand (Low *et al.*, 2015), Austria (Sánchez *et al.*, 2009), Spain (Sánchez and Elena, 2006; Cañibano and Sánchez, 2009; Ramírez, 2010; Ramírez Córcoles *et al.*, 2011), South Africa (Veltri and Silvestri, 2015), and the United Kingdom (Bezhani, 2010). As with other public sector bodies, public universities differ from private sector organizations in that their *raison d'être* is the production and diffusion of knowledge rather than profit generation. As recipients of both public and private funding, it is incumbent on universities to illustrate that these funds have been productively employed to generate or produce new knowledge useful to a range of societal stakeholders (Cañibano and Sánchez, 2009). As their primary investments are in research and human resources, individual universities as well as the overall university sector lends itself to what is described as third stage IC research (Guthrie *et al.*, 2012; Dumay and Garanina, 2013). Bezhani (2010) provides an indication of third stage research that could be usefully undertaken in the New Zealand university setting. This includes practical case study research in improving the design and implementation of performance measurement systems surrounding IC.

Other organizational types that form part of the public knowledge sector include Crown Research Institutes and schools. Stakeholders of the Crown Research Institutes rely on the research output of these organizations to maintain an internationally competitive advantage in a number of fields (for example, agriculture in the New Zealand context). These Crown Research Institutes play a central and critical role in the creation of new knowledge in New Zealand because as Ahn and York (2010) explain, they own nearly 70 per cent of intellectual properties and scientific publications (see also Lee *et al.*, 2012).

The setting of public and private schools as an area of IC research has largely been neglected (an exception is Kelly, 2004). That this is the case is unsurprising as IC is not something that has traditionally been associated with this knowledge area. Schools compete for local and foreign students and more committed and superior teachers whose knowledge and experience need to be managed. As with other organizational forms in the knowledge sector, IC management within schools focuses on knowledge creation and utilization. That is, research into how individual teacher and school knowledge is generated, and how individual experience communicated in teaching and administrative or management competencies is used to add value to consumers (students, parents, and communities) of education (Kelly, 2004) could prove insightful.

How Crown Research Institutes and schools deal with or manage IC in the New Zealand context has yet to be considered. As with the university sector, these knowledge sector organizations lend themselves to case study type research that fits in with third stage IC research "based on a critical and performative analysis of IC practices in action" (Guthrie *et al.*, 2012, p. 69).

State-owned entities

In their study, Veltri and Silvestri (2015) set out to critically evaluate the integrated report of a South African public university and compare it with the International Integrated Reporting

Council (IIRC) framework. They wished to establish whether the university's integrated report matched the IIRC framework's main aim: to integrate IC and non-IC information within a single report. The state-owned entity, New Zealand Post, was a participant in the IIRC's pilot program, and produced the country's first integrated report in 2013. As such, a critical examination of public sector integrated reports and how human, social and relationship, natural, and intellectual capital integrate with financial and manufacturing capital to create value in the public sector is a worthwhile endeavour (Guthrie and Dumay, 2015) and consistent with stage three IC research.

Big data

The various public sector organizations, including local government, health, social service, education, law enforcement, and security services, now collect extensive data on individuals with "greater granularity and frequency" Wielki (2013, p. 985). As Tene and Polonetsky (2013, p. 240) explain, these data sources and means of collection include:

> [o]nline transactions, email, video, images, clickstream, logs, search queries, health records, and social networking interactions; gleaned from increasingly pervasive sensors deployed in infrastructure such as communications networks, electric grids, global positioning satellites, roads and bridges, as well as in homes, clothing, and mobile phones.

The databases associated with this data harvesting by public sector organizational forms are likely to play an increasingly pivotal societal role. However, the transactional format of the current accounting framework means that a financial value is seldom ascribed to these data sources. A consistently reported element in the disclosure indices featured in prior research (see, for example, Appendix A and Appendix B) is databases or information systems. The challenge facing public sector organizations is how big data 'exchange' value, represented by its reusable IC (Sahay, 2016, p. 421), can be used to address local problems, develop and improve service performance, and generate value.

Health sector

Several studies have examined the New Zealand health sector, particularly in the aftermath of the public sector reforms of the 1980s and 1990s (Lawrence *et al.*, 1994; Boston *et al.*, 1996, 1999; Boston and Pallot, 1997; Bale and Dale, 1998; Boston, 1998; Pallot, 1998; Guthrie *et al.*, 1999; Hay, 2001; Jones *et al.*, 2001; Newberry, 2001). Despite a number of international studies focusing on IC research in the health sector (see, for example, Habersam and Piber, 2003; Yang and Lin, 2009; Veltri *et al.*, 2011; Vagnoni and Oppi, 2015) there are no studies that have focused on this sector in the New Zealand context. This is surprising given the extensive investment in specialist knowledge required for the effective operation of these organizational forms. A fruitful avenue for future research is how the big data generated, collected, managed, and used by the New Zealand health sector can be used to generate and leverage value and provide services.

Local government sector

An increase in the use of big data goes hand in hand with the continued evolution of digital or smart cities. Although the concept of smart cities or digital cities has gained traction in the academic literature, it has yet to be incorporated into the accounting literature (Dameri *et al.*, 2014; Dameri and Ricciardi, 2015 are exceptions). The advent of smart cities or digital cities has the potential to play a major role in future IC research. This is likely to provide a fruitful area of local government research as local government bodies,[3] as well as a state-owned entity in the form of Land Information New Zealand, are involved in the process of using smart city technologies. The benefits of these collaborations according to Land Information New Zealand (2016) include:

- access to more data that will help us form new policies and improve planning and decision making at a local, regional, and national level;
- more resilience in how we plan for, manage, and fund our city assets through improved maintenance planning, and better understanding of how we should use these assets;
- attraction of international talent to experiment and develop technologies in our cities as 'living laboratories';
- creation of new business opportunities, employment, and export earning through supporting existing and start-up companies to use sensor technologies and data services;
- collaborative ways of working and a multi-city approach help to keep things moving and overcome obstacles, enabling a 'fast fail' approach.

The benefits of smart cities detailed by Land Information New Zealand (2016) are consistent with what Dameri and Ricciardi (2015, p. 860) describe as the creation of strong social, economic, and environmental ecosystems comprising a "network of different actors and subjects rooted in different countries, cities and communities". It is clear that smart cities are organizational forms with multiple objectives, in which "complexity and multidimensionality represents a scientific challenge" (Abella *et al.*, 2017, p. 51). This will require researchers to move beyond how organizations manage the traditional structural, human, and relational capital, to consider and include institutional, social, environmental, renewable, natural, as well as IC at the individual level. Future IC research at the individual local government level has the potential to contribute to the fourth stage of IC research envisaged by Dumay (2013) and Dameri and Ricciardi (2015). For example, how smart cities can improve their big data management processes to develop cooperative operations that encourage its ecosystems (including citizens, private companies, and social organizations) to create public value is worthy of in-depth research (Abella *et al.*, 2017).

Conclusion

This chapter has highlighted the IC research that has been undertaken in conjunction with New Zealand academics and those studies using New Zealand data. This was the precursor to an overview of IC research conducted in the New Zealand public sector. The studies were then positioned within the four stages of IC research. This analysis provided a platform from which the future direction and outlook for IC research in the New Zealand public sector could be examined.

IC research has captured the imagination of a cadre of academics in a number of countries including New Zealand. However, this chapter has highlighted the relatively underdeveloped state of IC research undertaken in New Zealand to date. The majority of studies co-authored with New Zealand academics focused on the private sector and, in particular, China. Given its size, dynamic economy, and the composition of the author team, this is unsurprising. Prior research has largely focused on accounting using disclosure studies, while the intersection of accounting and management issues surrounding IC has been largely neglected.

The studies using New Zealand specific data provided slightly more variety, in that the use of CA using disclosure indices as a data collection technique was supplemented with questionnaires, interviews, and a case study. However, as with the studies co-authored with New Zealand academics, the majority of articles using local data examined the extent of disclosures, rather than examining how these organizations explicitly manage or enhance IC (Gibb, 2007; Steenkamp and Northcott, 2007 are exceptions). The different jurisdictional settings and different reporting periods notwithstanding, the similarity of the findings in the studies renders it questionable whether further studies of this nature would provide a meaningful contribution to the IC literature. That is, these studies reinforce the second stage of IC research rather than extending the frontiers of the discipline.

Other than studies using local government data by Schneider and Samkin (2008a, 2008b) and university data by Low *et al.* (2015), the absence of New Zealand public sector IC studies is disappointing. Although New Zealand was a leader with its reform of the public sector in the 1980s, IC research in this space has failed to progress beyond the relatively narrow focus of that which was first introduced in the early 2000s (Guthrie and Petty, 2000). The over-emphasis on the use of CA using a disclosure index as a method means that unless there is an appetite for change, the outlook for IC research in the New Zealand public sector appears bleak.

Given the absence of prior public sector IC research that has been undertaken in New Zealand, and Dumay's (2016) declaration that disclosure studies are dead, there is a clean slate for IC public sector research in the New Zealand context as this field is not clouded by what has gone before. While the link between IC and public value is being made in overseas jurisdictions by academics (Dumay *et al.*, 2017), this has not yet filtered down into the New Zealand public sector.

In order to broaden the field of IC research from its current narrow, Euro-centric focus and to understand it in a variety of contexts (Dumay *et al.*, 2017, p. x) a number of possible future avenues of research are introduced in this chapter. These include research situated in different organizational settings including, but not limited to, the knowledge sector, state-owned entities, health sector, and local government sector. Additionally, there is potential for research that provides additional insights into how IC and public value is measured, managed, and accounted for in the different public sector organizational settings. Finally, while Dumay (2016) and Dumay *et al.* (2017) have suggested the death of traditional annual report disclosure studies, research into 'involuntary disclosure' (Dumay and Guthrie, 2017) and disclosure in non-tradition formats is likely to provide fertile ground for future public sector IC research.

The broad range of organizational sites, coupled with the limited body of in-depth research into particular organizational forms, means that ample research opportunities abound for astute New Zealand academics to undertake IC research within the New Zealand public sector setting. This research will take IC research to the next frontier and move away from 'what is' research, towards a critical examination of IC practices in action.

Appendix A: Intellectual capital research undertaken jointly with New Zealand academics

Authors	Country	Stage of IC research	Data	Method	Findings
Shareef and Davey (2006)	England	Second stage	2002 annual reports of 19 listed professional football clubs	CA and disclosure index	IC reporting was generally poor. A significant correlation was found between club size and performance and IC disclosure. External capital had the highest disclosure score followed by human capital and internal capital.
Davey et al. (2009)	North America and Europe	Second stage	2005 annual reports of 15 European and 15 North American fashion companies	CA and disclosure index	External capital items were the most frequently reported followed by internal and human capital.
Yi and Davey (2010)	China	Second stage	2006 annual reports of 49 dual-listed A and H share Chinese (mainland) companies	CA and disclosure index	External capital reporting amounted to almost half of the total IC disclosures followed by internal and human capital. 'Business partnerships' was the most frequently reported external capital attribute, with 'management processes' the most frequently reported internal capital and 'employee' the most frequently reported human capital attributes.
Yi et al. (2011a)	China	Second stage	Construct a comprehensive theoretical framework based on agency, stakeholder, signalling, and legitimacy theory for interpreting voluntary IC disclosure practices	Theoretical	Applications of theoretical framework include: to explain and predict voluntary IC disclosure practices by firms; to investigate the drivers (or perceptions) of managers of firms as to voluntary IC disclosure in certain institutions or jurisdictions; to deduce hypotheses regarding determinants of voluntary IC disclosure, such as profitability, leverage, firm age, auditor type, board composition, ownership structure; and to explain other voluntary disclosure practices of information.

(continued)

(continued)

Authors	Country	Stage of IC research	Data	Method	Findings
Yi *et al.* (2011b)	China	Second stage	2006 annual reports of 49 dual-listed A and H share Chinese (mainland) companies were used to examine the associations between IC disclosures and the three most commonly used explanatory variables, namely industry type, firm size, and performance.	CA and disclosure index	Industry type did not have a significant influence on IC reporting practices of Chinese firms. Larger firms generally reported more IC information than smaller firms. There was also a positive relationship between corporate performance and IC disclosure.
Clarke *et al.* (2011)	Australia	Second stage	Quantitative data collected from Australian companies listed between 2004 and 2008	IC measured using Public's value added intellectual coefficient and human, structural, and capital employed efficiencies. Direct and moderating relationships analysed statistically	A direct relationship between value added intellectual coefficient and performance of Australian publicly listed firms, particularly with capital employed and to a lesser extent with human capital. A positive relationship existed between human and structural capital in the prior year and performance in the current year. Evidence also suggests the possibility of an alternative moderating relationship between the IC components of human and structural with physical and financial capital which impacts on firm performance.
Whiting and Woodcock (2011)	Australia	Second stage	Quantitative data collected from the annual reports of 70 publicly listed Australian for 2006	CA. Correlation and regression analysis used to statistically tests a theoretically motivated explanatory model of IC disclosures	IC disclosures low with external capital being the most frequently disclosed category. Companies that operate in high technology-based or knowledge-intensive industries, and companies with large Big Four auditing firms show more extensive IC disclosure than those in other industries and without Big Four auditors. Ownership concentration, leverage level, and listing age did not influence the occurrence of IC disclosures.

Liao *et al.* (2013)	China	Second stage	50 largest Chinese companies by market capitalization that are dual-listed on the Chinese Mainland and Hong Kong stock markets	CA and disclosure index	The level of IC disclosure in Chinese version annual reports was different from that contained in the English version. The Chinese version of the annual reports include more internal capital information, while the English version annual reports include more external capital information. The effect of industry type and size on IC disclosure was also significantly positive.
Yi *et al.* (2015)	China	Second stage	2009 annual reports of the top 100 Chinese A-share listed companies	CA and disclosure index	No significant information gap existed between the expectation of Chinese stakeholders and the actual disclosure practice of Chinese firms. The overall IC disclosure was good. The three most highly reported items were 'management processes', 'customers', and 'employees'. External capital was the most disclosed category followed by internal and human capital. Human capital achieved the highest quality score followed by internal and external capital.
Wang *et al.* (2016)	China and India	Second stage	2014 annual reports of 20 publicly listed Indian, and 20 publicly listed Chinese, information technology companies	CA and disclosure index	The level of disclosure by these companies was relatively good. Indian IT companies tended to perform better than Chinese IT companies in level and quality of disclosures. External capital was the most frequently reported disclosure category in India, while the least frequently disclosed category was human capital. In the English versions of Chinese annual reports, external capital was the most frequently disclosed, while internal capital was the least frequently disclosed category.

Appendix B: IC research using New Zealand data

Authors	Stage of IC Research	Data	Method	Findings
Wong and Gardner (2005)	Second stage	2003 annual reports of 60 randomly selected firms (30 high-tech, 30 traditional) listed on the New Zealand Stock Exchange	CA and disclosure index	Level of voluntary IC disclosure was generally low. Industry type did not have an impact on the level of IC disclosure in NZ firms. External capital reporting amounted to almost half of the total IC disclosures followed by human and internal capital. 'Customers' was the most frequently reported external capital attribute, with 'employee' the most frequently reported human capital attribute and 'information/networking systems' the most frequently reported internal capital attribute.
Gibb (2007)	Third stage	Interviews conducted with 15 staff members across the intermediary firm, 12 tenant firms and 3 recipient firms of a science park. Additional data included literature findings and internet data	Case study of a single organization	A model of how IC is generated in a science park was produced from the case study findings which combined interview findings, internet data and literature findings. The model identified how science park management adopt a brokering role between tenant and recipient firms, via innovation enabling links that span across the network, to encourage shared problem solving and the creation of new ideas. Comparison of case study with two other similar firms in Helsinki show similarities in the development of specialist knowledge and network promotion, due to the niche areas in which the firms operate. The model developed in the paper can be used by other science park managers to gauge current innovation capacity levels.
Steenkamp and Northcott (2007)	Second stage	Based on pilot study examining voluntary IC reporting in the 2003 annual reports of the ten largest NZ companies by market capitalization as at 22 January 2004	CA and disclosure index	The paper identified and illustrated three practical challenges of applying the CA methodology to a selection of NZ annual reports. The paper suggests strategies that may be helpful in overcoming similar challenges in future IC research.

Whiting and Miller (2008)	Second stage	2003 annual reports of 70 companies (35 high-tech, 35 traditional) listed on the New Zealand Stock Exchange	CA and disclosure index. Database retrieval of independent variable data. Correlation and regression analysis	New Zealand companies' average number of IC disclosures of 26 compares favourably with Ireland and other surveyed countries, but is not as high as found in Italy and Australia. NZ firms most commonly reported external IC structure elements (47%; brands and marketing information such as customers and business collaborations), followed by human capital (33%; employee information), and internal structure (21%; information and networking systems). High levels of hidden value (a proxy for IC) are not related to high levels of voluntary IC disclosure. New Zealand firms showed lower figures of hidden values compared to Irish companies reported by Brennan (2001). However, the results show that for firms that revalue their tangible assets, voluntary IC disclosure is important and related to hidden value.
Hooks et al. (2010)	Second stage	Questionnaire surveying 85 third-year financial accounting students as a proxy for 'informed investors' and structured interviews with individuals who prepared material included in the questionnaire from the annual reports of five large NZ listed companies	Questionnaires and interviews	Preparers and users bring multiple meanings to figures used in annual reports. Users overlooked some messages which were complex and symbolic and also perceived more messages than intended by the preparers. The two respondent groups generally perceived brands, corporate image building, and aspects related to employees as the IC items best portrayed in the selected figures. Most users and some preparers perceived the main reason for using figures was their strength as a marketing tool. The authors suggest the findings may be helpful to annual report preparers in understanding rhetorical impact of images, and choosing figures which are effective and persuasive to user engagement with annual reports.
Steenkamp and Kashyap (2010)	Second stage	New Zealand SMEs to investigate managers' perceptions about	Questionnaire survey with 30 usable responses	The majority of respondents perceive intangible asset components contribute to the success of their business. Customer satisfaction ranked as the most important followed by customer loyalty, corporate reputation, product

(continued)

(continued)

Authors	Stage of IC Research	Data	Method	Findings
		the importance of the contributions that IC components make to their businesses		reputation, and employee know-how. The least important component of IC are distribution agreements, followed by employee education and relationships with investors.
Steenkamp and Hooks (2011)	Second stage	2007 annual reports (including pictorial information) of 28 largest New Zealand firms (based on market capitalization)	CA and disclosure framework	A significant proportion (42%) of IC reporting is made in picture form. The majority of pictures included (66%) communicated messages about IC resources. The volumes of IC items disclosed by firms changes significantly when pictures are included. Many firms used pictures to disclose their IC resources, particularly employees and brands which may indicate that these are their most important IC items. The exclusion of pictures in previous IC reporting research may have under-reported the level of IC disclosure and may have led to a partial understanding of what IC items firms considered as being important.
De Silva et al. (2014)	Second stage	2004, 2007, and 2010 annual reports of ten companies (five knowledge-intensive and five traditional product-based) listed on the NZ Stock Exchange during 2004–2010	CA and disclosure framework	Although there was an increase in IC reporting from 2004 to 2010, there was no strong pattern reflecting a marked increase in reporting over the time period. The level of IC reporting cannot be determined by the type of organization. The majority of IC reporting was found to be in discursive rather than numerical form, and only a small percentage of reporting conveyed negative news.
Whiting et al. (2017)	Second stage	MYOB's customer list of small business owners to develop a tool for scoring relational capital components of IC	Discrete choice experiment applying the PAPRIKA[4] method via an online survey	Of the individual relational capital components of IC, New Zealand SME owners and employees perceive the most important indicator to be 'captured' customer opinions about the business such as online reviews and testimonials.

Public sector research

Low et al. (2015)	Second stage	2011 annual reports of 91 Universities: 8 from New Zealand, 39 from Australia, and 44 from United Kingdom	CA and disclosure framework	New Zealand and Australian universities disclosed higher levels of IC than the UK universities. Moderate increases in the levels of IC disclosures were found over the period of the study. The quality of IC disclosures by New Zealand universities was generally higher than their Australian and UK counterparts. Internal capital and human capital were the most disclosed categories, with external capital being the least frequently disclosed in all three countries. However, the quality of external capital disclosures was higher than internal and human capital. Finally, most IC disclosures were narrative in nature.
Schneider and Samkin (2008a)	Second stage	2005 annual reports of 82 local government authorities	CA and disclosure index constructed using a Delphi panel. Correlation and regression analysis	The reporting of IC by local government authorities in NZ was varied but generally low. The most reported category of IC was internal capital, followed by external capital. Human capital was the least reported category. The most reported items were 'joint ventures/business collaborations' and 'management processes', while the least reported items were 'intellectual property' and 'licensing agreements'.
Schneider and Samkin (2008b)	Second stage	2005 annual reports of 82 local government authorities	CA and disclosure index constructed using a Delphi panel	Annual report extracts presented to demonstrate examples of IC disclosures found in the study.

Notes

1 These three components are often described as human capital, external capital, and internal capital.
2 These organizations included the Ministry of Business, Innovation and Employment; the Ministry of Health; Crown Research Institutes (Landcare Research and National Institute of Water and Atmospheric Research); the Institute of Environmental Science and Research Limited; a state-owned enterprise (*New Zealand Post*); and the Controller and Auditor General of New Zealand.
3 Particularly in the larger areas such as Auckland, Wellington, and Christchurch.
4 Potentially All Pairwise RanKing of all possible Alternatives.

References

Abella, A., Ortiz-de-Urbina-Criado, M., and De-Pablos-Heredero, C. (2017), "A model for the analysis of data-driven innovation and value generation in smart cities' ecosystems", *Cities*, Vol. 64, pp. 47–53.

Abeysekera, I. and Guthrie, J. (2005), "An empirical investigation of annual reporting trends of intellectual capital in Sri Lanka", *Critical Perspectives on Accounting*, Vol. 16, No. 3, pp. 151–163.

Ahn, M. J. and York, A. (2010), "A resource-based view of innovation, technology transfer and commercialization", in United States Association for Small Business and Entrepreneurship. Conference Proceedings (p. 1106), United States Association for Small Business and Entrepreneurship.

April, K.A., Bosma, P., and Deglon, D. A. (2003), "IC measurement and reporting: establishing a practice in SA mining", *Journal of Intellectual Capital*, Vol. 4, No. 2, pp. 165–180.

Bale, M. and Dale, T. (1998), "Public sector reform in New Zealand and its relevance to developing countries", *The World Bank Research Observer*, Vol. 13, No. 1, pp. 103–121.

Bezhani, I. (2010), "Intellectual capital reporting at UK universities", *Journal of Intellectual Capital*, Vol. 11, No. 2, pp. 179–207.

Bontis, N. (2003), "Intellectual capital disclosure in Canadian corporations", *Journal of Human Resource Costing & Accounting*, Vol. 7, No. 1, pp. 9–20.

Boston, J. (1998), "Public sector management, electoral reform and the future of the contract state in New Zealand", *Australian Journal of Public Administration*, Vol. 57, No. 4, pp. 32–43.

Boston, J. (2000), "The challenge of evaluating systemic change: The case of public management reform", *International Public Management Journal*, Vol. 3, No. 1, pp. 23–46.

Boston, J. and Pallot, J. (1997), "Linking strategy and performance: Developments in the New Zealand public sector", *Journal of Policy Analysis and Management*, Vol. 16, No. 3, pp. 382–404.

Boston, J., Dalziel, P., and St. John, S. (Eds). (1999). *Redesigning the Welfare State in New Zealand*, Oxford University Press, Auckland, New Zealand.

Boston, J., Martin, J., Pallot, J., and Walsh, P. (1996), *Public Management: The New Zealand Model*, Oxford University Press, Auckland, New Zealand.

Bozzolan, S., Favotto, F., and Ricceri, F. (2003), "Italian annual intellectual capital disclosure", *Journal of Intellectual Capital*, Vol. 4, No. 4, pp. 543–558.

Brennan, N. (2001), "Reporting intellectual capital in annual reports: Evidence from Ireland", *Accounting, Auditing & Accountability Journal*, Vol. 14, No. 4, pp. 423–436.

Cañibano, L. and Sánchez, P. M. (2009), "Intangibles in universities: Current challenges for measuring and reporting", *Journal of Human Resource Costing & Accounting*, Vol. 13, No. 2, pp. 93–104.

Cinca, S. C., Molinero, M. C., and Queiroz, B. A. (2003), "The measurement of intangible assets in public sector using scaling techniques", *Journal of Intellectual Capital*, Vol. 4, No. 2, pp. 249–275.

Clarke, M., Seng, D., and Whiting, R. H. (2011), "Intellectual capital and firm performance in Australia", *Journal of Intellectual Capital*, Vol. 12, No. 4, pp. 505–530.

Collier, P. M. (2001), "Valuing intellectual capacity in the police", *Accounting, Auditing & Accountability Journal*, Vol. 14, No. 4, pp. 437–455.

Cuganesan, S. (2017), "Enabling relational capital through customer performance measurement practices: A study of no-for-profit organizations", in Guthrie, J., Dumay, J., Ricceri, F., and Nielsen, C. (Eds), *The Routledge Companion to Intellectual Capital*, Routledge, London, pp. XX–XX.

Cuganesan, S. and Lacey, D. (2011), "Developments in public sector performance measurement: A project on producing return on investment metrics for law enforcement", *Financial Accountability & Management*, Vol. 27, No. 4, pp. 458–479.

Cuganesan, S., Dunford, R., and Palmer, I. (2012), "Strategic management accounting and strategy practices within a public sector agency", *Management Accounting Research*, Vol. 23, No. 4, pp. 245–260.

Dameri, R. P. and Ricciardi, F. (2015), "Smart city intellectual capital: An emerging view of territorial systems innovation management", *Journal of Intellectual Capital*, Vol. 16, No. 4, pp. 860–887.

Dameri, R. P., Ricciardi, F., and D'Auria, B. (2014), "Knowledge and intellectual capital in smart city", *European Conference on Knowledge Management*, Vol. 1, pp. 250–257.

Dane-Nielsen, H. and Nielsen, C. (2017), "Value creation in business models is based on intellectual capital: and only intellectual capital! The critical path of intellectual capital", in Guthrie, J., Dumay, J., Ricceri, F., and Nielsen, C. (Eds), *The Routledge Companion to Intellectual Capital*, Routledge, London, pp. 418–434.

Davey, J., Schneider, L., and Davey, H. (2009), "Intellectual capital disclosure and the fashion industry", *Journal of Intellectual Capital*, Vol. 10, No. 3, pp. 401–424.

De Silva, T. A., Stratford, M., and Clark, M. (2014), "Intellectual capital reporting: A longitudinal study of New Zealand companies", *Journal of Intellectual Capital*, Vol. 15, No. 1, pp. 157–172.

Donato, F. (2008), "Managing IC by antennae: Evidence from cultural organizations", *Journal of Intellectual Capital*, Vol. 9, No. 3, pp. 380–394.

Dragonetti, N. C. and Roos, G. (1998), "Efficiency and effectiveness in government programmes: An intellectual capital perspective", paper presented at 2nd World Congress on Intellectual Capital, McMasters University, Hamilton, 21–23 January.

Dumay, J. (2009), "Intellectual capital measurement: A critical approach", *Journal of Intellectual Capital*, Vol. 10, No. 2, pp. 190–210.

Dumay, J. (2013), "The third stage of IC: Towards a new IC future and beyond", *Journal of Intellectual Capital*, Vol. 14, No. 1, pp. 5–9.

Dumay, J. (2014), "15 years of the *Journal of Intellectual Capital* and counting: A manifesto for transformational IC research", *Journal of Intellectual Capital*, Vol. 15, No. 1, pp. 2–37.

Dumay, J. (2016), "A critical reflection on the future of intellectual capital: From reporting to disclosure", *Journal of Intellectual capital*, Vol. 17, No. 1, pp. 168–184.

Dumay, J. and Cai, L. (2014), "A review and critique of content analysis as a methodology for inquiring into IC disclosure", *Journal of intellectual capital*, Vol. 15, No. 2, pp. 264–290.

Dumay, J. and Cai, L. (2015), "Using content analysis as a research methodology for investigating intellectual capital disclosure: A critique", *Journal of Intellectual Capital*, Vol. 16, No. 1, pp. 121–155.

Dumay, J. and Garanina, T. (2013), "Intellectual capital research: A critical examination of the third stage", *Journal of Intellectual Capital*, Vol. 14, No. 1, pp. 10–25.

Dumay, J. and Guthrie, J. (2007), "Disturbance and implementation of IC practice: A public sector organisation perspective", *Journal of Human Resource Costing & Accounting*, Vol. 11, No. 2, pp. 104–121.

Dumay, J. and Guthrie, J. (2017), "Involuntary disclosure of intellectual capital: Is it relevant?" *Journal of Intellectual Capital*, Vol. 18, No. 1, pp. 29–44.

Dumay, J., Guthrie, J., and Puntillo, P. (2015), "IC and public sector: A structured literature review", *Journal of Intellectual Capital*, Vol. 16, No. 2, pp. 267–284.

Dumay, J., Guthrie, J., and Rooney, J. (2017), "The critical path of intellectual capital", in Guthrie, J., Dumay, J., Ricceri, F., and Nielsen, C. (Eds), *The Routledge Companion to Intellectual Capital*, Routledge, London, pp. 21–39.

Farneti, F. and Dumay, J. (2014), "Sustainable public value inscriptions: A critical approach", in Guthrie, J., Marcon, G., Russo, S., and Farneti, F (Eds), *Public Value Management, Measurement and Reporting*, Emerald Group Publishing Limited, Bradford, pp. 375–389.

Farneti, F. and Guthrie, J. (2009), "Sustainability reporting by Australian public sector organisations: Why they report", *Accounting Forum*, Vol. 33, No. 2, pp. 89–98.

Firer, S., and Stainbank, L. (2003), "Testing the relationship between intellectual capital and a company's performance: Evidence from South Africa", *Meditari Accountancy Research*, Vol. 11, No. 1, pp. 25–44.

Fletcher, A., Guthrie, J., Steane, P., Roos, G., and Pike, S. (2003), "Mapping stakeholder perceptions for a third sector organization", *Journal of Intellectual Capital*, Vol. 4, No. 4, pp. 505–527.

Gibb, J. L. (2007), "Optimising intellectual capital development: A case study of brokering in a science park", *International Journal of Entrepreneurship and Innovation Management*, Vol. 7, No. 6, pp. 491–505.

Goebel, V. (2015), "Is the literature on content analysis of intellectual capital reporting heading towards a dead end?", *Journal of Intellectual Capital*, Vol. 16, No. 3, pp. 681–699.

Goh, C. P. and Lim, P. K. (2004), "Disclosing intellectual capital in company annual reports: Evidence from Malaysia", *Journal of Intellectual Capital*, Vol. 5, No. 3, pp. 500–510.

Guthrie, J. and Dumay, J. (2015), "New frontiers in the use of intellectual capital in the public sector", *Journal of Intellectual Capital*, Vol. 16, No. 2, pp. 258–266.

Guthrie, J. and Petty, R. (2000), "Intellectual capital: Australian annual reporting practices", *Journal of Intellectual Capital*, Vol. 1, No. 3, pp. 241–251.

Guthrie, J. and Russo, S. (2014), "Public value management: Challenge of defining, measuring and reporting for public services", in Guthrie, J., Marcon, G., Russo, S., and Farneti, F (Eds), *Public Value Management, Measurement and Reporting*, Vol. 3, Emerald Group Publishing Limited, Bradford, pp. 3–17.

Guthrie, J., Olson, O., and Humphrey, C. (1999), "Debating developments in New Public Financial Management: The limits of global theorising and some new ways forward", *Financial Accountability and Management*, Vol. 15, No. 3/4, pp. 209–228.

Guthrie, J., Ricceri, F., and Dumay, J. (2012), "Reflections and projections: A decade of Intellectual Capital Accounting Research", *The British Accounting Review*, Vol. 44, No. 2, pp. 68–82.

Habersam, M. and Piber, M. (2003), "Exploring intellectual capital in hospitals: Two qualitative case studies in Italy and Austria", *European Accounting Review*, Vol. 12, No. 4, pp. 753–779.

Hay, D. (2001), "Public sector decentralization, accountability and financial reporting in New Zealand", *Journal of Public Budgeting, Accountability & Financial Management*, Vol. 13, No. 2, pp. 133–156.

Hellström, T. and Husted, K. (2004), "Mapping knowledge and intellectual capital in academic environments: A focus group study", *Journal of Intellectual Capital*, Vol. 5, No. 1, pp. 165–180.

Hood, C. (1991), "a public management for all seasons", *Public Administration*, Vol. 69, No. 1, pp. 3–19.

Hooks, J., Steenkamp, N., and Stewart, R. (2010), "Interpreting pictorial messages of intellectual capital in company media", *Qualitative Research in Accounting & Management*, Vol. 7, No. 3, pp. 353–378.

Jones, L. R., Guthrie, J., and Steane, P. (2001), "Learning from international public management reform experience", in Jones, L. R., Guthrie, J., and Steane, P. (Eds), *Learning from International Public Management Reform: Part A*, Emerald Group Publishing Limited, Bradford, pp. 1–26.

Kamath, B. G. (2007), "The intellectual capital performance of the Indian banking sector", *Journal of Intellectual Capital*, Vol. 8, No. 1, pp. 96–123.

Kamath, B. G. (2008), "Intellectual capital and corporate performance in Indian pharmaceutical industry", *Journal of Intellectual Capital*, Vol. 9, No. 4, pp. 684–704.

Kelly, A. (2004), "The intellectual capital of schools: Analysing government policy statements on school improvement in light of a new theorization", *Journal of Education Policy*, Vol. 19, No. 5, pp. 609–629.

Kong, E. (2008), "The development of strategic management in the non-profit context: Intellectual capital in social service non-profit organizations", *International Journal of Management Reviews*, Vol. 10, No. 3, pp. 281–299.

Land Information New Zealand. (2016), "Smart Cities", Available at: www.linz.govt.nz/about-linz/what-were-doing/projects/smart-cities (Accessed 20 January 2017).

Lawrence, S., Alam, M., and Lowe, T. (1994), "The great experiment: Financial management reform in the NZ health sector", *Accounting, Auditing & Accountability Journal*, Vol. 7, No. 3, pp. 68–95.

Lee, S. M., Hwang, T., and Choi, D. (2012), "Open innovation in the public sector of leading countries", *Management Decision*, Vol. 50, No. 1, pp. 147–162.

Leitner, K. H. and Warden, C. (2004), "Managing and reporting knowledge-based resources and processes in research organisations: Specifics, lessons learned and perspectives", *Management Accounting Research*, Vol. 15, No. 1, pp. 33–51.

Liao, L., Low, M., and Davey, H. (2013), "Chinese and English language versions: Intellectual capital disclosure", *Journal of Intellectual Capital*, Vol. 14, No. 4, pp. 661–686.

Low, M., Samkin, G., and Li, Y. (2015), "Voluntary reporting of intellectual capital: Comparing the quality of disclosures from New Zealand, Australian and United Kingdom universities", *Journal of Intellectual Capital*, Vol. 16, No. 4, pp. 779–808.

Mouritsen, J., Thorbjørnsen, S., Bukh, P. N., and Johansen, M. R. (2004), "Intellectual capital and new public management: Reintroducing enterprise", *The Learning Organization*, Vol. 11, No. 4/5, pp. 380–392.

Mouritsen, J., Thorbjørnsen, S., Bukh, P. N., and Johansen, M. R. (2005), "Intellectual capital and the discourses of love and entrepreneurship in new public management", *Financial Accountability & Management*, Vol. 21, No. 3, pp. 279–290.

Newberry, S. (2001), "Network structures, consumers and accountability in New Zealand", in Lawrence R., Jones, L. R., Guthrie, J., and Steane, P. (Eds), *Learning from International Public Management Reform: Part A*, Emerald Group Publishing Limited, Bradford, UK, pp. 257–278.

New Zealand Government (2008), "Report on the efficiency and effectiveness of the Office of the Controller and Auditor General of New Zealand by an international peer review", Available from: www.oag.govt.nz/2008/peer-review/docs/peer-review-report.pdf.

Oliveras, E., Gowthorpe, C., Kasperskaya, Y., and Perramon, J. (2008), "Reporting intellectual capital in Spain", *Corporate Communications: An International Journal*, Vol. 13, No. 2, pp. 168–181.

Ordóñez de Pablos, P. (2003), "Intellectual capital reporting in Spain: A comparative view, *Journal of Intellectual Capital*, Vol. 4, No. 1, pp. 61–81.

Pallot, J. (1998), "New public management reform in New Zealand: The collective strategy phase", *International Public Management Journal*, Vol. 1, No. 1, pp. 1–18.

Petty, R. and Guthrie, J. (2000), "Intellectual capital literature review: Measurement, reporting and management", *Journal of Intellectual Capital*, Vol. 1, No. 2, pp. 155–176.

Pöyhönen, A. and Smedlund, A. (2004), "Assessing intellectual capital creation in regional clusters", *Journal of Intellectual Capital*, Vol. 5, No. 3, pp. 351–365.

Ramírez, Y. (2010), "Intellectual capital models in Spanish public sector", *Journal of Intellectual Capital*, Vol. 11, No. 2, pp. 248–264.

Ramírez Córcoles, Y., Santos Peñalver, J. F. and Tejada Ponce, Á. (2011), "Intellectual capital in Spanish public universities: Stakeholders' information needs", *Journal of Intellectual Capital*, Vol. 12, No. 3, pp. 356–376.

Sahay, S. (2016), "Big data and public health: Challenges and opportunities for low and middle income countries", *Communications of the Association for Information Systems*, Vol. 39, No. 1, pp. 419–438.

Sánchez, P. M. and Elena, S. (2006), "Intellectual capital in universities: Improving transparency and internal management", *Journal of Intellectual Capital*, Vol. 7, No. 4, pp. 529–548.

Sánchez, P. M., Elena, S., and Castrillo, R. (2009), "Intellectual capital dynamics in universities: A reporting model", *Journal of Intellectual Capital*, Vol. 10, No. 2, pp. 307–324.

Schiuma, G. and Lerro, A. (2017), "Understanding and exploiting intellectual capital grounding regional development: Framework and metrics", in Guthrie, J., Dumay, J., Ricceri, F., and Nielsen, C. (Eds), *The Routledge Companion to Intellectual Capital*, Routledge, London, pp. 67–75.

Schneider, A. and Samkin, G. (2008a), "Intellectual capital reporting by the New Zealand local government sector", *Journal of Intellectual Capital*, Vol. 9, No. 3, pp. 456–486.

Schneider, A. and Samkin, G. (2008b), "Narrative reporting of intellectual capital by New Zealand local government sector", *Journal of Economic and Financial Sciences*, Vol. 2, No. 2, pp. 115–138.

Sciulli, N., Wise, V., Demediuk, P., and Sims, R. (2002), "Intellectual capital reporting: An examination of local government in Victoria", *Accounting, Accountability & Performance*, Vol. 8, No. 2, pp. 43–60.

Shareef, F. and Davey, H. (2006), "Accounting for intellectual capital: Evidence from listed English football clubs", *Journal of Applied Accounting Research*, Vol. 7, No. 3, pp. 78–116.

Steenkamp, N. and Hooks, J. (2011), "Does including pictorial disclosure of intellectual capital resources make a difference?" *Pacific Accounting Review*, Vol. 23, No. 1, pp. 52–68.

Steenkamp, N. and Kashyap, V. (2010), "Importance and contribution of intangible assets: SME managers' perceptions", *Journal of Intellectual Capital*, Vol. 11, No. 3, pp. 368–390.

Steenkamp, N. and Northcott, D. (2007), "Content analysis in accounting research: The practical challenges", *Australian Accounting Review*, Vol. 17, No. 3, pp. 12–25.

Tene, O. and Polonetsky, J. (2013), Big data for all: Privacy and user control in the age of analytics", *Northwestern Journal of Technology and Intellectual Property*, Vol. 11, No. 5, pp. 240–273.

Vagnoni, E. and Oppi, C. (2015), "Investigating factors of intellectual capital to enhance achievement of strategic goals in a university hospital setting", *Journal of Intellectual Capital*, Vol. 16, No. 2, pp. 331–363.

Veltri, S. and Silvestri, A. (2015), "The Free State University integrated reporting: A critical consideration", *Journal of Intellectual Capital*, Vol. 16, No. 2, pp. 443–462.

Veltri, S., Bronzetti, G. and Sicoli, G. (2011), "Reporting intellectual capital in health care organizations: Specifics, lessons learned, and future research perspectives", *Journal of Health Care Finance*, Vol. 38, No. 2, pp. 80–97.

Villasalero, M. (2014), "University knowledge, open innovation and technological capital in Spanish science parks research revealing or technology selling?" *Journal of Intellectual Capital*, Vol. 15, No. 4, pp. 479–496.

Vishnu, S. and Gupta, K. V. (2014), "Intellectual capital and performance of pharmaceutical firms in India", *Journal of Intellectual Capital*, Vol. 15, No. 1, pp. 83–99.

Wang, Q., Sharma, U., and Davey, H. (2016), "Intellectual capital disclosure by Chinese and Indian information technology companies", *Journal of Intellectual Capital*, Vol. 17, No. 3, pp. 507–529.

Whiting, R. H. and Miller, J. C. (2008), "Voluntary disclosure of intellectual capital in New Zealand annual reports and the 'hidden value'", *Journal of Human Resource Costing & Accounting*, Vol. 12, No. 1, pp. 26–50.

Whiting, R. H. and Woodcock, J. (2011), "Firm characteristics and intellectual capital disclosure by Australian companies", *Journal of Human Resource Costing & Accounting*, Vol. 15, No. 2, pp. 102–126.

Whiting, R. H., Hansen, P., and Sen, A. (2017), "A tool for measuring SMEs' reputation, engagement and goodwill: A New Zealand exploratory study", *Journal of Intellectual Capital*, Vol. 18, No. 1, pp. 170–188.

Wielki, J. (2013), "Implementation of the Big Data concept in organizations-possibilities, impediments and challenges", in Computer Science and Information Systems (FedCSIS), 2013 Federated Conference, 985–989, IEEE.

Wong, M. and Gardner, C. (2005), "Intellectual capital disclosure: New Zealand evidence", in Accounting and Finance Association of Australia and New Zealand (AFAANZ), Conference, Melbourne, Australia, July.

Yang, C. C. and Lin, C. Y. Y., (2009), "Does intellectual capital mediate the relationship between HRM and organizational performance? Perspective of a healthcare industry in Taiwan", *The International Journal of Human Resource Management*, Vol. 20, No. 9, pp. 1965–1984.

Yi, A., and Davey, H. (2010), "Intellectual capital disclosure in Chinese (mainland) companies", *Journal of Intellectual Capital*, Vol. 11, No. 3, pp. 326–347.

Yi, A., Davey, H., and Eggleton, I. R. (2011a), "Towards a comprehensive theoretical framework for voluntary IC disclosure", *Journal of Intellectual Capital*, Vol. 12, No. 4, pp. 571–585.

Yi, A., Davey, H., and Eggleton, I. R., (2011b), "The effects of industry type, company size and performance on Chinese companies' IC disclosure: A research note", *Australasian Accounting Business & Finance Journal*, Vol. 5, No. 3, pp. 107–116.

Yi, A., Davey, H., Eggleton, I. R., and Wang, Z. (2015), "Intellectual capital disclosure and the information gap: Evidence from China", *Advances in Accounting*, Vol. 31, No. 2, pp. 179–187.

7

INTELLECTUAL CAPITAL IN THE CONTEXT OF HEALTHCARE ORGANIZATIONS

Does it matter?

Emidia Vagnoni

Introduction

Healthcare organizations differ from other organizations because of their fundamental mission to guarantee health protection to citizens, and therefore their management process is driven by different criteria. Mark (2006, p. 851) argues:

> [t]he scope of healthcare provision ranges from traditional healers in the developing world to medical consultants practising in the most sophisticated western hospitals. What they have in common is participation in an activity that requires trust between the parties concerned, to deliver a change in the patients' well-being.

Historically, healthcare organizations have been shaped by the way in which healthcare has been provided (Porter, 2003), For example, the purpose of hospitals has changed over time from quarantine to clinical intervention. However, the approach to provision of healthcare is dependent on the country context (Mark, 2006, p. 852). During the late 1980s and early 1990s, many Western countries changed the relationship between state provision and the private sector (Hood, 1991), consistent with the philosophy of new public management (Ferlie, 1999; Barzelay, 2002). These reforms were aimed at increasing efficiency and introducing managed care and managed competition criteria (Toth, 2010). They were frequently implemented in a range of country contexts with a 'one size fits all' approach. The reforms introduced the new role of clinical director and new accounting technologies, both to measure results and monitor the healthcare organizations' ability to challenge efficiency objectives (Llewellyn, 2001). Sheaff *et al.* (2003) highlights that measurement focuses only on what goes in and what comes out without looking at the process inside.

Health services' delivery is the result of a complex process; a number of knowledge exchanges occurs among the actors of the process, and many individuals participate in sharing values, routines, protocols, and so on. The accounting literature has often depicted healthcare organizations from a financial perspective, highlighting the role of accounting technologies for management control. As both the healthcare organization as a whole and its sub-units have been examined (Vagnoni and Oppi, 2015), clinical directors have been assessed on their ability to contain costs, and financial issues have sometimes become the main drivers of healthcare organizations' strategic management. However, many countries have recognized that the future of universal healthcare systems depends on the ability to respond to changing needs appropriately and in a way that is supported by the public. The ability of the healthcare organization to cope with innovation, knowledge management, and communication is crucial in a rapidly changing environment (Coulter and Jenkinson, 2005). Thus, intellectual capital (IC) is a comprehensive framework for valuing the particular characteristics of the healthcare environment. Specific to healthcare organizations is that the value creation process depends on a combination of both tangible and intangible assets, with the latter playing a dominant role. This means that managing IC helps the organization to create value and be responsive to health needs.

While there are many studies that examine IC and management, in terms of healthcare organizations IC is still a 'black box'. Costs and financial results are identified, but how IC interacts to share knowledge and create innovation and value, is not known or monitored. Despite efforts to mobilize knowledge and innovation to legitimize healthcare organizations' strategic role in society, the accounting literature has devoted surprisingly limited attention to these IC dimensions. This chapter aims to fill this gap.

The healthcare organization context

Both the managerial and medical literatures have pointed out the complexity of healthcare organizations (e.g. Mintzberg, 1983; Perrow, 1986; Institute of Medicine, 2001). Healthcare organizations are required to combine a wide range of production factors to deliver health services differentiated according to individual health needs. Furthermore, healthcare organizations' outcomes are the result of a continuous innovation process. The specific focus of an innovation (a new drug, computer system, clinical intervention, professional role, and so on) cannot be isolated from its social, technical, and spatial contexts and, therefore, innovations often involve highly organized and systematically regulated changes in the structure and delivery of services (May, 2013).

Plsek (2003) highlighted some 'properties' relevant to understanding the drivers of innovation in complex systems: interaction among agents; rules and mental models; structures, processes, and patterns; and constant adaptation. Furthermore, Plsek and Wilson (2001) emphasized the role of knowledge, capabilities, and skills to manage effectively healthcare organizations. They argued those:

> [w]ho seek to change an organization should harness the natural creativity and organizing ability of its staff and stakeholders through such principles as generative relationships, minimum specification, the positive use of attractors for change, and a constructive approach to variation in areas of practice where there is only moderate certainty and agreement (p. 746).

University hospitals play a key role in the health systems since they are affected by the logics of both healthcare and innovation (Miller and French, 2016). The university hospital model refers to an integrated organization in which academic, clinical, and research functions are performed. The activity of university hospitals involves patient care, teaching, and educational programmes for students, and research directed to the development of new diagnostic or therapeutic techniques. Therefore, the mission of university hospitals is the provision of a high-quality care, especially in the treatment of rare diseases and complex patients, the production of specialized services, the use of advanced technology, and conducting scientific research. University hospitals are focused on innovation, redesigning and improving models of care to respond to changing demand and integrating clinical activity with research and education. They include new skills developed through research into patient care, while students are taught how to practise.

While it is recognized in the literature that the university hospitals play a key role in the health care system (French and Miller, 2012) in terms of innovation and knowledge creation, their level of efficiency has been questioned (Lehrer and Burgess, 1995; Grosskopf *et al.*, 2004), with Huttin and De Pouvourville (2001) finding that they are more costly than their non-teaching counterparts.

However, beyond efficiency and cost, there are important elements in university hospitals that relate to their IC resources. One of these is experience, described by Lerro and Schiuma (2013) as one of the critical success factors of the organization, as it is the ability to act promptly and safely in a specific field (Joe *et al.*, 2013). Experience incorporates aspects of education, training, or competences and refers to the sphere of human capital, that is, those skills internal to the workforce and not obtainable from outside.

Another element, an important driver of competitive advantage, is the dissemination and sharing of knowledge within the organization, through the codification of skills and information, and their transmission to others in the form of explicit knowledge. This kind of knowledge is strongly linked to structural capital, as it allows the organization to enjoy internal capabilities that are shared and disseminated among professionals.

Finally, another element is the diffusion of knowledge within the organization both through networking among colleagues and with external professionals, which promotes what Gabbay and Le May (2004) defined as "mindlines". Mindlines is part of relational capital in which professionals tend to avoid formal sources of knowledge but seek out tacit knowledge created by interactions with colleagues.

Although university hospitals may be considered a privileged setting in which to investigate IC, all healthcare organizations rely on knowledge to create value. Thus, knowledge, skills, and abilities are the drivers of innovation, and the main IC resources used by healthcare organization to create value.

The role of knowledge

In service organizations, knowledge is considered one of the most important IC resources and the management of knowledge aims at maximizing the organization's knowledge-related effectiveness (Zhou and Fink, 2003). Successful management can give rise to a better allocation of work and activities, to more innovation, and to an environment that is receptive to change, particularly in competitive markets (Bishop *et al.*, 2008). Health organizations can particularly benefit from knowledge management in terms of cost reduction, job flexibility, and reaction to patients' needs, which can lead to better patient care (Zigan *et al.*, 2010).

According to Brailer (1999, p. 6), the management of knowledge-related elements in health services is linked to "any systematic process designed to acquire, conserve, organize, retrieve, display and distribute what is known". Reasons to deploy knowledge management in hospitals are the competitive differentiation with other organizations and the opportunity to improve quality of care, critical paths of care, collaborative care plans, evidence-based practice, and intra-organizational networks (Zigan *et al.*, 2010).

According to Magnier-Watanabe and Senoo (2008), the acquisition of knowledge involves all processes that support gaining new knowledge from either inside or outside the organization: in university hospitals, new knowledge may come from colleagues through informal and personal contacts, from books, journals, conferences, or from investment in training programmes. University hospitals are characterized by the constant generation of new knowledge through research activities and through the frequent rotation of medical staff in training.

Furthermore, as argued by Zigan *et al.* (2010), the codification of knowledge is relevant because it concerns identifying, capturing, indexing, and making explicit knowledge that is ready for use by professionals, and the distribution and the presentation of knowledge is important because it refers to the transfer and sharing of knowledge through formal and informal mechanisms, such as meetings, relationships, or dialogue between organizational members. Hospitals can share knowledge through formal educational programmes, such as seminars, or they can transfer knowledge through the development of good working relationships among staff. Sharing knowledge reduces training costs and builds better working relationships.

Knowledge is an organizational asset that is important to share. Typical features of knowledge contribute to influence its relocation (Joe *et al.*, 2013). In university hospitals, knowledge sharing behaviours are connected to the degree to which physicians share their knowledge and experience with others. Because their knowledge is indispensable to the care of patients in hospitals, physicians are considered a knowledge-intensive professional group. Sharing physicians' knowledge within hospitals is critical in a competitive environment, and to increasing the quality and efficiency of care in health organizations (Ryu *et al.*, 2003).

In research organizations such as university hospitals, knowledge can be categorized as implicit or explicit knowledge (Nonaka, 1994). Evidence-based healthcare imports explicit knowledge from research activities and incorporates it into practice, but it may underestimate the importance of implicit clinical knowledge. A study by Gabbay and Le May (2004) underlined the reluctance of physicians in the adoption of rigid formal sources of knowledge and their tendency to network with other professionals in order to develop "mindlines".

In organizations, only a few individuals can be classified as experts, so the organization benefits from the diffusion of knowledge to other employees through sharing. Joe *et al.* (2013) define expertise as the capability to act with excellence in a specific subject, involving intellectual and cognitive efforts for a long period. Experts are therefore a potent source of value creation within organizations as they have a deep knowledge of a subject, a variety of experiences, and have been rigorously tested and trained over the course of a long career. An expert demonstrates high levels of efficiency, accuracy, and ability and holds subject specific knowledge on, for example, methods and procedures, including knowledge of how to deal with problems and new situations. Traits of knowledge contribute to transfer; for example, explicit knowledge is more easily transferred than tacit knowledge (Joe *et al.*, 2013).

One of the main impacts from the departure of an expert may be the loss of credibility of the organization, as stakeholders may fear a reduction in the organization's performance. Another impact is the inability to replace the professional, especially if highly specialized, with the consequent loss of customers or users (Joe *et al.*, 2013).

Rondeau *et al.* (2009) investigated the negative effects of turnover among nursing staff. High turnover leads to higher workloads, negatively affects the morale of remaining staff, and reduces the productivity of those who have to train the new arrivals. Excessive turnover may also lead to workgroup conflict, decreased consensus and cohesion, and reduced job satisfaction due to changed communication patterns and social order. Turnover may lead to further turnover as otherwise satisfied employees consider leaving because of the increased stress of work, and excessive turnover may signal to remaining employees that there are better opportunities elsewhere. Kohn (2004) found that healthcare organizations need to enhance a good working atmosphere in order to attract excellent staff. They can achieve this, for example, by increasing autonomy and support staff and through investments in information and communication technology.

Although healthcare organizations can be considered late adopters of the knowledge management concept, some are starting to implement and evaluate knowledge management strategies (Kothari *et al.*, 2011). Some management practices in healthcare focus on the use of information and communication technologies including electronic libraries, repositories containing research articles, and clinical or best practice guidelines to assist organizations in managing knowledge. However, this ICT-based evolution does not support knowledge development and sharing, and knowledge-based initiatives in healthcare organizations "tend to focus on one solution instead of a comprehensive strategy" (Kothari *et al.*, 2011).

The clinical literature has shown the importance of knowledge, with studies discussing the relevance of capturing, sharing, and using knowledge within the daily work of health professionals (Chen, 2012; Lee *et al.*, 2014). The health policy literature has also shown growing interest in knowledge management and knowledge mobilization in the health context, as argued by Ferlie *et al.* (2012). In their work, based on a literature review, the authors highlight the shift in terms of knowledge mobilization models. However, the public management and accounting literatures have not focused on healthcare organizations to date.

Why consider IC for managing healthcare organizations?

Nowadays organizations manage knowledge and IC because they acknowledge that value is added through the development of expertise, knowledge, and intangible assets (Lerro and Schiuma, 2013). The relevance of IC to creating value and enhancing performance, and its interaction with the accounting dimension of the organization, is highlighted by Guthrie and Petty (2000).

Mouritsen *et al.* (2001a) argue that IC focuses on organizing knowledge resources in order to make knowledge manageable; it is about actions and activities linked to knowledge, which are not easy to represent. According to this view, managing knowledge means being able to represent what is personal, questioning the idea of knowledge as an individual phenomenon. The established IC framework in which IC is categorized as human, structural, and relational, is supported by this view.

Human capital can be defined as the combination of individuals' inherent qualities, education, experience, and attitudes (Hudson, 1993), and it includes knowledge, abilities, motivation, experience, and personal skills. Human capital is the principal source of innovation and strategic renewal (Bontis, 1998). In healthcare organizations, human capital refers to university education, training, professional experiences, but also to responsibility, to communicative abilities, to social competence, and 'personal touch' (Habersam and Piber, 2003).

Structural capital is defined as "the knowledge that stays within the firm at the end of the working day" (Meritum, 2002, p. 3). It is knowledge related to internal processes and structures, routines, procedures, systems, culture, technology, and databases.

Relational capital concerns all the resources external to the organization, such as consumers, users, research partners, funders, and other stakeholders. For an organization, it is "the value of its franchise, its ongoing relationships with the people or organizations to which it sells" (Stewart, 1997, p. 108).

Looking at these three dimensions separately does not provide a useful understanding of IC. It is important to note that IC does not consist of a stock of information, files, or paper, and it is not just what individuals know or how they work (Grantham *et al.*, 1997). It is not even in the sum of these capitals: human, structural, and relational capital can be useful for organizations only if they are linked through 'connectivity'. To this end, Habersam and Piber (2003) introduced connectivity as a fourth dimension of the IC framework, because it allows intensive-knowledge organizations, such as hospitals, to understand its IC as a whole, emphasizing the implications that the three dimensions have for each other. This is consistent with Bontis (1998), who considers IC as organizational learning flows, in which important knowledge cannot be transferred through education and training.

Guthrie *et al.* (2012) have underlined the importance of IC for management control and strategy areas. However, the focus on IC in regard to hospitals and healthcare organizations has been somewhat marginal, resulting in a lack of specific reporting models (Veltri *et al.*, 2011). Within the public sector, hospitals differ because of their special characteristics, as outlined earlier. Creating knowledge is a key issue with regard to hospitals, and even more so for university hospitals (French and Miller, 2012). In that context, the process of value creation involves the use of technological, human, and organizational resources to create knowledge. Research organizations and university hospitals primarily invest in IC determinants, combining them to provide knowledge-based outputs, such as innovative services, consultancies, publications, or clinical pathways.

Nowadays, these organizations are challenging the managerial approach when thinking about effective and efficient allocation of resources, which are knowledge-based, particularly in light of growing competition for funds and with the implementation of new instruments for measuring and managing knowledge (Leitner and Warden, 2004). In addition to budget constraints and perceived inefficiency, the culture of university hospitals also makes a management-integrated system more challenging because of the isolation of decision making. Schwartz and Pogge (2000) point out that in order to survive, university hospitals have to be better integrated, giving up their autonomy and working more effectively. In particular, it is essential to expand cultural change to stakeholders, stimulating innovation, supporting the development of a learning organization, and involving physicians and professionals in a patient-centred system.

Through a strong integration policy and a focus on the management of IC, intensive-knowledge healthcare organizations, such as university hospitals, may be able to mobilize their unique assets to develop long-term advantage. Robinson (1998) highlighted three actions: first, attract and train a new generation of physician leaders who can reconcile the conflicting expectations of doctors, customers, regulators, partners, and other stakeholders; second, through aggregation of physicians, organizations can improve innovation and sharing of best clinical practice; three, sharing best practice supports and develops quality and efficiency.

Similar to for-profit and other public sector organizations, the value generated by healthcare providers cannot be fully expressed by traditional financial measures, but requires innovative measurement models able to present qualitative elements, including numbers, narratives, and visualizations. In hospitals, the IC reporting activity has to take into account their system of values and operating context, which requires a considerable effort by management (Habersam and Piber, 2003). As a knowledge-based organization, hospitals' management can benefit from IC tools, which help to visualize the IC dimensions of the organizations. Any kind of measures and narratives related to IC determinants could be considered basic tools for depicting the IC of healthcare organizations.

Literature on IC in healthcare organizations

Habersam and Piber (2003) have pioneered the study of IC with regard to healthcare organizations, exploring the relevance and awareness of IC in the hospital setting through two qualitative case studies. While the IC accounting literature has mainly focused on for-profit organizations, discussing the contribution of IC to firms' performance and developing models to visualize and report IC dimensions and variables, Habersam and Piber investigated the IC framework in public healthcare organizations. Analysing the characteristics and the practices of the two case studies against different cultural backgrounds – Italy and Austria – the authors complement the widespread taxonomy of IC consisting of human, structural, and relational capital by introducing connectivity capital as a linking device. Identifying the dynamic character of interactions between IC components, they proposed a new comprehensive and dynamic framework of IC. This takes into account that IC is characterized by process-driven collective and individual capabilities in interaction. As a consequence, Habersam and Piber argue for a co-existence of financial metrics and non-metric rationalities in order to achieve transparency of IC.

Peng *et al.* (2007) analysed how hospitals view the importance of IC and performance in the healthcare sector. Based on a pilot study, the authors identify the elements and relative importance of IC and performance measurement in Taiwanese hospitals. The IC framework was operationalized in 54 variables, 7 of which referred to human capital, 32 to organizational capital, and 15 to relational capital. The authors expect this study to be a starting point for exploring healthcare IC and performance, by identifying relevant variables and measures of IC.

The clinical literature has often focused knowledge and IC, mainly from the perspective of a single professional group. For example, Covell (2008) developed the middle-range theory of nursing IC, conceptualizing the level of nursing knowledge available within healthcare organizations. Covell's work contributes to capturing the interrelationships between unit level variables within the work environment; nurses' knowledge, skills, and experience; knowledge structures; and patient and organizational outcomes. The author emphasizes the role of structural, human, and relational capital within the work environment, through a focus on social capital (Cohen and Prusak 2001; Prusak, 2001), human capital investment, and human capital depletion (Bontis and Fitz-enz, 2002), which influence the development of human capital. The propositions of IC theory identify the factors within the work environment that influence the development of nursing stocks of knowledge, and the relationship of this knowledge to patient and organizational outcomes. Covell (2008) suggests a model that is based on both nursing staffing and employer support to nurses' continuing professional development as the variables associated with nursing human capital; the latter affecting patients' outcomes and organizational outcomes, while nursing structural capital affects only patients' outcomes. The middle-range theory of nursing IC has strategic implications for healthcare organizations' management: it can be useful to governments and professional organizations in policy development, and it can support administrators to determine the cost–benefit of allocated resources to continuous professional development of nurses. While the cost of professional development may be high, its influence on patient and organizational outcomes may contribute to cost savings and improved performance for the organization.

Evans *et al.* (2015) presented a review of the IC literature in healthcare published between 1990 and 2014, in which they identified the following key terms: intellectual capital/assets, knowledge capital/assets/resources, and intangible assets/resources. As a result of the analysis, an outline of IC in healthcare is presented (see Table 7.1). The authors conclude that the framework of IC offers a means by which to study value creation in healthcare organizations, to systematically manage these IC resources together, and to enhance mutually their interactions with performance.

Table 7.1 IC in the healthcare organizations (Source: Evans *et al.*, 2015, p. 4)

IC dimensions	Definition	Variables (some examples)
Human capital	Knowledge, skills and experiences owned and used by individuals	Professional competencies and judgment Specialized skills Context-specific knowledge Leadership and managerial skills Personal dispositions
Structural capital	Institutionalized knowledge and codified experience stored in databases, procedures, and the organizational culture	Vision, mission, values, strategic plan Programs, tools, and information systems Ways of working together Best practice Routines
Relational capital	Knowledge available through networks of relationships internal and external to the organization	Patient/caregiver views and experiences Nature of internal clinical-managerial relations Contracts/agreements and partnerships with other service providers or with government, research institutions, consultants, etc. Brand, image, and reputation in the community

Evans *et al.* (2015) focus on the use of IC for managerial purposes, recommending both scholars and practitioners break down what it means to "manage IC" (p. 12). They recognize the important role of managing and measuring IC both within and across healthcare organizations, as the organizations in this context face innovation to improve quality of care, cost containment, and integrated services. They call for more effective methods to enhance IC management.

IC accounting theory has challenged the ability of IC to improve the effectiveness of managerial processes, decision making, and strategic management. Based on an empirical study using an action research approach in a university hospital setting, Vagnoni and Oppi (2015) develop and apply an IC framework to enhance the visualization of strategic IC. Furthermore, the authors investigate the ability of IC to root changes in a real setting, both from an information system perspective and from a strategic management process. The paper strengthens the case for the use of an interventionist research approach that would give more insight into organizational practice, proving the ability of IC theory to contribute to hospital management. Finally, the authors provide guidelines for both academics and practitioners applying IC management to a hospital setting.

Pirozzi and Ferulano (2016) addressed the need to integrate healthcare organizations' performance measurement systems with IC measures. Considering the gap between performance measurement approaches and the need to focus on both financial performance and clinical performance, the authors propose a model that provides a holistic representation of performance in healthcare organizations integrating different approaches stemming from intangible variables. Although the model could be used by administrators to manage and strategically control healthcare organizations more effectively, a discussion of the implications in practice is missing.

Most of the literature on IC in healthcare organizations aims at proposing new models, identifying IC variables, or proving the relevance of IC in the sector. Thus, authors have mainly analysed the literature to operationalize IC-related constructs or focused on case studies. Consequently, it can be argued that much of the literature related to IC in healthcare stems from the first and second stages of IC accounting studies (Guthrie *et al.*, 2012). What is missing is studies from the third stage of IC, focusing on IC managerial implications (Dumay and Garanina, 2013).

Conclusion

Considering the characteristics of healthcare organizations and of health service delivery, IC resources are drivers of performance, yet in this context much strategic decision making and management is focused on financial dimensions. The need to contain health expenditures as defined means that IC measures that can determine the value of the health service – both from the patient experience and from a social perspective – are overlooked. The accounting literature has examined the importance of measuring, visualizing, and reporting IC to improve performance in both private and public sector organizations (Borins, 2001; Mouritsen *et al.*, 2001b; Guthrie *et al.*, 2012). As healthcare organizations are complex, IC has a particular role to play in strategic management. Identifying IC variables, their relationships, and how to mobilize them, has the potential to contribute to achieving financial goals as well as clinical outcomes, and staff administration. It is also this complexity that makes the study of healthcare organizations more challenging and may be one reason why there are a limited number of accounting studies of the role of IC in that context; medical journals have more widely studied the IC framework and its operationalization in different dimensions, as well as criticizing the lack of methods and approaches to effectively use IC for management and strategy. Clinicians have emphasized the role of knowledge and IC for healthcare management, while directors of healthcare organizations are under pressure in relation to budget constraints. In this context, IC accounting scholars can play a key role in bridging the gap and contributing to management and accounting practice change in the healthcare organizations. Thus, studies related to the use of IC frameworks for managerial purposes at all levels of the organization can contribute to changes in practice and to closing the gap between administrative and healthcare roles, creating greater trust among healthcare professionals in accounting technologies.

References

Barzelay, M. (2002), "Origins of the new public management: An international view from administration/political science", in McLaughlin, K., Osborne, S. P. and Ferlie, E. (Eds), *New Public Management: Current Trends and Future Prospects*, Routledge, London, pp. 15–33.

Bishop, J., Boughlaghem, D., Glass, J., and Matsumoto, I. (2008), "Ensuring the effectiveness of a knowledge management initiative", *Journal of Knowledge Management*, Vol. 12, No. 4, pp. 16–29.

Bontis, N. (1998), "Intellectual capital: An exploratory study that develops measures and models", *Management Decision*, Vol. 36, No. 2, pp. 63–76.

Bontis, N. and Fitz-enz, J. (2002), "Intellectual capital ROI: A causal map of human capital antecedents and consequents", *Journal of Intellectual Capital*, Vol. 3, No. 3, pp. 223–247.

Borins, S. (2001), "Encouraging innovation in the public sector", *Journal of Intellectual Capital*, Vol. 2, No. 3, pp. 310–319.

Brailer, D. (1999), "Management of knowledge in the modern health care delivery system", *Journal on Quality Improvement*, Vol. 25, No. 1, pp. 6–19.

Chen, C. W. (2012), "Modelling and initiating knowledge management program using FQFD: A case study involving a healthcare institute", *Quality & Quantity*, Vol. 46, No. 3, pp. 889–915.

Cohen, D. and Prusak, L. (2001), *In Good Company: How Social Capital Makes Organizations Work*, Harvard Business School Press, Boston, MA.

Coulter, A. and Jenkinson, C. (2005), "European patients' views on the responsiveness of health systems and healthcare providers", *The European Journal of Public Health*, Vol. 15, No. 4, pp. 355–360.

Covell, C. L. (2008), "The middle-range theory of nursing intellectual capital", *Journal of Advanced Nursing*, Vol. 63, No. 1, pp. 94–103.

Dumay, J. and Garanina, T. (2013), "Intellectual capital research: A critical examination of the third stage", *Journal of Intellectual Capital*, Vol. 14, No. 1, pp. 10–25.

Evans, J. M., Brown, A., and Baker, G. R. (2015), "Intellectual capital in the healthcare sector: A systematic review and critique of the literature." *BMC Health Services Research*, Vol. 15, No. 1, pp. 556.

Ferlie, E. (1999), *The Rise of the New Public Management: Inaugural Professorial Lecture Imperial College Management School*, Imperial College, London.

Ferlie, E., Crilly, T., Jashapara, A., and Peckham, A. (2012), "Knowledge mobilisation in healthcare: A critical review of health sector and generic management literature", *Social Science & Medicine*, Vol. 74, No. 8, pp. 1297–1304.

French, M. and Miller, F. A. (2012), "Leveraging the 'living laboratory': On the emergence of the entrepreneurial hospital", *Social Science & Medicine*, Vol. 75, No. 4, pp. 717–724.

Gabbay, J. and Le May, A. (2004), "Evidence-based guidelines or collectively constructed mindlines? Ethnographic study of knowledge management in primary care", *British Medical Journal*, Vol. 329, pp. 1013–1017.

Grantham, C. E., Nichols, L. D., and Schonberner, M. (1997), "A framework for the management of intellectual capital in the health care industry", *Journal of Health Care Finance*, Vol. 23, No. 3, pp. 1–19.

Grosskopf, S., Margaritis, D., and Valdmanis, V. (2004), "Competitive effects on teaching hospitals", *European Journal of Operational Research*, Vol. 154, No. 2, pp. 515–525.

Guthrie, J. and Petty, R. (2000), "Intellectual capital Australian annual reporting practices", *Journal of Intellectual Capital*, Vol. 1, No. 3, pp. 241–251.

Guthrie, J., Ricceri, F., and Dumay, J. (2012), "Reflections and projections: A decade of intellectual capital accounting research", *British Accounting Review*, Vol. 44, No. 2, pp. 68–92.

Habersam, M. and Piber, M. (2003), "Exploring intellectual capital in hospitals: Two qualitative case studies in Italy and Austria", *European Accounting Review*, Vol. 12, No. 4, pp. 753–779.

Hood, C. (1991), "A public management for all seasons", *Public Administration*, Vol. 69, pp. 3–19.

Hudson, W. (1993), *Intellectual Capital: How to Build it, Enhance it, Use it*, John Wiley & Sons, New York.

Huttin, C. and de Pouvourville, G. (2001), "The impact of teaching and research on hospital costs", *The European Journal of Health*, Vol. 2, No. 2, pp. 47–53.

Institute of Medicine (2001), *Crossing the Quality Chasm: A New Health Care System for the 21st Century*, National Academy Press, Washington, DC.

Joe, C., Yoong, P., and Patel, K. (2013), "Knowledge loss when older experts leave knowledge-intensive organisations", *Journal of Knowledge Management*, Vol. 17, No. 6, pp. 913–927.

Kohn, L. T. (ed), (2004), *The Academic Health Center as a Modeller: The Patient Care Role*, The National Academies Press, Washington, DC.

Kothari, A., Hovanec, N., Hastie, R., and Sibbald, S. (2011), "Lessons from the business sector for successful knowledge management in health care: A systematic review", *BMC Health Services Research*, Vol. 11, No. 1, pp. 173.

Lee, E. J., Kim, H. S., and Kim, H. Y. (2014), "Relationships between core factors of knowledge management in hospital nursing organisations and outcomes of nursing performance", *Journal of Clinical Nursing*, Vol. 23, Nos 23–24, pp. 3513–3524.

Lehrer, L. A. and Burgess, J. F. (1995), "Teaching and hospital production: The use of regression estimates", *Health Economics*, Vol. 4, No. 2, pp. 113–125.

Leitner, K. H. and Warden, C. (2004), "Managing and reporting knowledge-based resources and processes in research organisations: Specifics, lessons learned and perspectives", *Management Accounting Research*, Vol. 15, No. 1, pp. 33–51.

Lerro, A. and Schiuma, G. (2013), "Intellectual capital assessment practices: Overview and managerial implications", *Journal of Intellectual Capital*, Vol. 14, No. 3, pp. 352–359.

Llewellyn, S. (2001), "Two-way windows': Clinicians as medical managers", *Organization Studies*, Vol. 22, No. 4, pp. 593–623.

Magnier-Watanabe, R. and Senoo, D. (2008), "Organizational characteristics as prescriptive factors of knowledge management initiatives", *Journal of Knowledge Management*, Vol. 12, No. 1, pp. 21–36.

Mark, A. L. (2006), "Notes from a small island: Researching organisational behaviour in healthcare from a UK perspective", *Journal of Organizational Behavior*, Vol. 27, No. 7, pp. 851–867.

May, C. (2013), "Agency and implementation: Understanding the embedding of healthcare innovations in practice", *Social Science & Medicine*, Vol. 78, pp. 26–33.

Meritum (2002), "Guidelines for managing and reporting on intangibles", in Cañibano, L., Sánchez, P., Garcia-Ayuso, M., and Chaminade, C. (Eds), *Meritum*, Fundación Airtel Móvil, Madrid.

Miller, F. A. and French, M. (2016), "Organizing the entrepreneurial hospital: Hybridizing the logics of healthcare and innovation", *Research Policy*, Vo. 45, No. 8, pp. 1534–1544.

Mintzberg, H. (1983), *Power In and Around Organizations*, Prentice-Hall, Englewood Cliffs, NJ.

Mouritsen, J., Johansen, M. R., Larsen, H. T., and Bukh, P. N. (2001a), "Reading an intellectual capital statement: Describing and prescribing knowledge management strategies", *Journal of Intellectual Capital*, Vol. 2, No. 4, pp. 359–383.

Mouritsen, J., Larsen, H. T., and Bukh, P. N. (2001b), "Intellectual capital and the 'capable firm': Narrating, visualising and numbering for managing knowledge", *Accounting, Organizations and Society*, Vo. 26, No. 7, pp. 735–762.

Nonaka, I. (1994), "A dynamic theory of organizational knowledge creation", *Organization Science*, Vol. 5, No. 1, pp. 14–37.

Peng, T. J. A., Pike, S., and Roos, G. (2007), "Intellectual capital and performance indicators: Taiwanese healthcare sector", *Journal of Intellectual Capital*, Vol. 8, No. 3, pp. 538–556.

Perrow, C. (1986), "Economic theories of organization", *Theory and Society*, Vol. 15, No. 1, pp. 11–45.

Pirozzi, M. G. and Ferulano, G. P. (2016), "Intellectual capital and performance measurement in health-care organizations: An integrated new model", *Journal of Intellectual Capital*, Vol. 17, No. 2, pp. 320–350.

Plsek, P. E. (2003), "Complexity and the adoption of innovation in health care", in *Proceedings of Accelerating Quality Improvement in Health Care: Strategies to Speed the Diffusion of Evidence-Based Innovations*, National Institute for Health Care Management Foundation, Washington, DC, 27–28 January 2003.

Plsek, P. E. and Wilson, T. (2001), "Complexity, leadership, and management in healthcare organisations", *British Medical Journal*, Vol. 323, No. 7315, pp. 746–749.

Porter, R. (2003), *Blood and Guts: A Short History of Medicine*, Allen Lane, London

Prusak, L. (2001), "Where did knowledge management come from?", *IBM Systems Journal*, Vol. 40, No. 4, pp. 1002–1007.

Robinson, J. C. (1998), "Financial capital and intellectual capital in physician practice management", *Health Affairs*, Vol. 17, No. 4, pp. 53–74.

Rondeau, V., Jacqmin-Gadda, H., Commenges, D., Helmer, C., and Dartigues, J. F. (2009), "Aluminum and silica in drinking water and the risk of Alzheimer's disease or cognitive decline: Findings from 15-year follow-up of the PAQUID cohort", *American Journal of Epidemiology*, Vol. 169, No. 4, pp. 489–496.

Ryu, S., Ho, S.H., and Han, I. (2003), "Knowledge sharing behavior of physicians in hospitals. Expert systems with applications", *Expert Systems with* Applications, Vol. 25, No. 1, pp. 113–122.

Schwartz, R.W. and Pogge, C. (2000), "Physician leadership is essential to the survival of teaching hospitals", *The American Journal of Surgery*, Vol. 179, pp. 462–468.

Sheaff, R., Schofield, J., Mannion, R., Dowling, B., Marshall, M., and McNally, R. (2003), *Organisational Factors and Performance: A Review of the Literature*, NCCSDO, London.

Stewart, T. A. (1997), *Intellectual Capital: The New Wealth of Organizations*, Nicholas Brealey Publishing, London.

Toth, F. (2010), "Healthcare policies over the last 20 years: Reforms and counter-reforms", *Health Policy*, Vol. 95, No. 1, pp. 82–89.

Vagnoni, E. and Oppi, C. (2015), "Investigating factors of intellectual capital to enhance achievement of strategic goals in a university hospital setting", *Journal of Intellectual Capital*, Vol. 16, No. 2, pp. 331–363.

Veltri, S., Bronzetti, G., and Sicoli, G. (2011), "Il Report del Capitale Intellettuale in Sanità: Specificità, Lezioni Apprese, Prospettive di Ricerca", *Mecosan*, Vol. 20, No. 78, pp. 101–112.

Zhou, A. Z. and Fink, D. (2003), "The intellectual capital web: A systematic linking of intellectual capital and knowledge management", *Journal of Intellectual Capital*, Vol. 4, No. 1, pp. 34–48.

Zigan, K., Macfarlane, F., and Desombre, T. (2010), "Knowledge management in secondary care: A case study", *Knowledge Process Management*, Vol. 17, pp. 118–127.

PART III

Stage 3
IC in practice

8

RETHINKING MODELS OF BANKS AND FINANCIAL INSTITUTIONS USING EMPIRICAL RESEARCH AND IDEAS ABOUT INTELLECTUAL CAPITAL

John Holland

Introduction

Traditional finance theory (TFT) provides established ways of developing theoretical models of financial firms, but is necessarily restricted to economic processes. However, in the post 2000 period, many of the economic problems faced by these financial firms have been located in their knowledge and social contexts, and in the (often negative) mutual and reciprocal interactions between knowledge, social, and economic factors. Problems have been encountered in using TFT to explain the phenomena. The aim of this chapter is to rethink models of banks and financial institutions (FIs) using ideas of intellectual capital (IC).

This chapter seeks to extend the explanatory framework for banks and FIs by using empirical (field) research and theoretical ideas about IC-based intangibles and social factors in financial firms and the world of finance. This concerns the role of knowledge-based intangibles and social factors in core economic processes or intermediation in financial firms. It concerns how top management in financial firms have responded to change, created knowledge and social factors, and mobilized these factors in their intermediation processes. It concerns how these interactions can become negative leading to major problems and financial firm failure (Holland, 2010). As a result, new ways of thinking about financial firms are required to analyse interactions between knowledge, and social and economic factors in FIs and their markets.

New developments in financial firm research, such as in IC, have occurred outside of the TFT paradigm and have been much constrained (Gendron and Smith-Lacroix, 2013). This research area has not made the same progress as IC accounting research (Guthrie *et al.*, 2012). Despite this, the progress broadly reflects the three stages of IC research in accounting outlined by Guthrie *et al.* (2012). The first stage reflects research to improve awareness of the role of IC in banks and FIs. Field work and literature are used in the chapter to explore the use and role of IC in banks and FIs. These sources are used to develop a field-based empirical narrative concerning knowledge (IC) and social and economic interactions in banks and

FIs, as well as change processes. The second stage reflects attempts to develop guidelines and theoretical views of IC in banks and FIs. The chapter develops a theoretical narrative to match the empirical results. It reveals work to develop grounded theory and to use alternative, non-finance theory to explain banks and FIs. Alternative theory includes sources such as literature on IC in financial firms and the theory of the firm. The first and second stages reflect attempts to develop and legitimize the field of IC research in financial firms as an area of multi-disciplinary and multi-focused research in a manner similar to IC accounting research (Petty and Guthrie, 2000; Guthrie *et al.*, 2012; Dumay and Garanina, 2013)

However, given the problems noted by Gendron and Smith-Lacroix (2013) in changing ideas in fields of finance academe and practice after the global financial crisis (GFC), the chapter also focuses on how to stimulate the third stage of more critically focused IC research identified by Guthrie *et al.* (2012). The chapter therefore identifies a core weakness of TFT arising from its inability to include IC thought in explaining banks and FIs. Such IC factors have been major influences on success and failure in bank and FI intermediation processes (Holland, 2010). The chapter illustrates how the above ideas from field work and empirical narrative and alternative theory narrative can be 'connected to' TFT. The combined set of ideas acts as a 'new theory frame for financial firms' (NTFF). It reveals new ways for critical thinking about financial firms and developing connections between broader social science and management literature and TFT. This creates new ways to critically evaluate the roles of banks and FI firms in the economy and society, develop a critical examination of IC in financial firm practice, and critically appraise the role of TFT in explaining financial firms.

Golden-Biddle and Locke (2007) distinguish between what they call 'field-based stories' and 'theoretical stories'. In this chapter 'field-based stories' or 'empirical narrative' refers to the empirical findings about the intermediation processes of banks and FIs in their markets. This includes 'basic economic models' of existing types of banks and FIs, as well as 'advanced models' that explicitly show the role of knowledge-based (or IC) intangibles and social contexts in economic processes. The empirical narrative also includes change processes and how they have stimulated knowledge creation and played a role in creating new, advanced forms of financial firms. The following section explores problems with existing bank/FI models and with theoretical interpretation using TFT. It highlights the need to include IC and learning ideas in explanation. This is followed by two further sections, which cover the main aspects of the empirical narrative. The first of these uses field-based research to explore the role of knowledge-based intangibles and social context in bank and FI intermediation processes, while the second notes that field-based ideas of change, learning, and knowledge creation are essential to understand the wider dynamics of bank/FI development. Two further sections develop the theoretical narrative, first by developing a theoretical narrative to match these empirical results. The combination of empirical and theoretical narratives form the NTFF conceptual framework to analyse and critically appraise the role of IC in financial firms, as well as the wider economic and social roles of these firms. Next, examples are provided of how this approach can be used to explain specialist financial firms such as retail banks, fund managers, and research analysts. The final section concludes and discusses how the analysis reveals new ways for critical thinking about the role of knowledge and social contexts in financial firms and new ways of developing connections between broader social science and management literature, and established finance theory.

Problems with existing bank/FI models and theoretical interpretations

The work of Revell (1973) and Lewis and Davies (1987) demonstrates how field-based research can be used to develop descriptions of new forms of banks and banking institutions (such as wholesale banks and commercial banks) in new kinds of financial markets (such as interbank markets for deposits and derivatives). These explanations focus on the basic economic processes in banks and FIs such as 'on balance' sheet and 'off balance' sheet financial intermediation as well as information intermediation. Bank/FIs financially intermediate and alter financial assets and their risks (both on and off balance sheet), and at the same time intermediate information about these transactions. All forms of intermediation can exist in a symbiotic relationship in the one financial firm or can operate at 'arm's length' through specialist financial firms and market mechanisms. The conventional literature has a strong emphasis on the economic processes of such intermediaries as they produce new information and transform financial assets (size, maturity, liquidity, function) and risks. This literature focuses primarily on the 'financial' and 'information' contexts of financial firms and their agents. These include contexts such as financial markets for the supply and demand of funds and financial services (Lewis and Davies, 1987), and markets for supply and demand for information (Barker, 1998). Conventional financial intermediation theory and finance theory are used as the sole means of interpretation (Buckle and Beccali, 2011) of empirical insights concerning economic processes in these contexts. However, many problems have been identified concerning the use of this theory. For example, it underplays the role of knowledge and social contexts, and change and knowledge creation (Holland, 2010).

Context also includes the social context in which agents of financial firms operate. The agents consisted of teams and individuals in bank/FI top management, their specialist research and information teams and individuals, specialist financial transaction teams, specialist asset portfolio and liability portfolio teams, and specialist teams for joint asset and liability management. Specialist 'front office' agents included financial actors such as bank lenders, fund manager investors, traders in markets, research analysts, and others. Context includes agents' 'relations' and network context with suppliers and users of funds, and financial and information services in financial markets. They include each agent's parent firm context and team context and individual agent's skill and behavioural contexts. These contextual areas function as a connected economic and social system.

Events immediately before and during the GFC, and analysis by many authors, have highlighted the importance of combined social, knowledge, and 'financial and information' contexts in the economic functions of financial firms and their agents (Holland, 2010; Holland *et al.*, 2012). They are the connected contexts in which agents in financial firms play an active role in intermediation processes. The GFC illustrated how knowledge of contexts and of economic processes in financial firms in these contexts is central to the work of agents in the firms. Knowledge-based intangibles (e.g. understanding of social or hierarchical positions, power, reputation, brands) in social contexts such as firm organization and external social networks (in markets) are major influences on success and failure in intermediation processes. Conventional theory and literature underplays or ignores the role of knowledge and social contexts in the decisions of financial firms and their agents (e.g. top management, middle management, front office staff).

In addition, before the GFC of 2007 to 2008, many authors identified problems in using finance theory alone in the world of finance (e.g. Holland 1998, 2005, 2006; Scholtens and Van Wensveen, 2003). After the GFC, authors such as, e.g. Holland, 2010 and Gendron and Smith-Lacroix, 2013, discussed how the crisis had exacerbated these problems and stimulated the need for a new approach. They included problems of change and limited learning and knowledge creation during change (Holland, 2010), and a lack of direct research on finance in action (Gendron and Smith-Lacroix, 2013).

Empirical narrative: central role of knowledge-based intangibles and social context in intermediation

In response to the above problems, this section uses field-based research to explore the role of knowledge-based intangibles in bank and FI intermediation processes. This research makes explicit the central role of knowledge in economic processes in new 'advanced models' of banks and FIs. It makes explicit the way in which management of financial firms mobilize knowledge and other resources to maximize their impact on wealth creation in economic processes such as intermediation.

These studies include Holland's (2005, 2016a) research into fund manager firms, Chen *et al.*,'s (2014) study of banking firms, Holland *et al.*'s (2012) research into venture capital firms, Chen *et al.*'s (2016) study of financial analysts in investment research firms, and Holland's (2016b) model of the 'market for information'. The GFC also revealed the central role of (failing) knowledge-based intangibles in wholesale banks and investment banks, as they developed risky and poorly understood new universal banks (Holland, 2010).

The field studies show the central role of unique combinations of many connected IC-based intangible resources in financial and information intermediation processes in banks and FIs. These included intangible resources such as knowledge or IC about financial firms (organization, hierarchy, process, culture, routines, teams) and the capabilities of bank/FI teams and individuals. They included knowledge of the financial needs of customers or clients, financial transactions, and of banking and financial markets. They also included knowledge about the external social networks and relations and the power and processes that banks and FIs have in relationships with customers and market participants. They included knowledge of pricing mechanisms in financial markets and the role of intangibles such as brand, reputation, and customer relations in supporting transactions in these markets. The tangible resources included financial resources, technology, and offices.

Each financial firm had a unique combination of resources, financial and intangible, integrated in a business model and driven by strategy. The special combination constituted a unique and sustainable competitive advantage (SCA) (Barney, 1991) for each financial firm. The intangibles and SCA were the basis for the bank/FI to construct specialized economies of scope and scale (Merton, 1995). Management mobilized the combined and special resources to enhance information production and support asset, liability, and risk management decisions by 'front office' teams and individuals. This enhanced ongoing intermediation processes, leading to success in transacting and in financial performance relative to competitors. Most banks and FIs operated as combined information and financial intermediaries, but specialist information intermediaries (investment banks, research firms), financial media, and database companies also existed.

More specifically, each bank/FI as an *information intermediary* involved economic, knowledge, and social processes in the search for production, exchange, and use of information. These processes occurred within the bank/FI firm as well as its specialist financial markets. For example, retail banks sought special insights (knowledge) into savings, spending, and borrowing behaviour by customers and by others in the retail banking market. This knowledge was the means to create special and private information about customers and close economic 'relationships', which together formed part of the competitive advantage for the retail bank. Bank learning over time created special knowledge about customer behaviour in markets and social settings. Similar processes occurred in other FIs such as pension funds, insurance companies, and fund managers.

Each bank/FI as a *financial intermediary* involved financial transformation processes *using the knowledge resources (intangibles) and information sources* (from information intermediation above) in balancing financial asset and liability risks to achieve a profit. Prior expert knowledge based on 'best practice' and many years of bank/FI management experience of success and failure in various connected areas of risk management (and often embodied in regulation and professional exams) was the means for effective management of the financial intermediation process. For example, in a 'basic' model of financial intermediation, financial risks were 'juggled' or managed in combination, in pursuit of profit, through well-tested and well-understood mechanisms and principles. The latter included contracting and diversification for both asset and liability transactions, asset/liability matching and mismatching for asset transformation, controlling asset and liabilities' interest rates or returns for positive margins, and the use of 'adequate' cash (liquidity) and equity capital as 'risk buffers' (Lewis and Davies, 1987). These were the combined basis for the transformation of the full set of assets and liabilities by size, maturity, and risk in financial firms such as banks, pension funds, insurance companies, fund managers, and venture capitalists (Buckle and Beccali, 2011). The ongoing 'front office' decisions about individual specialist financial assets and liabilities were conducted (in this controlled firm risk management context) in associated financial markets for savings, investment, and security exchanges.

Mobilizing resources: intangible and tangible

Knowledge-based intangibles were not static, passive dimensions of bank/FI economic activity. They had to be mobilized in a purposeful way by management to maximize their impact on intermediation and economic processes in banks/FIs. Top management used a combination of human and structural capital within the firm and relational capital in external networks as part of this mobilization. The human capital included the skills and capabilities of top management, middle management, and front office teams. Structural capital included knowledge of how to use bank/FI hierarchy, power, and organizational processes to mobilize resources. Relational capital involved knowledge of how to use social relationships and power to mobilize and exploit external financial resources.

In more specific terms, field studies revealed that each bank/FI firm was an organization made up of connected teams (e.g. Chen *et al.*, 2016; Holland, 2016a). They had a board and top management team with their own strategy and philosophy. They had a bank/FI firm hierarchy made up of top and middle management teams, which directed operational teams and individuals, both front and back office.

Each bank/FI firm had combinations of resources that were integrated in the bank/FI firm business model. For example, each bank/FI had expert knowledge for different kinds of specialist top management and for front and back office teams. These were key resources mobilized within the firm. Expert knowledge was the core of competitive advantage in ongoing bank/FI intermediation processes. In specific terms, bank/FI top management mobilized these knowledge-based intangibles via exercise of their power in the hierarchy and via their direction of organizational processes. These were used to support information production by front office staff dealing with new asset and liability decisions in financial intermediation.

We should also note that bank/FI intangibles such as quality of top management and front line and back office staff, of risk management methods and skills, and of board governance and accountability systems were increasingly the focus of regulation. Thus their coherent integration in the business model and effective mobilization relative to best practice became a compliance necessity for bank/FI management as much as a competitive and value creating issue. Poor compliance with regulatory requirements led to regulatory sanctions and subsequent negative impact on bank/FI reputation and value.

During this resource mobilization process, many bank/FI intangibles interacted in a purposeful way in bank and FI value creation processes. For example, Holland (2005) discusses how each case company (including banks and insurance firms) created value through careful management of its hierarchical, operational, and network value creation processes (Holland, 2004). In the case of banks and FIs, a specific group of intangible assets (or qualitative value creation factors such as top management quality, board governance capability, and quality of oversight of risk management), were critical hierarchical or top down drivers of the value creation process. Each case company also articulated a concept or idea of its 'operational' value creation process consisting of financial sourcing decisions and processes, financial asset and liability transformation decisions and processes, and financial outcomes (as in bank/FI financial and information intermediation). Within this intermediation process the top management of case financial firms exploited middle management and 'front office' employee human capital and other external intangibles such as customer and supplier relations and brands. They also exploited network value creation processes based on sharing of both tangible and intangible value drivers via customers, alliances, suppliers, and distributors. These were mainly employed at the boundary of the bank/FI firm. The nature of these value creation processes is discussed in detail in Holland (2004). The bank/FI cases discussed here were part of more general processes of intangibles in value creation in many different types of companies.

Bank/FI organizational processes for firm wide control (behaviour, risk, and so on) and information production were critical to resources mobilization (Cyert and March, 1963). They were driven by bank/FI aims and philosophy, based on bank/FI specialist financial roles and products. The organizational processes when combined with hierarchical power were the primary means for top management to mobilize resources within the bank/FI structure or hierarchy to support 'front office' team conditions, information production, and their financial asset, liability, and risk management decisions.

New value relevant information for these decisions was primarily created in organization processes and established decision routines from a variety of sources. These included combinations of soft and hard information sources (Stein, 2002), subjective judgements, and information from analysis of perceived regularities in markets for assets and liabilities. This information was the basis for active decision making by front office teams in financial asset, liability, and risk management areas. These included single financing and investment transactions (such as loans in banks or stock selection in fund managers). They included decisions about portfolios of large numbers of financial assets and liabilities, and they included joint asset liability risk management decisions (on and off balance sheet).

The above resource mobilization can also be interpreted from a risk management perspective. In the advanced model of financial intermediation (set in the bank/FI business model), top management 'juggled' tangibles risks (financial, technology) and intangibles risks to both balance and offset these combined risks in the search for profit. The intangibles risk concerned human capital as competence and skills, and with relational capital as reputation and brand power, and their impact on financial risks. This combined dynamic risk management created opportunities to mobilize bank/FI resources to ensure that the bank/FI could conduct financial and information intermediation in a highly competitive manner and thus add more value and make more profit than the competition. From a 'good practice' perspective, banks/FIs did this combined risk management first, and then sought profits. In the period before the GFC this was conducted the other way round by those banks that eventually failed.

Social contexts and bank/FI intermediation

The field studies reveal how various social contexts in the bank/FI and its external world were central to bank/FI economic processes. Knowledge of these contexts formed structural and relational types of IC (Meritum, 2002) which were developed by bank/FI top management during experiential learning during response to change. Within the firm, social context involved areas such as organization hierarchy and power (Stein, 2002), organizational culture (Schein, 1989), and organizational process (Cyert and March, 1963). For example, banks/FIs sought a balance between 'steep' and 'flat' organizational hierarchy to control decision costs or the costs of making decisions based on poor quality information. Stein (2002) argued that the steep hierarchy in established commercial banks maximized the use of hard numerical information (such as accounting information) but lost the benefits of 'soft' impressionistic or subjective information (such as information about people running firms). The 'flat' hierarchy used by financial firms such as investment banks and fund managers was intended to have the opposite decision costs and benefits, and to quickly exploit new impressionistic information. Banks/FIs used various types of hierarchy (steep, flat) and organization control process (centralize, high autonomy) to control decision costs and reduce behavioural biases in front office teams (Holland, 2016a). Banks/FIs also operated in external networks of social and economic relations (Stones, 2005). These networks supported information search and exchange. They were important in the control of behaviour and risky transacting and in further reducing decision costs for bank/FI agents. High power, reputation, and quality brands relative to external clients, customers, and suppliers in joint social and economic networks were expected to increase financial transaction success.

Management knowledge of, and power in, financial firm social contexts (internal and external), was the key to creating and using new information – both soft and hard – in specialist information intermediation processes. They were integrated means to cope with and reduce the uncertainty associated with financial asset, liability, and risk management decisions (Hellman, 2000, p. 236). When combined and mobilized they were important organizational means for uncertainty avoidance and conflict resolution in the manner suggested by Cyert and March (1963). Thus organizational and social contexts, agent knowledge of these, and power within contexts, were central to the bank/FI economic processes and decisions by their agents in financial markets.

Empirical narrative: change and bank/financial institution learning and knowledge creation

The previous section has discussed how knowledge-based intangibles and social contexts can be mobilized to play a role in bank/FI economic processes. It did not explain the origin and changing nature of knowledge and social factors. It did not explain changing bank/FI economic processes. Change has been a source of major problems and opportunities in banks/FIs. This section explores field research concerning how banks and other FIs respond to change and create knowledge. It argues that field-based ideas of change, learning, and knowledge creation are essential to understand the wider dynamics of bank/FI development.

Bank and financial institution learning: new knowledge and management and economic processes

Research by authors such as Harris (2002), Antonacopoulou (2006), Shih *et al*. (2010), Holland (2010), Holland *et al*. (2012), and Chahal and Bakshi (2015) illustrate how banks and other financial institutions respond to change, learn, and create knowledge-based intangibles of relevance to the effective functioning of the banking or FI firm. Top management and front office staff in financial intermediaries (banks and FIs) learnt over time to create knowledge to overcome, and at times create, market imperfections. They learnt how to develop IC (Meritum, 2002) to exploit the imperfections. This explanation is at odds with the TFT position whereby efficient markets and competition will erode imperfections and reduce the need for banks and FIs (Scholtens and Van Wensveen, 2003).

The above studies reveal how agents such as top management and front office staff learnt how to develop bank or FI organization and hierarchy (structural capital); the skills and capabilities of their teams and individuals (human capital); and their relationships, brands, and reputation with customers and other external agents (relational capital). The knowledge-intensive intangibles provided the means to create information for financial intermediaries to overcome market imperfections and to create financial products and services not available through markets. For example, agents learnt how to overcome imperfections associated with consumer preferences for funds (size, maturity, liquidity, risk), and consumer liquidity needs and shocks. They learnt how to reduce transaction costs and control adverse behaviour (before, after transactions) (Buckle and Thompson, 2005). They learnt how to use such knowledge to develop economies of scale and scope in financial transacting. In this frame, financial intermediaries existed because their agents learnt and created knowledge. However, banks and FIs did more than overcome market imperfections. In their search for value and profit, they used their knowledge to create competitive advantage in new products and services. These created new market imperfections which were best exploited by the bank/FI firm that created them.

For example, a study of Japanese FIs (fund managers and venture capital firms) by Holland *et al.* (2012) provides examples of how agent learning and knowledge creation were central to their response to change processes and hence to the way they formed new, valuable, and innovative economic processes in banks/FIs and financial markets. More generally, Shih *et al.* (2010, p. 74) comment:

> The ability to create knowledge is highly relevant to IC in the banking industry. Companies should define their own robust mechanisms for knowledge creation to improve their ability in knowledge creation. Knowledge creation in banks should focus on the exchange and sharing of information.

Knowledge management in this context is the key to superior value creation and performance relative to competitors. In this respect, Chahal and Bakshi (2015, p. 376) find many supportive relationships between change, learning, new IC formation, and innovation in banks. They note:

> The study finds that intellectual capital has direct and positive impact on the competitive advantage. It is also verified that innovation fully mediates the relationship between intellectual capital and competitive advantage. Further, the moderating effect of organizational learning on the relationship between intellectual capital and competitive advantage is also confirmed.

'Dynamic spirals' and change in banks and FIs

The major changes, learning, and knowledge creation noted above occurred in bank/FI firms over time as they learnt about new threats and opportunities. These were associated with reciprocal changes in customers, products, and markets in a "financial innovation spiral"

(Merton, 1995, p. 26). Despite changes in these elements, there was no fundamental change in the core risk management and intermediation roles of the banks/FIs in the real economy. The history of such change explains bank/FI success/failure as specialist intermediaries and as combinations of intermediaries. Merton's spiral provides a tentative explanation of how bank/FIs create knowledge and acquire new knowledge-based intangibles essential to SCA in financial intermediation.

However, major barriers to learning and knowledge creation also existed in banks/FIs and hindered constructive change. Harris (2002) and Antonacopoulou (2006) noted that problems can emerge in bank learning and knowledge creation. Harris (2002) provides evidence that learning from past mistakes, or even building upon past successes, continues to be the exception rather than the rule in major UK banks. Antonacopoulou (2006) argues that care must be taken in managing individual and team learning in bank organizational contexts.

The field studies above revealed a larger bank/FI 'change spiral' involving interactions within and between economic, knowledge, and social change processes in banks/FIs and their immediate markets. This involved mutual and reciprocal changes in these elements (Stones, 2005). This showed the central role of changing social context and forces in affecting bank/FI actions, at team and individual levels, and during ongoing decisions and long-term change periods.

Major events such as the GFC highlight how all of the above interactions (learning, knowledge, and role core functions) could go wrong and banks/FIs and markets could fail. In the period before the GFC, major (combinations of) bank/FI problems arose over time in intangibles, such as the quality of top management and their understanding of new risky bank models developed in a period of rapid change from 2000 to 2007. This led to high exposure to risk and excessive risk taking. When these coincided with major negative events (economic, political, and so on) in 2007 to 2008, they led to bank/FI firm failure and market problems (Holland, 2010). Major reasons for failure arose with problems with knowledge-based intangibles in banks/FIs in top management and front office staff. These created further problems with tangibles in intermediation processes. These intangibles' problems arose, inter alia, from joint social and economic issues such as top management abuse of reputation, knowledge, and power in financial firms and networks. They arose from problems with organization and with knowledge (Holland, 2010). These contributed to intangibles' problems with front office staff such as limited understanding of risk in new transactions and perverse incentives to sell these transactions. The above highlights the need to use the above ideas to develop ongoing diagnosis of change, 'innovation', and emerging problems with knowledge-based intangibles before they adversely affect the core intermediation processes in bank/FIs.

Developing an 'NTFF' using IC ideas

This section develops a theoretical narrative to match empirical results or narrative outlined in the previous two sections. This uses alternative, non-finance theory, to explain banks and FIs. Alternative theory includes sources such as literature on IC in financial firms and the theory of the firm. This section also illustrates how the ideas from field work and alternative theory can be 'connected to' TFT. The combined set of ideas acts as an NTFF.

Alternative theory to explain banks and FIs

The empirical narrative outlined in previous sections can be interpreted within a wider, non-finance theory literature, hence creating a broader theoretical narrative. This seeks to understand banks and FIs as profit-seeking businesses that organize their resources, tangible and intangible, to create an SCA matched to the needs of their markets, which allows them to conduct their specialist intermediation processes (information, financial) and risk management processes in more effective and valuable ways than similar specialist financial firms and in a superior way to individuals operating in markets. They sustain that advantage over time by the way they learnt and responded to change.

The empirical insights into 'real world' banks and FIs and the way they developed over time has revealed the importance of knowledge-based intangibles, such as bank/FI organization, hierarchy, capabilities (individual and team), social networks, and other factors in bank and FI intermediation processes, set in coherent business models, operating in competitive markets. Problems have been encountered in explaining banks and FIs using conventional theory (financial intermediation theory and finance theory) (Scholtens and Van Wensveen, 2003; Holland, 2010; Gendron and Smith-Lacroix, 2013). These problems become acute when new IC-based insights into banks and FIs are developed (Holland, 2005, 2006). As a result, a range of management theories and sociology of finance theories are combined with conventional theory (financial intermediation theory and finance theory) to interpret banks and FIs in their combined social, knowledge, and economic contexts.

The financial firms can be interpreted as evolutionary (Nelson and Winter, 1982) responses to uncertainty. Their organization structures and processes, external social networks, and shared firm wide knowledge, as knowledge-based intangibles, were developed by their agents learning in a common institutional setting (Scott and Meyer, 1994; Scott, 2001) during shared change processes. Holland *et al.* (2012) illustrates how these knowledge factors were the result of long-term learning and knowledge creation processes in financial firms during change processes. Knowledge in the firms changed over time via their activity as 'learning organizations' (Pedler *et al.*, 1997) hence maintaining, and at times enhancing, the firm's SCA (Teece, 2007).

Banks' and FIs' SCA was based on a unique, difficult to copy, combination of resources, both tangible and intangible. This idea is explained in the 'resource-based view of the firm' (Barney, 1991). Special combinations of resources with specific strengths matched to the external environment were the key to bank and FI success. A combination of unique knowledge-intensive intangibles and tangibles (with competitive advantages) were strategically matched to the external environment (customer needs, market conditions, competition, technology change, etc.) and were integrated in bank/FI business models and value creation chains (IIRC, 2013).

Bank and FI firms, and their top managers and 'front office' or decision teams, used organization processes and hierarchy to mobilize and exploit organizational resources such as knowledge, hierarchy, brand, and reputation in their financial decisions and financial intermediation processes (Cyert and March, 1963). The knowledge-based intangibles provided top management and 'front line' teams with organizational means and resources to focus on and interpret events and to produce new information during decisions (investment in financial assets, financing of financial liabilities, risk management of these). These intangible and tangible resources (and the SCA) were used by bank and FI teams to enhance information production and to support financing, investment, and risk management decisions by teams and individuals. They were the basis for effective and valuable intermediation (information, financial) and risk management by banks and FIs.

Connections to finance theory

Epistemological and ontological differences in the theory assumptions, core tenets, and views of the world create barriers to full integration of TFT and the above theories. However, the above alternative theory narrative can be connected to the TFT view (Buckle and Beccali, 2011) as follows. In TFT theory terms, the mobilization of resources and enhanced decision conditions for front office teams were expected to reduce information asymmetry, adverse selection, and moral hazard problems at single transaction and individual customer level as well as at aggregate portfolio levels. These conditions were intended to support front line staff to generate profitable transactions. The IC elements were seen as a primary means to aid senior management to manage aggregate transaction risk in the form of financial asset and liability portfolio risks and hence risks of intermediation processes in financial firms. The knowledge-intensive intangibles provided the means to manage joint asset liability portfolio risks through diversification, matching, and mismatching. Knowledge-based intangibles were the means to stabilize expected firm income. Enhanced knowledge of customers was the way for banks and FIs to manage and forecast their transaction flow for assets and liabilities. This improved the risk management and intermediation processes, and stabilized supply and demand, and costs and revenues, across market cycles. The size of a firm's cash reserves and equity levels as 'risk buffers', and preferred risk management methods were also determined by expert knowledge at top management level in the firm as well as by regulation (based on established expert knowledge). The combined impact of mobilized resources, improved team conditions, reduced information problems (at transaction, portfolio, firm levels), and improved risk management were the means to create value in the bank/FI through profitable transactions and secure financial intermediation.

The above theory narrative can also be extended to explain change in financial firms. The new conceptual framework viewed banks and FIs as profit-seeking businesses facing major change over time. Bank and FI learning and knowledge creation over time was the basis for the development of a dynamic version of SCA (Teece *et al.*, 1997) and for the creation of winners and losers between banks and between specialist FIs. The dynamic change in economic processes over time in the banks and FIs was an example of Merton's "financial innovation spiral" (1995), where key elements such as bank and FI business models, value creation chains, and competitive positions evolved together over time. At the same time, other elements such as the forms of financial and information intermediation, their financial and information products, their risk management services, product users and their needs, and the wider market for these bank and FI products, evolved together over time. Thus in terms of Merton's functional approach (1995), the financial functions of the financial system remained constant and stable, but the banks, FIs, and markets serving those functions evolved and changed over time.

From a TFT viewpoint, the role of knowledge in banks/FIs was to reduce agency costs and improve risk management. However, the empirical results reveal that banks' and FIs' primary aim was to create and use knowledge-based intangibles for value creation. Reduction of agency costs and transaction costs was achieved as a by-product of the main value creation purpose and activity, as suggested by Scholtens and Van Wensveen (2003). Thus, TFT by itself is inappropriate to explain the primary function, purpose, and behaviour of banks. It cannot explain the value creation process, the change process in banks, the creation of new knowledge, and emergence of new products and new transacting means. But these TFT sources (Buckle and Beccali, 2011) are important to explain the economic relationship between financial firms and markets once such change has occurred and the required knowledge has been created. Thus, current research requires the ideas from field work and alternative theory be 'connected to' TFT in a coherent way. The combined set of ideas acts as an NTFF.

Developing a meta theory framework

We should note that Stones' (2005) 'strong structuration theory' has been used in two complementary ways in the chapter. First, to explain observations of mutual, reciprocal, interactions between knowledge, social, and economic factors in banks and FIs. Second as a potential means to develop a meta theory approach.

In the first case, we use Stones' (2005) four elements of external structure, internal structure, actions, and outcome to structure the analysis of empirical insights into the intermediation role of agents in financial firms. Stones (2005) refers to active agency, in which agents such as top management or front line staff draw, routinely or strategically, on their internal structures (knowledge) to guide action in external contexts. Agents draw on their prior knowledge (general and specific) of external parent firm structures, of external market structures, and their socialization within these structures, to interpret events and circumstances, and to frame and direct their actions within the market and firm structures. The elements of structure, action, and outcomes are always present together in mutual reciprocal interactions. Economic processes in the form of agent experience of the supply of and use of funds, risk management, information exchanges (private, public), and stock market reactions to public information and actions by financial firm agents, provided rapid feedback stimuli during the interactions. The above is an ongoing economic process interacting with existing social and knowledge contexts, and is the means to reproduce social, knowledge, and economic structures on an ongoing basis.

The above reveals that Stones (2005) can also be potentially used as a 'meta' theory framework to guide choice from a 'menu' of theory and literature to match the empirical categories or narrative. Stones' (2005) strong structuration approach, and other relevant literature, can be used to interpret social structures in which agents operate in their parent financial firms (e.g. Chen *et al.*, 2014, 2016), and in social networks and relations in financial markets. The social and knowledge contexts are key areas where more explanation is required of the role of knowledge, social forces, and behaviour in purposeful agent economic processes and actions, and of how they contribute to structure in the agent financial firms and financial markets. This reflects the duality of structure and agency, whereby agents and structures (in financial firms and financial markets) mutually enact (or perform) social systems and social systems become part of that duality.

A new combined 'theory narrative': examples from field work

In this section, three examples are presented of how empirical insights, alternative theory, and finance theory can be combined in explaining specialist financial firms. The examples concern banks, research analysts, and fund managers (FMs). The alternative theory and literature view of banks/FIs is connected to (but not integrated with) the established finance theory view of banks/FIs. Together they offer a novel conceptual approach to analysing and interpreting the central role of knowledge-based intangibles in FIs.

A bank example of how to connect (expanded) theory and empirical sources

For example, Chen *et al.* (2014) outline a new theoretical narrative (Locke, 2001) corresponding to empirical findings on retail banks. Chen *et al.*'s (2014) views are briefly summarized in what follows.

Banks have business models (IIRC, 2013) that contain tangibles and knowledge-intensive intangibles (or human capital, structural capital, and relational capital as in Meritum, 2002).

The core tangibles of bank business models include financial assets, liabilities, and technology, and tangible processes such as risk management, intermediation, and technology-based processes. These tangibles are easily copied. Bank's intangibles, such as human capabilities or brands, are at the core of SCA in business models, as argued in the resource-based view of the firm (Barney, 1991). Intangibles are characterized as rare, inimitable, and difficult to copy sources of value (Barney, 1991). Combined intangibles and tangibles form bank business models (IIRC, 2013) and value creation chains (Porter, 1985). These are the means for banks to conduct risk management and financial intermediation in a more valuable way than competitors, and create higher financial performance. Use of intangibles in banking is expected to stabilize expected income. Enhanced employees' knowledge of customers can help banks better manage and forecast their transaction flow for assets and liabilities. This can improve the risk management and intermediation processes, and stabilize supply and demand, and costs and revenues, across market cycles.

Knowledge-intensive banks can reduce agency costs and problems of information asymmetry, and adverse selection and moral hazard at individual transaction (loan, deposits) levels and at aggregate portfolio levels. Knowledge-intensive intangibles provide the means to manage joint asset liability portfolio risks through diversification, matching, and mismatching and the use of equity capital and cash as risk 'buffers'. However, empirical studies such as Chen *et al.* (2014) reveal that the bank's primary aim was to create and use knowledge-based intangibles for value creation. Reduction of agency costs and transaction costs was achieved as by-products of the main value creation purpose and activity, as suggested by Scholtens and Van Wensveen (2003).

A research analyst example of how to connect (expanded) theory and empirical sources

In another example, Chen *et al.* (2016) outline a new theoretical narrative (Locke, 2001) corresponding to empirical findings on sell side analysts. This narrative can be constructed based on a combination of new literature and the conventional finance theory narrative. Chen *et al.*'s (2016) views are briefly summarized in what follows.

Analysts are concerned with knowledge-intensive intangibles that are rare, inimitable, non-substitutable sources of value (Barney, 1991). Analysts are also concerned with general knowledge about the external social and economic contexts of the firm, and with inter alia knowledge about the analyst parent, the company being analysed and valued, the fund manager client being served, and the wider market for information (MFI). At individual analyst level, these knowledge-based intangibles reflect special informal or experience-based capabilities allied with more conventional formal or professional capabilities. At analyst firm level, they reflect firm philosophy (on quantitative and qualitative research methods), and the degree of autonomy allowed for analysts. Analysts also rely on core tangible assets (e.g. technology, offices) and tangible processes (e.g. management, intermediation, technological). Knowledge-intensive intangibles are at the core of SCA for individual analysts, teams, and their parent firms, as noted in the resource-based view of the firm (Barney, 1991). These integrated and combined intangibles and tangibles form analyst value creation chains (Porter, 1985). These are the basis for analysts to conduct information intermediation (concerning information about company intangibles and their business models) more effectively than their competitors. This is expected to result in higher analyst performance in the provision of the combined information package of forecasting, valuation, explanation, and advice. Across many analysts and research teams it is expected to result in higher financial performance of the equity research function in parent investment banks. Such knowledge-intensive individual analysts, teams, and parent firms provide the means to reduce agency costs and associated problems of information asymmetry, adverse selection, and moral hazard between analysts, companies, and MFI actors, such as client FMs and small investors. Analyst intangibles provide the means to overcome imperfections by contributing to economies of information specialization, scale economies in information acquisition, and reduction in information search costs.

Analysts learn over time while making routine decisions and when responding to change pressures. This new knowledge contributes to changes in their information intermediation model, their outputs, and relations with companies and clients. These changes in information services, structure, and function in the MFI are interpreted through Merton's (1995) 'financial innovation spiral' (economic changes) and Stones' (2005) 'strong structuration theory' of social structure and change.

A fund manager example of how to connect (expanded) theory and empirical sources

Holland (2016a) outlines a new theoretical narrative (Locke, 2001) corresponding to empirical findings on FMs. These findings are summarized in what follows.

FMs have knowledge-intensive intangibles that are rare, inimitable, and non-substitutable sources of value (Barney, 1991). FMs are concerned with general knowledge about the external social and economic contexts and also with, inter alia, knowledge about the company being analysed, valued, and invested in, and about analysts and other information providers in the MFI. At individual FM level these knowledge-based intangibles reflect special informal or experience-based capabilities allied with more conventional formal or professional capabilities. At FM firm level, they reflect firm philosophy (on quantitative and qualitative research methods), and the degree of autonomy allowed for individuals and teams involved in investment decision making. They include organizational resources in the fund management firm such as organizational, hierarchical, team, and individual capabilities and processes. FMs also rely on core tangible assets (e.g. technology, offices) and tangible processes (e.g. management, intermediation, technological). The knowledge-intensive intangibles are at the core of SCA in individual FMs, teams, and their parent firms, as noted in the resource-based view of the firm (Barney, 1991). These integrated and combined intangibles and tangibles form FM value creation chains (Porter, 1985). These are the basis for FMs to conduct information intermediation (concerning information about investee company intangibles and their business models) more effectively than their competitors. These are the basis for FMs to conduct financial intermediation (concerning savers' funds and portfolio investment) more effectively than their competitors. These are expected to result in higher FM performance in the provision of saving services and investment portfolio services at team and FM firm levels.

For example, the behavioural theory of the fund management firm reveals much about the interaction of organizational intangibles (organizational, hierarchical, and individual/team processes) and tangibles in the FM economic process. FM firms created and mobilized intangible organizational resources to help investment decisions by teams and individuals in the FM firm. These intangibles were central to information production and risk management at firm, team, and individual levels.

The grounded theory was based on a set of relational concepts involving ongoing FM decision action, and broader organizational process and hierarchy. It was also based on a set of FM strategic and contextual resources and their properties. Immediate (investment) decision actions by individuals and teams were a goal-seeking structured task sequence and a process of sense making. These were different but related means to reduce the uncertainty associated with equity investments (Hellman, 2000, p. 236) and to find new information and investments of value.

The FM organizational processes were identified, first, as an integrated set of hierarchical processes or firm wide processes of control and influence over the allocation of resources, risk, and autonomy. Second, they existed as firm wide and team information production and exchange processes. FM firm wide organizational processes were key means for uncertainty avoidance and conflict resolution in the manner suggested by Cyert and March (1963). They were means to create and control FM hierarchy costs (Stein, 2002). They were also the base from which FM creativity could be stimulated. Both informal 'conversations' and formal communications were important in micro and macro processes. They were important in solving problems and making novel associations. The organizational processes mobilized FM resources in a dynamic and purposeful way to produce the desired influence on investment team conditions, ongoing investment decision processes, and investment success or failure.

Resources were interpreted as knowledge-based key properties of FM internal and external contexts. The external context of FMs consisted of various external 'networks' and markets. The internal context of FMs consisted of top management context, an organizational context, a team context, a personal context, and an immediate decision or action context. Each FM context had various knowledge-based properties and peer group relative strengths of these properties.

From the resource-based view of the firm (Barney, 1991) the FM contexts and their knowledge-based properties were resources mobilized by FM organizational processes to support investment team processes. The key resources were central to FMs exploiting investment opportunities and creating value, as well as in uncertainty avoidance and conflict resolution processes as outlined by Cyert and March (1963). These dynamic elements to FM firms can be interpreted as tentative organizational means to deal with major problems of behaviour, uncertainty, and information asymmetry at the heart of the valuation, investment, and performance problems facing FMs.

Summary

The aim of this chapter has been to rethink models of banks and FIs using ideas of IC. Problems have been encountered in using TFT to explain these financial firms, especially in the GFC and post GFC period. Many of the economic problems faced by these firms have been located in their misuse of their own expert knowledge and dependence on TFT to direct and explain these firms.

This chapter has extended the explanatory framework for banks and FIs by using empirical research and theoretical ideas about IC-based intangibles and social factors in financial firms and the world of finance. Golden-Biddle and Locke (2007) distinguish between what they call "field based stories" and "theoretical stories". The chapter has developed a novel empirical narrative to explain the role of knowledge-based intangibles in economic processes or financial intermediation in banks and FIs. The empirical narrative was extended to include issues of change, learning, and knowledge creation. The chapter has also developed a theoretical narrative to match these empirical results. The chapter illustrates how diverse but relevant literatures can be linked together via the analysis of the empirical patterns to form a coherent alternative 'theoretical narrative' for financial firms such as banks and FIs. The alternative literature base includes IC literature, 'management' theory, and theory of the firm relevant to financial firms. The chapter illustrates how the ideas from field work and alternative theory can be 'connected to' TFT. The combined set of ideas acts as an NTFF.

The analysis therefore reveals new ways to analyse and critically appraise the role of IC in financial firms. It reveals new ways for critical thinking about financial firms. It demonstrates new ways of developing connections between broader social science and management literature, and TFT. This provides a new form of intellectual flexibility designed to help practitioners and academics break out of dogma and "psychic prisons" (Morgan, 1986, p. 215) created by adherence to a single theoretical frame or intellectual viewpoint.

References

Antonacopoulou, E. P (2006), "The relationship between individual and organizational learning: New evidence from managerial learning practices", *Management Learning*, Vol. 37, pp. 455–473.

Barker, R. G. (1998), "The market for information: Evidence from finance directors, analysts and fund managers", *Accounting and Business Research*, Vol. 29, pp. 3–20.

Barney, J. (1991), "Firm resources and sustained competitive advantage", *Journal of Management*, Vol. 17, No. 1, pp. 99–120.

Buckle, M. and Beccali, E. (2011), *Principles of Banking and Finance*, University of London, London.

Buckle, M. and Thompson, J. L. (2005), *The UK Financial System: Theory and Practice*, Manchester University Press, Manchester, UK.

Chahal, H. and Bakshi, P. (2015), "Examining intellectual capital and competitive advantage relationship: Role of innovation and organizational learning", *International Journal of Bank Marketing*, Vol. 33, No. 3, pp. 376–399.

Chen, L., Danbolt, J., and Holland, J. (2014), "Rethinking bank business models: The role of intangibles, *Accounting, Auditing, & Accountability Journal*, Vol. 27, No. 3, pp. 563–589.

Chen, L., Danbolt, J., and Holland, J. (2016), *Analyst Information Intermediation and the Role of Knowledge and Social Forces in the 'Market for Information'*, Working Paper, Adam Smith Business School, University of Glasgow, UK.

Cyert, R. M. and March, J. G. (1963), *A Behavioral Theory of the Firm*, Prentice-Hall, New York.

Dumay, J. and Garanina, T. (2013), "Intellectual capital research: Critical examination of the third stage," *Journal of Intellectual Capital*, Vol. 14, No. 1, pp. 10–25.

Gendron, Y. and Smith-Lacroix, J. H. (2013), "The global financial crisis: Essay on the possibility of substantive change in the discipline of finance", *Critical Perspectives on Accounting*. Vol. 30, pp. 83–101.

Golden-Biddle, K. and Locke, K. (2007), *Composing Qualitative Research*, Sage Publications, Thousand Oaks, CA.

Guthrie, J., Ricceri, F., and Dumay, J. (2012), "Reflections and projections: A decade of intellectual capital accounting research", *British Accounting Review*, Vol. 44, No. 2, pp. 68–92.

Harris, L. (2002), "The learning organisation: Myth or reality? Examples from the UK retail banking industry", *The Learning Organisation*, Vol. 9, No. 2, pp. 78–88.

Hellman, N. (2000), *Investor Behaviour: An Empirical Study of How Large Swedish Institutional Investors Make Equity Investment* Decisions, PhD, Stockholm School of Economics.

Holland, J. (1998), "Private corporate disclosure, financial intermediation and market efficiency", *Journal of Business Finance and Accounting*, Vol. 25, Nos 1–2, pp. 29–68.

Holland, J. (2004), *Corporate Intangibles: Value Relevance and Disclosure Content*, ICAS Research Report, Edinburgh, UK.

Holland, J. (2005), "A grounded theory of corporate disclosure", *Accounting and Business Research*, Vol. 35, No. 3, pp. 249–267.

Holland, J. (2006), *A Model of Corporate Financial Communications*, ICAS Research Report, Edinburgh, UK.

Holland, J. (2010), "Banks, knowledge, and crisis: A case of knowledge and learning failure", *Journal of Financial Regulation and Compliance*, Vol. 18, No. 2, pp. 87–105.

Holland, J. (2016a), "A behavioural theory of the fund management firm", *European Journal of Finance*, Vol. 22, No. 11, pp. 1004–1039.

Holland, J. (2016b), *The Market for Information*, Working Paper, Adam Smith Business School, University of Glasgow, UK.

Holland, J., Henningsson, J., Johanson, U., Koga, C., and Sakakibara, S. (2012), "Use of IC information in Japanese financial firms", *Journal of Intellectual Capital*, Vol. 13, No. 4, pp. 562–581.

IIRC (2013), *The International Integrated Reporting Council, Business Model: Background Paper for Integrated Reporting*, The International Integrated Reporting Council, London.

Lewis, M. and Davies, K. T. (1987), *Domestic and International Banking*, MIT Press, Boston, MA.

Locke, K. D. (2001), *Grounded Theory in Management Research*, Sage Publications, London, UK.

Meritum (2002), *Guidelines for Managing and Reporting on Intangibles (Intellectual Capital Report)*, TSER Programme, MERITUM, Tucson, AZ.

Merton, R. C. (1995), "A functional perspective of financial intermediation", *Financial Management*, Vol. 24, No. 2, pp. 23–41.

Morgan, G. (1986), *Images of Organization*, Sage Publications, Newbury Park, CA.

Nelson, R. R. and Winter, S. G. (1982), *An Evolutionary Theory of Economic Change*, The Belknap Press, Harvard University Press, Cambridge, MA.

Pedler, M., Burgoyne, J., and Boydell, T. (1997), *The Learning Company: A Strategy for Sustainable Development*, McGraw Hill, London.

Petty, R. and Guthrie, J. (2000), "Intellectual capital literature review: Measurement, reporting and management, *Journal of Intellectual Capital*, Vol. 1, No. 2, pp. 155–176.

Porter, M. (1985), *Competitive Advantage: Creating and Sustaining Superior Performance*, The Free Press, New York.

Revell, J. (1973), *The British Financial System*, Macmillan, London,

Schein, E. H. (1989), *Organizational Culture and Leadership*. Jossey-Bass, San Francisco, CA.

Scholtens, B. and Van Wensveen, D. (2003), "The theory of financial intermediation: An essay on what it does (not) explain", SUERF, *The European Money and Finance Forum*, Vienna 2003, Number 2003/1.

Scott, W. R. (2001), *Institutions and Organizations*, Sage Publications, Thousand Oaks, CA.

Scott, W. R. and Meyer, J. W, (1994), *Institutional Environments and Organizations*, Sage Publications, Thousand Oaks, CA.

Shih, K. H., Chang, C. J., and Lin, B. (2010), "Assessing knowledge creation and intellectual capital in banking industry", *Journal of Intellectual Capital*, Vol. 11, No. 1, pp. 74–89.

Stein, J. C. (2002), "Information production and capital allocation: Decentralized versus hierarchical firms", *Journal of Finance*, Vol. 57, No. 5, pp. 1891–1921.

Stones, R. (2005), *Structuration Theory*, Palgrave Macmillan, Basingstoke, UK.

Teece, D. J. (2007), "Explicating dynamic capabilities: The nature and microfoundations of (sustainable) enterprise performance", *Strategic Management Journal*, Vol. 28, No. 13, pp. 1319–1350.

Teece, D. J., Pisano, G., and Shuen, A. (1997), "Dynamic capabilities and strategic management", *Strategic Management Journal*, Vol. 18, No. 7, pp. 509–533.

9

MOBILIZING INTELLECTUAL CAPITAL IN PRACTICE

A story of an Australian financial institution

Vijaya Murthy and James Guthrie

Introduction

Contemporary intellectual capital (IC) research has five stages (Dumay *et al.*, 2017). The first stage was raising awareness and the second stage was theory building and frameworks (Petty and Guthrie, 2000). The third stage was investigating IC in practice from a performative perspective (Guthrie *et al.*, 2012). A fourth stage is an ecosystem approach as outlined by Dumay and Garanina (2013). The fifth stage of IC research is identified as working towards reconciling the worth of IC to different people in different contexts, respecting that there will always be differences, and that one view should not always prevail (Dumay *et al.*, 2017). Our study attempts to explore the third stage.

An important turning point in IC research is the article by Guthrie *et al.* (2012), which reviews a decade of IC accounting research. They conclude that much of the past research into IC was commentary, and normative policy rather than empirical papers. This opened up the opportunity for more research examining IC practices. As Guthrie *et al.* (2012, p. 79) emphasize:

> We must challenge the status quo, employ innovative methodologies, experiment with the novel and take risks. We encourage you to watch the ICA space in the next decade for more critical field studies which will provide empirical studies of IC in action and help develop broader theoretical research.

Dumay *et al.* (2017, p. xx) state that to extend IC, researchers need to remove boundaries, and the question they ask needs changing from "what is IC worth to investors, customers, society and the environment?" to "is managing IC a worthwhile endeavour?" Asking the latter question removes the boundaries from IC research to include a much broader understanding of 'worth' and recognizes that IC is a substantial part of what impacts everyone on a day-to-day basis.

Different forms of IC value have different worths to different people. Dumay (2016, p. 169) highlights a distinction between IC 'value creation' and 'wealth creation', where wealth creation is about increasing the stock Demartini of money or something convertible to money. Managing IC is more than this as value creation is central and all activity cannot be measured just in monetary terms. Dumay (2016) defines value creation in four ways: monetary, utility, social, and sustainable value. We adopt this perspective of value creation in our case study, which explores how IC was mobilized and the consequences of this within an organization.

Motivated by Dumay *et al.* (2017) this chapter seeks to understand how IC theory translates into practice (e.g. to explore the impact of IC practices on the people and the organization). According to IC theory, the three elements of IC (i.e. human, structural, and relational capital) work together resulting in value creation. In practice, what happens when IC elements work together or independently? Is it true that when IC is managed it results in value creation?

The aim of this chapter is to examine how IC is mobilized in a large organization. We use data collected from an Australian financial institution to construct a narrative (a story with a beginning, middle, and end) to show that when managers mobilized IC elements expecting certain (intended) consequences, there were unintended consequences since elements of IC interacted, entangled, and acted with each other.

We use the narrative approach for the chapter as it endeavours to create an account of the process through stories to provide coherence and continuity to organizational experience (Lieblich *et al.*, 1998). Imposing a narrative structure containing a plot, a sequence, and actors (Bruner, 1990) onto fragmented material collected from various documents and interviews helped us in making sense of what was happening in the organization – the processes, the barriers, and the struggle to manoeuvre IC.

Literature review

Accounting researchers have long argued that there are drawbacks to relying exclusively on financial accounting information (Murthy, 2011) and that traditional accounting models (both financial and management accounting) do not capture the "value creation story" (Dumay *et al.*, 2017). While traditional accounting models have informed company management and other stakeholders about stocks and flows of financial value, IC consists of non-financial value.

In stage one of IC research, several authors argued that IC elements, such as customer loyalty, employee satisfaction, and internal processes, drive financial performance (Nowak and Anderson, 1999). According to Cumby and Conrod (2001), the activities that create shareholder value must be identified and managed, since IC plays a major role in performing this function. The success of this association depends on the way IC elements are used and managed within the organization (Joiner *et al.*, 2009; Reijonen and Komppula, 2007).

Since the early 2000s, IC researchers have been concerned with justifying IC theoretical assumptions through empirical testing (e.g. Marr *et al.*, 2003) and advocated for the research field to adopt empirical testing (Mouritsen, 2006). Andriessen (2004) believed that IC research was undertaken mostly by practitioners rather than academics and, among other concerns, called for research that could clarify how internal management used IC information.

In stage two of IC research, several IC researchers proposed models and guidelines (e.g. Roos, Sveiby, Mouritsen, and Edvinsson) and built a variety of IC toolboxes[1] to help organizations manage their knowledge. The common denominator among these toolboxes is that they acknowledge IC as necessary in the value creation process, but they tend to link the IC agenda with a financial agenda (Skoog, 2003).

With developments in the field of IC research, the third stage IC studies provided performative analysis, creating empirical evidence of 'IC in action'. For instance, Yu and Humphreys (2013) argued that IC components are interrelated and the implementation of IC management strategy was low within the engineering industry. They advocated moving away from a 'measuring' focus to a 'learning' focus by examining the flow of IC. Chiucci (2013) undertook interventionist research that showed that actors must complete an experiential learning cycle to mobilize IC. By doing so, companies introducing IC are more likely to become aware of barriers and levers to measuring and mobilizing IC.

Chiucchi and Dumay (2015) asked if it was possible for an organization to implement 'lock-in' IC accounting practices and subsequently 'un-lock' IC through a more strategic managerial approach. They concluded that at times a principal focus on accounting for IC is necessary to make sense of IC and manage it. Similarly, such studies were conducted with a performative research agenda to show the use of IC in managing organizations, how IC works, and how people and processes are mobilized (e.g. Cuganesan, 2005; Cuganesan *et al.*, 2007; Dumay and Guthrie, 2007).

IC in action type research has increased and matured in the third stage. However, as Dumay and Garanina (2013) point out, several of these studies seem to be stuck in an 'evaluatory trap' whereby they develop top-down ostensive IC research rather than taking a critical bottom-up approach. The critical approach has been labelled the fourth stage of IC research. Our study is an IC in practice study; it is unique in that we bring out the stories from the organization to show the complexities that managers face while trying to mobilize the network of IC resources. Also, the results of our study provide a flavour of the fifth stage of IC research as we can see evidence that the managerialist perspective is limiting and we explore impacts beyond intended consequences and highlight a perpective of IC in action.

Unintended consequences

This section briefly explores the theory of intended consequences, which is used to explain part of our story. Intended consequences of a purposive action are limited to those elements in the resulting situation that are exclusively the outcome of the action (Merton, 1936) and are relatively desirable to the actor. Unintended consequences (also known as unanticipated consequences or unforeseen consequences) are outcomes that are not those intended by a purposive action. For the purpose of this study, we label consequences that relate to the stated objectives 'intended consequences', or main effects, whereas consequences that do not relate to the stated objective are labelled 'unintended consequences' or side effects (Brüggemann *et al.*, 2013).

The theory of unintended consequences was popularized by Robert K. Merton in 1936. Merton's (1936) 'consequences' of purposive action are limited to those elements in a resulting situation that are exclusively the outcome of the action, that is, those elements that would not have occurred had the action not taken place. In an organization, attention is restricted to such situations that are immediately or directly the outcome of an action (Ashton, 1976). Nevertheless, due to the interdependence of organizational elements, there is a possibility that a change in one element may yield unforeseen consequences in other elements.

Unintended consequences should not be identified with consequences that are not necessarily undesirable (for the actor) (Merton, 1936). Though unintended, these consequences may be positive, negative, or perverse and are sometimes desirable. A positive unintended consequence is an unexpected benefit derived from an action, which we can refer to as luck or a windfall. A negative unintended consequence may result in unexpected adverse effects in addition to the intended effect of an action (e.g. while budgets help in increasing organizational efficiency, they may also reduce employee motivation). A perverse effect is a consequence contrary to what was originally intended, that is, when the intended solution makes a problem worse. Therefore, unintended consequences are NOT uniformly errors or mistakes that are not welcome; they are surprises that can vary on a scale from lucky to unfortunate (Campbell *et al.*, 2006).

Merton (1936) highlights five factors to a correct anticipation of consequences of action: ignorance, error, immediate interest, basic values, and self-defeating prediction. The first factor, given the existing state of knowledge, means that it is practically impossible to predict with certainty the results in any particular case. Also, incomplete knowledge, based on which action is carried out, could lead to a range of unexpected outcomes. This is categorized as ignorance that leads to incomplete analysis. The second factor that gives rise to unexpected consequence is an error. It is normal for human beings to err in any phase of action: an appraisal of the problem, selection of a course of action, or implementation of the action. Sometimes, an action can erroneously be taken based on the fact that it worked in the past, but may not prove successful under the current situation.

The third factor resulting in unintended consequence is immediate interest, which refers to situations where the actor looks for immediate results (short-run) neglecting the consideration of further consequences (in the long run) depending on a range of interests such as psychological needs, cultural values, economic needs, and so on. The fourth factor is that of basic values, which refer to situations where there is no consideration of further consequences because of being pressured by some basic values to perform certain actions. The final factor, self-defeating prediction, refers to instances when the public prediction of a social development proves false precisely because the prediction changes the course of history. Sometimes, people are scared of unfavourable unintended consequences of a particular act and want to avoid them.

Research method

Research using narrative methods enables researchers to place themselves at the interface between persons, stories, and organization (Czarniawska, 1998, 2005). Narrating is a mode of thinking and persuading that is as legitimate as calculating (Llewellyn, 1999, p. 220). Narratives can be defined in several ways. For instance, according to Riessman (1993, p. 17), narratives are discrete units, with clear beginnings and endings, detachable from the surrounding discourse rather than as situated events. Denzin (1989, p. 37) encapsulates the characters of 'narratives' as a story that tells a sequence of events that are significant for the narrator and his or her audience. Thus, for the purposes of this study, we define a narrative as a story that has a plot, a beginning, middle, and an end. It has an internal logic that makes sense to the narrator. A narrative relates events in a temporal, causal sequence and every narrative describes a sequence of events that has happened in the past. A narrative label can be applied at the personal, organizational, or societal level and allows multiple stories to be bundled together to form narratives (Hawkins and Saleem, 2012).

Narratives take different forms within organizational studies. This includes research that has been written in a story-like manner, research that collects stories, and research that looks at organizational life as story-making (Hawkins and Saleem, 2012). In this research, we use two forms of narratives. First, research is written in a story-like fashion. Second, stories were collected from the organizational members, reports, and newsletters (i.e. tales of the field, gathered from the field). Narrative accounts (coherent wholes) were constructed using parts supplied by organizational members and from those found in the reports and newsletters including the relevant and excluding the irrelevant (Llewellyn, 1999, p. 225). This helped to create some unified stories.

The narratives are constructed from raw and fragmented material obtained from the documents and transcripts of stories collected from interviews. The written and oral material complemented each other. The raw material thus obtained is organized with the help of a plot and characters. Thus, we perform narrative analyses by collecting descriptions of events, actions, and happenings, and synthesizing them using a plot into stories. The purpose of the narrative analysis is to produce stories as the outcome of the research. Narrative analysis studies rely on stories as a way of knowing, and stories emerge as data is collected and then are structured and rendered through an artistic and rigorous analytical process. Barone (2007, p. 456) calls this a 'narrative construction' because "recasting of data into a storied form is more accurately described as an act of textual arrangement". In this research, narrative analysis is used to analyse the empirical data collected by the financial institution (e.g. narrative construction is performed).

For this research, narrative analysis helps us answer the aims of this chapter, which are to examine how IC was mobilized in a large organization. In answering this question, a search was conducted for pieces of information from various sources such as interviews and different internal and external reports. Explanations based on evidence from the past were organized into a unified story in which the links between the events were developed (Polkinghorne, 1988). Written texts were considered not just as a collection of words but a sequenced discourse and a network of narratives that could be read in a variety of ways (Krippendorff, 2004, p. 63). The texts found in the written reports did not merely map, speak about, or indicate the features of the organization, but were considered to construct worlds for the people in the organization to see, enact, and live with (Krippendorff, 2004, p. 63). These texts were sequential in nature, and the narratives in each of the reports were not considered as individual silos but were integrated with each other to form a coherent story. Therefore the contents were read and re-read, compared and matched with interviews that helped the researcher to form the plot and sew the fragments of information collected to transform them into patterns of knowledge and to make sense of the organization.

Written texts are understood to be created within, and against, particular traditions and audiences (Riessman, 1993). Texts always stand on moving ground, and there is no master narrative (Clifford and Marcus, 1986). Nevertheless, written reports that represent the organization's practices were considered as the voice of the organization as a whole. The analysis and discussion sections of this study do not contain evidence (in the form of quotes) taken from reports and interviews, but consist of plotted stories that were configured by the researcher from the data collected.

The data was gathered from the back office of one Australian financial institution (known hereafter as the Bank) and included interviews and documents. These are all traces of past events of the organization that helped uncover how management mobilize IC in practice. Interviews took place with 14 senior executives and 45 employees of the back office (BO) of the organization. The documents gathered and analysed included both external and internal documents that managers use as tools that can be consulted for their future managerial activities. External documents analysed include annual reports and extended performance accounts for a five-year period. Internal documents included the strategy documents[2] of the BO for three years and employee newsletters for five years. In the case of interviews, each of them took approximately one to one-and-a-half hours. All interviews were tape recorded after obtaining the prior consent of the interviewees and were later transcribed.

The interviews started with a brief introduction of the purpose of the study and data required. The questions to executives were open ended and revolved around IC and strategy of the Bank, the effect of strategy in the working of the BO, strategic resources of the BO, challenges faced by the BO in implementing the strategy, IC indicators, and interviewees' individual role in the development of significant resources. The employees were asked to narrate stories on their work life experiences within the Bank, how performance measures helped and hindered their performance, and how work normally is done at the Bank. Leading questions were avoided, and the interviews were informal, building a rapport with the respondent. However, probing questions were asked during the process to access more information.

The BO of the Bank was chosen for the study because the senior management of this division wanted to examine its IC resources to understand if these could be measured, managed, and reported to demonstrate the BO's value to the senior management of the Bank. Therefore, the BO developed extended performance accounts (EPA), which highlighted using various measures to demonstrate the value it provided to the rest of the organization and the senior management of the Bank. The BO was a pilot study, and later the structure of the EPA was used to report on its IC to external parties. Thus the importance placed on the development of IC by BO made it an important research site. Covering data for five years in one organization revealed the uniqueness of this case and provided an understanding of its 'idiosyncrasy' and 'complexity' (Polkinghorne, 1988).

The investigation followed a path of narrative analysis that did not rely on standard methods. Peräkylä (2005) argued that qualitative researchers who use written texts or narrative interviews as their material should not try to follow any predefined protocol in executing their analysis. For them, it is necessary that the researcher has paid close attention to what the interviewer and the interviewees say to each other and how they say it. Also, the researcher must read and re-read the interview transcripts together with the gathered documents to ascertain key themes and give a fuller account of the connections between events and experiences.

The interviews in this study were treated as sessions of 'interrogation' in which the researcher was inquiring for 'facts and information' and not collecting 'views and opinions' of both managers and employees (Czarniawska, 2005, p.47). Being the interviewer and the researcher, the narrative researcher does not have the privilege of distancing him- or herself from the data. Finding the 'right distance' involves conscious work, but nevertheless, a degree of closeness to the data assists the researcher to interpret what is happening within the organization (Boyle, 1994, p. 166).

In this study narrative analysis was used to offer an account that transcends the individual voices of the participants (Llewellyn, 1999). The procedure adopted was to organize data elements into a coherent developmental whole by synthesizing data rather than separating it into its constituent parts. Events and actions that were related to one another were gathered from the reports and interviews and were contributing factors to the advancement of a plot. Commonalities were observed in the way evidence was generated – through interviews and searches in documents – by the researcher being immersed over the long term[3] in the social world of the organization (Coulter and Smith, 2009).

An understanding of the narrative structure was necessary to proceed with narrative analysis. As explained earlier, narratives have a beginning, middle, an end, and logic. The events gathered from the documents and interviews were not just temporal; it was found that they had a sequence where one event led to the next. As the papers and interviews were examined, it was found that a plot for each of them was being formed. Since a plot was emerging, the information collected was treated as plays and configured based on dramatic themes (Llewellyn, 1999) – romance, tragedy, comedy, and satire.

Romance is a form of narrative on a single character and his/her/its potentialities (Czarniawska, 2005, p. 21). It depicts a quest, a valiant tale, or a journey to a desired end and includes a heroic victory over adversity (Llewellyn, 1999, p. 225). In accounting research, the goal oriented decision usefulness story is a romantic plot that seems to be popular since it portrays a successful progression to the objective. Tragedy, according to Czarniawska (2005), views humankind as subjected to some laws of fate, laid bare through the central crisis that constitutes the hub of the narration. In accounting and management research, tragic plots are used as precursors to the main romantic plots (Llewellyn, 1999).

Comedy represents humankind not as subject to laws of fate, but forming parts of a higher unity, which despite setbacks and complications, works to resolve everything into harmony and a happy ending (Czarniawska, 2005, p. 21). The goal of comedy is the restoration of social order, and the hero must have the requisite social skills to overcome the hazards that threaten that order. Llewellyn (1999, p. 226) provides the example of "The evolution of management accounting" by Kaplan as a comic narrative that offers lessons for the future happy development of accounting techniques. Satire shows the absurdity of all that occurs and must reject the rational laws of fate in tragedy, the pursuit of common harmony in comedy, and self-fulfilment in romance (Czarniawska, 2005, p. 21). Llewellyn (1999, p. 226) points to accounting research that takes a post-modernism perspective as satire in describing how managers and organizations are inundated by chaos, ambiguity, and uncertainty.

Thus the 'plots' emerging from narratives helped in the organizational level analysis (macro) that had a structure of which the individual participating executives (managers) and employees were themselves not aware. As mentioned earlier, evidence in the form of quotations is not provided in our chapter, since the organization's management (micro) did not see its activities as tragic, comic, romantic, or satiric. Also, quotes from interviews and documents are not used as these can suppress the voice of the participants and at the same time ignore the role of the researcher. These plots are the interpretations of the researcher and not that of the participants, but nevertheless, participants can be heard in the stories.

The plot that the researcher discovered for the story displayed the connections between various types of information collected from the data. Also, based on these plots, the required information was carefully chosen from the data gathered to be included in the final storied account. Next, 'narrative smoothing' removed those elements that contradicted the plot or were not essential to its development (Spence, 1986). While performing narrative smoothing, care was taken not to impose a predetermined order on the data and to ensure that the final story fitted the data, while at the same time brought order and meaningfulness that was not apparent in each of the documents or interview transcripts in isolation. Thus, in the story form, narratives helped in bringing unintended consequences to the surface.

The scenario

Before narrating the stories, it is necessary to set the context in which the events happened. This section briefly describes the scenario and establishes the stage for the stories by providing information on the events that occurred at the research site when the Bank introduced a new customer charter.

Similar to any other large service organization, the Bank had a 'customer focus' strategy. The Bank trusted that it could provide value across its business through the 'service-profit chain model'[4] that could be established through the relationship between internal practices and employee commitment, customer satisfaction and loyalty, profitability, and value creation. These can be represented by the three IC categories (i.e. human, structural, and relational capital).

Based on its new customer focus strategy, the Bank launched a 'single point interface' customer charter to bring sweeping change focused on the customer rather than products. The senior managers believed that this new charter would reflect the expectations of the customers. Single point interface was a commitment from the Bank to its customers that it would provide an appropriate solution within an appropriate time. Thus, the Bank believed that it could create long-term shareholder value by committing to providing superior services to its customers.

To materialize this single point interface charter, management of the Bank decided to bring about two changes. First, it was agreed to automate the Bank's systems with the intention of enabling employees to have immediate access to information about the customer to deliver the single point interface commitment. Also, the Bank automated those ICT systems that could make more processes self-service for customers at all times, with a hope that this would help improve the customer experience and increase customer loyalty to the Bank. Second, it was decided to provide training to the Bank's employees to be able to deliver the single point interface commitment. The intention was to invest in training employees along the value chain to use the latest technology to be customer focused and develop their customer contact skills, expecting to provide effective service to customers at the first point of contact.

To aid and monitor its new customer focus strategy, the Bank proposed to organize its performance measures around the service-profit chain. This meant that management had to create, account, and focus on IC information, such as employee satisfaction, customer satisfaction, and customer loyalty, together with a concern for financial performance measures. This was present in the Bank's external reports called EPA, BO's internal reports called strategy documents (SD), its internal employee newsletters (ENL), and also in the conversations between employees within the BO.

At the time the interviews were conducted and the researcher was embedded in the BO of the Bank, the BO was at a transitional stage in the customer oriented strategy. The SD highlight that the focus of the BO was being shifted from efficiency and cost cutting to concentrating on enterprise-focused capability development and improving customer experience through customer focused service propositions. The BO, being the core service provider for the Bank's other business units, was responsible for making investments in automating the Bank's services and training the Bank's employees.

Interviews with senior executives revealed that this was also the time when the BO had been maintaining its costs flat for several years and was struggling with its image as a cost centre. The BO management found its cost cutting programs reasonable since it had demonstrated long and steady periods of incremental change in line with organizational objectives. So there was a tendency at the BO to stick with what was safe and predictable and still use cost reduction measures rather than experiment with other forms of transformational changes to prove their value. Thus, on the one hand, the BO management was attempting to move away from being a cost centre and at the same time clinging to cost cutting financial measures. On the other, the new customer focus strategy of the organization meant that the BO had the responsibility for spending large amounts of financial resources in automating processes and training employees.

Besides the significant financial investments required, automation had its challenges. From the interviews with the BO's executives, it was found that the process of automation was carried out with two aims: cost efficiency and customer satisfaction. These aims were pulling the BO in two different directions. For instance, when the BO managers had to decide and prioritize what to automate, based on the principles of the customer focused strategy, they preferred to automate processes that delivered the greatest results with customer satisfaction. This could not be materialized since it involved significant financial investment. Instead, they had to automate processes that were focused on particular products because of cost pressures. Thus while customer orientation was a broad agenda, cost efficiency forced the BO to cling to the economizing agenda.

The shift in the strategy on 'paper' resulted in unintended consequences within the BO. What follows is the narrative on what happened within the Bank's BO when the newly developed customer focus strategy was confronted with the existing systems, and when the BO management started using IC to help identify the knowledge resources that could prove the BO's intangible value to the Bank's other business units.

Narratives on mobilization of IC

The purpose of this section is to provide a thematic sequenced account, linking the parts collected from the interviews and the documents gathered, which convey meaning from the author to the reader on the manner in which managers of the Bank mobilize IC. Stories are constructed on events that happened in the organization before and during the study period. Thus three coherent stories are built, which lead to an understanding of the manner in which managers mobilize some aspects of IC.

Story 1: a tragedy

The single point interface and service-profit chain were reflected in three different spaces: internal documents (SD and ENL), external documents (EPA), and the conversations between the BO managers. The qualities of the service-profit chain (e.g. causality, identity, and influence) were present in all three spaces (i.e. both documents and among the BO managers), but the way they crafted the service-profit chain and customer focus was different. Senior executives used the proposals from the documents (i.e. toolbox) to increase or decrease resources (such as employees and technology), in a bid to move towards a customer focus.

The external EPAs provided a range of IC resources relating to the construction of customer needs. They indicated that customer focus was to provide new inexpensive (to customers) products and solutions, employees to provide immediate solutions, updated technology such as talking ATMs, e-statement initiatives and data security, branches with extended opening hours, helping the local community (such as rescue helicopters and surf lifesavers), and working towards sustainability – all of which were to increase shareholder value and financial resources. The EPAs enunciated the ambition of customer focus as expansion and perpetual investments along the service-profit chain. Thus the central discourse of the EPA was of expansion and abundant investment in intangible resources to increase shareholder value and financial capital, and this did not seem to be a concern.

While internal SDs shared a concern for the customer, this concern was overshadowed by the existing objective of the BO – cost efficiency. The SDs recommended investment in product transformation (products with heightened attention to customers) and technology development, with the main performance indicators centred on rationalization, economization, simplified processes, and expenditure reduction. SDs showed graphs predicting a decline in employee head count for a reduction in cost. Also, SDs supplied a comparison with competitors and demonstrated that products, technology, and IT were 'below rivals'. However, people and culture were 'above rivals'. Thus management was convinced that it was important to invest in technology and products and not necessarily in employees. Hence BO management decided to invest in advanced technology but decided to pay scant attention to employees, thus separating the resources by investing in one and disregarding the other.

The conversations at the BO also reflected customer orientation, but the BO managers struggled to craft their ideas about service-profit chain and customer focus. This was because the documents that were intended to guide management actions pulled customer orientation in opposite directions, mostly recommending disentanglement and separation of the resources. The BO managers were reluctant to make changes in technology for two reasons. First, such investments would be costly and risky when the effects of the investment's results were uncertain. Second, there was no guarantee that this new technology would make customers happy. Though EPAs proposed continued investments in technology, product, and employees, the BO inclined towards cost reduction and economization, and investing in technology, but not employees because their key performance indicators (as specified by SDs) were based on cost reduction. There was little synchronization between the IC of the BO, as reflected in their SDs, and the customer focus strategy of the Bank.

This is a tale that has a plot of classic 'tragedy' in which the Bank is subject to laws of fate. This story begins when the Bank management changed its strategy to customer focus and introduced its single point interface customer charter. The customer charter was translated differently in external and internal documents, which resulted in confusion among the BO management in making the choice of knowledge resources in which investments should be made (i.e. mobilizing non-financial resources). BO management had a (financial) crisis to be cost conscious; they were in a situation where they had to make a significant financial investment in technology for which they were forced to compromise on employee numbers. The crisis is not revealed in the EPA but is identified in the SDs that provides the solution of rationalization and economization.

The EPA enacts a fatalistic tragedy (Sköldberg, 1994, p. 229) by playing down the crisis and proposing continued investments in technology, products, and employees. Here the problem (of financial budgets) does not show up, but the solution (investments to enable customer focus strategy) comes to the forefront. The SD, on the other hand, plays the drama as a triumphant tragedy (Sköldberg, 1994, p. 229) where the emphasis is on the successful overcoming of the financial crises. The SD recommends a reduction in employee numbers and outsourcing, to free up money to fund the new customer focused technology.

The EPA dwelt mainly on ideals and brought a message of expansion and continuous investment in knowledge resources, while the SDs communicated on demands and conveyed a message on frugality, rationalization, economization, and efficiency, all of which were shaped by the financial budgeting process. The EPAs proposed a continual increase in all aspects of IC and the service-profit chain, providing positive correlation. However, in SDs the elements of service-profit chain were traded off and a negative correlation emerged. Thus, the internal and external documents' messages confused the managers, which led to the unintended consequences described in the story to follow.

Story 2: a satire

With the rising awareness of the importance of measuring IC, the BO sought to change its image from a cost centre. Also, the confusion created by the IC documents (EPA and SD) about investing in products, technology, and employees to enable customer focus, meant that management faced challenges in mobilizing IC resources. The appearance of causality found in the EPA appeared straightforward and uncomplicated since these included few non-financial performance indicators, were disentangled and separated, and projected no restrictions on financial investment. Similarly, the internal documents (SD) also recommended separating the IC elements despite limited money. Nevertheless, when management started to develop and mobilize non-financial resources, in particular IC, they experienced friction between the different categories of IC resources (i.e. human capital, structural capital, and relational capital).

It was arduous for the BO to completely adopt a customer focus strategy as it was not in direct contact with the Bank's customers and could reach customers only through other business units. Nevertheless, changes were made at the BO to transform the Bank's services to be customer focused. Technological upgrading commenced, but with some hesitation. To achieve the highest value from automation, those processes that promised delivery of customer satisfaction had to be automated. However, since the Bank had a legacy of product oriented technology, it was challenging and expensive to change to customer-oriented technology.

Investments were hesitantly made in new technology since the returns were doubtful and, even if expected, would emerge only in the long run. Also, budget restrictions forced the BO to automate processes that were focused on particular products. This left the BO to oscillate between (product oriented) processes and customers, and they faced the risk of pushing customer focus into second place behind the objective of cost focus.

Next, to support the working of new technology and use technology constructively in the delivery of customer focus, the BO had to work with the Bank's human capital by training employees and thereby improving their customer-facing skills. In other words, the BO had to simultaneously invest in people to make adequate use of new technology and move towards a customer focus. However, due to the cost focus of the BO and its budgetary process, two constraining factors emerged. First, technological change was partially developed and implementation was delayed. Second, to conserve financial cost, human capital was being reduced. Also, training of employees was not successful, since training was on partially developed technology.

At the time of interviews, the technological change had not yet been completed, but the BO had started its process of restructuring to eliminate process workers. Downsizing came rapidly, and in this process of restructuring, the Bank removed not only process workers, but also knowledge employees with capabilities and skills required by the Bank, therefore reducing IC resources. With incomplete automation and a reduced workforce, the BO now had to resort to outsourcing. Customer satisfaction was affected due to a combined effect of incomplete automation, untimely restructures, inappropriate training, and outsourcing. This in turn affected customer loyalty. Finally, despite investing in automation to enable customer satisfaction and employees being aware of the importance of customer focus, the Bank was struggling to meet its single point interface commitment.

This is a case of 'satire' with shifting ambiguities and complexities. The story starts with confusion created by the documents and the consequent challenges the BO managers faced in mobilizing IC resources. Management mobilization of non-financial IC elements caricatures the EPA and SD and shows the inconsistencies between the two. A general fragmentation or disassociation was identified and hence this story could be classified as fragmented satire (Sköldberg, 1994, p. 230). The disassociation differs in intensity but is all pervasive. It exhibits itself in many ways: between customer focus and automation of product oriented processes; between customer focus and reduction of employee numbers; between training and new technology; and between customer focus and outsourcing.

The BO managers had to cope with antagonistic signals that led to confusion – a satiric drama. In the setting of the BO, both documents (EPA and SD) were prevalent, and the BO managers separated the non-financial IC elements based on the documents. The BO managers were overwhelmed by chaos, ambiguity, and uncertainty due to the multiple and varied network effect of the non-financial IC elements and the influence of financial capital through the constrained budgetary process. The BO senior managers seemed to be challenged by the performance of the IC elements and were unable to use these effectively while constrained by financial resources. Moreover, the documents (EPA and SD) that were meant to guide them suggested disentangling of the non-financial IC elements, but in reality, this was not possible. By disentangling the IC elements, the BO management confronted negative unintended consequences in mobilizing IC because these items work well as a network and not separately. For instance, when technology was isolated from employees, and financial investments were made, it became expensive but little used because it was not supported by employee skills' development. Similarly, due to the budgeting process, when employee numbers had to be reduced substantially, the BO managers had to rely on the new technology and outsourcing, which were not functional without increased spending on employee capabilities via training.

Despite the problems faced by BO management in mobilizing the three categories of IC due to cost restrictions, the Bank was partly successful in mobilizing its human capital using various workplace flexibility discourses in the employee newsletters (ENL). This is described in the next romantic story.

Story 3: a romance

Though the Bank increased its automatic processes, it still had a substantial number of employees. Also, the Bank had to attract and retain people with the skills and expertise to deal with the processes that were being automated. This required knowledge workers, not process workers, who were looking for incentives beyond financial rewards, such as challenging jobs, career growth, and recognition and appreciation. Also, importantly, employees were keen to have flexibility at work to allow them to juggle the demands of work with other interests and needs, including family responsibilities.

Workplace flexibility arrangements already existed, but at the time of restructure, the Bank's management extensively publicised its workplace flexibility policies to its employees using the ENL. The intended purpose of workplace flexibility was essentially to motivate employees and regain employees' confidence with the Bank (impact human capital). Nevertheless, it had a positive unintended consequence too. Workplace flexibility not only helped managers to motivate employees (human capital), it also reflected on the internal culture of the organization (structural capital), impacted the community and customers (relational capital) positively, and reduced employee costs (financial capital).

The Bank used its ENL to highlight how employees could use flexible working arrangements to achieve efficiencies. The discourse in ENL was used to provide information on workplace flexibility to construct the employees' purpose at work. The discourses adopted in the newsletters seem to influence the attitudes of employees and shape employee behaviour, which positively impacted the culture of the organization. Employees' loyalty to the Bank increased since the Bank stated they provided flexible work options. Similarly, family and dependant care arrangements provided by the Bank also left employees with a feeling of gratitude and loyalty towards the Bank. Employees were ready to return the favour by working harder and longer.

The external reports (AR and EPA) indicated that workplace flexibility arrangements helped the Bank. Interviews (with managers and employees) and ENLs suggested that though not intended, this indirectly helped the BO in several ways. First, at the time when restructures were inevitable, flexible working arrangements allowed the Bank to retain skilled employees who were ready to work on a part-time basis. This enabled the BO to retain existing knowledge flows. Second, since the employees felt indebted to the Bank, they worked harder in their reduced working hours. Third, when employees had to care for their family at home, they were still willing to work from home, which was beneficial to the organization. Fourth, retention of employees was easier for the BO as employees felt loyal to the Bank. Fifth, the Bank paid employees who were adopting flexible working options for a lesser number of hours, which suited their cost cutting agenda.

The Bank actively promoted community volunteering as a part of its flexible workplace arrangements through ENL. Employees were encouraged to take up community activities of their choice for which they were given one day of leave in a year. As evidenced in the external reports, the Bank became involved in volunteering with an expectation of establishing a brand image as an institution that cared for the community. Also, community volunteering helped in building relationships with customers and the community. Through voluntary work, the employees were able to build deeper, stronger, and trusting relationships with clients and the community. Moreover, volunteering became the culture of the organization.

Though community volunteering did not directly reflect on the financial performance of the organization, it did so indirectly when management was able to use volunteering to mobilize different IC categories. As a result, the service-profit value chain appeared to work. At the BO, as community volunteering did not affect its cost strategy, the employees were encouraged to be involved in volunteering. All that the BO had to do was to release an interested employee for volunteering for just one day in a year. Employees were also encouraged to use their weekends for volunteering, which resulted in generating future business (by improving the relationship with the community and customers).

As intended, employees' involvement in community activities as representatives of the Bank promoted the organization's brand name among community and customers. ENL discourses showed that volunteering also built a positive reputation with clients and the community, lifting the Bank's profile. Also, the ENL demonstrated that employees' activities to support the community enabled reciprocal support to the organization from the community. The interviews with staff also revealed that employees were happy to be involved in volunteering and showed their loyalty to the Bank as they saw the Bank as an organization that cares.

The plot of this story is 'romantic'. This story starts at a time when the BO managers were trying to mobilize various IC elements by separating them due to constrained budgets. Managers searched for ways in which all three IC elements could be mobilized and realized that the discourse of workplace flexibility could help in this endeavour. It is a powerful tale about a transition from a complicated state of affairs (incomplete automation and untimely restructures), to a happy state of affairs (improved employee morale, loyalty, and support from community and customers). Instead of analysing why restructures and automation were proving difficult, the focus of ENL was on promoting workplace flexibility.

There is little emphasis on the original undesirable state of affairs, and the ENL concentrates on the final desirable state (Sköldberg, 1994). Through the significant emphasis on community volunteering, management attempted to increase the initiative of organizational members to achieve organizational performance. The BO managers had allowed their employees to express their self in choosing to do their preferred voluntary work, which is also the central message of the romantic mode. Thus by using discourse on workplace flexibility in ENL, the Bank achieved its (intended consequence) of putting all three IC elements to work together. It also had positive unintended consequences of changing the culture, increasing employee loyalty, and being able to retain existing knowledge flows.

Unintended consequences captured by narratives

By using narratives, we could show how the IC documents of the Bank led to management actions and how these actions produced consequences (both intended and unintended) in the form of organizational events (Llewellyn, 1999, p. 221). This analysis is one of many possible stories that could be told about the BO of the Bank. The narratives exhibit explanations rather than demonstrate them (Polkinghorne, 1988, p. 21), and by doing so, the unintended consequences of the managerial use of IC resources come to the surface.

Originally, at the Bank, management decided to make changes to technology and human capital, intending to aid the service-profit chain and achieve customer focus. The intended consequence was when new technology and trained employees worked together; it would result in superior service. Superior service would, in turn, make customers happy, who would be loyal to the Bank, which would then result in increased profits and improve shareholder value. This is a straightforward causal relationship envisaged by management, and if IC elements worked independently as planned, the intended consequences could be achieved. However, IC elements worked as a network and hence produced unintended consequences (positive, negative, and perverse), which the three narratives have highlighted. Also, the narratives help in understanding that there were several other factors (limitations) that led to unintended consequences.

Considering first ignorance, given the state of their knowledge and the different directions that the EPAs and SDs took, it was not possible for managers to predict with certainty that investments in technology would work. The managerial decision on investments in technology was based on assumptions based on different documents (Story 1). Their assumptions were based on a few verifiable (yet different) aspects as shown in the documents, which were only a tiny part of the reality existing at the Bank. The managers were not clear about the needs of the customers, had partial knowledge of customer needs, and carried out automation based on this knowledge. For instance, they assumed that the clients preferred the use of new technology that would aid self-service (such as ATMs, Internet banking). This was not supported by evidence and investments were made with some doubt. They had to wait for a long time to see the results from any new technology (Story 2).

Next, managers saw employees' skills in action on a daily basis, and since it was always available, they ignored its importance. They expected that their human capital could be replaced by automation (structural capital), which was not the case at the Bank. When they found that automation was expensive, they made people redundant to conserve cost, and this led to confusion, which was also not anticipated. New technology was available, but could not work on its own and needed employees' support to function. However, with redundancies and inappropriate training on new technology, employees could not efficiently support new technology, hence resulting in negative unintended consequences that surprised management (Story 2).

Another factor that led to unintended consequences was error. To achieve high value, processes that delivered customer satisfaction had to be automated. Nevertheless, based on SDs, management erroneously decided to invest in technology that was product oriented due to its cost focus (Story 1). Also, since the Bank already had the tradition of product oriented technology, it was considered safe to invest in existing technology, because it worked in the past and it was hoped that it would work in the current situation. This error had the perverse unintended consequence of driving customer focus behind cost focus. It is perverse because the solution (of investing in product oriented technology) made the problem (move towards customer focus) worse. Investment in product oriented new technology created more problems by pulling away from customer focus (Story 2).

Another error that was detected was (during the implementation stage) associated with the training of employees. Employees were supposed to understand new technology and use technology effectively to aid customer service. However, as the Bank was in a hurry to make employees redundant, the remaining employees were left with more work and did not have sufficient time for training on the new technology. Also, technological development was partially complete, and training was given on technology that was not tested properly. Training did not also correspond to real life situations, leaving employees confused rather than understanding the functioning of the new technology. Thus, although management intended to give due importance to training, unintentionally it had become expensive and ineffective (Story 2).

In terms of immediate interest, the BO was a cost centre that did not have income generation opportunity. Hence, to prove its value to the organization, the BO had to monitor its cost.

Its performance measures (as shown in SD) were based on economization and expenditure reduction. So the immediate interest of the BO was cost, which led to several negative unintended consequences. Investment in new technology was affected, employee head count was reduced, and work was outsourced. The BO management was interested in short-term cost efficiency and had to ignore the long-term strategy of customer focus because its performance measures were based on cost savings. Thus the Bank's cost control strategy seemed to be harsh and did not merge with the development of the organizational resources that added value in the long run (Story 1).

Another immediate interest for the Bank was workplace flexibility to attract and retain people by keeping them motivated. At the time of restructures, workplace flexibility was not just used to regain employee confidence; it also had a positive unintended consequence. Employees were happy with a bank that provided them with flexible options for working from home and part-time jobs, which made them loyal to the Bank. Unintentionally, the Bank was able to reduce its employee costs as it was paying for fewer work hours (part-time jobs) or employees were working longer (from home) for the same pay (Story 3).

Turning to basic values, the BO did not focus on customers of the Bank. Instead it focused on improving the Bank's operational efficiency. The BO was being pressured by its core value (of keeping a low cost profile) to achieve a significantly lower expense. Hence, it decided to invest in new technology and reduce head count at the same time with a subjective satisfaction of having kept costs low (by making employees redundant) and made investments in inappropriate (product oriented) new technology (Story 1).

The Bank valued community involvement and identified itself as a good citizen in Australian society. The Bank built a brand name as an organization that always endeavoured to build a deeper, stronger, and trusting relationship with the community. By doing so, it seemed to respond to social issues in the community, and from an IC perspective, the organization expanded its boundaries into the wider ecosystem (Dumay, 2016). This idea of community volunteering produced positive unintended consequences. The Bank not only improved its brand name but also improved its image among employees and customers. Employee morale was raised at a time when it was affected by restructures, and customers and the community also found the Bank to be a good corporate citizen (Story 3).

However, the Bank's management developed its customer focus strategy based on self-defeating predictions and found solutions for problems that were not present. For instance, management believed that customers were not happy with existing technology. So it invested in new technology, which rather than help customers, was found to be a hindrance. Also, employees did not have adequate knowledge of this new technology and were not able to help customers use it. Existing technology was probably not a problem at the Bank, but because of self-defeating management prediction that existing technology was not suitable for customer needs, they changed it unsuccessfully (Story 2).

Another instance where self-defeating predictions (leading to unintended consequences) were found was in SDs. As mentioned before, SDs highlighted cost rationalization as a principal aim of the BO. SD also showed that the Bank's human capital and culture were above rivals, but with the technology it was below rivals. This inference resulted in predicting that technology had to be improved. So to improve an underperforming resource such as technology, it decided to reduce head count as management's view was that it was better performing and would not have a negative impact. What could have been a solution to a self-prophesied problem, in fact made the problem worse, resulting in confusion at the BO that led to customer dissatisfaction (Story 1).

Conclusion

To understand the complex network of non-financial resources and to provide insights on the use of IC resources, an appropriate way to explore them would be by starting from observing them in action. Therefore, this chapter used narratives to inquire into the mobilization of IC in the Bank – a large Australian financial institution. By using a narrative structure, it was discovered that there was a deeper meaning hidden within this confusion and ambiguity in the effect of non-financial IC resources.

The BO management faced trials while using non-financial resources because these were constantly moderated by unacknowledged conditions (economized investments) and unintended effects (effects on various IC elements that were not anticipated).

The three stories of the BO of the Bank describe how managers mobilized various IC resources. In doing so, the stories brought out unintended consequences of managerial mobilization of IC. Story 1 was a tragedy where the EPA and SD constructed different meanings of customer needs and contradicted each other on the amount of financial investment that could be made on the different non-financial resources. As described in the previous section, a story that has a tragic plot highlights negative unintended consequences. The tragedy was then transformed into a satire in story 2 when managers struggled to mobilize the elements of IC within budgetary constraints. Here the story highlighted that there are possibilities of occurrence of both negative and perverse consequences. When the managers promoted operations that did not require significant financial resources, they could transform the story into a romance. This is the plot of story 3, which shows how the management of the BO was able to use the discourse on workplace flexibility within the ENL to (unintentionally) influence all three IC elements. A romantic story has positive unintended consequence. This story brings out the organization's intent to move from a managerialist perspective towards an ecosystem perspective (Dumay *et al.*, 2017).

We have argued in this chapter that it is important to pay attention to unintended consequences – positive, negative, or perverse. A tragic story focuses attention on problem areas and crises. The story highlighted negative unintended consequences that needed particular attention as these could result in chaos and confusion and ultimately break down the customer focus strategy if left unattended. Perverse consequences, as highlighted in the satiric story, also need managers' attention as organizations can avoid investing in (unnecessary) solutions that could make the problem worse. Thus, satiric plots are appropriate to locate decision points that direct attention to transitions where different actions lead to different results. Finally, positive unintended consequences as depicted in our romantic story could bring desirable solutions. So if managers pay attention to positive consequences, they could leverage the benefits derived out of it.

To conclude, unintended consequences occurred in part due to the contradicting aims and were fuelled by the prolonged time taken for the execution of the strategy. Unintended consequences could also be attributed to two other causes. First, the lack of congruence between the goal of the BO – cost focus – as moderated by the SDs and the actual goal of the Bank – customer focus. Second, the network effect when IC elements interact with each other. Thus, while not challenging the desirability of using IC resources independently by management, we conclude that the use of IC resources could be a liability if not understood. There is a danger that IC elements could fail unless management directs attention to the unintended consequences.

As with any body of research, this study using narrative analysis comes with a few limitations. First, the analysis has been performed as a complex transaction between the researchers and evidence, the results of which are provisional and translations may not be accurate. It is a story of the organization in action as interpreted by the researcher. Second, the results have to be judged based on characteristics of verisimilitude, fidelity, coherence, plausibility, useful-ness, and evidential warrant (Coulter and Smith, 2009). Triangulation of all data collected from the documents (both internal and external) and interviews (of executives and employees) was sought to produce confidence in the events that occurred at the BO. Recollection of past events was selective and produced from the perspective of the interviewees at the time of the interviews, which could be different on the date of the original experience. Finally, the study was conducted in the BO of an organization (i.e. the Bank) and does not show variations or comparisons with other organizations.

For the purpose of future research, to show variation or comparison more than one case study could be conducted. Second, narratives methods could be combined with other forms of quali-tative or quantitative analysis. Using a literary device such as narratives with other methods could bring out some interesting results. However, Riessman (1993) cautions that combining methods needs some creative epistemological footwork since the interpretive perspective of narratives is completely different to the realistic assumptions of qualitative and quantitative analysis. Third, though this study looks at non-financial information, it specifically pays atten-tion to IC elements (human, structural, and relational capital). Other non-financial resources such as social and natural capital are ignored and should be examined in detail in the future.

Notes

1 For example, Balanced Scorecard, Intangible Asset Monitor, Intellectual Capital Statement, Service profit chain, the Skandia Navigator, Meritum Schema, Ericsson Cockpit Communicator, Strategic Business Models, Extended Performance Accounts, VAIC, etc.
2 Strategy documents are highly confidential documents that were available only to the senior executives of the BO. We were given access to only three years of these documents due to confidentiality reasons. Therefore, analysis was conducted based on available documents.
3 The researcher spent a period of six months at the BO of the financial institution. This helped in observ-ing the regular functioning of the BO.
4 The 'service-profit chain model' establishes relationships between profitability, customer loyalty, and employee satisfaction, loyalty, and productivity. The links in the chain (which should be regarded as propositions) are as follows: profit and growth are stimulated primarily by customer loyalty; loyalty is a direct result of customer satisfaction; satisfaction is largely influenced by the value of services provided to customers; value is created by satisfied, loyal, and productive employees; employee satisfaction, in turn, results primarily from high-quality support services and policies that enable employees to deliver results to customers (Heskett *et al.*, 1994).

References

Andriessen, D. (2004), "IC valuation and measurement: Classifying the state of the art", *Journal of Intellectual Capital*, Vol. 5, No. 2, pp. 230–242.
Ashton, R. (1976), "Deviation-amplifying feedback and unintended consequences of management accounting systems", *Accounting, Organizations and Society*, Vol. 1, No. 4, pp. 289–300.
Barone, T. (2007), "A return to the Gold Standard? Questioning the future of narrative construction as educational research", *Qualitative Inquiry*, Vol. 13, No. 4, pp. 454–470.
Boyle, J. S. (1994), "Styles of Ethnography", in Morse, J. M. (Ed.), *Critical Issues in Qualitative Research Methods*, Sage Publications, Thousand Oaks, CA, pp. 159–185.
Brüggemann, U., Hitz, J. M., and Sellhorn, T. (2013), "Intended and unintended consequences: A review of extant evidence and suggestions for future research", *European Accounting Review*, Vol. 22, No. 1, pp. 1–37.
Bruner, J. (1990), *Acts of Meaning*, Harvard University Press, Cambridge, MA.

Campbell, E. M., Sittig, D. F., Ash, J. A., Guappone, K., and Dykstra, R. (2006), "Types of unintended consequences related to computerized provider order entry", *Journal of American Medical Informatics Association*, Vol. 13, No. 5, pp. 547–556.

Chiucchi, M. (2013), "Intellectual capital accounting in action: Enhancing learning through interventionist research", *Journal of Intellectual Capital*, Vol. 14, No. 1, pp. 48–68.

Chiucchi, M. and Dumay, J. (2015), "Unlocking intellectual capital", *Journal of Intellectual Capital*, Vol. 16, No. 2, pp. 305–330.

Clifford, J. and Marcus, G. E. (1986), *Writing Culture: The Poetics and Politics of Ethnography*, University of California Press, Berkeley, CA.

Coulter, C. A. and Smith, M. L. (2009), "The construction zone: Literary elements in narrative research", *Educational Researcher*, Vol. 38, No. 8, pp. 577–590.

Cuganesan, S. (2005), "Intellectual capital-in-action and value creation. A case study of knowledge transformations in an innovation project", *Journal of Intellectual Capital*, Vol. 6, No. 3, pp. 357–373.

Cuganesan, S., Boedker, C., and Guthrie, J. (2007), "Enrolling discourse consumers to affect material intellectual capital practice", *Accounting, Auditing & Accountability Journal*, Vol. 20, No. 6, pp. 883–911.

Cumby, J. and Conrod, J. (2001), "Non-financial performance measures in the Canadian biotechnology industry", *Journal of Intellectual Capital*, Vol. 2, No. 3, pp. 261–272.

Czarniawska, B. (1998), *A Narrative Approach to Organization Studies*, Sage Publications, London.

Czarniawska, B. (2005), *Narratives in Social Science Research*, Sage Publications, London.

Denzin, N. K. (1989), *Interpretive Interactionism*, Sage Publications, London.

Dumay, J. (2016), "A critical reflection on the future of intellectual capital: From reporting to disclosure", *Journal of Intellectual Capital*, Vol. 17, No. 1, pp. 168–184.

Dumay, J. and Garanina, T. (2013), "Intellectual capital research: A critical examination of the third stage", *Journal of Intellectual Capital*, Vol. 14, No. 1, pp. 10–25.

Dumay, J. and Guthrie, J. (2007), "Disturbance and implementation of IC practice: A public sector organisation perspective", *Journal of Human Resources Costing and Accounting*, Vol. 11, No. 2, pp. 104–121.

Dumay, J., Guthrie, J., and Rooney, J. (2017), "The critical path of intellectual capital", in Guthrie, J., Dumay, J., Ricceri, F., and Nielsen, C. (Eds), *The Routledge Companion to Intellectual Capital*, Routledge, London, pp. 21–39.

Guthrie, J., Ricceri, F., and Dumay, J. (2012), "Reflections and projections: A decade of intellectual capital accounting research", *The British Accounting Review*, Vol. 44, No. 2, pp. 68–92.

Hawkins, M. and Saleem, F. (2012), "The omnipresent personal narrative: story formulation and the interplay among narratives", *Journal of Organizational Change Management*, Vol. 25, No. 2, pp. 204–219.

Heskett, L. J., Jones, T. O., Loveman, G. W., Sasser, W. E., Jr. and Schlesinger, L. (1994), "Putting the service-profit chain to work", *Harvard Business Review*, Vol. 72, No. 2, pp. 164–170.

Joiner, T. A., Spencer, S. Y., and Salmon, S. (2009), "The effectiveness of flexible manufacturing strategies, The mediating role of performance measurement systems", *International Journal of Productivity and Performance Management*, Vol. 58, No. 2, pp. 119–135.

Krippendorff, K. (2004), *Content Analysis: An Introduction to its Methodology* (2nd Ed.), Sage Publications, Thousand Oaks, CA.

Lieblich, A., Tuval-Mashiach, R., and Zilber, T. (1998), *Narrative Research. Reading, Analysis and Interpretation*, Sage Publications, Thousand Oaks, CA.

Llewellyn, S. (1999), "Methodological themes. Narratives in accounting and management research", *Accounting, Auditing & Accountability Journal*, Vol. 12, No. 2, pp. 220–236.

Marr, B., Gray, D., and Neely, A. (2003), "Why do firms measure their intellectual capital?", *Journal of Intellectual Capital*, Vol. 4, No. 4, pp. 441–464.

Merton, R. (1936), "Unanticipated consequences of purposive social action", *American Sociological Review*, Vol. 1, No. 6, pp. 894–904.

Mouritsen, J. (2006), "Problematising intellectual capital research: Ostensive versus performative IC", *Accounting, Auditing & Accountability Journal*, Vol. 19, No. 6, pp. 820–841.

Murthy, V. (2011), *Narratives on Managerial Mobilisation of Non-Financial Performance Information in a Financial Institution*, PhD thesis, The University of Sydney.

Nowak, L. and Anderson, S. (1999), "The importance of non-financial performance measures in wine business strategy", *International Journal of Wine Marketing*, Vol. 11, No. 3, pp. 9–19.

Peräkylä, A. (2005), "Analyzing talk and text", in Denzin, N. K. and Lincoln, Y. S. (Eds), *The Sage Handbook of Qualitative Research*, Sage Publications, Thousand Oaks, CA, pp. 869–886.

Petty, R. and Guthrie, J. (2000), "Intellectual capital literature review: Measurement, reporting and management, *Journal of Intellectual Capital*, Vol. 1, No. 2, pp. 155–176.

Polkinghorne, D. (1988), *Narrative Knowing and the Human Sciences*, State University of New York Press, Albany, NY.

Reijonen, H. and Komppula, R. (2007), "Perception of success and its effect on small firm performance", *Journal of Small Business and Enterprise Development*, Vol. 14, No. 4, pp. 689–701.

Riessman, C. K. (1993), *Narrative Analysis*, Sage Publications, Thousand Oaks, CA.

Sköldberg, K. (1994), "Tales of change: Public administration reform and narrative mode", *Organization Science*, Vol. 5, No. 2, pp. 219–238.

Skoog, M. (2003), "Visualizing value creation through the management control of intangibles", *Journal of Intellectual Capital*, Vol. 4, No. 4, pp. 487–504.

Spence, D. P. (1986). "Narrative smoothing and clinical wisdom", in Sarbin, T. R. (Ed.), *Narrative Psychology: The Storied Nature of Human Conduct*, Praeger, New York, pp. 211–232.

Yu, A. and Humphreys, P. (2013), "From measuring to learning? Probing the evolutionary path of IC research and practice", *Journal of Intellectual Capital*, Vol. 14, No. 1, pp. 26–47.

10

INTELLECTUAL CAPITAL MANAGEMENT IN PUBLIC UNIVERSITIES?

*Jan Michalak, Joanna Krasodomska, Gunnar Rimmel,
Jesper Sort, and Dariusz Trzmielak*

Introduction

Traditional university management is closely related to what is thought of as the long-established values of universities. Traditional universities are primarily seen as communities of scholars where research, critical thought, and the dissemination of knowledge take place (Dearlove, 2002; Kok *et al.*, 2010). Therefore, university management needs to support and promote researchers to enable fulfilment of this traditional role by, for example, focusing on promoting academic freedom and autonomy (Kok *et al.*, 2010).

Universities are distinct from other educational institutions, being given university power to award academic degrees. This power enables university researchers freedom of inquiry and to teach with the purpose of seeking and further communicating the truths found in university research (Kok *et al.*, 2010). Hence, universities are regarded as centres of excellence both in education and research, which plays a role in attracting students and staff from all over the world. However, the original values and goals of knowledge generation, progressive inquiry, thought, and debate may be overwhelmed by new pressing issues of quantified quality (Bowden and Marton, 1998). As a result, the values of universities are changing (Mouwen, 2000; Kok *et al.*, 2010).

More recently, in addition to research and education, a third 'mission' of universities has emerged, which includes cooperation with business and other stakeholders towards the commercialization of research results. Furthermore, universities are engaging with multiple stakeholders. Secundo *et al.* (2016, p. 299) highlight that the activities of the third mission "comprise three dimensions in which universities engage externally: technology transfer and innovation; continuing education; and social engagement". The importance of the third role has increased together with the influence of new public management (Dearlove, 2002; Pollitt, 2002) and a push for more university–industry collaboration (Leydesdorff and Etzkowitz, 1996). Findings by Hazelkorn (2005) explain that, in recent years, more governments have begun to think strategically about the economic significance of academic knowledge production, asking how higher education can be restructured to become a more effective and efficient economic actor. This has an impact on how universities manage university IC (Veltri *et al.*, 2014).

Public universities have been facing major challenges in the second decade of the 21st century. The demographic downturn in many European countries has led to a lower number of students and more competition on the global educational market (Hemsley-Brown and Oplatka, 2006; Secundo *et al.*, 2015). Furthermore, the global financial crisis has resulted in an increase of public debt for most European countries, prompting governments to implement austerity policies (Morales *et al.*, 2014). Bracci *et al.* (2015, p. 882) stress that:

> The European Union appears to have been particularly stricken by austerity, as European member states have been required to adhere to new governance parameters, comply with fiscal compact rules, accept debt consolidation processes, pursue balanced budgets while still being expected to respect Maastricht treaty requirements.

Austerity policies translate into decreased public funding of both research and education as well as pressure for increased accountability for public spending (Claeys-Kulik Estermann, 2015; Fijałkowska, 2016). Additionally, universities are challenged by increased international student mobility, generating more global-scale competition. In such a setting, management of universities, and especially of university IC, is of particular importance.

University management cannot be abstracted from the whole ecosystem of university stakeholders. Burrows (1999) identified a broad range of university stakeholders: governing entities (state and local government), administration (rectors, chancellors, and senior administrators), employees (faculty, administrative staff, support staff), clients (students, parents, tuition reimbursement providers, service partners, employers), suppliers (secondary education providers, alumni, other colleges and universities, food purveyors, insurance companies, utilities, contracted services), donors, communities, regulators (both governmental and non-governmental), financial intermediaries, competitors, and joint venture partners. This group of competitors can be distinguished as direct distance providers – existing providers of post-secondary education and potential – and new ventures and substitutes, that is, employer-sponsored training programmes. As university resources become increasingly dependent on market decisions (like launching and pricing new educational programmes and research projects) and allocations based on metrics rather than institution oriented grants, universities are forced to decide how to prioritize and how to reconcile the contradictory interests of stakeholders (Slaughter and Leslie, 2001). Benneworth and Jongbloed (2010) stressed that in order to manage universities, university governing bodies should develop and, in some cases, influence the ranking of stakeholders based on impact. Well-developed IC management systems should include the impact of stakeholders and facilitate cooperation with them (Secundo *et al.*, 2015).

Researchers have divided IC research into three different stages (see Guthrie *et al.*, 2012; Dumay and Garanina, 2013; Dumay, 2014). During the first stage of IC research, emphasis was on practitioners' work in the 1980s and 1990s. At this stage, research focused mainly on the understanding and awareness that IC is of significance to organizations (among others, universities) and therefore should be measured and reported. Petty and Guthrie (2000) highlighted that during the first stage there was little empirical research. The second stage of IC research focused on strategic management. During this stage, a number of IC frameworks were applied in practice (e.g. the Danish IC Guidelines, Austrian Wissensbilanz) to show the potential of IC reporting for value creation. Different classifications were created, which helped to define and group various methods of IC evaluation (Boedker *et al.*, 2008; Ricceri, 2008). The third stage of IC research was inspired by Mouritsen's (2006) distinction between ostensive versus performative IC theocratization, followed by Guthrie *et al.*'s (2012, p. 69) call for more research focusing on "critical and performative analysis of IC practices in action". Dumay (2013) and Dumay and

Garanina (2013) enhanced this notion by analysis of the research that can be categorized as the third stage. The purpose of this chapter is to present the concept of IC in knowledge intensive organizations – public universities – by examining existing literature in the field at all three stages. IC in the public sector is a relatively unexplored area (Guthrie *et al.*, 2012, p. 74); however, public universities are relatively often researched (Dumay *et al.*, 2015).

New public management and intellectual capital management at universities

Changes in contextual factors mean that universities, regardless of type, have experienced the effects of managerialism and new public management (NPM) (Dearlove, 2002; Pollitt, 2002; Hood and Dixon, 2015). In other words, the ideals of learning and education as a public good may have been surpassed by new requirements for profitability and competitive survival (Bok, 2009). While these concepts are well-known aspects of running a company, they are not consistent with the traditional values of universities. Therefore, NPM, inevitably, has been changing management approaches at universities.

The introduction of NPM in universities has brought positive results in many cases, ensuring control, promoting accountability, and assessing performance. It has facilitated cooperation with business because universities have begun to follow similar principles. NPM has also raised awareness of IC in universities. However, at times, the results have led to severe strain on academic freedom and autonomy (Davies and Thomas, 2002; Banal-Estañol *et al.*, 2015). In turn, NPM is also believed to have forced scholars to engage in industry collaborations, further diminishing university freedom and forcing more applied science to be conducted at the cost of basic research.

Some critics argue that NPM – and the ideologies of performance measurement generally – are simply incompatible with the culture and mission of the public sector (Cavalluzzo and Ittner, 2004; Laegreid and Christensen, 2013). These critics believe that traditional performance measures of companies are not applicable at universities, as what is measured at universities – lecturing hours and publications – are indirect measures and do not show the real implications of knowledge generation and knowledge transfer on society (Bogt and Scapens, 2012).

Others believe that IC creation is the primary goal for universities and, hence, should not follow corporate measures and management styles (Warden, 2004; Van Dooren *et al.*, 2015). The advocates of IC are instead encouraging approaches from knowledge management to ensure the production and diffusion of knowledge (Elena, 2004; Secundo *et al.*, 2015). Although no 'one size fits all' solution has been found, different ideas about how to manage universities have been proposed, based on the knowledge management approach of letting knowledge work to create value (Roberts, 1999; Kianto *et al.*, 2014).

The knowledge management and IC management style emphasizes identifying and valuing the knowledge assets at universities and raising these assets through knowledge sharing and the creation of new knowledge (Holsapple, 2003; Elena-Perez *et al.*, 2015). Adopting this form of management should assist in the measurement, management, and diffusion of knowledge to improve transparency (Elena, 2004). The ambition of this management approach is to identify and support the knowledge assets of the university; for example, researchers need to show the value of university knowledge. This identification will thus help to illustrate the assets and to communicate university value to external stakeholders (Warden, 2003). In contrast to NPM, the idea is to enable an understanding of knowledge value for the stakeholder ecosystem rather than accepting the measures of traditional companies. In other words, identifying and communicating knowledge value rather than showing a positive bottom line.

The implementation of various knowledge management approaches has been studied from different perspectives and in different countries. The concepts underpinning the application of private sector notions of performance measurement to non-profit organizations rely on assumptions about the appropriateness of transferring management tools derived from a for-profit to a non-profit organization. If they are not appropriate, they must be adjusted (Speckbacher, 2003). Speckbacher (2003) presents three economic models for a firm and discusses them with respect to university adequacy for non-profit organizations. Of interest here is the third model, according to which a firm is understood as a combination of mutually specialized assets and people. It is a connection of incomplete contracts, and success depends on the importance of the specific investments that need to be managed. Balancing the contributions of all stakeholders against university share, and hence determining the extent to which implicit claims are fulfilled, is the core of performance measurement under this approach. Incomplete contracts and specific investments are transferrable to non-profit organizations. For example, university employment contracts usually state initial wages and other conditions but are incomplete with respect to other issues, such as the conditions for layoffs or promotions or timing and manner of determining salary increases. Students pay not only for their university education, but also for implicit claims, such as services and support, which are not legally enforceable. Likewise, universities may invest in graduate relations in the hope of gaining university loyalty, or creating conditions for future university–industry collaboration. The performance measurement system has to provide information about the nature of university stakeholders' claims, and it has to define trade-offs in the case of conflicting claims.

Universities are also organizations that increasingly use technology from external sources. Cooperation, as well as horizontal and vertical networking, have gained importance and are an important change in strategic management (Edler *et al.*, 2002, p. 161). A business network is understood as a set of two or more connected business relationships in which each exchange is between business firms that are conceptualized as collective actors (Emerson, 1981; Anderson *et al.*, 1994; Mattsson *et al.*, 2015). According to Sopińska (2014), knowledge management and IC management in a network organization should be carried out simultaneously at two levels: the level of the entire network and the level of a single link of the network. A knowledge management model should comprise the identification of the applied knowledge management strategy, a description of the knowledge exchange process, and a measurement of the level of formalization and centralization of the process. In the case of universities, networks are formed through government, individual, and department strategic initiatives (Jarratt *et al.*, 2014). The findings show a positive impact on IC, as the knowledge sharing occurring in networks allows sophisticated research, and for 'weaker' universities to contribute with university specific knowledge.

Knowledge and intellectual capital in universities

The components of a university's IC have been categorized in diverse ways. According to Ramírez and Gordillo (2014), the tripartite classification is the most widely accepted in the literature concerning universities (Leitner, 2004; Ramírez *et al.*, 2007; Sánchez *et al.*, 2009; Bezhani, 2010; Casanueva and Gallego, 2010; Secundo *et al.*, 2010). Relatively rarely, customer capital is distinguished (Kok, 2007). The three main components of IC are now discussed.

First, human capital is defined as the sum of the explicit and tacit knowledge of the university staff (teachers, researchers, managers, administration, and service staff), acquired through formal and non-formal education and the processes included in university activities. In other words, this is the knowledge that employees take with them when they leave the university. Examples of human capital include innovation capacity, creativity, know-how, previous experience, teamwork capacity, employee flexibility, tolerance for ambiguity, motivation, satisfaction, learning capacity, loyalty, formal training, and education (MERITUM, 2002, p. 10).

Second, structural (internal) capital is understood as explicit knowledge relating to the internal processes of dissemination, communication, and management of scientific and technical knowledge at the university. Structural capital may be divided into organizational capital and technological capital (Corcoles *et al.*, 2011; Ramírez and Gordillo, 2014). Organizational capital is the operational environment derived from the interaction between research, management, and organization processes, routines, culture, values, internal procedures, quality, scope of the information system, and so on. Technological capital includes the technological resources available at the university, such as bibliographical and documentary resources, archives, technical developments, patents, licences, software, databases, and so on.

Third, relational (external) capital is defined as all resources linked to the external relationships of the institution, such as customers, suppliers, R&D partners, and government. It also includes the perception that others have of the university. Examples of this category are image, students and other partner's loyalty and satisfaction, links with suppliers, commercial power, negotiating capacity with financial entities, environmental activities, and so on.

Within each category of IC we can differentiate between resources and activities. MERITUM (2002) defines these two categories as intangible resources (static notion) and intangible activities (dynamic notion). Both can be presented with the use of financial and non-financial indicators. Intangible resources are understood as the stock or current value of a given intangible at a certain moment in time. They may or may not be expressed in financial terms. The resources can be both inputs (researchers, for instance) or outputs (publications). The intangible activities imply an allocation of resources aimed at developing internally or acquiring new intangible resources, increasing the value of existing ones, or evaluating and monitoring the results of the former two activities (Sánchez *et al.*, 2006).

In order to measure and manage the above-mentioned types of categories of capital, the analysis of the university's stakeholder ecosystem is useful. Large, established universities in capital cities tend to have a stronger relational capital due to easier access to stakeholders, including state and local government, a wide range of employees, students, large employers, regulators, and joint venture partners. This advantage enables them to enhance university structural and human capital. Such universities are in a privileged position in acquiring the best researchers and 'celebrity lecturers', due to university budget, reputation, and proximity to the headquarters of large corporations, regulators, and so on. The superior infrastructure around them (including better IT infrastructure, laboratories, datacentres) enables them to expand university structural capital. However, such universities face more severe competition for some intangible resources, especially postgraduates who have better, well-paid career paths ahead of them.

Measurement and disclosure of university knowledge by diagnostic intellectual capital

IC measurement and disclosure is a widely researched and discussed topic, especially in the second stage of IC research (Petty and Guthrie, 2000, Guthrie *et al.*, 2012, Michalak, 2012; Dumay and Garanina, 2013). In the course of the dissemination of the IC concept, universities have tried to apply methods of IC measurement developed in the business environment, such as the Balanced Scorecard (Kaplan and Norton, 1996; Kaplan 2001; Philbin, 2011), Skandia Navigator, and the Skandia Value Scheme (Kok, 2007).

In addition, a growing number of IC measurement and reporting methods have been created specifically for universities. Examples of such methods are the IC Report of the Austrian Research Centre (Wissensbilanz, developed and implemented in Austria) and the ICU Report proposed by the Observatory of European Universities (OEU) (Sánchez and Elena, 2006).

In 1999, the Austrian Research Centre, Seibersdorf, was the first European research organization to publish a Wissensbilanz for the entire organization (Leitner and Warden, 2004). Shortly afterwards, the Wissensbilanz was made compulsory for universities in Austria. Mandatory implementation of Wissensbilanz was part of a series of reforms in Austria aimed at the creation of world-class universities, allowing universities to become more independent from state authority. It promoted differentiation of the higher education market, introduced more competition, increased accountability, and the use of negotiated performance-based contracts (Pechar, 2005; Sporn, 2015). The structure of the Wissensbilanz and the detailed list of its objectives were published in February 2006 (Altenburger *et al.*, 2006) and later updated.

The Austrian Wissensbilanz (Austrian Institute of Technology, 2012) consists of a set of indicators organized into typical IC categories (human, structural, and relational). It also presents measures of its core processes – strategic research, contract research and cooperative research – as well as university results. In the category of human capital, indicators embrace the number of researchers, the proportion of research staff (percentage headcount), the number of new employees hired, the percentage share of women in senior positions, total training days per employee, and so on. Examples of structural capital measures are the relation between capital investment and operating revenues, the amount of capital investment in large research equipment, and laboratory floor space. The number of international researchers and the number of international PhD students are used for relational capital measurement. In the area of core processes (research), Wissensbilanz embraces funding for strategic research and the number of projects with a budget over €70,000. Evaluation in the area of results includes total income from contract research in thousands of euros, incoming orders from industry (percentage), publications in peer-reviewed journals with a citation index, and the number of completed dissertations.

The Austrian Wissensbilanz also includes a narrative that covers the university structure and a commentary on obtained results.[1] The Austrian Wissensbilanz is also used for internal management purposes in order to produce disaggregated indicators and goals (Leitner and Warden, 2004). Recent study results have revealed that the Wissensbilanz is systematically coupled with the strategic management process, but is not fully utilized as a strategic tool (Wiedenhofer and Bornemann, 2016).

The mandatory nature of the Austrian IC report has both advantages and disadvantages. The advantages of mandatory IC reporting are the possibility of benchmarking between universities, the proliferation of IC awareness in universities, improvement in the development of public policies, and increased transparency of the whole system (Avkiran, 2006). The disadvantage of the mandatory approach may be the tendency to focus only on the measures that are obligatory while disregarding important aspects or processes that would have been developed otherwise (Altenburger *et al.*, 2006). Leitner (2004), quoting Davies (1999), even warns about "goal displacement", where the focus on performance-based assessment results in efforts towards meeting requirements rather than satisfying the institution's aims. Moreover, Leitner and Warden (2004) warn that the use of the Wissensbilanz for both external reporting and internal management may lead to concealing information, which will have negative consequences for funding.

The OEU was created in June 2004 with the aim of providing universities and research centres with the necessary tools and instruments for the governance of research activities (Sánchez and Elena, 2006, p. 538). Universities and research institutes from various European countries were involved in this project (Germany, Spain, France, The Netherlands, Hungary, Italy, Portugal, and Switzerland) (Dima, 2014, p. 36). The project ran until November 2006 and its primary outcome was a methodological guide to research measurement (Elena and Leitner, 2013, pp. 134–135).

The OEU identifies five 'thematic dimensions': funding, human resources, academic production, third mission, and governance. It also distinguishes 'transversal issues', which are autonomy, strategic capabilities, attractiveness, differentiation profile, and territorial embedding. As a result of the interactions of the aforementioned thematic dimensions, a 'strategic matrix' in each cell is created, in which fundamental questions and a set of indicators are included. As part of the OEU initiative, an *ICU Report* was developed. It provided a set of specific recommendations for European universities (Elena and Leitner, 2013, p. 135) aimed at an increase in the homogeneity of the disclosure of IC information on research activity in European universities.

According to the framework, an ICU Report should consist of three sections: the university's vision, a summary of intangible resources and processes, and a system of 43 financial and non-financial indicators related to human, organizational, and relational capital. The university's vision expresses its ambition to increase the value of the services it provides for the user. This (first) section is also called the knowledge narrative (Sánchez *et al.*, 2006, p. 230). The second section, a summary of intangible resources and activities, presents the intangible resources the institution can mobilize and the different activities undertaken to improve university value. In the third section, a system of indicators is proposed. These indicators allow the university's achievements to be compared with institutions (in space) and over time, which is useful to both external parties and management. From the 141 measures included in the OEU Matrix, only 43 were pre-selected, the remaining being identified by researchers during the project. In this process, strategic objectives, availability of data, and perceived willingness to disclose were taken into account and checked against the MERITUM characteristics.

The researchers participating in the OEU project identified the following barriers to IC measurement and disclosure within a university context:

1   No regulations, standards or norms related to the preparation of IC reports at the national level have been established by accounting bodies or government agencies.
2   Not all universities are at the same stage of development and IC awareness.
3   A vast diversity of institutions exists across Europe with an immense variety of models and initiatives.
4   Different definitions of strategic goals are used across universities; moreover, most European universities have individual functional internal structures, which makes it difficult to manage university research activity as a whole.
5   Most managers of individual faculties have little knowledge about research activities in other disciplines.
6   IC measurement is hindered by the typical departmental structure of universities, the consequences of which are discrepancies between departments.

In order to capture the dynamics of IC management, the Intellectual Capital Maturity Model (ICMM) was developed (Secundo *et al.*, 2015). Experts from eight different European countries (Austria, Greece, Italy, Latvia, Lithuania, Poland, Romania, and Spain) proposed a model based on seven levels of maturity: data collection, awareness, adjustment, measurement, reporting, interpretation and decision making, and strategy and planning. At level 0, collection activities are aimed at gathering and standardizing data. At level 1, university governing bodies identify key intangible assets of the university. At level 2, adjustments of the monitoring system are conducted in order to determine the intangible assets that are most important to stakeholders. Measurement of IC (level 3) requires systematic collection of ex ante defined measures. At the next level, a complete report on IC is prepared and publicized. The report should be based on previous activities as well as institutional pressures derived from laws and regulations of the country where the university is located. Interpretation and decision-making activities are undertaken at level 5. They can be conducted by various stakeholders including the faculty and researchers, technicians, the university board, local public institutions, and national funding bodies. At the sixth and final level, strategy and other plans are developed through the lens of IC asset dynamics, based on previous activities. These should focus on the more efficient use of the most valuable intangible assets (Secundo *et al.*, 2015).

Intellectual capital value for stakeholders and competitive advantage

University IC is created in many universities mainly based on scientific research that aims to discover new fields of knowledge and university application, e.g. new technologies. As Betz (1997) argues, the nature of work on university technologies embraces solutions at a very early stage of a technology and product life cycle. This knowledge is often completely new to the market, which could build a competitive advantage for both universities and potential buyers of this knowledge. However, researchers at universities consider the market potential and competitiveness of university created knowledge to a much lesser degree than is done in industry. Therefore, universities should additionally build specific knowledge and sources of competencies to be able to cooperate with business (Mazzoleni and Nelson, 1998). IC at universities should be built so that the university itself as an institution, scientists and purchasers of the knowledge, and technology created in universities (e.g. students, entrepreneurs) can compete in the market. The basic condition for the utilization of the transferred scientific research into intellectual value is generating a competitive advantage based on values important to potential buyers. A market approach is of great importance in transferring basic research into applied research.

Hendriks and Sousa (2013) stress that IC is not only the sum of the knowledge of an organization's members but also, perhaps primarily, knowledge transfer. Knowledge transfer from university stakeholders produces real IC value and competitive advantage. Additionally, relational capital is built, which creates the ability for the buyers of this knowledge to compete in the marketplace. Consequently, scientists should consider creating added value from their research for the buyers of knowledge from the very beginning of the project, which then provides the simultaneously generated scientific and commercial value that enables potential buyers and the organization itself to compete in the marketplace. The value of research work is determined by the method of implementation or granting of a licence, the value of the publication from a given organization, and scientists' and students' expert knowledge. The basic features of the competitive advantage of IC are a result of the specialist market orientation of knowledge, an understanding of stakeholders, the incubation of technology after assessment of its market potential, professional presentation of research results to the ecosystem of university stakeholders, and researchers' awareness of the added value to the target market before demonstrating and promoting the knowledge and technology to the market (Trzmielak, 2013).

The focal point of university management is that IC is a prominent source of competitive advantage. Viewing people, scientific research, and knowledge building as a cost centre is a fallacy that does not lead to a competitive position (Holton and Yamakovarenko, 2008). The specialization of knowledge makes an organization's intangible assets unique and increases its IC value in the marketplace. The conception of innovative knowledge may be an individual's activity (human capital), the implementation of new knowledge (know-how), or a collective achievement (structural capital) through social networks (Mura *et al.*, 2012). Specifically, we identify the understanding of stakeholders as the crucial point of the network. External and interactive network knowledge (relational capital) is necessary to exploit innovative market potential. Consistent with the needs of market potential assessment, competitive advantage is affected by demonstrating individuals' or organizational knowledge. The final challenge in defining IC value and competitive advantage is recognizing the IC value added before promoting the knowledge and technology to the market. The key to realizing the value of IC is to make sure that individuals and organizations enjoy a lasting presence in the market and create long-term value (Jolly, 1997).

Currently, developments of new products and services are characterized by their high degree of novelty. Highly novel and unique products derive from the principal sources of innovations. In this sense, IC aggregates these sources of innovations (Delgado-Verde *et al.*, 2016). They may be considered a fundamental base in creating a national and international competitive strategy. These features help to allocate IC at universities, to use the intangible assets (knowledge and intellectual property) intensively in this competitive market (Yassen *et al.*, 2016), and to differentiate university performance (Koçoğlu *et al.*, 2009).

Linking university intellectual capital with market value: the commercialization of knowledge

Universities face enormously difficult and complex decisions when commercializing university research results from an economic perspective. Changes within the university sector towards the marketization of the university's IC has not taken place at the same pace as shifts in requiring universities to be open to the needs of industry and innovative business support institutions. The mindset of researchers and other university staff cannot be changed in the short term, as this requires research and time. This creates a network of dependency, where the pace of building IC is dependent on its market value. Additionally, the authors of scientific research and technologies see the world very differently from entrepreneurs.

Dubinskas (1988, p. 201) describes the fundamental differences between entrepreneurs and the authors of university knowledge: "Realistic businessmen when facing challenges of the market have to deal with dreamers, who try to turn economically unfit ideas into the future wealth of companies".

There are several distinguishing features of the links between university IC and market value:

- creation of knowledge and research results;
- applications of research results in industry;
- utilization of research results;
- individual IC commercialization;
- increase of the value of IC.

The basic goal of a scientist is the creation of knowledge and research results that are new, revolutionary, and allow for a better understanding of the world. Individual academic and university philosophy not only needs to foster the idea of building IC with market value, but also the legal and financial conditions within the university, as well as specifications of system and structure (Potwora, 2011).

To consider university IC with market value requires a change in thinking of those who consider commercializing research results and preparing research projects in cooperation with scientists and entrepreneurs in contradiction to the goals of scientific work. According to this approach, an idea for scientific research should no longer be only an intellectual concept; it should also meet the requirements and needs of the market. The value of research results application depends on the quality and economic importance of the problems it solves (Wagner and Wakeman, 2016). Wissema (2009) provides numerous reasons for universities to create IC with market value. These include a massive increase in the number of students, globalization, interdisciplinary research, increase in the gains of revolutionary research, and a global culture which facilitates entrepreneurship (Wissema, 2009).

Collaboration between universities and industry has potential profits for both sides, and is encouraged by governments with the aim of promoting innovation and developing innovative, sustainable, and prosperous regional and national economies. Nielsen *et al.* (2013) present the potential benefits of, and barriers to, these collaborations, referring to studies by Lee (2000), Carayol (2003), and Bredillet *et al.*, (2008). University researchers are often encouraged to start collaboration because of the potential for testing the application of a theory in practice, the need for funds to conduct research, and the possibility of publications, which result in recognition within the scientific community. Companies are usually motivated to collaborate with universities by the opportunity to commercialize new knowledge in order to generate financial gain (Siegel *et al.*, 2003). From industry's perspective, collaborations with universities can result in the development and transfer of technology and expertise, enhanced reputation and image, skill development, enrichment of corporate values and culture, technology testing, and recruitment and retention (Nielsen *et al.*, 2013).

Within changes directed towards utilizing research results, it is necessary to introduce mechanisms of knowledge and technology commercialization that will make it possible to bring together centuries-old academic traditions, freedom of research, and generating a culture that can function within the market rules where companies now operate (Etzkowitz and Webster 1998; Matusiak and Guliński, 2010). Although the question of whether "a university should be an institution that should compete with other enterprises and institutions on the market, or should guard the traditional academic values, which are far from the market and commercial thinking" that Matusiak (2010, p. 179) proposes is still valid, an answer to it has been proposed by Gross and Allen (2003, p. 87): "Technology companies need new discoveries . . . the cost of the basic research program is formidable, and its value is difficult to assess". To overcome this, knowledge from industry should be integrated with university knowledge (Clauss and Kesting, forthcoming). Entrepreneurs require university IC in an equitable exchange and need well-defined university knowledge and technology licencing or acquisition. Nevertheless, they need to minimize the risk associated with invention and commercialization costs because the combination of university and company knowledge is the ideal creation (Pogue *et al.*, 2014). Utilization of IC can have a significant impact on human life in overcoming current issues we are facing (Bauer *et al.*, 2017), and may bring discoveries, health innovations, new treatments, and new pharmaceutical products with benefits to society (Nicol *et al.*, 2016).

Education has become a commodity, and many students seek opportunities for better employment. Finding a better job is a kind of 'individual IC commercialization'. Globalization has brought about the competitiveness of universities, and they have become subject to the world-wide education market. Revolutionary research is more and more often generated as a result of combining the knowledge and experiences of academics from different fields, and that is why they are increasingly expensive. Financing research requires both public and private funds. Individual IC value is also affected by informal learning (Weckowska, 2015). Therefore, there exists a profound sense in building the value of individual IC based on education value.

Students view university IC value somewhat differently from researchers. Students often want to commercialize university IC through employment after finishing university studies. This may be accomplished through university–industry collaboration, as this allows students to gain work experience in which students learn to apply theories in practice and assess business needs (Nielsen and Sort, 2013).

From the perspective of the researcher, there are several possibilities for increasing the value of the individual academic's IC. Given the assumption that IC can be mobilized, the primary objective of a researcher could be considered as enhancing university reputation (in both business and policy-making), having an impact on society, and publishing in academic journals (Siegel *et al.*, 2003; Bruneel *et al.*, 2010; Banal-Estañol *et al.*, 2015). Lee (2000) points out that collaborating with industry often gives researchers access to valuable research data and external funding. Furthermore, collaborations raise the possibility of the researcher being able to test the application of theories (Carayol, 2003). The university–industry collaboration, therefore, offers a way for the researcher to enhance the value of her/his IC by monetary or contextual research support. Moreover, as Vale *et al.* (2016) stress, in a meta-organization, IC is a function of both individual and collective IC dimensions. Changes in both individual IC and collective IC affect each other in various ways, strengthening and weakening mutually over time.

The application and utilization of research results and the increase in the value of IC can also be considered when it comes to cross-functional collaboration (Lin *et al.*, 2015). Cross-functional interactions are essential for the success of linking university IC with the market with regard to knowledge transfer, both personal and from results. Whereas knowledge transfer is more effective when a variety of channels is used, these pathways or mechanisms differ in terms of university capacity to transmit codified or tacit knowledge (Esquinas *et al.*, 2016).

Research published in academic journals may also be treated as an indicator of commercializing knowledge. Siegel *et al.* (2003) finds that researchers who collaborate with companies have a higher scholarly productivity. Furthermore, researchers have the possibility of directly commercializing university IC through spin-offs or patents, indicating the most direct route for the marketing of the potential value of university knowledge, even though this option is not always easily obtainable, as generating knowledge and commercializing it are two very different things (Zucker *et al.*, 2002; Boehm and Hogan, 2014).

In practice, however, there are a few barriers to successful collaboration between universities and industry (Karlsson *et al.*, 2007; Bruneel *et al.*, 2010; Tartari and Salter, 2015) which can be overcome by effective management. Nielsen *et al.* (2013) discuss the creation of tools for managing collaborative research and development projects, distinguishing between project management success and project success, and conclude that project management success is not intrinsically linked to project success. However, there is a link between project management success and ensuring the efficient use of resources in both companies and universities. According to the authors, project management is critical at all stages of university–industry collaborations. The research results also indicate that it is necessary to educate companies on how to work with universities. A good working relationship can generate extraordinary economic performance and has been described as the engine of IC value creation. Starting with a team of students or a small-scale research project can be effective and achievable, and universities may better support collaborations by structuring student contributions and supervision exercises through scouting, lab initiatives, and solution hubs, for example.

Conclusions

Universities are knowledge intensive organizations. They use knowledge as their primary input to create knowledge as an output. Consequently, universities are predestined to facilitate IC management. Public universities have been increasingly undertaking IC management activities in the face of pressures, including lower funding and the globalization of educational markets. This notion is influenced by NPM, which stresses the use of managerial and business methods in the public sector. Our literature review illustrates that NPM may have both positive and adverse impacts on IC creation and management at the university level. NPM tries to promote accountability by assessing performance, which establishes a stricter and more scrutinized form of administration. However, a stringent focus on results and performance evaluations sometimes leads to goal displacement, understood as aiming for easily attainable goals that enable one to get the most out of fund allocation formulas. IC management also faces significant challenges in commercializing research.

An increasing number of IC measurement and reporting methods have been developed specifically for universities. Examples of such methods are Wissensbilanz, formulated and implemented in Austria, the OEU and the ICU Report. Building on the experience from the above-mentioned IC measurement and reporting methods, the ICMM was developed. This model helps universities to evaluate university IC maturity and increase it incrementally from one level to the next.

Collaboration with stakeholders to increase IC for all is a central problem in IC management. Many public universities have the tendency to inwardly orientate, and changing this attitude will take time. In many cases, stakeholders, including business and local government, also find it difficult to start and maintain cooperation aimed at knowledge commercialization. Public universities are tied closely to university regions. The IC of the region and the university are often related in self-strengthening (or self-weakening) loops (Dumay and Garanina, 2013; Dumay, 2014). In a situation when the region loses its IC due to the transformation of economies, a similar trend affects the university.

In the area of IC management, various projects have aimed to enhance collaboration with partners from business. There is a need for more cohesion and alignment in the various actions aimed at IC management, particularly as some IC management practices do not succeed in becoming embedded in organizational routines and universities in the long term.

One more challenge in IC management at public universities is the collegial nature of their management. The election of rectors, deans, and senates enabling independence and autonomy of communities of scholars results in politicized decision making. In some cases, changes at the highest levels of authority lead to rapid development or, contrarily, abandonment of good practices in IC management. In a number of countries (e.g. Sweden), to overcome this problem, the majority of new rectors and deans that are appointed come from outside the university.

IC management in universities is likewise closely related to their country's policies on research and higher education (these vary among countries, even within the European Union). The main differences include the amount of money spent on public universities, priorities in national research strategies, share of public funding in the university budget, and procedures relating to how universities are evaluated and public funds allocated. Some countries spend vast amounts of money (both in absolute and relative terms) on higher education systems (i.e. Canada, Finland,

Sweden, Denmark spend more than 1.5 per cent of GDP), while other spend less (e.g. Italy and Slovakia spend less than 1 per cent of GDP) (UKA, 2015). The smaller the amount spent on universities the larger the challenge for IC management. In recent years, national research strategies seem to promote both certain disciplines (medicine, applied sciences) and university leading research universities (a country's 'champions'). The supported disciplines and universities have more incentives to measure and manage university IC.

The share of public funding in university budgets also affects the priorities in IC management at universities. In some countries, universities are entirely publicly funded (Iceland, Norway) while in others, like the UK, a significant part of university funding comes from tuition fees (Claeys-Kulik and Estermann, 2015, pp. 13–14). In systems where universities are entirely dependent on public funds, IC management is more oriented towards fulfilling the criteria of public funds allocation. Universities in the countries where tuition fees play a major role in funding tend to be focused, to a greater extent, on the fostering of university students' IC and place in the university ranking table.

The procedures for the allocation of funds vary between countries, especially performance-based funding, and constitute a key factor that either facilitates or hinders IC management at universities. In countries like Belgium or France, where block funding based on negotiation or historical determination prevails, IC management may be hampered due to the smaller external incentive. This hindrance may be further strengthened in systems where universities have little discretion in internal money allocation (i.e. Greece and Turkey). In contrast, performance-based funding, including the Danish taximeter, the Italian way of funding based on performance, or Austrian funding based fully on negotiated performance contracts, may foster IC management by adding external motivation. However, certain countries reduced or even abolished formula funding due to economic and financial crises (e.g. Spain, Portugal) (Claeys-Kulik and Estermann, 2015). Performance-based funds allocation may impede IC management in cases where it is based mainly on input metrics or when it leads to high volatility of funding. A significant decrease in financing often leads to substantial loss of IC by the given university, which may have been developed over many years.

There also exists substantial variations in the career development and evaluation of researchers between countries, which affects researchers' mobility and, consequently, IC management at the individual university level. In some countries, for example France, rotation of researchers between universities is mandatory. In others, including the UK or the US, rotation is a condition for career development. However, in Poland, Hungary, Austria, and the Czech Republic a three-stage career path, linked with researchers' remuneration, leads to considerably lower researcher mobility. Limited exchange of researchers means that IC development is mainly based on internal, organic growth. High mobility translates into the development of IC by competing for the most talented and renowned researchers.

Local management at universities likewise plays a significant role in how national policies are interpreted and translated into local IC management. Different strategies and performance measurement systems are implemented at universities, so that understanding IC management at universities is an arduous task, performed in isolation, as many institutional and contextual factors influence implementation at a local or individual level.

To conclude, more research in the area of IC management in the field of operationalizing strategies and development of skills is needed to manage IC at universities efficiently. The themes covered in this chapter provide inspiration for future research to explain how university IC is created and commercialized in cooperation with stakeholders where there are competing needs of various stakeholders. Also, further examination of the process of long-term embedding of IC management in the organizational routines and institutions of universities is required.

Recent research indicates that the limited use of NPM has been replaced by more value-based measures within the public sector, spurred by the critique of NPM. Future research may consider whether and how more value-based measures influence IC management at universities and the effect on employees. Frameworks to investigate IC management, like the ICMM or a collective intelligence approach (Secundo *et al.*, 2016), should be applied, explored, and explained in future research to understand the use of such frameworks both from a theoretical and practical perspective. Finally, it is useful to investigate both the influence of institutional factors as well as local contextual factors to give a more holistic view of IC management at universities. Following Dumay and Garanina's (2013) call for the third stage of IC research, more investigation is needed to explore how IC measurement and reporting is used for managing IC at the level of department, university, research consortia, country, and the whole of the European Union.

Note

1 www.oeaw.ac.at/fileadmin/NEWS/2013/pdf/intellectual_capital_report_2012a.pdf (accessed 15 September 2016).

References

Altenburger, O. A., Novotny-Farkas, Z., and Schaffhauser-Linzatti, M. M. (2006), "The order on the intellectual capital statements of Austrian universities", *Proceedings of the IFSAM: International Federation of Scholarly Associations of Management 8th World Congress*, 28–30 September, Berlin.

Anderson, J. C., Håkansson, H., and Johanson, J. (1994), "Dyadic business relationships within a business network context", *Journal of Marketing*, Vol. 58, No. 4, pp. 1–15.

Austrian Institute of Technology (2012), *Intellectual Capital Report of Austrian Institute of Technology 2012*, Vienna.

Avkiran, N. K. (2006), "Modelling knowledge production performance of research centres with a focus on triple bottom line benchmarking", *International Journal Business Performance Management*, Vol. 8, No. 4, pp. 307–327.

Banal-Estañol, A., Jofre-Bonet, M., and Lawson, C. (2015), "The double-edged sword of industry collaboration: Evidence from engineering academics in the UK", *Research Policy*, Vol. 44, No. 6, pp. 1160–1175.

Bauer, G., Abou-el-enein, M., Kent, A., Poole B., and Forte, M. (2017), "The path to successful commercialization of cell and gene therapies: Empowering patient advocates", *Cytotherapy*, Vol. 19, pp. 293–298.

Benneworth, P. and Jongbloed, B. W. (2010), "Who matters to universities? A stakeholder perspective on humanities, arts and social sciences valorisation", *Higher Education*, Vol. 59, No. 5, pp. 567–588.

Betz, F. (1997), "Academic government industry strategic research relationships", *Journal of Technology Transfer*, Vol. 22, No. 2, pp. 9–16.

Bezhani, I. (2010), "Intellectual capital reporting at UK universities", *Journal of Intellectual Capital*, Vol. 11, No. 2, 179–207.

Boedker, C., Mouritsen, J., and Guthrie, J. (2008), "Enhanced business reporting: International trends and possible policy directions", *Journal of Human Resource Costing and Accounting*, Vol. 12, No. 1, pp. 14–25.

Boehm, D. N. and Hogan, T. (2014), "A 'jack of all trades': The role of PIs in the establishment and management of collaborative networks in scientific knowledge commercialisation", *The Journal of Technology Transfer*, Vol. 39, No. 1, pp. 134–149.

Bogt, T. and Scapens, R. W. (2012), "Performance Management in Universities: Effects of the transition to more qualitative measurements system", *European Accounting Review*, Vol. 21, No. 3, pp. 451–497.

Bok, D. (2009), *Universities in the Marketplace: The Commercialization of Higher Education*, Princeton University Press, New Jersey.

Bowden, J. and Marton, F. (1998), *The University of Learning: Beyond Quality and Competence in University Education*, Kogan Page, London.

Bracci, E., Humphrey, C., Moll, J., and Stecconi, I. (2015), "Public sector accounting, accountability and austerity: More than balancing the books?" *Accounting, Auditing and Accountability Journal*, Vol. 28, No. 6, pp. 878–908.

Bredillet, C., Walker, D. H. T., Cicmil, S., Thomas, J., and Anbari, F. (2008), "Collaborative academic/ practitioner research in project management: Theory and models", *International Journal of Managing Projects in Business*, Vol. 1, pp. 17–32.

Bruneel, J., D'Este, P., and Salter, A. (2010), "Investigating the factors that diminish the barriers to university-industry collaboration", *Research Policy*, Vol. 39, No. 7, pp. 858–868.

Burrows, J. (1999), "Going beyond labels: A framework for profiling institutional stakeholders", *Contemporary Education*, Vol. 70, No. 4, pp. 5–10.

Carayol, N. (2003), "Objectives, agreements and matching in science-industry collaborations: Reassembling the pieces of the puzzle", *Research Policy*, Vol. 32, No. 6, pp. 887–908.

Casanueva, C. and Gallego, A. (2010), "Social capital and individual innovativeness in university research networks", *Innovation: Management, Policy and Practice*, Vol. 12, No. 1, pp. 105–117.

Cavalluzzo, K. S. and Ittner, C. D. (2004), "Implementing performance measurement innovations: Evidence from government", *Accounting, Organizations and Society*, Vol. 29, pp. 243–267.

Claeys-Kulik, L. and Estermann, T. (2015), *Define Thematic Report: Performance-based Funding of Universities in Europe*, European University Association, Brussels.

Clauss, T. and Kesting, T. (forthcoming), "How business should govern knowledge-intensive collaboration with universities: An empirical investigation of university professors", in *Industrial Marketing Management*.

Corcoles, Y. R., Penaver, J. S., and Ponce, A. T. (2011), "Intellectual capital in Spanish public universities: Stakeholders' information needs", *Journal of Intellectual Capital*, Vol. 12, No. 3, pp. 356–376.

Davies, A. and Thomas, R. (2002), "Gendering and gender in public service organizations: Changing professional identities under new public management", *Public Management Review*, Vol. 4, No. 4, pp. 461–484.

Davies, I. C. (1999), "Evaluation and performance management in government", *Evaluation*, Vol. 5, No. 5, pp. 150–159.

Dearlove, J. (2002), "A continuing role for academics: The governance of UK universities in the post-Dearing era", *Higher Education Quarterly*, Vol. 56, No. 3, pp. 257–275.

Delgado-Verde, M., De Castro, M., and Amores-Salvadó, J. (2016), "Intellectual capital and radical innovation: Exploring the quadratic effects in technology-based manufacturing firms", *Technovation*, Vol. 56, pp. 35–47.

Dima A. M., (2014), *Handbook of Research on Trends in European Higher Education Convergence*, IGI Global, USA.

Dubinskas, F. A. (1988), *Making Time: Ethnographics of High Technology Organizations*, Temple University Press, Pennsylvania, PA, pp. 201–202.

Dumay, J. (2013), "The third stage of IC: Towards a new IC future and beyond", *Journal of Intellectual Capital*, Vol. 14, No. 1, pp. 5–9.

Dumay, J. (2014), "Developing strategy to create a public value chain", in Guthrie, J., Marcon, G., Russo, S., and Farneti, F. (Eds), *Public Value Management, Measurement and Reporting*, Emerald, Bingley, UK, pp. 65–83.

Dumay, J. and Garanina, T. (2013), "Intellectual capital research: A critical examination of the third stage", *Journal of Intellectual Capital*, Vol. 14, No. 1, pp. 10–25.

Dumay, J., Guthrie, J., and Puntillo, P. (2015), "IC and public sector: A structured literature review", *Journal of Intellectual Capital*, Vol. 16, No. 2, pp. 67–284.

Edler, J., Mayer-Krahmer, F., and Reger, G. (2002), "Changes in the strategic management of technology: Results of a global benchmarking study", *R&D Management*, Vol. 32, pp. 149–164.

Elena, S. (2004), "Knowledge management and intellectual capital in European universities", paper presented at Entering the Knowledge Society Workshop, Institute for Science and Technology Studies, Bielefeld University, Bielefeld, Germany, 11–13 November.

Elena, S. and Leitner, K. H. (2013), "Coupling with standardisation and diversity: Intellectual capital reporting guidelines for European universities", in Garcia, L., Castellanos, R., and Barrutia-Guenaga, J. (Eds), *Proceedings of the 5th European Conference on Intellectual Capital: ECIC 2013*, Academic Conferences and Publishing International Limited UK, Bilbao, Spain, pp. 132–141,

Elena-Perez, S., Martinaitis, Ž., and Leitner, K. H. (2015), "An intellectual capital maturity model (ICMM) to improve strategic management in European universities", *Journal of Intellectual Capital*, Vol. 16, No. 2, pp. 419–442.

Emerson, R. M. (1981), "Social exchange theory", in Rosenberg, M. and Turner, R. (Eds), *Social Psychology: Sociological Perspectives*, Basic Books, New York, pp. 30–65.

Esquinas, M. F, Pinto, H., Yruela, M. P., and Pereira, T. S. (2016), "Tracing the flows of knowledge transfer: Latent dimensions and determinants of university-industry interactions in peripheral innovation system", *Technological Forecasting & Social Change*, Vol. 113, pp. 266–279.

Etzkowitz, H. and Webster, A., (1998), "Entrepreneurial Science. The Second Academic Revolution", in H. Etzkowitz, A. Webster, P. Healey (Eds), *Capitalizing Knowledge: New Intersections of Industry and Academia* (pp. 21–46). State University of New York Press, New York.

Fijałkowska, J., (2016), "Accountability of universities", in Sułkowski, L. (Ed.) *Management and Culture of the University*, Peter Lang International Academic Publishers, pp. 97–124.

Gross, C. M. and Allen, J. (2003), *Technology Transfer Entrepreneurs: A Guide to Commercializing*, Federal Laboratories Innovations, Praeger, London.

Guthrie, J., Ricceri, F., and Dumay, J. (2012), "Reflections and projections: A decade of intellectual capital accounting research", *British Accounting Review*, Vol. 44, No. 2, pp. 68–82.

Hazelkorn, E. (2005), *University Research Management, Developing Research in New Institutions*, OECD Publishing.

Hemsley-Brown, J. and Oplatka, I. (2006), "Universities in a competitive global marketplace: A systematic review of the literature on higher education marketing", *International Journal of public sector management*, Vol. 19, No. 4, pp. 316–338.

Hendriks, P. H. J. and Sousa, C. A. A. (2013), "Rethinking the liaison between intellectual capital management and knowledge management", *Journal of Information Science*, Vol. 39, No. 2, pp. 270–285.

Holsapple, C. W. (2003), *Handbook on Knowledge Management*, Springer, New York.

Holton, E. F. and Yamakovarenko, B. (2008), "Strategic intellectual capital development defining paradigm for HRD", *Human Research Development Review*, Vol. 7, No. 3, pp. 270–291.

Hood, C. and Dixon, R. (2015), "What we have to show for 30 years of new public management: Higher costs, more complaints", *Governance*, Vol. 28, No. 3, pp. 265–267.

Jarratt, D., Duncan, R., and Bossomaier, T. (2014), "It's not only what you know: Simulating research networks in the UK university sector", *Emergence: Complexity and Organization*, Vol. 16, No. 2, pp. 1–28.

Jolly, V. K. (1997), *Commercializing New Technology*, Harvard Business School Press, Boston, MA.

Kaplan, R. S. (2001), "Strategic performance measurement and management in nonprofit organizations", *Nonprofit Management and Leadership*, Vol. 11, No. 3, pp. 353–370.

Kaplan, R. S. and Norton, D. P. (1996), *The Balanced Scorecard: Translating Strategy into Action*, Harvard Business School Press, Boston, MA.

Karlsson, J., Booth, S., and Odenrick, P. (2007), "Academics' strategies and obstacles in achieving collaboration between universities and SMEs", *Tertiary Education and Management*, Vol. 13, pp. 187–201.

Kianto, A., Ritala, P., Spender, J. C., and Vanhala, M. (2014), "The interaction of intellectual capital assets and knowledge management practices in organizational value creation", *Journal of Intellectual Capital*, Vol. 15, No. 3, pp. 362–375.

Koçoğlu, İ., Manoğlu, S. Z. İ., and İnce, H. (2009), "The relationship between firm intellectual capital and the competitive advantage", *Journal of Global Strategic Management*, Vol. 6, pp. 181–208.

Kok, A. (2007), "Intellectual capital management as part of knowledge management initiatives at institutions of higher learning", *The Electronic Journal of Knowledge Management*, Vol. 5, No. 2, pp. 181–192.

Kok, S., Douglas, K., McClelland, A., and Bryde, D. (2010), "The move towards managerialism: Perceptions of staff in 'traditional' and 'new' UK universities", *Tertiary Education and Management*, Vol. 16, No. 2, pp. 99–113.

Laegreid, P. and Christensen, T. (2013), *Transcending New Public Management: The Transformation of Public Sector Reforms*, Ashgate Publishing Ltd, London.

Lee, Y. S. (2000), "The sustainability of university-industry research collaboration: An empirical assessment", *Journal of Technology Transfer*, Vol. 25, No. 2, pp. 111–133.

Leitner, K. H. (2004), "Valuation of intangibles. Intellectual capital reporting for universities: Conceptual background and application for Austrian universities", *Research Evaluation*, Vol. 13, No. 2, pp. 129–140.

Leitner, K. H. and Warden, C. (2004), "Managing and reporting knowledge-based resources and processes in research organizations: Specifics, lessons learned and perspectives", *Management Accounting Research*, Vol. 15, No. 1, pp. 33–51.

Leydesdorff, L. and Etzkowitz, H. (1996), "Emergence of a Triple Helix of university–industry–government relations", *Science and Public Policy*, Vol. 23, No. 5, pp. 279–286.

Lin Y., Wang Y., and Kung L. A. (2015), "Influences of cross-functional collaboration and knowledge creation on technology commercialization: Evidence from high-tech industries", *Industrial Marketing Management*, Vol. 49, pp. 128–138.

Mattsson, L. G., Corsaro, D., and Ramos, C. (2015), "Sense-making in business markets: The interplay between cognition, action and outcomes", *Industrial Marketing Management*, Vol. 48, pp. 4–11.

Matusiak, K. B. (2010), *Budowa powiązań nauki z biznesem w gospodarce opartej na wiedzy. Rola i miejsce uniwersytetu w procesach innowacyjnych*, Szkoła Główna Handlowa, Warsaw, Poland.

Matusiak, K. B. and Guliński, J. (2010), *Rekomendacje zmian w polskim systemie transferu technologii i komercjalizacji wiedzy*, Polish Agency of Enterprise Development, Warsaw.

Mazzoleni, R. and Nelson, R. R. (1998), "The benefits and cost of strong patent protection: A contribution to the current debate", *Research Policy*, Vol. 27, pp. 273–284.

Meritum (2002), "Guidelines for managing and reporting on intangibles", *Meritum*, Fundación Airtel Móvil, Madrid, Spanien.

Michalak, J. (2012), "Kapitał intelektualny: Trendy w pomiarze, prezentacji i badaniach", in Sobańska, I. and Kabalski, P. (Eds), *Współczesne nurty badawcze w rachunkowości*, Wydawnictwo Uniwersytetu Łódzkiego, Łódź, Poland, pp. 151–177.

Morales, J., Gendron, Y., and Guénin-Paracini, H. (2014), "State privatization and the unrelenting expansion of neoliberalism: The case of the Greek financial crisis", *Critical Perspectives on Accounting*, Vol. 25, No. 6, pp. 423–445.

Mouritsen, J. (2006), "Problematising intellectual capital research: Ostensive versus performative IC", *Accounting, Auditing and Accountability Journal*, Vol. 19. No. 6, pp. 820–841.

Mouwen, K. (2000), "Strategy, structure and culture of the hybrid university: Towards the university of the 21st century", *Tertiary Education and Management*, Vol. 6, pp. 47–56.

Mura, M., Lettieri, E., Spiller, N., and Radaelli, G. (2012), "Intellectual capital and innovative work behaviour: Opening the black box", *International Journal of Engineering Business Management*, Vol. 4, pp. 1–10.

Nicol, D., Critchley, Ch., McWhirter, R., and Whitton, T. (2016), "Understanding public reactions to commercialization of biobanks and use of biobank resources", *Social Science & Medicine*, Vol. 162, pp. 79–87.

Nielsen, C. and Sort, J. C. (2013), "Value exchange in university–industry collaborations", *International Journal of Technology Transfer and Commercialisation*, Vol. 12, No. 4, pp. 193–215.

Nielsen, C., Sort, J. C., and Bentsen, M. J. (2013), "Levers of management in university–industry collaborations: How project management affects value creation at different life-cycle stages of a collaboration", *Tertiary Education and Management*, Vol. 19, No. 3, pp. 246–266.

Pechar, H. (2005), "Backlash or modernisation? Two reform cycles in Austrian higher education", in Amaral, A., Kogan, M., and Gornitzka, A. (Eds), *Reform and Change in Higher Education. Analysing Policy Implementations*, Springer, Dordrecht, pp. 269–285.

Petty, R. and Guthrie, J. (2000), "Intellectual capital literature review: Measurement, reporting and management", *Journal of Intellectual Capital*, Vol. 1, No. 2, pp. 155–176.

Philbin, S. P. (2011), "Design and implementation of the balanced scorecard at a university institute", *Measuring Business Excellence*, Vol. 15, No. 3, pp. 34–45.

Pogue G. P., Lorenzini F., and Thomson K., (2014), "Technology transfer and the innovation reef", in Trzmielak, D. M. and Gibson, D. V. (Eds), *International Cases on Innovation, Knowledge and Technology Transfer*, Wydawnictwo Uniwersytetu Łódzkiego, Łódź, Poland, pp. 13–38.

Pollitt, C. (2002), "The new public management in international perspective", in McLoughlin, K., Osborne, S. P., and Ferlie, E. (Eds), *New Public Management: Current Trends and Future Prospects*, Routledge, London, pp. 274–292.

Potwora, W. (2011), "Innowacje (nie) innowacyjne: O współpracy nauki z gospodarką", in Trzmielak, D. M. and Żurawska, J. (Eds), *Zarządzanie innowacjami. Aspekty komunikacji, finansowania, badania rynku, psychologicznych uwarunkowań, polityki innowacyjnej i infrastruktury*, Publishing House of Silesian Institute, Opole, Poland, pp. 278–292.

Ramírez, Y. and Gordillo, S. (2014), "Recognition and measurement of intellectual capital in Spanish universities", *Journal of Intellectual Capital*, Vol. 15, No. 1, pp. 173–188.

Ramírez, Y., Lorduy, C., and Rojas, J. A. (2007), "Intellectual capital management in Spanish Universities", *Journal of Intellectual Capital*, Vol. 8, No. 4, pp. 732–748.

Ricceri, F. (2008), *Intellectual Capital and Knowledge Management: Strategic Management of Knowledge Resources*, Routledge, London.

Roberts, H. (1999), "The control of intangibles in the knowledge-intensive firm", paper presented at the 22nd Annual Congress of the European Accounting Association, Bordeaux, 5–7 May.

Sánchez, M. P. and Elena, S. (2006), "Intellectual capital in universities. Improving transparency and internal management", *Journal of Intellectual Capital*, Vol. 7 No. 4, pp. 529–548.

Sánchez, M. P., Castrilo, R., and Elena, S. (2006), "The intellectual capital report for universities", in *Strategic Management of University Research Activities, Methodological Guide, Observatory of European Universities (OEU)*, Prime, pp. 223–250, available at: www.finhed.org/media/files/01-THIRD_MISSION_poglavlje_125_169.pdf.

Sanchez, P., Elena, S., and Castrillo, R. (2009), "Intellectual capital dynamics in universities: A reporting model", *Journal of Intellectual Capital*, Vol. 10, No. 2, pp. 307–324.

Secundo, G., Dumay, J., Schiuma, G., and Passiante, G. (2016), "Managing intellectual capital through a collective intelligence approach: An integrated framework for universities", *Journal of Intellectual Capital*, Vol. 17, No. 2, pp. 298–319.

Secundo, G., Elena-Perez, S., Martinaitis, Ž., and Leitner, K. H. (2015), "An intellectual capital maturity model (ICMM) to improve strategic management in European universities: A dynamic approach", *Journal of Intellectual Capital*, Vol. 16, No. 2, pp. 419–442.

Secundo, G., Margheritam, A., Elia, G., and Passiante, G. (2010), "Intangible assets in higher education and research: Mission, performance or both?" *Journal of Intellectual Capital*, Vol. 11, No. 2, pp. 140–157.

Siegel, D. S., Waldman, D. A., Atwater, L. E., and Link, A. N. (2003), "Commercial knowledge transfers from universities to firms: Improving the effectiveness of university–industry collaboration", *Journal of High Technology Management Research*, Vol. 14, No. 1, pp. 111–133.

Slaughter, S. and Leslie, L. (2001), "Expanding and elaborating the concept of academic capitalism", *Organization*, Vol. 8, No. 2, pp. 154–161.

Sopińska, A. (2014), "Wiedza i kapitał intelektualny w nowych typach organizacji: w organizacjach sieciowych", *Research Papers of the Wroclaw University of Economics*, Vol. 340, pp. 788–798.

Speckbacher, G. (2003), "Performance management in non-profit organizations", *Non-Profit Management and Leadership*, Vol. 13, No. 3, pp. 267–281.

Sporn, B. (2015), "World class reform in Austria", *International Higher Education*, Vol. 29, pp. 18–19.

Tartari, V. and Salter, A. (2015), "The engagement gap: Exploring gender differences in university–industry collaboration activities", *Research Policy*, Vol. 44, No. 6, pp. 1176–1191.

Trzmielak, D. M. (2013), *Komercjalizacja wiedzy i technologii: Determinanty i strategie*, Wydawnictwo Uniwersytetu Łódzkiego, Łódź, Poland.

UKA (2015), *Educational Attainment and Economic Investment in the OECD. Tertiary Education from an International Perspective: A Comparison Based on Education at a Glance*, UKA, Swedish Higher Education Authority, Stockholm.

Vale, J., Branco, M. C., & Ribeiro, J. (2016), "Individual intellectual capital versus collective intellectual capital in a meta-organization", *Journal of Intellectual Capital*, Vol. 17, No. 2, pp. 279–297.

Van Dooren, W., Bouckaert, G., and Halligan, J. (2015), *Performance Management in the Public Sector*, Routledge, New York.

Veltri, S., Mastroleo, G., and Schaffhauser-Linzatti, M. (2014), "Measuring intellectual capital in the university sector using a fuzzy logic expert system", *Knowledge Management Research & Practice*, Vol. 12, No. 2, pp. 175–192.

Wagner, S. and Wakeman, S. (2016), "What do patent-based measures tell us about product commercialization? Evidence from the pharmaceutical industry", *Research Policy*, Vol. 45, pp. 1091–1102.

Warden, C. (2003), "Managing and reporting intellectual capital: New strategic challenges for HEROs", *IP Helpdesk Bulletin*, No. 8, April–May.

Warden, C. (2004), "New modes of self-description: Universities reaction in a changing environment", paper presented at the Towards a Multiversity? Universities between National Traditions and Global Trends in Higher Education workshop, Bielefeld, Germany, 11–13 November.

Weckowska, D. M. (2015), "Learning in university technology transfer offices: Transactions-focused and relations-focus approaches to commercialization of academic research", *Technovation*, Vol. 41–42, pp. 62–74.

Wiedenhofer, R. and Bornemann, M. (2016), "Bridging the gap from intellectual capital to quality and strategic management in higher educational institutions' governance: Experiences from Austria", Proceedings of the 12th EIASM Interdisciplinary Workshop on "Intangibles, intellectual capital & extra-financial information".

Wissema, J. G. (2009), *Uniwersytet Trzeciej Generacji Uczelnia XXI wieku*, Zante Publishing House, Zębice, Poland.

Yassen, S. G., Dajani, D., and Hasan, Y. (2016), "The impact of intellectual capital on the competitive advantage: Applied study in Jordanian telecommunication companies", *Computers in Human Behavior*, Vol. 62, pp. 168–175.

Zucker, L. G., Darby, M. R., and Armstrong, J. S. (2002), "Commercializing knowledge: University science, knowledge capture, and firm performance in biotechnology", *Management Science*, Vol. 48, No. 1, pp. 138–153.

11

INTELLECTUAL CAPITAL

A (re)turn to practice

Hannu Ritvanen and Karl-Erik Sveiby

Introduction

Intellectual capital (IC) research has come a long way since its first awareness raising stage (Guthrie *et al.*, 2012; Dumay, 2013; Dumay, 2014). The second and third theory stages have yielded one important insight, showing that the social reality for organizations is too complex to be squeezed into a single theoretical framework, where financial performance directly or indirectly is the norm. The IC triad seems to have taken on the notion of ontology in Gruber's (1993) sense, and much research effort has gone into proving various IC triad classifications' relevance for general financial performance. Our chapter contributes to the emerging stream of research, which broadens the perspective beyond the IC triad and beyond the narrow focus on financial value (Dumay *et al.*, 2017) and other authors in this volume. We suggest that the way forward is to shift scholarly attention from ontological issues to epistemological issues, that is, towards practices of understanding, learning, and searching how to generate knowledge and meaning for managers and stakeholders of their organizations.

We argue that this will expand the applicability of IC from the traditional managerial focus on firms' financial performance to management issues in general. Our proposition is that the IC triad will be seen as a visualization tool, a 'lens'; an essential part of a methodology for practitioners to guide research, select activities, and assess effects and consequences of managerial action in its broadest sense. We approach IC from a social constructivist perspective (Giddens, 1984), where individuals' activities and practices produce and reproduce structures in society. Individual action and social structure are in Giddens' theory seen as mutually dependent on each other – a duality – and form and reform continuously both intentionally and unintentionally. An organization is, according to this perspective, a place of social construction, where structuration occurs. It makes the classification and content of the IC triad contingent on the situation, the objective, and the task at hand. We define the concept of practice based on Bourdieu (1990) and illustrate our theoretical proposals through empirical research in the spirit of IC-as-practice.

The research object of the chapter is a business unit MT (fictitious name) within a large manufacturing company, where the top management team is facing a difficult management problem; a strategic decision under uncertainty. It is an example of a generic problem common to all practitioners. Managers and consultants are often forced to initiate change in a social environment without knowing how their objectives will be fulfilled and what the actual effects and consequences will be for them and their stakeholders. We invite the reader to follow the process of how the MT management team uses measurement of intangibles to frame their construction of meaning and objectives for action.

Management and the issue of uncertainty

Ever since the publication of organization scholar Thompson's (1967) classic *Organizations in Action*, coping with uncertainty has been seen as one of the fundamental management problems of complex organizations. We will here apply two theories dealing with the uncertainty problem. One is the economist Knight's (1921, p. 233) seminal distinction between 'uncertainty', which he defined as unmeasurable, and 'risk', which he considered possible to measure by assigning probabilities to objective outcomes. The other is Milliken's (1987, p. 136) definition of uncertainty, as "an individual's perceived inability to predict something accurately". Milliken's (1987) influential definition covers three types of uncertainty that managers may perceive in organizational settings. They experience 'state uncertainty' when they perceive the organizational environment or a part thereof, to be unpredictable. It is essentially unmeasurable due to lack of information, and hence is compatible with Knight's (1921) definition of uncertainty.

Managers, however, are generally in a less severe situation. The case highlights that the managers had access to plenty of information and good networks, but they experienced the two other Milliken (1987) types of risk. They were uncertain about cause–effect correspondences, and they had to respond to sudden events without sufficient information or knowledge about how to proceed. Milliken (1987) calls them 'effect uncertainty' and 'response uncertainty' respectively, and we approach them from the point of view of risk literature, which has devoted considerable effort to these issues.

Risk literature offers an approach to deal with both effect uncertainty and response uncertainty as deviations from objectives (ISO 31000, 2009). The benefit from our purpose is that it is a general approach and that deviations are not a priori labelled positive or negative. The potential effects of future events on objectives are heavily dependent on contingencies of the environment and business objectives, which tend to have a temporal reach extending over many years. Thus, some of the uncertainties identified can be calculable and thus be transformed to risk, whereas others (such as natural disasters), remain in the unmeasurable realm. A risk assessment similar to the ISO procedure focuses on the relationship[1] between our case company, MT, and a number of environmental factors, most of which are organizations or people whom we refer to as 'stakeholders' following Freeman (1984) and Freeman *et al.* (2010). What is measured is MT's relative resource dependency (Pfeffer and Salancik, 1978) on each stakeholder. The dependencies are assessed and evaluated according to the first order relationship (direct supplier-to-customer), while network effects are deliberately omitted. The relationships need to be categorized according to the purpose of the analysis; in the MT case, we classify them according to the IC triad.

In summary, the theories we apply to frame the case in this chapter are the notion of risk as a measurable plus/minus deviation from objectives and the measurement of this deviation as a relative resource dependency on each identified stakeholder. The relationship is symmetric (from them to us/from us to them). For the practice perspective we rely on Bourdieu, in particular his *Logic of Practice* (1990), which we consider in the discussion section.

The MT case

This section is divided into three parts. First, we briefly describe the MT organization and the visualization of its IC relationships. It is followed by the description of the risk assessment process, and third, the construction of meaning and the generation of action.

The MT organization

The case company MT is a business unit within a major European industrial corporation, which manufactures heavy-duty metal-based equipment. MT assembles machine parts, where the metallurgical specifications of the components are of crucial importance. MT has developed a unique in-house technology; however, the field is developing rapidly and cheaper substitutes are coming to the market. In 2002, MT changed the board and recruited a new CEO. The new CEO initiated a process in June 2002 for determining a new strategy and started with an assessment of the risks inherent in the existing business.

The new CEO identified two issues. First, MT did not have an in-house process for identifying risks, and second, MT needed a distinct easy-to-follow presentation format, which enabled a constructive discussion: "Our folks argue passionately and critically – they even shout in discussions. They do not accept anything at face value, and we needed something that was not just words on paper, but something that generates consensus and action".

The process the MT board decided to use was based on identifying stakeholders and the firm's relationships, categorized in a holistic way under four main headings. In Figure 11.1 these relationships are grouped according to the IC triad plus the fourth 'Environmental factors'. External and internal 'structures' are to be seen, consistent with Giddens' sense, and they are created by the activites and simultaneous influencing of the actors. The visualization is measured at a certain point in time, thus an ahistorical snapshot, whereas the description of the process and how MT resolved the problem is in line with Giddens – I influence but by the same token I get influenced – either directly or indirectly. In Figure 11.1 the case company MT is positioned in the middle as the focal point. The relative relationships between MT and the stakeholders are symbolized through lines. Arrows pointing in the direction of MT symbolize asymmetric dependencies that are riskier for MT than for the stakeholder. Double-edged arrows symbolize competition. Arrows with circles symbolize alliance. The thickness of the arrow symbolizes the strength of the asymmetry. The high dependency risk on the supplier that became identified as the urgent strategic issue is the thickest arrow. The numbers 1 to 10 in Figure 11.1 refer to the steps in the process described in the next section.

Assessing the risks

The risk assessment process consisted of two parts. The first part was the RealBiz assessment workshop. There the management team, including CEO, key managers, and members of the board participated. They had to create the context within which the risks were to be assessed and the group formulated a corporate strategy through lengthy discussion and the objectives. The stakeholders and the salience of their relationships from a risk perspective were set in the visualization tool (Figure 11.1).

The second part of the process started with assessment of the objectives against the risks in the stakeholder relationships. Since all stakeholders can potentially have relationships with all

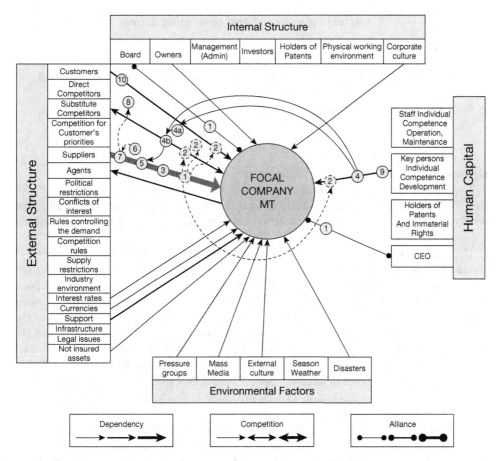

Figure 11.1   The visualization of the MT stakeholder environment and relationships, applying IC-terminology/classification

others, the full picture is a daunting task and impossible to visualize. The method developer's practical solution to reduce complexity was to visualize only the first order relationship of 31 'interested parties', most of which could be classified as stakeholder relationships, thus also IC elements. Each relationship was assessed by means of a set of question-and-answer alternatives, which were then calculated to give a score (degree of dependency, alliance, or competition). The software visualized only the relevant relationships as arrows. In total there were nearly 300 potential questions, which the management team had to answer (see Appendix for an example).[2] The management team was coached by two management consultants (none of the authors), who were trained by the developer of the method.

The structure in Figure 11.1 functioned as the agenda for the conversations; it determined the issues to be discussed. This structured and visual method of taking risks into consideration affected conversations considerably and hence the strategy process. Also the dense/prompt formulation of the risks, which comprised the essential elements, was important. In order to arrive at the consensual formulation, lengthy and thorough discussion was needed. After the data was collected, the system evaluated the severity of the identified risks.

Constructing meaning and generating action

Construction of meaning enabled action:

> The finding [supplier dependency] was not considered as important at first. Not until we articulated the issue in conjunction with the risk assessment [did] it become obvious that the identified risks must be acted upon [removed] in order to achieve the strategic objectives.
>
> *(CEO)*

The issue then, became what action to choose.

The following text is a synthesized excerpt from two three-hour open interviews with the CEO, based on one question: 'Tell me what did you do when you got the result of the assessment?' The numbers 1 to 10 in the process description below refer to the numbers in Figure 11.1.

The management team "awakened" (1) to the fatal supplier dependency (thick line in Figure 11.1). It was a known issue, but it had not been considered important. It was becoming a problem, however, since although MT's market was becoming more and more price sensitive, the supplier refused to reduce the price. Grounded in the new awareness, the management team's conversation became an attempt to understand (2) the implications of the dependency. The conversation synthesized the identified aspects into what we here call *the first renegotiation strategy*. Due to the lack of direct competition for its primary product (no link to the direct competitors in in Figure 11.1) the supplier was dependent on MT, and this would give MT leverage in future discussions about how to expand the market, and how to reduce costs. Based on this notion it [the team] made its first attempt (3) to renegotiate the contract with the supplier, *which failed*.

After the failure of the first renegotiation strategy, "we considered an aggressive response" and began searching for an alternative supplier in Eastern Europe. "We also mobilised our key persons (4) to do two things: to improve the production process of the primary product(4a); and to learn and master the technology of a secondary solution/product to compete with the substitutes" (4b). For the primary product (4a), the R&D department suggested a package of five methods. In that way MT could tailor its offering, achieving "20–30%, even 50% cost reduction". The conversation now changed nature: from argumentation about implications to action-oriented (we can and will survive).

The management team suddenly realized that only very few key persons (4) possessed the required development competence to achieve the R&D goal; the risk had been identified earlier, but now it became important to address. They also began to interpret the lack of direct competitors for MT's type of product differently. Rather than considering the situation of no competition for their primary product as 'good', their conversations now constructed the situation as 'bad'; a problem for market expansion. (If there is no competition for their primary product (4a), there is less 'noise' and potential customers are not aware of its existence). *These (4a and 4b) became part of MT's second strategy (5)* to renegotiate the supplier contract, *which failed again*.

By now the search for a second supplier brought results; the test results from East-European suppliers showed that the quality was adequate, at least for some of the methods in MT's new 'package', and the price was 90 per cent lower than its existing supplier's (6). "We never believed, the risk analysis would lead us to buying air tickets to Ukraine, Russia and countries in search for new partners". This added leverage and credibility to the management team's 'aggressive' strategy; instead of just saying we can survive, they now knew that they could expand their market with support of the other suppliers. This became the foundation for MT's *third strategy*. By now, MT was more than one year into the process and it was time for a final negotiation with its existing supplier (7), which was to include all aspects of what MT had found out so far. The *result was success*: it managed to reduce the price and even to make the supplier a closer ally, thus realizing the objectives in the first renegotiation strategy.

However, unexpectedly, a new competitor appeared (8); an East-European supplier had copied the technology that MT had developed and was trying to patent it. MT had not filed for patent protection, because its earlier analysis had not shown any dependency on intellectual property owners. The event triggered an immediate reassessment of MT's human capital side, in particular the dependence on key people (9), who might be attracted by the new entrant. They immediately discovered one unexpected benefit of the new alliance: "We had only one expert on welding and it was shared 50/50 with our main supplier. Suddenly, he decided to leave us to be employed 100% by the main supplier. We were lucky that no third party was involved". This made MT realize that: "Our brains are our absolutely biggest tool or production resource". As a consequence, MT initiated a program for improving the staff's physical safety, and it also led to a more careful attitude in terms of intellectual property, such as non-disclosure clauses in employment contracts.

Finally (10), having resolved the supplier dependency issue, MT could concentrate on the customer's needs and meet its requirements. They reduced the price level and the number of potential customers grew and two years later the bottom line had turned from red to black.

The CEO reflected on the experience a year later: "We would not have started these forceful activities unless it [the dependency] had not arisen so big and if the results had not been discussed on the board of director level".

Analysis of the case

The case highlights how the management team alternates between two typical management activities. One is intra-team assessment and conversations, where meaning is created and leads to a range of decisions; the other is when individual members go outside the team to execute the decisions. The place for IC-as-practice would be in supporting the first type of activities, where *identification and measuring* are only the initial steps. IC also generates (can generate) *consensus about the meaning* of the metrics; it enables (can enable), in fact enforces, a *holistic approach* to any issue under investigation; it may contribute to the *formulations of actions*; and it makes (can make) the *time span shorter* between talk and action. We see them all in the MT case.

The method for identifying and defining relevant metrics is an example of the *Logic of Practice* (Bourdieu, 1990): the designer's long experience of due diligence work (*habitus*; for more see the Discussion section). The metrics underlying the arrows in Figure 11.1 are hence not 'objectively true'; they are numbers (+1, 0, −1, etc) subjectively allocated by the software to subjective assessments, such as 'high', 'low', 'yes', 'no', expressed by the managers during the conversations. The function of numbers, mathematics, and presentation format is hence not to 'prove' anything in the scientific sense.

The function of metrics is to crystallize individual subjectivity into a meaningful whole; a consensus to which each individual team member knows that he/she is contributing. The format enforces holistic thinking, but the numbers and the meanings are fluid; the holistic approach sees each relationship in the context of other relationships. Several other relationships are required in order to complete the configuration[3] based on which strategic action can be formed, and we see how the managers create and re-create the meaning over and over again in light of new information, reflecting previous attempts. A successful solution to a complex issue, as in the MT case, is only rarely found where the problem is first identified. It requires an exploratory approach, which follows the logic of practice: a chain of activities and experiments that link into each other and the final outcome is unknown, because unintended consequences are generated along the way.

The dependency on key people is a measure of the value of human competence and the case shows two approaches to dealing with key-person dependency. One is the CEO's approach to regard key people as capable resources and to motivate them to stay by giving them attractive tasks and by mobilizing them to build new methods and products. The dependency becomes the impetus for a new line of business: to develop and sell software that enables customers to apply the technologies with less support from MT. The other approach is the owner group and its HR-department; they treat the dependency as a risk and try to contain it through non-disclosure agreements. This shows that each resource has a specific role, defined just for this particular attempt to achieve the objective, and that their role changes when circumstances are assessed differently. Thus, even though the metric stays the same, the meaning of the metric can shift from 'risk' to 'opportunity' in an instant.

The IC triad is sufficiently flexible to disregard the common notion that the firm's legal structure determines its boundaries. The choice of focus entity is crucial. If, for instance, the problem had been seen as a logistics issue or delegated to a logistics function, the solution would have been sought in terms of supplier relationships. The relevant boundary for resource dependency is around a program or project, where development competencies are needed most intensively. The case shows that boundaries may include 'parts' of many firms: customers, suppliers, even competitors. The project or the program fails or succeeds based on how well the participants are able to collaborate. Open access to information and other individuals' knowledge is essential. The event of the key person, who left to be employed by the supplier, highlights the inadequacy regarding the internal structure from a firm's legal perspective. Thanks to the new supplier alliance, MT still had access to the person's competence (a positive unanticipated consequence). Human capital, knowledge, and the capabilities to access information know no boundaries. It is hence counterproductive to require talented peoples' professional networks to be confined within firm boundaries, while at the same time demand superior performance from them. The above is quite a challenge for many managers; they must understand more than just the rules of financial accounting. For instance, how value is created through human participation. This is one area where an IC perspective can make a difference.

We finish this section by suggesting several generic questions that we consider essential, when the IC triad is used as a 'lens' in construction of metrics and meanings. The questions are specifically linked to the dynamic capabilities view of the firm (DCV).[4]

Questions for intellectual capital-as-practice

What is the purpose of the task?

The purpose in the empirical case was to formulate strategy and to assess its risks against 31 factors (26 could be considered as IC related relationships) for the focal entity MT. Dependencies were assessed symmetrically: the focal entity's dependency on a particular stakeholder and vice versa; the stakeholder's dependency on the focal entity.

What is the business logic of the firm/organization in focus?

There is a major difference, for instance, between the business logic of manufacturing and that of professional services, and performance requirements need to be tailored for the particular business logic. As the CEO noted: "We did not understand until after the process that we had different types of businesses: consulting and manufacturing". What is the appropriate focal entity for the identified issue? The case shows a total firm perspective; a sub-unit focus, such as the logistics department would have limited the perspective.

People: the dynamic force

'People are everywhere', in all three IC categories. People are the main dynamic force in all organizations. Hence, a useful distinction for determining people's contributions to the dynamic capability of the organization is between creation/development competences and maintenance/operation competences.

What are the roles of people and their competences?

What is labelled 'human capital' in Figure 11.1 is only those people whose competences contribute directly to the core of the organization's fundamental business, such as those who are in direct contact with customers or R&D. In human capital this is the distinction between the expertise to create deep customer relationships and change their offerings so they follow the needs of the customer and keep abreast of the competition, versus the ability to produce or sell predefined products or services. The distinction has relevance when reflecting on the relationships between human capital and structures. MT's CEO said: "We would not have been this successful without well organised external brainwork".

Who are the customers and what are our relationships with them?

The customer relationships generally tend to be considered the most important, but, as the case shows, the solution to customers' demands may have to be found elsewhere – and this is where a holistic perspective is essential.

Who are the competitors and what are our relationships with them?

MT had no direct competition for its primary product and had initially seen the cheaper substitutes as a mere nuisance. The owner's decision to change the board and CEO altered this. Yet, the new management team did not realize until far into the process that their core technology was being copied by one of their suppliers; a major change in the relationship.

Who are the other external stakeholders and what are our relationships with them?

The case shows that one particular supplier relationship was important. This was because they directly contributed to the core competence of MT.[5]

What are the roles of people and their competences in the external structure?

We see it as the distinction between the value of a personal relationship with the people of a demanding customer, who challenge our experts to create the 'impossible', versus the value of a faceless relationship with a corporation, which just generates a stream of orders.

Which processes are essential for sustaining the organization long term?

New processes which enhanced the effectiveness of the primary technology were developed. They were a means to improve the main objective 'to meet customer expectations' and to influence the supplier of the critical material to start producing solutions to the technology of substitute competition.

What are the roles of people and their competencies in internal structure?

The case shows how management 'discovered' that people had two roles requiring two types of important competencies: the key persons possessing the crucial competence to create new processes were in short supply, whereas MT was less dependent on the competence to use, apply, and maintain existing organizational routines and processes: "This [exercise] opened our eyes in a fundamental way that brains and competencies are our biggest resources".

Discussion and conclusion: towards a practice perspective on IC

Recent IC literature points towards a changing notion of IC; a "third stage" (Guthrie *et al.*, 2012; Dumay and Guthrie, 2012) or "IC2" (Mouritsen, 2006), which calls for IC research to become closer to practitioners. This is consistent with the 'practice turn', which has been emerging in the management literature since Mintzberg's (1971) classic work revealed the unheroic world of 'managerial work' inside organizations. Whittington's (1996) seminal work starts the lively strategy-as-practice stream in management literature, and a leadership-as-practice stream (Carroll *et al.*, 2008) is also emerging. So, who are the 'IC practitioners'?

IC literature gives several alternatives. The practitioners can be consultants (Yu and Humphreys, 2013) or internal practitioners/participants (Dumay and Guthrie, 2012). For some, the focus is on management practice of/in organizations (e.g. Mouritsen, 2006) or employed key people (e.g. Bontis and Serenko, 2009). There are also the practices and methods of the IC scholars who, as Polanyi (1962) pointed out, are as personal and dependent on tacit knowledge as any of the other two. The borders between the practitioner types are fuzzy and, therefore, it perhaps makes more sense to talk about them as 'roles' that a practitioner may play over time. The fuzziness in literature may have to do with the fact that many of the early first-stage contributions to IC theory originate from managers who tried to make sense of their practical experiences in knowledge intensive firms, which at the time were poorly understood. Some of them shifted roles to become consultants, in some cases also academic scholars, and wherever they went they brought their manager *habitus* with them.

The manager *habitus* is a considerable strength in the role of management consultant; one's own management experiences give an ability to understand the situation and they give credibility during coaching sessions. Manager *habitus* is "embodied history, internalized as a second nature and so forgotten as history . . . [it] is the active presence of the whole past of which it is the product" (Bourdieu, 1990, p.58). At MT, in their roles as managers, the management team had applied the logic of practice, which Bourdieu (1990) contrasts against the logic of science of the academic scholar (by which he means positivist science). Many issues that trouble IC scholarship may emanate from the difference between the two logics for acquiring knowledge, and the attempts by practitioners to justify their individually acquired *habitus* in terminologies that positivist scholarship can accept.

Practice unfolds in time and it has all the correlative properties, such as irreversibility, that synchronization destroys. Its temporal structure, that is, its rhythm, its tempo, and above all its directionality, is constitutive of its meaning. Because it is entirely immersed in the current of time, practice is inseparable from temporality, not only because it is played out in time, but also because it plays strategically with time and especially with tempo. A player who is involved and caught up in the game adjusts not to what he sees but to what he fore-sees, sees in advance in the directly perceived present. Science has a time which is not that of practice. For the [academic scholar] analyst, time disappears: not only because, as has often been repeated, arriving after the battle, the analyst cannot have any uncertainty as to what can happen, but also because he has the time to totalize, that is, to overcome the effects of time.

(Bourdieu, 1990 p. 81)

The practice perspective hence focuses on the unromantic realities of the micro level. It takes interest in *how*; how managers work with the nitty-gritty of budgeting, meetings, reporting, presentations, and so on. A practice perspective is concerned with how managers deal with the fact that action is irreversible and tends to have unexpected outcomes. Also, the practice perspective does not shy away from issues of power and ethics as Yu and Humphreys (2013) point out in their vision for "a transformed IC-in-Practice". This is where the practitioner roles separate. Also, when the IC consultants and the managers work and learn together, the external consultants will eventually leave the internal managers for the next client.

The managers, then, remain with the responsibility and are governed by the logic of practice; every action carries a risk and as the effects of their actions unfold in time they – and their stakeholders – will have to re-act, when the (Giddens-)structures return the unintended consequences of their actions. Our study highlights how managers shifted in interpretation; the meanings attributed to the individual elements in the IC triad were contingent on position (CEO versus owners versus key people); in time (early in the process versus later); and on relationships (direction of dependency), of which their actions changed the relative dependencies.

For the academic IC scholar a perspective is a challenge. As Bourdieu points out, what unfolds over time cannot be understood 'after the battle', or studied from a distance with the aim of producing generic theory. Thus history is crucial when attempting to understand how managers work. If the full implications of IC-as-practice are accepted, IC scholars will have to do more than analysing IC statements or manipulate large databases. It signals a commitment to sociological theories of practice (Vaara and Whittington, 2012) and close-up methods, such as ethnographic methods and action research. The (often implicit) notion in IC literature that value is synonymous with financial performance does not hold in the MT case. The key determinant for performance is contingent on what particular business they are in. In MT, the performance of the volume business (which follows a standardized production routine) is measured by metrics that emphasize financial aspects, whereas the Knightian uncertainties that reside in R&D practices cannot be measured, only subjectively assessed. There, best available assessment is hence the management's subjective 'faith and judgment', to use Knight's (1921) expression.

Summary and implications

Our proposal for IC-as-practice builds on seeing the IC triad's weakly structured elements as an opportunity and on Mouritsen's (2006) suggestions for the new direction of IC research that he calls IC2. We suggest expanding his notion and hence the applicability of IC from the traditional issue of firm performance to management issues in general, such as the vexing problem managers are dealing with in the MT case: how to accomplish a complex management task under uncertainty and how to generate consensus around the activities to undertake. We have shown how different constructions of a social world can emerge from intense interaction between metrics and narratives and how this enables both managerial action and preparedness to deal with unanticipated consequences. The case illustrates how the strategic issue – resource dependency – the performative purpose to reduce uncertainty, and the constructed metrics may stay the same over time, while the conversations change their meanings, and hence the managers' constructions of this particular slice of their social world.

We conclude the chapter by listing three existing advantages that have accumulated from more than 20 years of IC research that give IC a unique position to accomplish a (re)turn to practice.

First, the holistic perspective of the IC triad combined with the triad's weakly constructed structure is a unique feature of IC. We suggest that the primary value of the IC triad lies in being used as the epistemological lens when studying organizational and managerial issues. The lens is flexible, yet firm in maintaining the holistic perspective also when the lens is combined with other concepts. The opportunity is that the IC triad can with this perspective be a 'tool' for managers; a 'structuration lens'. We distinguish two basic purposes for the structuration. One is epistemological, to acquire knowledge. The other is performative, to influence the construction of the social structure of which their organization is part.

Second, the theory of the resource-based view of the firm, in particular its extension, the dynamic competencies perspective (DCV) is implicitly or explicitly one of theoretical bases of most IC research (Teece *et al.*, 1997; Eisenhardt and Martin, 2000). IC research is, in fact, one of the liveliest streams of DCV-based scholarship, albeit not recognized as such. Making the DCV more explicit in studies would add theoretical strength to arguments and it would increase IC scholarship's relevance for the academic community.

Third, the methodology of measuring intangibles is another unique feature of IC scholarship. The construction of indicators for ephemeral phenomena is the first IC practice, and it has a strong legacy by now. We suggest that the purpose of measuring should not be control, but learning, to complement language for increasing the precision in strategy conversations, and for speeding up impetus for action.

As final notes, the authors contribute two personal reflections.

Author's reflections

Ritvanen reflecting on discovering IC

I have devoted a large part of my working life to measurement issues attempting to bridge the understanding/communication gap between business and computer technology. When I started my IC and IC management related doctoral studies, I was astonished to discover that I had unknowingly been working with IC related phenomena all the time. I believe that many of the managers and experts that I have been working with over the years are still in a situation similar to mine before my 'enlightenment'; they are working with IC related elements, often unknowingly. This 'bilingual' or 'multilingual' role assumes the understanding of both 'worlds', which is difficult without work experience in them. My turn from practitioner to scholar has been a lengthy transition, much learning, but probably more unlearning.

In the 1990s I was working as a knowledge engineer with Expert systems and there I met Per-Erik Kihlstedt and his issue of formalizing the inference logic of his tacit knowledge in a software, which eventually became the RealBiz risk assessment system. The challenge was to arrive at a standardized score that took all the selected environmental factors into account in a coherent way. We arrived at the solution described in the MT case earlier.

This kind of work, where one has to acquire and formalize expertise, certainly leaves traces in one's thinking and I picked out Sveiby's (largely unread) book, *Kunskapsföretaget* (*Managing Knowhow*), from my book shelf to read it from a new perspective. I then realized that while working as a marketing manager in a large Finnish ICT service company some 30 years ago in the 1980s, I had actually been working in a 'knowledge company'.

During the early 2000s I worked with another ICT company known for its analytics technology. Sadly, the unfortunate result from our highly efficient report generators was that managers were often overwhelmed by reports, because the simple question about the purpose of the measurements was rarely asked. Today I believe that the purpose of measurement is all-important and it should be made explicit and clear before the measurement work is even started. The clearer the purpose, the smaller the number of indicators and reports. This also makes it easier to cancel reports, when a purpose changes.

As the MT case shows, risks constitute the proverbial 'devil', because they affect the aggregate, the 'whole', but they reside hidden in the detail. This is where visualization may function as a multidimensional tool and IC is perfectly suited for this, if we allow for flexibility. When I conducted the interviews with the CEO, we used the same visualization as they did during the process we describe in this chapter. It was a considerable help during the communication between interviewer and interviewee. Compared to a 'normal' question/answer situation, the interview became a progressive dialogue with two 'controlled' dimensions. One was to focus on the selected relationship and problems in it (supplier dependency), the other was to discuss the focal relationship in context – that is, its relationship to other relationships. This holistic view 'lifted' the discussion to address the second-order dimension of the relationships, where the problems were resolved. I, as the outsider, came closer to what the insider might have experienced – an invaluable extra dimension.

Finally, I wish to emphasize the experience of an old practitioner scholar: IC allows and requires a close collaboration between theory and practice. IC was born in practice but it has for too long been a theoretical exercise. Practitioners are always on the hunt for something useful and will gladly accept an IC theory that is built squarely on practice. It is not either/or but the synthesis, that is, both/and. In the spirit of Vermeulen (2005), "Relevance is then found in the question, rigor in the method applied to provide the answer" (p. 979).

Sveiby reflecting on the purpose of it all . . .

Approaching a half-century of working life, I have had the fortune to experience all three roles in Figure 11.2, and Bourdieu's (1990) *Logic of Practice* describes quite well my own experience. As a manager I had to act and make decisions that had a direct impact on the welfare of my firm and the working life of employees, despite not fully knowing the impact and indirect consequences for those affected by the activities. In an increasingly complex world, therefore, it is no wonder that many managers rely heavily on the strongly structured concepts of financial accounting and economics for guidance. The enormous performative power of measuring human activity in economic terms is, however, dehumanizing organizations; it reduces human agency to petty conversations about budgets, euros, dollars, and cents.

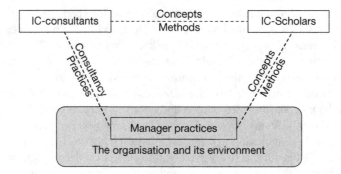

Figure 11.2   Three practitioner roles and three types of practices

My interest in what has become known as 'intellectual capital' and 'knowledge management' (Sveiby and Risling, 1986; Sveiby and Lloyd, 1987) started as frustration with this situation (I was then a manager and co-owner of a publishing firm), and I found that I was not alone. Hence, I took the initiative to gather a handful of Swedish practitioners to form the Konrad group, in the late 1980s. It turned public in Sweden ('Konradgruppen', 1990) and spread globally (Edvinsson and Malone, 1997). There were both managers and consultants among us, and the common purpose was to do something about the inadequacy of financial accounting as guidance in our jobs. We represented two kinds of practices – line management and management consulting – and our purpose was explicitly performative: to develop something that could help us to manage our businesses better and to give better advice to our customers. The performative power of the IC metaphor has since supported the practices of many management consultants and also produced a proliferation of scholarly measuring models; there were more than 30 of them in 2010, mine included.

The purpose of my consulting practice was and still is to help make organizations better for people and to help managers see metrics as a language with the purpose of learning (Sveiby, 2004). However, I have come to realize that measuring intangibles serves two other purposes in most organizations: one is public relations, to support the executives' optimistic statements in annual reports; the other is to be part of the internal systems for performance control. In my experience, and again confirmed by the MT case, indicators of intangibles and their meanings are subjective and are as fluid as normal language. This makes them invalid for PR and far too dangerous to be used for control, because how they are constructed and how they are interpreted depend entirely on context, and context changes over time as a consequence of managerial action. For scientific purposes the validity of intangible indicators is hence generally quite poor. If the managerial purpose is to measure for rewarding or punishing individual performance, their application can be outright counterproductive, and seen from the perspective of the measured individuals they can even be debasing. When I came to understand how IC measuring was actually used in organizations and how easily the fine line between learning and control was crossed into a full-on control purpose, I turned critical. I stopped my measuring consulting practice and turned my attention to IC's 'sister discipline', knowledge management.

So, was IC measuring as used in the MT case, learning or control? The managers were, of course, controlled by their own construction of meaning – intangible indicators and visualization are effective performative tools. However, they controlled the measurement tool and the continuously changing meanings were their own, no one else's. That is where the border line goes. When measuring intangibles, make sure that you will control the meaning. If not, it is better having no metric at all than applying a correctly calculated but invalid indicator.

Appendix: An example of questions and coding of answers.

MT applied an approach for risk assessment 'RealBiz' developed by the Swedish executive Per-Erik Kihlstedt

Stakeholder	Variable	Question	QA1	QA2	QA3	VA1	VA2	VA3
Agents	Agent damage	AGENTS How much would the profit before tax of the business area "{businessidea}" drop in the case where the agent it is most dependent on stops its business? Include loss of revenues, non-recurring costs as well as remaining increases of costs.	1 A change would not cause a drop in profit that is bigger than "{currency}" "{damagesmall}".	2 A change would not cause a drop in profit that is bigger than "{currency}" "{damagelarge}".	3 A change would cause a drop in profit that is bigger than "{currency}" "{damagelarge}".	1	2	3
Agents	Agent problem	THE BUSINESS AREA "{businessidea}"'s IMPORTANCE TO THE AGENTS What would happen to the agent on whom the business area "{businessidea}" is most dependent if the relation were to be broken?	1 The relation between the agent and the business area "{businessidea}" can be broken without serious damage to the agent.	2 The relation between the agent and the business area "{businessidea}" cannot be broken without serious damage to the agent.	3 The agent would not survive if the relation to the business area "{Businessidea}" were broken.	1	2	3

(continued)

(continued)

Stakeholder	Variable	Question	QA1	QA2	QA3
Staff	Existence of key persons	KEY PERSONS Does the business area "{businessidea}" have any key persons among the employees? Exclude the leader. For definition of the concept key person consult the help text	Yes	No	
Staff	Key person alternative	ALTERNATIVE TO KEY PERSONS Is there a person inside or outside the company who is identified as the potential successor for every key person in the business area "{businessidea}" if the present key person were to leave or become unable to work?	1 For every key person in the business area "{businessidea}" there is a person identified who is able to succeed. Alternative normal recruitment.	2 It is difficult to find a successor for at least one key person in the business area "{businessidea}".	3 It is very difficult to find a successor for at least one key person in the business area "{Businessidea}".
Staff	Key person mobility	THE MOBILITY OF THE KEY PERSONS Could the key persons of the business area "{businessidea}" easily find other jobs outside the company if it were necessary?	1 The key persons can easily find other jobs outside the company.	2 The key persons can find other jobs outside the company with some difficulties.	3 The key persons can find other jobs outside the company only with great difficulties.
Staff	Key person exch cost	THE COSTS TO CHANGE KEY PERSON By how much would the earnings decrease during the next 12 months if the key person who is most difficult to replace in the business area "{businessidea}" suddenly needed to be replaced? Include potential costs to hire a consultant and a new key person and exclude the costs of the present leader. The result is:	1 The costs to change a key person in the business area "{businessidea}" are less than "{currency}" "{damagesmall}".	2 The costs to change a key person in the business area "{businessidea}" are less than "{currency}" "{damagelarge}".	3 The costs to change a key person in the business area "{Businessidea}" are greater than "{currency}" "{damagelarge}".

Notes

1 Following Freeman (1984) and ISO 31000:2009 we define relationships as mutual, two-ways.
2 The act of measuring the uncertainty in the relationships transformed them to 'risk' in Knight's (1921) sense.
3 Configuration expresses how things are put (or just are) together, often for some purpose. Here it is used in Mintzberg's (1979) sense, as the basis for describing structural transitions: "to help us to understand how and why organizations undertake transitions from one structure to another".
4 Teece *et al.* (1997, p. 516): We define dynamic capabilities as the firm's ability to integrate, build, and reconfigure internal and external competences to address rapidly changing environments. Dynamic capabilities thus reflect an organization's ability to achieve new and innovative forms of competitive advantage given path dependencies and market positions.
5 From Teece *et al.* (1997, p. 516): Core competences define a firm's fundamental business as core. Core competences must accordingly be derived by looking across the range of a firm's (and its competitors') products and services. The value of core competences can be enhanced by combination with the appropriate complementary assets. The degree to which a core competence is distinctive depends on how well endowed the firm is relative to its competitors, and on how difficult it is for competitors to replicate its competences. N.B. initially the notion core competence stems from Prahalad and Hamel (1990).

References

Bontis, N. and Serenko, A. (2009), "A causal model of human capital antecedents and consequents in the financial services industry", *Journal of Intellectual Capital*, Vol. 10, No. 1, pp. 53–69.
Bourdieu, P. (1990), *The Logic of Practice*, Polity Press, Cambridge, UK.
Carroll, B., Levy, L., and Richmond, D. (2008), "Leadership as practice: Challenging the competency paradigm", *Leadership*, Vol. 4, No. 4, pp. 363–379.
Dumay, J. (2013), "The third stage of IC: Towards a new IC future and beyond", *Journal of Intellectual Capital*, Vol. 14, No. 1 pp. 5–9.
Dumay, J. (2014), "15 years of the *Journal of Intellectual Capital* and counting", *Journal of Intellectual Capital*, Vol. 15, No. 1, pp. 2–37.
Dumay, J. and Guthrie, J. (2012), "IC and strategy as practice: A critical examination", in *ePub-Proceedings of the 4th European Conference on Intellectual Capital: ECIC 2012*, Academic Conferences Limited, pp. 156.
Dumay, J., Guthrie, J., and Rooney, J. (2017), "The critical path of intellectual capital", in Guthrie, J., Dumay, J., Ricceri, F., and Nielsen, C. (Eds), *The Routledge Companion to Intellectual Capital*, Routledge, London, pp. 21–39.
Edvinsson, L. and Malone, M. S. (1997), *Intellectual Capital: Realizing Your Company's True Value by Finding Its Hidden Brainpower*, Harper Business, New York.
Eisenhardt, K. M. and Martin, J. A. (2000), "Dynamic capabilities: What are they?", *Strategic Management Journal*, Vol. 21, Nos 10–11, pp. 1105–1121.
Freeman, E. R. (1984), *Strategic Management: A Stakeholder Approach*, Pitman Publishing Inc, Marshfield, MA.
Freeman, E. R., Harrison, J. S., Wicks, A. C., Parmar, B. L., and De Colle, S. (2010), *Stakeholder Theory. The State of the Art*. Cambridge University Press, Cambridge, UK.
Giddens, A. (1984), *The Constitution of Society: Outline of the Theory of Structuration*, University of California Press, Berkeley, CA.
Gruber T. R. (1993), "A translation approach to portable ontologies", *Knowledge Acquisition*, Vol. 5, No. 2, pp. 199–220.
Guthrie, J., Ricceri, F., and Dumay, J. (2012), "Reflections and projections: A decade of intellectual capital accounting research", *British Accounting Review*, Vol. 44, No. 2, pp. 68–92.
Knight, F. H. (1921), *Risk, Uncertainty and Profit*. Augustus M. Kelley, New York.
'Konradgruppen' (Sveiby, K. E., Annell E., Axelsson S., Emilsson, P. M., Karlsson, H., Wangerud C. J., and Vikström, S.) (1990), *The 'Invisible Balance Sheet': Key Indicators for Accounting, Control and Evaluation of Know-How Companies*. Original in Swedish: *Den osynliga balansräkningen*, Affärsvärlden Förlag, Stockholm (English translation available from www.sveiby.com).

Milliken, F. J. (1987), "Three types of perceived uncertainty about the environment: State, effect, and response uncertainty", *Academy of Management Review*, Vol. 12, No. 1, pp. 133–143.

Mintzberg, H. (1971), "Managerial work: Analysis from observation", *Management Science*, Vol. 18, No. 2, pp. B-97–B-110.

Mintzberg, H. (1979), *The Structuring of Organizations. A Synthesis of the Research*, Prentice-Hall, Inc., Englewood Cliffs, NJ.

Mouritsen, J. (2006), "Problematising intellectual capital research: Ostensive versus performative IC", *Accounting, Auditing & Accountability Journal*, Vol. 19, No. 6, pp. 820–841.

Pfeffer, J. and Salancik, G. R. (1978), *The External Control of Organizations. A Resource Dependance Perspective*, Harper and Row, New York.

Polanyi, M. (1962), *Personal Knowledge: Towards a Post-critical Philosophy*, University of Chicago Press, Chicago, IL.

Prahalad, C. K. and Hamel, G. (1990), "The Core Competence of the Corporation", *Harvard Business Review*, May–June 1990, pp. 79–91.

Sveiby, K. E. (2004), "When measuring fails: Try learning", *International Journal of Learning and Intellectual Capital*, Vol. 1, No. 3, pp. 370–376.

Sveiby, K. E. and Lloyd, T. (1987), *Managing Know-how: Add Value By Valuing Creativity*, Bloomsbury, London.

Sveiby, K. E. and Risling, A. (1986), *Kunskapsföretaget. "The Know-how Company"*, Liber, Malmö, Sweden.

Teece, D. J., Pisano, G., and Shuen, A. (1997), "Dynamic capabilities and strategic management", *Strategic Management Journal*, Vol. 18, No. 7, pp. 509–533.

Thompson, J. D. (1967), *Organizations in Action: Social Science Bases of Administrative Theory*, Transaction Publishers, New Brunswick.

Vaara, E. and Whittington, R. (2012), "Strategy-as-practice: Taking social practices seriously, *The Academy of Management Annals*, Vol. 6, No. 1, pp. 285–336.

Vermeulen, F. (2005), "On rigor and relevance: Fostering dialectic progress in management research", *Academy of Management Journal*, Vol. 48, No. 6, 978–982.

Whittington, R. (1996), "Strategy as Practice", *Long Range Planning*, Vol. 29, No. 5, pp. 731–735.

Yu, A. and Humphreys, P. (2013), "From measuring to learning? Probing the evolutionary path of IC research and practice", *Journal of Intellectual Capital*, Vol. 14, No. 1, pp. 26–47.

12

INTELLECTUAL CAPITAL AND INNOVATION

Jim Rooney and John Dumay

Introduction

Innovation has been identified as "the principal determinant of competitiveness" (Petty and Guthrie, 2000, p. 157). However, research has also shown that it is multi-faceted and multi-dimensional (Tidd, 2001, p. 169). In particular, the innovation process is "power and value-laden" (Dumay *et al.*, 2013, p. 609) with outcomes that are difficult to predict (Tidd, 2001). Further, the literature on innovation in strategic practice identifies gaps between perceptions of innovation and awareness of the common characteristics of successful innovation (Cooper and Kleinschmidt, 1993, p. 74). Here, researchers find that the role of subjective judgment and its behavioural implications have strong links to innovation and its management (Bisbe and Otley, 2004; Chenhall and Moers, 2015).

According to the Oslo Manual issued by the OECD/Eurostat (2005, p. 46), "Innovation is the implementation of a new or significantly improved product (good or service), process, new marketing method or a new organisational method in business practices, workplace organ-isation or external relations". Thus, innovation is a broad concept encompassing all levels of product, service, and process improvement from the smallest change to the most radical invention. Quite simply, innovation is doing something different today than you did yesterday (Smith *et al.*, 2005).

Intellectual capital (IC), in its various guises (including processes and capabilities), has also been identified in the management literature as a source of innovation (for example, Benner and Tushman, 2003, p. 242). However, past interest has been on linking IC and innovation from an ostensive perspective (Mouritsen, 2006), along with continued efforts to justify these links empirically (Martín de Castro and López Sáez, 2008; Delgado-Verde *et al.*, 2011).

It is worth noting that the tendency in such research has been to focus on the positive aspects of innovation (Dumay *et al.*, 2013, p. 612). For example, in the economics literature, "inno-vation has been included in the capital accumulation concept" (Galindo and Mendez-Picazo, 2013, p. 502). Despite this research, the relationship between IC and innovation is considered, in many aspects, to be "unresolved" (Delgado-Verde *et al.*, 2016, p. 35).

In this chapter, the focus is on research that explores the behavioural influences on innova-tion practice and their association with IC, especially through narratives, which are associated with communication of IC inside and outside organizations (Dumay, 2008; Dumay and

Roslender, 2013). We examine performative interactions between IC and innovation practice, including how IC contributes towards innovation based on a continuum including radical, evolutionary, and incremental innovation. As identified by Dumay *et al.* (2013, p. 627), "different types of IC influence different forms of innovation". Understanding the implications and influences of these types of IC has theoretical as well as practitioner benefits.

An overview of the link between IC and innovation

In the academic literature, the recursive contribution of innovation to business competitiveness has been widely investigated (Teece *et al.*, 1997). Following Schumpeter, several authors have considered innovation as a critical source of competitive advantage in the context of an ever-evolving business and technological environment (Tushman and O'Reilly, 1996, p. 36; Christensen and Raynor, 1997, p. 31). Therefore, understanding how firms achieve and sustain competitive advantage in this environment is fundamental (Tsai and Yang, 2013). As Teece *et al.* (1997, p. 509) argue, this "is especially relevant in a Schumpeterian world of innovation-based competition". Given the relationship between IC and value creation through innovation (Hermans and Kauranen, 2005, p. 183), this understanding is also an IC story.

Unfortunately, not all innovations are successful, with many failing to live up to the promised outcomes. Even firms acknowledged for past innovation (for example, Apple) have had their fair share of unsuccessful products, such as the Newton PDAs, PiPPiN game consoles, and Macintosh TVs (see Gardiner, 2008). Further, such companies can easily lose their way if they do not keep up with changes in their product markets. Witness the profit demise of Nokia, which until the introduction of the iPhone was the leading manufacturer of mobile phones at a considerable profit. However, Nokia's profits soured, losing €487 million in the second quarter of 2011 as it felt the sting of competition from the iPhone and Android-based smartphones (Nokia Press Release, 2011–04–21).[1] The rest is history, and now, Nokia is no more.

This mixed outcome highlights a problem in understanding the different factors that enable innovation due to the gap between managers' perceptions of innovation and awareness of criteria for successful innovation (Cooper and Kleinschmidt, 1993, p. 74). Compounding this problem is the difficulty in establishing a relationship between measures of innovation and firm performance (Tidd, 2001, p. 169), a problem in common with management accounting research (Pitkanen and Lukka, 2011, p. 125). Similar to IC, making a link between innovation and a firm is difficult because the innovation process is unpredictable, making the measurement of its inputs and outputs challenging.

Some authors go as far as claiming that successful innovations are a result of luck (Barney, 1986). Borrowing from the resource-based-view of the firm, Dierickx and Cool (1989, p. 1508) take this one step further and outline the "jackpot" model of R&D in relation to radical innovation as "firms sink R&D flows in projects with highly uncertain outcomes, and only a few firms actually 'hit the jackpot' by bringing out highly successful products". Therefore, the literature does not advocate one best way to strategize, manage, or measure innovation. Rather, the strategic approach to innovation is contingent on a range of factors such as the business environment, organizational performance, organizational structure, and the design and type of innovation (Tidd, 2001, pp. 173–4).

Early practitioner implementations of IC practice identified innovation as being central to justifying investment in measuring, managing, and reporting IC. For example, innovation capital is featured in the original Skandia Navigator and is defined as the "Renewal strength in a company, expressed as protected commercial rights, intellectual property, and other intangible assets and values" (Skandia, 1996, p. 22). The link between IC and innovation gained more prominence after Skandia entitled its subsequent report *Power of Innovation* and declared "Innovation is now understood as the driving force behind increases in wealth" (Skandia, 1996, p. 3).

At the turn of the millennium, the link between IC and innovation through practice was embraced by governments and policy-makers interested in promoting innovation within national economies as a source of growth and economic prosperity. As outlined in the Meritum Project (2002, p. 59):

> [t]he disclosure of a greater amount of reliable information on the firm's intangible investments may help overcome the problems currently affecting the validity of the results of innovation studies. For it will facilitate the design and implementation of public policies aimed at increasing economic growth and social welfare by promoting innovation.

Over time, policy-making progressed to lauding the power of IC to promote innovation through the refinement of internal company processes. The policy link is exemplified in the Danish IC guidelines, developed with the support of the Danish Ministry of Science, Technology and Innovation (Mouritsen *et al.*, 2003, p. 11):

> Processes relate to the knowledge content embedded in the company's stable procedures and routines. These can be the company's innovation processes and quality procedures, management and control processes and mechanisms for handling information.

There have been several other IC initiatives linking the development of IC to innovation. A prime example is the European Commission (EC) sponsored RICARDIS report, whereby the authors advocate that:

> Intellectual Capital is a key element in an organization's future earning potential. Theoretical and empirical studies show that it is the unique combination of the different elements of Intellectual Capital and tangible investments that determines an enterprise's competitive advantage. R&D and innovation can be regarded as one element of Intellectual Capital. However, research intensive enterprises invest not only in R&D and innovation, but also in other forms of Intellectual Capital. Empirical studies provide evidence for the tight link and contingency between investments in R&D, Innovation, Human Resources and Relational Capital.
>
> *(European Commission, 2006, p. 10)*

A more contemporary example can be found in another EC sponsored project, InCAS (Intellectual Capital Statement: Made in Europe). In line with the RICARDIS argument, the authors advocate the link between IC, innovation, and competitive advantage (Humphreys *et al.*, 2010, p. 4):

> As a result of constant changes caused by globalization, emerging technologies and shorter product life-cycles, knowledge and innovation have already become the main competitive advantages of many companies … Intellectual Capital (IC) forms the basis for high quality products and services as well as for organizational innovations. So far, conventional management instruments and balance sheets do not cover the systematic management of IC.

As can be seen in the evolution of these IC statement guidelines, policy-makers were seeking to convince themselves and others of the need to develop IC by promoting the 'grand theory' that IC is necessary for innovation (Llewellyn, 2003; Dumay, 2012). However, it seems that policy-makers have yet to achieve this end. Despite continuing exhortations for organizations to develop IC to promote innovation that will lead to competitive advantage and the arguments to disclose innovation in IC reports, it seems that the propensity of organizations to publish IC statements is at a low ebb, and has even been declared dead (Dumay, 2016). Thus, the public disclosure of innovation and IC is now lower than when the guidelines were developed. So how can organizations implement and control innovation through an IC lens?

Linking innovation and IC through narrative

Borrowing from the strong tradition of IC narratives (Dumay, 2008; Dumay and Roslender, 2013), we argue that to implement and control innovation through an IC lens innovation narratives can be used as a coordination device as "they have the power to explain innovation processes so that they are comprehensible and appear legitimate" (Bartel and Garud, 2009, p. 107). Innovation narratives act as a sense-making device designed to create a common understanding of what the organization is trying to achieve. They act to persuade people involved in innovative processes "to take cognizance of the . . . consequences of their decisions" (Llewellyn, 1999, p. 239). Thus, managers who can deploy innovation narratives effectively can potentially control the process of innovation.

Here the role of narrative in the process of controlling for innovation is also related to how innovation is measured because narratives are crucial in conveying the meaning of numbers (Dumay and Rooney, 2016). As Llewellyn (1999, p. 220) observes, "people reason, learn and persuade in two distinct modes – through stories (narration) and by numbers (calculation)" and "in everyday life narration is privileged over calculation". Narrative predominates in sense-making because people have what is known as "narrative capacity and can judge probability and fidelity" of arguments made in a narrative (Weick and Browning, 1986, p. 249). The problem with relying solely on the calculation of numbers is that most people who participate in innovative processes are not accountants or 'experts' at measuring. As a result, Weick and Browning (1986, p. 249) contend:

> In a rational paradigm that undergirds argumentation (calculations), only experts can debate experts, which means that non-experts are spectators. In the narrative paradigm, when the topic is nontechnical, experts are storytellers just like everyone else, which means that non-experts can be more active participants.

The participation of interested people who are not IC or measurement experts is essential to innovation processes because, as Bartel and Garud (2009, p. 107) espouse, "innovation requires the coordinated efforts of many actors to facilitate" generating ideas, solving problems, and linking past experiences to future ambitions. Similar findings emanate from later research on collaborative networks (Kolleck and Bormann, 2014) and knowledge sharing between professional communities (Kimble *et al.*, 2010). In response, Bartel and Garud (2009, p. 108) identify two specific types of innovation narrative, provisional and structured. The narratives promote the coordinated action of actors during the innovation process, symbolize the boundaries of acceptable behaviour, are a mechanism for sharing information about past innovations, and inspire new ideas.

Provisional innovation narratives are used to enable real-time problem solving to help coordinate the efforts of different actors. These narratives are emergent in nature and unlike fully formed stories replete with a plot, protagonist, and outcomes. Provisional narratives are based on innovations in progress and are speculative about the outcome of the innovation at hand. These narratives help to coordinate the efforts of those involved in the innovation process by framing the problem definition to find solutions. Thus, unlike fully formed stories, they are fleeting, ever-evolving, and are more than likely to be communicated in the day-to-day conversation of the actors involved rather than being recorded. Being conversations, they can enrol the interest of listeners and alter their conception of how the innovation relates to the rest of the organization (Bartel and Garud, 2009, pp. 112–13). Related research on the use of ethnographic methodologies in studying innovation processes (Hoholm and Araujo, 2011, p. 938) posit that "This real-time tracking of processes enabled the systematic development of analytical frame-works and theorizing, taking controversy and uncertainty of how to relate the innovation to other networks and processes as a starting point".

In contrast, structured innovation narratives coordinate the past, present, and future of innovation processes to allow the organization to learn from its experiences. These narratives preserve "actors and their activities, material artefacts and how they are transformed during the innovation process" (Bartel and Garud, 2009, p. 113). From an academic perspective these narratives are related to the case study papers found in academic journals that tell the story of how specific innovation challenges were tackled and overcome from a historical context (see Blundel, 2006). Structured narratives also help to highlight the complexity of innovation processes and capture the tensions between emerging ideas and current operations to highlight how innovative processes are non-linear and do not guarantee success (Bartel and Garud, 2009, pp. 113–14). Structured innovation narratives also provide a rich source of research data and have been used to build models of innovation in particular contexts (see Ellonen and Karhu, 2006). It is these structured innovation narratives that would be found in IC reports, especially the original reports developed by Skandia (1996). However, as discussed previously, these reports are no longer commonly found externally, so there also needs to be a further way of understanding how innovation works inside an organization from an IC perspective beyond the grand theory linking IC and innovation.

The differing roles of IC across the innovation continuum

Researchers continue to seek evidence to prove the grand theory linking IC to innovation. The problem with any grand theory is that it represents "meta-narratives formulated at a high level of generality and reflect[s] ideas that have been arrived at by thinking through the issues and relationships in an abstract way – rather than being derived from empirical research" (Llewellyn, 2003, p. 676).

In response, many studies attempt to demonstrate that developing IC and innovation is beneficial and this is almost never questioned (Sveiby *et al.*, 2012). For example, Delgado-Verde *et al.* (2011, p. 5) claim that "Organizational knowledge assets are key organizational factors responsible for firm innovation, as well as effective management". In their article, they declare "The main contribution of the empirical findings of this research is precisely providing evidence that supports that organizational [structural] capital is one of the main sources for firm innovation" Delgado-Verde *et al.* (2011, p. 14). Research, as exemplified by Delgado-Verde *et al.* (2011), is needed to develop more "differentiation theories" (Llewellyn, 2003, p. 672) of IC practice, whereby researchers establish the "meaning and significance" of innovation "through setting up contrasts and categories" to link specific IC elements to innovation.

An example of how specific IC categories link to innovation is provided by Dumay *et al.* (2013), who investigated impediments to innovation practice using an IC lens. In their research, Dumay *et al.* (2013) challenge the notion that all aspects of IC are equally important in developing innovation and that innovation is multi-faceted and not all innovations are successful. To conduct their research, Dumay *et al.* (2013) gathered structured innovation narratives in semi-structured interviews with 27 Australian executive managers. The interviews elicited structured innovation narratives about successful and unsuccessful innovations to identify both enablers and impediments to innovation.

One important aspect of the Dumay *et al.* (2013) research is that they place different types of innovation on a continuum, rather than just consider innovation to be radical or incremental. They explain the continuum as follows (Dumay *et al.*, 2013, pp. 614–5).

- Radical innovation relates to the classical notion of Schumpeterian innovation (Schumpeter, 1934), in that managers recognize that what is developed represents a discontinuity/disruption of what was before (Dosi, 1982, p. 147). Radical innovation is associated with breakthrough ideas (Gundling, 2000; O'Connor and Rice, 2001) and with the development of new business or product lines based on new ideas or technologies or substantial cost reductions that transform the economics of a business (Leifer *et al.*, 2000).
- Evolutionary innovation is typically an expansion of, or significant change to, current products and services, vertical integration, expansion of core competencies or exploring a significantly new market (see Pascale, 1984; Kay and Goldspink, 2013). In contrast to radical innovations, evolutionary innovation does not "re-write the rules of the competitive game, creating a new value proposition" and is more than "continuous movement in the cost/performance frontier" (Tidd *et al.*, 2005).
- Incremental innovation represents an improvement to current business models not involving significant change. It often involves fixing problems with current operations rather than creating new operations. There is a high level of certainty about the internal and external business environments. Incremental innovation is a gradual change and improvement, and product and processes are modified starting from what there was before (McGuigan and Henderson, 2005, p. 199).

Overall, the findings of Dumay *et al.* (2013) are consistent with the grand theory linking IC to successful innovation because all forms of successful innovation require human, structural, and customer capital. However, if different IC elements are not recognized for what they contribute to specific innovation types, then this could lead to innovation failures. Thus, the Dumay *et al.* (2013) findings also contrast with the grand theory, by finding that a mix of IC components leads to a nuanced understanding of the IC-innovation relationship as shown in Table 12.1.

Based on the findings of Dumay *et al.* (2013), we briefly examine the categories of innovation highlighted earlier in this chapter and their links to IC as presented in Table 12.1.

Table 12.1 Links between IC and innovation

	Relational capital	*Structural capital*	*Human capital*
Radical innovation	Key success factor	Mitigating factor	Mitigating factor
Evolutionary innovation		Key success factor	Mitigating factor
Incremental innovation			Key success factor

Source: Adapted from Dumay *et al.*, 2013, p. 626

Radical innovation

Although all three IC types are useful in encouraging radical innovation, relational capital appears to be the most significant regarding an effective relationship between IC and innovation practice. Here two factors emerge from the findings of Dumay *et al.* (2013). First, selection of the 'right' partner is perhaps the most important success factor in order to ensure cooperation and support for a common vision. Indeed this appears to be substantially more important than commonly discussed factors such as entrepreneur personality and organizational culture (Colombo *et al.*, 2015). There are, however, differences between the related factors dependent on the life cycle stage of the individual firm (Ripolles and Blesa, 2016). Second, a focus on 'unseen' customer needs is critical to radical innovation. In the business literature, this factor has been identified as important for both start-up (Lumkin and Dess, 2001; Paradkar *et al.*, 2015) and mature firms (Tripsas, 2008). The importance of this factor cannot be considered in isolation, as Dumay *et al.* (2013, p. 622) identify "the process of uncovering the unseen needs is developed as a portfolio of ideas with the help of partners who contribute capabilities, capacity or social capital, [and] uncertainty is gradually and systematically reduced over time".

From a strucural capital perspective, it is also a mitagating factor because developing rigid processes is not seen as a key success factor for developing successful innovations. In fact Dumay *et al.* (2013, p. 622) find that the need to balance rational considerations of likely success before committing to an individual innovation is detrimental to, rather than enabling of, innovation. Here, the innovation process followed is more akin to Dierickx and Cool's (1989, p. 1508) 'jackpot' model of innovation, which advocates that "Firms sink R&D flows in projects with highly uncertain outcomes, and only few firms actually 'hit the jackpot' by bringing out highly successful products". Therefore, while organizations are not entirely laissez faire about innovation, many successful innovations were not developed using overly rigid innovation processes, as bureaucracy could actually hamper rather than promote innovation.

Interestingly, human capital is identified as a mitigating factor for successful radical innovation rather than being critical to it. Dumay *et al.* (2013, p. 621) find that there is a relative absence of personality and organizational culture as factors in successful radical innovation, which is in contrast to the belief that human capital drives innovation. While it is true that some people can drive innovation at this level, for example Steve Jobs at Apple, human capital seems to play a secondary role to developing relationships with external actors who help to influence the success or failure of an innovation. Additionally, relying on just one or two people to drive innovation can have devastating results should that one person leave or run out of ideas. As Dumay *et al.* (2013, p. 621) conclude, what the "results highlight is that the role of individual personalities in radical innovation is more subtle than the leadership literature would suggest, but that does not mean it is unnecessary".

Evolutionary innovation

Given a focus on 'top-down impetus' for evolutionary innovation (Dumay *et al.*, 2013, p. 622), the exercise of internal power relationships becomes more critical to this category of innovation (for example, see Ratten, 2015, p. 318). However, in common with other IC/innovation relationships outlined earlier, the interaction is multi-level and contextual (for example, see Lees and Sexton, 2014). As highlighted by Dumay *et al.* (2013, p. 627), IC in the form of human capital is important in evolutionary innovation, particularly in the form of leadership "personality and internal communication within the innovating firm". However, as with radical innovation, it can be a mitigating factor because unless the person driving the innovation can inspire the team to follow, then success is not guaranteed.

With evolutionary innovation, forms of structural capital, such as technology, provide essential support to existing human capital. Additionally, Dumay *et al.* (2013, p. 627) find that there needs to be an organizational environment for innovation that is not just cultural, but also requires clearly outlined organizational structures that include requisite management controls essential for enabling innovations to develop.

Incremental innovation

In relation to this final category of innovation, the focus is on product and process enhancement, which requires a greater need for "human capital in the form of organisational culture" (Dumay *et al.*, 2013, p. 627). In incremental innovation, the problem and viable solution are already clearly identified and require human resources to implement the solution, as a manager from the Dumay *et al.* (2013, p. 627) study outlines:

> So what we realized was for us to be good collectively, we had to change the individual view of success from a context of "me" to "we". Once we did that and we created an understanding that it's the bigger picture.

Unlike radical innovation, which does not occur in all organizations, incremental innovation is found in the day-to-day operations of organizations as they strive to improve processes. It is only through the constant interactions of employees and managers working on improving organizational processes and products that incremental innovations take place, and a strong organizational culture is needed to support such change.

Conclusions and implications for theory and practice

In this chapter, we have examined innovation practice and its association with IC, especially through narratives, rather than numbers. These associations were examined across a continuum including radical, evolutionary, and incremental innovation. Our exploration is based on the literature linking IC and innovation practice associated with the use or implementation of these concepts. In contrast to the prior literature, however, we have explored empirical findings beyond the grand theory linking IC and innovation. From the discussions in this chapter, we demonstrate and conclude that the relationships between IC and innovation are substantively more nuanced than the IC-innovation grand theory suggests. We conclude that different types of IC are more effective for different categories of innovation, and can also be mitigating factors in developing innovations, going some way to explaining the mixed empirical results of prior IC-innovation studies.

These findings have a number of implications for IC and innovation practice, research, and policy-making. First, for practitioners, there is an imperative to resist the temptation to apply quantitative frameworks based on grand IC theories without critical review of the nuanced relationship between IC type and innovation categories. Given that innovation is, to a considerable extent, driven by strategy, there is a need for clarity on the desired strategic outcomes. Second, for researchers there is a need to consider the influences on innovation failure as well as success. As for practitioners, this requires a more critical and nuanced understanding of the various relationships between IC type and the continuum of innovation categories not usually examined in grand theories of IC. Finally, for policy-makers, there is a need to critically analyse past preferences for 'one size fits all' innovation policies. All forms of innovation have a role in achieving national and global economic goals.

Note

1 Nokia Press Release (2011-04-21), http://press.nokia.com/2011/07/21/nokia-q2-2011-net-sales-eur-9-3-billion-non-ifrs-eps-eur-0-06-reported-eps-eur-0-10/. (accessed 27 December 2011).

References

Barney, J. B. (1986), "Strategic factor markets: Expectations, luck, and business strategy", *Management Science*, Vol. 32, No. 10, pp. 1231–1241.

Bartel, C. A. and Garud, R. (2009), "The role of narratives in sustaining organizational innovation", *Organization Science*, Vol. 20, No. 1, pp. 107–117.

Benner, M. J. and Tushman, M. L. (2003), "Exploitation, exploration, and process management: The productivity dilemma revisited", *Academy of Management Review*, Vol. 28, No. 2, pp. 238–256.

Bisbe, J. and Otley, D. (2004), "The effects of the interactive use of management control systems on product innovation", *Accounting, Organizations and Society*, Vol. 29, pp. 709–737.

Blundel, R. (2006), "'Little ships': The co-evolution of technological capabilities and industrial dynamics in competing innovation networks", *Industry & Innovation*, Vol. 13, No. 3, pp. 313–334.

Chenhall, R. H. and Moers, F. (2015), "The role of innovation in the evolution of management accounting and its integration into management control", *Accounting, Organizations and Society*, Vol. 47, pp. 1–13.

Christensen, C. and Raynor, M. (1997), *The Innovator's Solution. Creating and Sustaining Successful Growth*, Harvard Business Review Press, Cambridge, MA.

Colombo, M. G., Franzoni, C., and Veugelers, R. (2015), "Going radical: Producing and transferring disruptive innovation", *The Journal of Technology Transfer*, Vol. 40, No. 4, pp. 663–669.

Cooper, R. G. and Kleinschmidt, E. J. (1993), "Screening new products for potential winners", *Long Range Planning*, Vol. 26, No. 6, pp. 74–81.

Delgado-Verde, M., Castro, G. M.-D., and Amores-Salvadó, J. (2016), "Intellectual capital and radical innovation: Exploring the quadratic effects in technology-based manufacturing firms", *Technovation*, Vol. 54, pp. 35–47.

Delgado-Verde, M., Castro, G. M.-D., and Navas-López, J. E. (2011), "Organizational knowledge assets and innovation capability: Evidence from Spanish manufacturing firms", *Journal of Intellectual Capital*, Vol. 12, No. 1, pp. 5–19.

Dierickx, I. and Cool, K. (1989), "Asset stock accumulation and sustainability of competitive advantage", *Management Science*, Vol. 35, No. 12, pp. 1504–1511.

Dosi, G. (1982), "Technological paradigms and technological trajectories", *Research Policy*, Vol. 11, No. 3, pp. 147–162.

Dumay, J. (2008), "Narrative disclosure of intellectual capital: A structurational analysis", *Management Research News*, Vol. 31, No. 7, pp. 518–537.

Dumay, J. (2012), "Grand theories as barriers to using IC concepts", *Journal of Intellectual Capital*, Vol. 13, No. 1, pp. 4–15.

Dumay, J. (2016), "A critical reflection on the future of intellectual capital: From reporting to disclosure", *Journal of Intellectual Capital*, Vol. 17, No. 1, pp. 168–184.

Dumay, J. and Rooney, J. (2016), "Numbers versus narrative: An examination of a controversy", *Financial Accountability & Management*, Vol. 32, No. 2, pp. 202–231.

Dumay, J. and Roslender, R. (2013), "Utilising narrative to improve the relevance of intellectual capital", *Journal of Accounting & Organizational Change*, Vol. 9, No. 3, pp. 248–279.

Dumay, J., Rooney, J., and Marini, L. (2013), "An intellectual capital based differentiation theory of innovation practice", *Journal of Intellectual Capital*, Vol. 14, No. 4, pp. 608–633.

Ellonen, H.-K. and Karhu, P. (2006), "Always the little brother? Digital-product innovation in the media sector", *International Journal of Innovation and Technology Management*, Vol. 3, No. 1, pp. 83–105.

European Commission (EC) (2006), *RICARDIS: Reporting Intellectual Capital to Augment Research, Development and Innovation in SMEs*, European Commission, Directorate-General for Research, Brussels.

Galindo, M-A. and Mendez-Picazo, M-T. (2013), "Innovation, entrepreneurship and economic growth", *Management Decision* Vol. 51, No. 3, pp. 501–514.

Gardiner, B. (2008), "Learning from failure: Apple's most notorious flops", *WIRED*, Available at: www. wired.com/gadgets/mac/multimedia/2008/01/gallery_apple_flops, (accessed 27 December 2011).

Gundling, E. (2000), *The 3M Way to Innovation*, Kodansha International, New York.

Hermans, R. and Kauranen, I. (2005), "Value creation potential of intellectual capital in biotechnology: Empirical evidence from Finland", *R&D Management*, Vol. 35, No.2, pp. 171–185.

Hoholm, T. and Araujo, L. (2011), "Studying innovation processes in real-time: The promises and challenges of ethnography", *Industrial Marketing Management*, Vol. 40, No. 6, pp. 933–939.

Humphreys, P., Liasides, C., Garcia, L., Roser, T., Viedma Marti, J., and Martins, B. (2010), *InCaS: Intellectual Capital Statement Made in Europe*, InCAS Consortium, Brussels.

Kay, R. and Goldspink, C. (2013), *What Public Sector Leaders Mean When They Say They Want to Innovate*, Incept Labs, Sydney.

Kimble, C., Grenier, C., and Goglio-Primard, K. (2010), "Innovation and knowledge sharing across professional boundaries: Political interplay between boundary objects and brokers", *International Journal of Information Management*, Vol. 30, pp. 437–444.

Kolleck, N. and Bormann, I. (2014), "Analyzing trust in innovation networks: Combining quantitative and qualitative techniques of social network analysis", *Zeitschrift für Erziehungswissenschaft*, Vol. 17, No. 5, pp. 9–27.

Lees T. and Sexton, M. (2014), "An evolutional innovation perspective on the selection of low and zero-carbon technologies in new housing", *Building Research & Information*, Vol. 42, No. 3, pp. 276–287.

Leifer, R., McDermott, C., O'Connor, G., Peters, L., Rice, M., and Veryzer, R. (2000), *Radical Innovation: How Mature Companies Can Outsmart Upstarts*, Harvard Business School Press, Boston, MA.

Llewellyn, S. (1999), "Narratives in accounting and management research", *Accounting, Auditing & Accountability Journal*, Vol. 12, No. 2, pp. 220–237.

Llewellyn, S. (2003), "What counts as 'theory' in qualitative management and accounting research? Introducing five levels of theorizing", *Accounting, Auditing & Accountability Journal*, Vol. 16, No. 4, pp. 662–708.

Lumkin, G.T and Dess, G.G (2001), "Linking two dimensions of entrepreneurial orientation to firm performance: The moderating role of environment and industry life cycle", *Journal of Business Venturing*, Vol. 16, pp. 429–451.

Martín de Castro, G. and López Sáez, P. (2008), "Intellectual capital in high-tech firms: The case of Spain", *Journal of Intellectual Capital*, Vol. 9, No. 1, pp. 25–36.

McGuigan, M. and Henderson, J. (2005), "Organizational strategic innovation: How is government policy helping?", *International Journal of Innovation and Technology Management*, Vol. 2, No. 2, pp. 197–215.

Meritum Project (2002), *Guidelines for Managing and Reporting on Intangibles (Intellectual Capital Report)*, European Commission, Madrid.

Mouritsen, J. (2006), "Problematising intellectual capital research: Ostensive versus performative IC", *Accounting, Auditing & Accountability Journal*, Vol. 19, No. 6, pp. 820–841.

Mouritsen, J., Bukh, P. N., Flagstad, K., Thorbjørnsen, S., Johansen, M. R., Kotnis, S., Larsen, H. T., Nielsen, C., Kjærgaard, I., Krag, L., Jeppesen, G., Haisler, J., and Stakemann, B. (2003), *Intellectual Capital Statements: The New Guideline*, Danish Ministry of Science, Technology and Innovation (DMSTI), Copenhagen.

O'Connor, G. C. and Rice, M. P. (2001), "Opportunity recognition and breakthrough innovation in large established firms", *California Management Review*, Vol. 43, No. 2, pp. 95–116.

Organisation for Economic Co-Operation and Development (OECD) and Statistical Office of the European Communities (Eurostat) (2005), *Oslo Manual: Guidelines for Collecting and Interpreting Innovation Data*, Paris.

Paradkar, A., Knight, J., and Hansen, P. (2015), "Innovation in start-ups: Ideas filling the void or ideas devoid of resources and capabilities?" *Technovation*, Vols 41–42, pp. 1–10.

Pascale, R. T. (1984), "Perspectives on strategy: The real story behind Honda's success", *California Management Review*, Vol. 26, No. 3, pp. 47–72.

Petty, R. and Guthrie, J. (2000), "Intellectual capital literature review: Measurement, reporting and management", *Journal of Intellectual Capital*, Vol. 1, No. 2, pp. 155–176.

Pitkanen, H. and Lukka, L. (2011), "Three dimensions of formal and informal feedback in management accounting", *Management Accounting Research*, Vol. 22, pp. 125–137.

Ratten, V. (2015), "Healthcare organisations innovation management systems: Implications for hospitals, primary care providers and community health practitioners", *International Journal of Social Entrepreneurship and Innovation*, Vol. 3, No. 4, pp. 313–322.

Ripolles, M. and Blesa, A. (2016), "Development of interfirm network management activities: The impact of industry, firm age and size", *Journal of Management & Organization*, Vol. 22, No. 2, pp. 186–204.

Schumpeter, J. A. (1934), *The Theory of Economic Development*, Harvard University Press, Cambridge, MA.

Skandia (1996), *Power of Innovation: Intellectual Capital Supplement to Skandia's 1996 Interim Report*, Skandia Insurance Company Ltd., Sveavägen 44, SE-103 50 Stockholm.

Smith, J. A., Morris, J., and Ezzamel, M. (2005), "Organisational change, outsourcing and the impact on management accounting", *The British Accounting Review*, Vol. 37, No. 4, pp. 415–441.

Sveiby, K.-E., Gripenberg, P., and Segercrantz, B. (Eds) (2012), *Challenging the Innovation Paradigm*, Routledge, New York & London.

Teece, D. J., Pisano, G., and Shuen, A. (1997), "Dynamic capabilities and strategic management", *Strategic Management Journal*, Vol. 18, No. 7, pp. 509–533.

Tidd, J. (2001), "Innovation management in context: Environment, organization and performance", *International Journal of Management Reviews*, Vol. 3, No. 3, pp. 169–183.

Tidd, J., Bessant, J., and Pavitt, K. (2005), *Managing Innovation: Integrating Technological, Market and Organizational Change*, John Wiley & Sons, Chichester, UK.

Tripsas, M. (2008), "Customer preference discontinuities: A trigger for radical technological change", *Managerial and Decision Economics*, Vol. 29, Nos 2–3, pp. 79–97.

Tsai, K. H. and Yang, S. Y. (2013), "Firm innovativeness and business performance: The joint moderating effects of market turbulence and competition", *Industrial Marketing Management*, Vol. 42, No. 8, pp. 1279–1294.

Tushman, M. and O'Reilly (1996), "Ambidextrous organizations: Managing evolutionary and revolutionary change", *California Management Review*, Vol. 38, No. 4, pp. 36–37.

Weick, K. E. and Browning, L. D. (1986), "Argument and narration in organizational communication", *Journal of Management*, Vol. 12, No. 2, pp. 243–259.

13

INTELLECTUAL CAPITAL DISCLOSURE IN DIGITAL COMMUNICATION

Maurizio Massaro and John Dumay

Introduction

This chapter contributes to the field of intellectual capital (IC) disclosure by analysing how IC is disclosed in digital communication channels. According to Lipiäinen *et al.* (2014, p. 276) "literature classifies new digital communications channels in various ways. Recently, the terms 'social media' and 'new media' have been used to describe a changing communications landscape". In digital communication, investors who are traditionally considered consumers of information provided by companies now become actors that actively contribute the production and diffusion of such information (Dumay and Guthrie, 2017). Digital communication channels are complex and redefine "the concept of media as a medium that disseminates information" (Zhang, 2016, p. 3). In IC research, most studies examine companies' traditional approaches to IC disclosure (ICD), and less attention is on new digital communication channels. As Dumay and Cai (2014, p. 276) state "there is a general acceptance of the annual report as the main source of data for analysing ICD, and we note how there is a very little critique of this fact". Therefore, digital communication channels represent new media where investors discuss IC and represent new venues for ICD.

To explore ICD in digital communication, this study focuses specifically on Internet Stock Message Boards (IMBs) that represent a digital communication channel where investors can discuss specifically listed companies. The study analyses 60,996 messages posted by investors about the top 10 companies by market capitalization listed on the New York Stock Exchange in the period 1 October 2014 to 30 September 2015. Three specific research questions are investigated to understand the key IC elements discussed in IMBs. This study is novel since it focuses on ICD assuming an investor perspective and investigates if and how much investors discuss IC.

Literature review and research questions

The development of the Internet generated a democratization process of information (Jones, 2006) not only for private persons but also for business contexts. Valuable knowledge originally restricted to small privileged groups of people such as bankers and professional investors is now available for a larger part of the business population (Lund and Nielsen, 2017) at a reasonable price or even for free (Ojala, 2006, p. 42). According to Sabherwal *et al.* (2011, pp. 1209–10): "In addition to trading via online discount brokers, traders often seek information online from paid sources such as ValueLine and Zacks and free sources". Zhang (2016, p. 9) argues that digital communication channels such as blogs and social media are a good venue for investors to learn about other people's opinions about securities and markets. The opinions expressed by investors about the future development of the market price is usually called 'sentiment', and according to Kim and Kim (2014, p. 708), it has predictive power for stock returns, volatility, and trading volume. Therefore, technology opens new digital communication opportunities for disclosing, discussing, and learning other investors' opinions about the future stock market price.

Several digital communication channels such as social media allow users to express their opinion about other messages using tools such as likes and dislikes. Therefore, digital communication channels not only allow investors to express their opinions about specific companies but they also allow investors to comment on other opinions showing agreement or disagreement. As suggested by Berger and Milkman (2012, p. 192) emotional aspects of a message (such as likes and emoticons) may affect whether users share specific messages. Indeed, "People may share emotionally charged content to make sense of their experiences, reduce dissonance, or deepen social connections" (Berger and Milkman, 2012, p. 192). Therefore, the use of specific tools such as like and dislike may affect information sharing processes.

Digital communication channels move the approach from a traditional top-down information scheme to a model that allows companies and investors "to be more interactive, to connect with more people, to be consistent and flexible and to benefit from the opportunity of speed" (Liu and Kop, 2015, p. 128). Traditional approaches consider information to be company owned and require companies to manage and disclose it. For example, Curado *et al.* (2011, p. 1080) propose a six-step model that enables "firms to more accurately describe their intangible assets". However, in digital communication, every participant can introduce new information based on direct observation or personal beliefs. Additionally, investors can create discussions using digital communication tools such as blogs and social media to deepen and better understand specific topics. This form of dialogue is thus used by people "to construct versions of the world which are variant, functional and consequential" (Crane, 2012, p. 449). Therefore, digital communication channels provide new and faster ways for companies to disclose information and creates new communities where different actors engage in a discussion that contributes to creating and disseminating information.

Traditional ICD research focuses on company owned information communicated to the market mainly through annual reports (Dumay and Cai, 2014, p. 265). Several studies developed a critique of this approach. For example, Abeysekera (2006, p. 66) observes that few studies acknowledge that annual reports might not reflect the objective reality of the firm. Additionally, Lardo *et al.* (2017, p. 65) recognize that "annual reports are backward-looking, and contain limited information about the prospects of a company, as would be expected in an IC report". According to Dumay and Guthrie (2017, p. 30), "How IC information and its communication emanate from sources other than the traditional media associated with a corporation's IC disclosure and reporting is of growing interest". Therefore, digital communication channels offer a new perspective to analyse ICD.

Digital communication channels allow for the investigation of investor opinions, measuring topics discussed by investors, measuring their ability to attract attention regarding likes and dislikes, and comparing them with topics analysed and traditionally communicated in annual reports. Scholars use IC research frameworks with checklists of IC related items for analysing the ICD of companies, and some of these frameworks have been reused over time, with some adjustments to adapt them to specific contexts (Goebel, 2015, p. 683). According to Guthrie *et al.* (2012, p. 76) reusing existing frameworks is a sign that IC research is "maturing and becoming entrenched as a discipline". The development of digital communication channels allows researchers to compare frameworks developed by scholars using a company oriented perspective to the topics discussed by investors.

Several recent studies critique the traditional approach to ICD, for example Schaper *et al.* (2017) and Dumay (2016, p. 168), the latter stating specifically that "IC reporting appears to have died for listed companies. From promising beginnings at Skandia in 1994, I can no longer find any evidence of listed companies reporting their IC". Similarly, Abeysekera (2006, p. 66) states "most listed firms use the annual report as a document to publicise the firm rather than as merely a way of complying with accounting standards and corporate law". However, digital communication channels have generated relevant changes in the way companies and investors interact (Pisano *et al.*, 2017, p. 102) providing new opportunities of ICD that need to be addressed. Moving from this premise we draw our general research question:

RQ: What are the key IC elements discussed in digital communication channels?

To answer the general research question, we want to focus on three main aspects of ICD in digital communication channels:

RQ 1. How much is IC discussed in digital communication channels?

RQ 2. What is the difference between traditional ICD frameworks and investors' discussions?

RQ 3. In which way is ICD used by investors to justify their sentiment?

Methodology

Research context

To analyse ICD in digital communication channels, we focus on IMBs that represent online communities where investors discuss specific companies listed on stock exchanges. IMBs are normally distinguished in topic-generic and topic-specific message boards (also known as stock trading boards and trading boards, respectively) (Zhang, 2016, pp. 27–32). In topic-generic message boards, messages are shown in chronological order and focus on all companies (Zhang, 2016, pp. 27–32). Examples are TheLion,[1] HotCopper,[2] and Trade2Win.[3] By contrast, topic-specific message boards mainly focus on target companies, and therefore discussions are organized by the company itself. Examples are Yahoo! Finance Message Board[4] and Raging Bull.[5] Focusing on the different message boards, Sabherwal *et al.* (2011, p. 1210) report that TheLion attracts more than 250 million monthly page views. Similarly, focusing on Yahoo Message Board, Das and Chen (2007, p. 1375) report the high growth in the number of messages on this platform. Therefore, this chapter uses Yahoo Message Board and TheLion as important IMBs to study.[6]

Within the IMBs sources, this chapter analyses the ten most capitalized companies listed on the New York Stock Exchange: Apple, Microsoft, Walmart, IBM, JP Morgan, Oracle, Alphabet, Pfizer, Citigroup, and BP. For each company, we develop and use a web-scrapping script to download messages posted in a one-year period from 1 October 2014 to 30 September 2015, resulting in 60,996 messages. The downloaded messages are first included in an Excel spreadsheet and then imported into the software NVivo for coding. For each company the following details are obtained: title, text, author, date of posting, number of likes and dislikes, and sentiment provided (e.g. sell, buy, hold).

Data analysis

To answer the research questions, this chapter employs a mixed method approach first based on a content analysis to determine if the messages contain any IC information (Krippendorff, 2013), and then we develop quantitative analysis on the messages coded. To conduct the analysis, we follow four main steps.

First, we define the framework representing the analytical construct to develop the content analysis. According to Krippendorff (2013, p. 40), "analytical constructs operationalize what the content analysis knows about the context, specifically, the network of correlations that are assumed to explain how available texts are connected to the possible answers to the analyst's questions". To analyse existing frameworks, this study focuses on papers published in previous peer-reviewed journals. This analysis builds on the framework presented by Goebel (2015, p. 686). We updated the original framework adding recent studies not considered at the time of the original framework. According to Goebel (2015, p. 681) "widely used IC items capture the majority of IC reporting". Therefore, this study relies on previous studies on ICD to measure the key IC topics discussed by the literature.

Second, we performed an extensive coding of all the messages. According to Krippendorff (2013, p. 127) "coding is the term content analysts use when this process is carried out according to independent observer rules". Due to the high number of messages, we trained a group of young researchers to code the messages. A manual coding selection was developed on the total of 60,996 messages downloaded to delete irrelevant or only market focus messages. As a result, we selected 18,076 messages representing 30 per cent of the whole sample.

Third, we focused on the 18,076 relevant messages applying the ICD framework developed at step one. To assure reliability of results, one author independently performed a computer-aided coding based on a "word search" and results were compared to the manual coding to calculate the Krippendorff's Alpha. According to Krippendorff (2013, p. 325) researchers can "rely only on variables with reliability above a = 0.800; consider variables with reliabilities

Table 13.1 Methodology followed

Step	Activities	Examples of the results
1 Identify IC frameworks used in previous studies	Start with the Goebel's (2015) framework and update it with more recent studies	Human capital: 24 papers discuss employee education, 14 about employee training
2 Download all the messages and delete not-relevant messages	Manually code all the messages to exclude messages not related to the company	60,996 messages downloaded 18,076 messages are company-related
3 Apply a content analysis to the 18,076 messages that are company related	Develop a manual coding system and support it using a word search strategy	Human capital: 1,466 messages and 137 specifically focus on management quality
4 Deepen the analysis analysing specific aspects of each message	Develop basic statistical analysis to search for differences between the companies, sectors, and messages	Companies of the new economy disclose more information about human capital rather than other companies

between 0.667 and a = 0.800 only for drawing tentative conclusions". The results of this analysis show a Krippendorff's Alpha over 0.8 in all instances, and therefore we claim reliability of the results.

Fourth, we use the results of the content analysis to develop descriptive statistics. More precisely, findings of the ICD framework discussed within the literature are compared to the content analysis of the relevant messages. The main differences are discussed, searching for differences between items discussed by investors and items analysed by the literature.

Fifth, results are deepened focusing on some specific aspects such as differences between companies belonging to different sectors and the ability of the ICD messages to attract likes. Table 13.1 summarizes the steps of the analysis.

Findings

This section presents the main results of the analysis. The first subsection presents results of the content analysis with the aim of answering *RQ1: How much is IC discussed in digital communication channels?* The second subsection deepens the analysis focusing specific items for each IC component with the aim of answering *RQ 2: What is the difference between traditional ICD frameworks and investors' discussions?* The third subsection presents some further insights with the aim of answering *RQ 3: In which way is ICD used by investors to justify their sentiment?*

RQ 1: IC discussions in IMBs

This subsection provides descriptive statistics about the ICD. The results depicted in Table 13.2 show that IMBs are widely used by investors who posted 60,996 messages, but only 18,076 messages focus on the company. The majority of the messages are general discussions on the stock price, the stock market, or out of topic. Focusing only on company-based messages, Table 13.2 shows that 14 per cent of the messages contain ICDs with 2,581 messages. Interestingly, 1,466 (57 per cent) messages contain discussions on relational capital. Flöstrand (2006, p. 457) finds similar results in the analysis of 250 financial analyst reports of randomly selected S&P 500 companies. Therefore, relational capital is widely discussed in IMBs and widely disclosed in analyst reports.

Our sample companies arise from more innovative sectors usually connected with the new economy rather than more traditional sectors. According to Lohr (2001, p. 1) the term new economy, is "a symbolic shorthand for the power of technology to transform the economy, investment strategy, business thinking, even modern culture". Businessdictionary.com refers to the new economy as being strongly connected with ICT[7] and usually labelled high-tech companies. Following this definition, in our sample, Apple, IBM, Oracle, Microsoft, and Google are considered high-tech companies.

Findings show that 37 per cent of the messages of high-tech companies (respectively: 38 per cent for Apple, 33 per cent for Microsoft, 44 per cent for Oracle, and 31 per cent for Google) discuss structural capital, while the total average is only 27 per cent. Thus, investors discuss more structural capital when high-tech companies are analysed. Similarly, Dumay and Tull (2007, p. 250) find that structural capital information has a different impact on stock prices when compared to other disclosures. Therefore, high-tech companies that produce higher ICD on structural capital can potentially have a relevant impact on stock prices.

To test the validity of these results, we performed a logistic regression with the dependent variable being the ICD based only on structural capital, and the independent variable being

Table 13.2 Descriptive statistics for ICD in IMBs

Code	(A)	(B)	(C)	(D)	(D/C)	(E)	E/C	(F)	(F/C)
	No. of messages	*No. of company based*	*IC*	*Human capital*	*% of IC*	*Relational capital*	*% of IC*	*Structural capital*	*% of IC*
AAPL	9,716	4,815	737	52	7%	473	64%	283	38%
MSFT	7,999	1,959	377	31	8%	258	68%	126	33%
WMT	8,008	1,912	567	336	59%	268	47%	22	4%
IBM	4,605	3,720	415	194	47%	157	38%	132	32%
JPM	4,250	641	39	16	41%	22	56%	3	8%
ORCL	7,981	161	9	4	44%	3	33%	4	44%
GOOG	4,717	1,445	135	10	7%	99	73%	42	31%
PFE	1,971	323	48	1	2%	26	54%	27	56%
C	5,715	1,318	77	18	23%	58	75%	10	13%
BP	6,034	1,782	177	42	24%	102	58%	42	24%
Total	**60,996**	**18,076**	**2,581**	**704**	**27%**	**1,466**	**57%**	**691**	**27%**
Krippendorff's Alpha		**0.986**	**0.930**	**0.828**		**0.975**		**0.987**	

Note. The sum of human capital, relational capital and structural capital can be different from the sum of IC since one message coded as IC could have one or more IC determinants.

the fact that the company belongs to the new economy group. Results confirm that in IMBs, messages of high-tech companies have a higher probability of containing structural capital information compared to low-tech companies with a p-value of less than 0.001. These results build on Abdolmohammadi (2005, p. 412) who states that:

> [t]he new economy sector discloses more about its intellectual property and informa-tion systems categories than the old economy sector … [and this] may indicate that the companies in the new economy either possess more of these IC categories or are more willing to disclose them.

The higher level of discussions based on structural capital suggests that investors perceive this element as more important for these companies.

Additionally, Table 13.2 shows that innovative firms based on the new economy show a lower level of ICD based on human capital. To test the validity of these results, we performed a logistic regression with ICD based on human capital as the dependent variable and the fact that the company belongs to the new economy group as the independent variable. Results confirm with a p-value of less than 0.001 that companies of the new economy disclose less information about human capital compared to other companies These results contradict Bellora and Guenther's (2013, p. 265) findings where "Human capital is the category with most INC [Innovation Capital Disclosure]". As suggested by Alex Mandl, interviewed by Carey (2000, p. 146), "the plain fact is that acquiring is much faster than building. And speed – speed to market, speed to positioning, speed to becoming a viable company – is essential in the new economy". According to Geis (2015, p. 42), Google and Apple and other players such as Facebook, Yahoo!, and Microsoft will join in an acquisition fray and engage in many respon-sive merger and acquisition operations. Therefore, these results suggest that investors could be less interested in human capital, and more in companies with a strong merger and acquisition strategy such as Google, Apple, and Microsoft.

RQ 2: IC items discussed in IMBs

Focusing on the IC elements results show that there is a discrepancy between the most analysed IC items depicted in Table 13.2 and the most discussed IC items in IMBs. Figure 13.1 depicts the main findings and shows the most important items comparing how much an item is used in previous studies and how much the item is discussed within IMBs. The main differences are connected with human capital. While items such as training, employee retention, and skills are heavily used by scholars in previous studies, they are barely discussed in IMBs. More precisely, comparing the two groups, items that are commonly used in at least ten studies of the total of 37 studies analysed, count for less than 10 per cent of all the items discussed in human capital ICD, 51 per cent of all the items discussed in relational capital ICD, and 31 per cent of all the items discussed in structural capital ICD. Therefore, results show that shared items that see scholars in agreement about their importance regarding ICD, account for a minimal part of the whole discussion about ICD.

Items recognized only by some scholars and that do not show agreement among scholars about their relevance to IC still account for a large part of ICD. Some of the most under-considered

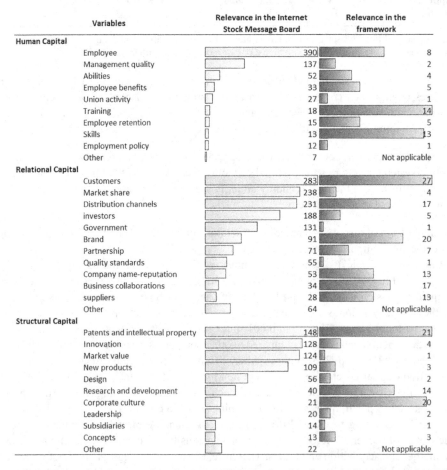

Variables	Relevance in the Internet Stock Message Board	Relevance in the framework
Human Capital		
Employee	390	8
Management quality	137	2
Abilities	52	4
Employee benefits	33	5
Union activity	27	1
Training	18	14
Employee retention	15	5
Skills	13	13
Employment policy	12	1
Other	7	Not applicable
Relational Capital		
Customers	283	27
Market share	238	4
Distribution channels	231	17
investors	188	5
Government	131	1
Brand	91	20
Partnership	71	7
Quality standards	55	1
Company name-reputation	53	13
Business collaborations	34	17
suppliers	28	13
Other	64	Not applicable
Structural Capital		
Patents and intellectual property	148	21
Innovation	128	4
Market value	124	1
New products	109	3
Design	56	2
Research and development	40	14
Corporate culture	21	20
Leadership	20	2
Subsidiaries	14	1
Concepts	13	3
Other	22	Not applicable

Figure 13.1   Comparison between the relevance of IC Items found in the analysis and in previous ICD studies

items are management quality, market share, and new products. These results confirm the findings of Sakakibara *et al.* (2010) and Abhayawansa and Guthrie (2014), who focus on analyst's needs and find that several types of IC information had not been examined previously in capital markets research. Additionally, ICD not focused on investors' needs can be detrimental to market functioning. Indeed, according to Nielsen *et al.* (2015, p. 83), "the efficient functioning of capital markets is dependent upon the flow of information between companies and investors, either directly or indirectly through financial intermediaries".

The above results build on Goebel's (2015, p. 693) findings where "companies seem to focus on the same widely used IC items as IC researchers because corporate IC reporting mainly refers to these items for each IC category". However, most of the items used for developing previous research are for analysing annual reports. As Dumay (2016) states "it is highly unlikely that any information contained in the annual report would be price-sensitive because annual reports detail periodic rather than current information". IMBs are "closely watched by investors who seek inputs to enhance their trading profits" (Sabherwal *et al.*, 2011, p. 1210). Therefore, investors widely discuss new products or figures about market share because it is more price-sensitive information in comparison to information about employee training or retention. These results confirm Holland's (2003, p. 42) observation "that qualities of key executives, and changes in top management, have affected stock prices" and call for a re-discussion of top IC items in ICD.

RQ 3: IC disclosure and sentiment provided

Focusing on the role of ICD in justifying the sentiment provided (e.g. buy, hold, sell), the results show that 9,071 messages provide a sentiment that represents 18 per cent of all messages. Additionally, results show that there is a statistical significance difference between messages that provide sentiment and messages that do not provide it. IC focused messages show that 22 per cent of the messages provide investor's sentiment (e.g. buy, hold, sell) while only 15 per cent of the messages that do not contain IC information provide investor's sentiment. To test differences, we perform a statistical test developed using a logistic regression with the dependent variable a dummy variable (1 if the messages provide sentiment and 0 if it does not) and the independent variable the fact that the message contains IC (1 if the messages contain ICD and 0 if it does not). Findings show that with a *p*-value less than 0.001, messages that contain IC have a probability higher than 63 per cent of providing sentiment. Therefore, investors refer to IC to justify their opinion about the future development of company's stock market prices. IC determinants are therefore more important than other elements not related to IC to justify investor opinions about the future development of company's share price.

In addition, findings show that ICD is used to justify sell or buy sentiment rather than hold. Even though there is not a statistically significant difference among sell and buy, "strong sell" and "strong buy" together account for more than 84 per cent of the total ICD messages with sentiment. These results confirm Kim and Kim's (2014, p. 712) findings that "retail investors tend to reveal extreme sentiments such as Strong Buy and Strong Sell rather than moderate sentiments such as Buy and Sell".

Finally, in IMBs investors can comment on other investors' messages and express their agreement or disagreement expressing likes and dislikes. Likes and dislikes show how much investors are involved in specific discussions. Results show that investors react more to strong sentiment (e.g. strong buy or strong sell) with higher levels of likes and dislikes. Additionally, our analysis shows that messages that contain ICD are more able to attract discussions with a

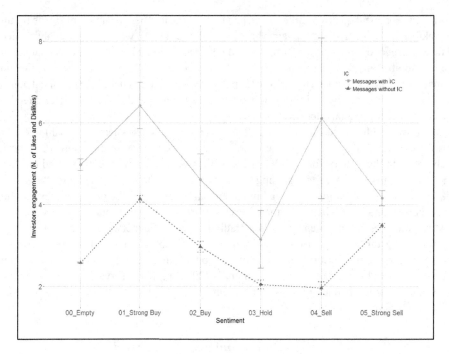

Figure 13.2   ICD and message engagement

higher level of likes or dislikes expressed by other investors independently by the sentiment expressed (buy, hold, or sell). Therefore, the results show that investors are more engaged in messages that contain ICD considering both positive sentiments (buy and strong buy), negative sentiments (sell and strong sell), or neutral sentiment (empty or hold). Figure 13.2 depicts the main findings.

Discussion

This chapter contributes to the field of IC by analysing the role of stock message boards for disclosing IC as a new form of digital communication. Following this premise, this research allows the building of some implications for ICD research.

Implication 1. Digital communication channels provide new venues to disclose IC

According to Bismuth and Tojo (2008, p. 242), "providing the market with sufficient and appropriate information about intellectual assets improves decision-making by investors and helps discipline management and boards with positive economic consequences". The study investigates an alternative form of disclosure in IMBs, not traditionally analysed in the IC literature.

Analysing alternate forms of disclosure is important because, as Dumay (2016, p. 168) outlines, there is no "evidence of listed companies reporting their IC". Furthermore, the most traditional document used in ICD research is the annual report, and this document is not designed to include ICD and is arguably used in ICD research because few, if any, IC reports exist (Dumay and Cai, 2014). Additionally, IC reports and/or disclosures that emanate from the company are often biased, focusing on good news, and thus cannot be trusted as a reliable source of ICD. Therefore, we need to uncover company unbiased sources of ICD to understand how IC information affects investor decision-making processes because annual reports are not the sole source of information for investors. IMBs offer the potential to give us company unbiased information because the posts are not created by the companies, but rather by investor participants of the IMBs

The most significant aspect of the messages posted in IMBs is that they are an example of what Dumay and Guthrie (2017) call 'involuntary disclosure', whereby the messages are created by external stakeholders who disclose information about a company. Therefore, unlike traditional ICD research, which examines company-created and voluntary ICD, we can now analyse the response to company ICD through these messages. Examining messages from market participants is important because ICD research has always espoused the benefits of ICD, but few studies have ever analysed the response to IC reporting and disclosure (Abhayawansa and Abeysekera, 2009; Abhayawansa, 2011; Abhayawansa and Guthrie, 2012).

Implication 2. IC disclosure should focus on investor IC needs rather than perpetuating existing frameworks

The results of this study show that IC is an important topic discussed in IMBs. Interestingly, specific topics discussed by investors do not match frameworks previously published in ICD research. While some elements strongly discussed in previous studies, such as employee skills, are barely discussed by investors, other elements, such as management quality, are heavily commented on. Therefore, the results of this study show the need to update current frameworks on ICD, since some topics are less discussed within the literature but are heavily considered by investors.

According to Guthrie *et al.* (2012, p. 76), reusing existing frameworks is a sign that IC research is maturing as a research field. However, when frameworks do not focus on investors' information needs, there is a divide between IC research that produces research knowledge and stakeholders that use that knowledge. Therefore, several studies claim the existence of an academic–practitioner divide (Wofford and Troilo, 2013, p. 41), with academics sometimes closed in their ivory towers (Cuozzo *et al.*, 2017, p. 9) ignoring innovation provided by digital communication channels. The results of this study provide evidence that there are new ways for companies and investors to discuss IC and that IC researchers should question existing frameworks rather than perpetuate existing models.

Implication 3. IC disclosure should focus on different company characteristics since one suit does not fit all

Our findings show that within companies that belong to different industries, ICD is differently discussed by investors. Indeed, human capital is less discussed in very dynamic sectors such as in the new economy-based companies. The need to acquire and adapt makes other IC elements, such as relational capital, more relevant to investors. Therefore, ICD frameworks cannot be drawn without considering the specific sector in which the company operates.

According to Ardley (2008, p. 533), "Scholars desire to reduce real world activity to overarching explanations has led to the simplification of theory". Understanding "how IC works" (Dumay and Garanina, 2013, p. 20) requires developing focused analysis avoiding the risk of developing "grand theories" (Dumay, 2012), suggestive for scholars but hardly useful for practitioners. As a result of this divide according to Van De Ven and Johnson (2006, p. 802), "academic research has become less useful for solving practical problems and [therefore] the gulf between theory and practice in the professions is widening". Results of this study show that ICD cannot be drawn without considering the specific industrial sector where the companies analysed work. Therefore, for researchers to adapt their ICD research strategy, as well as managers, they need to adapt their ICD models to address the specific needs of investors.

Implication 4. IC disclosures as not only roses and sunshine

Results show that ICD discussed by investors has an important impact on the sentiment provided. Interestingly, IC information is used by investors to disclose sentiment to buy, hold, or even sell. These results build on Santis and Giuliani's findings that investing in IC has both negative and positive effects and therefore ICD is not all sunshine and roses. The results show that investors are worried not only about the wealth creation myth but also with the idea of wealth destruction and intellectual risks or obligations (Santis and Giuliani, 2013, p. 213).

According to Dumay (2013, p. 7), "managers must monitor and manage intellectual liabilities to control the possible negative effects generated by IC". Results show that investors carefully discuss these topics and use ICD to justify critical positions such as sell or strong sell. Interestingly, as suggested by Dumay and Cai (2014, p. 276), managers tend to overlook negative effects and therefore understanding intellectual liabilities in traditional communication channels is difficult. Digital communication channels such as IMBs offer new opportunities to investigate these intellectual liabilities.

Conclusion

In concluding this chapter, we recall some of the reasons that motivated it. This chapter starts with the observation that digital communication channels provide new venues for ICD. The paper focuses on IMBs analysing 60,996 messages posted on two message boards in one year for the 10 most capitalized companies on the New York Stock Exchange. The high number of messages confirms that investors use new media to acquire, discuss, and share information about companies. Interestingly, discussions concentrate on different IC elements according to the sector of the company. More precisely, our results show that high-tech companies are more focused on relational capital and less on human capital. Additionally, the findings show that topics discussed by investors do not match previous frameworks used in ICD research. Indeed, some topics highly discussed by scholars are almost ignored by investors (e.g. employee training) and others almost ignored by scholars are heavily discussed by investors (e.g. management quality). Finally, the results show that messages that contain ICD more likely disclose investor's sentiment (e.g. hold, buy, or sell), showing that IC matters to investors and is often used to justify their opinion about a company's future.

The study has several implications for practitioners. First, IMBs represent an interesting discussion arena. Managers can understand market concerns about a company's IC by analysing investors' discussions. By understanding what users talk about in IMBs, managers can see if and how the information about their company's IC is received by investors. Additionally, executives can analyse the main doubts expressed by investors and therefore analyse the effectiveness of their communication. In other words, through IMB analysis, managers can understand the long- and short-term impact of ICD. Managers should consider that ICD is evolving and social media offers new ways to communicate. This moves communication from a traditional one-way top-down communication (where managers communicate things to the market) to a more complex process. Technology provides new ways to analyse text, and text mining projects can help managers in understanding investors' doubts and beliefs. Automated tools for theme extraction and semantic analysis could be added or used. These tools can help managers in making sense of investors' perceptions of IC. In this context, ICD is moving from a one-way communication approach to an interactive approach, where the doubts of the market are analysed by managers, and ICD and company communications are consequently adjusted.

Second, IMBs, like many new digital communication tools, allow users to express their engagement, posting comments to messages, and likes or dislikes. This interaction provides the opportunity to influence other investors' perceptions. Indeed, according to Roelens *et al.* (2016, p. 25), there is a "growing acceptance of the fact that people are highly influenced by information received from others". Communication in social media assumes new ways and can be affected by specific users called a "social media influencer" (Freberg *et al.*, 2011, p. 90). Managers should analyse the behaviours of these social media influencers who with their opinions can influence other behaviours.

Third, the ability for social media to influence investors has also gained the attention of regulators. For example, in the US, the Securities Exchange Commission (SEC) is monitoring social networks and has charged several brokers for posting fake information on IMBs to manipulate stock prices (SEC, 2009). However, digital communication tools provide new ways to also influence others without posting fake information. Besides the social media influencers, Zhang (2016, pp. 42–55) identifies a subgroup of investors that use IMBs called 'trolls' who repeatedly and deliberately break the etiquette by posting inflammatory, extraneous, and off-topic messages. Those users can lead discussions and contribute to shaping investors' opinions even without posting fake information. Based on our findings, we argue that regulators should extend their monitoring activity on IMBs, not only focusing on the communication of false information to prevent potential frauds (e.g. pump and dump schemes)[8] but also consider the role of social media influencers and trolls.

Fourth, the results can be used by IMB managers. Considering the high number of messages posted, investors need to find a way to filter relevant messages ignoring the noise produced by off-topic or not-company-based messages. At present, search tools of most of the IMBs are very basic. Therefore, developing new methods for filtering messages (e.g. by sentiment provided, by the number of likes or dislikes) could help investors to search for specific messages.

This research opens new research opportunities. First, this study focuses only on variables that affect ICD. New research lines could focus on the impact that IMBs have on the market, such as the relationship between ICD and market volatility or stock market prices. Second, new perspectives could be derived from event studies (e.g. Dumay and Tull, 2007). For example, new research lines could analyse how IMBs react to specific price-sensitive information delivered to the market. Third, the role of users could be deepened to include interviews to understand their motivation to post information and their actual ability to influence market prices. Fourth, IMBs are only one of the new social media tools available in the market. For example, micro-blogging using Twitter is another example of a social media tool that can be considered to expand upon, and compare with, the findings of this study.

To conclude this chapter, it is important to point out that this study has its limitations. First, considering the high number of messages, this study focuses only on ten companies for one year. Several extraordinary political and catastrophic events happened during the period of analysis (e.g. the Greek debt crisis, the immigrant crisis, and other mass media events), as well as company related events (e.g. the launch of new products for one company), which could have influenced the results of the analysis. Additionally, subjectivity in applying manual content analysis should be considered. To confirm these results, this study should be repeated in the future. Additionally, this study focuses on companies listed on the New York Stock Exchange with a high capitalization, a dimension that could affect the results, and thus we could also extend this study to smaller companies, and companies listed in different countries.

Notes

1 See www.thelion.com/ (accessed 19 April 2016).
2 See http://hotcopper.com.au/postview (accessed 19 April 2016).
3 See www.trade2win.com/boards/ (accessed 19 April 2016).
4 See, for example, http://finance.yahoo.com/mb/YHOO/ (accessed 19 April 2016).
5 See http://ragingbull.com/ (accessed 19 April 2016).
6 Since the beginning of this study in 2015, TheLion has introduced new features to the platform. TheLion now collects messages from all other IMBs, becoming a Board of Boards (Zhang, 2016). At the time of the last access on 24 April 2016 the old functions were still available under the menu Forum on the platform. Results discussed in this chapter refer to the old version of the platform.
7 See: www.businessdictionary.com/definition/new-economy.html (accessed 22 August 2016).
8 A pump and dump scheme works by pumping the market with false information to dump it when the maximum price is reached (Zhang, 2016).

References

Abdolmohammadi, M. J. (2005), "Intellectual capital disclosure and market capitalization", *Journal of Intellectual Capital*, Vol. 6, No. 3, pp. 397–416.

Abeysekera, I. (2006), "The project of intellectual capital disclosure: Researching the research", *Journal of Intellectual Capital*, Vol. 7, No. 1, pp. 61–75.

Abhayawansa, S. (2011), "A methodology for investigating intellectual capital information in analyst reports", *Journal of Intellectual Capital*, Vol. 12, No. 3, pp. 446–476.

Abhayawansa, S. and Abeysekera, I. (2009), "Intellectual capital disclosure from sell-side analyst perspective", *Journal of Intellectual Capital*, Vol. 10, No. 2, pp. 294–306.

Abhayawansa, S. and Guthrie, J. (2012), "Intellectual capital information and stock recommendations: Impression management?", *Journal of Intellectual Capital*, Vol. 13, No. 3, pp. 398–415.

Abhayawansa, S. and Guthrie, J. (2014), "Importance of intellectual capital information: A study of Australian analyst reports", *Australian Accounting Review*, Vol. 24, No. 1, pp. 66–83.

Ardley, B. (2008), "A case of mistaken identity: Theory, practice and the marketing textbook", *European Business Review*, Vol. 20, No. 6, pp. 533–546.

Bellora, L. and Guenther, T. W. (2013), "Drivers of innovation capital disclosure in intellectual capital statements: Evidence from Europe", *The British Accounting Review*, Vol. 45, No. 4, pp. 255-270.

Berger, J. and Milkman, K. L. (2012), "What makes online content viral?", *Journal of Marketing Research*, Vol. 49, No. 2, pp. 192–205.

Bismuth, A. and Tojo, Y. (2008), "Creating value from intellectual assets", *Journal of Intellectual Capital*, Vol. 9, No. 2, pp. 228–245.

Carey, D. (2000), "Lessons from master acquirers: A CEO roundtable on making mergers succeed", *Harvard Business Review*, Vol. 78, No. 3, pp. 145–154.

Crane, L. (2012), "Trust me, I'm an expert: Identity construction and knowledge sharing", *Journal of Knowledge Management*, Vol. 16, No. 3, pp. 448–460.

Cuozzo, B., Dumay, J., Palmaccio, M., and Lombardi, R. (2017), "Intellectual capital disclosure: A structured literature review", *Journal of Intellectual Capital*, Vol. 18, No. 1, pp. 9–28.

Curado, C., Henriques, L., and Bontis, N. (2011), "Intellectual capital disclosure payback", *Management Decision*, Vol. 49, No. 7, pp. 1080–1098.

Das, S. R. and Chen, M. Y. (2007), "Yahoo! for Amazon: Sentiment extraction from small talk on the web", *Management Science*, Vol. 53, No. 9, pp. 1375–1388.

Dumay, J. (2012), "Grand theories as barriers to using IC concepts", *Journal of Intellectual Capital*, Vol. 13, No. 1, pp. 4–15.

Dumay, J. (2013), "The third stage of IC: Towards a new IC future and beyond", *Journal of Intellectual Capital*, Vol. 14, No. 1, pp. 5–9.

Dumay, J. (2016), "A critical reflection on the future of intellectual capital: From reporting to disclosure", *Journal of Intellectual Capital*, Vol. 17, No. 1, pp. 168–184.

Dumay, J. and Cai, L. (2014), "A review and critique of content analysis as a methodology for inquiring into IC disclosure", *Journal of Intellectual Capital*, Vol. 15, No. 2, pp. 264–290.

Dumay, J. and Garanina, T. (2013), "Intellectual capital research: A critical examination of the third stage", *Journal of Intellectual Capital*, Vol. 14, No. 1, pp. 10–25.

Dumay, J. and Guthrie, J. (2017), "Involuntary disclosure of intellectual capital: Is it relevant?", *Journal of Intellectual Capital*, Vol. 18, No. 1, pp. 29–44.

Dumay, J. and Tull, J. A. (2007), "Intellectual capital disclosure and price-sensitive Australian Stock Exchange announcements", *Journal of Intellectual Capital*, Vol. 8, No. 2, pp. 236–255.

Flöstrand, P. (2006), "The sell side: Observations on intellectual capital indicators", *Journal of Intellectual Capital*, Vol. 7, No. 4, pp. 457–473.

Freberg, K., Graham, K., McGaughey, K., and Freberg, L. A. (2011), "Who are the social media influencers? A study of public perceptions of personality", *Public Relations Review*, Vol. 37, No. 1, pp. 90–92.

Geis, G. T. (2015), *Semi-Organic Growth: Tactics and Strategies Behind Google's Success*, Wiley, London.

Goebel, V. (2015), "Is the literature on content analysis of intellectual capital reporting heading towards a dead end?", *Journal of Intellectual Capital*, Vol. 16, No. 3, pp. 681–699.

Guthrie, J., Ricceri, F., and Dumay, J. (2012), "Reflections and projections: A decade of intellectual capital accounting research", *The British Accounting Review*, Vol. 44, No. 2, pp. 68–82.

Holland, J. (2003), "Intellectual capital and the capital market. Organisation and competence", *Accounting, Auditing & Accountability Journal*, Vol. 16, No. 1, pp. 39–48.

Jones, L. A. (2006), "Have internet message boards changed market behavior?", *Info*, Vol. 8, No. 5, pp. 67–76.

Kim, S.-H. and Kim, D. (2014), "Investor sentiment from internet message postings and the predictability of stock returns", *Journal of Economic Behavior & Organization*, Vol. 107, pp. 708–729.

Krippendorff, K. (2013), *Content Analysis. An Introduction to Its Methodology*, Sage Publications, Thousand Oaks, CA.

Lardo, A., Dumay, J., Trequattrini, R., and Russo, G. (2017), "Social media networks as drivers for intellectual capital disclosure. Evidence from professional football clubs", *Journal of Intellectual Capital*, Vol. 18, No. 1, pp. 63–80.

Lipiäinen, H. S. M., Karjaluoto, H. E., and Nevalainen, M. (2014), "Digital channels in the internal communication of a multinational corporation", *Corporate Communications: An International Journal*, Vol. 19, No. 3, pp. 275–286.

Liu, R. and Kop, A. E. (2015), "The usege of social media in new product development process", in Hajli, N. (Ed.), *Handbook of Research on Integrating Social Media into Strategic Marketing*, IGI Global, New York, pp. 120–135.

Lohr, S. (2001, 8 October), "The new meaning of new economy", *New York Times*, pp. 1–5.

Lund, M. and Nielsen, C. (2017), "Making intellectual capital matter to the investment community", in Guthrie, J., Dumay, J., Ricceri, F., and Nielsen, C. (Eds), *The Routledge Companion to Intellectual Capital*, Routledge, London, pp. 435–449.

Nielsen, C., Rimmel, G., and Yosano, T. (2015), "Outperforming markets: IC and the long-term performance of Japanese IPOs", *Accounting Forum*, Vol. 39, No. 2, pp. 83–96.

Ojala, M. (2006), "Finance portals and their impact on information professionals", *The Dollar Sign*, pp. 42–44.

Pisano, S., Lepore, L., and Lamboglia, R. (2017), "Corporate disclosure of human capital via LinkedIn and ownership structure: An empirical analysis of European companies", *Journal of Intellectual Capital*, Vol. 18, No. 1, pp. 102–127.

Roelens, I., Baecke, P., and Benoit, D. F. (2016), "Identifying influencers in a social network: The value of real referral data", *Decision Support Systems*, Elsevier B.V., Vol. 91, pp. 25–36.

Sabherwal, S., Sarkar, S. K., and Zhang, Y. (2011), "Do internet stock message boards influence trading? Evidence from heavily discussed stocks with no fundamental news", *Journal of Business Finance and Accounting*, Vol. 38, No. 9–10, pp. 1209–1237.

Sakakibara, S., Hansson, B., Yosano, T., and Kozumi, H. (2010), "Analysts' perceptions of intellectual capital information", *Australian Accounting Review*, Vol. 20, No. 3, pp. 274–285.

Santis, F. De and Giuliani, M. (2013), "A look on the other side: Investigating intellectual liabilities", *Journal of Intellectual Capital*, Vol. 14, No. 2, pp. 212–226.

Schaper, S., Nielsen, C. and Roslender, R. (2017), "Moving from irrelevant intellectual capital (IC) reporting to value-relevant IC disclosures: Key learning points from the Danish experience", *Journal of Intellectual Capital*, Vol. 18 No. 1, pp. 81–101.

SEC (2009), "SEC charges New York broker for manipulating stock prices through fake press releases and internet postings", *Press Release*.

Van De Ven, A. H. and Johnson, P. E. (2006), "Knowledge for theory and practice", *Academy of Management Review*, Vol. 31, No. 4, pp. 802–821.

Wofford, L. and Troilo, M. (2013), "The academic-professional divide: Generating useful research and moving it to practice", *Journal of Property Investment & Finance*, Vol. 31, No. 1, pp. 41–52.

Zhang, Y. (2016), *Stock Message Boards. A Quantitative Approach to Measuring Investor Sentiment*, Palgrave Macmillan, New York.

14

ENABLING RELATIONAL CAPITAL THROUGH CUSTOMER PERFORMANCE MEASUREMENT PRACTICES

A study of not-for-profit organizations

Suresh Cuganesan

Introduction

The not-for-profit (NFP) sector is an important and growing component of modern economies. In the US, those NFPs that collect more than $25,000 in annual receipts reported collectively a total of $1.9 trillion in revenue and $4.3 trillion in assets (Wing *et al.*, 2009). Worldwide the NFP sector represents approximately 10 per cent of non-agricultural employment in developed economies and even larger proportions in developing regions (United Nations, 2003). Recent analysis also identifies significant growth trends, with the NFP sector outgrowing the for-profit sector in the US during 2000–2010 (Salamon *et al.*, 2012), and it is expected to grow by 4.1 per cent per annum over the five years to 2015–16 in Australia to reach $124.25 billion by the end of the period (Wilson, 2010).

While the growth projections for the NFP sector are significant, so too are the challenges it faces. In particular, many NFPs face financial sustainability problems, with forces of change and competition threatening their viability. Reduced government funding and more competition for the philanthropy dollar has created an imperative to seek external funding sources, both to diversify sources of revenue and seek financial sustainability (Dees, 1998). Meanwhile profit-oriented organizations increasingly participate and compete in sectors traditionally dominated by NFPs (Salamon *et al.*, 2012). This has led many NFPs to sell services or goods through 'earned income' activities that compete with for-profit businesses in attempting to generate commercial sources of revenue (Bolton and Mehran, 2006).

Building and managing relational capital is therefore critical for NFPs. In particular, identifying those customers of earned income activities that represent the best avenues to financial sustainability, prioritizing these, and managing them effectively are important activities if entrepreneurial NFPs are to be successful in enhancing their financial sustainability (Peredo and McLean, 2006; Weerawardena *et al.*, 2010). In this regard, measuring customer performance offers significant benefit through providing information for planning and resource allocation purposes, as well as for monitoring and identifying when corrective action is required (Guilding and McManus, 2002). Indeed, prior research on customer performance measurement has shown that its use can be positive for performance (O'Connor and Cheung, 2007). However, research to date on customer performance measurement practices has focused exclusively on the for-profit sector, overlooking the significance of the NFP sector and the differences between for-profit and NFP organizations. Hence this study examines customer performance measurement practices in NFPs attempting to generate commercial sources of revenue through earned income activities.

In particular, the study examines the extent to which the market and relational orientation influences the use of customer performance measurement practices. Prior research establishes not only the importance of market orientation and the utilization of market intelligence as a means of competing for commercial sources of revenue (Kohli and Jaworski, 1990) but also its influence on some customer performance measurement approaches (Guilding and McManus, 2002). However, research to date has yet to examine whether this finding applies to the NFP sector, with some research suggesting against the adoption of formal measurement approaches (Parker, 2001, 2002). Also, quite distinct to market orientation is the continued and widespread adoption of relational approaches to managing customers that emphasize customization and long-term perspectives (Payne and Frow, 2005; Plakoyiannaki *et al.*, 2008). Despite this, accounting research to date has not explored the influences of relational orientation on customer performance measurement practices. Consequently, "the research investigating the links between customer-focused strategies and performance measures is very limited" (Hyvonen, 2007, p. 345).

The study also examines the effects of customer performance measurement practices on the NFP organization in terms of impacts on customers receiving earned income goods and services, social outcomes, and indicators of financial sustainability. The adoption of management approaches that are more commercial in nature in NFPs has been fiercely debated, with concerns over whether their effects are likely to have negative impacts on the generation of social value (Kong, 2008). Despite this, the NFPs' need to pursue financial self-sufficiency is broadly acknowledged (LeRoux, 2009). Together, these attributes suggest uncertainty around the effects of customer performance measurement practices for the achievement of social goals, their interactions with recipients of their services, and their financial sustainability in the NFP context.

The influences and effects of customer performance measurement practices

The importance of customers to business success is widely recognized (refer to Peters and Waterman, 1982), most recently evolving into a concern with how organizations can structure themselves horizontally to deliver greater customer value (Chenhall, 2008). Concurrently, measurement practices relating to customers have increased in importance (Cuganesan, 2008; Vaivio, 1999). Customer performance measurement practices comprise the measurement of value provided to customers through indicators such as customer satisfaction, customer retention, and complaints, as well as the measurement of value extracted from customers through techniques such as customer profitability analysis and customer lifetime valuation (Boyce, 2000). This study examines both of these dimensions to measuring customer performance. The sub-sections below review literature that examines influences on their use and their effects.

Influences on use of customer performance measurement

Market orientation

Market orientation is one organizational characteristic that is proposed as influencing customer performance measurement (Guilding and McManus, 2002). Market orientation comprises the approach to generating, disseminating, and responding to market intelligence (Kohli and Jaworski, 1990). It involves collecting and analysing information about customers, the industry, and competitive forces through both formal and informal means (Wood *et al.*, 2000).

While market orientation is broader in the external objects on which it focuses, comprising also consideration of industry dynamics and competitor actions, market oriented organizations are expected to engage in greater marketing expenditure and demand information about customers (Slater and Narver, 1994; Guilding and McManus, 2002). Prior research has found that amongst private-sector organizations, market orientation influences the use of customer performance measurement. Specifically, Guilding and McManus (2002) found that the use and perceived merit of practices that measure the value extracted from customers – practices they label 'customer accounting' – is higher in firms with high market orientation than in those with low market orientation. Furthermore, Cadez and Guilding (2008) also found a positive association between market orientation and strategic management accounting techniques, one of which includes the measurement of value extracted from customers.

Although prior research indicates that market orientation is positively associated with use of customer performance measurement, the NFP context problematizes this link. Given the preference for other than formal modes of managing in NFPs (as noted in the previous section), informal approaches to collecting and analysing information may occur in market oriented NFPs. NFPs may also lack the skill-sets and capabilities to engage in formal measurement practices (Dees, 1998), such as customer performance measurement, even if they desire to do so. Hence, this chapter examines the following null hypothesis:

H1: The extent of market orientation of the NFP is not associated with the (a) measurement of value provided to customers or (b) the measurement of value extracted from customers.

Relational orientation

Over time, marketing scholars have noted a shift in how firms interact with their customers, moving from what has been termed a transactional orientation to a relational orientation, or engaging in relationship marketing approaches. Adopting a relational orientation and engaging in relational rather than arms-length transactional exchanges is widely suggested in business research as a means to enhance organizational profitability (Boulding *et al.*, 2005). It has also been prescribed for NFPs as a means of securing financial sustainability (Weerawardena *et al.*, 2010).

In contrast to market orientation, which denotes an external focus, a relational orientation comprises decisions to focus on key customers, understand their specific needs, and engage in the delivery of customized products and services (Payne and Frow, 2005; Plakoyiannaki *et al.*, 2008). It also includes the adoption of a long-term perspective in customer interactions, where the goods or service provider shifts from an episodic transactional perspective to a forward-looking and relationship focus (Ganesan, 1994; Boulding *et al.*, 2005). These aspects of customization and making relationship specific investments based on understanding individualized needs as well as the adoption of long-term thinking characterize relational orientation as a particular value creation approach (Srivastava *et al.*, 1999; Pillai and Sharma, 2003).

The implication of these propositions is that the adoption of a relational orientation creates an environment and demand for customer performance measurement practices. Adoption of this approach requires decisions about on which customers to focus and how to manage the cost-benefits of customization across the life of the relationship. Measurement of value provided to, and extracted from, customers is important here. Supporting these arguments, the accounting literature acknowledges the possibility of linkages between relational approaches to managing customers and measurement of value from customers (Guilding and McManus, 2002). However, these have rarely been examined. Adding further complexity, studies of how accounting is used to manage customers have documented approaches to managing customers grounded in qualitative information that competes with quantitative measurement practices (see Vaivio, 1999; Cuganesan, 2008). The previously mentioned particularities of the NFP context (see discussion on Hypothesis 1) also apply in relation to whether a formal or informal approach to assessing value is preferred or if the capabilities exist for applying customer performance measurement as part of a relational approach. Given this, the following null hypothesis is tested:

H2: The extent of relational orientation of the NFP is not associated with the (a) measurement of value provided to customers or (b) the measurement of value extracted from customers.

In addition to the above influences on customer performance measurement, NFP size needs to be accounted for. Cadez and Guilding (2008) found that organizational size is associated significantly with SMA use (including the measurement of value from customers). The notion that larger organizations adopt more sophisticated management accounting techniques is also well established through prior research (Chenhall, 2003). Hence, the impact of organizational size will be controlled for in the analysis of results.

Performance effects

Numerous arguments can be mounted for the positive impacts of customer performance measurement practices on customer and financial performance. High value customers may respond to the extra and targeted attention and become more satisfied and loyal. Also, targeted marketing and relationship building efforts can shift unprofitable relationships into becoming more profitable. For example, customers may be encouraged to modify their behaviour or discontinue the relationship with the organization. Overall, the analysis that can be facilitated through customer performance measurement can enable organizations to attain a competitive advantage in the market (Foster *et al.*, 1996). This is consistent with the notion that better information leads to more effective managerial decisions, which leads to greater organizational performance (Baines and Langfield-Smith, 2003; Chenhall, 2003).

Empirical support also exists for the positive performance consequences of customer performance measurement. O'Connor and Cheung (2007) found that banks in Hong Kong measuring the profitability and value of customers – that is, measuring the value extracted from customers – improved their return-on-asset performance when they were early product adopters. Similarly, Cadez and Guilding (2008) found that greater strategic management accounting use (of which customer profit and lifetime value measurement practices is one dimension) is positively associated with performance, comprising both non-financial (such as customer satisfaction, product quality, new product development, market share) and financial dimensions (return on investment, margin on sales). These findings specific to customer performance measurement are supported by a broader literature investigating non-financial performance measurement. These studies typically find positive performance effects in firms from the use of non-financial measures, including indicators that assess the value provided to customers (Ittner and Larcker, 1995; Said *et al.*, 2003).

In summary, studies of for-profit organizations find that the use of customer performance measurement, whether measuring value provided to or value extracted from customers, has positive effects for performance. These include enhancements to non-financial performance in terms of product and service delivery processes and their impact on customers, as well as for financial performance in terms of profits and margins.

Drawing parallels with the NFP context, it can be argued that the use of customer performance measurement will have positive effects for non-financial performance dimensions, such as for processes that achieve social outcomes as well as impact recipients of earned income activities, and financial sustainability through the generation of revenues and cash. However, given the previously noted concerns about the applicability of such techniques in the NFP context (Chetkovich and Frumkin, 2003; Kong, 2008), it is also possible that customer performance measurement could have negative effects for NFP performance (Dees, 1998; Peredo and McLean, 2006). Indeed, even in the broader for-profit studies that have occurred to date examining accounting and performance generally, Cadez and Guilding (2008, p. 843) observed "[prior] studies' mixed outcomes" although there is a tendency for findings of a positive relationship. As such, this chapter examines the non-financial performance (comprising social outcomes and impact on customers of earned income activities) and financial sustainability effects of customer performance measurement techniques through the following null hypotheses:

H3: The extent of measurement of value provided to customers is not associated with NFP (a) non-financial performance and (b) financial sustainability.

H4: The extent of measurement of value extracted from customers is not associated with NFP (a) non-financial performance and (b) financial sustainability.

In examining the performance effects of customer performance measurement practices it is important to acknowledge the direct effects that market orientation and relational orientation may have for performance. Market orientation has been associated with business profitability (Kohli and Jaworski, 1990; Narver and Slater, 1990) and non-financial performance dimensions, such as capacity utilization, customer satisfaction, market share, and product development and quality (Cadez and Guilding, 2008). Empirical evidence exists of market orientation's positive association with performance in an NFP context, albeit limited to hospital settings only (see Wood *et al.*, 2000). Similarly, the adoption of relational orientation is prescribed as a means of improving customer interactions and both non-financial and financial performance. There is also empirical evidence that demonstrates that the adoption of a relational orientation has positive effects on firm performance, such as customer satisfaction, customer retention, and profitability (Boulding *et al.*, 2005). Hence the following directional hypotheses are examined:

H5: The extent of market orientation of the NFP is positively associated with NFP (a) non-financial performance and (b) financial sustainability.

H6: The extent of relational orientation of the NFP is positively associated with NFP (a) non-financial performance and (b) financial sustainability.

Turning to financial performance, the logic that non-financial performance is positively associated with financial performance underpins popular concepts and frameworks such as the service-profit-chain (Heskett *et al.*, 1997) and the balanced scorecard (Kaplan and Norton, 1992, 2004). Studies indicate the presence of positive relationships between customer and financial performance, although the empirical evidence is mixed. Smith and Wright (2004) found customer loyalty explains relative revenue growth, profitability, and competitive advantage in the personal computer industry, while Malina *et al.* (2007) found an absence of causal relationships in their case study of a Fortune 500 company. Bryant *et al.* (2004), in a study of 125 firms across multiple years, found positive relationships between customer satisfaction and financial performance, but only when a mixed performance measurement system is used. Earlier studies also suggest a contingent relationship. Ittner and Larcker (1998) found positive relationships between customer measures, such as satisfaction and retention, and financial measures, such as revenue and revenue growth, although these do not extend across all firms studied. Links between customer satisfaction and firm value likewise do not extend across the entirety of their sample. Similarly, mixed evidence for the financial performance effects of customer satisfaction is also found by Banker *et al.* (2000).

Adding further complexity to the relationship that we might expect in NFP settings, concerns exist that financial sustainability occurs at the expense of achieving the NFP entity's mission and social objectives, all of which suggest a negative relationship. Yet no accounting research on the relationships between non-financial and financial performance in the NFP context has been done. Based on the mixed evidence about the relationship between non-financial and financial performance in private-sector contexts and unclear expectations as to how this is likely to manifest in NFP settings, the following null hypothesis is tested:

H7: NFP non-financial performance is not associated with NFP financial sustainability.

Research method

NFP setting: disability enterprises

To test the hypothesis developed, a particular sector of NFPs was chosen, comprising disability enterprises in Australia. Australian disability enterprises (ADEs) perform an important social function, providing supported employment services for people with disability who are unable to obtain work in the open labour market or who need significant ongoing support in order to obtain and retain gainful employment. The core business of ADEs is described as "helping people with disability to take part in quality, appropriately paid employment, develop their capabilities and promote their participation in community life" (Commonwealth of Australia, 2008, p. 61). This employment is provided through ADEs' operations in commercial enterprise, delivering services in areas such as packaging, horticulture, animal husbandry, laundry, catering, and woodwork.

Economic indicators reveal that the provision of social assistance services such as employment services is not only a sizeable component of the NFP sector (United Nations, 2006; Commonwealth of Australia, 2009) but also that this NFP sub-sector has experienced significant competition from for-profit firms (Kong, 2008; Salamon *et al.*, 2012). Within Australia, government funding to ADEs to offset the costs of providing supported employment has reduced in recent times (National Disability Services Australia, 2010).

Customer relationships can enhance or detract from an ADE's financial sustainability in terms of whether it generates funds through earned income activities that can be reinvested in managing and developing the organization. Importantly, these social and financial sustainability objectives can conflict from time to time. ADEs not only have to appropriately manage customer relationships in order to achieve their social goal of providing supported employment services, but need to do so at sufficient profit to ensure that their economic independence and financial sustainability are not threatened. Managing this tension arguably requires information about the value that is provided to, and generated from, customer relationships, and customer performance measurement practices offer potential benefit in this regard. Hence the ADEs represent an appropriate setting to investigate how customer performance measurement practices operate in NFP organizations attempting to become more focused on their managing of customer relationships.

Interview and survey sample

A series of interviews was conducted with selected ADEs as part of familiarizing the researcher with the NFP and ADE research context, and to obtain an understanding of the issues they faced in managing and measuring customer relationships. Selection of ADEs for interview occurred on the basis of size and location. Discussions with the national industry association for ADEs (National Disability Services Australia) identified these criteria as providing a sufficiently diverse perspective on the issues faced by the industry in relation to managing and measuring customer relationships.

Six interviews were held with CEOs and General Managers in charge of ADEs of differing characteristics. Table 14.1 presents an overview of the size and nature of these organizations. Interview themes comprised: (1) a discussion of the objectives of the ADE and the main challenges faced in achieving these; (2) the approach taken by the ADE to managing its customer relationships; (3) the measurement of customer relationships that the ADE undertook, if any; and (4) the effects/impacts of the approach taken to managing and measuring customer relationships. Two researchers independently coded the interview data with a particular focus on the extent to which the approaches evidenced exhibited market orientation and/or relational orientation, the types of customer performance measures that were used, and the effects of approaches and measurement practices for the ADE in question.

Table 14.1 Overview of interviewed ADEs

Organization (interviewee)	Nature of business
ADE 1 (CEO)	Small regional ADE operating exclusively in rural and regional areas. Providing services such as document shredding, car cleaning, lawn and gardening services, amongst others
ADE 2 (General Manager)	Large metropolitan ADE specializing in the manufacture of light wooden items/furniture, assembly services, and contract packing. Employs approximately 150 people with disability
ADE 3 (CEO and General Manager)	Small metropolitan ADE offering mail fulfilment, light wooden items/furniture manufacture, packaging, assembly services
ADE 4 (CEO)	Medium-sized ADE providing cleaning, catering, document shredding, packaging and assembly, and gardening services
ADE 5 (CEO)	Medium-sized ADE providing assembly, packaging, collating and labelling services
ADE 6 (General Manager)	Large ADE operating in predominantly regional locations. Operates catering, packaging, landcare, hospitality, and industrial labour services

The quantitative data for this study was collected via an electronic survey. Discussions were held with National Disability Services Australia to pilot test the survey and identify the most suitable respondents. Based on these, the survey was targeted at either the CEO of the organization or the General Manager most responsible for managing customer relationships. These discussions also indicated that some ADEs employed dedicated business managers, whose main responsibility was managing customers. In these cases, the business manager was targeted as the desired survey respondent.

Information about the survey was disseminated via National Disability Services Australia. One week later, an email containing a link to the survey webpage was emailed to the 177 ADEs on the membership list of National Disability Services. Given that a single ADE typically operates multiple disability outlets, this represented a sizeable coverage of the ADE population (see Commonwealth of Australia (2009), which identifies approximately 362 outlets in Australia). A reminder email also containing the survey link was subsequently sent to the membership list.

Eighty responses were initially received for a response rate of 45 per cent. Examining responses indicated 15 responses with multiple missing values (where respondents ticked a 'Don't know/Not Applicable' response) on items relating to independent or dependent variables. These were excluded from further analysis. For the remainder of the sample, the pattern of missing data was examined using the Little's missing completely at random (MCAR) test. The pattern of missing values was found not to depend on the values of observed data (χ^2 = 295.059, d.f. = 290, Sig. = 0.407), and individual missing values were replaced with mean values for subsequent analysis. This procedure resulted in 65 usable responses for a final response rate of 37 per cent.

To test for possible non-response bias, non-parametric tests of differences in the responses provided by early and late survey respondents were conducted. This comprised testing both the first and last 25 per cent and the first and last 33 per cent respectively. In addition, responses between the 15 cases excluded and the 65 that were included were also compared. In all cases, no significant differences ($p < 0.05$) were obtained for either dependent or independent variable items. Table 14.2 presents the demographics of the final sample.

Table 14.2 Sample demographics

Category	Number of responses [% of responses]
Panel A: Respondent type	
CEO	25 (39%)
General Manager	24 (37%)
Director	1 (2%)
Business Manager	15 (23%)
Panel B: Revenue size	
> $500,000	44 (68%)
$350,000–$500,000	8 (12%)
$200,000–$349,999	7 (11%)
$100,000–$199,999	3 (5%)
< $100,000	3 (5%)
Panel C: Number of management and support staff	
> 40	15 (23%)
11–40	24 (37%)
6–10	15 (23%)
< 6	11 (17%)

$N = 65$

Variable measurement

Survey items are presented in Appendix A. All questions utilized a seven-point Likert scale with an additional option for a 'Don't know/Not Applicable' response. Respondents were asked about the extent of their agreement with statements about market and relational orientation. Questions relating to customer performance measurement asked about the extent of measurement of value provided to customers and value extracted from customers, while performance related questions solicited self-reported performance relative to peers.

Market orientation was measured using the four-item market orientation scale used by Guilding and McManus (2002) and Cadez and Guilding (2008). Discussions with National Disability Services Australia representatives and interviews indicated that these items would be interpreted appropriately.

Based on a review of marketing literature, a scale for relational orientation was developed using items from two sources. First, items developed by Hong-Kit *et al.* (2005) to assess the extent to which organizations engage in 'Focusing on Key Customers' and 'Managing (Customer) Knowledge' were selected. These provided items linked to the customization aspect of a relational orientation. The Hong-Kit *et al.* (2005) instrument was also oriented towards the business-to-business context, which matched the ADE setting given the focus of these organizations on servicing other businesses. Second, given that a significant aspect of relational orientation involves shifting from a transactional to a long-term relational approach, items from the long-term relationship orientation scale of Ganesan (1994) were also incorporated. The combined set of items was reviewed in discussions with National Disability Services Australia representatives. This indicated that two items from the Hong-Kit *et al.* (2005) scale pertaining to establishing dedicated channels for two-way dialogue with customers were problematic on the grounds of their lack of applicability and impaired interpretability in the ADE setting. One item from the Ganesan (1994) long-term relationship orientation scale was also dropped as it was based on the presumption that profit was the sole outcome to be sought from long-term relationships. Consequently, it was considered to be inappropriate for the NFP context. The remaining relational orientation scale thus comprised six items from the Hong-Kit *et al.* (2005) instrument and three items from the Ganesan (1994) scale.

Measuring value provided to the customer comprises non-financial indicators that assess how the organization is performing in providing goods or services to customers. A diverse range of potential indicators has been suggested by researchers, consultants, and organizations. Potential items were sourced by comparing and aggregating customer performance measurement lists from Edvinsson and Malone (1997), Kaplan and Norton (1996), and Niven (2002). These were then reduced through the removal of duplicate or overlapping indicators and further rationalized through discussions with National Disability Services Australia and ADE interviews in terms of which indicators would best represent the spectrum of measurement practices. The result was a scale comprising four items.

A scale for the measurement of value extracted from customers was initially sourced from Guilding and McManus (2002), given their focus on measuring customer profitability and lifetime value. Here, discussions with industry participants indicated that the more sophisticated practices, such as lifetime customer profitability analysis, valuation of customers, or customer groups as assets, were not used in the industry. Also, the holistic notion of 'customer accounting' was identified as an item that respondents would find difficult to interpret. Hence, these items were dropped. However, measuring the revenue extracted from individual customers through earned income activities was identified as a practice that would vary across the industry as a number of ADEs would focus on measuring only total earned income revenue and/or revenue by earned income activity. As this indicator represents value extracted from customers, it was added to the scale.

For organizational performance, respondents were asked to rate the performance of their organization relative to peers, following a procedure similar to Cadez and Guilding (2008). Specific items relating to the NFP context were drawn from Parsons (2003, 2007). These comprised non-financial performance dimensions, such as customer satisfaction and achievement of mission, and financial sustainability indicators, such as diverse revenue sources and operating margins. The remaining items for each of the non-financial performance and financial sustainability categories were identified in workshops and pilot testing of the survey with representatives from National Disability Services Australia.[1]

Other questions in the survey elicited responses on the participant's position in the organization, the size of the organization in terms of the amount of revenue earned from customer relationships, and the number of employees in managerial and support/administrative positions.

Data analysis

An analysis was conducted of the internal reliability of the scale items given that these had been constructed or adapted for each construct for the purposes of the study (with the exception of market orientation). An exploratory factor analysis using principal component analysis and oblique rotation was conducted, and Cronbach alphas were calculated for all constructs using IBM SPSS Statistics 20.[2] The results of the factor analysis are presented in Table 14.3.

As indicated in Table 14.3, single factor solutions were obtained for all constructs with all loadings well in excess of the minimum 0.5 threshold (Hulland, 1999). This also included the

Table 14.3 Internal reliability tests: factor analysis and Cronbach alphas

Construct and item	Dimension I
Market orientation	Eigenvalue = 2.687; % of variance = 67.16%; α= 0.831
MO Item 1	.755
MO Item 2	.874
MO Item 3	.811
MO Item 4	.833
Relational orientation	Eigenvalue = 6.480; % of variance = 72.00%; α= 0.949
RO Item 1	0.855
RO Item 2	0.843
RO Item 3	0.886
RO Item 4	0.851
RO Item 5	0.822
RO Item 6	0.882
RO Item 7	0.868
RO Item 8	0.882
RO Item 9	0.739
Measuring value to customers	Eigenvalue = 2.680; % of variance = 66.99%; α= 0.831
MVTC Item 1	0.761
MVTC Item 2	0.875
MVTC Item 3	0.812
MVTC Item 4	0.823
Measuring value from customers	Eigenvalue = 2.126; % of variance = 70.88%; α= 0.793
MVFC Item 1	0.829
MVFC Item 2	0.880
MVFC Item 3	0.816

Non-financial performance	*Eigenvalue = 2.290; % of variance = 76.33%; α= 0.842*
NFinP Item 1	0.885
NFinP Item 2	0.924
NFinP Item 3	0.807

Financial sustainability	*Eigenvalue = 2.052; % of variance = 68.40%; α= 0.760*
FS Item 1	0.866
FS Item 2	0.739
FS Item 3	0.869

Notes: MO = Market Orientation. RO= Relational Orientation. MVTC = Measuring Value to Customers. MVFC=Measuring Value from Customers. NFinP=Non-financial Performance. FS=Financial Sustainability.

relational orientation construct, where items related to customization and long-term perspectives were combined for the purposes of the factor analysis. All single factor solutions achieved Cronbach alphas of 0.760 or greater, exceeding the 0.70 threshold that is prescribed for acceptable internal reliability (Nunnally, 1981). Thus the latent variables examined are considered to be internally consistent and reliable.

The remainder of the analysis is conducted using the partial least squares (PLS) technique for structural equation modelling using SmartPLS 2.0 (Ringle *et al.*, 2005). The PLS approach has been used in recent accounting studies, including those investigating the impact of information systems (Chapman and Kihn, 2009) and performance measurement systems (Chenhall, 2005; Hall, 2008). The use of PLS is appropriate for this study given that it does not require large sample sizes as well as making minimal data assumptions (Wold, 1980; Chin, 1998). As such, PLS is used to test the hypotheses outlined in this study.

The PLS approach consists of both a measurement model and a structural model and simultaneously estimates these. The measurement model specifies relations between observed values on survey items and the latent constructs that they represent. The structural model specifies the relations between the latent constructs. Both models are usually analysed sequentially, with the measurement model reliability and validity assessed first before turning attention to hypothesis testing and the relationships between latent constructs (Hulland, 1999). In this section, the measurement model is assessed while the next section presents the results of estimating the structural model.

Factor loadings and cross-loadings were initially examined. Table 14.4 presents the factor loading results of the PLS measurement model. In terms of the relationships between survey items and the latent variables, all factor loadings were high with the exception of Financial Sustainability Item 2 – Diverse Revenue Sources. This was 0.687, but is well above the 0.50 threshold (Hulland, 1999) and can be considered acceptable for the purposes of the analysis. Comparing cross-loadings also shows sufficient differences between an item loading onto its own construct vis-à-vis another latent variable. All differences exceeded 0.25 with the exception of Measuring Value to Customers Item 1 – Acquisition of New Customers (difference of 0.2361) and Non-Financial Performance Item 1 – Customer Satisfaction (difference of 0.2425).

Table 14.5 presents the composite reliability and average variance extracted (AVE) statistics for each latent variable. Assessing the composite reliability of each construct indicates high reliability (ranging from 0.8636 to 0.9582). Examining the AVE statistics enables an assessment of the convergent validity of the constructs, with the criterion value being 0.50 or greater to demonstrate adequate convergent validity (Chin, 1998). All latent variables achieve this with a minimum of 0.6695 (for Market Orientation). The results of the final PLS measurement model, as presented in Tables 14.4 and 14.5, satisfy the statistical requirements of composite reliability and convergent reliability.

To assess the discriminant validity of the measurement model, the square root of the AVE statistic is compared to the correlations between the latent variables. This comparison is presented in Table 14.6. This test allows an assessment of whether a latent construct shares more variance with its measures than it shares with other constructs (Fornell and Larcker, 1981), and the square root of each construct's AVE statistic should be much larger than its correlation

Table 14.4 Factor loading results from the PLS measurement model

item	MO	RO	MVTC	MVFC	SP	FS	Size
MO item 1	**0.7012**	0.1134	0.3606	0.3755	0.2726	0.1366	0.0678
MO item 2	**0.8421**	0.2431	0.5040	0.4684	0.2894	0.2600	−0.0240
MO item 3	**0.8518**	0.4379	0.4984	0.4126	0.5626	0.5022	0.2748
MO item 4	**0.8633**	0.3521	0.5001	0.4980	0.4498	0.3777	0.3811
RO item 1	0.3628	**0.8609**	0.4129	0.1692	0.5582	0.3670	0.0758
RO item 2	0.4299	**0.8556**	0.5650	0.2519	0.5384	0.3360	0.0772
RO item 3	0.2681	**0.8801**	0.4101	0.2698	0.4786	0.2881	0.0678
RO item 4	0.3072	**0.8551**	0.3886	0.1655	0.5632	0.3988	−0.1303
RO item 5	0.4035	**0.8316**	0.4472	0.2855	0.5523	0.4185	−0.1815
RO item 6	0.4111	**0.8943**	0.5293	0.1887	0.6059	0.3094	−0.0931
RO item 7	0.0743	**0.8486**	0.2943	0.1360	0.3283	0.2373	−0.0023
RO item 8	0.2667	**0.8683**	0.3373	0.1561	0.4501	0.3378	−0.030
RO item 9	0.1676	**0.7230**	0.2589	0.1204	0.3607	0.3184	0.1130
MVTC item 1	0.5038	0.3334	**0.7453**	0.5092	0.3427	0.2381	0.1570
MVTC item 2	0.5779	0.4670	**0.8820**	0.4498	0.5223	0.4078	0.1310
MVTC item 3	0.3643	0.4559	**0.8138**	0.4877	0.5559	0.2791	−0.0177
MVTC item 4	0.4368	0.3477	**0.8262**	0.3842	0.5026	0.4310	−0.0107
MVFC item 1	0.4722	0.1607	0.4716	**0.8264**	0.1247	0.2192	0.1572
MVFC item 2	0.4526	0.2701	0.5101	**0.8774**	0.2526	0.2007	−0.0806
MVFC item 3	0.4318	0.1609	0.4128	**0.8206**	0.1235	0.3207	0.1823
NFinP item 1	0.4819	0.5512	0.6350	0.2459	**0.8775**	0.3879	−0.0739
NFinP item 2	0.3429	0.4822	0.4505	0.0732	**0.9109**	0.4532	−0.0306
NFinP item 3	0.4747	0.5241	0.4622	0.1943	**0.8290**	0.5593	0.0746
FS item 1	0.2943	0.3624	0.4088	0.2385	0.5336	**0.8857**	0.2702
FS item 2	0.3928	0.2338	0.2783	0.3038	0.2137	**0.6870**	0.2939
FS item 3	0.3780	0.3721	0.3459	0.2179	0.5148	**0.8875**	0.1909
Size item	0.2375	−0.0218	0.0770	0.0996	−0.0097	0.2922	1

Notes: MO = Market Orientation. RO= Relational Orientation. MVTC = Measuring Value to Customers. MVFC = Measuring Value from Customers. NFinP = Non–financial Performance. FS = Financial Sustainability.

Table 14.5 Latent variables: descriptive statistics, reliability, and convergent validity

Latent construct	Mean	Standard deviation	Composite reliability	Average variance extracted
MO	5.54	0.97	0.8897	0.6695
RO	5.90	1.10	0.9582	0.7185
MVTC	5.58	1.20	0.8898	0.6696
MVFC	4.93	1.35	0.8794	0.7087
NFinP	5.77	0.93	0.9057	0.7623
FS	4.57	1.31	0.8636	0.6814

Notes: MO = Market Orientation. RO= Relational Orientation. MVTC = Measuring Value to Customers. MVFC = Measuring Value from Customers. NFinP = Non-financial Performance. FS = Financial Sustainability.

Table 14.6 Latent variable correlations and square root of AVE [in diagonal]

	MO	RO	MVTC	MVFC	SP	FS	Size
MO	0.8182						
RO	0.3740	0.8476					
MVTC	0.5758	0.4936	0.8183				
MVFC	0.5369	0.2356	0.5526	0.8418			
SP	0.5007	0.5973	0.5937	0.1998	0.8731		
FS	0.4160	0.4000	0.4217	0.2928	0.5376	0.8255	
Size	0.2375	-0.0218	0.0770	0.0996	-0.0097	0.2922	1

with any of the other constructs in the model (Chin, 1998). The results of Table 14.6 show that the square roots of the AVE statistics of all constructs are greater than their correlations with other constructs, indicating satisfactory discriminant validity in the measurement model.

Results and discussion

PLS structural model

The PLS structural model is assessed using standardized β-statistics as the path coefficients generated by SmartPLS, with the R^2 statistic used to evaluate the PLS model on the basis of the

Table 14.7 PLS structural model results

	Path Coefficient	R2
Panel A: Paths to measuring value provided to customers		
Market orientation -> Measuring value provided to customers	0.4622**	0.4222
Relational orientation -> Measuring value provided to customers	0.3201*	
Size -> Measuring value provided to customers	-0.0258	
Panel B: Paths to measuring value extracted from customers		
Market orientation -> Measuring value extracted from customers	0.529**	0.2903
Relational orientation -> Measuring value extracted from customers	0.0372	
Size -> Measuring value extracted from customer	-0.0253	
Panel C: Paths to non-financial performance		
Market orientation -> Non-financial Performance	0.3235	0.5367
Relational orientation -> Non-financial Performance	0.4762*	
Measuring value provided to customer -> Non-financial performance	0.3995*	
Measuring value extracted from customer -> Non-financial performance	-0.2511	
Size -> Non-financial performance	-0.004	
Panel D: Paths to financial sustainability		
Market orientation -> Financial sustainability	0.3111*	0.3366
Relational orientation -> Financial sustainability	0.2836*	
Measuring value provided to customer -> Financial sustainability	0.1665	
Measuring value extracted from customer -> Financial sustainability	0.0295	
Non-financial performance -> Financial sustainability	0.4027*	
Size -> Financial sustainability	-0.005	

* $p < 0.05$ (two-tailed test)
** $p < 0.01$ (two-tailed test)

variance it explains (Chin, 1998). Bootstrapping (500 samples with replacement) was used to assess the significance of the path coefficients. The path coefficients, along with the R^2 for each endogenous construct in the PLS model, are presented in Table 14.7.

Antecedents to customer performance measurement

As Table 14.7 indicates, both null Hypotheses 1a and 1b are rejected. Market orientation is positively associated with customer performance measurement practices, comprising both measurement of value provided to, and value extracted from, customers. This extends the findings of Guilding and McManus (2002) and Cadez and Guilding (2008) in two ways. First, the finding is extended into the NFP sector, indicating that these organizations engage in new performance measurement practices as they seek to know more about their external environments and their customers. Second, market orientation was found to influence a broader set of customer performance measurement practices than those found in Guilding and McManus (2002), where influences on the measurement of value extracted from customers were found, comprising lifetime profitability, valuation, and generic customer accounting techniques. Here, market orientation influenced both value provided to customers (indicated by customer acquisition, retention, complaints, and satisfaction) as well as the measurement of value extracted from customers (sales and profit). Thus, NFPs that are externally oriented in their outlook are more likely to measure both non-financial/lead and financial/lag measures of their customer relationships.

Evidence also exists to reject the null Hypothesis 2a but not Hypothesis 2b. A statistically significant and positive relationship was observed between relational orientation and the measurement of value provided to customers. However, no relationship was obtained between relational orientation and the measurement of value extracted from customers. These findings highlight the influence of relational orientation on performance measurement practices aimed at evaluating how customers perceive the services and earned income activities performed. It also indicates that relational orientation amongst the sample of NFPs surveyed does not extend to influencing the measurement of economic outcomes from specific customer relationships such as sales and profitability.

Customer performance measurement practices and performance

In relation to the effects of customer performance measurement, measuring value provided to customers was associated with non-financial performance only, with no direct effects on financial sustainability. Measuring value extracted from customers was not found to have any direct effects on either dimension of performance. Hence, the null Hypothesis 3a is rejected but no support was found for rejecting the null Hypotheses 3b, 4a, or 4b. This is in contrast to Cadez and Guilding (2008), who found a positive relationship between the measurement of value from customers (albeit as part of a broader strategic management accounting construct) and performance.

The directional Hypothesis 5b was supported, with a positive association between market orientation and financial sustainability. In contrast, Hypothesis 5a positing a positive relationship between market orientation and non-financial performance was not supported. This contrasts with Cadez and Guilding (2008), where significant positive relationships were found between market orientation and performance in the private sector, comprising both financial and non-financial elements. Relational orientation was found to be positively associated with both non-financial performance and financial sustainability. Hence Hypothesis 6 is supported.

Finally, non-financial performance was found to influence financial performance. Hence, the null Hypothesis 7 is rejected. The significant work examining the relationships between these two constructs has almost exclusively occurred in the for-profit sector. This finding extends the applicability of a positive relationship between impacting customers through earned income activities and financial sustainability. The non-financial performance latent variable also included an item examining achievement of mission, indicating that a focus on financial sustainability is consistent with the achievement of social outcomes for this class of NFP.

Overall summary of results

Figure 14.1 presents the PLS structural model obtained in terms of significant paths. Note that while size was controlled for in the analysis, it was found not to have a significant influence on both customer performance measurement latent variables.[3] In terms of the explained variance in the endogenous variables, just over 40 per cent of the variation in measurement of value provided to customers and close to 30 per cent of the variation in measurement of value extracted from customers, is explained by the independent variables. Over half and approximately one-third of variation in non-financial performance and financial sustainability is explained through the PLS model. To explore these relationships further, data from the interviews conducted is presented in the next section.

Interview analysis

The main themes of ADE interviews comprised: (1) challenges facing ADEs; (2) ADE approaches to managing customers and evidence of market and/or relational orientation; (3) customer performance measurement; and (4) effects of customer performance measurement. Each sub-section below aligns to these themes.

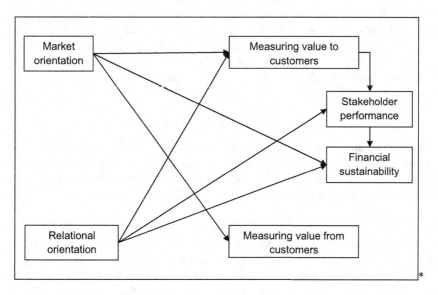

Figure 14.1 Final path model

Note: All hypothesized paths are positive.

Challenges facing ADEs

All ADEs interviewed had experienced changes in terms of the need to become more commercial. The CEO of ADE 1 described it as:

> Really that was the biggest change ... getting staff to understand that while we remain client focused, if we actually don't make money in business services there ain't going to be no business services. And so that's been the biggest thing. I think staff now do understand that you know, love it, hate it, this is the world we're in.

While the CEO of ADE 4 described how he had emphasized the need for profitability as a way of operating:

> I met with the staff and I said "If we don't push the pendulum far to the business end of the spectrum for the next two to three years, you can have all the fantastic service outcomes you like, you know, you'll be telling people about it over a cup of tea while you're standing in the unemployment queues". I said "None of us will have a job". You know, we've got to get more business like. One of the staff members said to me "What will that look like on the ground? What does that mean?" And I said, "Well, for a start, we're going to get out of any jobs that aren't profitable".

Indeed, an ongoing challenge for the organizations interviewed was the balance between commercial focus and social outcomes. As the General Manager of ADE 6 explained, efficiency concerns and keeping disabled individuals employed presented a tension with which he grappled:

> The decisions that you would normally make in a business sense, aren't the ones that we always make here. So some of the ways that I can make our business more viable and more profitable wouldn't reflect what we're here to do from a service provision point of view. For example, reducing people's hours, getting in the packaging, getting machinists in to help assemble components quicker because that would take the work away from what we do. The normal business efficiencies that you would make to make a business viable, we don't because we can't and that's not what we're here to do. So ... viability will always be an ongoing challenge for us.

Market and relational orientation

The challenges of managing the need to ensure employment for disability clients as well as ensure that sufficient profits are earned by the business for its viability led a number of interviewed ADEs to increase their focus on external markets. The General Manager of ADE 2 discussed this tension and the implication for its need to focus externally:

> We are very reluctant to retrench our supported workforce and that means our profit margins are often impacted by that decision because in the end of the day that's our main game, to maintain the employment of people with disabilities ... that's the other problem I think disability enterprises face and that is that if they work with external customers, businesses, who provide their work to the disability enterprises, quite often the reduction in work or reduction in contracts is quite sudden. There's no warning that this might happen.

Needing to ensure continuity of employment for people with disabilities translated into a need for ADEs to focus on markets and industries that were viable and growing. Exemplifying the notion of market orientation, the CEO of ADE 3 talked about how her organization was targeting different markets to those it had previously:

> For us, literally, we've got 40 people turning up for work and if our customers don't send us work, you know, we're in a bad way. So I think the main challenges are work going offshore. Any manufacturing people will tell you that, it's just all going bad. So we've got stuff going off to China, we've got manufacturing downsizing. So we've got changes in the markets we need to target, that traditional stuff with packaging and assembly for manufacturers, we're not going to get any growth from that.

Similar processes were in evidence at ADE 6. Providing catering services for other businesses was identified as a stable business that would allow it to offer a new avenue of steady employment for people with disability:

> We are desperately trying to grow because we know to continue to be viable we need to be growing. We're currently looking at a few different options. The food is – an area at the moment that we're very interested in and we've just started doing catering. It's been very successful … Food is something that is constant. People are still going to eat. So we see it as – probably a good growth area for us at the moment. So we're doing a fair bit of work around that.

Relational orientation was also evidenced in the interview data. Interviewees discussed how they had begun to focus and prioritize selected customers with a view to understanding them better. The CEO of ADE 1 explained how his organization had begun to focus on those customers that offered significant potential for employment:

> We've targeted some larger institutes, we're quite good in building in partnerships and relationships with councils. When you're in rural areas they are probably the biggest employer in the areas.

Also reflecting elements of a relational orientation, the General Manager of ADE 3 explained a focus on selected customers and understanding trends and issues in their business:

> I talk to major customers at least every week, and ask, "how's business going? How are your sales?" Before, 10 years ago, I never asked my customers that. It was more just "when are you sending me work and when do I need to get it done?" And now, they say "our business is growing, our sales are up over the last month, over the last three months our sales are up and increasing".

Customer performance measures

There were varying extents of customer performance measurement practices in the ADEs interviewed. While there was a general consensus that larger ADEs were better able to put in more sophisticated customer management systems and processes, size by itself did not appear to be a clear discriminator in terms of customer performance measurement practices.

This provides some support for size not being significantly associated with the extent of customer performance measurement. The practices of ADE 1 (small ADE) and ADE 4 (medium ADE) were very similar:

> So no, we're not good at tracking. We're not good at anything in terms of customer relationships, except with our existing contracts to do with ADEs. And we've never had the ability to afford somebody like a relationships manager to do that.
>
> *(CEO ADE 1)*

> I've got all the data there. It comes into my computer every month. But nobody has actually looked at the longitudinal, you know, relationship from one month to the next, or centre by centre, or whatever.
>
> *(CEO ADE 4)*

Also supporting the notion that size was not a clear driver of customer performance measurement practices, ADE 3 (also a small organization) engaged in measurement of value provided to customers as well as value extracted from customers. Indeed, what appeared to distinguish the smaller sized ADE 3 from ADE 1 was the former's market orientation and focus on selected customers (as indicated by the previous comments presented for ADE 3).[4] Interestingly, ADE 3 also evidenced a transition from these customer performance measures to include profitability:

> So we track who we've targeted per month, which ones were successful, what industry they're from? What was the sales value? And then, yeah, we track repeat customers. So if they were a customer here in January 09, when did they come back, what's their frequency, what are they spending per visit? But now we're trying to get to the next level of trying to analyse that, who are our most profitable? We know who our top 10 and our top 20 are. [Another manager] and I do a lot more surveillance now on which of our customers are growing their business, are they going into new markets? If they've got a business opportunity how can we leverage that to get in there and help?
>
> *General Manager ADE 3*

Performance effects

The comments in the preceding sub-section suggest explanations for the statistically significant relationships between the measurement of value provided to customers and non-financial performance. The interviews indicated that these measurement practices enabled ADEs to take operational actions to improve or extend specific customer relationships. In turn, this enabled the employment of more people with disabilities and the generation of social outcomes as the comments of the following ADE representatives indicate:

> We're constantly looking to grow and that's not always a whole lot of fun. But we're doing it for a few reasons. One, because I think if we stop growing we're going to go backwards because we tend to take hits every now and again. And if we don't have something around the corner, when one thing closes we'd not have another door ready to open. And there's still so many people out there that want a job.
>
> *(ADE 6)*

People now are very much focused on their work and the customer, this awareness now that these things we're packaging or producing are going to a customer, and we try and educate our workforce on who we're doing work for and why and how it needs to go … It hasn't been at the cost of our employees. In fact, the focus on business has actually improved their skills, given them more variety and made them feel like they have a real job. So it's actually had a lot of other spin offs.

(ADE 3)

Interview discussions also contained potential reasons for the absence of a direct relationship between measuring value extracted from customers and financial sustainability. Typical prescriptions for organizations that measure customer sales and profit are to increase prices for unprofitable customers or drop them if price increases are not obtainable (Howell and Soucy, 1990; Foster *et al.*, 1996). While these prescriptions are not the only ones offered, they are the most consistent with a direct link between the measurement of value extracted from customers and financial performance. However, interviewees indicated that both of these actions were problematic in the ADE context. Increasing prices was a challenge due to the price sensitivity of customers and perceptions that businesses that employed individuals with disabilities would offer low-priced services. The comments of ADE 1, ADE 3, and ADE 5 best exemplified this:

Everything we do is price sensitive.

(ADE 1)

There's a lot of managing expectations and our prices are very low and they [customers] still have this mentality that "you're a sheltered workshop, you've got people with a disability, we know you're not paying them $20 an hour. You must be able to do it for these rock bottom prices".

(ADE 3)

I'm hearing of contracts going for what I reckon would – would be more than the cost of production which is crazy.

(ADE 5)

The high price sensitivity of customers, their perceptions of ADEs, and the level of price competition in the industry evidenced by these comments indicate a level of difficulty in increasing prices even if ADEs identify particular customers as unprofitable. The need to preserve revenue levels (rather than profit levels) in order to offer employment and achieve social goals were reasons for not increasing prices and risking loss of customers.

Examples of dropping customers who were unprofitable were not provided by any of the interviewees, despite being questioned on whether they had rationalized their customer base. Instead a number of ADEs talked about the need to grow their customer base to reduce the risk of dependency on a few clients:

And in fact, in terms of exposure to single clients, one of those is about 67% of our income in packaging. So, that's something that we have identified as a real problem. If they suddenly pulled the pin on us, or shift their, transfer their products to China, which is always a possibility, that's going to leave a big hole.

(ADE 4)

> Our two biggest customers, one I think has gone into receivership or they've taken –
> withdrawn their products. And in one case, the big one, they've taken back all their
> work and they're doing it in house to try to retain their own existing staff. And with
> all the eggs in the one basket we aren't in a very good position to survive.
>
> *(ADE 5)*

Again, the ability to act on customer profitability information appears to be limited given that customer bases were not sufficiently large for ADEs to refuse business and prioritize. Thus, opportunities to improve profits by dropping unprofitable customers appear to be limited given the specific characteristics of ADEs.

Conclusion

This study examined the influences on customer performance measurement practices and their effects on performance in the context of social service NFP organizations. The study's main contributions are as follows.

First, the study adds to knowledge of customer performance measurement practices and how these operate in NFP settings. The study finds that measurement of value provided to customers positively and directly contributes to performance in terms of customer impact from earned income activities and the achievement of social mission, while also having indirect benefits on financial sustainability through these non-financial performance effects. Those NFPs that were looking to generate 'earned income' to complement government funding benefited from measuring how they performed in their customer relationships. Hence, there is support for the argument that the adoption of private-sector approaches to managing and measuring customers can have positive effects on both non-financial and financial dimensions of performance in NFPs despite concerns that the opposite might occur (Peredo and McLean, 2006; Kong, 2008).

Second, and following on from the above, the study provides insights into the nature of the benefits obtained from customer performance measurement in the NFP context. These appear to be operational in terms of enhancing individual customer relationships, rather than strategic (changing the portfolio of customers) or pricing related (charging unprofitable customers higher prices). The absence of relationships between the measurement of value extracted from customers and either non-financial performance or financial sustainability support this, as does the qualitative data from interviews. Interview data in particular indicated an inability by ADEs to shift pricing or drop customers due to firm image (perceptions of NFPs), social objectives (the need to provide supported employment), and the size of customer base (ADEs interviewed focused on diversifying the customer base rather than dropping unprofitable customers). Further research focusing on NFP managerial decision making is required to examine how performance is enhanced through the use of customer performance measurement information.

Third, the study extends prior research findings on the role of market orientation in explaining use of customer performance measurement practices from the for-profit to the NFP context. In addition, it highlights the influence of relational orientation on the use of practices that examine the measurement of value provided to customers. To date, research examining the influences on customer performance measurement practices has not considered the impact of relational orientation.

Finally, the study adds to the limited research on customer performance measurement's influence on organizational performance. Studies have found positive relationships (see O'Connor and Cheung, 2007). Other research suggests that the pursuit of customization and customer-focused strategies make contemporary performance measurement difficult to use and does not improve performance (Hyvonen, 2007). In contrast, the findings here are that the measurement of value provided to customers is associated with non-financial performance, which in turn is positively associated with financial performance. Measuring value extracted from customers to reprice and manage customer portfolios to improve financial performance directly are opportunities that are not accessible for the surveyed NFPs given broader industry dynamics and characteristics. Overall, however, the study supports the thesis that customer performance measurement practices generate decision-making benefits and contribute to organizational performance.

For practitioners, findings that market orientation and relational orientation has effects for performance have implications for customer management. Specifically, becoming much more externally focused and adopting a more commercial approach in analysing which markets to provide earned income activities into (within the framework of their NFP constitution and context), the size and potential growth of customer bases, and the extent of competition are likely to translate into benefits for financial sustainability. Being able to segment customer bases and focus on particular segments through customization and taking long-term approaches to managing relationships is also beneficial, not just in terms of those involved in the provision and receipt of earned income goods and services but also for the financial resources of the organization.

The findings also have practical implications in terms of how NFP organizations should support their adoption of market and relational orientation. Measuring value provided to customers translates into performance benefits for the organization through the generation of information that allows for operational improvements and problem correction. While in this study the measurement of value extracted from customers was not found to have performance effects, this may not be the case in other NFP settings. Here, NFP managers need to consider their capacity to take action in terms of repricing earned income activities and/or rationalizing their customer base to focus on valuable customers in terms of earned income activities. It is likely that measuring the value extracted from customers will have performance benefits.

In closing, the study's limitations need to be considered. First, only one sub-sector of social service NFPs was examined. The context of ADEs, where profit-generating activities can also support the social mission of providing employment to individuals with disability, may limit the generalizability of findings relating to the effects of customer performance measurement and the observed positive relations between non-financial performance and financial performance. Second, the interviews and discussions with National Disability Services Australia indicated that this was an NFP sector that was in transition in relation to its acceptance of the need to become more commercial in orientation. Hence, a 'timing' effect is likely to exist where other NFP sectors might differ in their use of customer performance measurement and strategic management accounting practices more generally, depending on how long they have sought alternative sources of funding. Finally, given the state of the sector and their experience with customer performance measurement, it is likely that some survey respondents did not possess enough information to answer these questions. However, the effects of this on the survey results are mitigated through the pilot testing and adaptation processes utilized as well as by excluding those responses where participants had selected multiple 'don't know' or 'not applicable' options to the survey questions.

Appendix A: survey questions

Market orientation

1   My organization has a strong understanding of our Disability Enterprise customers.
2   The functions in my organization work closely together to create superior value for our Disability Enterprise customers.

3　Management in my organization thinks in terms of serving the needs and wants of well-defined markets chosen for their long-term growth and profit potential for the company.

4　My organization has a strong market orientation.

Relational orientation

1　My organization provides customized services and products to our key customers.

2　My organization makes an effort to find out what our key customer needs are.

3　When my organization finds that customers would like to modify a product/service, the departments involved make coordinated efforts to do so.

4　All people in my organization treat customers with great care.

5　Customers can expect exactly when services will be performed.

6　My organization fully understands the needs of our key customers.

7　Maintaining a long-term relationship with our customers is important to us.

8　We focus on long-term goals in our relationships with customers.

9　We are willing to make sacrifices to help customers from time to time.

Measuring value provided to customers

1　Acquisition of new customers.

2　Retention of existing customers.

3　Customer complaints.

4　Customer satisfaction.

Measuring value extracted from customers

1　Annual sales per customer.

2　Profitability of individual customers.

3　Profitability of customer segments/groups.

Non-financial performance

1　Customer satisfaction.

2　Customer loyalty.

3　Achievement of mission.

Financial sustainability

1　Cash flow.

2　Diverse revenue sources.

3　Operating margins.

Notes

1 Other measures relating to the social objectives of NFPs were explored, but it was decided to retain the 'achievement of mission' item on the basis that this captured objectives relating to the placement of individuals in employment whilst also being general enough to be applicable across the sample. For example, a specific item such as 'Amount of time an individual was in actual employment' was

seen as being impacted by the severities of the individual employee's disabilities and demographic of the ADE's employee base. Financial sustainability was not directly assessed as National Disability Australia representatives and interviewees indicated that they struggled to assess this. Thus an 'indirect approach' was taken where cashflow, margins, and diversity of revenue sources were examined.

2 Bartlett's test of sphericity indicated non-zero correlations existed for all variables ($p = 0.000$) while Kaiser-Meyer-Olkin (KMO) measures of sampling adequacy were equal to or greater than 0.657 in all cases.

3 This result may have been driven by the manner in which the size variable was measured. However, interview results (see next section) indicate that size was not a significant influence of sophisticated customer accounting practices.

4 ADE 5, also a medium-sized organization, did not engage in significant customer measurement.

References

Baines, A. and Langfield-Smith, K. (2003), "Antecedents to management accounting change: a structural equation approach", *Accounting, Organizations and Society*, Vol. 28, pp. 675–698.

Banker, R. A., Potter, G., and Srinivasan, D. (2000), "An empirical investigation of an incentive plan that includes nonfinancial performance measures", *The Accounting Review*, Vol. 75, No. 1, pp. 65–92.

Bolton, P. and Mehran, H. (2006), "An introduction to the governance and taxation of not-for-profit organizations", *Journal of Accounting and Economics*, Vol. 41, No. 3, pp. 293–305.

Boulding, W., Staelin, R., Ehret, M., and Johnston, W. J. (2005), "A customer relationship management roadmap: what is known, potential pitfalls and where to go", *Journal of Marketing*, Vol. 69, pp. 155–166.

Boyce, G. (2000) "Valuing customers and loyalty: The rhetoric of customer focus versus the reality of alienation and exclusion of (devalued) customers", *Critical Perspectives on Accounting*, Vol. 11, No. 6, pp. 649–689.

Bryant, L., Jones, D., and Widener, S. (2004), "Managing value creation within the firm: an examination of multiple performance measures", *Journal of Management Accounting Research*, Vol. 16, pp. 107–131.

Cadez, S. and Guilding, C. (2008), "An exploratory investigation of an integrated contingency model of strategic management accounting", *Accounting, Organizations and Society*, Vol. 33, Nos 7–8, pp. 836–863.

Chapman, C. S., and Kihn, L. A. (2009), "Information system integration, enabling control and performance", *Accounting, Organizations and Society*, Vol. 34, pp. 151–169.

Chenhall, R. H. (2003), "Management control system design within its organizational context: findings from contingency-based research and directions for the future", *Accounting, Organizations and Society*, Vol. 28, No. 127–168.

Chenhall, R. H. (2005), "Integrative strategic performance measurement systems, strategic alignment of manufacturing, learning and strategic outcomes: An exploratory study", *Accounting, Organizations and Society*, Vol. 30, pp. 395–422.

Chenhall, R. H. (2008), "Accounting for the horizontal organization: A review essay", *Accounting, Organizations and Society*, Vol. 33, pp. 517–550.

Chetkovich, C. and Frumkin, P. (2003), "Balancing margin and mission: Non-profit competition in charitable versus fee-based programs", *Administration and Society*, Vol. 35, No. 5, pp. 564–596.

Chin, W. W. (1998), "The partial least squares approach for structural equation modelling", in: Marcoulides, G. A. (Ed.), *Modern Methods for Business Research*, Lawrence Erlbaum Associates, New Jersey, pp. 295–336.

Commonwealth of Australia (2008), *Australian Government Disability Services Census 2007*, Commonwealth of Australia, Canberra.

Commonwealth of Australia (2009), *The Way Forward: A New Disability Policy Framework for Australia*, Commonwealth of Australia, Canberra.

Cuganesan, S. (2008), "Calculating customer intimacy: Accounting numbers in a sales and marketing department", *Accounting, Auditing & Accountability Journal*, Vol. 21, No. 1, pp. 78–103.

Dees, J. (1998), "Enterprising non-profits", *Harvard Business Review*, Jan–Feb, pp. 55–67.

Edvinsson, L. and Malone, M. S. (1997), *Intellectual Capital*, Piatkus, London.

Fornell, C. and Larcker, D. F. (1981), "Evaluating structural equation models with unobservable variables and measurement error", *Journal of Marketing Research*, Vol. 18, pp. 39–50.

Foster, G., Gupta, M., and Sjoblom, L. (1996), "Customer profitability analysis: Challenges and new directions", *Journal of Cost Management*, Spring, pp. 5–17.

Ganesan, S., (1994), "Determinants of long-term orientation in buyer–seller relationships", *Journal of Marketing*, Vol. 58, pp. 1–19.

Guilding, C. and McManus, L. (2002), "The incidence, perceived merit and antecedents of customer accounting: An exploratory note", *Accounting, Organizations and Society*, Vol. 27, pp. 45–59.

Hall, M. (2008), "The effect of comprehensive performance measurement systems on role clarity, psychological empowerment and managerial performance", *Accounting, Organizations and Society*, Vol. 33, pp. 141–163.

Heskett, J. L., Sasser Jr., W. E., and Schlesinger, L. A. (1997), *The Service Profit Chain*, Free Press, New York.

Hong-Kit, F., Anderson, R., and Swaminathan, S. (2005), "Customer relationship management: Its dimensions and impact on customer outcomes", *Journal of Personal Selling and Sales Management*, Vol. 24, No. 4, pp. 265–280.

Howell, R. A., and Soucy, R. (1990), "Customer profitability: As critical as product profitability", *Management Accounting*, October, pp. 43–47.

Hulland, J. (1999), "Use of partial least squares (PLS) in strategic management research", *Strategic Management Journal*, Vol. 20, pp. 195–204.

Hyvonen, J. (2007), "Strategy, performance measurement techniques and information technology of the firm and their links to organizational performance", *Management Accounting Research*, Vol. 18, pp. 343–366.

Ittner, C. D. and Larcker., D. F. (1995), "Total quality management and the choice of information and reward systems", *Journal of Accounting Research*, Vol. 33, pp. 1–34.

Ittner, C. D. and Larcker., D. P. (1998), "Are non-financial measures leading indicators of financial performance? An analysis of customer satisfaction", *Journal of Accounting Research*, Vol. 36, pp. 1–35.

Kaplan, R. S. and Norton, D. P. (1992), "The balanced scorecard: Measures that drive performance", *Harvard Business Review*, Vol. 70, No. 1, pp. 71–79.

Kaplan, R. S. and Norton, D. P. (1996), *The Balanced Scorecard: Translating Strategy into Action*, Harvard Business School Press, Boston, MA.

Kaplan, R. S. and Norton, D. P., (2004), *Strategy Maps: Converting Intangible Assets into Tangible Outcomes*, Harvard Business School Press, Boston, MA.

Kohli, A. K., and Jaworski, B. J. (1990), "Market orientation: The construct, research propositions, and managerial implications", *Journal of Marketing*, Vol. 54, pp. 1–18.

Kong, E. (2008), "The development of strategic management in the non-profit context: Intellectual capital in social service non-profits", *International Journal of Management Reviews*, Vol. 10, No. 3, pp. 281–299.

LeRoux, K. (2009), "Managing stakeholder demands balancing responsiveness to clients and funding agents in non-profit social service organizations", *Administration Society*, Vol. 41, No. 2, pp. 158–184.

Malina, M. A., Norreklit, H., and Selto, F. H. (2007), "Relations among measures, climate of control and performance measurement models", *Contemporary Accounting Research*, Vol. 24, No. 3, pp. 935–982.

Narver, J. C. and Slater, S. F. (1990), "The effect of a market orientation on business profitability", *Journal of Marketing*, Vol. 54, pp. 20–35.

National Disability Services, Australia (2010), "Budget decision jeopardises jobs of workers with disability", Media Release 12 May. Available from: www.nds.org.au/media (accessed 17 July 2010).

Niven, P. R. (2002), *Balanced Scorecard Step-by-Step*, John Wiley & Sons, New York.

Nunnally, J. C. (1981), *Psychometric Theory*, McGraw-Hill, New York.

O'Connor, N. G. and Cheung, C. L. K. (2007), "Product/service adoption strategies and bank customer accounting in Hong Kong", *Pacific Accounting Review*, Vol. 19, pp. 31–46.

Parker, L. D. (2001), "Reactive planning in a Christian bureaucracy", *Management Accounting Research*, Vol. 12, pp. 321–356.

Parker, L. D. (2002), "Budgetary incrementalism in a Christian bureaucracy", *Management Accounting Research*, Vol. 13, pp. 71–100.

Parsons, L. M. (2003), "Is accounting information from non-profit organizations useful to donors? A review of charitable giving and value-relevance", *Journal of Accounting Literature*, Vol. 22, pp. 104–129.

Parsons, L. M. (2007), "The impact of financial information and voluntary disclosures on contributions to not-for-profit organizations", *Behavioral Research in Accounting*, Vol. 19, pp. 179–196.

Payne, A. and Frow, P. (2005), "A strategic relationship framework for customer relationship management", *Journal of Marketing*, Vol. 69, pp. 167–176.

Peredo, A. M. and McLean, M. (2006), "Social entrepreneurship: A critical review of the concept", *Journal of World Business*, Vol. 41, pp. 56–65.

Peters, T. and Waterman, R. (1982), *In Search of Excellence*, Harper, New York.

Pillai, A. and Sharma, K. (2003), "Mature relationships: Why does relational orientation turn into transaction orientation?", *Industrial Marketing Management*, Vol. 32, pp. 643–651.

Plakoyiannaki, E., Tzokas, N., Dimitratos, P., and Saren, M. (2008), "How critical is employee orientation for customer relationship management? Insights from a case study", *Journal of Management Studies*, Vol. 45, No. 2, pp. 267–293.

Ringle, C. M., Wende, S., and Will, A. (2005), SmartPLS 2.0 (beta). Available from www.smartpls.de.

Said, A. A., HassabElnaby, H. R., and Wier, B. (2003), "An empirical investigation of the performance consequences of nonfinancial measures", *Journal of Management Accounting Research*, Vol. 15, pp. 193–223.

Salamon, L. M., Sokolowski, S. W., and Geller, S. L. (2012), "Holding the fort: Non-profit employment during a decade of turmoil", *Non-Profit Employment Bulletin No. 39*. John Hopkins University, Baltimore, MD.

Slater, S. F. and Narver, J. C. (1994), "Market orientation, customer value, and superior performance", *Business Horizons*, April, pp. 22–28.

Smith, R. E. and Wright, W. F. (2004), "Determinants of customer loyalty and financial performance", *Journal of Management Accounting Research*, Vol. 16, pp. 183–205.

Srivastava, R. K., Shervani, T. A., and Fahey, L. (1999), "Marketing, business processes and shareholder value: An organizationally embedded view of marketing activities and the discipline of marketing", *Journal of Marketing*, Vol. 63, pp. 168–179.

United Nations (2003), *Handbook on Non-profit Institutions in the System of National Accounts*, Department of Economic and Social Affairs Statistics Division, United Nations, New York.

United Nations (2006), *ISIC Annex: International Classification of Non-Profit Organizations (ICNPO) Revised*, Department of Economic and Social Affairs Statistics Division, United Nations, New York.

Vaivio, J. (1999), "Examining 'the quantified customer'", *Accounting, Organizations and Society*, Vol. 24, No. 8, pp. 689–715.

Weerawardena, J., McDonald, R. E., and Mort, G. S. (2010), "Sustainability of nonprofit organizations: An empirical investigation", *Journal of World Business*, Vol. 45, No. 4, pp. 346–356.

Wilson, C. (2010), *Charities and Not-for-Profit Organizations in Australia*, IBISWorld Industry Report X0021, IBISWorld, Melbourne.

Wing, K. T., Roeger, K. L., and Pollak, T. H. (2009), *The Non-Profit Sector in Brief: Public Charities, Giving and Volunteering 2009*, Urban Institute's Center on Nonprofits and Philanthropy, Washington, DC.

Wold, H. (1980), "Model construction and evaluation when theoretical knowledge is scarce", in Kmenta, J. and Ramsey, J. B. (Eds), *Evaluation of Econometric Models*, Academic Press, New York, pp. 47–74.

Wood, V. R., Bhuian, S., and Kiecker, P. (2000), "Market orientation and organizational performance in not-for-profit hospitals", *Journal of Business Research*, Vol. 48, pp. 213–226.

15

SUSTAINED COMPETITIVE ADVANTAGE AND STRATEGIC INTELLECTUAL CAPITAL MANAGEMENT

Evidence from Japanese high performance small to medium sized enterprises

Jun Yao and Chitoshi Koga

Introduction

Intellectual capital (IC) management is not new to Japanese companies. Japan has a long-term commitment to the resource-based view, with Itami's (1987) *Mobilizing Invisible Assets* one of the earliest and most significant contributions to IC research (Sullivan, 2000). Later, Nonaka and Takeuchi's (1995) *The Knowledge-Creating Company* promoted interest in Japanese style knowledge management (KM). However, the IC and KM literature, including these well-known works, mostly focus on large companies. Previous studies have identified that small to medium sized enterprises (SMEs) manage IC in a different way from large companies (Hutchinson and Quintas, 2008; Demartini and Del Baldo, 2015; Marzo and Scarpino, 2016). SMEs have also attracted less research interest, despite being economically important – in Japan 99.7 per cent of companies are SMEs.

However, in recent years, Japan has been involved in initiatives to promote a *new* model of growth, which places high-value-added intangible assets or IC at its core. In 2005, the Ministry of Economy, Trade and Industry of Japan (METI) published the first guidelines for IC management reporting. In the following years, IC policies were developed and in some regions (Kansai Area) or prefectures (Kyoto Prefecture), local governments promoted IC management, reporting, and financing especially for SMEs.

Japanese IC management differs from that in western countries (Uchida and Roos, 2008), while the IC reporting models recommended by the Japanese government are borrowed from western countries. Japanese organizations often find preparing IC reports based on western models difficult and Japanese financial institutions, despite acknowledging IC as critical to value creation, find it difficult to evaluate IC. There is a lack of understanding of IC management and its relationship to firm performance among managers, investors, and other stakeholders. It is against this background that this chapter attempts to analyse the third stage of IC research – how organizations implement IC in practice from a critical and performative perspective (Guthrie *et al.*, 2012; Dumay and Garanina, 2013) – and how IC management is implemented in practice in Japanese SMEs. We analyse five case companies over ten years to explore how IC contributes to sustained competitive advantage.

Ricceri (2008) called for the integration of strategitization into IC management. Strategy is thought to affect developing IC, which affects how an SME performs (Cohen *et al.*, 2014), thus, "discussing strategy helps with understanding how IC practices contribute to competitive advantage" (Dumay and Guthrie, 2012). Also, the new reporting initiative, Integrated Reporting, suggests disclosing strategy to help information users understand sustainable value creation (IIRC, 2013). Therefore, we focus our analysis on the strategy and compare 'winners' and 'losers' to find out whether these companies strategically manage IC and how they formulate strategies and convert IC into competitive advantage and improved performance.

Theoretical framework and key concepts

Although the resource-based view regards the organization as a bundle of resources, not all businesses with superior capabilities and resources can obtain improved market position and performance. For example, some famous companies like Sharp, despite owning numerous technology and patents, faced a crisis in recent years. How IC contributes to sustained competitive advantage remains in the 'black box'. To analyse and compare the case companies, we utilize a framework constructed based on a review of the strategy literature. The key terms used in the framework, such as competitive advantage, capabilities, and resources including IC and strategy (both competitive strategy and KM strategy), will be defined and explained.

Framework used for analysis

There is no widely accepted definition of competitive advantage in the practice and management literature. Some research focuses on the relative advantage of the market position, and high performance is thought to be gained by providing customers with products of higher quality, better design, faster service, or at a lower cost (Porter, 1985). Some research focuses on the sources of competitive advantage, which is defined as relative superiority in terms of capabilities and resources. For example, Coyne (1986) considers the sources of competitive advantage to be: positional, for example, customer loyalty as a result of past action; regulatory or legal entities such as patents and contracts; functional, which is created from the competence of employees and others in the value chain; and cultural, which comprises, for example, organizational habits, attitudes, beliefs, and value. Others focus on more specific KM factors, connecting KM to innovation, which in turn leads to competitive advantage (Egbu *et al.*, 2005; Lee *et al.*, 2016).

Day and Wensley (1988) argue that none of the above views provides a whole picture; rather, combined they define both the state of competitive advantage and the process of how it is gained. Therefore, he proposed an integrative framework connecting capabilities, resources, position, and performance for diagnosing competitive advantage. In this study, we adopt an integrated framework as shown in Figure 15.1 based on Day and Wensley (1988), but expand it to enable more detailed analysis of IC management. The key components of the framework such as positional and performance superiority (results of IC management), superior capabilities and resources (source of competitive advantage), and strategy (what leads IC to competitive advantage) are explained in the following section (Day and Wensley, 1988; Barney, 1991; Rangone, 1999; Takahashi, 2012; Lee *et al.*, 2013).

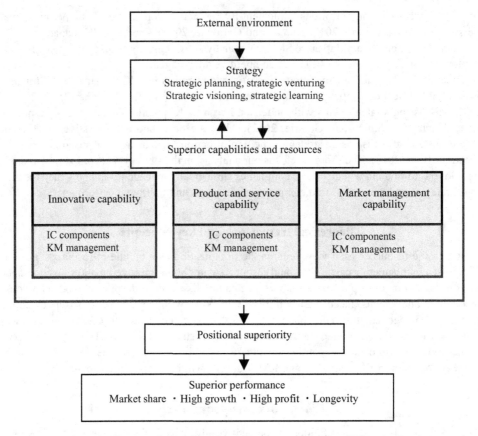

Figure 15.1   Integrated framework for competitive advantage, strategy, and IC management

Key components of the framework

Positional and performance superiority

Competitive advantage is often demonstrated as superiority in market position. In an existing market, the company's relative superior position may be represented either as the cost edge or the differentiation in product function, branding, reputation, or business model, or a new market based on current technology. It may also refer to an expanding market based on revolutionary technology (Takahashi, 2012). SMEs' strategic position may affect the composition of IC either developed or acquired (Aragón-Sánchez and Sánchez-Marín, 2005; St-Pierre and Audet, 2011). There are many ways to measure performance. Superior performance may refer to high growth rate, profit, or market share. In the case of SMEs, long-term survival can also be regarded as superior performance because, according to the Teikoku Databank, the average life span of an SME is 30 years. Many SMEs, instead of focusing on growth, see longevity as their primary goal.

Superior capability and resources

Competitive advantage derives from deeply rooted capabilities (Prahalad and Hamel, 1990). There are three basic capabilities. Innovation capability is the ability to develop new products and process and achieve superior technology. Production and service capability is the ability to produce and deliver differentiated products and service to the customer regarding quality, flexibility, time, and cost. Market management capability is the ability to market and sell products and services efficiently and effectively (Rangone, 1999). An organization needs to hold appropriate complementary resources and manage them effectively to obtain and enhance these capabilities. Research based on the resource-based view regards a company's resources as the source of competitive advantage (Teece *et al.*, 1997). Resources may be both tangible and intangible, with the latter often described as IC in the management literature. IC includes human capital, structural capital, and relational capital (Swart, 2006). To be identified as the source of competitive advantage, IC items should have the following characteristics: (1) valuable to differentiate the company to its competitors (in extreme cases, to prevent competitors entering the market); (2) rare compared to the competition; (3) inimitable, that is, difficult for competitors to imitate or imitable but at a high cost, which causes inefficiency; (4) unsubstitutable by other resources (Barney, 1991; Collis and Montgomery, 1995; Rangone, 1999).

Strategy: competitive strategy and KM strategy

Strategy is the key concept in competitive advantage. IC management and KM must be integrated at an early stage to monitor progress and "keep the body of knowledge alive and vibrant to secure the enterprise's well-being and long-term viability" (Wiig, 1997, p. 405). To understand how IC is strategically managed to obtain a competitive edge, it is significant to look at two different strategies: competitive strategy and KM strategy.

The concept of competitive strategy has been the subject of extensive research since the 1960s. In the past 50 years, it has been extended, examined, and redefined in many ways. There are two contrasting theories of strategy: prescriptive and descriptive theory. The prescriptive theory defines strategy as the process of determining the organization's long-term goals and objectives, of adopting a course of action, and allocating sufficient resources (Chandler, 1962). Alternatively, it is defined as a fundamental pattern of present and planned objectives, resource deployments, and interactions of an organization with markets, competitors, and other environmental forces (Kerin *et al.*, 1990). In the SME literature, the definition of strategy includes five components. They are "planned activities being carried out to achieve stated objectives, resources and capabilities being deployed to a strategic decision, markets being entered, explored and learned from, competitors being engaged and benchmarked, and environments providing signals filtered through personal and entrepreneurial networks" (Burke and Jarratt, 2004, p. 129). In contrast, descriptive theory, based on practice, shows that strategy does not need to be deliberately planned, react to the external environment, or benchmark competitors.

Mintzberg *et al.* (2008) summarized descriptive and prescriptive strategy theory, arguing that strategy should require a number of definitions, and five in particular: a strategy is a plan that means a direction, a guide, or course of action into the future; a strategy is a pattern that refers to the consistency in behaviour over time; a strategy is a position showing the location of particular products in particular markets; a strategy is a perspective that directs the fundamental way of doing things; moreover, a strategy is a ploy – a particular manoeuvre intended to outwit an opponent or competitor. While the first and the second are two different processes of strategic formulation, the third and fourth represent different strategic content.

Figure 15.2, proposed by Mintzberg *et al.* (2008), combines plan and pattern with position and perspective to analyse strategy formation. According to Mintzberg *et al.* (2008), the definition of strategy as a plan represents a view that strategy is made for the future with previously determined objectives. Along with this line of definition, the strategy is intended and

Strategic theory	Prescriptive theory	Descriptive theory
Strategy formation	Deliberate plans	Emergent patterns
	Strategic planning (Tangible position)	Strategic venturing (Tangible position)
	Strategic visioning (Broad perspective)	Strategic learning (Broad perspective)

Figure 15.2   Types of strategy theory and strategy formulation

Source: Adapted from Mintzberg, 2008, p. 16

deliberately planned. In contrast, the definition of strategy as a pattern that evolves in the past implies that strategy emerges over time as intentions collide with and accommodate a changing reality. Strategy formed in this way is called *emergent* strategy, and is formulated in the learning process.

Compared with competitive strategy, KM strategy has a more focused content. The KM literature focuses on the identification, acquisition, sharing, conversion, and utilization of knowledge. KM strategy includes the following dimensions (Hansen *et al.*, 1999; Choi and Lee, 2002; Bierly and Daly, 2007; Greiner *et al.*, 2007; Choi *et al.*, 2008):

1   *KM objective*. KM may aim to improve efficiency or improve innovation.
2   *Knowledge source*. KM strategy can be classified as internal or external oriented depending on the source of knowledge.
3   *Knowledge sharing and transfer*. KM strategy can be divided into codification and personalization with the former focusing on the reuse of knowledge so that knowledge is usually codified by application of technology, while the latter features face to face communication where knowledge is tacit.

Research method

Some researchers criticized the top-down approach to guiding IC reporting, calling for more research on what works (and does not) in specific organizational contexts from a bottom-up perspective (Mouritsen, 2006; Dumay, 2012). In this study, we selected five companies from a large sample to analyse the contribution of their IC management to competitive advantage from 2005 to 2016. First, 3,000 enterprises, revenues of which increased over the period 2005 to 2007 were selected from 78,000 SMEs. Those with fewer than ten employees were then excluded. A survey was conducted via a questionnaire sent to the selected sample companies to explore the following three questions.

1   What kind of IC do you consider a source of competitive advantage?
2   How do IC elements interact to create corporate value?
3   How do companies manage and assess intellectual assets?

Based on the questionnaires received, we approached 21 companies with active IC management or specific KM. Among them, eight companies accepted our interview request.

Table 15.1 Profiles of the case companies

Company	Years of operation as of 2016	Business segment	Performance from 2008 to 2016
A	13 years	Engineering and manufacturing	High growth in sales and market share
B	24 years	Engineering and manufacturing	Slow but continuous growth in sales and employee number
C	15 years	Engineering and manufacturing	Significant fluctuation in sales and profits, downsized
D	107 years	Wholesale (mainly steel raw materials) and other business	Keeping top transaction volume in the business segment; growth in sales and profit but not in size
E	17 years	Planning and sales of character products	Restructured and downsized

The first interviews were undertaken in 2008.[1] We followed these up regularly and additional interviews were conducted in 2016. Information about these companies was collected from various sources including interviews, the company webpage, word of mouth, and databases. Three companies were excluded because of inaccessibility, leaving a sample of five companies (see Table 15.1).

All the case companies had high growth in sales and profit from 2005 to 2007. Company A is a 'development-based' engineering company with image processing technologies as its core technology. Despite the effects of the global financial crisis, it had high growth until 2015, with its capital tripling and number of employees doubling.

Company B was founded in 1992 by its current three executives, formerly technicians at a synthetic leather manufacturer. The successful development of new technologies based on plastic film sheet moulding pushed rapid growth from 2005 to 2007, with sales growth of 191 per cent, and an earnings growth rate of 145 per cent. Although this rate of growth could not be maintained in later years, the company's growth was continuous with the number of employees increasing from 18 in 2007 to 30 in 2016.

Company C specializes in the processing of glass products for semiconductors. It is a wholly-owned subsidiary of a major semiconductor and printing manufacturer. In the fiscal year 2005, the company emerged as the global leader in quartz glass tanks. However, after 2008, the company's growth stalled and sales, profits, and total assets decreased from 2010 to 2015, with a small recovery in 2016. It has 85 employees as at 2016, a 25 per cent decrease from 2008.

Company D is a wholesaler of raw materials for steel established in 1909 as a privately-owned enterprise. The growth rates of net profits from 2005 to 2007 were 169 per cent, 181 per cent, and 131 per cent respectively. The company has continued to show steady growth in profit in recent years.

Company E was founded in 1999. It is involved in the planning, development, and wholesale of limited area character-related goods for popular tourist destinations. The company grew rapidly from 2005 to 2008 with sales increasing tenfold due to the successful development and marketing of a popular character product. It aimed to list on the Tokyo Stock Exchange in 2009, but since 2008 the company has been contracting and in 2016, was one-third of its peak size.

Findings of the case analysis

Snapshot of competitive advantage and intellectual capital 2008

The case companies were divided into three groups based on their specific capabilities: (1) technology-based production capability; (2) information capability; and (3) marketing capability. Table 15.2 summarizes what the case companies indicated were the drivers of competitive advantage and the strategy they adopted to obtain advantage in position and performance.

Type 1: Technology-based production capability

The first group of companies shares similarities in that they are in a niche market with specific demands for products, they are in competition with very large companies in this market, and they were founded based on the experience and know-how of the founders and staff in the same industry. The three companies each adopted different strategies to survive and win in such a market.

Table 15.2 Competitive advantage and IC management of case companies as of 2008

Company	Positional superiority and strategy	Capability and resources superiority		
		Human capital	Structural capital	Relational capital
A	Differentiation by developing high value-added product	Production capability based on technology		
		Abilities and skills of engineers/ developers and marketing staff	Computer-based product model	Collaboration with the rival company
B	Differentiation by developing product with special function	Production capability based on technology		
		Leadership of managers; skilled technicians	Patent for technology	Good relationship with business partners
C	Differentiation by producing high-quality product	Production capability based on technology		
		Craftsmanship of skilled workers	Division-of-labour production system; quality management system; craftsmanship cultivation system	Close relationship with parent companies
D	Differentiation by speed (matching seller and buyer; searching new business chance based on information)	Information capability		
		Leadership of managers	Unique organizational structure and culture, on demand system	Relationship with various stakeholders
E	Differentiation by new marketing model	Marketing capability		
		Sense and planning ability of managers and planners	–	Collaboration with business partners

Company A differentiates itself from rivals by providing high value-added products at a higher price than those of its rivals. Its innovative product is developed based on an idea of the CEO, and its high-end product strategy was formulated when the company was established. However, this strategy could not be successfully implemented without the efforts of the key world-class technicians who have five years or more practical experience in image processing, and with accumulated knowledge and experience in image processing algorithms, optical technologies, and electricity and machinery in the same industry, and who jointly established the company. A stock option system was introduced to motivate technicians and developers. Company A's success stems from its win-win relationship with its rival, the top company in the market. By entering a licence agreement with this company, which has a library of application tools, Company A can make the best use of the rival company's technology and convert it to its advantage.

In contrast to Company A, Company B has no specific idea or objective for product development. Instead, its specific product and unique film sheet processing technology were developed as a result of customers' specific requests. This customer-oriented development strategy is a typical emergent strategy.

> If a customer says they want to do something, then we try, without any special consideration of the cost. You could say we enjoy this. We try plenty of things, one of which will tie into some interesting technological development.
>
> *(CEO of Company B)*

The standard processing techniques only allow for high performance film sheets to be produced at a thickness of 0.4mm and are traditionally used in stationery manufacturing and packaging manufacturing. However, the company was able to produce an ultra-thin, highly transparent film sheet that is one-tenth the thickness of 0.04mm. This processing technology was revolutionary and is used in new areas like LCDs and plasma screen displays. To protect its technology, Company B has applied for a patent. In the interview, the company executives summarized the critical resources contributing to Company B's success as key technicians, unique technology, and intellectual property, as well as the close relationship with customers and business partners.

Company C's differentiation lies in its high-quality product guaranteed by the craftsmanship of skilled workers, quality management system, and division of labour. The company has earned a worldwide reputation in quartz glass processing technology, driven by the presence of skilled workers at the company who contributed to its founding and who are regarded as critical IC. On-the-job training helps apprentices to learn the craftsmanship required, which takes seven to ten years to master, hence the technology is difficult to imitate. The subsequent development of the company has been based not only on the craftsmanship of these individual workers but also on the company's efforts to significantly improve efficiency, reducing errors and costs by transitioning its production system to a system of division of labour and adopting ISO.

Type 2: Information capability

Company D has positioned itself as an 'information trading company' despite its core business being distributing and wholesaling steel raw material. This creates customer value through swift action based on its high power of information acquisition. The competitive advantage that Company D has derived from this strategy is its ability to respond rapidly to customers' demands and requests. While large companies seek huge-volume transactions with a small number of business partners with the aim of efficient management, Company D carries out small-volume decentralized transactions with many trading partners. At a glance, this appears to be an inefficient approach that increases costs. However, Company D is seeking "inefficient efficiency" rather than short-term profit, underpinned by long-term relationships of trust, consistent with traditional Japanese business practices. This has boosted Company D's ability to gather information, increasing the efficiency of business, thereby enabling economy of speed. The IC that contributes to Company D's growth includes its unique management philosophy, strong leadership by the CEO, organization culture and structure, processes that support rapid information gathering and matching, and long-term relationships with various business partners.

Type 3: Marketing capability

Company E's dramatic growth in financial performance from 2005 to 2008 was achieved by successfully planning and selling character goods designed especially for the region's souvenir market. The character is unique and popular among both men and women, old and young. The character-themed goods are designed with their styles showing regional characteristics and sold to retailers specializing in tourist merchandise. After a successful trial in Okinawa, this marketing model was copied and successfully applied to other regions. The CEO summarized the IC that supported the company's competitive advantage as the exceptional ability of management coupled with the experience and capabilities of the person in charge of planning, the prioritization of relationships with regional retailers, the close cooperative supply system, and the small scale of production, which reduces problems associated with base-stock inventory.

Sustained superiority, strategy and IC management: winners versus losers

The prior literature has provided few case studies considering whether and how IC contributes to high performance (for example, Marzo and Scarpino, 2016), in particular, empirical studies that demonstrate whether and how IC can help sustain competitive advantage over time. Hence we followed up the companies in 2016 to see if their performance had been sustained over time. Not all the companies in our sample had sustained high performance and we have separated the companies on the basis of winners – those that sustained competitive advantage – and losers – those that did not. We re-examined the IC elements regarded as critical success factors to see whether they remained relevant, and analysed and compared the companies' competitive strategy and KM strategy to explore the factors that lead to sustained organizational success (Table 15.3).

Winner group

Common to the winner group companies is that the IC items identified in 2008 as the source of competitive advantage still work well. We found that winner companies successfully combined competitive strategy with KM strategy; this may have been intended or unintended. For example, the competitive advantage of both Company A and Company B is their innovative technology. To maintain their position, Company A focused on one type of product and

Table 15.3 Competitive strategy and KM strategy

Company		Competitive strategy	KM objective	Knowledge source	Knowledge sharing and transferring
Winner group	D	Strategic visioning and strategic learning (combination of deliberate and emergent strategy)	Innovation and efficiency	Combination of internal and external	Personalization
	A	Strategic planning and learning (combination of deliberate and emergent strategy)	Innovation	Combination of internal and external	Personalization
	B	Strategic learning (emergent strategy)	Innovation	Mainly internal	Personalization
Loser group	C	Strategic visioning	Efficiency	Internal	Personalization
	E	Strategic learning (emergent strategy)	No clear objective	Internal	Personalization

continuously renewed the technology to make the product easier to use while maintaining precision and versatility. In contrast, Company B had no deliberate plan but continued its customer demand-based development strategy, which also helped the company to grow.

On the other hand, these companies' KM strategy is more open, actively utilizing external expertise, experience, and knowledge, which helps to overcome the inherent shortages in resources. To continuously develop the high value-added product, Company A collaborates with large companies to utilize their technology and convert them into a new product. Like Company A, Company D attached great importance to external intelligence. The significance of the network was emphasized by the CEO and openly disclosed on the company's webpage. A network club was created to provide a 'ba' – a shared context in which knowledge is shared, created, and utilized so that people from outside the company can share experience, and ideas and business opportunities can be jointly explored. In knowledge creation, generation and regeneration of ba are key, as ba provides the energy, quality, and place to perform individual conversions and to move along the knowledge spiral (Nonaka *et al.*, 2000). By doing so, Company D established a strategy combining internal- and external-oriented KM. In contrast, Company B has a more internal-oriented KM strategy, in which development was conducted based on the explicit or implicit needs of customers, but was realized based on the expertise and know-how of technicians. This may be why Company B, though considered successful, only grew slowly.

Company D's competitive advantage was maintained over the long term because it relies on management philosophy, work processes, and organizational structure, characteristics considered as KM infrastructure for knowledge management and impossible for other companies to copy. Company D's philosophy is that instead of benchmarking competitors to formulate strategy, it focuses on its own corporate value, what kind of company it wants to be, and how to do business in the long term. Its work processes encourage information exchange between employees so that new business opportunities can be taken, and problems identified and solved in a timely fashion. Employees write a daily report, which is then summarized and disclosed so that silos between different districts are broken down and knowledge acquired, accumulated, and utilized company-wide. The organization's structure is also designed to be very flat to allow information sharing and business opportunity identification.

Loser group

The loser group shares similar characteristics in that the IC items identified by their managers as value drivers have lost value in the later years. For example, Company C did not lose its technology advantage in the current market. While it is still the world leader in quartz processing, with a high level of efficiency achieved through mass production and good customer relations, its focus on efficiency meant that it did not respond to changing markets, and relied too heavily on orders from the parent company, which is facing a contracting market, especially after the financial crisis. Meanwhile, Company C's KM appears to be very internal-oriented, lacking channels to external knowledge resources. While it has been exploring new markets where its technologies can be employed, it needs to integrate its current knowledge with new knowledge from the different industries in order to realize new opportunities.

Similarly, Company E has downsized as its performance has decreased while its IC remains static. The company's success was based on one excellent idea and no hot commodity can have longevity without value being constantly added. Company E did not use any value-added activities to strengthen the brand of the character goods it designed and its business model could not prevent other companies from entering the market and copying their methods. More importantly, Company E had no strategy to improve the capability of planning and design. The employee who was regarded as the source of competitive advantage in this instance becomes a disadvantage to the company.

Discussion

What kinds of IC deliver sustained competitive advantage for SMEs?

In the IC literature, dozens of IC components have been proposed as the source of competitive advantage. For example, Gallego and Rodriguez (2005) investigated 39 Spanish companies using a questionnaire to analyse 25 items of IC. They found that IC such as customer relationships, employee experience, information technologies, brand image, procedures, and systems are most relevant, and the number of indicators used by companies is about 20. Steenkamp and Kashyap (2010) surveyed 30 New Zealand SMEs using 23 items of IC components. They had similar results, finding that most of the IC items are important, including customer satisfaction, customer loyalty, corporate reputation, product reputation, and employee know-how. However, as revealed by our study, some of these will not necessarily lead to future success.

Barney (1991) identified resources that are valuable, rare, inimitable, and unsubsitutable as key to competitive advantage. However, can these kinds of resources deliver sustainable competitive advantage that persists despite variable economic and market conditions? To answer the question, Peteraf (1993) offered the following requirements as necessary for transforming resources with the above characteristic into sustainable competitive advantage: resource heterogeneity, which means resource bundles vary from firm to firm; ex ante limits to competition-barriers that deter or prevent other firms from attempting to develop the same resource bundle; ex post limits to competition – barriers that make it difficult for competitors to imitate what the pioneer is doing effectively; and resource immobility. When it comes to SMEs, in the long run, the most important measure is to prevent imitation to defend existing advantage or renew resources advantage through innovation.

From our analysis, inimitability not only means it is impossible to imitate a resource technically but also legally, efficiently, and culturally. For SMEs, legal protection of patents and trademarks is one of the most effective ways to protect themselves from larger rivals. For example, Company B learned the importance of patents from a painful lesson in the past in which a larger company copied its technology. Organizations can also prevent imitation by focusing on a specific area through which they obtain the technology advantage that makes imitation more costly, as did Company A. While large enterprises have the capacity to develop the same technology, buying the product may be more cost efficient. Organizational culture is also a barrier to imitation, as can be seen in the case of Company D. Its CEO is not concerned that employees will give away the secret of their success because "it is hard to describe, even if they can describe they cannot copy it". The employee who leaves cannot help a competitor replicate what is unique about the organization.

How does KM facilitate sustained competitive advantage?

Preventing imitation may work in an existing market; however, maintaining the resource-based advantage can be achieved through renewing resources and capabilities through KM. However, this can only be achieved when some conditions are met. First, as some researchers indicate, an organization managing knowledge well has the potential to obtain competitive advantage and create significant value, but only if it is linked to its overall strategy and strategic decisions (Egbu *et al.*, 2005; Lai and Lin, 2012; Lee *et al.*, 2013). Company A is an example of this. Second, KM with an objective of innovation rather than efficiency is essential, especially in a changing market. For example, Company B, despite having the most advanced technology, lost its advantage because it focused on quality and efficiency instead of development of revolutionary technology or innovative ways to use the technology when facing a shrinking market. Third, instead of relying on the knowledge inside the organization, the utilization of external technologies and expertise is critical because SMEs often have a bottleneck of resources. Company D overcame this because it did not see employees as success factors and therefore higher turnover did not lead to a competitive disadvantage. Company D worked in a holistic way to act as a knowledge creation facilitator.

The findings of our study are consistent with previous studies (for example, Wong and Aspinwall, 2005) which find that KM is conducted in an informal way in SMEs without the use of the language and concepts of KM, specific staff, and formal KM structures. Regardless of whether KM is informally or formally conducted, if properly integrated with overall strategy, with a more open source and directed towards creation of new capabilities, it should ultimately lead to long-term competitive advantage.

How to incorporate strategization into IC management

Mintzberg *et al.* (2008) summarized ten schools of strategy theories in their popular book *Strategy Safari*. Strategic IC management cannot be described using a simplified model considering the existence of a variety of strategy theories and practices; however, IC theory is easier to incorporate into some schools of strategy than others. The idea of IC combines the resource-based theory and dynamic capabilities approach. The former implies that the capabilities of the firm are rooted in the evolution process of the organization while the latter regards them as developed through strategic learning. These two views, though different, are related with their focus on sustaining and developing internal capabilities, that is, the inside-out view, rather than the outside-in view (Mintzberg *et al.*, 2008). Therefore, resource-based theory is often criticized because it is difficult to incorporate into the position school of strategy, while fitting well with the culture school of strategy.

Moreover, prescriptive strategy theory cannot explain practice entirely. Ricceri (2008) called for the incorporation of strategization within the management of IC. Both proper strategy formulation and execution are needed to link IC to performance. This separation of formulation and implementation is central to the design school of strategy and convenient for a business school case study. However, in practice, strategy formation is a long, subtle, and difficult process of learning. If managers:

> [d]etach thinking from acting, remain in their headquarters instead of getting into factories and meeting customers where the real information may have to be dug out, then it may be a cause of some of the serious problems faced by some of the today's organizations.
>
> *(Mintzberg et al., 2008, p. 41)*

Third, strategy at its essence is integrative. Though some schools of strategy are more popular than others, all of them are just a part of a big 'animal'. The problem with the resource-based is that it explains too easily what already exists, rather than tackling the tougher question of what can come into being – just as our study found that some IC developed as a past strategy will not necessarily lead to future success. A combination of other perspectives to form a holistic view of strategic IC management may help to predict the future. Our study reveals that those in the winner group like Company A and Company D adopted an integrated rather than specific approach to formulating strategy. The integrated approach strengthens the causal link between IC, positions, and final company performance. This holistic view of strategic IC management is consistent with the way information users evaluated IC. For example, in 2008, a committee organized by the Organization for Small & Medium Enterprises and Regional Innovation in Japan investigated perceptions of IC reporting among 439 Japanese banks (Yosano and Koga, 2008). The result shows that the lenders have difficulties in judging internal resources, as well as corporate strategy, as isolated information. Rather, they use integrated information that is tightly correlated with both internal resources and strategy, and incorporate other data regarding the company's relationship with other businesses and society.

Does the Japanese style of IC management exist in SMEs?

Uchida and Roos (2008) compared large companies using the western style of intellectual resources management and the Japanese style. The former was labelled as strategy rationality style, while the latter was described as resource rationality style. The western IC management with strategic rationality relied on external environment analysis and utilized intellectual resources according to strategic goals, featuring deliberate strategy and an indirect management of intellectual assets. In contrast, the Japanese style of IC management or resource rationality based its activities on the company's internal resources. Resource rationality is formulated in the process of utilizing IC and is a direct management of intellectual assets (Yao and Bjurström, 2014). Therefore, sometimes Japanese companies are criticized for their lack of strategic views from the western perspective of strategy (deliberate strategy), which is based more on the analysis of external competition and environment. The strategic formulation of Japanese companies is more internally oriented and resource-based (emergent strategy). Our study is consistent with this, finding that of the five companies, four showed an emergent pattern of strategy formation and attached great importance to learning from the process.

The other characteristic of Japanese SMEs is that IC management is conducted based on a broad perspective instead of position analysis. Instead of relative value, some of the Japanese companies have a propensity for pursuing absolute value, which is regarded as the essence of innovation (Nonaka and Katsumi, 2004). These kinds of Japanese companies try to differentiate themselves from others with unique intellectual resources that only exist within themselves. This perspective-based strategy formulation can be seen in all five case companies.

Conclusion

IC is more important as a source of competitive advantage in SMEs than large companies because SMEs have fewer tangible resources, and should compete through IC (Jardon and Martos, 2012, p. 463). However, the lack of understanding of IC management in SMEs and the application of prescription strategy theory to explain the link between IC and firm performance has caused practice difficulties, with investors and creditors finding it difficult to evaluate IC and use it to predict future performance, and managers losing interest in IC reporting. In this situation, the so-called third stage of IC research that examines what works in practice is needed. This chapter attempts to explore how IC contributes to sustained competitive advantage through strategic management in Japanese SMEs.

Our research reveals that not all IC can deliver competitive advantage in the long run. SMEs' technology and business know-how can be copied by rivals, especially large companies. The winner group in our study focus on technology, legal protection, efficiency, and culture to sustain a competitive advantage. Only by combining with overall competitive strategy could KM facilitate long-term competitive advantage. High performance companies tend to adopt a KM strategy that aims at innovation instead of efficiency, and more positively utilize the external resources of capability, expertise, know-how, and technology. There are different ways to incorporate strategy into IC management and, when compared to the loser group, the winners adopted a more integrated approach to formulating strategy. The Japanese style of IC management is more internally oriented with the strategy formulation process featuring an emergent pattern rather than a deliberate plan.

Our research has practice and policy implications. As the case companies we chose for analysis were all high growth companies in the first three years, understanding the reason for the difference in performance in the later years may help managers to take measures to prevent imitation and mobility of their capability and resources, and to review and modify their KM and strategy formation so that competitive advantage can be sustained for a longer period. Meanwhile, our results will also help investors and others who need to evaluate IC management to predict the future performance of SMEs. Furthermore, the government may provide more support for SMEs to develop, protect, and improve IC by taking into account the features of the Japanese style of management.

Instead of applying one strategy definition and theory, we analyse strategy formation based on Mintzberg *et al.*'s (2008) idea that strategy may include many definitions and approaches, all of which together provide a whole picture of a big animal. We revealed that strategic IC management in practice takes various forms that leads to different performance in the long term. This implies that the strategy theory researchers choose to study in relation to IC management should be carefully examined to avoid fragmentation and prejudice. To uncover the secret inside the black box, more sophisticated research design and bold exploration are needed.

Note

1 We appreciate the Small and Medium Enterprise Agency for assisting us in the case study, which is a part of the OECD high-growth project 2008. We are also thankful to T. Yosano of Kobe University for assisting in the interviews.

References

Aragón-Sánchez, A. and Sánchez-Marín, G. (2005), "Strategic orientation, management characteristics, and performance: A study of Spanish SMEs", *Journal of Small Business Management*, Vol. 43, No. 3, pp. 287–308.

Barney, J. (1991), "Firm resources and sustained competitive advantage", *Journal of Management*, Vol. 17, No. 1, pp. 99–120.

Bierly, P. E. and Daly, P. S. (2007), "Knowledge strategies, competitive environment and organizational performance in small manufacturing firms", *Entrepreneurship Theory and Practice*, Vol. 31, No. 4, pp. 493–516.

Burke, G. I. and Jarratt, D. G. (2004), "The influence of information and advice on competitive strategy", *Qualitative Market Research*, Vol. 7, No. 2, pp. 126–138.

Chandler, A. (1962), *Strategy and Structure: Chapters in the History of American Enterprise*, MIT Press, Cambridge, MA.

Choi, B. and Lee, H. (2002), "Knowledge management strategy and its link to knowledge creation process", *Expert Systems with Applications*, Vol. 23, pp. 173–187.

Choi, B., Poon, S. K., and Davis, J. G. (2008), "Effects of knowledge management strategy on organizational performance: A complementarity theory-based approach", *Omega*, Vol. 36, pp. 235–251.

Cohen, S., Naoum, V. C., and Vlismas, O. (2014), "Intellectual capital, strategy and financial crisis from a SMEs perspective", *Journal of Intellectual Capital*, Vol. 15, No. 2, pp. 294–315.

Collis, D. J., and Montgomery, C. (1995), "Competing on resources: Strategies in the 1990s", *Harvard Business Review*, Vol. 73, pp. 119–128.

Coyne, K. P. (1986), "Sustainable competitive advantage: What it is, what it isn't", *Business Horizons*, Vol. 29, No. 1, pp. 54–61.

Day, G. S. and Wensley, R. (1988), "Assessing advantage: A framework for diagnosing competitive superiority", *Journal of Marketing*, Vol. 52, No. 2, pp. 1–20.

Demartini, P. and Del Baldo, M. (2015). "Knowledge and social capital: Drivers for sustainable local growth", *Chinese Business Review*, Vol. 14, No. 2, pp. 106–117.

Dumay, J. (2012), "Grand theories as barriers to using IC concepts", *Journal of Intellectual Capital*, Vol. 13, No. 10, pp. 4–15.

Dumay, J. and Garanina, T. (2013), "Intellectual capital research: A critical examination of the third stage", *Journal of Intellectual Capital*, Vol. 14, No. 1, pp. 10–25.

Dumay, J. and Guthrie, J. (2012), "IC and strategy as practice", *International Journal of Knowledge and Systems Science*, Vol. 3, No. 4, pp. 28–37.

Egbu, C. O., Hari, S., and Renukappa, S. H. (2005), "Knowledge management for sustainable competitiveness in small and medium surveying practices", *Structural Survey*, Vol. 23, No. 1, pp. 7–21.

Gallego, I. and Rodríguez, L. (2005), "The situation of intangible assets in Spanish firms: An empirical analysis", *Journal of Intellectual Capital*, Vol. 6, No. 1, pp. 105–126.

Greiner, M. E., Bo'hmann, T., and Krcmar, H. (2007), "A strategy for knowledge management", *Journal of Knowledge Management*, Vol. 11, No. 6, pp. 3–15.

Guthrie, J., Ricceri, F., and Dumay, J. (2012), "Reflections and projections: A decade of intellectual capital accounting research", *The British Accounting Review*, Vol. 44, No. 2, pp. 68–92.

Hansen, M., Nohria, N., and Tierney, T. (1999), "What's your strategy for managing knowledge?" *Harvard Business Review*, Vol. 77, No. 2, pp. 106–116.

Hutchinson, V. and Quintas, P. (2008), "Do SMEs do knowledge management? Or simply manage what they know?" *International Small Business Journal*, Vol. 26, No. 2, pp. 131–154.

International Integrated Reporting Council (IIRC) (2013), *The International <IR> Framework*, International Integrated Reporting Council, London.

Itami H. (1987), *Mobilizing Invisible Assets*, Harvard University Press, Cambridge, MA.

Jardon, C. M., and Martos, M. S. (2012), "Intellectual capital as competitive advantage in emerging clusters in Latin America", *Journal of Intellectual Capital*, Vol. 13, No. 4, pp. 462–481.

Kerin, R. A., Mahajan, V., and Varadarajan, P. R. (1990), *Contemporary Perspectives on Strategic Market Planning*, Allyn and Bacon, Boston, MA.

Lai, Y. L. and Lin, F. J. (2012), "The effects of knowledge management and technology innovation on new product development performance an empirical study of Taiwanese machine tools industry", *Procedia-Social and Behavioural Sciences*, Vol. 40, pp. 157–164.

Lee, V. H., Foo, A. T. L., Leong, L. Y., and Ooi, K. B. (2016), "Can competitive advantage be achieved through knowledge management? A case study on SMEs", *Expert Systems with Applications*, Vol. 65, pp. 136–151.

Lee, V. H., Leong, L. Y., Hew, T. S., and Ooi, K. B. (2013), "Knowledge management: A key determinant in advancing technological innovation?" *Journal of Knowledge Management*, Vol. 17, No. 6, pp. 848–872.

Marzo, G. and Scarpino, E. (2016), "Exploring intellectual capital management in SMEs: An in-depth Italian case study", *Journal of Intellectual Capital*, Vol. 17, No. 1, pp. 27–51.

Mintzberg, H., Ahlstrand, B., and Lampel, J. B. (2008), *Strategy Safari: The Complete Guide Through the Wilds of Strategic Management*, Pearson Education, Toronto, ON.

Mouritsen, J. (2006), "Problematising intellectual capital research: Ostensive versus performative IC", *Accounting, Auditing & Accountability Journal*, Vol. 19, No. 6, pp. 820–840.

Nonaka, I. and Katsumi, A. (2004), *The Essence of Innovation* (in Japanese), Nikkei BP.

Nonaka, I. and Takeuchi, H. (1995), *The Knowledge-Creating Company: How Japanese Companies Create the Dynamics of Innovation*, Oxford University Press, New York.

Nonaka, I., Toyama, R., and Konno, N. (2000), "SECI, ba and leadership: A unified model of dynamic knowledge creation", *Long Range Planning*, Vol. 33, No. 1, pp. 5–34.

Peteraf, M. A. (1993), "The cornerstones of competitive advantage: A resource-based view", *Strategic Management Journal*, Vol. 14, No. 3, pp. 79–191.

Porter, M. E. (1985), *Competitive Advantage*, The Free Press, New York.

Prahalad, C. K. and Hamel, G. (1990), 'The core competence of the corporation", *Harvard Business Review*, Vol. 68, No. 3, pp. 79–91.

Rangone, A. (1999), "A resource-based approach to strategy analysis in small-medium sized enterprises", *Small Business Economics*, Vol. 12, No. 3, pp. 233–248.

Ricceri, F. (2008), *Intellectual Capital and Knowledge Management: Strategic Management of Knowledge Resources*. Routledge Advances in Management and Business Studies: Routledge, London.

Steenkamp, N. and Kashyap, V. (2010), "Importance and contribution of intangible assets: SME managers' perceptions", *Journal of Intellectual Capital*, Vol. 11, No. 3, pp. 368–390.

St-Pierre, J. and Audet, J. (2011), "Intangible assets and performance: Analysis of manufacturing SMEs", *Journal of Intellectual Capital*, Vol. 12, No. 2, pp. 202–223.

Sullivan, P. H. (2000), *Value-driven Intellectual Capital: How to Convert Intangible Corporate Assets into Market Value*, John Wiley & Sons Inc., New York.

Swart, J. (2006), "Intellectual capital: Disentangling an enigmatic concept", *Journal of Intellectual Capital*, Vol. 7, No. 2, pp. 136–159.

Takahashi, T. (2012), *Strategy for the Age of Knowledge-Organization*, Diamond Books, India.

Teece, D. J., Pisano, G., and Shuen, A. (1997). "Dynamic capabilities and strategic management", *Strategic Management Journal*, Vol. 18, No. 7, pp. 509–533.

Uchida, Y. and Roos, G. (2008), *Intellectual Capital Management for Japanese Firms* (in Japanese). Chuokeizai-sha, Inc.

Wiig, M. K. (1997), "Integrating intellectual capital and knowledge management", *Long Range Planning*, Vol. 30, No. 3, pp. 399–405.

Wong, K. Y. and Aspinwall, E. (2005), "An empirical study of the important factors for knowledge management adoption in the SME sector", *Journal of Knowledge Management*, Vol. 9, No. 3, pp. 64–82.

Yao, J. and Bjurström, E. (2014), "Trends and challenges of future IC reporting experiences from Japan", in P. Ordoñes de Pablo and L. Edvinsson (Eds), *Intellectual Capital in Organizations, Non-Financial Reports and Accounts*, Routledge, New York, pp. 277–296.

Yosano, T. and Koga, C. (2008), "Influence of intellectual capital information on credit risk rating process criterion and credit conditions: Survey analysis of Japanese financial institutions", *Proceedings of 4th Workshop on Visualizing, Measuring and Managing Intangibles and Intellectual Capital*, 22–24 October.

16

TOWARDS AN INTEGRATED INTELLECTUAL CAPITAL MANAGEMENT FRAMEWORK

Ulf Johanson

Background

In recent years intellectual capital (IC) has been subject to criticism for a number of reasons. Dumay (2014), for example, expressed the opinion that IC has been too focused on reporting and not enough on IC management. The same criticism was raised by Bukh and Johanson (2003) in relation to the Meritum project. More recently, Japanese initiatives have downplayed the IC management issue (Johanson and Koga, 2015; Yao and Bjurström, 2015), despite the development of the Intellectual Asset Based Management (METI, 2005) guideline.

This chapter aims to address this criticism by developing an integrated IC management framework to understand how public and private organizations handle their IC management. Referring to Gröjer and Johanson (1998), the chapter is also a contribution to the practice turn in IC (Guthrie *et al.*, 2012; Dumay *et al.*, 2017). The framework incorporates management control (MC) and performance management research and aims to increase understanding of how work environment management was performed in about 250 Swedish organizations (Frick and Johanson, 2013). To further check the usefulness of the framework, it was applied to understand IC management in a successful medium-sized Swedish IT consultant group (Johanson and Skoog, 2015). The use of the concept 'integrated' refers to the need for cohesion between different management items classified in four categories (i.e. management ideal, content, supporting processes, and continuous evaluation).

Initiatives addressing IC management

Several initiatives with respect to previous IC guidelines will be addressed here: the Meritum guideline; the Danish guideline; the Austrian legislation; and the Japanese guidelines.

After several years of discussion within the OECD and EU during the 1990s, an extensive European R&D project addressing IC management and reporting was undertaken. The project, which was labelled Meritum, was divided into four sub-projects: classification of concepts; capital market aspects; MC issues; and the development of a guideline. The Guideline for Managing and Reporting on Intangibles (Meritum, 2002) was built on the knowledge acquired from the three earlier projects and divided into three sections. In the first section the basic concepts of IC, human capital, structural capital, and relational capital are defined. In the second section, which concerns the management of intangibles, the clear relationship between measurement, reporting, and management is addressed. The last section contains an IC report model comprising three parts: vision of the firm; summary of intangible resources and activities; and a system of indicators.

In the late 1990s, the Danish government encouraged an R&D project that in 2001 culminated in the Danish IC guideline (DATI, 2001). It focused on the preparation of IC statements for external publication, in which four elements together express the company's knowledge management. The four elements link users of the company's goods or services with the company's need for knowledge resources. They include the acknowledgement of the need for expressing the knowledge narrative of the company, the management challenges to improve knowledge management, and a set of indicators to define, measure, and follow up different initiatives.

Since 2007, Austrian universities and research institutions have had a legal obligation to set up a 'Wissenbilanz', similar to the Meritum IC report (Piper and Pietsch, 2006). The report should include a narrative and indicators addressing goals, strategies, resources, planned research, and education activities as well as results. The legislation originates from a demand to increase transparency with respect to how universities and research institutions exploit tax-based funding. However, even before the Wissenbilanz became a legal obligation its likely impact on internal management process was questioned.

Finally, Japan has been one of the most ambitious countries with respect to trying to adapt the ideas of IC. Since the turn of the century, a number of METI guidelines have been launched. One of these is the Intellectual Asset based Management (IAbM) (METI, 2005). In the Kansai region, IC seems to have been adopted more so than elsewhere in Japan. In 2008, the Kyoto prefecture created its own Chie management evaluation and certification system, which refers to the technology and know-how that cannot be registered as intellectual property. It also includes other intangible business resources that bring about corporate value, such as human resources, customer base, and brand. In other words, Chie equals the strength of companies and their management (Yao and Bjurström, 2015).

Initially, the expectations from METI as well as from financial market actors was high (Johanson and Koga, 2015). IC was regarded as highly important with respect to comparative advantages for firms. However, after several years, firms were hesitant to disclose IAbM reports. There were not many firms in Japan that adapted the guidelines. The IAbM guideline was not used by big firms, and a study of SMEs (Johanson *et al.*, 2009) revealed some concerns with respect to its usefulness. Even the interest in the Chie system declined (Yao and Bjurström, 2015).

How can this decline in interest in IC be understood? It seems that this decline is not restricted to Japan; global interest in producing IC statements has been declining (Dumay, 2014), including for the Meritum and the Danish guidelines (Nielsen *et al.*, 2014). As Dumay (2014) suggested, the production of a report does not necessarily say anything of what is going on inside firms or in internal discussions between fund managers, analysts, and banks. Neither is it significant for what is going on with respect to communication between firms and the financial market, which may happen through other channels like the internet and meetings. An early interview study with SMEs (Johanson *et al.*, 2009), as well as a study of four fund management firms (Holland *et al.*, 2012), were attempts to achieve an understanding of the learning and decision processes taking place.

The four initiatives are not the sole, but are probably the most influential, guidelines to have been launched. They have focused global attention on IC management and reporting, but have not shed light on how IC management should be tackled. In this respect, the Japanese and the

Danish guidelines are the most advanced. The Japanese IAbM guideline explicitly addresses IC management. The guideline is detailed but the theoretical foundation is not obvious, which makes the guideline unclear. However, despite declining interest, it may be too early to draw any conclusions. Even if the number of external IC reports is reduced, firms have perhaps learnt something about IC resources and IC management that is not easily understood from simply counting reports. For example, in the Japanese context we do not know enough about the role of IC and IAbM inside firms as well as in communication with stakeholders. This could be established from the kind of mature second phase studies for which Dumay (2014) advocates. As Bjurström (2012) proposed, the Japanese context is probably well positioned for a more profound understanding. The diffusion of IC ideas by means of different fairly well-prepared guidelines has taken place over more than ten years. Johanson and Bjurström (2015) suggested that this probably means that the adoption of the IC idea will move into another phase. Instead of diffusion of the IC idea, it could be a matter of re-invention (Rogers, 1995). In the Japanese context, there is a strong change agent (i.e. METI, as part of the national system of innovation).

Dumay's (2014) second phase studies require a critical mass of interest. This may still exist in Japan, where there may be possibilities for gaining a deeper understanding of the interactive re-invention phase. It is important to unlock the black box and try to gain a deeper understanding of what is happening inside firms with respect to IC management. The aim of this chapter is to suggest a framework that may be useful in furthering this understanding.

Theoretical background to the IC management framework

Before developing the IC management framework, which will be called an integrated IC management framework, it is necessary to summarize briefly the theoretical background.

Accounting has traditionally used formal systems to focus financial resources. The basic idea is to represent reality objectively and transparently. MC is a top-down process by means of 'command and control'. However, over the last decades, there has been criticism from both practitioners and researchers (Johnson and Kaplan, 1987; Johnson, 1992) of management accounting and control practices and their lack of relevance and usefulness. It has been suggested that perceptions of management accounting and control tools and techniques have changed during this discourse (Johanson *et al.*, 2006). From having previously been seen as instruments for supporting top management in making complex organizational activities and transactions more intelligible to managers in general, the tools are regarded as separating top management from the organization by being too abstract, short-sighted, money-oriented, and simplified. Another important argument concerns the transformed approach to organizational value creation, where industrial logic has been challenged. Industrial logic and the traditional tools of management accounting and control do not lend themselves to addressing crucial value-creating aspects, including intangible resources such as knowledge and customer relations (Sveiby and Lloyd, 1987). It has been suggested that these intangible resources are the only truly sustainable competitive advantage of a firm (Mouritsen *et al.*, 2001). Health and work environment, as valuable organizational resources, are further examples of problems that are normally considered in other arenas within the enterprise rather than in the MC and accounting function. Organizations of various kinds have realized that the traditional means of control, which have often involved mutually isolated financial and non-financial measures, objectives, and targets, can no longer be legitimized (Johanson *et al.*, 2001a, 2001b).

Several authors have suggested that a new approach to accounting and MC is required and two pathways have been identified. First is the development of completely new non-financial models like balanced scorecard, intangible assets monitor, health statements, IC, and integrated reporting. The second is traditional accounting where MC is the point of departure in attempts to extend its borders. The framework to be suggested later in this chapter is based on a combination of these two pathways.

MC has been defined as "the process by which managers assure that resources are obtained and used effectively and efficiently in the accomplishment of the organization's objectives" (Anthony, 1965, p. 17). MC is supposed to be the link between strategy and operations. However, Anthony´s definition has been criticized by Ferreira and Otley (2009, p. 264) for encouraging a narrow view "that falls short of capturing the richness of issues and relationships implicated in MC systems design and use. In particular, it concentrated on formal (and usually accounting) controls without setting them in their wider context". Additionally, Simons (1995) holds that MC is, and should be, an interactive communication process as opposed to just a diagnostic one-way information tool. One-way hierarchic communication has often been linked with command and control behaviour (Bjurström *et al.*, 2010) where processes are the main concern. This might be dysfunctional because organizational vision and goals may be forgotten. Lapsley (2009) adds that a strong focus on measurability has supported a 'tick-box mentality' where audits are performed by 'accountocrats' (Power, 1997).

Hofstede (1978) complained that MC and accounting suffer from philosophical poverty. The latter facilitates an instrumental approach to MC where basic values and visions can be forgotten. Dean (1999) holds that there is a need to reconsider the regimes of government behind MC and to investigate and address basic MC values. Following the same kind of reasoning, Hasselbladh *et al.* (2008) used the concept of ideals instead of values. The term ideal here refers to a basic intention shared by a collective of individuals which is the rationale for the existence of a specific organization. If the governance ideal is not supported by the complete MC system, the MC process will fail to reach its aims. MC may end up in a box-ticking ritual. Andersson (2014) demonstrated a conflict between two kinds of values with respect to providing home help service for elderly people in a Swedish local authority. The ideal of accurate care held by employees (and by politicians) was in sharp contrast to an ideal of administrative and economic efficiency promoted by the management of the organization. Middle managers find themselves under pressure when they have to satisfy both of these ideals.

MC has also been accused of being too focused on obtaining a representation of objective facts by using exact and precise measures. In opposition to this, mainstream MC and accounting accepts the idea that because objective facts are hard to achieve when it comes to accounting, the focus needs to be shifted towards mobilizing action by means of 'good enough' measures (Johanson *et al.*, 2001b; Mouritsen *et al.*, 2001). MC is about influencing the behaviour of involved actors, and MC processes are located in a system of complexity where single causalities seldom exist. It is rather a system of complex mutual causalities (Bjurström, 2012).

As a consequence of the criticism of MC systems, Ferreira and Otley (2009) prefer the concept performance management system. They view:

> [p]erformance management systems as the evolving formal and informal mechanisms, processes, systems, and networks used by organizations for conveying the key objectives and goals elicited by management, for assisting the strategic process and ongoing management through analysis, planning, measurement, control, rewarding, and broadly managing performance, and for supporting and facilitating organizational learning and change.
>
> *(p. 264)*

Based on a theoretical framework comprising evolutionary action, organizational learning, and structuration theories, Johanson *et al.* (2001a, 2001b) performed an explorative qualitative

Table 16.1 Routines

Recognition and measurement routines	• human capital surveys • market capital surveys • accounting practices
Reporting routines	• continuous internal reports • informal information to the financial market
Evaluation routines	• evaluation of single human capital and market indicators by each manager • statistical analysis
Attention routines	• meetings
Motivation routines	• top management demand • benchmarking between departments • dialogues • salary bonus related to change in human capital and market capital index
Commitment routines	• ownership of each indicator • contract between managers at different levels to act upon the indicators
Follow up routines	• statistical analysis of the complete performance management system

study of the performance management practices addressing intangibles in several Swedish companies. They identified different routines that facilitate learning and the transformation of attention and knowledge into action. Routines additional to surveys include statistical analysis, benchmarking, dialogues, salary bonuses, and contracts. A classification of the routines is highlighted in Table 16.1.

Johanson *et al*. (2001b, p. 731) conclude that the routines are listed above direct managers' and employees' attention to the results from measurements:

> These results, in combination with statistical analysis, affect knowledge. Motivation is further addressed by a clear top-management demand, benchmarking, and salary bonuses. Finally, commitment to change is made possible by means of a contract between managers at different levels. The empirical data reveals that organizational learning processes have been affected in the way that dominating cognitive schemes and coordinated action have been obtained.

Referring to Giddens (1984), management control of intangibles provides new practices of domination structures through motivation and commitment routines. The signification (i.e. the collective cognitive schemes), as well as the legitimization (the shared sets of values and ideals) structures are gradually transformed into new structures (Johanson *et al.*, 2001b).

To analyse the design and the use of performance management systems, Ferreira and Otley (2009, p. 266) suggest a framework comprising 12 issues that need to be considered. These issues are:

1 the *vision* and *mission* of the organization and how this is brought to the attention of managers and employees, including the mechanisms, processes, and networks that are used to convey the organization's overarching purposes and objectives to its members;
2 the *key factors* that are believed to be central to the organization's overall future success and how they are brought to the attention of managers and employees;
3 the *organization structure* and what impact it has on the design and use of the performance management system;

4   the *strategies and plans* that the organization has adopted and the processes and activities that it has decided are required for it to ensure its success, that is, how are strategies and plans adapted, generated, and communicated to managers and employees?

5   the organization's *key performance measures* deriving from its objectives, key success factors, and strategies and plans, that is, how these are specified and communicated and the role they play in performance evaluation;

6   the *level of performance* that the organization needs to achieve for each of its key performance measures;

7   the processes that the organization follows for evaluating individual, group, and organizational performance;

8   the *rewards or penalties*, financial or non-financial, which managers and other employees gain by achieving or failing to meet performance targets;

9   the *information flows and systems* that the organization has in place to support the operation of its performance management system;

10 the type of *use of information* and of the various *control mechanisms* that are in place;

11 the *alteration of the performance management systems* in the light of the change dynamics of the organization and its environment, that is, have the changes in performance management system design or use been made in a proactive or reactive manner?

12 the strength and cohesion *between the components* of performance management systems and the ways in which they are used.

Primarily based on the proposals by Ferreira and Otley (2009), Hofstede (1978), Hasselbladh *et al.* (2008), and Johanson *et al.* (2001a, 2001b), the construction of the framework will be presented in the next section.

Developing an integrated IC management framework

The integrated IC management framework was originally constructed by Frick and Johanson (2013) for the purpose of analysing work environment management – also later extended by Johanson and Skoog (2015) when analysing IC management in a couple of firms. All the applications have been performed in Sweden.

Ferreira and Otley's performance management systems framework is adjusted and further developed to underline the importance of: (1) the communication process as opposed to the information process, that is, emphasizing the interactive as opposed to the diagnostic approach (Simons, 1995); (2) the basic values or the performance management systems ideal as suggested by Hofstede (1978) and Hasselbladh *et al.* (2008); (3) the supporting routines as proposed by Johanson *et al.* (2001a, 2001b); and (4) finally the learning aspect with respect to the continuous adjustment of the performance management system in accordance with what has been suggested by, for example, Nonaka and Toyama (2005).

To improve the usefulness of a framework, overlapping issues should be clarified and, if necessary, deleted. A grouping of the elements into different categories might also be useful. Therefore, the issues are classified into Ideal, Content, Support, and Evaluation. The performance management system framework is outlined in Table 16.2.

Each of these elements will now be explored. In relation to vision, Ferreira and Otley (2009) claim that vision and mission are comprised of core values. They hold that "Vision and mission statements are landmarks that guide the process of deciding what to change and what to preserve in strategies and activities" (p. 268). To distinguish between these concepts, we prefer to separate the core value – which we label ideal – and the vision. In accordance with Hasselbladh

Table 16.2 Performance management system framework

Ideal	• Vision
Content	• Strategies, plans, goals
	• Critical success and risk factors
	• Key performance measures
	• Follow-up
Support	• Reward processes
	• Responsibility and contract processes
	• Supporting communication
Evaluation	• Cohesion between ideal, content, and supporting processes
	• Learning and adjustment of the performance management system

et al. (2008), we suggest that ideal is a part of the belief system that is sometimes unknown to employees as well as stakeholders. Vision is often, but not necessarily, a written statement that works as a guiding principle. When it works as expected the vision is broken down into strategies, plans, and goals. During this process, critical success and risk factors are identified and subject to measurements. Follow-up is equivalent to Ferreira and Otley's evaluation. We prefer to instead use the concept of evaluation in relation to the evaluation of the complete performance management system. Follow-up refers in our framework to the content elements.

Ferreira and Otley discuss reward processes and supporting organization and communication structure but do not give attention to responsibility and contract processes. In the Swedish firms analysed by Johanson *et al.* (2001a, 2001b), responsibility and contract processes were important components influencing managerial behaviour in accordance with issues labelled ideal and content in our framework. The Swedish companies in Johanson's *et al.* study were keen to allocate responsibility for certain actions that were assumed necessary and these responsibilities and actions were outlined in some kind of contract, written or un-written, between different hierarchical managerial levels. The contracts encouraged managers' commitment to visions, strategies, and goals.

Concerning cohesion between ideal, content, and support, Ferreira and Otley (p. 275) claim that "Although the individual components of the performance management systems may be apparently well-designed, evidence suggests that when they do not fit well together (either in design or use) . . . failures can occur". This means that it is important that (4) key performance measures link back to (3) key success/risk factors and to (2) strategies and objectives, and finally to (1) the vision and the ideal. Even the supporting processes should be cohesive with ideal and content. However, cohesion is not enough. A learning process is also needed to adjust the performance management system to changed conditions – a kind of double-loop learning process where reflection about the relevance of the performance management system in relation to its ideal is challenged. If necessary, the performance management system is adjusted. The latter refers to a kind of self-renewal process that Nonaka and Toyama (2005) call "kata". The need for adoption of the performance management system with respect to changes in the organization or its surroundings is also addressed by Ferreira and Otley.

The framework is not a manual that prescribes what should be addressed when analysing or developing performance management. Neither does the framework prescribe anything about linear causality. The issue at stake, performance management, is probably a matter of a number of mutual causalities that may vary in different contexts. Further, we want to add the word 'integrated'. Integrated has here another meaning than in the Integrated Reporting initiative (IIRC, 2012). As it is used here, it has nothing to do with ecology and sustainability, but rather is a way to underline the importance of coherence between ideal, content support, and evaluation.

It remains to be seen if the performance management framework presented now could be used in different contexts. It was originally developed when analysing texts summarizing about 250 Swedish work environment management cases (Frick and Johanson, 2013).

Applying the performance management framework in two contexts

To demonstrate how the framework was used, this section will first contain an analysis of the work environment management cases and, second, the IT consultancy firm case. There are many similarities between IC and work health/work environment. Work health and work environment are important elements influencing competitive advantage (Johanson *et al.*, 2001a). However, they are rarely addressed in the IC literature. When trying to understand the effects of Swedish legal working environment provisions, Frick and Johanson (2013) constructed an analytical framework based on earlier proposals by Ferreira and Otley (2009), Hofstede (1978), and Johanson *et al.* (2001a, 2001b). After a revision of the framework it was used to understand IC management in a medium-sized Swedish IT company, Stretch (Johanson and Skoog, 2015). Both these cases are presented in this section.

The work environment management cases

A two-step procedure was used when the performance management system framework was applied to the empirical context. First, the framework was applied to a rich case description of the work environment management in a Swedish local authority. The aim of this first step was to find out if the theoretically developed performance management framework was useful for an extended analysis of the other 250 Swedish cases on work environment management that were found in database searches. It is important to note that the approach to the analysis was explorative, seeking to ascertain if it is possible to deepen the common understanding of why work environment management works or otherwise, and which are the critical factors if work environment management is integrated in organizational management? The need for integration of work environment management with general organizational management is explicitly called for in the Swedish mandatory provisions of systematic work environment management.

One researcher selected and analysed the 270 cases from a completely different perspective from the performance management framework. The performance management system framework was unknown even to that researcher. The results were written down and handed over for a performance management system framework analysed by a second researcher. After that the second researcher presented the performance management system framework and the analyses to the first researcher in order to avoid misunderstandings or shortcomings with respect to interpreting the text provided by the first researcher.

Before presenting the outcome of this two-step analysis, it is necessary to emphasize that in the final report (Frick and Johanson, 2013) the focus is on employers' shortcomings in their work environment management to a significantly greater extent than their successes. The aim of the explorative analysis was not to grade the work environment practices in the different organizations but to understand how these practices could be improved and also to understand the usefulness of the framework for future research and development of work environment management.

In the local authority case, the analysis reveals that the work environment ideal appears to be unclear. A work environment vision (issue (1) above) exists, but this vision is not supported by other performance management system issues. Critical factors (3) are vaguely described. Strategies and goals (2) exist, but these are not consistent with existing performance measurements (4).

The latter means that follow-ups (5) are difficult to perform. The formal treatment of the provision requirements is good, and in accordance with the provisions, but still the achievement of the ideal of a healthy work environment is not convincing. Budget issues seem to be more important than improving the work environment. This probably due to insufficient or vague responsibility and contract processes (7), as well as rewarding processes (6) that prohibit necessary work environment investments when these investments exceed the budget.

An analysis of all of the other 250 case studies shows the same pattern; most of the larger organizations strive to fulfil the requirements of formal routines required by the provisions, but without necessarily obtaining a healthy workplace with low risks. Identification of risk factors (3), actions plans (2), and follow-ups (5) are more developed and effective in reducing accidents than in relation to other technical risks (e.g. noise and heavy lifting), and particularly so for abating organizational risks (psycho-social issues).

Regarding the content of the work environment management, the performance measurements (4) are poor and more oriented towards formal provision routines than related to achieving a healthy work environment with low risks. The lack of or inadequate performance measures complicate the essential follow-up (5) and self-improvement of the work environment management itself. The responsibility and contract processes (7) are not sufficient, which reduces the organization's commitment to change. The latter also refers to (8) the communication processes, that is, the internal work environment dialogue that is supposed to take place between management and unions. Cooperation by means of dialogues, that is, interactivity (Simons, 1995), is a central issue in the work environment legislation. When dialogues and cooperation are suffering – that is, formal meetings but with a limited content – learning about how the work environment management promotes a good work environment (10), becomes complicated. To conclude, the practices we found seem to be in conflict with different ideals, that is, on the one hand an ideal that is limited to a 'tick-box mentality' and on the other a more profound work environment ideal of abolishing or at least reducing health risks in the workplace.

The IT consultant firm case

In this case the aim was to understand how the founder, main owner, and chairman of the board was thinking about integrated IC management in the successful medium-sized Swedish IT consultant company, Stretch. Also it was to explore if the framework was useful as a guideline for a semi-structured interview. Before the interview a number of questions were developed covering different items in the framework. The interview guideline is presented in the Figure 16.1.

Stretch's webpage says:

> Stretch is an innovative consultancy company … Together we spend our days finding new ways to simplify processes and "stretching" businesses with awesome technology. This is a winning approach that lets us maximize the resources available to our customers' core business – where the true business value is found. We are the large small consultant that delivers with personality and creates business value. We promise to care. We are curious about you, your business and the global market. We are driven by achieving results. Curiosity is for us about continuously moving forward and breaking new ground, beyond obstacles that will arise along the way. As such, a close dialogue is essential to us at Stretch, one in which we listen to our customers and then provide expert advice.[1]

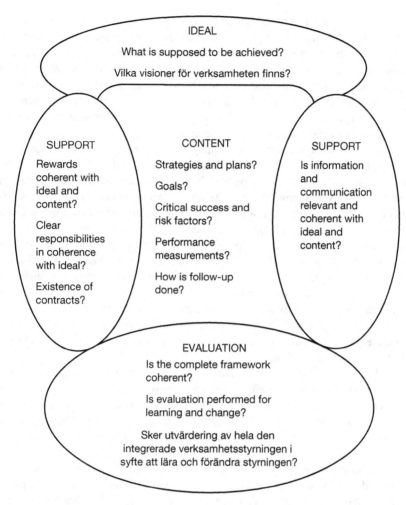

Figure 16.1   Interview guideline

Our case study organization Stretch was founded in 2002. The Group operates on the Scandinavian market with companies in Stockholm and five other cities and has approximately 170 employees. To be the "large small consultant" it must separate itself from its competitors, many of which have technical competence but not the ability to create value for customers. The idea of being the "large small consultant" is also behind the company's division into seven subsidiaries (strategy).

During his interview, the founder, principal owner, and chairman of the board said that he is driven by the ambition to 'win' (ideal). Money is not the primary driving force, although profitability is important (ideal). Stretch is to be considered as very competent (strategy) and should also be able to lead the development of the business. "I believe that we are that competent. Many are watching us". A basic value is always to be able to choose (ideal). The possibility of choice creates opportunities and freedom. The opposite would be dependence. Therefore, it is important to the founder that the enterprise has a long-term perspective (strategy) and is operated profitably (ideal) so that their investments can be self-financed (strategy).

How to become a competent and profitable industry leader? The following four strategies were identified by the founder as important at the time of start up and continue to be so. First, customer focus, quality, and customer value. Stretch shall "make a difference together with the customers". To fulfil and exceed customer expectations, not only structured processes and delivery precision are required; the customer must also understand that the company is listening, is interested, and acts in the customer's best interests – it is a question of customer-perceived quality. In a recent survey, customers suggested that the culture of commitment, competence, and fun at work is infectious and that quality contributes to customer value. Second, organic growth through profitability – most of the company's profits should be used for growth. Third, entrepreneurship and creativity, in which at least 20 per cent of the company's turnover three years ahead should come from something that the company does not do today: "If employees grow even the company will grow". Fourth, the most attractive workplace – in 2014 Stretch was ranked as the eighth most attractive workplace among medium-sized companies in Sweden. The company has been among the top ten companies for the last ten years.

An important task as a leader is to promote what employees are good at. According to the Stretch founder: "Most people have greater demands on themselves than others have on them". Therefore, employees should set their own objectives (strategy, reward) within certain frames. For example, Stretch only operates in the Scandinavian market (strategy). In addition to mobilizing creativity and entrepreneurship, an important task for managers is to maintain certain strategies and objectives (responsibilities, contracts). The Stretch founder also emphasizes the importance of differentiating between desire and ability. Ability can be gained, but desire is more difficult.

Stretch subsidiaries are expected to develop a three-year vision. The business plan (plan, target) is built from the bottom up and provides a framework for the business. All employees should participate in developing the business plan (strategy); while the founder's task is to emphasize the frames for the future, he is not expected to come up with new ideas. Rolling forecasts replace budgets and critical key ratios are formulated (performance measurement), referring, for example, to potential employees and customers.

Some of the strategic and operative processes are coordinated between subsidiaries. This includes, in addition to common customers, recruitment and competence development processes. When employees commence their employment, it is made clear that all consultants are expected to work a certain number of hours internally to contribute to the business planning process and to participate in spring and autumn conferences as well is in monthly meetings.

It is essential to promote understanding of what business means (strategy), and to support this training, addressing culture, leadership, and sales models are mandatory for all leaders. Participation in competency networks is also common throughout the organization.

The individual consultants' billing, as well as time spent with customers, is continuously followed up. Development talks take place twice a year and are documented and approved by the responsible manager and the employee (reward, responsibilities, contracts). The basic salary is fixed with an individual bonus as well as a company bonus paid. The individual bonus is related to the individual's billing and the company bonus to the subsidiaries' profitability. Generally, the salaries are high (reward).

When an employee is considered to have contributed to the four strategies mentioned earlier, he or she can be proposed to become a partner of the subsidiary (reward). Two partners should be on the board of directors of each company. To date there are 40 partners.

Stretch seems to be a very efficient company with customers that are satisfied with the competent, creative, and results-oriented consultants. The growth of the company is good and well planned; the idea of 20 per cent new operations within three years creates a creative and entrepreneurial climate in accordance with the four strategies. Employees enjoy their work and develop their competencies, and profitability is good.

According to the founder, the different management items appear to interact effectively, probably because the ideal of freedom of choice and the profitability to maintain freedom of choice interacts with a high level of competence. The strategies of customer quality and value, organic growth, attractive workplace, entrepreneurship, and support for creativity are underpinned by the ideal to be "the big small consultant that combines personality and value creation". Supporting processes like rewards, responsibilities, and contracts further leverage the ideal. Finally, the continuous learning process demonstrates that the founder at least has a good overview with respect to what is needed to achieve an integrated IC management system.

Of course, this example does not give a full picture of how integrated IC management is performed in the organization. It is the perception of one person, the chairman of the board. However, it provides a good view of what he wants to obtain and how he wants to run the company to achieve management ideals.

Conclusions

The integrated IC management framework outlined and applied in this chapter is a further development of the performance management systems framework suggested by Ferreira and Otley (2009). It attempts to classify the different IC management items into four classes (management ideal, content, supporting processes, and evaluation). The issue of ideal is a response to Hofstede's (1978) view about the hidden ideology of MC systems, whereas the concept of supporting processes is further developed from our own findings (Johanson *et al.*, 2001a, 2001b). Finally, evaluation is inspired by Nonaka and Toyama's (2005) suggestion that it is of uttermost importance that every management system is subject to adjustment based on reflection and learning.

The framework is not intended as a manual that prescribes what items have to be addressed to achieve successful IC management. It is not intended as a tick-box tool and it does not suggest a causal relationship between the items. Rather the management issues that it aims to address probably consist of a number of mutual causalities. The goal is to increase understanding of the obstacles to improving performance management irrespective of any concerns about IC management or working environment management. This means that the framework can benefit from further development.

Existing IC guidelines do not sufficiently address IC management and therefore a deeper understanding of how IC management is performed is needed for policy makers to be able to improve guidelines and for big private and public organizations to improve their understanding of the role of IC in their own operations.

Because of the ageing population and the lack of a competent workforce in many Western countries, there is also a great need to improve understanding of how work environment and work health affect and are affected by competitive advantage, as well as a need to consider sustainability at an individual, organizational, and societal level. Policy makers need the knowledge that research can provide from across a range of academic disciplines. The title of our *Accounting, Auditing & Accountability Journal* article (Gröjer and Johanson, 1998) still resonates: "Reality present – but where is the knowledge?"

Note

1 www.stretch.se.

References

Andersson, M. (2014,) *Välfärdssektorn, en arena för makt och motstånd: Studier av sjukvård och hemtjänst*, Mälardalen University, Västerås, Sweden.

Anthony, R. N. (1965), *Planning and Control Systems: A Framework for Analysis*, Harvard Business School Press, Boston, MA.

Bjurström, E. (2012), "Japan: Third generation intellectual capital", *The Japan Intellectual Capital Management Journal*, August, pp. 65–80.

Bjurström, E., Enkvist, T., and Roxström, G. (2010), "A harmonization marketplace: C2 goes social", paper presented at the *15th ICCRTS International Command and Control Research and Technology Symposium*, Santa Monica, California, 22–24 June.

Bukh, P. N. and Johanson, U. (2003), "Research and knowledge interaction: Guidelines for intellectual capital reporting", *Journal of Intellectual Capital*, Vol. 4, No. 4, pp. 576 – 588.

DATI (2001), *Guideline for Intellectual Capital Statements: A Key to Knowledge Management*, Danish Agency for Trade and Industry, Copenhagen.

Dean, M. (1999), *Governmentality: Power and Rule in Modern Society*, Sage, London.

Dumay, J. (2014), "15 years of the *Journal of Intellectual Capital* and counting: A manifesto for transformational IC research", *Journal of Intellectual Capital*, Vol. 15, No. 1, pp. 2–37.

Dumay, J., Guthrie, J., and Rooney, J. (2017), "The critical path of intellectual capital", in Guthrie. J., Dumay, J., Ricceri, F., and Nielsen, C. (Eds), *The Routledge Companion to Intellectual Capital*, Routledge, London, pp. xx–xx.

Ferreira, A. and Otley, D. (2009), "The design and use of performance management systems: An extended framework for analysis", *Management Accounting Research*, Vol. 20, No. 4, pp. 263–282.

Frick, K. and Johanson, U. (2013), *Systematiskt arbetsmiljöarbete: Syfte, inriktning, hinder och möjligheter i verksamhetsstyrningen*, Del I: *En analys av svenska fallstudier*. Rapport 2013:11. Arbetsmiljöverket, Stockholm.

Giddens, A. (1984), *The Constitution of Society: Outline of the Theory of Structuration*, University of California Press, Los Angeles.

Gröjer, J. E. and Johanson, U. (1998), "Current development in Human Resource Costing and Accounting: Reality present – Researchers absent?" *Accounting, Auditing & Accountability Journal*, Vol. 11, No. 4, pp. 495–506.

Guthrie, J., Ricceri, F., and Dumay, J. (2012), "Reflections and projections: A decade of intellectual capital accounting research", *The British Accounting Review*, Vol. 44, No. 2, pp. 68–92.

Hasselbladh, H., Bejerot, E., and Gustafsson, R. Å. (2008), *Bortom new public management: Institutionell transformation i svensk sjukvård*, Academia adacta, Lund, Sweden.

Hofstede, G. (1978), "The poverty of management control philosophy", *Academy of Management Review*, Vol. 3, No. 3, pp. 450–461.

Holland, J., Henningsson, J., Johanson, U., Koga, C., and Sakakibara, S. (2012), "Use of IC information in Japanese Financial Firms", *Journal of Intellectual Capital*, Vol. 13, No. 4, pp. 562–581.

IIRC (2012), *Prototype Framework*. London. Available at www.theiirc.org/wp content/uploads/2012/10/DraftPrototypeFramework.pdf (20130308).

Johanson, U. and Bjurström, E. (2015), "Following the adoption of Japanese IC-guidelines during 10 years", *The Japan Intellectual Capital Management Journal*, August, pp. 65–80.

Johanson, U. and Koga, C. (2015), "Intellectual capital in Japan: Governmental guidelines, financial market perceptions and company practice", in Ordónez de Pablos, P. and Edvinsson, L. (Eds), *Intellectual Capital in Organizations: Non-Financial Reports and Accounts*. Routledge, New York, pp. 203–230.

Johanson, U. and Skoog, M. (2015), *Integrerad verksamhetsstyrning*, Studentlitteratur, Lund, Sweden.

Johanson, U., Koga, C., Almqvist, R., and Skoog, M. (2009), "'Breaking taboos': Implementing intellectual assets-based management guidelines", *Journal of Intellectual Capital*, Vol. 10, No 4, pp. 520–538.

Johanson, U., Mårtensson, M., and Skoog, M. (2001a), "Mobilising change by means of the management control of intangibles", *Accounting, Organisations and Society*, Vol. 26, Nos 7–8, pp. 715–733.

Johanson, U., Mårtensson, M., and Skoog, M. (2001b), "Measuring to understand intangible performance drivers", *European Accounting Review*, Vol. 10, No. 3, pp. 1–31.

Johanson, U., Skoog, M., Almqvist, R., and Backlund, A. (2006), "Balancing dilemmas of the balanced scorecard", *Accounting, Auditing & Accountability Journal*, Vol. 19, No. 5, pp. 842–857.

Johnson, H. T. (1992), *Relevance Regained: From Top-Down Control to Bottom-Up Empowerment*, Free Press, New York.

Johnson, H. T. and Kaplan, R. S. (1987), *Relevance Lost: The Rise and Fall of Management Accounting*, Harvard Business School Press, Boston, MA.

Lapsley, I. (2009), "New public management: The cruelest invention of the human spirit?" *Abacus*, Vol. 45, No. 1, pp. 1–21.

Meritum (2002), "Guidelines for managing and reporting on intangibles", *Meritum*, Fundación Aritel Móvil, Madrid, Spanien.

METI (2005), *Guidelines for Disclosure of Intellectual Assets Based Management*, Japanese Ministry of Economy, Trade and Industry.

Mouritsen, J., Larsen, H. T., and Bukh, P. N. D. (2001), "Intellectual capital and the 'capable firm': Narrating, visualizing and numbering for managing knowledge", *Accounting, Organizations & Society*, Vol. 26, pp. 735–762.

Nielsen, C., Roslender, R., and Schaper, S. (2014), The rise (and fall) of the IC statement: Whatever happened to the legitimacy of IC reporting in Denmark? Unpublished.

Nonaka, I. and Toyama, R. (2005), "The theory of the knowledge-creating firm: Subjectivity, objectivity and synthesis", *Industrial and Corporate Change*, Vol. 14, No. 3, pp. 419–436.

Piper, M and Pietsch, G. (2006), "Performance measurement in universities: The case of knowledge balance sheets analyzed from a new institutionalist perspective", *Studies in Managerial and Financial Accounting*, Vol. 16, pp. 379–401.

Power, M. (1997), *The Audit Society: Rituals of Verification*, Oxford University Press, Oxford, UK.

Rogers, E. M. (1995), *Diffusion of Innovations*, The Free Press, New York.

Simons, R. (1995), *Levers of Control: How Managers Use Innovative Control Systems to Drive Strategic Renewal*, Harvard Business School Press, Boston, MA.

Sveiby, K. E. and Lloyd, T. (1987), *Managing Knowhow: Add Value by Valuing Creativity*, Bloomsbury, London.

Yao, J. and Bjurström, E. (2015), "Trends and challenges in future IC reporting: Experiences from Japan. Part VII" in Ordónez de Pablos, P. and Edvinsson, L. (Eds), *Intellectual Capital in Organizations: Non-Financial Reports and Accounts*, Routledge, New York.

17

ENABLING INTELLECTUAL CAPITAL MEASUREMENT THROUGH BUSINESS MODEL MAPPING

The Nexus case

Marco Montemari and Maria Serena Chiucchi

Introduction

Over the past few decades, research into intellectual capital (IC) accounting has gone through three stages, which have gradually changed its aims and shape. This path has led IC accounting from raising awareness (first stage) and theory building (second stage) to investigating IC in practice from a critical and performative perspective (third stage) (Guthrie *et al.*, 2012; Dumay, 2013, 2014). During the first and the second stage, IC accounting researchers have developed several frameworks and guidelines for measuring and reporting IC (Andriessen, 2004a; Sveiby, 2010), the aim being to foster management practices that would increase the competitiveness of companies and improve IC disclosure. Despite an abundance of these frameworks and guidelines, their adoption is not widespread in practice (Dumay, 2009a, 2009b, 2012; Lönnqvist *et al.*, 2009; Chiucchi, 2013; Chiucchi and Montemari, 2016). Within the third stage of IC accounting research, interventionist research has been promoted in order to understand why IC measurement is more preached than practised (Chiucchi and Dumay, 2015, p. 326). IC measurement frameworks have been criticized, among other things, because of their atomistic focus on IC and their limited ability to capture the relationships between IC and value creation (O'Donnell *et al.*, 2006; Dumay and Cuganesan, 2011; Beattie and Smith, 2013; Montemari and Nielsen, 2013). This atomistic focus signifies that IC measurement frameworks support only IC management rather than the management of the business as a whole. Moreover, these frameworks are inadequate to show the impact of IC on the company performance.

Recently the business model concept has been identified as a platform within which to refocus the IC debate (Beattie and Smith, 2013), thus helping reduce the gap between theory and practice in IC accounting research. The business model can be considered the framework through which companies can operationalize and execute their strategy (Nielsen *et al.*, 2009; McGrath, 2010; Nielsen and Montemari, 2012), thus enabling the understanding of how value is actually created and captured (Osterwalder and Pigneur, 2010; Arend, 2013).

Despite there being several conceptual linkages between IC and business model concepts, the IC accounting literature, on the one hand, makes little use of the business model concept (Beattie and Smith, 2013) and the business model literature, and on the other, is silent on how to move from business model to measurement (Magretta, 2002; McGrath, 2010; IIRC, 2013). Thus, both the contribution of the business model to IC measurement and the process that leads from business model to building measures need to be explored. Therefore, this chapter aims to contribute to filling these research gaps by investigating the following intertwined research questions: 1) how can the business model support and foster IC measurement? 2) How can the transition from business model to measurement be executed?

To answer these research questions, we present a reflective analysis of a single in-depth case study of an Italian company, Nexus, which used its business model to design and implement IC measures. The actual research project was conducted adopting an interventionist approach.

This chapter contributes to the IC accounting literature by identifying the benefits of using the business model to build IC measures. In particular, the chapter shows that the business model sheds light on the flow and context for value creation by clarifying which IC elements are of utmost importance and what role they play in the company's value creation process, along with tangible and financial assets. Therefore, the business model ensures that IC indicators are tightly connected to the company's conception of value creation, thus offering an overarching focus to IC and supporting not only IC management, but also the management of the business as a whole.

Moreover, the chapter unveils the process that leads from business model to measurement. More specifically, the chapter brings to light that in order to move from business model to measurement, strategic themes should be identified as they play a crucial role by acting as a bridge between the business model and the items to be measured. Strategic themes serve as the *fil rouge* of the measurement system, thus supporting and fostering the design and implementation of measures. In addition, the chapter shows an additional contribution of the business model to the measurement process; the business model and related strategic themes ensure a high level of integration and consistency between departmental and company-wide measurement systems, and among the departmental measurement systems themselves.

Literature review

The performative and critical research agenda aims to investigate how IC is understood and implemented in practice (Dumay, 2012, 2014; Guthrie *et al.*, 2012), in order to understand the role and the effects of IC in companies in which it is measured, reported, and managed (Giuliani, 2016; Giuliani *et al.*, 2016), by providing insights on what works and does not work using a bottom-up approach (Mouritsen, 2006). Within the third stage of IC accounting research and consistent with its aims, there has been a call for more interventionist research to explore IC in action by bringing together academics and practitioners (Dumay, 2010, 2013; Cuozzo *et al.*, 2017). In this regard, Dumay (2014, p. 20) states that "as IC researchers, we need to walk the talk by working inside organizations with practitioners and managers in real time, implementing IC and then share these experiences . . . so others can learn both from our success and from our mistakes".

One of the reasons for promoting interventionist research is the ambition to understand why IC measurement is more preached than practised (Chiucchi and Dumay, 2015, p. 326), thus helping to reduce the gap between theory and practice. In fact, while many frameworks and guidelines for measuring and reporting IC have been developed (Andriessen, 2004a; Sveiby,

2010) with the aim of fostering management practices that increase the competitiveness of companies and improve IC disclosure, their adoption is not widespread in practice (Dumay, 2009a, 2009b, 2012; Lönnqvist *et al.*, 2009; Chiucchi, 2013; Chiucchi and Montemari, 2016).

IC measurement frameworks have been criticized as not fully able to display the contribution of IC to the value creation process of companies (O'Donnell *et al.*, 2006; Dumay and Cuganesan, 2011). Many are grounded on IC categories (Edvinsson and Malone, 1997; Sveiby, 1997), which place the measurement focus only on IC, thus hindering the measurement of IC 'in action': the resources are detached from the specific organizational setting in which they are exploited and they are measured while "on hold" (Mouritsen, 2004, p. 61). This stock approach does not explicitly consider the relationships between IC elements or the link between them and the creation of value. These stock-based IC measurement frameworks adopt an atomistic focus on IC rather than an overarching approach to highlighting how IC is actually employed in the company's value creation process in order to gain a competitive advantage. Even when IC measurement frameworks adopt a flow approach in order to capture the process by which value is created by IC (Mouritsen *et al.*, 2003; InCaS, 2008), the measurement focus ends up being almost exclusively on IC; the relationship between IC and value creation is only partially captured as the links between IC, tangible, and financial resources are not explicitly considered (Beattie and Smith, 2013; Montemari and Nielsen, 2013). To sum up, the aim of IC measurement frameworks is to support IC management rather than the management of the business as a whole.

Recently, the business model concept has entered into the discourse concerning IC accounting. In particular, the business model has been identified as a holistic and overall platform upon which to refocus the IC debate (Beattie and Smith, 2013, p. 243). The business model can be considered the framework through which companies can operationalize and execute their strategy (Nielsen *et al.*, 2009; McGrath, 2010; Nielsen and Montemari, 2012), thus enabling the understanding of how value is actually created and captured (Osterwalder and Pigneur, 2010; Arend, 2013). The business model concept allows entrepreneurs and managers to conceptualize the company as a set of interrelated strategic choices (Morris *et al.*, 2005; Massa *et al.*, 2017) concerning a range of key elements. For instance, the target customers, the value proposition to be offered to the target customers, the channels for reaching them, the relationships to develop with them, the key activities and the key resources needed to create the value proposition, and the partners needed to access key activities and key resources. The connectivity among these key elements is an integral part of the model itself (Nielsen and Montemari, 2012, p. 147; Wirtz *et al.*, 2016, p. 41).

Several conceptual linkages exist between IC and business model concepts. Some business model components related to relational capital (customer relationships, key channels, and key partnerships) are IC in nature (Tikkanen *et al.*, 2005, p. 790; Bini *et al.*, 2016, p. 86). Moreover, IC elements play a crucial role in some other business model components: key activities and key resources needed to create the value proposition are often intangible in nature (Amit and Zott, 2001, p. 511; Osterwalder and Pigneur, 2010, pp. 34–37), in other words, linked to human capital (competences, capabilities, know-how) and structural capital (databases, intellectual property).

Different business model configurations have different value creation logics and thus require different sets of IC elements (Liang *et al.*, 2013). For instance, "channel maximization" (Linder and Cantrell, 2000) refers to a business model configuration in which the offering is distributed through as many channels as possible in order to create a broad distribution (e.g. Coca Cola, Nestlé, Budweiser). This is generally done not only through a company's own channels, but also through an extensive network of partner channels such as those with larger reseller chains. Apart from channels and strategic partnerships, this configuration also affects the other business model components: the key activities refer primarily to network construction (channel scouting and channel contracting) and outbound logistics management. Therefore, in this configuration, customer and network relationships and all the activities related to their development are the key intangibles. 'Inside-out' (Osterwalder and Pigneur, 2010), instead, is a business model configuration through which a company generates revenues by selling or licensing its own R&D to companies operating in other industries, that is, intellectual properties or technologies that are not used or are underused inside the company for strategic or operational reasons (e.g. GlaxoSmithKline, BASF, IBM). This configuration is suitable in knowledge-intensive and technology-intensive contexts and it allows the company to monetize intellectual properties or technologies that cannot be directly applied to new products in the core business. A strong patenting strategy is crucial for this business model configuration to work. Therefore, from an IC perspective, human capital (competences and knowledge to perform R&D activities) and structural capital (intellectual properties) are crucial intangibles for value creation in this configuration.

Thus, the business model concept offers an overarching focus to IC. Avoiding the risk of an atomistic analysis of IC has the potential to foster IC measurement and management by providing justifications for why companies should measure and manage IC. In fact, individual IC indicators, taken in isolation, may end up being disconnected from the company's conception of value creation; in turn, this entails the risk of managers considering them "solutions in search of a cause" (Andriessen, 2004b, p. 230).

Despite the acknowledgment of the conceptual linkages between IC and the business model, the IC accounting literature makes little use of the business model concept (Beattie and Smith, 2013, p. 249) on the one hand and, on the other, the business model literature is silent on how to move from business model to measurement (Magretta, 2002; McGrath, 2010; IIRC, 2013), while recognizing that the business model can favour the "entangling of the indicators" (Nielsen *et al.*, 2009, p. 9; Nielsen and Roslender, 2015, p. 265). Thus, both the contribution of the business model to IC measurement and the process that leads from business model to measures need to be investigated. In this regard, Bromwich and Scapens (2016, p. 6), acknowledging that the business model is a "hot topic" in practice, state:

> While much of the content of these models is based on management accounting information, accounting researchers do not seem to be particularly interested in the area. If researchers are to contribute to new practical innovations they need to become involved earlier in the life of those innovations.

Our chapter aims to contribute to this research stream by investigating how the business model can support and foster IC measurement and how the transition from business model to measurement can be executed.

Method

In order to answer the research questions, we present a reflective analysis (Arnaboldi, 2013; Suomala *et al.*, 2014) of a single, in-depth case study of an Italian company, Nexus, which leveraged on its business model to design and implement IC measures.

The case study method was chosen to answer the research questions because it makes it possible to follow the process that led from the business model design to measurement, to focus on the dynamics among actors, and to highlight levers and obstacles in this process.

The intention is not to generalize, but rather to explore the potentialities and criticalities of using a company's business model to support IC measurement and management.

The case is based on an interventionist research project conducted by a team of researchers that included one of the authors (Jönsson and Lukka, 2006; Dumay, 2010). During the time period focused on in this chapter (2015–16), the company was facing the need to improve its management accounting system, which was not able to reveal the contribution of the company's intangibles to the Group's value creation process. Because Nexus is IC intensive, the management felt the need to thoroughly understand the company IC and measure its impact on the Group's performance and on value creation. In order to achieve this aim and remain in line with the integrated thinking that characterizes Nexus, the researchers decided to develop an integrated measurement system, inspired by the Framework (IIRC, 2013) and which had, at its core, the company business model.

Data was predominantly collected through document analysis, interviews, and participant observation carried out during meetings between the researchers and the company actors involved in the project, that is, the President of the Group, the General Manager, the Group Controller, and top management (the R&D Manager, the Market Development Manager, the Communications Manager, the Human Resources Manager). All interviews and meetings were recorded with the permission of the company. Participating in the measurement project also provided the opportunity to gather empirical data through informal talks, emails, and phone calls. The use of a variety of methods to collect data allowed the researchers to cross-validate the information collected and to capture different dimensions of the phenomenon under analysis (Ryan *et al.*, 2002).

A qualitative data analysis was applied to the interview and observational data as this made it possible to focus on what had happened as well as to maintain sensitivity to the context (Denzin and Lincoln, 2000; Patton, 2002). Some of the company actors' verbatim quotes will be provided throughout the chapter to support the reflections and findings.

The case study

The case company

Nexus is the parent company of a group that designs and manufactures turnkey tailor-made solutions for the automatic measurement and quality control of customers' products and processes. The Group is headquartered in Italy, but it sells its solutions all over the world. Nexus is a highly IC intensive entity as it develops, manages, and provides services related to human resources, research and innovation, administration and control, marketing and business development, to all Group companies. The mission of Nexus is to think and plan the future of the Group through its intangible resources, activities, and outcomes. Consistent with its aims, Nexus is made up of four business departments: 1) R&D develops the know-how and the technologies of the Group through incremental and radical innovation; 2) market development identifies, analyses, and develops new market opportunities and new customers; 3) communications strengthens the company culture and image by spreading them inside and outside the Group; and 4) human resources performs recruitment, training, and evaluation activities concerning the human resources of the Group.

At the outset of the project, Nexus' management accounting system was focused predominantly on financial performance (i.e. financial KPIs, cost accounting system, variance analysis). The other (non-financial) dimensions of company performance were mainly assessed through the perceptions of managers. The intangible outcomes of Nexus' activities (new customer relationships, new competences, new technological solutions) were not measured by the management accounting system, which was not able to reveal their size, their growth, or decline nor, overall, their impact on the Group value creation process.

Because Nexus is so IC intensive, the management felt the need to understand IC and measure its impact on the Group's performance and on value creation. In the words of the CEO, "Managing Nexus is like throwing a stone into the water; thus, we need to control what ripples arise when we throw some stones in". In order to improve the management accounting system in this direction, an interventionist research project involving a group of university researchers was launched.

When the project was started, it immediately came to light that Nexus was characterized by strongly integrated thinking. Integrated thinking takes place when there is constant interplay between financial and non-financial dimensions of the business; when all operating and functional units break down internal barriers and work together to achieve the company's strategic objectives; when decision-making and actions consider the creation of value not only over the short term but also over the medium and long term (IIRC, 2013). At Nexus, the decision-making process and actions usually incorporate non-financial considerations in order to simultaneously achieve advantages in the long term that go beyond the financial dimension. For instance, the company cooperates with a wide range of external partners (universities, research centres, customers, and suppliers) to develop EU projects. Beyond obtaining funding, these projects are used to contact and collaborate with 'number one' players in specific industries in order to grow new competences and broaden the network of technological partners in the medium and long term. Following along these lines, the company develops networking activities that aim to create not only new business opportunities and to get new customers, but also to strengthen the visibility of the Group on the market and to make the Group's values stronger in the eyes of a broad variety of stakeholders (customers, employees, partners, competitors, suppliers, local communities, and universities). Even when potential customers do not buy the Group's solutions after the first contact, thus not generating a short-term financial outcome, the company carries on nurturing the relationship in order to keep the door open for collaborations in the medium and long term (obtaining new knowledge, obtaining new technologies, co-creating solutions). This constant search for opportunities involves a focus beyond the short-term financial dimension of the business as it also aims to achieve medium and long-term non-financial benefits. It is worth noting that the company's business departments work in close contact with each other, and their competences, activities, and operations are integrated in order to develop different facets of the relationships with customers and all stakeholders in an effort to create the aforementioned opportunities.

Consistent with the integrated thinking that characterizes Nexus, the researchers decided to develop an integrated measurement system, inspired by the principles of the Framework (IIRC, 2013), aimed at identifying and measuring the tangible and the intangible resources and activities developed to create value and the resulting tangible and intangible outputs and outcomes. Indeed, an IR should show "a holistic picture of the combination, interrelatedness, and dependencies between the factors that affect the organization's ability to create value over time" (IIRC, 2013, p. 5).

During the development of the IR for the company, a specific information need gradually emerged at the departmental level. More specifically, every department expressed the desire to have its own report that could support the decision-making process in keeping with the company's business strategy. Therefore, besides the preparation of a company IR, departmental reports were also designed in such a way that they would be consistent in their structure and logic with the company IR. In order to ensure a high level of consistency, the company business model acted as the pivot point for the design of the whole system of departmental and company integrated reports.

Business model mapping

Consistent with the content elements of an IR (IIRC, 2013, p. 5), the researchers decided to leverage on the development of the company's business model since they believed that business model mapping could match the company's integrated thinking well and that it could drive IC measurement. In the literature, the business model has been proposed as a framework through which companies can operationalize and execute their strategy (McGrath, 2010; Nielsen and Montemari, 2012), thereby enabling the understanding of how value is actually created and captured (Osterwalder and Pigneur, 2010; Arend, 2013). Thus, the business model was identified by the researchers as a suitable platform from which to select the relevant intangibles and to understand their role in the value creation process. During one of the meetings, the controller underlined how business model mapping was crucial to the success of the measurement process:

> If there is something wrong in the business model mapping, we will identify KPIs which are not consistent with the value creation process, and are useless for the decision making process ... business model mapping helps us to keep track of the reasons why we choose some KPIs and discard other ones.

The researchers mapped the company's business model using the portfolio of business model configurations, thus following the process suggested by Gassmann *et al.* (2014) and Taran *et al.* (2016). This mapping technique was chosen after the analysis of the literature on business model designing and mapping, because of its flexibility and completeness. It offers several business model options to choose from and it gives a frame of reference for the different value creation logics (the tangible and intangible value drivers) that can be adopted by companies and how they can coexist. Business model configurations can be defined as "cognitive instruments that embody important understanding of causal links between traditional elements in the firm and those outside" (Baden-Fuller and Mangematin, 2013, p. 418). A business model configuration is a mode of doing business that depends on how the different business model building blocks are set and aligned to achieve overall consistency (Taran *et al.*, 2016).

Since Nexus is the parent company of a group and it takes part in the value creation process of the Group as a whole, the mapping process was divided into two steps: 1) mapping the Group's business model; and 2) understanding how Nexus influences the Group's business model through the resources and activities of its business departments, that is, through its intangibles.

The Group's business model mapping process was carried out by the researchers and the Group Controller, through interviews and meetings with key company figures who had in-depth knowledge of the Group's strategy and operations. None of the business model configurations proposed in literature was able, per se, to capture the multiple facets and value creation logics that coexisted in the Group. In the words of one of the researchers, "It is not easy to identify just one business model configuration that includes all the different facets of the Group; we need to craft a tailor-made solution for the Group". Therefore, it was decided to design a hybrid business model composed of a mix of the following business model configurations: solution provider, open business model, systems integrator, layer player, outside-in (see Figure 17.1).

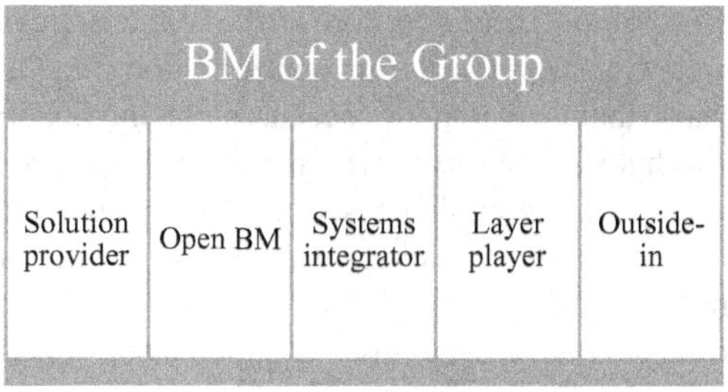

Figure 17.1   The hybrid BM of the Group

Solution provider aims to provide a total and complete coverage of products and services in one particular area of expertise (e.g. financial, health) in order to offer the customers an all-inclusive package (product sales, installation, consulting services, after-sales services, spare parts, and maintenance) able to satisfy a wide range of needs in a particular domain. By establishing close relationships with its customers, a company can understand their needs and habits and thus improve its solutions. Accordingly, the Group under analysis offers its customers an all-inclusive package of products and services in the area of automatic measurement and quality control. This implies that the relationships with customers go beyond the mere sales of products, and that they also include close collaboration aimed at satisfying specific needs and identifying the most suitable solution. As a result, customer relationships are very strong, being grounded on mutual trust and information exchange.

Open business model aims to create an 'ecosystem' by establishing its technologies as the basis for value chain innovation. The ecosystem develops around the focal firm's technologies, the disappearance of which would destroy the whole ecosystem. A vital issue concerns the identification of the areas in the value creation process where external parties can contribute, so that a win–win solution can be achieved. Consistent with this configuration, the involvement of external partners (suppliers, customers, competitors, universities, high schools, associations, and local governments) is deeply rooted in the Group culture. These relationships go beyond the core business of the Group and they include recruitment and training projects as well as social responsibility projects. Implicit in this ecosystem is the building of win–win relationships so that both the Group and the partners involved can benefit from the cooperation. Following from this concept of mutual benefit, the Group also takes care of the area where its plants are located; for instance, for several years the Group has been carrying out maintenance of the riverbanks located near the headquarters in order to avoid overflows, thus redeveloping a neglected area to create value for the Group as a whole. Therefore, the relationship with the human and non-human actors belonging to the ecosystem is very strong.

Similar to solution provider, systems integrator offers an all-inclusive package of highly customized products and services. However, the focus here is on the ability to coordinate and integrate internal and external sources of tangible and intangible components in order to develop novel combinations of solutions for customers. Accordingly, the Group not only takes the lead for the assembly or piecing together of a solution but also for the design of the components that make up the solution itself. Thus, the value that the Group adds to the solution relies specifically on the ability to coordinate and integrate internal technologies and know-how with external competences to achieve superior performance.

Layer player focuses on a specific function in the value chain, such as electronic payments or logistics, with the intent to serve a number of different value chains in several industries. Indeed, specific competences on a core area of expertise can be used as a platform to serve several industries. Consistent with this configuration, the Group focuses on a specific area of the value chain, that is, automatic measurement and quality control. Then it uses its in-depth know-how in this field to serve customers operating in several industries (automotive, healthcare, transport, home appliances, pharmaceuticals, and energy). Everything that is measurable can be a potential business for the Group, the mission of which is to convert the measures into value.

Outside-in obtains R&D from external entities and builds on it in order to shorten time-to-market and increase internal R&D productivity. Moreover, this business model configuration exploits external sources of technology and knowledge to complement internal sources in order to be able to serve broader markets. Consistent with this configuration, the Group is the 'knowledge hub' of a network of knowledge (customers, universities, research centres, high schools, and partners), the aim being to obtain technological competences from outside and bring them in to increase the Group's cache of know-how.

Choosing this mix of business model configurations allowed the researchers to discover and clarify the value creation logics of the Group. In particular, this business model mapping process made it possible to identify some strategic themes closely linked to the mix of business model configurations and considered crucial for the value creation process of the Group. Table 17.1 shows the outcome of this matching process between business model configurations and strategic themes.

The hybrid business model solution and the strategic themes were discussed with the President of the Group, the CEO, and top management of Nexus over the course of three meetings. After a series of minor refinements, which did not change the overall content and meaning of the business model configurations and the strategic themes, the company actors approved the outcomes of the mapping process, thus kicking off the second step of the process, that is, understanding how Nexus influences the Group's business model through resources, activities, and outcomes of its business departments. This second step revealed that the IC elements of the four departments strongly support and influence the accomplishment of the strategic goals linked to the hybrid business model of the company.

For example, the R&D Department supports 'Aptitude for collaboration' and 'Ability to acquire new knowledge' through its strong relational capital: it cooperates with a range of external partners (universities, research centres, customers, and suppliers) to carry out EU projects, to develop new competences and broaden the network of technological partners. The structural capital and human capital of this department are leveraged to support the 'Ability to develop ad hoc solutions for customers': new technologies are acquired from external partners in order to be integrated with its internal technologies and know-how so that specific solutions for customers can be crafted. For the sake of this strategic theme, the human capital of the Market Development Department also plays a crucial role; indeed,

Table 17.1 The Group's BM configurations and the related strategic themes

BM configurations	Group's strategic themes
Open Business Model; Systems Integrator	Aptitude for collaboration
Open Business Model; Systems Integrator	Ability to create new knowledge
Open Business Model; Outside-In	Ability to acquire new knowledge
Systems Integrator; Solution Provider	Ability to develop ad hoc solutions for customers
Open Business Model; Layer Player	Ability to diversify

employees in this department have to understand and analyse customers' problems and needs so that the company can improve its solutions.

The IC (human, structural, and relational capital) of the Human Resources Department and the Communications Department has an across-the-board influence over all the strategic themes. Recruitment and training, as well as initiatives to strengthen commitment and team spirit, produce direct and indirect effects on all of the business model configurations on which the Group's business model is founded.

In addition, the business model mapping process triggered a strategic dialogue among participants, thus going beyond the initial measurement purposes for which it was designed. In particular, the business model mapping process provided the participants with a simple shared language that enabled dialogue on strategic issues, on the importance of IC for accomplishing the business strategy, and on potential new initiatives. For example, during one meeting, the CEO leveraged the business model configurations and the five strategic themes to show top management the strategic direction to follow:

> These business model configurations tell us that we have to always be up-to-date on four dimensions: 1. new measurement technologies, the foundation of our success; 2. new business segments, as we want to be a continuous start up; 3. new business Departments, as we need to change our organization according to the challenges we have to face – ten years ago we did not have the R&D and the Communications Departments; 4. new geographic areas, we have 3 business units and 40 people in other parts of the world and we need to carry on strengthening our international profile. For each business Department, let's try to identify the main partners who will help us to stay up-to-date on these four dimensions. Who did we talk to over the last five years? And who will we have to talk to in the next five years? We have to zoom in on our crucial partners.

During another meeting, the President spotlighted the theme of human capital:

> Measurement is relevant, but we need to reach a balance between things that can be counted and things that count. These strategic themes tell us that we have to secure human capital in order to ensure the continuity of the business. This can be done in two ways. First, by training on the job: we have people who have been working in the Group for more than 20 years, and they have to transfer their experience, their knowledge, their competences as well as the culture of the Group to young employees. This has to be done methodically, otherwise this human capital will disappear in the short run and we will have to build it up from scratch in the future. Second, by promoting ourselves and recruiting: high schools, universities, and research centres are our target. We have to make sure that students know our company, our culture so that they can understand us … I want to see that employees work here not just because they want a job, but I want them to feel part of something bigger.

Following along the lines of the President, the Communications Manager suggested trying to map the specific behavioural competences (openness, networking ability, and so on) of potential new-hires.

During the second step of the project, that is, when investigating how Nexus influences the Group's business model through the resources and activities of its business departments, it gradually came to light that every business department needed to have its own departmental report, able to support its decision-making process. The researchers decided to satisfy these needs for several reasons. First, it would ensure consistency between the decision-making process at the departmental level and the company business strategy. Second, it permitted the researchers to build trust with the company actors, thus obtaining commitment and additional information needed to carry out the project. Third, giving way to departmental needs allowed the researchers to keep managerial attention on the project. Fourth, the development of departmental measurement systems was used as a lever to develop the company IR; a selection of KPIs included in the departmental reports was inserted in the company IR, along with brand new KPIs developed ad hoc for the company-wide measurement system. All in all, satisfying departmental needs added credibility to the measurement project and gave it a boost towards the achievement of the final objective (i.e. the development of the company IR).

To sum up, the Group's business model and the strategic themes were considered the frame of reference for identifying how Nexus' resources, activities, and outcomes (its intangibles) affected these strategic themes and contributed to the value creation process of the Group as a whole. This step was a prerequisite to drawing up a set of KPIs linked to the relevant intangibles of each business department. The next section will follow the development of the measurement system for the R&D Department.

The development of the measurement system

This need for departmental reports was felt most strongly by the R&D Department. Over the years, its members had already carried out some initiatives to develop new KPIs able to improve the internal decision-making process and to express and disclose to the rest of the company how R&D outcomes contributed to the overall Group performance. The measurement system of the R&D Department, similarly to that of Nexus as a whole, was centred on financial KPIs, with a particular focus on the analysis of the department's expenses. The monthly variance analysis was aimed at ensuring alignment between actual and standard expenses. Moreover, a quarterly analysis monitored the progress of the research projects in order to ensure alignment between actual and standard timing. Thus, the departmental measurement system was focused on R&D project timeliness and expenses and it was not able to reveal the intellectual and technological outputs of the R&D Department. These outputs are intangible in nature and the assessment of their current and potential value was perceived as being 'at risk' because of the lack of appropriate KPIs. As stated by the R&D manager during one interview:

> We need to improve on the KPI side. We have to highlight the outputs that we produce here. For example, publications cannot be measured in euros, but they are very relevant because it means that we are considered innovative and expert out there. They are pieces of new knowledge that we create here.

Moreover, a time lag often occurred before these intangible outputs started to generate revenues. In the words of the R&D manager:

> R&D designs and creates a functioning prototype which works in a real environment. This is our output. Then, another two years are needed before selling the product and seeing the "tangible" results of our activities ... We must get this message across: investing in R&D generates results in the long-term [sic].

Table 17.2 The contribution of the R&D Department to the Group's strategic themes

Group's strategic themes	Contribution of the R&D Department
Aptitude for collaboration	The R&D Department cooperates with a range of external partners (universities, research centres, customers, and suppliers) to carry out specific projects. In particular, the Department develops EU projects to grow new competences and broaden the network of technological partners. Beyond obtaining funding, these projects are used to collaborate with 'number one' players in specific industries.
Ability to create new knowledge	The creation and the development of the core competence of the Group (automatic measurement and quality control) is the main aim of the R&D Department.
Ability to acquire new knowledge	This theme is closely linked to 'Aptitude for collaboration'. New knowledge is acquired from external partners whenever the R&D Department needs to integrate its internal knowledge in order to craft specific solutions for customers. Partners are mapped according to the type of knowledge that they can provide. Then, depending on the knowledge gap that the R&D Department aims to fill, a specific partner is contacted and external knowledge is brought in and integrated with the internal knowledge.
Ability to develop ad-hoc solutions for customers	The R&D Department develops deep relationships with customers through intensive interactions; the customers commission feasibility studies to the R&D Department which crafts and directs its innovative activities towards 'tailor-made' technologies and solutions for customers.
Ability to diversify	Once internal and external knowledge are integrated, the next step for the R&D Department is to convert this integrated knowledge in order to make it scalable, i.e. easy to expand or upgrade on demand. The aim of the R&D Department is to enable the implementation of the core competence of the Group (automatic measurement and quality control) in as many industries as possible, in other words, expanding the core competence and making it scalable to enter new industries.

The members of the R&D Department did not want it to be treated simply as a cost centre, but they wanted to highlight their department's real contribution to the value creation process of the Group. R&D needed other kinds of numbers able to physically show the "returns on investments" of the research activity and to answer questions like "What are the outcomes of the activities performed? What is the return on the money invested in these activities?"

The measurement project, then, provided the opportunity for the R&D Department to develop a departmental measurement system (and a related departmental report) able to moni-tor the intellectual and technological outputs resulting from the research activity. To develop the measurement system, pivoting on the Group business model and consistent with Step 2 of the business model mapping process, R&D personnel reflected on how the R&D Department influences the Group's business model and strategic themes through its resources, activities, and outcomes (see Table 17.2).

These reflections guided the identification of KPIs, which should express how the R&D Department contributes to the accomplishment of the strategic themes through its resources, activities, and outcomes. Table 17.3 shows a selection of the KPIs designed for the R&D Department.

KPIs are predominantly non-financial, related to intangible dimensions of performance. In a nutshell, these KPIs were chosen in consideration of the contribution made by the R&D

Table 17.3 A selection of the KPIs designed for the R&D Department

Group's strategic themes	KPIs for the R&D Department
Aptitude for collaboration	• Number of European and national projects • Number of conference attendances • Number of non-disclosure agreements • Number of hosted partners
Ability to create new knowledge	• Number of patents • Number of publications • Number of employees transferred to other departments
Ability to acquire new knowledge	• Number of partnerships aimed at acquiring know-how
Ability to develop ad-hoc solutions for customers	• Number of visits to customers • Number of feasibility studies for customers' specific needs
Ability to diversify	• Number of new customers to be served through new competences • Number of long-standing customers to be served through new competences

Department to the business model of the Group. For instance, in order to express the contribution to the theme 'Ability to create new knowledge', beyond traditional KPIs like 'Number of patents' and 'Number of publications', a particular emphasis was put on 'Number of employees transferred to other departments', by monitoring the number of employees who left the R&D Department to start working in other departments. This measure stands for the competences developed by the R&D Department and handed over to other business units, thus representing the way in which the R&D Department supports the business model of the Group, that is, by offering 'injections' of innovation and competences. Two KPIs were selected in order to measure the 'Ability to diversify'; they were 'Number of new customers to be served through new competences' and 'Number of long-standing customers to be served through new competences'. These KPIs are designed to highlight the ability of the department to create innovations able to serve the customers in new ways and/or to enter new business areas. Moreover, as the R&D Department crafts and directs its innovative activities towards tailor-made technologies and solutions for customers, developing close intensive contacts with clients is crucial for the research process as a whole. For this reason, the KPI 'Number of visits to customers' was inserted into the report in order to monitor this aspect. This entire set of KPIs is calculated quarterly and is included in a departmental report, along with pre-existing financial measures (expenses, funding from research projects, and so on).

The new departmental report provides a thorough representation of the R&D Department's contribution to the value creation process of the Group. It goes beyond the short-term perspective of simply monitoring expenses and financial results by introducing forward-looking measures related to the non-financial dimensions of performance. It also provides management with information on IC, which is strategically relevant from a business perspective, as regards human capital (new competences created, number of employees transferred to other departments), relational capital (number of new customers to be served through new competences, number of long-standing customers to be served through new competences, number of visits to customers), and structural capital (number of patents).

This process was repeated for the remaining business departments in Nexus, so that each department could have a departmental dashboard of KPIs strictly linked to the value creation process of the Group and consistent with the activities of the other departments. Thus, the business model was used as a shared platform to enrich the departmental reports (at the department level), to design the IR (at the company level), and to guarantee consistency and fluid movement between them.

Discussion and conclusion

This chapter analyses a case study adopting an interventionist research approach to explore how a business model favoured the design and the implementation of IC measures, thus permitting us to answer the research questions: RQ1: How can the business model support and foster IC measurement? and RQ2: How can the transition from business model to measurement be executed?

The case shows that the business model provided managers with a simple shared language that triggered dialogue on the most relevant IC elements needed to carry out the business strategy, thus highlighting the role that they played in the Group's value creation process. The business model became the centre of the measurement system by providing the logic through which IC was mapped and measured within the company. Figure 17.2 shows the process that led from business model mapping to IC measurement.

First, the process started from the identification of a mix of business model configurations able to clarify the value creation logics of the Group. Second, the business model configurations drove the identification of the strategic themes considered crucial for the value creation process of the Group. Third, the strategic themes helped to clarify which IC elements were of utmost importance and what role they played in the Group's value creation process. Fourth, KPIs were identified according to the role that IC elements played in value creation, along with tangible and financial assets. This process shows that strategic themes acted as a bridge between business model and IC and became the *fil rouge* of the measurement system, thus supporting and fostering the design and the implementation of IC measures.

This process made it possible to identify the intangible levers of value creation and to match these levers with relevant KPIs so that management could control the leading factors

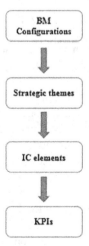

Figure 17.2   The process leading from BM mapping to IC measurement

that affect the performance of the Group as a whole. Borrowing a metaphor from the CEO, the designed measurement system had the potential to monitor "what ripples arise when we throw some stones in".

In turn, using the business model as a pivot provided the measurement system with three strong attributes. First, a high level of consistency with the value creation logic of the Group was reached as KPIs were able to grasp the strategic themes identified from business model configurations. Second, a high level of selectivity was achieved because only the KPIs strictly connected to the value creation logic of the Group were designed and calculated. Third, a high level of integration between financial and non-financial KPIs was accomplished given that the measurement system was able to show the constant interplay between the financial and non-financial dimensions of the business.

Moreover, the case shows an additional contribution made by the business model to the measurement process. Business model configurations and the strategic themes were used not only to design the company IR, but also to build and/or enrich the departmental reports. Business model configurations and strategic themes were used as a shared platform that ensured, on the one hand, a high level of integration and consistency between departmental measurement systems and the company-wide measurement system and, on the other, a high level of integration and consistency among the departmental measurement systems as they were founded on the same set of strategic themes, so that the designed KPIs made it possible to highlight relationships, synergies, and frictions among the different business departments.

This interventionist case study offers theoretical and practical contributions (Jönsson and Lukka, 2005). From the theoretical point of view, the chapter contributes to filling two distinct but intertwined research gaps identified. The first research gap is connected to RQ1 and concerns the contribution of the business model to IC measurement. In this regard, the chapter shows how the drawback related to the atomistic focus of IC measurement frameworks can be overcome by using the business model to build IC measures. In particular, the business model sheds light on the flow and context for value creation by clarifying which IC elements are of utmost importance and what role they play in the company's value creation process, along with tangible and financial assets. This avoids the risk of making an atomistic analysis of IC and prevents the design of KPIs considered "solutions in search of a cause" (Andriessen, 2004b, p. 230). Indeed, the business model clearly identifies the "cause" of KPIs as it favours the "entangling of the indicators" (Nielsen *et al.*, 2009, p. 9; Nielsen and Roslender, 2015, p. 265). In other words, the business model ensures that IC indicators are tightly connected to the company's conception of value creation. Such a business model-based measurement system offers an overarching focus to IC, thus supporting not only IC management, but also the management of the business as a whole.

Moreover, the chapter contributes to filling a second research gap, which is related to RQ2 and regards the process leading from business model to measurement. In this regard, the chapter shows how the business model can be the pivotal element of a measurement system. More specifically, in order to move from business model to measurement, the intermediate level of analysis of strategic themes has been proven to play a crucial role. Indeed, strategic themes act as a bridge between business model and the items to be measured; on the one hand, strategic themes are identified from business model configurations, and, on the other, they help to frame the role and the contribution of the items to be measured for the sake of the value creation process.

Additionally, the chapter sheds light on the relevant role that business model and strategic themes have in ensuring a high level of integration and consistency between departmental measurement systems and a company-wide measurement system, on the one hand, and among the departmental measurement systems themselves, on the other.

From the practical point of view, the managerial problems that pushed the company to undertake an interventionist project were solved by first, switching from a management accounting system focused predominantly on financial performance to an integrated management accounting system that also took into consideration the other company (intangible) key value drivers (i.e. human, structural, and relational capital). Moreover, the traditional stock-flow approach was abandoned and replaced by a focus on strategic themes. Second, the company's managerial problems were also solved by spreading the logic of strategic control inside Nexus through the implementation of a measurement system that focused managerial attention on strategic themes and that challenged the company's strategic assumptions.

Finally, it is important to acknowledge the limitations of this chapter. Although the use of a single case study provides in-depth and rich data, it also limits the generalizability of the observations to other companies. Concerning avenues for future research, it could be interesting to investigate if and why using alternative business model mapping techniques from that of business model configurations, for example Business Model Canvas (Osterwalder and Pigneur, 2010), leads to different outcomes in terms of items to be measured and, consequently, in terms of KPIs to be established. This would allow the comparison of different outcomes, potentially explaining why different outcomes arise and the testing of the effectiveness of different business model mapping techniques from a measurement perspective. Moreover, it could be interesting to delve into the role of the business model in the integration between departmental measurement systems and company-wide measurement systems. By focusing on the dynamics between actors, levers and barriers that can arise in this process could be highlighted.

Regarding policy implications stemming from our focus on business model mapping and IC measurement, by highlighting that the transition from business model to measures is a very complex process, this chapter shows that the effectiveness of this transition often depends on the competences and the skills of IR developers who actually design and implement IR in companies. Therefore, we consider it essential that all measurement and reporting models such as, for instance, the IR proposed by the IIRC (which has inspired the case studied), should provide developers with detailed guidance on how to perform this process (e.g. the choice and the implementation of a business model mapping technique, how to identify the items to be measured, and so on). Without this guidance, comparability of different IRs in time and space could be at risk.

References

Amit, R. and Zott, C. (2001), "Value creation in e-business", *Strategic Management Journal*, Vol. 22, No. 6–7, pp. 493–520.

Andriessen, D. (2004a), *Making Sense of Intellectual Capital. Designing a Method for the Valuation of Intangibles*, Elsevier Butterworth-Heinemann, Burlington, MA.

Andriessen, D. (2004b), "IC valuation and measurement: Classifying the state of the art", *Journal of Intellectual Capital*, Vol. 5, No. 2, pp. 230–242.

Arend, R. J. (2013), "The business model: Present and future: Beyond a skeumorph", *Strategic Organization*, Vol. 11, No. 4, pp. 390–402.

Arnaboldi, M. (2013), "Consultant–researchers in public sector transformation: An evolving role", *Financial Accountability & Management*, Vol. 29, No. 2, pp. 140–160.

Baden-Fuller, C. and Mangematin, V. (2013), "Business models: A challenging agenda", *Strategic Organization*, Vol. 11, No. 4, pp. 418–427.

Beattie, V. and Smith, S. J. (2013), "Value creation and business models: Refocusing the intellectual capital debate", *British Accounting Review*, Vol. 45, No. 4, pp. 243–254.

Bini, L., Dainelli, F., and Giunta, F. (2016), "Business model disclosure in the Strategic Report", *Journal of Intellectual Capital*, Vol. 17, No. 1, pp. 83–102.

Bromwich, M. and Scapens, R.W. (2016), "Management accounting research: 25 years on", *Management Accounting Research*, Vol. 31, pp. 1–9.

Chiucchi, M. S. (2013), "Intellectual capital accounting in action: Enhancing learning through interventionist research", *Journal of Intellectual Capital*, Vol. 14, No. 1, pp. 48–68.

Chiucchi, M. S. and Dumay, J. C. (2015), "Unlocking intellectual capital", *Journal of Intellectual Capital*, Vol. 16, No. 2, pp. 305–330.

Chiucchi, M. S. and Montemari, M. (2016), "Investigating the 'fate' of intellectual capital indicators: A case study", *Journal of Intellectual Capital*, Vol. 17, No. 2, pp. 238–254.

Cuozzo, B., Dumay, J. C., Palmaccio, M., and Lombardi, R. (2017), "Intellectual capital disclosure: A structured literature review", *Journal of Intellectual Capital*, Vol. 18, No. 1, pp. 9–28.

Denzin, N. K. and Lincoln, Y. S. (2000), "Introduction: The discipline and practice of qualitative research", in Denzin, N. K. and Lincoln, Y. S. (Eds), *Handbook of Qualitative Research*, Sage Publications, Thousand Oaks, CA, pp. 1–28.

Dumay, J. C. (2009a), "Reflective discourse about intellectual capital: Research and practice", *Journal of Intellectual Capital*, Vol. 10, No. 4, pp. 489–503.

Dumay, J. C. (2009b), "Intellectual capital measurement: A critical approach", *Journal of Intellectual Capital*, Vol. 10, No. 2, pp. 190–210.

Dumay, J. C. (2010), "A critical reflective discourse of an interventionist research project", *Qualitative Research in Accounting & Management*, Vol. 7, No. 1, pp. 46–70.

Dumay, J. C. (2012), "Grand theories as barriers to using IC concepts", *Journal of Intellectual Capital*, Vol. 13, No. 1, pp. 4–15.

Dumay, J. C. (2013), "The third stage of IC: Towards a new IC future and beyond", *Journal of Intellectual Capital*, Vol. 14, No. 1, pp. 5–9.

Dumay, J. C. (2014), "15 years of the *Journal of Intellectual Capital* and counting", *Journal of Intellectual Capital*, Vol. 15, No. 1, pp. 2–37.

Dumay, J. C. and Cuganesan, S. (2011), "Making sense of intellectual capital complexity: Measuring through narrative", *Journal of Human Resource Costing & Accounting*, Vol. 15, No. 1, pp. 24–49.

Edvinsson, L. and Malone, M. (1997), *Intellectual Capital: The Proven Way to Establish Your Company's True Value by Measuring Its Hidden Brain Power*, Piatkus, London.

Gassmann, O., Frankenberger, K., and Csik, M. (2014), *The Business Model Navigator*, Pearson, Harlow, UK.

Giuliani, M. (2016), "Sensemaking, sensegiving and sensebreaking. The case of intellectual capital measurements", *Journal of Intellectual Capital*, Vol. 17, No. 2, pp. 218–237.

Giuliani, M., Chiucchi, M. S., and Marasca, S. (2016), "A history of intellectual capital measurements: From production to consumption", *Journal of Intellectual Capital*, Vol. 17, No. 3, pp. 590–606.

Guthrie, J., Ricceri, F., and Dumay, J. (2012), "Reflections and projections: A decade of intellectual capital accounting research", *British Accounting Review*, Vol. 44, No. 2, pp. 68–82.

InCaS (2008), *InCaS: Intellectual Capital Statement - Made in Europe*, available at: www.incas-europe.org (accessed 1 July 2016).

International Integrated Reporting Council (IIRC) (2013), *The International <IR> Framework*, International Integrated Reporting Council, London.

Jönsson, S. and Lukka, K. (2005), *Doing Interventionist Research in Management Accounting*, Gothenburg Research Institute, Gothenburg, Sweden.

Jönsson, S. and Lukka, K. (2006), "There and back again: Doing interventionist research in management accounting", in Chapman, C. S., Hopwood, A. G., and Shields, M. D. (Eds), *Handbook of Management Accounting Research*, Elsevier, Oxford, UK, pp. 373–397.

Liang, C. J., Chen, T. Y., and Lin, Y.L. (2013), "How do different business models affect intellectual capital?", *Journal of Intellectual Capital*, Vol. 14, No. 2, pp. 176–191.

Linder, J. and Cantrell, S. (2000), *Changing Business Models: Surveying the Landscape*, Accenture Institute for Strategic Change, available at: http://course.shufe.edu.cn/jpkc/zhanlue/upfiles/edit/201002/20100224120954.pdf (accessed 1 July 2016).

Lönnqvist, A., Kianto, A., and Sillanpää, V. (2009), "Using intellectual capital management for facilitating organizational change", *Journal of Intellectual Capital Journal of Intellectual Capital*, Vol. 10, No. 10, pp. 559–572.

Magretta, J. (2002), "Why business models matter", *Harvard Business Review*, Vol. 80, No. 5, pp. 86–92.

Massa, L., Tucci, C., and Afuah, A. (2017), "A critical assessment of business model research", *Academy of Management Annals*, Vol. 11, No. 1, pp. 73–104.

McGrath, R. G. (2010), "Business models: A discovery driven approach", *Long Range Planning*, Vol. 43, No. 2–3, pp. 247–261.

Montemari, M. and Nielsen, C. (2013), "The role of causal maps in intellectual capital measurement and management", *Journal of Intellectual Capital*, Vol. 14, No. 4, pp. 522–546.

Morris, M., Schindehutte, M., and Allen, J. (2005), "The entrepreneur's business model: Toward a unified perspective", *Journal of Business Research*, Vol. 58, No. 6, pp. 726–735.

Mouritsen, J. (2004), "Measuring and intervening: How do we theorise intellectual capital management?", *Journal of Intellectual Capital*, Vol. 5, No. 2, pp. 257–267.

Mouritsen, J. (2006), "Problematising intellectual capital research: Ostensive versus performative IC", *Accounting, Auditing & Accountability Journal*, Vol. 19, No. 6, pp. 820–841.

Mouritsen, J., Bukh, P. N., Flagstad, K., Thorbjørnsen, S., Johansen, M. R., Kotnis, S., Larsen, H. T., *et al.* (2003), *Intellectual Capital Statements: The New Guideline*, Danish Ministry of Science, Technology and Innovation, Copenhagen.

Nielsen, C. and Montemari, M. (2012), "The role of human resources in business model performance: The case of network-based companies", *Journal of Human Resource Costing & Accounting*, Vol. 16, No. 2, pp. 142–164.

Nielsen, C. and Roslender, R. (2015), "Enhancing financial reporting: The contribution of business models", *British Accounting Review*, Vol. 47, No. 3, pp. 262–274.

Nielsen, C., Roslender, R., and Bukh, P. N. (2009), "Intellectual capital reporting: Can a strategy perspective solve accounting problems?", in Lytras, M. and Ordóñez de Pablos, P. (Eds), *Knowledge Ecology in Global Business: Managing Intellectual Capital*, Information Science Reference, Hershey, PA, pp. 174–191.

O'Donnell, D., Henriksen, L. B., and Voelpel, S. C. (2006), "Becoming critical on intellectual capital", *Journal of Intellectual Capital*, Vol. 7, No. 1, pp. 5–11.

Osterwalder, A. and Pigneur, Y. (2010), *Business Model Generation: A Handbook for Visionaries, Game Changers, and Challengers*, John Wiley & Sons, Hoboken, NJ.

Patton, M. Q. (2002), *Qualitative Research and Evaluation Methods*, Sage Publications, Thousand Oaks, CA.

Ryan, B., Scapens, R. W., and Theobald, M. (2002), *Research Method and Methodology in Finance and Accounting*, Thomson Learning, London.

Suomala, P., Lyly-Yrjänäinen, J., and Lukka, K. (2014), "Battlefield around interventions: A reflective analysis of conducting interventionist research in management accounting", *Management Accounting Research*, Vol. 25, No. 4, pp. 304–314.

Sveiby, K. E. (1997), *The New Organizational Wealth: Manageing and Measuring Knowledge-Based Assets*, Berrett-Koehler Publishers Inc., San Francisco, CA.

Sveiby, K. E. (2010), "Methods for measuring intangible assets", available at: www.sveiby.com/ articles/ IntangibleMethods.htm (accessed 1 July 2016).

Taran, Y., Nielsen, C., Montemari, M., Thomsen, P., and Paolone, F. (2016). "Business model configurations: A five-V framework to map out potential innovation routes", *European Journal of Innovation Management*, Vol. 19, No. 4, pp. 492–527.

Tikkanen, H., Lamberg, J. A., Parvinen, P., and Kallunki, J. P. (2005), "Managerial cognition, action and the business model of the firm", *Management Decision*, Vol. 43, No. 6, pp. 789–809.

Wirtz, B. W., Pistoia, A., Ullrich, S., and Göttel, V. (2016), "Business models: Origin, development and future research perspectives", *Long Range Planning*, Vol. 49, No. 1, pp. 36–54.

18

INTELLECTUAL CAPITAL DISCLOSURE

What benefits, what costs, is it voluntary?

Sarah Jane Smith

Introduction

This chapter addresses the disclosure of intellectual capital (IC). It is possible to identify the three stages in the development of IC research in terms of IC disclosure. During the first stage, specific disclosures came to be identified as IC disclosures, thus raising awareness. During the second stage, generic disclosure theories were applied in the IC context. The third stage investigates the disclosure of IC in practice. Within the literature, IC disclosure has been examined from a range of philosophical perspectives: positivist, interpretivist, and critical.

IC refers to intangible resources that create corporate value (Ashton, 2005). IC is embedded within a spectrum of corporate activities, and has been generally categorized into human, structural, and relational capital (Meritum, 2002). Human capital encapsulates the knowledge, skills, experiences, and abilities of people. Structural capital includes the value embedded in organizational routines, procedures, systems, cultures, and databases. Elements of structural capital may be legally protected and become intellectual property rights, legally owned by the company under separate title. Relational capital refers to all resources linked to the external relationships of the firm, such as relationships with investors, creditors, customers, and suppliers. Relational capital also comprises the perceptions that stakeholders hold about the company. Numerous components or elements have been associated with these three categories of human, structural, and relational capital.[1]

Under contemporary international financial reporting regulations, many IC elements are not recognized in the financial statements, and are historically not subject to extensive mandatory narrative reporting requirements. However, the narrative reporting context is constantly changing and, beyond the regulatory environment, the opportunity to voluntarily disclose IC does exist within the narrative sections of the corporate annual report and other channels of corporate communication.

A variety of incentives are suggested in relation to the disclosure of IC information that is not captured by the traditional financial reporting framework. The incentives to voluntarily disclose information, in general, can be explained in terms of a variety of economic and managerial theories, each of which focuses on a different aspect of corporate behaviour. Establishing trustworthiness with stakeholders and providing a valuable marketing tool (Van Der Meer-Kooistra and Zijlstra, 2001) are prime concerns.

Capital market incentives, such as the opportunity to increase transparency to capital markets, reduce information risk, lead to strong benefits in the form of a lower cost of capital, increased share price, and increased liquidity (Richardson and Welker, 2001; Verrecchia, 2001; Lundholm and Van Winkle, 2006). The more social exposure a company receives, the more it needs to legitimize its existence (Patten, 1991). Through information disclosure, external perceptions of legitimacy can be altered and the costs arising from non-legitimacy avoided (Deegan, 2000). Additional economic costs in the form of loss of competitive advantage, litigation exposure, and the direct costs of collecting, processing, and disseminating information, act as disincentives (Elliott and Jacobson, 1994). The competitive disadvantage to disclosure is particularly pertinent in the IC context given that IC is a prime source of competitive edge in a global market place (Edvinsson and Malone, 1997; Lev, 2004). Value creation processes are potentially highly sensitive, and thus disclosing such information would be a serious burden. Importantly, therefore, the management of IC and the disclosure of IC are mutually dependent activities in the value creation process with disclosure in itself having the potential to create or destroy value (Beattie *et al.*, 2013). In theory, voluntary disclosure of IC information will occur if the benefits exceed the costs (Heitzman, *et al.*, 2010). However, due to bounded rationality, not all potential benefits and costs might be taken into consideration by corporations.

The purpose of this chapter is to explore the benefits, costs, restrictions, and alternative perspectives to IC disclosure. This is achieved through a synthesis of the evidence obtained from a direct survey investigation of, and follow up interviews with, UK listed companies (228 questionnaire responses and 17 interviews) across finance, marketing, and human resource specialists.[2] This chapter contributes an analysis of this evidence with additional interpretative commentary, particularly in relation to recent developments in the narrative reporting arena, providing a platform from which the IC disclosure decision may be deliberated.

IC disclosure prior research

Prior studies have extensively investigated the extent and nature of IC disclosure in corporate annual reports. The majority of such studies use content analysis to capture indirectly the extent to which different IC components are disclosed to infer their relative importance. Prior studies have focused either on a single country setting (for example, Guthrie and Petty, 2000; Brennan, 2001; April *et al.*, 2003; Bontis, 2003; Bozzolan *et al.*, 2003; Goh and Lin, 2004; Abdolmohammadi, 2005; Abeysekera and Guthrie, 2005; Unerman, *et al.*, 2007; Li *et al.*, 2008; Campbell and Rahman, 2010) or across countries (for example, Vandemaele *et al.*, 2005; Vergauwen and Van Alem, 2005; Bozzolan, *et al.*, 2006; Guthrie *et al.*, 2007). Findings suggest that relational capital is generally the most extensively reported IC category (Abeysekera, 2006). In their pioneering study, Guthrie and Petty (2000) investigated IC disclosure in the annual reports of 20 Australian companies. They found 40 per cent and 30 per cent of IC disclosures relate to relational capital and human capital respectively, although overall disclosure was evaluated as 'low'. Employing the same framework, similar studies were conducted in Ireland (Brennan, 2001) and Italy (Bozzolan *et al.*, 2003). Bozzolan *et al.* (2003) found relational capital to comprise just under half of IC disclosures, with particular attention given to customers, distribution channels, business collaboration, and brands. Human capital made up a smaller proportion, 21 per cent, of total disclosure. Guthrie and Petty (2000) related the low IC disclosure levels found to the lack of reporting frameworks and the lack of initiative in measuring and externally reporting. The potential loss of competitive advantage to disclosure has also been suggested as an explanation (Bozzolan *et al.*, 2003).

Subsequent studies have developed and extended the range of components of IC investigated, for example Abeysekera and Guthrie (2005). UK studies of this type are relatively few. Unerman *et al*. (2007) and Striukova *et al*. (2008) use content analysis to investigate IC disclosure across a range of corporate media for 15 UK companies operating in four different industry sectors. Relational capital was found to account for 61 per cent of such disclosures with information relating to customers making up 20 per cent of total disclosure and being disclosed by all companies. Human capital accounted for 22 per cent, including informa-tion on work-related knowledge and employee information. For a sample of 100 UK listed companies, Li *et al*. (2008) found, based on word count, relational capital to account for 38 per cent and human capital 28 per cent of total IC disclosures. The most frequently disclosed components were found to be customers, relationships with suppliers and stakeholders, market presence, customer relationships, and market leadership, with over 90 per cent of sampled firms having disclosures of such items. The significance of relational capital was further emphasized in a longitudinal study by Campbell and Rahman (2010), who reviewed the annual reports of the major UK retailer Marks and Spencer over the period 1978 to 2008. The proportion of relational capital was found to vary between 45 per cent and 70 per cent of total IC disclosure, making it the most disclosed category of IC throughout the 31-year period. Since 2001, rapid growth in relational capital disclosure has been observed, with information on brands, distribution channels, customers, and corporate image building being the most frequently disclosed.

The importance and disclosure of IC has also been explored directly using case studies and semi-structured interviews on limited occasions (for example, Van Der Meer-Kooistra and Zijlstra, 2001; Chaminade and Roberts, 2003; Roslender and Fincham, 2004; Unerman *et al*., 2007). Roslender and Fincham (2004) conducted a series of interviews with senior managers in six UK knowledge-based companies. Whilst they note a growing importance attached to the long-term value creation aspirations of organizations, they find that understanding, meas-urement, and reporting of IC was generally under-developed. Further, external reporting was not considered, irrespective of any recognition of the contribution to sustained value creation. Unerman *et al*. (2007) conducted 15 in-depth interviews with UK finance directors. Despite some evidence to suggest a balance between informing capital markets and ensuring competi-tive advantage is not compromised, they concluded that the costs to external disclosure were not a significant obstacle. Abeysekera (2008) conducted 11 case study interviews when inves-tigating human capital disclosure in the annual reports of firms in Sri Lanka, and concluded it is made to reduce tension between the firm and their stakeholders in the interest of further capital accumulation. The questionnaire survey method has seldom been used in the IC con-text. However, Gunther and Beyer (2003) obtained insights from 54 German listed companies where limited IC disclosure was associated with reluctance to damage competitive position. In summary, from prior research relational capital could be perceived as the most important IC category to value creation given the extent of observed disclosure. The IC disclosure decision-making process also appears to have the foundations for a cost-benefit trade-off, the benefits from putting value creation information into the hands of various stakeholders versus the cost of loss of competitive position.

Research methods: who provides the evidence for this chapter?

IC questionnaire survey evidence referred to in this chapter comes from 93 finance direc-tors, 55 from companies listed on the London Stock Exchange main market and 38 from large companies listed on the Alternative Investment Market (AIM) market. The industry

profile of these companies is shown in Table 18.1. The industrial goods and services industry is most represented. Whilst certain small industries, namely automobiles and parts,
food and beverage, and telecommunications are not represented, overall industry profile
is closely aligned with the population of domestic UK main market companies and the
sample of AIM companies surveyed. The average annual sales and number of employees
for these 93 companies was £561m and 3,108 respectively. Human and relational capital
disclosure was further explored with 67 human resource specialists (87 per cent of whom
indicated they held the positions of director or manager of human resources) and 68 marketing specialists (64 per cent of whom indicated they held positions of director, head or
manager of marketing/business development). Both human resource and marketing specialists held their positions in main market companies. With the exception of automobiles and
parts, all of the industry classifications are represented in the human resource specialists'
companies (Table 18.1). There are no marketing specialists from companies representing
automobiles and parts, basic resources, food and beverage, media, and personal and house-
hold goods. Nevertheless, industry profiles are not significantly different from that of the
population. Human resource specialists come from companies with average annual sales
of £2,931m and average number of employees of 4,337. The marketing specialists come
from companies with average annual sales of £1,552m and average number of employees of 7,561. Five interviews were conducted with finance directors from main market
companies included in either the FTSE 100 or FTSE 250, and six interviews were with

Table 18.1 Industry classification for the companies of the key functional specialists providing
questionnaire survey evidence

Industry sector	Finance directors (n = 93)	Human resource specialists (n = 67)	Marketing specialists (n = 67)
Automobiles & parts	—	—	—
Banks	1	2	1
Basic resources	2	2	—
Chemicals	3	2	2
Construction & material	2	4	3
Financial services	9	3	6
Food & beverage	—	2	—
Healthcare	7	3	5
Industrial goods & services	26	24	20
Insurance	2	4	1
Media	8	1	—
Oil & gas	5	4	4
Personal & household goods	1	3	—
Real estate	6	3	8
Retail	6	3	1
Technology	9	1	7
Telecommunications	—	1	1
Travel & leisure	4	4	7
Utilities	2	1	1
Total	**93**	**67**	**67**

Note: n = 67 because one marketing questionnaire was returned anonymously companies listed on the AIM market. Two interviews were conducted with human resource specialists and four interviews with marketing specialists, all from main market companies. All interviewees appeared hold senior relevant corporate positions.

What elements of IC are most important to value creation?

The relative importance of the three categories of IC – human, relational, and structural capital, and their respective components – to value creation is considered in this section. The overall importance of IC to finance directors is emphasized by the finding that over 57 per cent of them believe IC contributes to 50 per cent or more of shareholder value. Human capital was ranked as providing the highest contribution of all three IC categories with no significant difference between structural and relational capital. Various components of these three categories were found to contribute to value creation to some extent. However, four components (customer relationships, employee skills and education, competitive edge in terms of quality of product/service, and company reputation) were considered the most valuable by a clear margin. According to the finance director of a FTSE 250 company in industrial goods and services: "The only assets we have in our business are our people . . . our main route to market is a combination of our people and their ability to convince clients" (Beattie and Thomson, 2010, p. 50). It is apparent though that the IC concept is not always considered in terms of the individual components that create value. A number of companies appeared to focus on how the components come together under a strategy for creating company value. This supports what Habersam and Piper (2003) term "connectivity capital", a linking pin between human, structural, and relational capital. Mouritsen et al. (2001) highlight the importance of converting human capital into structural capital in the value creation process. This was evident from finance director responses: "All our products are based on years of research and developed knowledge and for practically everything we sell, we depend on patenting and protecting that knowledge" (Group Financial Reporter, FTSE 100 Healthcare company; Beattie and Thomson, 2010, p. 51). Irrespective, the human contribution to company value appears paramount, given that 75 per cent of finance directors viewed a low level of employee turnover as providing a moderate to very strong contribution "You can have all kind of intellectual property protections you want but basically the knowledge is in the people and therefore our ability to retain those people is really key" (Group Finance Director, FTSE 100 industrial goods and services company; Beattie and Thomson, 2010, p. 51).

Within the human capital category, employee skills and education were viewed as making the most important contribution by human resource specialists. This was followed by employee commitment, positive employee attitudes, positive employee behaviour, and employee motivation. Not surprisingly, human resource specialists attach even more importance to employee skills and education than finance directors: "Human capital actually starts with the people that we have, the calibre of skills, competencies and experiences that they either bring with them or that they evolve and create by the type of work they do with us" (Group HR Director of a FTSE Small Cap company operating in the industrial goods and services sector; Beattie and Smith, 2010, p. 270).

Within the relational capital category, all of the components investigated contribute to generating value to some extent according to marketing specialists. The top four components (customer relationships, company reputation, competitive edge in terms of quality of product/service, and data/knowledge of customers) were thought to be more important than anything else. Communication with which to build relationships and knowledge of customers appeared to be at the forefront of value creation for the marketing specialists:

Knowledge of customers is critical to understanding how our customers sell their products to their customers and how they market them. So the more you understand about how customers use our technology as part of their overall marketing message, the better we can actually promote our next technologies to them.

(VP of Marketing, FTSE Small Cap company operating
in the Technology sector; Beattie et al., 2013, p. 34)

Relationships and communication with customers also appears to have additional benefits in acquiring knowledge essential to the development of a competitive edge: "Customers are incredibly willing to offer information about competitors' products. So most of it comes from informal feedback from a customer" (Director of Business Development, main-market company operating in the technology sector; Beattie *et al.*, 2013). Marketing specialists attach more importance to the contribution of individual relational capital components compared to finance directors, especially in terms of data/knowledge of customers and marketing strategies. Such differences in views are not surprising, and are likely to reflect the customer-orientated perspective of marketing specialists compared to the shareholder-orientated perspective of finance directors.

Benefits and costs of IC disclosure

This section considers both the benefits and costs of IC disclosure and the existence of a benefit versus cost trade-off.

Benefits of IC disclosure

According to the UK finance directors surveyed, the capital market benefits of IC disclosure dominate. Disclosing IC information to correct an undervalued share price was considered more important than anything else. According to the group financial report of a FTSE 100 healthcare firm:

The attitude of our senior management is to maintain clear communication with our investors so that there are no surprises ... they want our share price to correctly value the business ... it's a very different culture from some aggressive corporates of the past where communication has been about enhancing share price beyond what it should be.

(Beattie and Thomson, 2010, p. 55)

Increasing the predictability of future prospects was next in terms of importance, with increasing price/earnings ratio and reducing information risk both being at least fairly important. The importance of capital market benefits documented here are not, however, unique to the IC context since previous research in the US has found voluntary disclosure in general is made in order to reduce information risk and boost stock price (Graham *et al.*, 2005). UK finance directors have previously been found to voluntarily disclose for the benefit of obtaining a reputation for openness (Armitage and Marston, 2007). However, in the IC context in general, disclosure to promote a reputation for transparent and accurate reporting was considered below capital market considerations in terms of importance by finance directors. In the words of the group financial controller of a FTSE 250 firm operating in industrial goods and services, "We do pride ourselves on being, within reason, as transparent as possible to the market, and we hope that stands us in good stead, in terms of the value that the market attributes to us" (Beattie and Thomson, 2010, p. 55).

Certain companies were driven by the reputational benefits of IC disclosure in terms of responding to perceived unethical corporate behaviour. Communicating IC information to customers and other stakeholders was important where the nature of business encouraged it. As the group finance director of one FTSE 100 industrial goods and services company put it:

> We get attacked by various pressure groups outside the organization saying [the nature of our business] is unethical. We have put it [ethics] higher up on the corporate agenda. We engage now you know, and we listen and ... we change. In the early 90's the test was if it's legal that's alright. The test isn't that anymore, the test is how would it read on the front page of the Daily Mail, and would I be happy explaining this to my mum? The test for all businesses is much different from where the law sits ... so you end up having to try and inform all those opinion formers.
>
> *(Beattie and Thomson, 2010, p. 56)*

According to human resource specialists, attracting and retaining high calibre employees are the most important two benefits gained from disclosing human capital information. The disclosure of existing employee reputation is valuable to future recruitment. In this manner, value is created "through enhanced reputation and disclosure influences the external perception of reputation" (Toms, 2002, p. 258). As the assistant head of employee engagement at a FTSE 100 firm operating in the banking sector put it:

> It's very important that [the company] has as strong an external perception and reputation as we can have ... we have done some work in the area of employer branding ... the more people know about the good employee practices we do, the more they are hopefully likely to work for us.
>
> *(Beattie and Smith, 2010, p. 278)*

The majority of finance directors did not rate creating trustworthiness with other stakeholders such as employees and customers as a significant benefit to IC disclosure. However, such benefits vary according to the type of IC information disclosed, being of more importance in relation to human and relational capitals, but not structural capital. According to the marketing specialists, the disclosure of customer relational capital information is most beneficial when creating trustworthiness with customers. It is also important in both retaining and attracting new customers. Trustworthiness with potential customers can be achieved by disclosing information about current customers. According to the director of business development for a main market company operating in the technology sector:

> [t]he most powerful way to sell to a customer is a reference. You'll typically always be asked for references within an industry. The most credible thing you can do with a customer is say we've done the same thing for somebody else in the same industry.
>
> *(Beattie et al., 2013, p. 41)*

Through disclosure companies can, therefore, borrow their customer's reputation to add value to their own (Helm and Salminen, 2010).

Costs of IC disclosure

A significant cost of IC disclosure is loss of competitive advantage in terms of divulging company secrets or otherwise harming competitive position, according to finance directors:

> I'll describe it [processes, our life cycle, management process] in the generality to investors but the forms we use and how we go about this is proprietary so we keep it ... The sector is prone to industrial espionage by nations, not necessarily by individuals but by nations.
>
> *(Group finance director, FTSE 100 firm in industrial*
> *goods and services; Beattie and Thomson, 2010, p. 60)*

> We find ourselves in the fortunate position where we are probably sort of number one or number two in most of the markets we operate in ... so we set the precedent for the development of the market ... so we don't want to give too much of what we are trying to achieve to our competitors.
>
> *(Group financial controller, FTSE 250 firm in industrial*
> *goods and services; Beattie and Thomson, 2010, p. 60)*

The importance attached to the cost of loss of competitive advantage reinforces the findings of prior studies in both the UK (Armitage and Marston, 2007; Unerman *et al.*, 2007) and elsewhere (Van Der Meer-Kooistra and Zijlstra, 2001; Gunther and Beyer, 2003; Graham *et al.*, 2005).

The potential costs associated with creating unrealistic expectations and a disclosure precedent that is potentially difficult to maintain are also considered important. This is consistent with previous findings where Unerman *et al.* (2007) found that UK finance directors were concerned that investors and analysts would develop overly optimistic/pessimistic expectations from IC disclosures. The cost of information provision in terms of information collection and auditor opinion was also generally viewed as important.

Although the majority of finance directors surveyed viewed IC disclosure to be fairly to very important in terms of marketing their company products, being overtly seen to market via IC disclosure created a cost to be avoided in certain sectors. As the financial controller of a financial services company on the AIM market observed:

> We're not allowed to market ... we cannot market ... we need to be careful on our annual report about marketing ... the FSA could clamp down on us and say you are marketing to the general public ... talking up [your] products too much.
>
> *(Beattie and Thomson, 2010, p. 56)*

The group financial reporter in a FTSE 100 company operating in healthcare had similar concerns: "The promotion and marketing of medicines is something that's very regulated . . . legal obligations in terms of selling and marketing and promotion of our products . . . makes it different" (Beattie and Thomson, 2010, p. 57). These quotes serve to illustrate why it is important to avoid attracting unwanted scrutiny from regulators and other stakeholders when disclosing IC information.

Human resource specialists indicated that loss of competitive position was the most important cost to disclosing human capital information. As the group HR director of a FTSE Small

Cap industrial and services firm acknowledged: "We report in our annual report and accounts carefully, because if you have got good people then other people want them" (Beattie and Smith, 2010, p. 276). The assistant head of employee engagement of a FTSE 100 Bank echoed such concerns:

> We have a strong reputation externally and we place a very high value on our human capital team and our human capital strategy, that's a competitive advantage for us. So we would be cautious to some degree in the level of information, the level of detail we would share with our competitors externally.
>
> *(Beattie and Smith, 2010, p. 276)*

Marketing specialists were also most concerned with the costs associated with loss of competitive position when disclosing customer relational capital information. "With our competitors . . . we don't actually want to tip them off . . . we don't necessarily want to beat the drum and allow our competitors to go in to win them [new customers] over instead of working with us" (VP of Marketing, FTSE Small Cap company operating in the technology sector; Beattie *et al.*, 2013, p. 43).

> You do get some organizations that will put up an entire list of the entire customer base. I'll never do that. All I do is go to my competitors and I copy those people and I go target them, because I now know they use those products.
>
> *(Director of Business Development, main market company operating in the Technology sector; Beattie et al., 2013, p. 43)*

A further cost of disclosing customer relational capital exists in terms of eroding trustworthiness and relationships with existing customers who wish associated relationships to remain private. This was a major concern raised by the VP of Marketing of a FTSE Small Cap technology company:

> We'll only disclose stuff that is consistent with how they [the customers] are going to market and that is very, very important. In principal [sic], the more relationships we can talk about the better. However, it's rather more complex because a lot of the time leading brands [our customers] do not want to disclose ... the moment they start saying "well we got this technology from here and that technology from there", that is diluting the strength of their brand.
>
> *(Beattie et al., 2013, p. 41)*

Benefit versus cost trade-off?

Beattie and Smith (2012), through a statistical analysis of the finance director responses to a long list of benefits and costs associated with IC disclosure identified in previous academic literature, conclude that a limited set of benefits and costs are traded-off. In contrast to previous research (Van Der Meer-Kooistra and Zijlstra, 2001), the evidence does not suggest strongly that the costs of providing IC information outweigh the benefits.

Finance directors recognize that the benefits from disclosing IC information to investors in the capital market must be weighed against putting that same information in the hands of competitors. Sixty-two percent agreed or strongly agreed that "informing capital markets in relation to IC is balanced with the need to ensure that competitive advantage is not compromised" (Beattie and Smith, 2012, p.12). As the finance director and company secretary of a chemical company listed on the AIM market articulated:

> I think it needs to be recognized in financial reporting that there is a fundamental conflict between confidentiality and competitively sensitive information, and providing information to investors … investors want to know what that is [competitive advantage] because that helps them to value the business, but competitors want to know … in order that they can knock it down and get around it somehow.
>
> *(Beattie and Thomson, 2010, p. 60)*

The existence of a trade-off between the benefits of informing capital markets and the cost of loss of competitive advantage is also consistent with previous findings (for example, Unerman *et al.*, 2007).

When specifically disclosing human capital information, the benefits in terms of acquiring new human capital are weighed against the cost of losing existing human capital to competitors. The benefits of disclosing customer relational capital information are recognized in the form of attracting new customers, building trust with those customers, and enhancing corporate reputation. However, the trade-off is the associated cost of delivering the sensitive information of customer identity straight into the hands of competitors. The director of business development for a main market technology company summarized this as follows: "You want to have as much information in the hands of your customers as possible and you want to have as little information in the hands of your competition as possible" (Beattie *et al.*, 2013, p. 43). However, customer relational capital disclosure not only costs in terms of competitors, it costs in terms of damaged relationships with existing customers in situations when there is a desire to keep associations private.

To what extent is IC disclosure voluntary?

This section considers the extent to which IC disclosure is voluntary. An analysis of both financial reporting and narrative reporting requirements is provided. External restrictions outside of financial and narrative reporting requirements are also highlighted.

Financial reporting requirements

According to Roslender and Fincham (2001), it is unlikely that traditional financial reporting will be capable of accommodating IC. In the UK, international accounting standards are mandatory for listed companies when producing consolidated group accounts. New UK regulation in the form of Financial Reporting Standard 102 is an option for individually listed companies. For IC assets to be included in the statement of financial position (balance sheet), the IC assets would have to meet certain recognition criteria, namely that it is probable that expected future economic benefits attributable to the asset will flow to the entity and the cost or value of the asset can be measured reliably. Additionally, to be recognized, intangible assets (defined as 'an identifiable non-monetary asset without physical substance') must meet an identifiability criterion. This also has two aspects. First, the asset must be separable from the entity and second arise from a contractual or legal right (*International Accounting Standard 38*, IASB, 2004; *Financial Reporting Standard 102*, FRC, 2015). Consequently,

IC is generally excluded from the traditional financial reporting framework because major components do not meet several of these criteria (Roos *et al.*, 1998). On average, finance directors disagreed that IC reporting could be improved if the capitalization rules for intangible assets were made less restrictive. As the financial controller of a financial services AIM company protested: "Not on the balance sheet, because it's just going to be too subjective and everyone's going to have a different answer".

Narrative reporting requirements

Given the exclusion of IC from the financial statements, a narrative disclosure approach has become accepted as an appropriate route to take (DATI, 2000, 2002). The financial statements are embedded within the annual corporate report which, despite the availability of various alternative communication channels, remains a key reporting document (Beattie, 1999).

It has been increasingly asserted, especially in the aftermath of the 2008 banking crisis, that financial statements should be complemented with narrative information that provides context for the financial information. This narrative information should inform stakeholders of the company's business model in terms of what creates corporate value, including key risks, resources, and relationships, and also includes key performance indicators already used by management to manage the business. This term 'business model' increasingly features in the business reporting debate. According to Teece (2010), a business model conveys how a company converts resources into economic value. It captures all forms of a company's capital, including physical, financial, and intellectual, so both the IC concept and the business model concept are mutually concerned with value creation. Therefore, IC disclosure is made, at least to some degree, through business model description and disclosure. Beattie and Smith (2013) describe the business model as the higher-level concept in value creation, driving IC disclosure in terms of what IC components are most crucial. This emphasis on narrative reporting, including business model reporting, has become increasingly global as more countries adopt International Financial Reporting Standards (FASB, 2009; ICAEW, 2009; EFRAG, 2010; BIS, 2011; IIRC, 2013). Indeed, the business model is central to the ever-evolving integrated reporting debate where the future of corporate reporting is said to depend on the ability to communicate how all forms of capital (financial, manufactured, intellectual, human, social, and natural) come together to create value.

In 2010, the IASB issued a Practice Statement on "management commentary", which recommends that IC resources should be disclosed, significant relationships should be identified and discussed, with appropriate performance measures also disclosed (IASB, 2010). However, mandatory compliance is not currently required and, in the absence of any detailed rules or guidance, the nature and degree of any IC information voluntarily disclosed has the potential to exhibit significant variation across companies. A European Commission (EC) directive on the disclosure of non-financial information introduced in 2014 has future implications for around 6,000 large companies listed on EU markets.[3] The directive requires the disclosure of relevant social, environmental, and board diversity information in annual reports from financial year 2017 onwards, capturing a degree of IC components. Guidelines are expected to be published by the EC in spring 2017. However, the guidelines are to be 'non-binding'.

In the UK, the Corporate Governance Code, which is mandatory for listed companies under London Stock Exchange rules, requires company directors to "include in the annual report an explanation of the basis on which the company generates or preserves value over the longer term (the business model) and the strategy for delivering the objectives of the company" (UK Corporate Governance Code, FRC, September 2014, p. 16). This has been the case since 2010 and, on this basis, IC disclosure could be interpreted as mandatory. However, the mandatory business review required prior to 2013 included no specific requirements in relation to business models and IC. The UK Narrative Reporting Statement (ASB, 2006), which continued to influence corporate reporting in the UK, also encouraged discussion of resources such as IC. Subsequently, the Department for Business, Innovation and Skills (BIS) issued a consultation document in 2011 subsequently proposing that the reporting statement be revised to replace the business review and directors' report with a high-level strategic report and annual directors' statement. In August 2013, the government amended company law and UK listed companies must include a description of strategy and their business model in this new strategic report (The Companies Act 2006 (Strategic Report and Director's Report) Regulations 2013, s. 414C,). BIS requested that the UK Financial Reporting Council prepare non-mandatory guidance supporting the new legal requirements for the strategic report. This guidance was subsequently published in 2014. As the EC requirements are similar to those of the strategic report, UK companies may also use this guidance to accommodate the EC directive.[4] Although preparing a strategic report is mandatory, the FRC itself acknowledges that these regulations "represent a relatively modest change to pre-existing legal requirements" (FRC, 2014, p. 3). With both the UK strategic report and the EC directive, where the requirement for mandatory disclosure is accompanied by non-mandatory guidance on how to do so, the distinction between mandatory and voluntary is blurred.

Finance directors in the study described here viewed the narrative sections of the annual report as being highly appropriate for IC disclosure. Approximately 53 per cent viewed the annual report as an effective form for communicating human and structural capital, with 46 per cent considering it effective for communicating relational capital. Investor and analyst presentations and one-to-one meetings were thought to be even more effective for communicating all IC forms. Approximately 73 per cent of human resource specialists indicated the annual report was effective, and it was viewed by them as the most effective form for human capital disclosure. Although 66 per cent of marketing specialists viewed the annual report as effective in terms of marketing/customer relations information disclosure, its limitations were widely acknowledged: "Well it's not the case of it [the annual report] isn't effective, but it only reaches certain people" (VP of marketing for a FTSE Small Cap technology company; Beattie and Thomson, 2010, p. 127). "I absolutely view it [the corporate annual report] as a marketing document. But I understand the audience who it's talking to is very limited to those who want to invest in your company, rather than take products out with you" (Head of marketing and UK retail marketing for a FTSE 250 financial services company; Beattie and Thomson, 2010, p. 127). Marketing specialists viewed company web pages as more effective than the annual report, with press releases a close contender. "Press releases are bread and butter for us and particularly when you look at how the web feeds have developed now. The press release will get quickly dropped into any number of e-newsletters and e-zines" (VP of marketing for a FTSE Small Cap technology company; Beattie and Thomson, 2010, p. 128).

For finance directors, the preferred nature of disclosure regulation governing the annual report was via a best practice statement, rather than mandatory requirements and via principles-based guidance, rather than detailed guidance/standardization. The finance director of an AIM chemical company explained why:

> You can have fifteen companies making soap powder, and the soap powder may be almost identical to one another in terms of how clean they make your socks; but what will make fifteen companies different, and what will make some of them profitable and some of them unprofitable? It will be, how well do they treat their employees, do

they have good employees, and do they value their good employees? If employees come up with good ideas do they implement them? If they have good formulations for new types of soap powder, are they effective in getting them into the market as new products, within innovative claims that then win market share? All these things are what creates value and each one of them will be unique, and that's going to make it very difficult to quantify or to reflect in an annual report in any other way than through some sort of principal narrative disclosure.

The FRC has subsequently conducted a study on the impact of the Strategic Report (FRC, 2015). They conclude that business model reporting is still evolving, variation exists across companies, and although some companies provide good examples of disclosures explaining how corporate value is generated, there is a need for better explanation on what makes companies different. Such calls are without doubt aimed at "providing the information necessary for shareholders to assess the entity's performance, business model and strategy" (FRC, 2014, p. 8). However, the evidence discussed previously in this chapter has already underlined that the benefits of IC disclosure to investors are balanced with the cost of loss of competitive advantage. On that basis, it is hardly surprising that the FRC finds companies reluctant to highlight what that competitive advantage is in their strategic reports. It has indicated that in the absence of mandatory rules, IC disclosure remains predominantly voluntary. Further, introducing mandatory rules could be viewed in terms of a 'double-edged sword'. Investor stakeholders may indeed benefit from additional IC disclosure but at what ultimate cost to their pockets when loss of proprietary information diminishes value creation and potential competitors jump on the corporate band wagon? Consequently, it is well documented in the disclosure literature that one of the principal reasons why mandatory rules are resisted is the concern regarding the commercial sensitivity of disclosures.

External restrictions outside financial and narrative reporting regulations

When considering the costs of IC disclosure earlier in this chapter, it was highlighted that industry regulations restricted the voluntary disclose of certain IC information. Examples in point were the financial services industries and healthcare where companies were restricted in terms of product promoting. The healthcare sector also seems somewhat restricted in terms of disclosing who it provides products to. This was emphasized by the group development director of a FTSE Small Cap company:

> We work with [a particular government department], we provide services to the [government department], the [government department] as a brand is hugely valuable to us but it's hugely valuable to the [government department] and they will therefore in contracts often limit, or try to limit, what we are allowed to say and how we are allowed to use the [government department's] brand in our own materials.
>
> *(Beattie et al., 2013, p. 41)*

In certain contexts, national legislation prevents the disclosure of, for example, customer relationships. The group finance director of a FTSE 100 company operating in the industrial goods and services sector provides an illustration: "We operate on the Official Secrets Act and the various classifications that come back with that with various work. So we know what we can disclose and we know what we can't" (Beattie *et al.*, 2013, p. 44). Further, finance directors indicated that they are increasingly finding themselves in situations where legal restrictions imposed by individual customers prevent customer relationships being disclosed:

> Most of our North American customers will now contractually explicitly forbid us to ever use their name or the fact that they'd done business with us in any communica-tion without prior consent. Constraints placed on us by customers as to how/where/when we are allowed to use information about our relationship with them. Typically, this is part of the contract agreement and has changed from unusual to normal over the past few years.
> *(Director of Business Development, main market technology company; Beattie et al., 2013, p. 44)*

However, the existence of non-disclosure agreements is not necessarily an absolute barrier. As the VP of marketing for a FTSE Small Cap technology company indicated: "You can't hang everything back to a contract. The reality is these things are never black and white and you've just got to understand and toe the line" (Beattie *et al.*, 2013, p. 44). These various external restrictions and regulations placed on the IC disclosure decision, arising from cus-tomer-specific non-disclosure agreements and generic legislation, make mandatory disclosure rules impossible, as two inconsistent sets of legal imperatives would result.

Concluding remarks

Prior indirect content analysis research, based on the extent of its observed disclosure, suggests that relational capital is the most valuable IC category. In the study reported here, using ques-tionnaire survey responses from UK finance directors, human capital was ranked as providing the highest contribution to value creation overall. Further, employee skills and education was in the top four components with three relational capital components (customer relationships, competitive edge in terms of product/service quality, and company reputation). The overall importance of human capital is consistent with the position taken by the DTI (2003) in the *Accounting for People* Task Force. However, it sits in stark contrast to the findings from con-tent analysis studies, where disclosure is focused on relational capital.

This chapter focuses on benefits, costs, and restrictions and finds that they are unequally associated with disclosure across the spectrum of IC information. This explains why IC com-ponents observed to be disclosed are not necessarily those which are the most important in the value creation process. There is strong evidence to confirm the existence of a trade-off between benefits of informing capital investors versus the cost of loss of competitive advan-tage. However, the corporate disclosure decision is not entirely within the remit of the external financial reporting function, since other functional specialists such as marketing and human resources also play a central role in the corporate communication process. The benefits of attracting new human capital are traded against the cost of losing existing human capital to com-petitors. Disclosing customer relationship information attracts new customers and enhances trust and reputation, but these benefits must be traded-off against delivering sensitive customer information to competitors and damaging trust and relationships with existing customers.

The extent to which IC disclosure is voluntary depends on the existence of specific mandatory narrative reporting requirements. The IASB's management commentary is not mandatory and, in the UK, although there is a mandatory requirement for a strategic report, the accompanying guidance is non-mandatory. The same can be said in relation to the EC directive on the disclosure of non-financial information. The existence of mandatory reporting requirements is, therefore, blurred and IC reporting in corporate annual reports is perceived as predominantly voluntary. However, IC disclosure cannot be said to be voluntary, if private disclosure agreements or other legal restrictions/regulations, outside the narrative reporting arena are in place to safeguard highly sensitive information from the public domain. Further, in this modern communication era, Dumay and Guthrie (2017) highlight that both risks and opportunities arise outside the reporting entity via "involuntary disclosures produced by stakeholders and stakeseekers" (p. 40).

In short, IC disclosure decisions are increasingly complex given the spectrum of different benefits, costs, trade-offs, restrictions, risks, and opportunities in place. This chapter has served to emphasize that IC disclosure in itself has the power to enhance corporate value through the benefits it brings. However, IC disclosure needs to be carefully managed given the associated costs that potentially destroy value. IC disclosure appears to involve successfully negotiating a fine line indeed; a fine line that separates value creation and value destruction in this brave new narrative reporting world. At the heart of this new narrative reporting world sits IC through its contribution to the business model central to the integrated reporting debate, and through new narrative disclosure regulation such as the EC directive and the UK strategic report. Future research presents the opportunity to understand how the most important IC components identified in this chapter contribute to the overall business model itself. The opportunity also arises to explore the extent to which it is possible to manage the disclosure benefits and costs identified, particularly in terms of disclosing competitive advantage in a manner that is both understood and satisfies investors, whilst inhibiting replication by competitors. The latter appears to be a pivotal issue going forward in the regulation of business model disclosures. Investigating the management of 'involuntary' disclosures in the value creation process has also been advocated as a fruitful new future IC research direction (Dumay and Guthrie, 2017).

Notes

1 See Appendix 1 of Beattie and Thomson (2010) for a list of 128 such components.
2 This evidence is currently fragmented across several publications (Beattie and Smith, 2010, 2012; Beattie and Thomson, 2010; Beattie et al., 2013) which individually address separate aspects. This chapter brings a holistic analysis of this evidence with new interpretative commentary, particularly in relation to recent developments in the narrative reporting arena. Previously unpublished interview material extends the illustration of key points being made.
3 Companies with more than 500 employees.
4 www.frc.org.uk.

References

Abdolmohammadi, M. J. (2005), "Intellectual capital disclosure and market capitalization", *Journal of Intellectual Capital*, Vol. 6, No. 3, pp. 397–416.
Abeysekera, I. (2006), "The project of intellectual capital disclosure: Researching the research", *Journal of Intellectual Capital*, Vol. 7, No. 1, pp. 61–77.
Abeysekera, I. (2008), "Motivations behind human capital disclosure in annual reports", *Accounting Forum*, Vol. 32, No. 1, pp. 16–29.
Abeysekera, I. and Guthrie, J. (2005), "An empirical investigation of annual reporting trends of intellectual capital in Sri Lanka", *Critical Perspectives on Accounting*, Vol. 16, No. 3, pp. 151–163.

Accounting Standards Board (ASB) (2006), "Reporting Statement 1: Operating and Financial Review", available at: www.frc.org.uk/images/uploaded/documents/Reporting%20Statements%20OFR%20web.pdf (accessed 15 January 2012).

April, K. A., Bosma, P., and Deglon, D. A. (2003), "IC measurement and reporting: Establishing practice in SA mining", *Journal of Intellectual Capital*, Vol. 4, No. 2, pp. 165–180.

Armitage, S. and Marston, C. (2007), *Corporate Disclosure and the Cost of Capital: The Views of Finance Directors*, ICAEW Centre for Business Performance, London.

Ashton, R. H. (2005), "Intellectual capital and value creation: A review", *Journal of Accounting Literature*, Vol. 24, pp. 53–134.

Beattie, V. (1999), *Business Reporting: The Inevitable Change?* Institute of Chartered Accountants of Scotland, Edinburgh, UK.

Beattie, V. and Smith, S. J. (2010), "Human capital, value creation and disclosure", *Journal of Human Resource Costing & Accounting*, Vol. 14, No. 4, pp. 262–285.

Beattie, V. and Smith, S. J. (2012), "Evaluating disclosure theory using the views of UK finance directors in the intellectual capital context", *Accounting and Business Research*, Vol. 42, No. 5, pp. 1–24.

Beattie, V. and Smith, S. J. (2013), "Value creation and business models: Refocusing the intellectual capital debate", *British Accounting Review*, Vol. 45, No. 4, pp. 243–254.

Beattie, V. and Thomson, S. (2010), *Intellectual Capital Reporting: Academic Utopia or Corporate Reality in a Brave New World?*, Institute of Chartered Accountants of Scotland, Edinburgh, UK.

Beattie, V., Roslender, R., and Smith, S. J. (2013), "Balancing on a tightrope: Customer relational capital, value creation and disclosure, *Financial Reporting*, Vol. 3–4, pp. 17–50.

BIS (2011), *The Future of Narrative Reporting: A Consultation*, Available at: http://bis.gov.uk/Consultations/future-of-narrative-reporting-further-consultation (accessed 6 January 2012).

Bontis, N. (2003), "Intellectual capital disclosure in Canadian corporations", *Journal of Human Resource Costing and Accounting*, Vol. 7, No. 1–2, pp. 9–20.

Bozzolan, S., Favotto, F., and Ricceri, F. (2003), "Italian annual intellectual capital disclosure", *Journal of Intellectual Capital*, Vol. 4, No. 4, pp. 543–558.

Bozzolan, S., O'Regan, P., and Ricceri, F. (2006), "Intellectual capital disclosure (ICD): A comparison of Italy and the UK", *Journal of Human Resource Costing & Accounting*, Vol. 10, No. 2, pp. 92–113.

Brennan, N. (2001), "Reporting intellectual capital in annual reports: Evidence from Ireland", *Accounting, Auditing & Accountability Journal*, Vol. 14, No. 4, pp. 423–436.

Campbell, D. and Abdul Rahman, M. R. (2010), "A longitudinal examination of intellectual capital reporting in Marks & Spencer annual reports, 1978–2008", *British Accounting Review*, Vol. 43, No. 1, pp. 56–70.

Chaminade, C. and Roberts, H. (2003), "What it means is what it does: A comparative analysis of implementing intellectual capital in Norway and Spain", *European Accounting Review*, Vol. 12, No. 4, pp. 733–751.

Danish Agency for Trade and Industry (DATI) (2000), *A Guideline for Intellectual Capital Statements: A Key to Knowledge Management*, DATI, Copenhagen.

Danish Agency for Trade and Industry (DATI) (2002), *Intellectual Capital Statements in Practice: Inspiration and Good Advice*, DATI, Copenhagen.

Deegan, C. (2000), *Financial Accounting Theory*, McGraw-Hill, Sydney, Australia.

Department for Trade and Industry (DTI) (2003), *Accounting for People*, Task Force Report, Department for Trade and Industry, London.

Dumay, J. and Guthrie, J. (2017), "Involuntary disclosure of intellectual capital: Is it relevant?" *Journal of Intellectual Capital*, Vol. 18, No. 1, pp. 29–44.

Edvinsson, L. and Malone, M. (1997), *Intellectual Capital: The Proven Way to Establish your Company's Real Value by Measuring It Hidden Brain Power*, Piatkus, London.

EFRAG (2010), *The Role of the Business Model in Financial Reporting*, European Financial Reporting Advisory Group, Brussels.

Elliott, R. K. and Jacobson, P. D. (1994), "Costs and benefits of business information disclosure", *Accounting Horizons*, Vol. 8, No. 4, pp. 80–96.

FASB (2009), *Disclosure Framework*, Financial Accounting Standards Board, Norwalk, CT.

FRC (2014), *Guidance on the Strategic Report*, available at www.frc.org.uk/Our-Work/Publications/Accounting-and-Reporting-Policy/Guidance-on-the-Strategic-Report.pdf (accessed 4 July 2016).

FRC (2015), *Clear Concise Developments in Narrative Reporting*, available at: www.frc.org.uk/Our-Work/ Publications/Accounting-and-Reporting-Policy/Clear- Concise-Developments-in-Narrative-Reporti.aspx (accessed 4 July 2016).

Goh, P. C. and Lin, K. P. (2004), "Disclosing intellectual capital in company annual reports Evidence from Malaysia", *Journal of Intellectual Capital*, Vol. 5, No. 3, pp. 500–510.

Graham, J. R., Harvey, C. R., and Rajgopal, S. (2005), "The economic implications of corporate financial reporting", *Journal of Accounting and Economics*, Vol. 40, No. 1–3, pp. 3–73.

Gunther, T. and Beyer, D. (2003), *Hurdles for the Voluntary Disclosure of Information on Intangibles: Empirical Results for New Economy Industries*, Dresden Papers of Business Administration, No. 71/03, Germany.

Guthrie, J. and Petty, R. (2000), "Intellectual capital: Australian annual reporting practices", *Journal of Intellectual Capital*, Vol. 1, No. 3, pp. 241–251.

Guthrie, J., Petty, R., and Ricceri, F. (2007), *External Intellectual Capital Reporting: Evidence from Australia and Hong Kong*, Institute of Chartered Accountants of Scotland, Edinburgh, UK.

Habersam, M. and Piper, M. (2003), "Exploring intellectual capital in hospitals: Two qualitative case studies in Italy and Austria", *European Accounting Review*, Vol. 12, No. 4, pp. 753–779.

Heitzman, S., Wasley, C., and Zimmerman, J. (2010), "The joint effects of materiality thresholds and voluntary disclosure incentives on firm's disclosure decisions", *Journal of Accounting and Economics*, Vol. 49, No. 1–2, pp. 109–132.

Helm S. and Salminen R. T. (2010), "Basking in reflected glory: Using customer reference relationships to build reputation in industrial markets", *Industrial Marketing Management*, Vol. 39, No. 5, pp. 737–743.

IASB (2004), *Intangible Assets, International Accounting Standard No. 38*, IASB, London.

IASB (2010), *Management Commentary, Practice Statement*, available at: www.ifrs.org/Current+Projects/ IASB+Projects/Management+Commentary/IFRS+Practice+Statement/IFRS+Practice+Statement. htm (accessed 6 January 2012).

ICAEW (2009), *Developments in New Reporting Models*, Institute of Chartered Accountants in England and Wales, London.

International Integrated Reporting Council (IIRC) (2013), *The International <IR> Framework*, International Integrated Reporting Council, London.

Lev, B. (2004), "Sharpening the intangibles edge", *Harvard Business Review*, Vol. 82, No. 6, pp. 109–116.

Li, J., Pike, R., and Haniffa, R. (2008), "Intellectual capital disclosure and corporate governance structure in UK forms", *Accounting and Business Research*, Vol. 38, No. 2, pp. 127–159.

Lundholm, R. and Van Winkle, M. (2006), "Motives for disclosure and non-disclosure: A framework and review of the evidence", *Accounting and Business Research*, International Accounting Policy Forum, Vol. 36, pp. 43–48.

Meritum, (2002), "Guidelines for managing and reporting on intangibles", *Meritum*, Fundación Aritel Móvil, Madrid.

Mouritsen, J., Larsen, H. T., and Bukh, P. N. D. (2001), "Intellectual capital and the 'capable firm': Narrating, visualising and numbering for managing knowledge", *Accounting, Organizations & Society*, Vol. 26, No. 7–8, pp. 735–762.

Patten, D. M. (1991), "Exposure, legitimacy and social disclosure", *Journal of Accounting and Public Policy*, Vol. 10, No. 4, pp. 297–308.

Richardson, A. J. and Welker, M. (2001), "Social disclosure, financial disclosure and the cost of equity capital", *Accounting, Organizations and Society*, Vol. 26, No. 7–8, pp. 597–616.

Roos, G., Roos, J., Edvinsson, L., and Dragonetti, D. C. (1998), *Intellectual Capital Navigating in the New Business Landscape*. New York University Press, New York.

Roslender, R. and Fincham, R. (2001), "Thinking critically about intellectual capital accounting", *Accounting, Auditing & Accountability Journal*, Vol. 14, No. 4, pp. 383–399.

Roslender, R. and Fincham, R. (2004), "Intellectual capital accounting in the UK: A field study perspective", *Accounting, Auditing & Accountability Journal*, Vol. 17, No. 2, pp. 178–209.

Striukova, L., Unerman, J., and Guthrie, J. (2008), "Corporate reporting of intellectual capital: Evidence from UK companies", *British Accounting Review*, Vol. 40, No. 4, pp. 297–313.

Teece, D. J. (2010), "Business models, business strategy and innovation", *Long Range Planning*, Vol. 43, No. 2–3, pp. 172–194.

Toms, J. S. (2002), "Firm resources, quality signals and the determinants of corporate environmental reputation: Some UK evidence", *British Accounting Review*, Vol. 34, No. 3, pp. 257–282.

Unerman, J., Guthrie, J., and Striukova, L. (2007), *UK Reporting of Intellectual Capital*, ICAEW Centre for Business Performance, London.

Van der Meer-Kooistra, J. and Zijlstra, S. M. (2001), "Reporting on intellectual capital", *Accounting, Auditing & Accountability Journal*, Vol. 14, No. 4, pp. 456–476.

Vandemaele, S. N., Vergauwen, P. G. M. C., and Smits, A. J. (2005), "Intellectual capital disclosure in the Netherlands, Sweden and the UK: A longitudinal and comparative study", *Journal of Intellectual Capital*, Vol. 6, No. 3, pp. 417–426.

Vergauwen, P. G. M. C. and Van Alem, F. J. C. (2005), "Annual report IC disclosures in The Netherlands, France and Germany", *Journal of Intellectual Capital*, Vol. 6, No. 1, pp. 89–104.

Verrecchia, R. E. (2001), "Essays on disclosure", *Journal of Accounting and Economics*, Vol. 31, No. 1–3, pp. 97–180.

19

WISSENSBILANZ MADE IN GERMANY

Twelve years of experience confirm a powerful instrument

Manfred Bornemann

Introduction and motivation

In this chapter, I report on the state of the discipline of intellectual capital (IC) reporting and management in Germany. The chapter reflects the last 15 years of IC reporting starting with the new millennium and explains the social, political, and economic context, which in many aspects differs from other parts of the world. I will describe the method of Wissensbilanz (IC reporting and management) briefly and discuss strengths and weaknesses from the perspective and hindsight of several years of application in industry, government institutions, and non-profit organizations.

The second section after this brief introduction highlights some key characteristcs of the German speaking economies. In order to understand their knowledge orientation, the concept of family owned Mittelstand companies is discussed in the context of the general political orientation of Agenda 2010 and its emphasis on innovation as well as efforts to increase transparency, the management of IC, and the organizational knowledge base.

The third section covers the conceptual foundations of Wissensbilanz, a management instrument for strategic organizational development as well as communication. It highlights the bottom up approach and the special role of skilled labour and knowledge workers in leveraging IC. The implicit nature of experience becomes strategically increasingly relevant in organizations with employees who give (and expect) long-term (lifetime) commitment. For the management of intangible assets or IC, a sound understanding of the strategic priorities of top management as well as the interdependencies with corporate culture, business processes, and market dynamics is essential.

The fourth section reflects on the strengths and weaknesses of Wissensbilanz after 12 years of experience. Interfaces and compatibility with established management models and a strong focus on development and learning as an organization are the key strengths, while indicators – even though they are supported – seem to be crucial for family enterprises.

The fifth section discusses the conceptual limitations of Wissensbilanz, such as the qualitative assessment of IC and the company specific orientation towards strategy requirements. For this purpose, a financial perspective seems to be less beneficial, even though it would support inter-company benchmarking. Another limitation is the Mittelstand requirement for simplicity in application in order to support a do-it-yourself approach. Compared to other scientific approaches, compromising generalization in favour of organizational relevance seems to be justified and constitutes an advantage. A limitation in international reach and more general application of the ideas of Wissensbilanz is the national branding; while its conceptual ideas have been well received in other European countries, this has not been without some reservations.

Context

Management stereotypes in Germany

The practice of IC management is an integral part of the German Mittelstand way of management, which is based on ideas of long-term committed strategic use and development of resources. Employees stay on average more than ten years with the same enterprise and show high levels of loyalty to their organizations. Both organizations and employees show high regional embeddedness and low mobility, particularly in rural areas. This has implications for IC, which can be described as sticky and changing slowly over time.

Even though Germany and alpine regions of Europe (Austria and Switzerland) are associated with a culture of "low context" (Hofstede, 2001), the technical knowledge for production and value creation seems to be "high context". One explanation might be a specific education model that combines theoretical education and practical training in a three-year long apprenticeship (dual education). This creates strong ties between (young) employees and their trade, a very strong connection between theoretical and conceptual (explicit) knowledge and tacit knowledge based on several years of experience within one trade. Apprentices spend more than three years with one organization, which provides their training. That allows high specialization as well as "efficient communication" between workers of the same trade but in distinct organizations (Federal Ministry of Education and Research).[1]

In many organizations, IC is implicit and does not benefit from a dedicated management function. In many organizations IC is not on the radar of managers, who consequently do not take full advantage of IC in strategic planning or decision making. Even though communities of practice for knowledge management and IC management have been established for over 15–20 years, they are not yet mainstream. However, this is changing, as quality management (with the reform of ISO 9001), accounting and management reporting (with integrated reporting), and project management are using these ideas.

Germany's Agenda 2010: the goal to succeed in the knowledge economy

The general motivation for identifying methods and instruments for the management of knowledge and IC for German enterprises emerged from the German Federal Ministry for Economic Affairs' (Hochreiter, 2005)[2] interest in the knowledge society (European Commission/OECD; Drucker, 1959) at the beginning of the millennium.

The historic and social context was defined by a government led by social democrats and supported by the green political party while working on "Agenda 2010".[3] Their general objective was to make Germany once again the economic and political powerhouse of Europe and overcome the struggles and costs of reunification. This policy proved to be effective and prepared the ground for current developments of "digitalization" in technology and the "internet of things".

The economic backbone of the German economy historically was and still is the Mittelstand, which comprises more than 200,000 enterprises with more than 500 employees. It does not include large listed companies. These Mittelstand companies employ 60 per cent of the national work-force, generate 35 per cent of turnover, and train and educate more than 80 per cent of skilled labour in the dual education model (IFM, 2016)[4]. Equity in these predominantly family owned enterprises is around 15 per cent compared to about 30 per cent for very large listed organizations. The overwhelming share of the remaining capital is provided by banks in the form of long-term loans, giving these financial institutions a powerful position as principal bank ('Hausbank').

Fostering innovation, transparency, and investment

Mittelstand managers typically subscribe to risk-averse growth models, competing on quality and technological leadership in the premium market segment. Because of generally high labour costs, high social standards, and a generous welfare system, competition on price is of lower importance in Germany. A typical strength of Mittelstand companies is their focus on innovation, which needs to be nurtured by a well-trained workforce (human capital) and up-to-date organizational structures. Agenda 2010 focused – among other priorities – on improving the innovation capabilities of small and medium sized enterprises (SMEs).

One objective was to increase management awareness of intangible drivers of corporate performance and to provide easy access to appropriate management instruments. Knowledge management and instruments to visualize and assess IC in order to improve value creation were selected from existing approaches as well as specifically adjusted to the needs and requirements of SMEs and Mittelstand companies. One of these instruments is Wissensbilanz.

Another objective was to comply with the the then new requirements of the financial market and the concept of Basel II and later Basel III. 'Basel' (a city in Switzerland) refers to the minimum equity to guard against the financial risks of banks and its introduction required companies to provide more transparent reporting. Two of the supporting – and still relevant and valid – arguments for the initiative of the German government were first, to increase transparency on intangible assets of enterprises based on the efficient market hypothesis (Fama, 1965), and second to lower transaction costs. Companies with 'valuable intangible assets' and 'efficient utilization of intangibles in their business models' should pay lower interest rates than companies that fail to do so. Productive organizations therefore should get benefit from improved financing arrangements with banks, if they report on the status and management of IC.

In an era of low to sometimes negative interest rates (2016), this second motivation is not as important but may become relevant sooner than expected. A problem is the already mentioned comparatively high reliance of Mittelstand companies on their banks, who – as a consequence of the tighter regulations related to Basel II and III – find that taking account of the intangible assets of organizations can be difficult and thus systematically underestimate their credit rating. This limits investment by enterprises and – on a macro scale – leads to lost chances for growth in GDP. Accounting, reporting, and managing IC and intangible assets[5] were considered as likely to improve this situation for Mittelstand companies by improving transparency on these resources and thus supporting innovation.

Key elements of IC reporting and management: Made in Germany (M.i.G.)

The theoretical concept of IC reporting m.i.G (Wissensbilanz) emerged gradually from a series of projects[6] (Bornemann and Leitner, 2002; Bornemann and Sammer, 2002; Leitner *et al.*, 2002) and was discussed by Bornemann and Alwert (2007). Further refinements were tested in international projects[7] and supported by several guidelines and case studies,[8] but the majority of these are so far available only in the German language. Given the original motivation to strengthen the German economy, the local focus made sense – even though there was no indication that the ideas would not work in general. On the contrary, the InCaS project (Intellectual Capital Statements – Made in Europe) provided plenty of evidence that Wissensbilanz could be applied without constraints in the international context.[9] The following paragraphs illustrate the key ideas of Wissensbilanz but are not detailed due to space constraints. For a full explanation, please refer to Bornemann and Alwert (2007).

Focus on knowledge workers

If a knowledge organization depends on the competence and contribution of (all of) its employees, it needs to identify its knowledge priorities, the status quo of the corporate knowledge base, and the path of future development. Therefore, a team representing the competence and knowledge of the IC of the system at stake (the organization) is defined. Team members *negotiate* on the assumption of 'self-organization', the priorities to improve the knowledge base, and to optimize the future ability to act. They present arguments for favourable as well as negative assessment and balance these among each other and relative to their interpretation of strategic requirements.

This is a significant difference to specialized financial accountants, who form a group of specialists and work relatively independently from the rest of the organization. Taking advantage of representative teams from all functional and hierarchical origins constitutes one of the central levers for organizational learning.

Customized IC drivers: based on templates

Which intangibles really drive business performance? This is the guiding question for cross-functional teams in knowledge intensive organizations to come up with strategically relevant drivers and capabilities (Grant, 2013). In hundreds of empirical settings (action research as well as consulting), IC teams regularly identified several hundred items that later could be aggregated into more general terms and together represent the knowledge base of the system. From analysing the earliest 44 case studies of IC reporting in SMEs (Alwert *et al.*, 2004), a set of general drivers for IC could be identified (see Appendix). More than 500 additional surveys confirmed them to be of relevance for 'a typical organization'. Non-profit organizations (e.g. supporting social welfare) or some administrative units or schools (e.g. kindergarten or primary schools) with particular needs could not relate to all of them, but selected and amended according to their own requirements (e.g. 'relations to the capital market' was not relevant but was adjusted to 'relations to funding institutions').

This approach of simply asking a team of relevant experts clearly deviates from other concepts that offer the top 3, 7, or essential 100 drivers of performance according to scientific literature surveys or theoretical concepts. Even though this was – of course – not an original accomplishment, it can be explained in the historic context of the time, where – at least in German speaking areas – only very limited prior research on the relevant dimensions of IC was available. The dominant approach of those days was – influenced by quantitative methods pioneered, for example, from Bontis *et al.* (2000) – to look into existing data of management information systems and (cor)relate them to performance. The obvious limitation of this research was not only the restriction to dimensions that were already in the focus of management and therefore available for number crunching, but the total lack of publicly available (large and valid) databases in Germany to do this analysis.

In order to create context and to relate to the tacit or implicit knowledge of employees and the organization, an organization-specific definition of IC drivers was developed. It helps to explain what is represented by the head line or key word of an IC driver. Most experts might agree that the culture of the organization impacts productivity. But what exactly is "our corporate culture"? What more than "the way we do things over here" constitutes the culture of a specific enterprise? Is it informal social interaction? Or is it a shared discipline, such as the problem-and-solution driven culture of engineers or the 'give me the numbers' mentality of consultants? Or something else?

Coming up with a specific answer proved to be a very tangible result in most of the organizations I worked with and gave them a better understanding of "who we are" and "what makes us special". It is hard work – but the effort always paid off. Useful shortcuts provide templates as in the Appendix, but only as a reference that needs to be adapted.

Strategic assessment: portfolios and contextual reasoning

For assessing intangible assets, two dimensions help to describe the current status quo, while an additional one reflects on future developments:

- quantity – to accomplish a strategic objective, a certain quantity of IC is necessary or appropriate, for example, the number of employees needed for accomplishing a strategic objective;
- quality – the employees available should have a certain skill level to accomplish the strategic objective, for example, they need a portfolio of certificates or technical trainings to have the legal eligibility to actually do their jobs;
- systematic development focuses on all activities to maintain these capabilities; related to quality management, a PDCA-cycle (plan-do-check-act) proved to be useful to cover activities for development in a systematic way.

To support a visualization of these dimensions in a management portfolio, they need to follow a very strict formula of questions and refer to the same yard stick or reference. As the core idea is to identify the status quo of IC relative to strategic priorities, the strategy is this reference. Sometimes, the strategy does not provide sufficient details to assess all dimensions of IC. Therefore, this approach of reflecting quantity, quality, and systematic management of IC supports a systematic reflection and amendment of the strategy by the IC team. This group should deliver according to the strategy and thus have an excellent opportunity to clarify IC, what and where exactly it is needed.

Indicators and KPIs for reality checks

Many small organizations as well as companies representing Mittelstand lack a defined set of indicators and up-to-date reporting instruments. Management decisions are based on gut feeling, intuition, or randomly available data. For small organizations with a management-owner involved in daily business this makes a lot of sense, as it helps to cut costs. The owner him- or herself decides most of the strategic as well as operational issues and thus knows from daily business about the status quo of IC. But growing organizations quickly reach a size that qualifies for management instruments.

In order to keep barriers to applying IC management and reporting instruments as low as possible, requirements for the quality of indicators are set very modestly. Management models have varying degrees of reliance on formal reporting and indicators. Thus we observe a wide spread between data available only from financial accounting to fully integrated management information systems. Mittelstand companies are high context organizations with a stable workforce (Hofstede, 2001). Typically, they use indicators much less than low context organizations. Regarding both cost of data collection and the quality of data collected (validity), asking for the quick assessment of an expert provides a more than sufficient substitute.

The larger the organization, the more arguments support a sound management information system. Turbulent business environments, high staff fluctuation, and high paced technology changes are additional arguments to increase the professionalization of reporting.

Business model reconstruction to visualize and align human capital

The business model of many SMEs remains tacit and is not regularly subject to systematic reflection. This can constitute a deficit, as employees might not have a clear understanding of how their skills and activities optimally contribute to accomplishing strategic objectives. This applies particularly for established members of the workforce who might not be aware of changes in the organizational environment (e.g. the specific demands for change with respect to "digitalization").

One very effective approach to making the business model explicit among employees builds on visualizing the impact of IC (and other value drivers such as financial capital or tangible assets) on business processes and results. A sensitivity analysis (Forrester, 1961; Sterman, 2000) proved to be a very powerful learning set-up to transfer implicit knowledge across business units as well as to share implicit knowledge within teams. The workshop setting involving representatives of all business units supports alignment of teams and thus improves internal communication and generally speeds up all activities.

Software tools help to visualize the data from sensitivity analyses as business models and to test the emerging value patterns against strategy. The resulting "Aha" (as Edvinsson describes it in much of his work) or learnings immediately support the improvement of the business model and identify "white spots of understanding". Top management can use this opportunity to clarify and emphasize its vision and to involve knowledge workers to support their vision. Improved understanding directly changes the organizational culture and allows for self-organized coordination of knowledge workers.

Focus on where the organization can change and improve

For many organizations the typical priority is to 'satisfy customers' (Drucker, 1954). Given the logic of cause and effect, this objective becomes a 'result' only after a series of prior actions are accomplished. The list of potential interventions and measures for improvement is – almost by definition – longer than what could be accomplished with limited resources in a given time frame. For small enterprises, a prioritized list of what actually would impact the organization at all and what creates the best ratio of costs and benefit is obviously highly valuable.

The formal structure to identify drivers of IC with the highest priority to change is the IC management portfolio. It takes advantage of the two dimensions we already assessed:

- the status quo of IC as the average of quantity, quality, and systematic management for each driver (x-axis);
- and the relative influence to the system from the sensitivity analysis (y-axis).

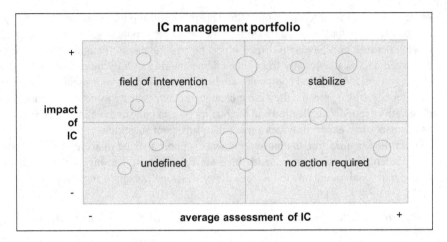

Figure 19.1   The IC management portfolio shows priorities

IC drivers with a comparatively low current status quo according to strategic requirements and, simultaneously, a high impact on the system and the accomplishment of the strategy should be developed (see Figure 19.1).

Depending on who is asked, different priorities to take action emerge. When focusing on the requirements of the financial markets (as an example), financial returns and relations to investors are urgent (Alwert *et al.*, 2009). When focusing on the experts of the organization – employees represented in the IC team – German SMEs report other priorities such as the urgency for improving leadership or internal communication. These two drivers of IC are highly generic and thus most likely affect almost all organizations.

Continuing management of IC

Instruments for managing IC and intangible assets are available for many years and help to improve overall productivity. Once the most urgent bottlenecks are identified, they need to be fixed with these instruments (which are not covered here) and checked for sustainable improvement. Implementing these measures requires long-term oriented change management as described in standard text books (e.g. Hayes, 2010) and need regular follow up. Defining goal-oriented indicators that help to monitor the status of implementation supports the accomplishment of strategic goals.

Following up regularly on reviewing IC in an organization helps to establish awareness for this resource and to better understand the strategic implications of IC. Crucial change agents are the members of the IC assessment team, who meet again and learn to relate the current situation to the historic one and to imagine what should be done to accomplish strategic objectives. Gradually, they contribute to establishing a corporate culture that actively leverages intangible assets and – eventually – become new core capabilities that on their own differentiate the organization.

Communicate to internal and (selected) external stakeholders

Reporting externally on the status quo of IC is a delicate task. The main benefit is to improve transparency for stakeholders. But the same benefit raises concern among entrepreneurs who fear loss of competitive advantage if the strategy and the status quo of core capabilities and IC become transparent. This dilemma has no simple solution, but allows for a general recommendation: being transparent to key stakeholders is a requirement in order to support their decision making and to help them accomplish their objectives. Lack of transparency more often than not has a negative impact on decisions, as factors to one's advantage remain invisible. Thus, it makes sense to communicate as openly as possible.

Human resource development, as well as education sciences, has a long history of describing the difficulty of transferring knowledge. These observations might help to diffuse concerns against transparency. Giving competitors a lead on one's ambitions might pose a risk, but we are still one or two steps ahead. Knowing about this challenge might even improve the odds for implementing the strategic measures for development and improvement.

Strength and weakness: a critical reflection after 12 years

When starting with the prototype for Wissensbilanz in 2004, several assumptions regarding its appropriate implementation were formulated, discussed, refined, and – many of them – rejected. Among the most relevant were the following:

- SMEs and Mittelstand organizations prefer to work with existing instruments and avoid implementation of additional management instruments;
- even though monitoring of business processes is clearly supported by indicators, only few small and not all large organizations have an integrated management information system, thus, Wissensbilanz should take advantage of management information systems, if available, but not define them as mandatory;
- Wissenbilanz is primarily a learning event that helps to reflect strategic developments and to elaborate risks and deficits and it should be supported by tools – but not be fully automated;
- Wissenbilanz should build on the business models of organizations and contribute to improve them and should not cover every detail of daily routines;
- primary stakeholders are internal and some selected external partners in order to improve strategic decision making and development of IC with an additional but distinct target group being the financial market.

Utilization of established management models

SMEs have a limited capacity and acceptance for very complex management instruments. Suggesting "another new and specific approach" therefore is less welcome than building on what is already in place and familiar to employees and management.

The general assumption of Wissensbilanz builds on established strategic models, business models, and process models and takes advantage of team-based (agile) ideas. Even if some of them are not yet implemented in a particular organization, they are generally accepted and established, thus not creating any systematic barrier or resistance to change. Respecting the established instruments and – gradually – adjusting them for current requirements seems to support the idea of a learning organization and – maybe even more important – leverages existing capabilities and assets.

Support of indicators: but not as an end in itself

Since the mid 2000s, the scientific literature (e.g. *Journal of Intellectual Capital*) has come up with a complex lists of IC indicators. Some of them support a very convincing rationale (e.g. a large number of patents indicates innovation). But a large number of indicators has no general rationale (e.g. gender ratios indicate innovation capability). Particularly in public organizations (e.g. universities in Austria), these lists of indicators sometimes reflect more a political desire than a rational strategy hypothesis. The 'measures' have limited impact on strategy.

Most SMEs still lack integrated management information systems and thus are challenged to present up-to-date indicators. This will be overcome in time, but does it make sense to buy a management information system 'off the shelf' for managing IC? Maybe not, as empirical observations reveal that the costs of collecting the data for a single indicator are substantial: more than one day of labour is – on average – required to (systematically) update the data. This easily keeps one employee busy for a year – and frequently proves to be the killer argument against indicator-based monitoring for SMEs.

To accomplish the need for governing and monitoring the implementation of development action, very few, but specific indicators might be better suited. While benchmarking is interesting for several organizations, it is not required to manage IC or to accomplish a strategic objective. Tailored indicators that specifically focus on following up a defined management action earn extremely high approval rates among managers and employees.

IT tools with strong emphasis on complementary coaching

In order to cut costs for IC management and to automate as much as possible, some organizations make use of web-based IT solutions. The benefit of decentralized (and sometimes asynchronous) technologies allows the simple challenge of organizing a physical meeting for a workshop to conduct an IC assessment to be overcome.

While this certainly is an option to support the data-gathering process and to improve the level of representativeness of data, it poses the risk of sabotaging the intended effects on the social and contextual alignment of teams and of developing strong ties among employees. A balanced approach that builds on the advantages of a people strategy and a document strategy (Hansen *et al.*, 1999) might make most sense.

Reflecting on the practice of IC management in Germany shows several cases where organizations tried to improve the process. In many cases, the focus shifted from developing a learning organization to conducting 'another survey' and creating 'another database'. Discussions of staff units concentrated on abstract models and sometimes quite irrelevant details instead of simply addressing those who are experts in their domain and actually 'know'.

Focus on development and learning versus benchmarking

Managers are generally competitive and thus like to use management instruments for benchmarking. This helps to learn, if the 'bench' is supporting the expectation. Interesting cases for benchmarking and bench learning can be reported from large companies, who have a joint strategic objective and allow their divisions to break these objectives down to business units. A shared set of IC drivers and a strategic framework programme provide almost perfect conditions for comparing IC management routines, in particular for the dimension of systematic management of IC.

For almost all other organizations, the odds for benchmarking opportunities are less favourable, as either the strategy or the set of IC drivers is not sufficiently similar. Several of the pioneers who implemented Wissensbilanz were disappointed in this perspective. Others tried to report "impressively high scores" with averages above 90 per cent. This is – of course – unrealistic as not even a world market leader would be able to accomplish 'all' his or her strategic objectives – and if he or she did, one might ask if the target was not sufficiently challenging.

A final observation relates to time series of Wissensbilanzen. If the quality of assessment is high, a spread of scores will become evident for each period. Measures for improvement will lead to better scores in the following period while some IC drivers that had a satisfactory level might gradually score lower. That can be the consequence of the shift of management attention or the result of a changed environment. Whatever the reason, IC managers need to adjust again in order to keep their strategic gap between internal assessment and requirements.

Conceptual limitations of Wissensbilanz and their impact on application

The framework presented in the second section of this chapter meets the requirements presented in the first section. But there are several conceptual limitations that need to be addressed and considered when applying the concept.

Rigid formulation of assessment questions

The decision to maximize flexibility regarding the definition of IC and its components and the intention to support portfolio visualizations had an impact on how the assessment of IC was conducted. The strict application of essentially only three questions allows the comparison of results and avoids misleading presentation. The negative side effect is that these questions are generic and sometimes need clarification and elaboration to create shared context. In the preferred setting of a workshop, this is no problem as the joint creation of shared mental models on the strategy is considered a valuable benefit. But in the context of a survey, this crucial element easily creates confusion and thus runs the risk of diluting the quality of data.

Strategy as reference and objective of measurement

Choosing the corporate strategy as the reference for assessing the status quo of IC certainly boosts the relevance of the results. But for many small organizations, the strategy is not defined or generally agreed upon. Small organizations frequently 'muddle through', taking advantage of market opportunities and cutting costs once the business cycle contracts. As a consequence, the 'numbers' for the assessment of IC might fluctuate – not because the IC changed dramatically, but because the environment forced a change of strategy. This has negative effects on external comparisons, while in the internal interpretation the shifts can be understood and accepted.

Alternative approaches come up with financial values for IC drivers that help to immediately gain an understanding on the scale or dimension of the monetary stock (Guthrie *et al.*, 2012). But these approaches are not free from substantial changes of evaluations – depending on the beta for risk, interest rates, or the estimates for future market opportunities. A more serious disadvantage stemming from monetary valuation is that it does not give any hints which of the many different intangible assets needs management attention, or what exactly is the most promising approach to develop IC.

Dilemma of three masters: simplicity – validity – generality

Weick (1969) was among the first to identify a theoretical problem that also applies to Wissensbilanz. A theory – and in analogy a management instrument – can support only two of three requirements simultaneously:

- the concept could be simple, but that is generally not supporting validity of results or generalization;
- the concept could provide valid results, but this comes with increasing complexity; or
- the concept could be applicable in general.

According to the requirements of Mittelstand, simplicity in application is the highest priority. The second priority is to deliver valid and relevant insight to come up with the right priorities to develop IC – and to avoid misallocation of (scarce) funds. Thus, generalization, which would be possible by some financial assessments of IC that support benchmarking or other general comparison, could not be accomplished.

National branding

The utilization of the globally positively associated reference 'Made in Germany' served to raise acceptance among German organizations. The international business community was less impressed; some were explicitly repelled by the national branding. In hindsight – and not being a German myself – the motivation to create a method that works and is cost efficient was genuine and might have been accomplished quite well. This view is supported by the level of application (more than 100,000 software installations). But the branding created an emotional barrier in other regions of Europe and certainly did not contribute to global dissemination and application.

Conclusion and summary

Wissensbilanz – Made in Germany has been implemented and tested in Mittelstand companies since 2004. Both, the initiators in the Federal Ministry for Economic Affairs as well as the target group of SMEs have been impressed by its powerful contribution to managing IC and to communicating with stakeholders. The concept has become part of training for consultants by prestigious institutions and is being incorporated gradually into business school education. Wissensbilanz is a recommended management instrument by various industry groups.

The concept of Wissensbilanz aims to meet the requirements of the knowledge society in general and enterprises in particular:

- already established management instruments are leveraged and thus minimize the cost of change for the organization as well as the employees;
- the approach of involving not only a specialized task force but a representation of experts from all over the organization is consistent with current discussions on participation, inclusion, crowd intelligence, and self-organization of knowledge professionals;
- economic efficiency seems to be very high as are the strategic orientation and validity of results.

However, there is still room for further improvement as discussed earlier. The strengths come at the cost of limited comparability with IC reports. To understand an IC report correctly, one needs either deep knowledge of the context of the organization or an extended narrative that explains the context and makes the implications explicit for the (external) reader. Depending on the strategic intention to manage or to communicate IC, such documents are usually available internally, but not regularly made accessible externally.

The future challenge for IC management and reporting will be to support the current transformation of businesses to global and digital business models, utilize the internet of things, and handle demographic change. IC management covers all these dimensions with its categories of relations, structures, and – most crucial according to the sensitivity analysis – human capital and is therefore destined to diagnose strategic requirements on all corporate levels as well as to support organizational change and learning.

Appendix: Sample definition of drivers for IC

ID	Driver	Definition
Human Capital		
HK-1	Professional competence	The expertise gained within the organization or in the employee's career: professional training, higher education, training courses and seminars, as well as practical work experiences gained on-the-job.
HK-2	Social competence	The ability to get on well with people, communicate and discuss in a constructive manner, nurturing trust-enhancing behaviour in order to enable a comfortable cooperation. Furthermore, the learning ability, the self-conscious handling of critique and risks, as well as the creativity and flexibility of individual employees are embraced in the term 'social competence'.
HK-3	Employee motivation	The motivation to play a part within the organization, to take on responsibility, committed to the fulfilment of tasks and the willingness for an open knowledge exchange. Typical sub-areas are, for example, satisfaction with the labour situation, identification with the organization, sense and participation of achievement.
HK-4	Leadership ability	The ability to administer and motivate people. Develop and communicate strategies and visions and their empathic implementation. Negotiation skills, assertiveness, consequence, and credibility, as well as the ability to create a scope of self-dependent development belong to this IC factor.
Structural Capital		
SK-1	Internal cooperation and knowledge transfer	The manner in which employees, organizational units, and different hierarchy levels exchange information and cooperate (e.g. conjoint projects). The focused knowledge transfer between employees. Furthermore, the focused knowledge transfer between generations is noticeable.
SK-2	Management instruments	Tools and instruments supporting the efforts of the leadership and therefore have an impact on the way decisions are made and what information paths are incorporated in the decision-making process.
SK-3	Explicit knowledge	Explicit knowledge includes, for example, specific technical operating principles and documentation, networks, content of intra- and extranet, database, etc.
SK-4	Product innovation	Innovations of great importance for the future of the organization. Characterized by bringing new products into being or fundamentally changing existing products that eventually result in a patent application.

(continued)

(continued)

ID	Driver	Definition
SK-5	Process optimization and innovation	Optimization and improvement of internal procedures and processes, e.g. continuous improvement of all business processes as well as idea management in order to gather suggestions of improvement.
SK-6	Corporate culture	The business culture comprises all values and norms, influencing joint interaction, knowledge transfer, and the nature of the work. Compliance to rules, good manners, 'Do's and Don'ts' and the handling of failures are important aspects in the process.

Relational Capital

ID	Driver	Definition
BK-1	Customer relationships	The relationship to former, current, and potential customers. The management of these relationships comprises activities like sales and marketing, CRM, and face-to-face customer cultivation by employees.
BK-2	Supplier relationships	The relationship to former, current, and potential suppliers. The management of these relations comprises activities concerning purchases and the cultivation of suppliers.
BK-3	Public relationships	Relationship to the public. Including the relationship to former and potential employees and the public in general, all activities of public relationship management as well as corporate citizenship, e.g. supporting regional activities.
BK-4	Investor relationships	All relations to investors – external and internal investors – i.e. banks, owners, stockholders. The management of these relations comprises all activities providing specific information to the group, e.g. accountability.
BK-5	Relationship to cooperation partners	All relationships with professional associations, bodies, and societies. The management of these relationships comprises activities like joint acquisition of customers, suppliers, and investors as well as an active knowledge transfer on R&D partnerships, best-practice transfer, and networking activities.

Notes

1 See www.bmbf.de/en/the-german-vocational-training-system-2129.html to gain an impression of the German vocational training system.
2 See Hochreiter (2005).
3 Agenda 2010 was first presented in the German Bundestag in 2003. The speech can be downloaded here: http://dipbt.bundestag.de/doc/btp/15/15032.pdf.
4 Source: Institut für Mittelstandforschung, www.ifm-bonn.org/statistiken/mittelstand-im-ueberblick/#accordion=0&tab=0 (September 2016).
5 The difference between IC and intangible assets is explained by Reinhardt and Bornemann (2001).
6 Building on conceptual ideas (OECD) and experiences in Scandinavian countries (Scandia, Sveiby, Edvinsson) and the early projects of Meritum and the Danish Guidelines (Mouritsen), the Austrian Research Centers started a three-year development project to report on intangibles in research organizations that was quickly adopted by industry (Hribernik *et al.*) and clusters (e.g. Nanonet and Noest, which represent two research clusters in Austria).
7 The European Commission funded two projects to transfer the method "intellectual capital reporting – made in Germany" to other EU countries. It was in 2007 that the first was started under the project name "intellectual capital statements – made in Europe" (InCaS), and this was followed in 2013 by "Cross-Organizational Assessment and Development of Intellectual Capital" (Cadic).

8 The German Guideline for Intellectual Capital Reporting was published by the German Federal Ministry BMWI (2004); an English document is available here: www.akwissensbilanz.org/Infoservice/ Infomaterial/Leitfaden_english.pdf. Case Studies can be downloaded from: www.akwissensbilanz.org/ Infoservice/Wissensbilanzen.htm.

9 The InCaS results are reported here: www.psych.lse.ac.uk/incas/page114/page114.html.

References

Alwert K., Bornemann M., and Kivikas, M. (2004), *Intellectual Capital Statement: Made in Germany. Guideline*, Federal Ministry for Economy and Labor, BMWA, Berlin.

Alwert, K., Bornemann, M., and Will, M. (2009), "Does intellectual capital reporting matter to financial analysts?" *Journal of intellectual Capital*, Vol. 10, No. 3, pp. 354–368.

BMWI (2004), *Guideline for IC Reporting*, Berlin.

Bontis, N., Keow, W. C. C., and Richardson, S. (2000), "Intellectual capital and business performance in Malaysian industries", *Journal of Intellectual Capital*, Vol. 1, No. 1, pp. 85–100.

Bornemann, M. and Alwert, K. (2007), "The German guideline for intellectual capital reporting: Method and experiences", *Journal of Intellectual Capital*, Vol. 8, No. 4, pp. 563–576.

Bornemann, M. and Leitner, K. H. (2002), "Measuring and reporting intellectual capital: The case of a research technology organization", *Singapore Management Review*, Vol. 24, pp. 7–19.

Bornemann, M. and Sammer, M. (2002), *Anwendungsorientiertes Wissensmanagement*, Gabler, Wiesbaden, Germany.

Drucker, P. F. (1954), *The Practice of Management*, Harper and Row, New York.

Drucker, P. F. (1959), *The Landmarks of Tomorrow*, Harper and Row, New York.

Fama, E. (1965), "The Behavior of Stock Market Prices", *Journal of Business*, Vol. 38, pp. 34–105.

Forrester, J. W. (1961), *Industrial Dynamics*, MIT Press, Boston, MA.

Grant, R. (2013), *Contemporary Strategy Analysis*, John Wiley & Sons, Inc, New York.

Guthrie, J., Ricceri, F., and Dumay, J. (2012), "Reflections and projections: A decade of intellectual capital accounting research", *British Accounting Review*, Vol. 44, No. 2, pp. 68–92.

Hansen, M. T., Nohria, N., Tierney Th. J. (1999), "What's your strategy for managing knowledge?" *Harvard Business Review*, Vol. 77, No. 2, pp. 106–116.

Hayes, J. (2010), *The Theory and Practice of Change Management*, Palgrave, New York.

Hochreiter, R., (2005), "Vorwort", in Mertins, K., Heisig, P., and Alwert, K. (Eds), *Wissensbilanzen. Intellektuelles Kapital Erfolgreich Entwickeln*, Springer, Berlin.

Hofstede, G. (2001), *Culture's Consequences: Comparing Values, Behaviors, Institutions, and Organizations Across Nations* (2nd ed.), Sage Publications, Thousand Oaks, CA.

Leitner, K. H., Bornemann, M., and Schneider, U. (2002), "Development and implementation of an intellectual capital report for a research technology organization", in Bontis, N. (Ed.), *World Congress of Intellectual Capital Readings*, Butterworth Heinemann, Massachusetts, pp. 266–286.

Reinhardt, R. and Bornemann, M. (2001), "Intellectual capital and knowledge management: The measuring perspective", in Child, J., Dierkes, M., Nonaka, I., and Berthoin, A. (Eds), *Handbook on Organizational Learning*, Oxford University Press, Oxford, UK, pp. 794–820.

Sterman, J. (2000), *Business Dynamics. Systems Thinking and Modeling for a Complex World*, McGraw-Hill, Boston, MA.

Weick, K. E. (1969), *The Social Psychology of Organizing*, Addison-Wesley, Boston, MA.

20

A MANAGEMENT CONTROL SYSTEM FOR ENVIRONMENTAL AND SOCIAL INITIATIVES

An intellectual capital approach

Paola Demartini and Cristiana Bernardi

Introduction

Over recent decades, commitment to corporate sustainability has been gaining prominence worldwide. In response to recent corporate scandals there has been increasing pressure on enterprises to integrate into organizational management the three pillars of sustainability: economic, environmental, and social. As a consequence, many companies have strengthened their commitment to provide external stakeholders, such as fund providers, customers, suppliers, employees, local communities, and government, with supplementary non-financial statements, along with traditional accounting reporting (e.g. Gray and Milne, 2002; Kolk, 2004, 2008; Guthrie *et al.*, 2008; Dumay *et al.*, 2016). The main aim of such voluntary disclosure is to shed light on firms' value creation/destruction and distribution processes (Gray, 2006).

In addition, these sustainability reports can be regarded as a means of communication to those investors who determine their portfolios' asset allocation on the basis of a company's commitment to the concept of sustainability. Environmental and social initiatives (also called socially responsible investments) provide investors with further insight into corporate sustainability performance. Within this context indices linked to financial markets that systematically assess the environmental, social, and economic performance of corporations have been developed (e.g. Lòpez *et al.*, 2007; Searcy and Elkhawas, 2012). Among these, of particular prominence are the Dow Jones Sustainability Indices and the FTSE4Good Index (Cerin and Dobers, 2001; Knoepfel, 2001; Chatterji and Levine, 2006).

In our chapter, attention is focused on a company operating in the global aerospace and defence industry, the top management of which had planned to increase its committment to corporate sustainability. The analysed entity, entirely owned by a listed multinational Italian company, is an international leader in electronic and information technology and designs and develops large systems for homeland protection, systems and radars for air defence, battlefield management, naval defence, air and airport traffic management, and coastal/maritime surveillance. Expertise and knowledge are crucial to the firm's success, as the work is highly specialized. Moreover, companies in the industry are obliged to adhere to strict regulations involving national security, export restrictions, and licensing for military goods, accounting rules, and safety requirements. Detailed information about the company, which is not necessary for the discussion of our findings, is not provided. Authorization for access to the company and its data was obtained with the proviso of guaranteeing anonymity of the company and its personnel.

In 2010 the holding company of the high-tech group, the shares of which are listed on the Milan Stock Exchange and on the New York Stock Exchange, was selected as an index component of the Dow Jones Sustainability Indices (DJSI), and has maintained its membership for seven years in a row. As a consequence, top management decided to issue a master plan so as to implement specific sustainability initiatives while looking for a financial rationale to justify this decision. Each initiative was subject to measurement, evaluation, and reporting through the intellectual capital (IC) lens. Therefore, our research aims to answer the following question: how can environmental and social initiatives be identified, assessed, and monitored to improve corporate performance?

In order to answer the research question, we propose a management control system that provides a link between sustainability-oriented projects and corporate intangible assets (hereafter referred to as IC) in order to create value for sustainable development. In particular, we argue that the adoption of a management control system might have a positive impact not only on firms' financial performance, but also on the assessment process companies are subject to for inclusion in sustainability indices. From a methodological point of view, the investigation is the result of a research project carried out together with the top management of the analysed company. Therefore, it takes an action research perspective.

Literature review and research framework

In order to establish the framework underpinning the proposed model for a mangement control system, the following three streams of research are considered. First, managing IC for organizational value creation. Second, developing sustainability management control systems. Third, managing socially responsible investments and sustainability indices.

Managing IC for organizational value creation

The construct of IC – defined by Stewart (1997) as knowledge, information, intellectual property, and experience, which can be exploited in order to generate wealth – offers a means to visualize, assess, and measure the knowledge accumulated within the firm, also referred to as 'intangible resources' or 'intangible assets'. In line with Dumay (2016), we maintain that IC should also encompass environmental and social knowledge, as well as the information and IC to be managed for the purposes of meeting social requirements, improving business competitiveness, and enhancing corporate performance.

In the current globalized competitive arena, IC is a source of competitive advantage as it improves innovation, competitive differentiation, and organizational learning (e.g. Petty and Guthrie, 2000, p. 155; Guthrie, 2001; Marr *et al.*, 2004a, 2004b; Mouritsen and Larsen, 2005; Subramaniam and Youndt, 2005; Ricceri, 2008; Schiuma *et al.*, 2008; Montemari and Nielsen, 2013; Dumay and Roslender, 2013; Zakery *et al.*, 2017). IC is categorized into three subcomponents: human capital, structural capital, and relational capital (Saint-Onge, 1996; Roos *et al.*, 1997; Stewart, 1997; Sveiby, 1997; Bontis, 1998). Human capital is defined as the knowledge acquired from people's experiences, capabilities, skills, creativity, and innovativeness

(Sveiby, 1997). It has been argued that it comprises the knowledge that employees take with them when they leave the firm; however, even if not owned or even controlled by the firm, it is considered as the most significant element of IC, since it is the driving force of the other two components. By contrast, structural capital is referred to as "what is left in the organization when people go home in the evening" (Roos and Roos, 1997, p. 415), the storehouses of knowledge that are embedded in systems, databases, and programs (Edvinsson and Malone, 1997). Lastly, relational capital reflects the idea that firms are not isolated systems, rather they depend, to a great extent, on the continuous interplay with the external environment. Therefore, relational capital consists of all the knowledge embedded in relationships with external parties such as customers, suppliers, partners, and other external stakeholders (Roos *et al.*, 1997). Brand, image, and corporate reputation, for example, fall into this category.

Researchers and consultants have studied the advantages of IC management on companies' organizational value creation (Guthrie *et al.*, 2001; Dumay, 2016, pp. 169–171; Dumay *et al.*, 2017). However, the effectiveness of IC management on organizational performance, both financial and non-financial, is difficult to achieve and assess (Dumay, 2012). Thus, our investigation aims to contribute to the debate concerning the impact of IC management on organizational business performance.

Sustainability management control systems

The development of environmental and social accounting has contributed to sustainability management and reporting (Bebbington and Gray, 2001; Gray, 2010). Many academics and practitioners have developed performance measurement systems, including the Performance Pyramid (Lynch and Cross, 1991), Balanced Scorecard (Kaplan and Norton, 1992), Performance Prism (Neely *et al.*, 2002) and Sustainability Balanced Scorecard (Figge *et al.*, 2002; Dias-Sardinha and Reijnders, 2005; Schaltegger and Wagner, 2006; Hubbard, 2009).

Management control is essential in promoting corporate sustainability (Schaltegger and Wagner, 2006; Gond *et al.*, 2012) and academics are increasingly calling for empirical research on the role of management control systems in relation to environmental and social activities undertaken by organizations (e.g. Ferreira *et al.*, 2010; Henri and Journeault, 2010; Schaltegger, 2011; Gond *et al.*, 2012). Accordingly, Perez *et al.* (2007) claim that sustainability-oriented activities must be integrated into the firm's strategic processes in order to translate environmental and social performance into long-term shareholder value. Nevertheless, to date few empirical studies have investigated how management control systems have been deployed in practice to promote corporate sustainability (e.g. Perego and Hartmann, 2009; Henri and Journeault, 2010; Riccaboni and Leone, 2010; Arjaliès and Mundy, 2013).

The purpose of this chapter is the proposal of a management control system that attempts to embed an IC perspective to identify, measure, and manage environmental and social initiatives (e.g. environmental protection, gender equality initiatives, charity, and wealth projects). An assumption underlying our investigation is that embedding environmental and social aspects into corporate strategy supports firms in the process of IC accumulation, such as skills and competencies, knowledge and innovation, legitimacy, trust, and reputation (Perrini *et al.*, 2011). More specifically, we posit that IC plays a crucial role in mediating the relationship between the management of sustainability-oriented activities and corporate financial performance (Surroca *et al.*, 2010; Demartini *et al.*, 2014, 2015; Lin *et al.*, 2015; Ferrero *et al.*, 2016).

The literature review carried out by Guthrie *et al.* (2012, p. 75) reveals that management accounting has been the most popular focus of IC accounting research since the mid 2000s, covering a wide range of management-related subjects. In their conclusions, the authors call for "more critical field studies which will provide empirical studies of IC in action and help develop broader theoretical research" (p. 79). The need for a bottom-up performative approach to IC has also been advocated by Dumay and Garanina (2013) and Dumay (2013). It has indeed been contended that the adoption of such a perspective would benefit researchers and practitioners alike, since it would enable them to gain greater insights into how IC works within a specific organization (Mouritsen, 2006). Hence, our research aims to contribute to the ongoing debate on IC practices in action.

Managing socially responsible investments and sustainability indices

The phenomenon of socially responsible investment reflects the increasing concerns of investors towards environmental, social, ethical, and corporate governance issues. The growing awareness that 'sustainable' investments might produce better financial performance has indeed prompted numerous companies to publish voluntarily sustainability reports with the aim of guiding, at least in part, investment decisions (e.g. Magness, 2010; Berthelot *et al.*, 2012). Quoting Boiral (2013, p. 1036), "Sustainability Reporting has become an increasingly common practice in companies' attempts to respond to expectations, pressures and criticisms from stakeholders who want to be better informed about the environmental and social impacts of business activities".

With the aim of providing guidance for investors seeking further insight into sustainability performance, many sustainability indices have been designed to measure the performance of those firms that set industry-wide best practices with regard to sustainability. Sustainability indices provide meaningful signals of social legitimacy in the attempt "to verify that a firm's goals and actions align with societal values such as environmental sustainability, labour and human rights, anti-corruption practices, and community engagement" (Hawn *et al.*, 2011, p. 3). It has indeed been argued that they serve as informational intermediaries between companies and their stakeholders (such as analysts, brokers, and financial institutions) by evaluating the disclosed sustainability related information (Robinson *et al.*, 2011). From the investor's point of view, such indices allow the identification of the world's sustainability leaders for different industries, thus enabling regional and global benchmarking.

Within the realm of sustainability indices, the most widely recognized are the DJSI Family and the FTSE4Good. Established in 1999 and maintained collaboratively by RobecoSAM and S&P Dow Jones Indices, the DJSI family tracks the performance of the world's largest companies leading the field in terms of corporate sustainability, defined by RobecoSAM (2013) as "a company's capacity to prosper in a hypercompetitive and changing global business environment". Since its inception, RobecoSAM has been conducting the annual Corporate Sustainability Assessment, which consists of an analysis of the sustainability performance of more than 2,500 companies covering the major indices. The assessment, based on information provided by the companies through the online questionnaire, is built on a range of financially relevant sustainability criteria covering the economic, environmental, and social dimensions. Nevertheless, as pointed out by Fowler and Hope (2007) and more recently by Searcy (2012), little is currently known about what impact sustainability indices have, in practice, on management control systems and what steps corporations have taken to be or remain included in the DJSI.

As a second assumption, we deem that a sustainability-oriented management control system could have a significatively positive impact on the assessment process companies are subject to for inclusion in the DJSI. Drawing on the above considerations, the joint team,

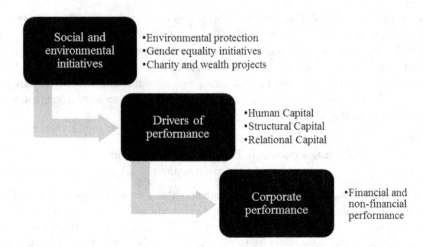

Figure 20.1   The model to assess and monitor environmental and social initiatives

made of professionals and academics, designed a management control system focusing particularly on i) the process by which environmental and social initiatives increase IC, and ii) how this might have a positive impact on corporate performance. In Figure 20.1, we sketch the model that will be analysed later in this chapter.

Research method

The selection of a company belonging to the aerospace and defence sector is consistent with our research aim, since the field comprises high-tech global firms whose products and services result from investments in financial, human, structural, and relational capital. In particular, we focus on the case of a large company headquartered in Italy. Specifically, the analysed entity, entirely owned by a listed multinational Italian company, designs and develops large systems for homeland protection systems and radars for air defence, battlefield management, naval defence, air and airport traffic management, and coastal and maritime surveillance.

In recent years, the company's top management has shown an interest in enhancing the company's IC potential. To this end, an organizational unit was established entirely devoted to promoting product innovation, increasing patents and trademarks, strengthening personnel competencies, and enabling academic relationships. Moreover, the company's top management expressed willingness to adopt an IC measurement approach through collaborations with researchers, and this allowed us to be involved in a business project that aimed to identify, measure, and manage the firm's intangible resources. As a consequence, the investigation was conducted as action research (Dumay, 2010; Dumay and Baard, 2017). Given the strategic sector within which the company operates, detailed information about the company profile – not relevant in order to discuss our findings – will not be provided.

According to Reason and Bradbury (2006, p. 1), action research is a process that "seeks to bring together action and reflection, theory and practice". Consistent with the interpretative approach, this is a case study whereby the researchers cooperate with the host organization, promoting solutions to actual problems and contributing to theory at the same time (Jönsson and Lukka, 2005; Dumay, 2010). In its traditional sense, action research "involves a collaborative change management or problem solving relationship between researcher and client aimed at both solving a problem and generating new knowledge" (Coghlan and Brannick, 2010, p. 44). Action research adopts a scientific approach to studying the resolution of social or organizational issues together with those who experience these issues directly. One of its main objectives is to increase understanding on the part of the researcher or the client personnel, or even both. Therefore, the researcher is intended to act in concert with the host organization: s/he observes the whole process and the related outcomes, and analyses the findings in light of the relevant literature.

Action research as a methodology not only reflects on the observations of the researcher, but also on the impact the interventions have on the organization. The main benefit for the researcher is the ability to develop insights into the implementation of new management innovations within organizations. For practitioners, the benefit is to gain the assistance and knowledge of academics as a resource in the implementation process (Dumay, 2010). Therefore, action research contributes to both research and practice.

There is not an agreed set of methodological protocols, or rules, shared by all researchers; however, action research usually begins with the establishment of initial contact between the researcher(s) and the representatives of the organization (Entry Stage). Diagnosis is a pivotal stage in action research, as the researcher(s) may introduce organizational members to conceptual schemes and/or theories that enable them to reinterpret how they perceive their situation. The ultimate goal of this phase is to develop a conscious understanding among organizational members and to co-determine and plan possible interventions. The intervention stage follows, during which both practitioners and researchers try to implement management innovation within the organization.

The research project lasted for five years (from 2010 to 2014). The project team was made up of three professionals belonging to the organizational unit devoted to the enhancement of IC (project controllers or 'go-to' persons) and three academics. Among the latter were the supervisors of this project, who were its sponsors and 'gatekeepers' (Dumay, 2010, p. 54). The supervisors helped facilitate access to the company. The 'go-to' persons helped the researchers become 'insiders', thus facilitating their taking part in the everyday processes and activities and working to "develop participatory interactions more akin to the interventionist process required for the conduct of interventionist research", consistent with Dumay (2010, p. 55). Table 20.1 summarizes the steps undertaken by the joint team to develop the project, the information collected, and the main outcomes.

The researchers were involved in decisions and actions aimed at achieving objectives with the managers. The researchers' involvement is consistent with an interventionist approach, in which participant observation is the main 'research weapon' used (Chiucchi and Dumay, 2015). Nevertheless, data was also collected through interviews and the review of internal documents (Jönsson and Lukka, 2005; Dumay, 2010). Between January 2010 and December 2013, the researchers attended 48 meetings running on average for 4 hours each. Additionally, the researchers recorded and transcribed semi-structured interviews along with field notes.

The research began with the identification of the problems perceived within the organization, before recognizing the 'the client/stakeholder' figure, and the agreement on who, how, where, and when they would take part in the research. The first issue was the identification of the main user of IC information, which in the analysed case study was identified as the company's top management. Although the disclosure of IC information to external stakeholders is a further important aim, it was not taken into consideration since the research mainly focused on the managerial decision-making process (if only because the company is a subsidiary that does not produce separate financial statements for public consumption).

Table 20.1 Activities and main outcomes

Steps	Period	No. joint group meetings (hours)	Practitioners' data/ information gathering	Researchers' data/information gathering	Main outcomes
STEP 1 Entry stage	January 2010– May 2010	8 meetings lasting on average 4 hours Key interviews/ discussions with CFO, HR and R&D	Internal data collection (e.g. Strategic plan; managerial reporting, procedures, protocols, etc.)	Literature review	2 presentations of the project's state of art to the CEO and the company's top management
STEP 2 Diagnosis	May 2010– August 2012	25 meetings lasting on average 4 hours Key interviews with CFO	Internal data collection (e.g. DJSI assessment questionnaire)	Competitors' benchmarking	3 presentations of the project's state of art to the CEO and the company's top management
STEP 3 Plan of interventions	September 2012– December 2013	15 meetings lasting on average 4 hours Key interviews with CFO	Internal data collection about specific initiatives to be launched in 2014	Updating literature review	1 presentation of the project's state of art to the CEO and the company's top management

The primary role of researchers was to introduce the IC conceptual scheme and related theories to organizational members (thus enabling them to reinterpret how they understood their company). The main role of practitioners was the assessment of their usefulness in practice. The ultimate goal of the joint research group was proposing to the company's top management a model for the measurement and management of the firm's intangible assets within a sustainability framework. Both the researchers and the controllers shared the responsibility of delivering the project's output. Such a model, deriving from the joint effort of the research team, could therefore be integrated into managerial practices in support of the decision-making process.

Analysis and findings

In this section we present the model for the measurement and management of the company's IC that the company's top management decided to implement in order to control the specific sustainable management initiatives planned for 2014.

Managing IC within a sustainability framework

In this case study, the researchers' involvement occurred in two distinct periods. From 2010 to 2012 the researchers were involved in designing and developing an IC measurement system leading to the publication of an internal IC report to manage intangible resources that had to be reinforced or acquired in response to the management's suggestions and that support the strategic objectives of the company (see Demartini and Paoloni, 2013).

From late 2012 to the end of 2013, the functionality of the model outlined for measuring, reporting, and managing IC was broadened in order to take into account sustainability. In fact, following the changes in the parent company's top management team and the inclusion of the holding company in the DJSI, sustainability became a primary strategic objective of the group. Thus, in 2013, management issued a master plan to implement specific sustainability initiatives while looking for a financial rationale to justify this decision. Each initiative was subject to measurement, evaluation, and reporting through the IC lens. Each project launched by the company that had a relevant impact on IC underwent calculation, evaluation, and reporting.

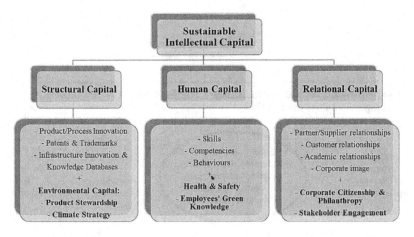

Figure 20.2   Implementing sustainability categories as per the DJSI in the company's IC map

The traditional vision of IC was used in the three areas represented by structural, human, and relational capital (see Figure 20.2). On the one hand, the application of the model represents a managerial innovation for the company's single unit, whereas on the other, it offers a powerful reporting tool for the firm as a whole. It is worth noting that while the management control system design was completed in 2013, its deployment in practice was carried out in 2014.

Managing environmental and social initiatives

The research group elaborated a process for the identification of an efficient management tool to implement the new model into the management control of specific initiatives. The benefits of these initiatives (i.e. the projects launched by the company to foster sustainability performance, but not only these) should not be only measured by current financial indicators, because their output impacts intangible resources that are 'mediating variables' for expected financial benefits in the longer term.

The process follows an annual cycle starting from strategic planning, and then develops into subsequent stages, as shown in Figure 20.3. The circular process means the results return to the firm's management through a feedback report that can be used in order to make changes where and if necessary.

Specifically, the activities are:

- identification of the main initiatives that have a significant impact on IC, including sustainability aspects and analysis of their related expected benefits;
- IC measurement, which implies the identification of the relevant resources that will be reinforced and/or acquired through the development of specific activities;
- implementation of the initiatives and data gathering; and
- reporting, that is, a document containing the results of the measurement and assessment activity of the projects to be sent to the firm's top management at the end of the year.

This is a process approach which goes beyond the company's functions since it works transversally within the firm. Such a mechanism will be successful only if there is general awareness and understanding of the central role intangible resources (including sustainability aspects) play within a highly competitive and technological sector.

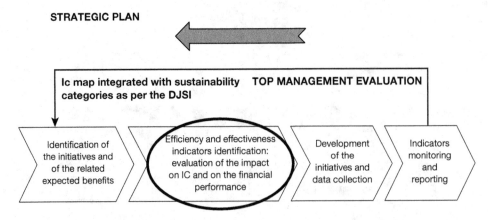

Figure 20.3 The delineated process

The pilot project the research group was responsible for concerns the implementation of the outlined model for a series of specific initiatives that the company planned for 2014 in line with sustainable management, namely: Life Cycle Assessment (Eco Design), Eco Recycling, Age Diversity Management, Green Communication, Green Procurement, and Charity and Welfare.

The IC measurement model implies the identification and use of a tailor-made measurement system. In order to monitor each single initiative, a set of performance indicators is available:

- effectiveness indicators (to monitor if the organization has reached the planned goals);
- efficiency indicators (to monitor the related costs);
- indicators to measure the impact the initiative has on the company's IC; and
- indicators to measure financial performance.

Indicators are defined by personnel in charge of specific initiatives with the support of experts on intangible management control, whose task is to gather data for management reporting.

To give an example, we concentrate only on the first of the aforementioned initiatives, that is, Life Cycle Assessment (Eco Design) – LCA. The aim of LCA is to carry out a feasibility study

Table 20.2 Indicators for life cycle assessment (eco design) initiative

Effectiveness and efficiency indicators of the initiative
Effectiveness
With respect to the fixed goals
Efficiency
Incurred costs vs estimated costs

Impact on intellectual capital

Structural capital

Product innovation

- R&d costs*
- Collaboration with external partners in the r&d field (no. And €)
- New products /'green' components to be included in the company's database (no. And % of costs and revenues)*

Number of patents and trademarks/ipr (intellectual property rights)

- Number of new trademarks
- Environmental certifications

Processes

- Number of implemented portals*
- Number of new processes integrated into the company*
- New management software

Environmental capital*

- Product strategy
    - Reduction of the volume of hazardous substances (€ or %)
    - Reduction of volumes/reduction of packaging and transport costs (€ or %)

(continued)

Table 20.2 (continued)

Impact on intellectual capital

- Climate strategy
  - Reduction of CO_2 emissions (€ or %), recovery of recyclable materials from waste electrical and electronic equipment (€ or %)

Human capital

Competence

- On-the-job-training (no. of hours)

Skills

- No. of employees who acquired specific skills (e.g. Use of specific tools, knowledge of regulatory requirements)

Corporate behaviour

- No. of employees involved in the project

Relational capital

Supplier relationship

- No. of suppliers that meet 'green requirements'*
- Required standards for suppliers (e.g. Audit)
- Training initiatives addressed to suppliers (no. And €)

Relations with the scientific community

- No. of collaborations and € invested in them

Effects on financial performance (short and medium/long term)

Revenues increase

- Increased revenues (greater value in use for customers in the medium/short term)
- Capitalization of patents and of environmental certifications (ad hoc evaluation)

Cost reduction

- Reduction of volumes/reduction of packaging and transport costs (€ or %) in the medium/long term

* Key performance indicators relevant for the Dow Jones Sustainability Index (DJSI) questionnaire

(concerning methods, timing, and costs) on the implementation of an environmental impact assessment with respect to the company's whole life production process. Possible indicators – useful for the Life Cycle Assessment (Eco Design) project – are listed in Table 20.2.

Discussion and conclusions

The assessment process to which companies are subject for inclusion in sustainability indices is built on a wide array of financially relevant sustainability criteria concurrently covering the economic, environmental, and social dimensions. Within this context, intangible resources and capabilities are broadly recognized as the most influential sources of value creation and competitive advantage. Therefore, it seems reasonable to posit that the evaluation of firms' IC represents a promising starting point for the incorporation of environmental and social aspects into the general management system.

We argue that intangibles can be regarded as the mediating variables between sustainability management and corporate financial performance. Accordingly, a management control system that enhances sustainability performance by measuring and managing the firm's IC – such as skills and competencies, knowledge and innovation, values, legitimacy, trust and reputation – has been depicted. More specifically, we posit that accounting for environmentally and socially responsible activities through the effect of mediating contingent variables (i.e. firm-specific intangibles) allows managers to be aware of what drivers of performance can lead to both revenue and cost-related outcomes.

The top management's willingness to integrate IC and corporate social responsibility perspectives into the company's management system and communication process arose following changes that occurred in the management team and the inclusion of the company in the DJSI. This was the first step, which motivated sustainability performance measurement; consequently, the development and implementation of sustainability initiatives required the support of appropriate mechanisms such as management accounting and control. Indeed, these events have contributed to the topic of sustainability becoming a primary strategic objective. To this end, the company's CEO has demonstrated his interest in building an organizational unit entirely devoted to promoting sustainability. Commitment to sustainability is communicated both externally (through formal claims) and internally (by progressively including sustainability principles into organizational culture).

Thanks to our methodological approach – action research – we have an inside perspective on the process that involved the managers of the analysed company in planning environmentally and socially responsible activities for 2014. Our investigation aims to demonstrate that measurement is not the main goal of managerial accounting, but is rather a means to manage and create value (Catasús *et al.*, 2007). As Mouritsen and Larsen (2005) point out, there is an additional management control agenda where information is an input to management activities. This means, to be able to understand the relationships existing between measurement and operational activities on the one hand, and strategies and context on the other. We find that it is extremely important for managers to be aware of the mechanism that allows environmental and social initiatives to increase specific intangibles (operational-side), and which intangibles need strengthening in order to increase the competitive advantage of a firm (strategy-side) within a particular context. Yet, we deem that the extent of such a change and the level of a real strategic renewal depends on an organization's commitment to sustainability and the role ascribed to, and actual use of, management control systems (Gond *et al.*, 2012).

To date, the main critical factor arising from the intervention plan is the accurate identification of the actors involved in the reporting process. The process mentioned earlier provides a comprehensive view of IC practices within the company; nevertheless, in order to make it work, the cooperation of all owners of the information is required. Retrieving data involves identifying such individuals, which is not always easy in a big business reality; it also implies interacting with the various parties to obtain all contributions. What is also important is the way in which managerial reporting is related to the reward system. This is not straightforward, since the management control system is still at an experimental stage and not yet widely accepted in the business management system.

To overcome these obstacles that might impede the implementation of IC management procedures within the firm, we suggest pilot projects are a good starting point so that emerging problems and opportunities can be dealt with as they arise by personnel involved in day-to-day activities. The chance that a new reporting system is effective relies also on its 'value in use' as perceived by the 'owners' of the information. Therefore, the study represents a preliminary approach to understanding whether and to what extent a management control system might foster sustainability performance, thus enabling companies to meet the stringent criteria required for inclusion in the DJSI.

Since sustainability management is as yet in its infancy, its integration poses significant organizational challenges. The management control system proposed in this chapter, which to our knowledge has not been addressed in any previous publication, offers a framework for systematically incorporating sustainability thinking into corporate practice.

References

Arjaliès, D. L. and Mundy, J. (2013), "The use of management control systems to manage CSR strategy: A levers of control perspective", *Management Accounting Research*, Vol. 24, No. 4, pp. 284–300.

Bebbington, J. and Gray, R. H. (2001), "An account of sustainability: Failure, success and a reconceptualization", *Critical Perspectives on Accounting*, Vol. 12, No. 5, pp. 557–587.

Berthelot, S., Coulmont, M., and V. Serret (2012), "Do investors value sustainability reports? A Canadian study", *Corporate Social Responsibility and Environmental Management*, Vol. 19, No. 6, pp. 355–363.

Boiral, O. (2013), "Sustainability reports as simulacra? A counter-account of A and A+ GRI reports", *Accounting, Auditing & Accountability Journal*, Vol. 26, No. 7, pp. 1036–1071.

Bontis, N. (1998), "Intellectual capital: An exploratory study that develops measures and models", *Management Decision*, Vol. 36, No. 2, pp. 63–76.

Catasús, B., Ersson, S., Gröjer, J., and Yang Wallentin, F. (2007), "What gets measured gets... on indicating, mobilizing and acting", *Accounting, Auditing and Accountability Journal*, Vol. 20, No. 4, pp. 505–521.

Cerin, P. and Dobers, P. (2001), "What does the performance of the Dow Jones Sustainability Group Index tell us?", *Eco-Management and Auditing*, Vol. 8, No. 3, pp. 123–133.

Chatterji, A. and Levine, D. (2006), "Breaking down the wall of codes: Evaluating nonfinancial performance measurement", *California Management Review*, Vol. 48, No. 2, pp. 29–51.

Chiucchi, M.S. and Dumay, J. (2015), "Unlocking intellectual capital", *Journal of Intellectual Capital*, Vol. 16, No. 2, pp. 305–330.

Coghlan, D. and Brannick, T. (2010), *Doing Action Research in Your Own Organisation*, Sage, London.

Demartini, P. and Paoloni, P. (2013), "Implementing an intellectual capital framework in practice", *Journal of Intellectual Capital*, Vol. 14, No.1, pp. 69–83.

Demartini, P., Paoloni, M., and Paoloni, P. (2015), "Sustainability and intangibles: Evidence of integrated thinking", *Journal of International Business and Economics*, Vol. 15, No. 2, pp. 107–122.

Demartini, P., Paoloni, M., Paoloni, P., and Bernardi, C. (2014), "Managerial integrated reporting: Evidence from practice", *Management Control*, No. 3, pp. 37–58.

Dias-Sardinha, I. and Reijnders, L. (2005), "Evaluating environmental and social performance of large portuguese companies: A balanced scorecard approach", *Business Strategy and the Environment*, Vol. 14, No. 2, pp. 73–91.

Dumay, J. (2010), "A critical reflective discourse of an interventionist research project", *Qualitative Research in Accounting and Management*, Vol. 7, No. 1, pp. 46–70.

Dumay, J. (2012), "Grand theories as barriers to using IC concepts", *Journal of Intellectual Capital*, Vol. 13, No. 1, pp. 4–15.

Dumay, J. (2013), "The third stage of IC: Towards a new IC future and beyond", *Journal of Intellectual Capital*, Vol. 14, No. 1, pp. 5–9.

Dumay, J. (2016), "A critical reflection on the future of intellectual capital: From reporting to disclosure", *Journal of Intellectual Capital*, Vol. 17, No. 1, 168–184.

Dumay, J. and Baard, V. (2017), "An introduction to interventionist research in accounting", in Hoque, Z., Parker, L. D., Covaleski M., and Haynes, K. (Eds), *The Routledge Companion to Qualitative Accounting Research Methods*, Routledge, Oxford, UK.

Dumay, J. and Garanina, T. (2013), "Intellectual capital research: A critical examination of the third stage", *Journal of Intellectual Capital*, Vol. 14, No. 1, pp. 10–25.

Dumay, J. and Roslender, R. (2013), "Utilising narrative to improve the relevance of intellectual capital", *Journal of Accounting and Organizational Change*, Vol. 9, No. 3, pp. 248–279.

Dumay, J., Bernardi, C., Guthrie, J., and Demartini, P. (2016), "Integrated reporting: A structured literature review", *Accounting Forum*, Vol. 40, No. 3, pp. 166–185.

Dumay, J., Guthrie, J., and Rooney, J. (2017), "The critical path of intellectual capital", in Guthrie, J., Dumay, J., Ricceri, F., and Nielsen, C., (Eds), *The Routledge Companion to Intellectual Capital*, Routledge, London, pp. 21–39.

Edvinsson, L. and M. Malone (1997), *Intellectual Capital: Realizing your Company's True Value by Finding its Hidden Brainpower*, Harper Business, New York.

Ferreira, A., Moulang, C., and Hendro, B. (2010), "Environmental management accounting and innovation: An exploratory analysis", *Accounting, Auditing & Accountability Journal*, Vol. 23, No. 7, pp. 920–948.

Ferrero, I., Fernández, M. Á., and Muñoz, M. J. (2016), "The effect of environmental, social and governance consistency on economic results", *Sustainability*, Vol. 8, p. 1005–1021.

Figge, F., Hahn, T., Schaltegger, S., and Wagner, M. (2002), "The sustainability balanced scorecard. linking sustainability management to business strategy", *Business Strategy and the Environment*, Vol. 11, No. 5, pp. 269–284.

Fowler, S. and Hope, C. (2007), "A critical review of sustainable business indices and their impact", *Journal of Business Ethics*, Vol. 76, No. 3, pp. 243–252.

Gond, J. P., Grubnic, S., Herzig, C., and Moon, J. (2012), "Configuring management control systems: Theorizing the integration of strategy and sustainability", *Management Accounting Research*, Vol. 23, No. 3, pp. 205–223.

Gray, R. H. (2006), "Social, environmental and sustainability reporting and organisational value creation? Whose value? Whose creation?" *Accounting, Auditing & Accountability Journal*, Vol. 19, No. 6, pp. 793–819.

Gray, R. H. (2010), "Is accounting for sustainability actually accounting for sustainability... and how would we know? An exploration of narratives of organisations and the planet", *Accounting, Organizations and Society*, Vol. 35, No. 1, pp. 47–62.

Gray, R. H. and Milne, M. (2002), "Sustainability reporting: Who"s kidding whom?" *Chartered Accountants Journal of New Zealand*, Vol. 81, No. 6, pp. 66–70.

Guthrie, J. (2001), "The management, measurement and the reporting of intellectual capital", *Journal of Intellectual Capital*, Vol. 2, No. 1, pp. 27–41.

Guthrie, J., Cuganesan, S., and Ward, L. (2008), "Industry specific environmental and social reporting: The Australian Food and Beverage Industry", *Accounting Forum*, Vol. 32, No. 1, pp. 1–15.

Guthrie, J., Petty, R., and Johanson, U. (2001), "Sunrise in the knowledge economy: Managing, measuring and reporting intellectual capital", *Accounting, Auditing & Accountability Journal*, Vol. 14, No. 4, pp. 365–384.

Guthrie, J., Ricceri, F., and Dumay, J. (2012), "Reflections and projections: A decade of intellectual capital accounting research", *The British Accounting Review*, Vol. 44, No.2, pp. 68–82.

Hawn, O., Chatterji, A., and Mitchell, W. (2011), "Two coins in one purse? How market legitimacy affects the financial impact of changes in social legitimacy: Addition and deletion by the Dow Jones Sustainability Index", Working Paper, Duke University, NC.

Henri, J. F. and Journeault, M. (2010), "Eco-control: The influence of management control systems on environmental and organizational performance", *Accounting, Organizations and Society*, Vol. 35, No. 1, pp. 63–80.

Hubbard, G. (2009), "Measuring organizational performance: Beyond the triple bottom line", *Business Strategy and the Environment*, Vol. 18, No. 3, pp. 177–191.

Jönsson, S. and Lukka, K. (2005), *Doing Interventionist Research in Management Accounting*, Gothenburg Research Institute, Gothenburg, Sweden.

Kaplan, R. and Norton, D. (1992), "The balanced scorecard: Measures that drive performance", *Harvard Business Review*, Jan-Feb, pp. 71–79.

Knoepfel, I. (2001), "Dow Jones Sustainability Group Index: A global benchmark for corporate sustainability", *Corporate Environmental Strategy*, Vol. 8, No. 1, pp. 6–15.

Kolk, A. (2004), "A decade of sustainability reporting: Developments and significance", *International Journal of Environment and Sustainable Development*, Vol. 3, No. 1, pp. 51–64.

Kolk, A. (2008), "Sustainability, accountability and corporate governance: Exploring multinationals' reporting practices", *Business Strategy and the Environment*, Vol. 17, No. 1, pp. 1–15.

Lin, C. S., Chang, R. Y., and Dang, V. T. (2015), "An integrated model to explain how corporate social responsibility affects corporate financial performance", *Sustainability*, Vol. 7, No. 7, pp. 8292–8311.

Lòpez, M. V., Garcia, A., and Rodriguez, L. (2007), "Sustainable development and corporate performance: A study based on the Dow Jones Sustainability Index", *Journal of Business Ethics*, Vol. 75, No. 3, pp. 285–300.

Lynch, R. L. and Cross, K. F. (1991), *Measure Up: The Essential Guide to Measuring Business Performance*. Mandarin, London.

Magness, V. (2010), "Environmental disclosure in the mining industry: A signaling paradox?" in Freedman, M. and Jaggi, B. (Eds), *Sustainability, Environmental Performance and Disclosures, Advances in Environmental Accounting and Management*, Vol. 4, pp. 55–81, Emerald Group Publishing Limited (UK).

Marr, B., Gray, D., and Schiuma, G. (2004b), "Measuring intellectual capital: What, why, and how", in Bourne, M. (Ed.), *Handbook of Performance Measurement*, Gee Publishing, London.

Marr, B., Schiuma, G., and Neely, A. (2004a), "The dynamics of value creation: Mapping your intellectual performance drivers", *Journal of Intellectual Capital*, Vol. 5, No. 2, pp. 312–325.

Montemari, M., and Nielsen, C. (2013), "The role of causal maps in intellectual capital measurement and management", *Journal of Intellectual Capital*, Vol. 14, No. 4, pp. 522–546.

Mouritsen, J. (2006), "Problematising intellectual capital research: Ostensive versus performative IC", *Accounting, Auditing & Accountability Journal*, Vol. 19, No. 6, pp. 820–841.

Mouritsen, J. and Larsen, H. T. (2005), "The 2nd wave of knowledge management: The management control of knowledge resources through intellectual capital information", *Management Accounting Research*, Vol. 16, No. 3, pp. 371–394.

Neely, A., Adams, C., and Kennerley, M. (2002), *The Performance Prism: The Scorecard for Measuring and Managing Business Success*, Prentice Hall, London.

Perego, P. and Hartmann, F. (2009), "Aligning performance measurement systems with strategy: The case of environmental strategy", *Abacus*, Vol. 45, No. 4, pp. 397–428.

Perez, E. A., Correa Ruiz, C., and Carrasco Fenech, F. (2007), "Environmental management systems as an embedding mechanism: A research note", *Accounting, Auditing & Accountability Journal*, Vol. 20, No. 3, pp. 403–422.

Perrini, F., Russo, A., Tencati, A., and Vurro, C. (2011), "Deconstructing the relationship between corporate social and financial performance", *Journal of Business Ethics*, Vol. 102, Issue 1 Supplement, pp. 59–76.

Petty, R. and Guthrie, J. (2000), "Intellectual capital literature review: Measurement, reporting and management", *Journal of Intellectual Capital*, Vol. 1, No. 2, pp. 155–176.

Reason, P. and Bradbury, H. (2006), *Handbook of Action Research: The Concise Paperback Edition*, Sage, London.

Riccaboni, A. and Leone, E. L. (2010), "Implementing strategies through management control systems: The case of sustainability", *International Journal of Productivity and Performance Management*, Vol. 59, No. 2, pp. 130–144.

Ricceri, F. (2008), *Intellectual Capital and Knowledge Management: Strategic Management of Knowledge Resources*. Routledge, London.

RobecoSAM, (2013), Measuring intangibles: RobecoSAM's corporate sustainability assessment methodology, available at: www.sustainability-indices.com (accessed May 2014).

Robinson, M., Kleffner, A., and Bertels, S. (2011), "Signaling sustainability leadership: Empirical evidence of the value of DJSI membership", *Journal of Business Ethics*, Vol. 101, No. 3, pp. 493–505.

Roos, G. and Roos, J. (1997), "Measuring your company"s intellectual performance", *Long Range Planning*, Vol. 30, No. 3, pp. 413–426.

Roos, J., Roos, G., Dragonetti, N., and Edvinsson, L. (1997), *Intellectual Capital: Navigating in the New Business Landscape*. Macmillan, London.

Saint-Onge, H. (1996), "Tacit knowledge the key to the strategic alignment of intellectual capital", *Planning Review*, Vol. 24, No. 2, pp. 10–16.

Schaltegger, S. (2011), "Sustainability as a driver for corporate economic success: Consequences for the development of sustainability management control", *Society and Economy*, Vol. 33, No. 1, pp. 15–28.

Schaltegger, S. and Wagner, M. (2006), "Integrative management of sustainability performance, measurement and reporting", *International Journal of Accounting, Auditing and Performance Evaluation*, Vol. 3, No. 1, pp. 1–19.

Schiuma, G., Lerro, A., and Sanitate, D. (2008), "Intellectual capital dimensions of Ducati"s turnaround: Exploring knowledge assets grounding a change management program", *International Journal of Innovation Management*, Vol. 12, No. 2, pp. 161–193.

Searcy, C. (2012), "Corporate sustsainability performance measurement systems: A review and research agenda", *Journal of Business Ethics*, Vol. 107, No. 3, pp. 239–253.

Searcy, C. and Elkhawas, D. (2012), "Corporate sustainability ratings: An investigation into how corporations use the Dow Jones Sustainability Index", *Journal of Cleaner Production*, Vol. 35, pp. 79–92.

Stewart, T. (1997), *Intellectual Capital. The New Wealth of Organisations*, Doubleday, New York.

Subramaniam, M. and Youndt. M. A. (2005), "The influence of intellectual capital on the types of innovative capabilities", *Academy of Management Journal*, Vol. 48, No.3, pp. 450–463.

Surroca, J., Tribó, J. A., and Waddock, S. (2010), "Corporate responsibility and financial performance: The role of intangible resources", *Strategic Management Journal*, Vol. 31, No. 5, pp. 463–490.

Sveiby, K. E. (1997), *The New Organisational Wealth: Managing and Measuring Knowledge-Based Assets*, Berrett-Koehler, San Franciso, CA.

Zakery, A., Afrazeh, A., and Dumay, J. (2017), "Analysing and improving the strategic alignment of firms' resource dynamics", *Journal of Intellectual Capital*, Vol.18, No. 1, pp. 217–240.

21

LEVERS AND BARRIERS TO THE IMPLEMENTATION OF INTELLECTUAL CAPITAL REPORTS

A field study

*Maria Serena Chiucchi, Marco Giuliani,
and Stefano Marasca*

Introduction

Intellectual capital (IC) has been debated for decades. The first of three stages of IC research was focused on raising awareness of IC, and on new methods for measuring it. The second stage was aimed at building theory while the third stage has aimed to investigate IC from a critical and performative perspective, by challenging taken-for-granted assumptions (Dumay, 2013; Guthrie, *et al.*, 2012). By analysing the evolution of the IC discourse, we can see that both scholars and practitioners have proposed a plethora of IC concepts (Chaminade and Roberts, 2003; Meritum Project, 2002; Mouritsen, *et al.*, 2001; Stewart, 1997) and reporting frameworks (Andriessen, 2004; Sveiby, 2010) none of which can be considered as generally accepted, implying that individual organizations have defined their own specific IC reporting agenda according to their particular purposes (Abeysekera, 2008, p. 39; Sveiby, 2010).

There are two different perspectives on IC (Brännström *et al.*, 2009; Brännström and Giuliani, 2009; Roslender and Fincham, 2001, 2004). The first is focused on IC management and the second on IC disclosure. In the first, the underlying idea is that measuring and reporting IC enables the firm to manage its resources and activities and to deliver sustainable competitive advantage. In the second, the disclosure of IC can lead to more efficient capital markets and company valuations. These two perspectives are the foundation for different approaches to reporting IC (Andriessen, 2004; Gröjer and Johansson, 2000; Marr, *et al.*, 2003). Table 21.1 summarizes the main reasons for analysing and measuring IC as suggested by the extant literature. These reasons can coexist and change over time according to internal or external contexts (Giuliani, 2009, 2015a).

Despite the various benefits attributed ex ante, the implementation of IC reporting frameworks is not widespread in practice (Dumay, 2009, 2012; Lönnqvist *et al.*, 2009; Chiucchi, 2013a). More specifically, early adopters, such as Skandia, have abandoned IC reporting and a recent study of companies that participated in the Danish project has shown

Table 21.1 Reasons for analysing and measuring IC

Gröjer & Johansson (2000)	Marr et al. (2003)	Andriessen (2004)
• Corporate governance • Insider gains • Investor decisions • Merger and acquisitions • Credit decisions • Tradability • National accounts • Management control	• Strategy formulation • Strategy assessment and execution • Strategic development, diversification and expansion • Compensation • Communication to external stakeholders	• Improving internal management • Improving external reporting • Transactional and statutory motives

that few of them continued to report IC after the end of the project (Schaper, 2016). This makes urgent a reflection on how measuring IC can help to realize the benefits attributed to it and an examination of what are the levers and barriers that can influence the successful implementation of an IC report and its long-term fate (Catasús *et al.*, 2007; Catasús and Gröjer, 2006; Chiucchi, 2013b; Chiucchi and Montemari, 2016; Dumay, 2012; Giuliani *et al.*, 2016; Lönnqvist *et al.*, 2009).

Several studies have highlighted some of the levers and barriers to the adoption of IC reports. The barriers include:

- the existence of grand theories, such as that which represents IC as the difference between market and book value and that which maintains that IC disclosure leads to efficiency in capital markets, which can be misleading (Dumay, 2012);
- the complexity of the data collection and calculation processes (Catasús and Gröjer, 2006; Demartini and Paoloni, 2013);
- the fact that IC indicators may be perceived as 'provocative', as they give visibility to local practices (Vaivio, 2004), or 'rapidly obsolete', because of the changes in the competitive environment and/or users' needs (Chiucchi, 2013b; Dumay and Rooney, 2011), or as 'fragile', due to their lack of completeness and isomorphism (Chiucchi and Montemari, 2016);
- specific qualities of IC measurements (not self-evident, ambiguity, not fully comparable, etc.) (De Santis and Giuliani, 2013; Giuliani, 2014; Giuliani *et al.*, 2016; Mårtensson, 2009);
- the fact that IC scores may not confirm the users' perceptions or expectations (Chiucchi and Montemari, 2016);
- the 'lock in' or 'accountingization' phenomenon (Chiucchi and Dumay, 2015; Dumay, 2009; Habersam *et al.*, 2013) that occurs when IC measurement dominates IC management and consequently the production of numbers is not followed by their use.

Recently, Schaper (2016, p. 66–68) investigated why companies that implemented the Danish Intellectual Capital Statements (Mouritsen *et al.*, 2003) have abandoned this practice. The author highlights the following principal factors: no purpose or value perceived; organizational change; other priorities; difficulties in implementation; IC statements managed merely as a project; low interest from management; abandonment by key employees; and no completion of the first project.

Studies have shown that levers to the implementation and diffusion of IC reporting frameworks can be attributed to:

- the ambiguity of the IC concept, which makes it more likely that managers will make sense of IC and engage with it by applying it to corporate concerns so that IC can be enacted and used as a solution to issues (Cuganesan *et al.*, 2007; Dumay, 2008; Dumay and Rooney, 2016);
- the involvement of managers in designing IC frameworks so that they engage with IC (Chiucchi, 2013b; Chiucchi and Dumay, 2015);
- the creation of tailor made solutions and the rejection of the one-size-fits all approach (Dumay, 2009);
- the 'dramatization' of IC indicators (Catasús and Gröjer, 2006);
- the visualization of the value creation and destruction processes (Cuganesan, 2005; Cuganesan and Dumay, 2009; Giuliani, 2013, 2015b);
- the linkages between numbers and specific organizational challenges (Dumay and Guthrie, 2007).

Levers and barriers can also relate to the actors involved in the process of production and use of IC measurements and to their engagement (Dumay and Rooney, 2011). In particular, two types of actors seem to be particularly important, as they determine the design, implementation, and development trajectories of IC projects and, consequently, can act as levers or as barriers (Chaminade and Roberts, 2003; Chiucchi, 2013a, 2013b). These are the project sponsor and the project leader. The project sponsor can be defined as the person who promotes the relevance of IC within the organization, supports the development of the project, and gives legitimation to the IC project. The project leader is the person that develops the IC project in practice, that is, the person actually involved in the design and implementation of the IC reports.

The aim of this chapter is to analyse the levers and barriers to the implementation of IC reports from a longitudinal perspective, thus contributing to the third stage of IC research.

Research method

In order to gather insights into levers and barriers to the implementation of IC reports, we conducted a field study, which is "a research design that embraces a relatively small number of companies, as opposed to a wide-ranging survey or intensive case enquiries in two or three companies" (Roslender and Hart, 2003, p. 262). This method is considered suitable to explore "complex phenomena in a confined domain" (Lillis and Mundy, 2005, p. 131).

We focused on Italian firms because "Italy has become the new, hot bed of IC research, especially aimed at working side by side with managers inside organizations in developing IC practices" (Dumay, 2013, p. 6). Furthermore, different from other countries, such as for instance Denmark (Schaper, 2016), where national projects on measuring and reporting IC have been launched, there have been no national or large-scale projects in Italy and companies began to measure IC on their own initiative, in different points in time, with different aims, and adopting different frameworks.

Our sample is composed of companies that prepared at least one IC report for disclosure and/or managerial aims. Therefore we included in our research only companies that reported IC according to the system of intangible resources categorized as human, organizational, and relational capital (Edvinsson and Malone, 1997; Sveiby, 1997). This means that we excluded companies that report only specific IC resources, such as human capital or relational capital, for instance.

Considering the ad hoc implementation of IC reporting practices, the name and number of companies that have ever produced an IC report in Italy is unknown. Therefore, in order to

Table 21.2 Interview's main themes

1	General information on the first IC report and reasons for reporting IC
2	Technical and organizational characteristics of the IC report's projects
3	Barriers and levers in reporting IC
4	Benefits and drawbacks of the IC report
5	Use of the IC report (managerial and/or disclosure purposes)
6	Evolution and/or abandonment of the IC report

identify them, we adopted a step-by-step process. First, a review of national and international publications within the IC field was carried out using SCOPUS, Google books, and Google libri (Italian version of Google books). Second, we searched Google to collect data about companies not mentioned in publications but which have declared that they report or have reported IC. Third, in order to integrate the results of steps one and two, several people familiar with the Italian IC field were interviewed to ensure the list produced after steps one and two was complete and, if not, identify missing firms. The result was a list of 34 companies being identified, representing the majority of Italian firms producing IC reports. Of these, 16 companies agreed to be involved in this research project (hereafter named with letters from 'A' to 'P').

Semi-structured interviews with preparers were conducted (Kreiner and Mouritsen, 2005; Qu and Dumay, 2011) to determine levers and barriers and also to compare different practical experiences of IC reporting. Semi-structured interviews are well suited for the exploration of the perceptions and opinions of respondents regarding complex and sometimes sensitive issues. In addition, they also allow the interviewer to probe for more information and elicit clarification of answers. A list of questions was submitted to the interviewees beforehand, but we also allowed open discussion to emerge. The interview was piloted in two companies around the themes listed in Table 21.2.

The 16 analysed companies differed in size and mainly belonged to the private sector (69 per cent), with public sector (19 per cent) and non-profit sector (12 per cent) companies also represented in the sample.[1]

We interviewed those people in the organization who had guided the IC reporting project; in all, we interviewed 18 people. In seven cases, the interviewees were also the projects' promoters (those who were first interested in IC, promoted, and supported the IC report).

Interviews were conducted during the spring and summer of 2014, lasting from one to two hours each, were all tape-recorded, and then transcribed for analysis. In order to overcome bias, the analysis was carried out through triangulation (Patton, 1990; Yin, 2003); thus, it was designed in such a way that one of the researchers was responsible for data collection, while the others examined the interview material and notes. Post-interview communication with the respondents helped the authors to ensure the accuracy of collected data.

Results

Reasons for introducing an IC report

The majority of the companies in our sample declared to have undertaken IC reporting projects both for managerial and disclosure reasons (69 per cent) or exclusively for managerial reasons (31 per cent). None prepared an IC report only for disclosure aims. Among the analysed companies, 13 have continued measuring and reporting IC for some years whereas 3 stopped after the first experience. 'Meteors' are therefore of marginal relevance in our sample. The average duration of the experience is 6.38 years with a maximum of 16 to a minimum of 1 year (see Table 21.3).

Table 21.3 Data overview

Company	Years of experience (measuring IC)	Stopped producing an IC report (Y/N)	Stopped measuring IC (Y/N)	Initial aims (MGT-management /DIS-disclosure)
A	11	N	N	MGT/DIS
B	8	N	N	MGT/DIS
C	6	Y	Y	MGT/DIS
D	5	Y	Y	MGT/DIS
E	14	N	N	MGT/DIS
F	12	Y	N	MGT
G	4	N	N	MGT/DIS
H	9	Y	N	MGT
I	2	Y	Y	MGT
J	5	Y	Y	MGT/DIS
K	1	Y	Y	MGT/DIS
L	5	Y	Y	MGT/DIS
M	1	Y	Y	MGT/DIS
N	2	Y	Y	MGT/DIS
O	1	Y	Y	MGT
P	16	Y	N	MGT

All interviewees declared they reported IC for several reasons. Some of the interviewees pointed out that when their projects started there was uncertainty about what an IC report was and which aims an IC report could expect to realize.

At the beginning we had no ideas about this type of projects... (A)

Various interviewees said they had decided to report IC to improve disclosure. Sometimes, interviewees talked in general terms about "communicating company value" (C, N) or about "improving transparency" (B, L). In some cases, the reasons given were more specific and referred to filling the gaps in the typical financial statement with information that could better illustrate company strategy, activities, and characteristics (A, E, J, K, L), and permitted a more complete and realistic picture of the company.

[b]efore transparency became mandatory or a "big issue", we used to publish on our website our Corporate Social Responsibility report where our stakeholders could understand what we do, our activities, the benefits we generate for them, etc. In 2007 we decided to include in our report also these aspects related to human, relational and organizational capital. (B)

Surely the IC report has information that are [sic] not reported in typical financial statements and that give a better picture of our "non-financial activities", that is the results achieved and the activities carried out that do not have a financial accounting impact. Thus, this kind of reporting fits much better with an organization like ours ... it offers a more appropriate perspective for non-traditional companies like us. (A)

I have two main reasons. The first reason is the improvement of the information flow towards our stakeholders, establishing a kind of a dialogue, a way of sharing relevant information ... The second reason is that by publishing this panel of indicators ... by representing our culture and by disclosing our commitment to our stakeholders and the society, it would be difficult to ignore them in case of a change of the management or of the ownership. In this way, we wanted to define our long-term perspective. (E)

We tried to understand what we could do to give to our stakeholders a more complete picture of what we actually do. So, we started thinking how to do it ... We noticed that several information [sic] of the IC report were [sic] complementary to the financial ones and they allowed us to show to our stakeholders how and why we spend our money, what we have done for them, etc. They allow [us] to disclose a more reliable and realistic picture of our business. (J)

In some cases, IC reports were produced to improve communication aimed at specific stakeholders. Here the idea was to give emphasis to the role of the company in the value chain of customers or suppliers (G), to show the "real company value" to financial institutions (N), or to produce information that could be useful in mergers and acquisitions and which went beyond financial numbers (L).

We have tried to make the prospective partner understand who we are and what we expect from him ... and that we are a delicate organism and there are some elements that have to be considered when merging together: our employees, the way we manage them, the way knowledge is disseminated, the way we are used to doing our job. All in all, the IC statement should help our 'Chieftain' make the colonizers understand that we are not exactly cavemen. (L)

In other cases, there was also the will to show that the company was innovative (K, L).

[w]e had, to some extent, satisfaction by showing that we were interested in these issues and that were doing things that only some big firms were doing. (K)

In other cases, the IC report was produced to enrich existing voluntary disclosure, made through Corporate Social Responsibility (CSR) reports (Bilancio Sociale), with information on intangibles and to give emphasis to some labour issues. (G)

As far as managerial aims are concerned, projects were aimed at promoting a better understanding of the company and of its performance by:

- filling the gaps of financial information (C, D, K, N);
- showing the company's ability to implement strategy and accomplish projects (E);
- providing information on key success factors; and
- depicting how the company used resources and competences to build relationships with suppliers and to develop processes and technologies (P).

In some cases, the aims were also related to the project leader's aim to legitimize his or her actions and decisions. This was done by providing evidence to the rest of the company or to the board of directors/owner that company value was higher than book value (H) or showing the activities done over the years by a specific department (L).

I need to give a sort of authority to the new Department I am heading, which I think stems from a great intuition from an organizational point of view: put together all the *non-financial* activities, all the support activities. It is crucial to show that this new Department has its usefulness, that it uses *scientific tools* and that it promotes coordinated actions within the company. This project is useful also to me (emphasis added) (L).

337

In other instances, the aims for reporting IC were related to human resources and include gaining a more in-depth understanding of the personnel, to producing information to support decisions related to them. The IC report was produced to understand people and their competencies (D, I) and the risks associated with their management (E), and to acquire knowledge on workplace relationships to support and guide personnel policies (L). At the same time, the IC report was also aimed at stimulating certain behaviours and actions related to personnel. Companies pointed out that by reporting IC they aimed to improve organizational consciousness and integration among people (B, G, J) and alignment to company values (J). IC reporting was considered useful also to satisfy top management's desire to undertake stimulating and innovative projects (I, M).

Finally, other reasons reported related to specific objectives such as supporting change management processes (A) or improving effectiveness and efficiency (O).

The frameworks adopted to report IC

As there has not been any large-scale IC reporting projects in Italy and, consequently, companies have decided to implement them on an ad hoc basis, in different time-points and under the guidance of different consultants or researchers, the frameworks used to report IC differed from respondent to respondent.

In 13 cases, IC reports were standalone documents while in the other 3 cases they were part of CSR reports where there was a specific section referring to IC. In one case, after a few years, the IC report ceased to be a standalone document and was integrated with the company's quality report.

When IC reports were standalone documents, they were predominantly inspired by famous and widely used frameworks, mainly the Intangible Asset Monitor (Sveiby, 1997) and the Meritum guidelines (Meritum Project, 2002).

While for all companies the experience of reporting IC started with the production of an IC report, it did not necessarily end in the same form. Among the companies that stopped producing an IC report, four continued measuring specific dimensions of IC using only some parts of the initial IC report that became part of corporate and/or departmental control systems.

The practice of reporting IC as a part of the CSR report deserves some further discussion. In the Italian context, sustainability and social and environmental reports have a long history and several initiatives on CSR have taken place, both at private and public level (Borga *et al.*, 2009; Hinna, 2002). More specifically, the Italian "Gruppo di Studio per il Bilancio Sociale" (Italian Group for Studies on Social Reporting) has published guidelines for preparing social reports, the so-called 'GBS model', in 2001, with the latest version released in 2013 (GBS, 2013). In 2003, the Italian Ministry of Labour and Social Affairs launched the CSR-SC Project, presented as "the Italian contribution towards the promotional campaign of CSR throughout Europe" (Baldarelli, 2007, p. 8), aimed at spreading CSR culture among companies and public institutions and guaranteeing citizens that CSR communication is not misleading. Within this project a Social Statement is promoted that firms can adopt on a voluntary basis and which aims to guide the reporting of CSR performance (Baldarelli, 2007).

Although IC reports and CSR reports have been developed as independent models of reporting, research suggests some similarities. Cordazzo (2005) analysed 83 environmental and social reports of Italian companies and found similarities between these reports and IC reports. The author concluded that environmental and social reports could support the development of IC reporting in Italy and also that "the IC report could be a useful tool for generalizing these two sets of accounts by interpreting (and visualizing) the 'society' and the 'environment' as part of the new value-drivers of a company" (p. 459). Del Bello (2006) analysed a local government sustainability report, suggesting two possible integration processes between this document and the IC report: a weak integration process, leading to a set of common indicators, and a strong integration process, which could generate a new form of single reporting. Similarly, Pedrini (2007), by observing that IC and CSR reports have several convergence points (e.g. methodology, issues covered, such as human resources), proposed the reports be integrated into a 'Global or Holistic Report', which would show how CSR strategy has been developed, how it influences intangible resources, and the company's commitment to orient CSR strategy to maximize the firm's value. More recently, Cinquini *et al.* (2012) investigated the content, frequency, and quality of IC disclosure and the changes that took place over two years (2005 and 2006) in 37 sustainability reports published by Italian listed companies. The authors, by showing that sustainability reports present a range of information on IC, confirmed the findings of studies that have demonstrated that sustainability reports could be useful for providing some information on IC. Schaper *et al.* (2017), by examining the Danish context, identified a trend towards more integrated forms of reporting, motivated in part by the need to reduce reporting overload. To conclude, all these studies, while recognizing that IC reports and CSR reports have different objectives and stakeholders, highlight that a convergence between the two is possible and even desirable.

Levers to the implementation of IC reports

In the interviews, we explicitly formulated questions regarding the perceived conditions that can favour the implementation of IC reports, that is, IC reporting levers. From the interviews it emerged that levers can be related both to technical (e.g. frameworks, indicators, etc.) and organizational (e.g. actors involved, personnel involvement, commitment, etc.) aspects of IC projects.

In term of technical aspects, the main levers can be identified as follows:

- the existence of a quality system, of a well-developed management accounting system, and of existing databases as well as of a business intelligence system;
- the possibility to concentrate and directly control the production of indicators in one department;
- the managers' familiarity with using non-financial indicators;
- the strong connection between the IC report initiative and company strategy.

Size is considered a lever, as smaller companies are better able to communicate with staff and therefore can more easily explain the meaning of the project, obtain data, and secure staff involvement.

Four of the analysed companies reported IC as a separate section of their CSR report and one as a part of its quality report. These companies are among those still reporting IC, suggesting that combining the IC report and other voluntary reports seems to be successful. Nevertheless, in those cases in which the IC report is a separate section of the CSR report, the experience of measuring IC seems to merge with that of CSR reporting. Even if we asked questions specifically referring to the IC project and the IC report, interviewees frequently answered referring to the social report and to social/sustainability accounting. In support of this, we counted the times the interviewees used the words 'social', 'sustainable/sustainability', 'intangible(s)', and 'intellectual capital' (see Table 21.4).

Table 21.4 Use of terms during interviews

	B	E	G	J
Social	32	6	32	11
Sustainable/sustainability	0	6	0	0
Intangible(s)	0	3	11	7
Intellectual	19	10	0	0

All but one company used the words 'social' and 'sustainable/sustainability' more so than 'intangibles' and or 'intellectual capital'; in company E, their use is almost equal.

With regard to organizational aspects, the interview data suggests that three types of actors emerge as relevant: project leaders, project sponsors, and external partners (consultants and university researchers). These have a fundamental role in undertaking these projects, in determining their aims, in carrying out the projects, and in continuing and/or in abandoning them. For instance, in those cases in which the project leader was the CFO/controller the IC report was used for management aims, and even if some of the companies stopped producing an IC report, specific parts of it were then included in departmental or corporate management accounting systems. Therefore, specific dimensions of IC continued to be analysed in different forms and with different tools. In this sense, the competences of the project leader influenced the development trajectories of the IC projects.

In general, the sponsorship of the board of directors and/or of the entrepreneur has been identified as a key lever by all interviewees and it appears that all projects could benefit from this sponsorship. Similarly, specific managers' sponsorship, for example, the heads of human resources and/or marketing departments, has been identified as a lever.

External partners appear to be particularly relevant: almost all companies (15) undertook the IC reporting project under the guidance of consultants and/or university researchers. However, in one company, the president had the initiative to undertake the project and guided it because he had already participated in the preparation of an IC report in the company in which he was previously working. External partners played different roles; as 'coach' they guided and cooperated actively in measuring and reporting IC during the first years. In those cases in which companies became autonomous in producing IC reports, external partners continued to be consulted from time to time to discuss the evolution of the IC reports. The relevance of the consultants in some cases went far beyond this and they not only cooperated and/or guided the project but were referred to as the "real promoters" of the projects. Some interviewees admitted that before the project began they did not even know what IC was. Therefore, they trusted the consultants and the idea of IC; two respondents referred to one of the consultants as a "guru".

Barriers to the implementation of IC reports

We also specifically asked about perceived barriers to reporting IC. In terms of technical aspects, interviewees stressed the following:

- producing an IC report is a time-consuming activity as it requires a specific and complex data collection and data analysis process;
- the need to devote personnel to the project (and the expenses connected to this);
- the need for high commitment and cooperation by those who collect and process information;

- the need to obtain the cooperation of other departments for the production of indicators;
- the difficulties in understanding the IC frameworks, in selecting the 'right' IC indicators, in understanding and 'trusting' the IC indicators, and in linking the IC performance with financial performance.

Some of these technical barriers relate to organizational aspects: in several cases, the design and implementation phases seem to be predominantly circumscribed to the project leader, to his/her department, and to the consulting companies. Company managers were rarely involved as permanent members of the project teams (only in 4 of 16 cases) and their participation ranged from providing the necessary information to designing the system, to producing the data needed for calculating indicators. Sometimes, they did not participate at all. It is worth noting that managers' involvement in the design and implementation processes was not identified by most interviewees as either a lever (if low) or as a barrier (if high).

The role played by the sponsor, leader, and external partners can also be perceived as a double-edged sword. In fact, if it is true that these actors can contribute to the success of the IC project, it is also true that a change in the role of one of these key actors likely meant a (negative) change in the fate of the IC reports. If this key figure quit the company or changed his/her priorities, the IC report was abandoned. In one case, the interviewee considered the failure of the consulting company as the reason for abandoning the IC report. Respondents offered different reasons for the abandonment of IC reports, including: restructuring processes; the financial crisis and the related need to cut costs; and the inability of IC reports to fulfil their initial aims.

The specialization of the consultant determined the fate of the IC project. When the consultant was a quality systems consultant, even if the IC report initially was a standalone document, over time it became a section of the quality report. When the consultant had already guided the production of a social report, the IC report was or became a section of the social report. Likewise, when the IC report was proposed by a strategy consultant, the IC project had a strong managerial aim and the IC report usually was used to support managerial actions. Finally, when the consultant changed, the IC project failed.

Discussion and conclusions

By presenting a field study of companies that have adopted IC reports, levers and barriers to IC reporting were identified from an empirical perspective. Our study confirms and supports many of the levers and barriers that have been highlighted in the prior literature. The complexity of the data collection and calculation processes, the 'provocative' and 'fragile' nature of IC indicators, the lack of correspondence between IC measures' scores and users' perceptions and expectations, the absence of linkages between IC indicators and financial performance (thus, the limited knowledge of value creation processes) have all been identified as barriers. Elements that make the collection and calculation processes straightforward have been specifically identified as levers: databases, quality and management accounting systems, and software such as business intelligence. Related to this is also the role of the project leader in controlling the collection and calculation processes.

However, the intensity of each of these levers and barriers can vary in space and time. In other words, the intensity is not perceived as the same in all companies and it can change over time depending on the technical and organizational specificities of each company (e.g. culture, size, accounting system, etc.).

Two specific aspects need to be detailed further: the role of ambiguity and of grand theories. Regarding ambiguity, consistent with Giuliani (2009), we show that the reasons for deciding to measure and report IC vary. Interviewees referred to them in general terms (e.g. improve communication towards stakeholders, improve company performance) and, sometimes, also in very specific terms (e.g. emphasize labour issues such as the ability to offer job opportunities). The term 'ambiguity' recurred frequently during the interviews in relation to how the IC reports and the initial aims of the IC project were perceived. This seems to be reinforced by the fact that some interviewees said that consultants were the "real sponsors" and that they (project leaders and company personnel) did not know at the beginning of the project what IC and an IC report was. IC ambiguity is fundamental to the implementation of IC reporting practices, since it is more likely that managers will make sense of IC and engage with it by applying it to corporate concerns or to the project leader's or sponsor's concerns (e.g. give authority to a certain department, emphasize specific labour issues, etc.) (Cuganesan *et al.*, 2007; Dumay, 2008; Dumay and Rooney, 2016). Our data shows how this ambiguity can act as a double-edged sword since some projects were undertaken without understanding what companies could expect from the projects and without general aims. Ambiguity, therefore, can act as a lever or as a barrier depending on how the sensemaking and sensegiving processes (Giuliani, 2016) are carried out by the project leader and by the organization.

In terms of grand theories (Dumay, 2012) to justify the implementation of these reports, the evidence suggests that theories appear to support the initial stage of the process and allow for the natural initial distrust related to a new project and/or to new accounts to be overcome (Catasús, 2008; Gray, *et al.*, 1997). At the same time, when the IC report has been implemented, if the expectation created by grand theories, such as performance or the market value improvement, is not fulfilled, grand theories can become one of the reasons for abandoning the IC reporting project. Therefore, grand theories can act as levers or as barriers depending on the organizational context and experience.

While Giuliani (2009, 2015a) shows that IC reporting methods and tools can change in space and over time, we demonstrate that from a technical perspective, levers and barriers can change in space and over time and due to the technical specifics and dynamics of IC reporting methods and tools. Our study suggests that some aspects, such as ambiguity of aims or indicators and the existence of grand theories, can act both as levers and as barriers depending on aspects of the organization and of the development, over time, of the IC reporting project.

Our study also highlights that in Italy, the IC report experience seems to have been linked to that of CSR reporting. While the prior literature has investigated the content, frequency, and quality of IC disclosure in CSR reports (Cinquini *et al.*, 2012; Oliveira *et al.*, 2010; Pedrini, 2007), here we analyse the relationship between these two reports. Our empirics show that the existence of a CSR report can be a lever both to start and to continue IC reporting. At the same time, our data also show that there is a risk that IC reports are subsumed by CSR reports. Our interviewees frequently confused IC reports and information with CSR reports; while this is not necessarily a barrier to the diffusion of IC reporting practices, it becomes a barrier if IC practices are undertaken to reach objectives that differ from those of the CRS reports. The predominantly disclosure nature of CSR reports can be misleading and represent a barrier when IC reporting practices are undertaken to manage IC.

In relation to organizational levers and barriers, consistent with Chiucchi (2013a, 2013b), our study confirms the roles of project leaders and project sponsors as key in undertaking these projects, in determining their aims, in carrying out the projects, and in continuing and/or in abandoning them. Nevertheless, our study adds to this by showing the relevance of the external partners (consultants and in a few cases university researchers) that seem to be in several cases the *deus ex machina* of the projects. They have a key role in the sense-making and sense-giving processes (Giuliani, 2016) and their specialization influences the way IC is perceived within the company and the fate of the IC report. External partners transferred to companies their own meaning of IC and the IC report and of what organizations could expect from it. This means that the capabilities of the external partners to give sense to the IC report and to allow the organization to make sense of it is relevant in determining the success or failure of IC projects. At the same time, there is the risk of an excessive 'personalization', that is a dependence of the project on the external partner (barrier).

In our interviews, technical barriers are more stressed by interviewees than organizational barriers. The low participation of managers in the design and implementation phase was not generally (but not ever) perceived as a problem. Frequently, the limited participation of managers was perceived as a problem related to the difficulty of collecting and processing data and rarely as a problem related to the use of IC frameworks and measures. Therefore, the initiatives undertaken to solve these problems were usually (even if not always) aimed at solving technical aspects, with the risk of the organizational aspects being overlooked. In this sense, our study confirms that the 'accountingization' phenomenon, which occurs when practitioners (and researchers) focus their attention on fitting a company IC into a measurement framework, instead of focusing on its practices Dumay (2009, pp. 205–6), is a relevant barrier to the use of IC concepts and to the realization of their potential.

Finally, the longitudinal perspective of our analysis allows speculation as to the persistence and status of levers and barriers over time. Barriers can be overcome by adopting specific actions, for example, better communication. Barriers can also be superficially overcome but at the cost of depth, for example, the complexity of data calculation and processing was 'solved' by reducing indicators. However, barriers can be 'latent' and reappear if, for example, key actors consider them a priority.

These findings have both theoretical and practical significance. This study enriches the IC literature based on a performative approach. The results show what happens after IC concepts, methods, and tools are introduced within an organization. The study contributes to the literature on IC "in practice" (Dumay, 2012, p. 12; Guthrie *et al.*, 2012, p. 79) as the analysis is developed *in vivo* and not *in vitro*. Finally, this study offers a longitudinal perspective with reference to organizational and technical levers and barriers.

There are two main potential limitations to the study. First, the results can be affected by the typical limitations of the design adopted for the study, that is, generalization is not possible, and the results may be subject to both interviewee and interviewer bias and interpretation. Nevertheless, considering the exploratory nature of the study, generalization on some aspects is possible. Further, while it was not possible to interview all the companies adopting IC reporting, we believe that we provided enough data to make useful observations.

This study calls for more IC research to be carried out by adopting a performative approach in order to understand in greater depth the technical and organizational dimensions of IC, what they are influenced by, and how they determine the success or failure of an IC project. Moreover, it can be interesting to investigate how companies can face and overcome barriers or use levers in practice. Analysing the Italian context can also open up future research avenues by comparing the research findings to similar studies conducted in other country contexts in order to understand if and how the IC reporting *genesis* can influence its evolution.

Note

1 For privacy reasons, we are not allowed to disclose more information than is reported in this chapter (e.g. sector, dimension, etc.) in order to protect the anonymity of the companies.

References

Abeysekera, I. (2008), "Intellectual capital practices of firms and the commodification of labour", *Accounting, Auditing & Accountability Journal*, Vol. 21, No. 1, pp. 36–48.

Andriessen, D. (2004), *Making Sense of Intellectual Capital: Designing a Method for the Valuation of Intangibles*, Elsevier Butterworth–Heinemann, Burlington, MA.

Baldarelli, M. G. (2007), "New prospectives in inter-company relations, social responsibility (CSR) and social, ethical and environmental accounting in Italy by way of the government CSR-SC project: Theory and praxis", *Economia Aziendale Online*, Vol. 1, pp. 1–26.

Borga, F., Citterio, A., Noci, G., and Pizzurno, E. (2009), "Sustainability report in small enterprises: Case studies in Italian furniture companies", *Business Strategy and the Environment*, Vol. 18, No. 3, pp. 162–176.

Brännström, D. and Giuliani, M. (2009), "Accounting for intellectual capital: A comparative analysis", *VINE: The Journal of Information and Knowledge Management Systems*, Vol. 39, No. 1, pp. 68–79.

Brännström, D., Catasús, B., Gröjer, J.-E., and Giuliani, M. (2009), "Construction of intellectual capital: The case of purchase analysis", *Journal of Human Resource Costing & Accounting*, Vol. 13, No. 1, pp. 61–76.

Catasús, B. (2008), "In search of accounting absence", *Critical Perspectives on Accounting*, Vol. 19, No. 7, pp. 1004–1019.

Catasús, B. and Gröjer, J.-E. (2006), "Indicators: On visualizing, classifying and dramatizing", *Journal of Intellectual Capital*, Vol. 7, No. 2, pp. 187–203.

Catasús, B., Errson, S., Gröjer, J.-E., and Wallentin, F. Y. (2007), "What gets measured gets... On indicating, mobilizing and acting", *Accounting, Auditing & Accountability Journal*, Vol. 20, No. 4, pp. 505–521.

Chaminade, C. and Roberts, H. (2003), "What it means is what it does: A comparative analysis of implementing intellectual capital in Norway and Spain", *European Accounting Review*, Vol. 12, No. 4, pp. 733–751.

Chiucchi, M. S. (2013a), "Intellectual capital accounting in action: Enhancing learning through interventionist research", *Journal of Intellectual Capital*, Vol. 14, No. 1, pp. 48–68.

Chiucchi, M. S. (2013b), "Measuring and reporting intellectual capital: Lessons learnt from some interventionist research projects", *Journal of Intellectual Capital*, Vol. 14, No. 3, pp. 395–413.

Chiucchi, M. S. and Dumay, J. (2015), "Unlocking intellectual capital", *Journal of Intellectual Capital*, Vol. 16, No. 2, pp. 305–330.

Chiucchi, M. S. and Montemari, M. (2016), "Investigating the 'fate' of intellectual capital indicators: A case study", *Journal of Intellectual Capital*, Vol. 17, No. 2, pp. 238–254.

Cinquini, L., Passetti, E., Tenucci, A., and Frey, M. (2012), "Analyzing intellectual capital information in sustainability reports: Some empirical evidence", *Journal of Intellectual Capital*, Vol. 13, No. 4, pp. 531–561.

Cordazzo, M. (2005), "IC statement vs environmental and social reports: An empirical analysis of their convergences in the Italian context", *Journal of Intellectual Capital*, Vol. 6, No. 3, pp. 441–464.

Cuganesan, S. (2005), "Intellectual capital-in-action and value creation. A case study of knowledge transformation in an innovation process", *Journal of Intellectual Capital*, Vol. 6, No. 3, pp. 357–373.

Cuganesan, S. and Dumay, J. (2009), "Reflecting on the production of intellectual capital visualisations", *Accounting, Auditing & Accountability Journal*, Vol. 22, No. 8, pp. 1161–1186.

Cuganesan, S., Guthrie, J., and Boedker, C. (2007), *How Mutable Discourse Shapes Material Practice: An Accounting of Intellectual Capital*, Macquarie Graduate School of Management, Sydney.

Del Bello, A. (2006), "Intangibles and sustainability in local government reports: An analysis into an uneasy relationship", *Journal of Intellectual Capital*, Vol. 7, No. 4, pp. 440–456.

Demartini, P. and Paoloni, P. (2013), "Implementing an intellectual capital framework in practice", *Journal of Intellectual Capital*, Vol. 14, No. 1, pp. 69–83.

De Santis, F. and Giuliani, M. (2013), "A look on the other side: Investigating intellectual liabilities", *Journal of Intellectual Capital*, Vol. 14, No. 2, pp. 212–226.

Dumay, J. (2008), "Narrative disclosure of intellectual capital: A structurational analysis", *Management Research News*, Vol. 31, No. 7, pp. 518–537.

Dumay, J. (2009), "Intellectual capital measurement: A critical approach", *Journal of Intellectual Capital*, Vol. 10, No. 2, pp. 190–210.

Dumay, J. (2012), "Grand theories as barriers to using IC concepts", *Journal of Intellectual Capital*, Vol. 13, No. 1, pp. 4–15.

Dumay, J. (2013), "The third stage of IC: Towards a new IC future and beyond", *Journal of Intellectual Capital*, Vol. 14, No. 1, pp. 5–9.

Dumay, J. and Guthrie, J. (2007), "Disturbance and implementation of IC practice: A public sector organisation perspective", *Journal of Human Resource Costing and Accounting*, Vol. 11, No. 2, pp. 104–121.

Dumay, J. and Rooney, J. (2011), "'Measuring for managing?' An IC practice case study", *Journal of Intellectual Capital*, Vol. 12, No. 3, pp. 344–355.

Dumay, J. and Rooney, J. (2016), "Numbers versus narrative: An examination of a controversy", *Financial Accountability & Management*, Vol. 32, No. 2, pp. 202–231.

Edvinsson, L. and Malone, M. S. (1997), *Intellectual Capital*, Harper Business, New York.

GBS (2013), *Gruppo di studio per il bilancio sociale: Il bilancio sociale. Standard. Principi di redazione del bilancio sociale*, Giuffrè, Milan, Italy.

Giuliani, M. (2009), "Intellectual capital under the temporal lens", *Journal of Intellectual Capital*, Vol. 10, No. 2, pp. 246–259.

Giuliani, M. (2013), "Not all sunshine and roses: Investigating intellectual liabilities 'in action'", *Journal of Intellectual Capital*, Vol. 14, No. 1, pp. 127–144.

Giuliani, M. (2014), "Accounting for intellectual capital: Investigating reliability", *International Journal of Finance and Accounting*, Vol. 3, No. 6, pp. 341–348.

Giuliani, M. (2015a), "Intellectual capital dynamics: Seeing them 'in practice' through a temporal lens", *Vine*, Vol. 45, No. 1, pp. 46–66.

Giuliani, M. (2015b), "Rome wasn't built in a day… Reflecting on time, intellectual capital and intellectual liabilities", *Journal of Intellectual Capital*, Vol. 16, No. 1, pp. 2–19.

Giuliani, M. (2016), "Sensemaking, sensegiving and sensebreaking: The case of intellectual capital measurements", *Journal of Intellectual Capital*, Vol. 17, No. 2, pp. 218–237.

Giuliani, M., Chiucchi, M. S., and Marasca, S. (2016), "A history of intellectual capital measurements: From production to consumption", *Journal of Intellectual Capital*, Vol. 17, No. 3, pp. 590–606.

Gray, R., Dey, C., Owen, D., Evans, R., and Zadek, S. (1997), "Struggling with the praxis of social accounting: Stakeholders, accountability, audits and procedures", *Accounting, Auditing & Accountability Journal*, Vol. 10, No. 3, pp. 325–364.

Gröjer, J. E. and Johansson, U. (2000), *Accounting for Intangibles at the Accounting Court*, available at: www.fek.su.se (accessed 22 December 2007).

Guthrie, J., Ricceri, F., and Dumay, J. (2012), "Reflections and projections: A decade of intellectual capital accounting research", *The British Accounting Review*, Vol. 44, No. 2, pp. 68–82.

Habersam, M., Piber, M., and Skoog, M. (2013), "Knowledge balance sheets in Austrian universities: The implementation, use, and re-shaping of measurement and management practices", *Critical Perspectives on Accounting*, Vol. 24, No. 4, pp. 319–337.

Hinna, L. (2002), *Il bilancio sociale*, Il sole 24 ore, Milan, Italy.

Kreiner, K. and Mouritsen, J. (2005), "The analytical interview: Relevance beyond reflexivity", in Tengblad, S., Solli, R., and Czarniawska, B. (Eds), *The Art of Science*, Liber & Copenhagen Business School Press, Kristianstad, Denmark, SW, pp. 153–176.

Lillis, A. M. and Mundy, J. (2005), "Cross-sectional field studies in management accounting research:Closing the gaps between surveys and case studies", *Journal of Management Accounting Research*, Vol. 17, No. 1, pp. 119–141.

Lönnqvist, A., Kianto, A., and Sillanpää, V. (2009), "Using intellectual capital management for facilitating organizational change", *Journal of Intellectual Capital*, Vol. 10, No. 4, pp. 559–572.

Marr, B., Gray, D., and Neely, A. (2003), "Why do firms measure their intellectual capital?", *Journal of Intellectual Capital*, Vol. 4, No. 4, pp. 441–464.

Mårtensson, M. (2009), "Recounting counting and accounting: From political arithmetic to measuring intangibles and back", *Critical Perspectives on Accounting*, Vol. 20, No. 7, pp. 835–846.

Meritum Project (2002), *Guidelines for Managing and Reporting on Intangibles (Intellectual Capital Report)*, European Commission, Madrid.

Mouritsen, J., Bukh, P. N., Flagstad, K., Thorbjørnsen, S., Johansen, M. R., Kotnis, S., Larsen, H. T., Nielsen, C., Kjærgaard, I., Krag, L., Jeppesen, G., Haisler, J., and Stakemann, B. (2003), *Intellectual Capital Statements: The New Guideline*, Danish Ministry of Science, Technology and Innovation (DMSTI), Copenhagen.

Mouritsen, J., Larsen, H. T., and Bukh, P. N. D. (2001), "Intellectual capital and the 'capable firm': Narrating, visualising and numbering for managing knowledge", *Accounting Organizations and Society*, Vol. 26, Nos 7–8, pp. 735–762.

Oliveira, L., Lima Rodrigues, L., and Craig, R. (2010), "Intellectual capital reporting in sustainability reports", *Journal of Intellectual Capital*, Vol. 11, No. 4, pp. 575–594.

Patton, M. Q. (1990), *Qualitative Evaluation and Research Methods*, Sage, Newbury Park, CA.

Pedrini, M. (2007), "Human capital convergences in intellectual capital and sustainability reports", *Journal of Intellectual Capital*, Vol. 8, No. 2, pp. 346–366.

Qu, S. Q. and Dumay, J. (2011), "The qualitative research interview", *Qualitative Research in Accounting & Management*, Vol. 8, No. 3, pp. 238–264.

Roslender, R. and Fincham, R. (2001), "Thinking critically about intellectual capital accounting", *Accounting, Auditing & Accountability Journal*, Vol. 14, No. 4, pp. 383–398.

Roslender, R. and Fincham, R. (2004), "Intellectual capital accounting in the UK: A field study perspective", *Accounting, Auditing & Accountability Journal*, Vol. 17, No. 2, pp. 178–209.

Roslender, R. and Hart, S. J. (2003), "In search of strategic management accounting: Theoretical and field study perspectives", *Management Accounting Research*, Vol. 14, No. 3, pp. 255–279.

Schaper, S. (2016), "Contemplating the usefulness of intellectual capital reporting: Reasons behind the demise of IC disclosures in Denmark", *Journal of Intellectual Capital*, Vol. 17, No. 1, pp. 52–82.

Schaper, S., Nielsen, C., and Roslender, R. (2017), "Moving from irrelevant intellectual capital (IC) reporting to value-relevant IC disclosures: Key learning points from the Danish experience", *Journal of Intellectual Capital*, Vol. 18, No. 1, pp. 81–101.

Stewart, T. A. (1997), *Intellectual Capital*, Bantam Doubleday Dell Publishing Group, New York.

Sveiby, K. E. (1997), *The New Organisational Wealth: Managing and Measuring Knowledge-Based Assets*, Berrett-Koehler, San Francisco, CA.

Sveiby, K. E. (2010), "Methods for measuring intangible assets", available at: www.sveiby.com/portals/0/articles/IntangibleMethods.htm (accessed 22 August 2010).

Vaivio, J. (2004), "Mobilizing local knowledge with 'provocative' non-financial measures", *European Accounting Review*, Vol. 13, No. 1, pp. 39–71.

Yin, R. K. (2003), *Case Study Research: Design and Methods*, Sage Publications, Newbury Park, CA.

22

REVIVAL OF THE FITTEST?

Intellectual capital in Swedish companies

Gunnar Rimmel, Diogenis Baboukardos, and Kristina Jonäll

Introduction

In today's globalized and interconnected world, the negative impacts of past financial crises have resulted in a growing need for financial stability and sustainability development among investors and stakeholders around the world (International Integrated Reporting Council (IIRC), 2013). It is argued that there is a gap between current corporate reporting and investors' demands (KPMG, 2013a, 2013b). The traditional way of disclosing only historical financial information has started to lose its importance as investors become more concerned about the future outlook and how to manage the risks and opportunities that organizations will face in the future (IIRC, 2013; KMPG, 2013a). New forms of reporting required by stakeholders, including investors, incorporate narratives about non-financial voluntary information on the broad issue of sustainability (IIRC, 2015).

The integration of voluntary information on sustainability in annual reports can be traced back to the 1960s, when experiments with social reporting were conducted in the US and Europe (Global Reporting Initiative (GRI), 2010). It is 30 years since the World Commission on Environment and Development (1987) released what is known as the 'Brundtland report', where sustainable development was defined as "development that meets the needs of the present without compromising the ability of future generations to meet their own needs" (p. 41). Various frameworks such as Green Accounting, Social Reporting, Triple Bottom Line Reporting, and the GRI have since evolved. All of these frameworks are devoted to disclosing sustainability information (Higgins *et al.*, 2014).

However, many of today's sustainability reporting frameworks have been criticized as purely symbolic. What companies claim to do in their reports is in many cases not actually implemented in the organization (Melloni *et al.*, 2016). Usually, the reports do not mediate how economic, environmental, and social factors are interrelated and how these factors affect the organization (Gray and Milne, 2002; Moneva *et al.*, 2006; De Villiers *et al.*, 2014). In order to solve this problem several actors, such as standard setters, regulators, and investors, have developed the concept of integrated reporting. The most eminent organization in this area is the IIRC, which has developed the <IR> Framework (Higgins *et al.*, 2014).

The <IR> Framework is considered to be the next step in the evolution of globally harmonized corporate reporting (Monterio, 2015). The aim of the framework is to close the gap between current corporate reporting and investors' demands by focusing on conciseness, relevance, and future orientation. The goal is to create a more holistic reporting of how an organization creates value in the short, medium, and long term. It should be a clear and concise description of the organization's strategy, governance, performance, and forecasts. The key principle, "integrated thinking", should, according to the <IR> Framework, lead to a higher degree of integration (IIRC, 2013).

The cornerstones in the <IR> Framework are six capitals: financial, manufactured, intellectual, human, social and relationship, and natural. These capitals are considered as stocks of value that the organization uses and transforms through its activities. The description of the interconnection between the different capitals provides a picture and understanding of value creation over time in an organization (IIRC, 2013). The IIRC states in its discussion paper from 2011 that integrated reporting will give investors and other stakeholders a deeper explanation of organizational performance and value creation compared to traditional corporate reporting (IIRC, 2011).

Although the concept of integrated reporting is a relatively new phenomenon to corporate reporting, its practice has grown and research about its effects on corporate reporting has recently emerged (De Villiers *et al.*, 2014). South Africa is one of the early adopters of integrated reporting. Since 2011 all organizations listed on the Johannesburg Stock Exchange are required to adopt integrated reporting on a "comply or explain" approach (Baboukardos and Rimmel, 2016). The implementation of integrated reporting has resulted in an improvement in traditional annual reporting with an increased disclosure of non-financial information (Atkins and Maroun, 2015). Studies show evidence of an increase in disclosures about human, social, natural, and intellectual capital (IC) (Setia *et al.*, 2015). Baboukardos and Rimmel's (2016) study found that mandatory integrated reporting information is value relevant to the South African capital market.

As in the rest of the world, in Sweden the concept of integrated reporting is a new but hotly debated phenomenon. Supporters of integrated reporting within the corporate reporting sector in Sweden drive the debate about the <IR> Framework and its contribution to value creation and improved reporting behaviour among organizations. In international surveys, Sweden is mentioned as one of the top countries when it comes to organizations publishing integrated reports, but only some of these organizations refer to the <IR> Framework (KPMG, 2015). This is not surprising, as Swedish companies demonstrated their interest in extending traditional financial reporting to include voluntary disclosure of non-accounting information some 20 years ago.

In the 1990s, Swedish companies were among the forerunners of IC reporting. Skandia had been one of the leading companies globally within the IC field. Since the IIRC aims to create a global framework for integrated reporting and specifically focus on IC as one key capital, it is interesting to study the ways in which listed companies disclose IC information.

Although a large stream of research on IC has been generated since the late 1990s, whether there is a difference in IC disclosure between companies that apply integrated reporting and those that issue traditional annual reports has not yet been examined. Sweden has a long tradition in IC. In the 1990s, IC reporting was widespread among Swedish companies. Skandia with its Navigator had been one of the leading companies within IC. Although there has been no accepted IC reporting practice in Sweden, IC reporting is still a vital issue among Swedish companies.

Hence, in this chapter the amount of IC disclosure in the annual reports of Swedish companies is analysed. The level of Skandia's IC disclosure in the late 1990s is compared with the current level of reporting in the top 30 companies. How different is the level of IC disclosure in Swedish companies now (2017) in comparison with the leading company in the late 1990s? Has integrated reporting led to a revival of IC reporting?

Consequently, the aim of this chapter is threefold. First, to give an indication of the importance of IC information in current reporting practice. Second, to investigate the level of disclosure of IC in the leading IC company in the late 1990s. Third, to assess these findings to establish to what extent there is a difference in the current level of disclosure of IC in comparison to the leading practice in the late 1990s.

The evolution of integrated reporting and the role of IC

Since the late 1990s, the interaction between reporting systems and performance measurement, and company's control systems and managements' strategic positions, have been analysed and four different frameworks have been developed: the Balanced Scorecard, Triple Bottom Line, Sustainability Disclosures, and Integrated Reporting (De Villiers *et al.*, 2014). The first to emerge was the Balanced Scorecard, which mainly measures internal performance and integrates internal financial and non-financial measures. In contrast to the Balanced Scorecard's internal focus, the Triple Bottom Line, introduced by John Elkington in 1997, focuses on external reporting. The Triple Bottom Line brought in external disclosures of social and environmental information together with financial performance (Elkington, 1997). This was the starting point for the GRI with the objective "to make sustainability reporting standard practice by providing guidance and support to organizations" (Eccles and Serafeim, 2011, p. 75). In more recent times there has been a trend towards including social and environmental disclosures as Sustainability Disclosures instead of using the Triple Bottom Line (Eccles and Serafeim, 2011; De Villiers *et al.*, 2014).

South Africa developed the practice of integrated reporting long before the formation of the IIRC (Cheng *et al.*, 2014; De Villiers *et al.*, 2014; Baboukardos and Rimmel, 2016). In 1994, South Africa released its first King report (King I) on corporate governance, issued by the King committee on corporate governance chaired by professor Mervyn E. King. The report consisted of recommended standards of conduct and was applicable to listed companies, banks, and certain state-owned enterprises. King I focused on the interests of stakeholders, aiming to improve financial, social, ethical, and environmental practice (SAICA, 2010).

Several weaknesses within King I led to a second report, King II, which was released in 2002. King II aimed for further integration of sustainability reporting and the first indication of integrated reports emerged through the notion of an "integrated sustainability report". The King II report was applicable to companies listed on the Johannesburg Stock Exchange (JSE), banks, financial and insurance entities, and public sector enterprises governed by the Public Finance Act and the Municipal Finance Management Act. King II was applicable on a voluntary basis, giving the companies the option of a comply or explain basis, meaning that companies had to comply with the principles or explain possible deviations (Atkins and Maroun, 2014).

In September 2009, the King Code of Governance Principles for South Africa (King III) was published (IODSA, 2009). King III has become a milestone. By implementing the principles of King III into JSE listing, South Africa became the first country to implement mandatory application of integrated reporting (IRCSA, 2011; Atkins and Maroun, 2014; Eccles and Krzus, 2014; Baboukardos and Rimmel, 2016). The GRI is acknowledged by King III as the accepted international standard for reporting non-financial information (Solomon and Maroun, 2012).

The IIRC was founded in 2010 by the International Federation of Accountants, the GRI, and the Prince's Accounting for Sustainability Project (A4S), with the aim of creating a globally accepted integrated reporting framework (Rowbottom and Locke, 2016). The IIRC consists of a wide group of representatives, including investors, firms and organizations, academics, regulators, accounting practitioners, sustainability groups, and other stakeholders (IIRC, 2013).

After the formation of the IIRC, the discussion paper *Towards Integrated Reporting* was released in September 2011 and explained the reasoning behind the creation of the IIRC and the shift towards integrated reporting. It also contained the fundamental ideas for the <IR> Framework (IIRC, 2011). The IIRC (2011) describes integrated reporting as five guiding principles: (1) strategic focus; (2) connectivity of information; (3) future orientation; (4) responsiveness and stakeholder inclusiveness; (5) conciseness, reliability, and materiality. These principles should interconnect with six content elements: (1) organizational overview and business model; (2) operating context, including risks and opportunities; (3) strategic objectives and strategies to achieve those objectives; (4) governance and remuneration; (5) performance; and (6) future outlook.

The <IR> Framework was released in December 2013 (IIRC, 2013) and is based on the existence of six different capitals: (1) financial capital; (2) manufactured capital; (3) IC; (4) human capital; (5) social and relationship capital; and (6) natural capital.

Differing views on IC in the literature

As noted, the IIRC approach draws on bringing together different factors that materially affect the ability of an organization to create value over time (IIRC, 2013). By specifically including IC as one of the core capitals, the IIRC inevitably has brought the reporting of IC back onto the agenda, which had been mostly dormant since the development of a range of IC frameworks and models in the mid-1990s.

There are many generic definitions of IC, as many companies, authors, and researchers eagerly develop their own individual version. Therefore, it is not often clear what is incorporated in IC. Terms such as 'intangibles', 'intangible assets', 'intellectual knowledge', 'intangible property', 'intangible resources', and 'intellectual capital' often refer to the same things (Meritum, 2002; Rimmel, 2003; Dumay *et al.*, 2015). Several researchers conclude that IC is the difference between an organization's book value and its market value (Edvinsson and Malone, 1997; Sveiby, 1997; Mouritsen *et al.*, 2001). However, some researchers consider this gap between the book and market value only as goodwill (Holthausen and Watts, 2001), while other researchers believe that goodwill, as an intangible asset, is not sufficient to explain IC, as the term goodwill is too vague and broad (Choong, 2008).

Organizations cannot recognize IC in their balance sheets and its value remains hidden. Hence, it is a means of explaining the gap between market and book value (Mouritsen *et al.*, 2001). This is consistent with how many researchers defined IC in the mid-1990s. The most common way of defining IC is as something that possesses value to the company or will generate future benefits, but unlike traditional assets it is without physical substance and is a non-monetary asset (Choong, 2008).

Researchers often divide IC into two categories to further explain the term. These categories are internal (structural) capital and employee benefits (human) capital. One of the first authors to divide IC this way was Karl-Erik Sveiby in 1997. Since then numerous researchers have accepted, added, or renamed these categories but in general they remain the same (Edvinsson and Malone, 1997; Sveiby, 1997; Rimmel, 2003; Choong, 2008; Rimmel *et al.*, 2009). Internal structure refers to the value in, for example, organizational management, research, and development, legal structures, patents, technology, and software. The external structure emphasizes the relationships with customers and suppliers, branding, trademarks, and reputations. Employee benefits focus on the skills, level of education and training, and the experience of the organization's workforce (Rimmel, 2003; Petty and Cuganesan, 2005; Rimmel *et al.*, 2009). However, Beattie and Thomson (2007) illustrate that the concept of IC is rather broad as they identified a total of 128 different sub-categories across the IC literature.

Recently, IC as a research field is said to contain three stages of development (see Guthrie *et al.*, 2012; Dumay, 2013, 2014). The first stage is the raising of awareness and understanding of IC and the second, to establish IC as a research field, which led to a great number of different guidelines, for example, Meritum, the Danish Intellectual Capital Guidelines, or the Japanese IC reporting. Nevertheless, none of these frameworks was adopted widely and disappeared in practice in many cases after a few years (Rimmel *et al.*, 2012). According to Dumay (2014), the third stage of IC research focuses on critically examining the practice of IC reporting.

The latest 'trend' likely to become the next stage for IC research is the impact that the <IR> Framework may have on IC reporting. Since IC is one of the six capitals emphasized in the <IR> Framework, this opens up new research opportunities, as companies that apply integrated reporting have to consider IC and its reporting. Therefore, a fruitful avenue for research is examining and comparing existing IC models and frameworks with the <IR> Framework.

The development of IC reporting in Sweden and Skandia

Swedish companies have a long history of various methods for issuing IC disclosures in annual reports. In the mid-1980s, research and practical efforts were conducted to attempt to measure knowledge in what was known as the Swedish Community of Practice (Sveiby, 1997). In 1987, the Swedish Konrad group (1988), which included members from several Swedish knowledge companies as well as Karl-Erik Sveiby, developed a theory about measuring intangible assets. This group was elaborating on the invisible parts of a company that did not show up on the balance sheet. The Konrad Assets Theory became broadly recognized in Scandinavia during the late 1980s. It divided the intangible parts of a company into three different categories: individual competence, internal structure, and external structure. In the report, a set of 38 key indicators were defined ranging from common financial performance indicators to new aspects of capturing non-financial factors measuring intangible assets. The group worked on high-lighting non-financial indicators with the purpose of improving external communication and internal monitoring. They introduced 'The Intangible Assets Monitor', which was composed of indicators measuring external structure (customers and suppliers), internal structure (organi-zation), and people's competence. They also tried to encourage knowledge-based companies to improve their non-financial reporting. In 1994, 43 Swedish companies reported at least some of their intangible assets using the Konrad model. Among these knowledge-based companies was the insurance and financial management company Skandia, which moved on to become an international leader in the field (Sveiby, 1997).

A team from the Skandia Future Center, headed by Leif Edvinsson, pioneered a system for visualizing and developing intellectual, intangible, and organizational business assets, which resulted in the Skandia Navigator (see Figure 22.1), which attracted worldwide attention and has been continuously refined (Stewart, 1997).

The Skandia Navigator consists of five focus areas, which aim to help a company navigate into the future and by this means advance business renewal and development. In May 1994, Skandia launched the first IC annual report, using its Navigator model for reporting a set of knowledge measurements (Skandia, 1994).

Skandia (1994) promoted IC as a term, innovation, and complete system of measurement and management. Skandia (1994) claimed the Navigator to be a systematic application of common sense, arguing that IC reporting illustrates both the organization's value-generating

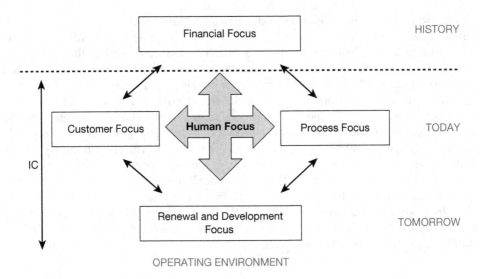

Figure 22.1 The Skandia Navigator (source: adapted from Edvinsson and Malone, 1997)

resources and its future earnings potential, which are not shown in the balance sheet. In its view, IC represents the margin between the book value and the market prices of the company's share (Skandia, 1994).

The Navigator model of Skandia was firmly established in the widespread Balance Scorecard approach launched in 1992 by Kaplan and Norton (1992). The Balanced Scorecard approach retains traditional financial measures, which reflect past organizational achievements, but adds three new measures of future performance considered necessary in this information age with its focus on customer relationships and long-term capabilities: customer, internal business process, and learning and growth. With these perspectives providing the framework for the Balanced Scorecard, organizations measure how they create value for customers, how they can enhance internal competencies, and how they must invest in people, systems, and procedures to improve future performance.

Even if other companies developed their own specialized concept of IC, the idea basically remains the same (Stewart, 1997). The right balance of different elements will generate the most IC, which results in the best way to utilize assets. Building on almost the same basic definitions, Skandia identified and categorized areas of the company where IC can be found. In general, the same categories of IC are adopted as applied in the Skandia Navigator's value scheme (see Figure 22.2).

Following Skandia's market value scheme, IC can be defined and classified as IC assets, that is, knowledge, experience and technical infrastructure, customer relations, routines, and professional competencies that create future earnings potential. Market value includes both financial capital and IC. The latter consists of human and structural capital. Human capital is the capabilities of the company's employees to provide necessary solutions to customers, to innovate, and to renew. Structural capital is the infrastructure of human capital, including the organizational capabilities to meet market requirements. Infrastructure includes the quality and reach of information technology systems, company images, databases, organizational concepts, and documentation. Customer capital is the relationship with people with whom a company does business. Although this usually means clients and customers, it can also mean suppliers. It has also been referred to as relationship capital. The interaction between human,

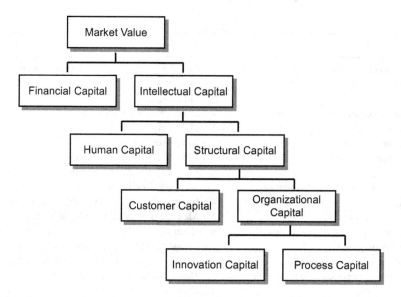

Figure 22.2   The Skandia Market Value Scheme (adapted from Edvinsson and Malone, 1997)

structural, and customer capital helps to determine the value of a company's IC. According to Skandia (1994), IC can be described as an assessment of a company's future prospects.

Skandia was the first company in the world to establish an IC function and to appoint a director of IC. In 1994, Leif Edvinsson became IC Manager at Skandia. He was awarded 'brain of the year' in 1998 for his work at Skandia (Rimmel, 2003). However, IC reporting lost its momentum after the 1990s and disappeared at Skandia at the turn of the millennium, even before Skandia had been acquired by Old Mutual.

Even so, in the 1990s, Swedish companies were among the forerunners of IC reporting. And IC is still a focus for Swedish companies. With the introduction of integrated reporting, and hence a renewed interest in IC, it is topical to investigate how listed companies disclose IC information. A direct comparison might seem problematic at first sight, as Skandia's value scheme shows that human capital is included as one category within IC whereas the <IR> Framework separates human and intellectual capitals. Yet, being aware of these different categorizations should not hamper a comparative study as, for example, disclosure scoreboards can be adjusted for these differences. Swedish listed companies have no mandatory requirement to produce integrated reports or to follow the recommendations from the IIRC. However, companies are starting to adapt and adopt the concept of integrated reporting.

Studying the level of IC disclosures in annual reports

In the empirical part of this chapter, a disclosure index is used to quantify the amount of information regarding IC included in annual reports. There is an extensive amount of accounting literature relating to the use of disclosure scoreboards to measure the amount of information that is contained in corporate reports. We follow previous disclosure scoreboard studies, replicating the disclosure scoreboard originally developed by Bukh *et al.* (2005) in relation to Danish IPO prospectuses and subsequently applied in a number of disclosure studies analysing Japanese companies (Rimmel *et al.*, 2009; Nielsen *et al.*, 2015), Italian companies (Cordazzo, 2007), and Singaporean companies (Singh and Van der Zahn, 2007). Our disclosure scoreboard consists of 78 items, grouped into 6 different categories as illustrated in Table 22.1.

Table 22.1 The disclosure index

Employees (27 items)		IT (5 items)	
1	Staff breakdown by age	1	Description & reason for investments in IT
2	Staff breakdown by seniority	2	IT systems
3	Staff breakdown by gender	3	Software assets
4	Staff breakdown by nationality	4	Description of IT facilities
5	Staff breakdown by department	5	IT expenses
6	Staff breakdown by job function		**Processes (8 items)**
7	Staff breakdown by level of education	1	Efforts related to the working environment,
8	Rate of staff turnover	2	Information and communication within the company
9	Comments on changes in number of employees	3	Working from home
		4	Internal sharing of knowledge and information
10	Staff health and safety	5	Measure of internal or external failures
11	Education and training expenses/ number of employees	6	External sharing of knowledge and information
		7	Fringe benefits and company social programs
12	Staff interview	8	Environmental approvals and statements/policies
13	Statements of policy on competence development		**Research & Development (9 items)**
		1	Statements of policy, strategy and/or objectives of R&D activities
14	Description of competence development program and activities	2	R&D expenses
15	Education and training expenses	3	R&D expenses/sales
16	Absence	4	R&D invested in basic research
17	Employee expenses/number of employees	5	R&D invested in product design/development
18	Recruitment policies	6	Future prospects regarding R&D
19	HRM department, division or function	7	Details of company patents
20	Job rotation opportunities	8	Number of patents and licenses etc,
21	Career opportunities	9	Patents pending
22	Remuneration and incentive systems		**Strategic statements (15 items)**
23	Pensions	1	Description of new production technology
24	Insurance policies	2	Statements of corporate quality performance
25	Statements of dependence on key personnel	3	Strategic alliances
26	Revenues/employee	4	Objectives and reason for strategic alliances
27	Value added/employee	5	Comments on the effects of the strategic alliances
	Customers (14 items)	6	Description of the network of suppliers and distributors
1	Number of customers	7	Statements of image and brand
2	Sales breakdown by customer	8	Corporate culture statements
3	Annual sales pr, segment or product	9	Best Practise
4	Average customer size	10	Organisational structure
5	Dependence on key customers	11	Utilisation of energy, raw materials and other input goods
6	Description of customer involvement		
7	Description of customer relations	9	Best Practise
8	Education/training of customers	10	Organisational structure
9	Customers/employees	11	Utilisation of energy, raw materials and other input goods
10	Value added pr, customer or segment		
11	Market share (%)	12	Investment in the environment
12	Relative market share	13	Description of community involvement
13	Market share, breakdown by country/ segment/product	14	Information on corporate social responsibility and objective
14	Repurchase	15	Description of employee contracts/contractual issues

This particular research design was selected as the disclosure scoreboard approach represents a proxy for the quality of disclosure of IC disclosures in corporate reports. In order to increase the reliability of the results and the objectivity of the study, the present study had clear instructions in the coding process. The coding was verified through separate coding by multiple researchers. The content of each annual report was compared to the items on the disclosure scoreboard and coded as 1 or 0, depending upon whether the annual report contained or did not contain the item disclosure. The analysis of the disclosure scoreboard for this study is additive and unweighted following the path of the studies conducted by Cooke (1989), Meek *et al.* (1995), Adrem (1999), Rimmel (2003), and Rimmel *et al.* (2009). Hence, either a company discloses an item in its annual report or not, which shows that the number of items measures the amount of disclosure. No ranking list for the importance of different items is applied neither is the number of words about an item used. While some argue that the amount of disclosure might not be an exact indicator of disclosure quality (Beattie *et al.*, 2004; Rimmel and Baboukardos, 2016), this study is concerned with extent of disclosure, so the disclosure scoreboard method fulfils these requirements satisfactorily.

In selecting a sample, we limited it to include only companies listed on the Nasdaq Stockholm OMXS30, at 1 February 2016. The OMXS30 includes the 30 most traded shares on the Swedish stock market (see Table 22.2). The OMXS30 list includes companies from various business sectors. Since these companies' stocks are the most frequently traded on the Swedish stock market they tend to be under greater pressure from stakeholders to be held responsible and accountable for their actions. Also, companies on the OMXS30 are those most likely to have interpreted the concept of integrated reporting and produced a report accordingly. The OMXS30 comprises 30 different stocks but only 29 companies, because 1 company, Atlas Copco AB, has both its A and B shares listed. Thus, this company is counted as one, resulting in a research sample of 29 companies (see Figure 22.3).

Of the 29 companies, six state that they have integrated reports as their 2015 annual report. These companies are AstraZeneca, Atlas Copco, Boliden, SKF, Swedbank, and Tele2. Of the 23 companies that do not mention integrated reporting, eight have combined reports, which means that they publish their annual report and sustainability report in the same document, but without indicating that the information is integrated. Traditional annual reports, with no mention of a separate sustainability report, have been adopted by 15 companies.

Since this study wants to compare the level of Skandia's IC disclosure in the late 1990s with the current level of IC disclosure in Sweden's top 30 companies, Skandia's 1996 annual report has been used as a basis for comparison. The study by Rimmel (2003) illustrates that the 1996 annual report had the highest level of IC disclosure, as well as being the last one in which Skandia presented its Navigator and mentioned IC explicitly. Skandia is no longer listed on

Table 22.2 30 Most traded shares on the Swedish stock market

Basic materials	Assa Abloy; Boliden; SSAB
Communication services	Tele2; TeliaSonera
Consumer cyclical	H&M
Consumer defensive	SCA; Swedish Match
Energy	Lundin Petroleum
Financial services	Investor; Kinnevik; Nordea SEB; Sv. Handelsbanken; Swedbank
Healthcare	AstraZeneca; Getinge
Industrials	ABB; Alfa Laval Atlas; Copco Sandvik; Securitas Skanska; SKF; Volvo
Technology	Electrolux Ericsson; Fingerprint Nokia

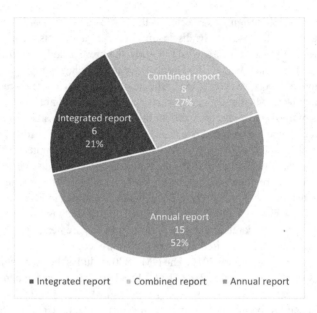

Figure 22.3   Report type at OMXS30 for reporting year 2015

the Swedish stock exchange. In 2005, Skandia was sold to Old Mutual and in 2011 was bought back by Skandia Liv.

Empirical findings regarding IC in Swedish annual reports

Figure 22.4 shows each company's total number of IC disclosures, aggregating the scores from the six categories Employees, Customers, IT, Processes, Research & Development, and Strategic Statements. The maximum number of scores attainable for the total scoreboard

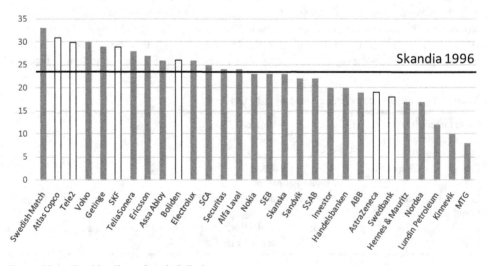

Figure 22.4   Total intellectual capital disclosure

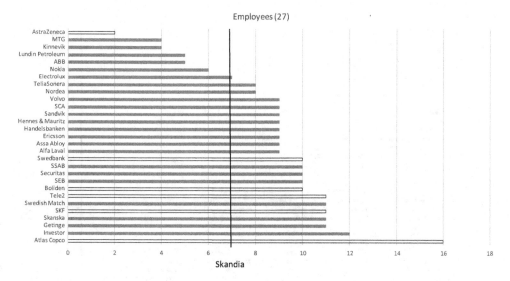

Figure 22.5   Disclosure category: employees

amounts to 78 items. Skandia's annual report for the year 1996 achieved a total score of 24 items, which corresponds to 30.8 per cent of the maximum score.

Adding up the total scores of all 29 OMXS30 companies, from Swedish Match with the highest score of 33 items (42.3 per cent) to the lowest score of 8 items (10.3 per cent) by MTG, would give a mean value of 22.79. This implies that benchmarking the average of all OMXS30 companies from 2015 with Skandia from 1996, Skandia would even after 20 years still be on top. The mean value for all six integrated reporting companies (Atlas Copco, Tele2, SKF, Boliden, AstraZeneca, Swedbank) is 25.50. The mean value for the traditional annual report companies is 21.26. This would imply that comparing these three groups, the group of integrated reporting companies on average disclose more information on IC in comparison to Skandia, while traditional companies tend to disclose slightly less.

The category Employees about employee information is the largest category in the disclosure scoreboard with a total of 27 items. In their 1996 annual report Skandia disclosed seven items about their employees scoring seven items, indicating 25.9 per cent of the maximum Employees score (see Figure 22.5).

The mean value for all 29 OMXS30 companies is 8.75, which represents 32.4 per cent of the maximum score. Atlas Copco had the highest score of 16 items (59.3 per cent) with the lowest score of 2 items (7.4 per cent) for AstraZeneca, which is interesting as both companies are applying integrated reporting. Dividing all companies into different groups, the mean value of the integrated reporting companies is 10.00 and the mean value for the traditional annual reporting companies is 8.43. Comparing these values shows that Skandia disclosed on average less employee related information than the OMXS30 companies. In direct comparison, only ABB, Lundin Petroleum, Kinnevik, MTG, and AstraZeneca are disclosing less. Of the 27 items only 1 item 19, HRM department, division or function had been disclosed by all companies. Very few companies provided information regarding staff breakdown, whereas the second most mentioned item was related to pensions. None of the analysed reports of either OMXS30 or Skandia made available information on value added/employee.

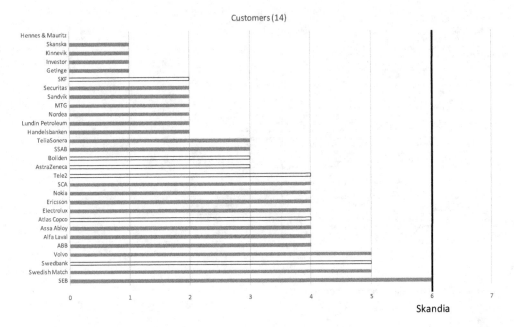

Figure 22.6 Disclosure category: customers

The category Customers consists of 14 items to evaluate voluntary disclosure information about customers, including items about market share. As Figure 22.6 illustrates Skandia's 1996 annual report contained six items, which represents 42.9 per cent of the maximum score in this category.

The mean value of the total scores of all 29 OMXS30 companies is 3.00, with SEB having the highest score of six items (42.9 per cent) and Hennes & Mauritz the lowest score of 0 items. Only SEB had the same score as Skandia. Comparing the mean value all OMXS30 companies 3.00, with the mean value for all six integrated reporting companies 3.50, and the mean value for the traditional annual report companies 2.87, shows that Skandia leads this category. However, the integrated reporting companies disclose on average more information than the companies that report in traditional annual reports. None of the 14 items in the category Customers had been disclosed by every company. The most frequent item disclosed was Repurchase followed by Average customer size. However, none of the companies, not even Skandia, had disclosed the item Number of customers. Worth mentioning is that Hennes & Mauritz as one of the largest apparel companies in the world but did not make any voluntary disclosure regarding customers.

The category IT consist of five items and is the smallest category in the disclosure scoreboard. In its 1996 annual report Skandia disclosed all five information items, which is 100 per cent of the maximum IT score (see Figure 22.7).

Figure 22.7 illustrates that Skandia is the only company that provided all voluntary information in this category. On the contrary, 12 companies did not make any voluntary disclosure available. It can be seen that not even telecom companies like Tele2, TeliaSonera, or Nokia provided more information. The most equally frequently disclosed items were regarding Software and IT expenses. The mean value of the total scores of all 29 OMXS30 companies is 1.00. The mean value for all six integrated reporting companies is 1.50 and the mean value

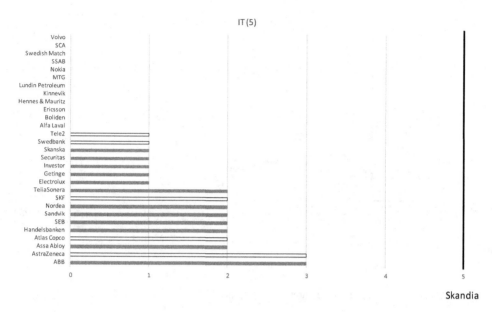

Figure 22.7 Disclosure category: IT

for the traditional annual report companies is 0.87. As already mentioned, only 15 out of 29 OMXS30 companies provide voluntary information in the IT category.

The category Processes evaluates the amount of information that a company voluntarily discloses about processes in their company with the help of eight items. In Figure 22.8, it is evident that in Skandia's 1996 annual report five items were disclosed or 62.5 per cent of the maximum score. Only Swedish Match scored as high as Skandia. However, it can be seen that three companies (ABB, SEB, SCA) do not provide voluntary information in this category.

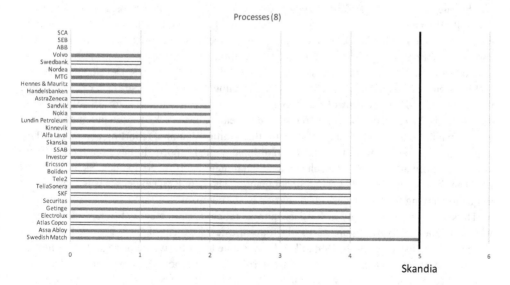

Figure 22.8 Disclosure category: processes

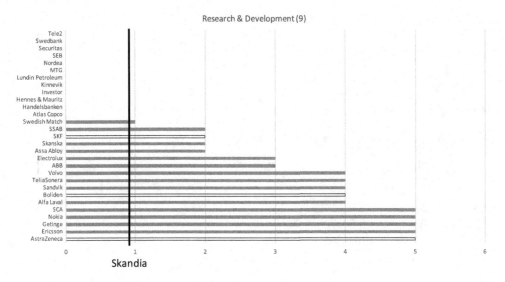

Figure 22.9   Disclosure category: research & development

The mean value for all 29 OMXS30 companies is 8.75, which is 32.4 per cent of the maximum score. The mean value for the integrated reporting companies is 2.83. In this group Atlas Copco, SKF, and Tele2 scored four items each but not the same items. The mean value for the traditional annual reporting companies is 2.26. Comparing the mean values, it is clear that Skandia and the companies that apply integrated reporting disclosed on average more process related information than the OMXS30 companies. In direct comparison, only ABB, Lundin Petroleum, Kinnevik, MTG, and AstraZeneca disclose less. The equally most frequently disclosed items are Information and communication within the company and Environmental approvals and statements/policies by 15 companies.

The category Research & Development measures a total sum of nine items. Figure 22.9 shows that in its 1996 annual report Skandia scored one item. Twelve companies did not provide additional information about R&D. Although the same number of companies, these are not the same companies not providing IT information. However, three of the companies that apply integrated reporting are among those companies not disclosing additional Research & Development items.

Five companies (Alfa Laval, SCA, Nokia, Getinge, Ericsson, AstraZeneca) score five items, which is 55.6 per cent of the maximum score. The mean value for all 29 OMXS30 companies is 2.07 and can be compared with the mean value of 1.83 for the integrated reporting companies and the mean value of 2.13 for the traditional annual reporting companies. This implies that the companies that produce traditional annual reports do have on average more voluntary information on R&D disclosed than integrated reporting companies. Skandia scored less than the average of all 29 OMXS30 companies. The item R&D expenses was scored most frequently among the 9 items as was disclosed by 12 companies.

The second largest category in the disclosure scoreboard is the category Strategic Statements, which includes 15 items. Figure 22.10 illustrates the development of the aggregated scores for these items in this category. In 1996, Skandia was able to score five items regarding voluntary information about strategic statements in the 1996 annual report. However, this is less than half in direct comparison with Volvo and Swedish Match, which scored the most with 11 items each (73.3 per cent).

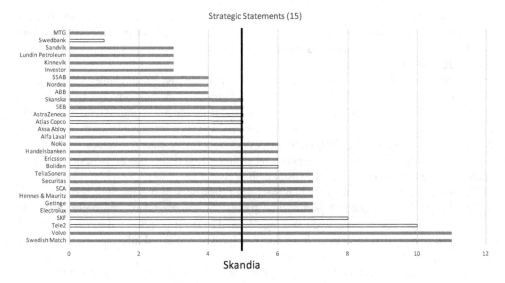

Figure 22.10   Disclosure category: strategic statements

Although Volvo and Swedish Match provided most voluntary disclosure on strategic statements, the mean value for the traditional annual reporting companies is 5.52. In comparison, this score is less than the mean value for the integrated reporting companies, which is 5.83 or the mean value of 5.58 for all 29 OMXS30. The companies that disclose least in this category are MTG and Swedbank with one score each (6.7 per cent). Worth mentioning is that the item Information on corporate social responsibility and objective and investments in the environment had been disclosed by 27 companies each.

Conclusions

This study revealed that the level of Skandia's IC disclosure in the late 1990s is on average above the level of IC items contained in current corporate reports by OMXS30 companies. One could argue that the overall level of disclosure in this study might be low in relation to the total number of disclosures in the disclosure scoreboard. However, the level of disclosure is somewhat higher than in previous studies applying the same disclosure scoreboard (e.g. Cordazzo, 2007; Singh and Van der Zahn, 2007; Rimmel *et al.*, 2009; Nielsen *et al.*, 2015). Nonetheless, the finding that Skandia is on average above the disclosure level for IC reporting is interesting from two perspectives. First, from a historical perspective it is interesting that Skandia in the mid-1990s had developed a high level of voluntary disclosure reporting for IC that still holds after 20 years of possible advancement on the understanding of reporting IC. Second, despite a formal IC reporting framework there is a high level of IC disclosure prominent in today's corporate annual reports. Just by looking at Figure 22.4, which illustrates the total IC disclosures, the findings show that more than one-third of all companies do provide more IC disclosure than Skandia.

Another interesting finding in this study is that IC disclosures in integrated reporting companies do differ from companies that do not report according to integrated reporting and rely on traditional annual reports. Reading all the statements from the IIRC's website, one could perceive that integrated reporting would result immediately in great differences in reporting and therefore also higher IC disclosures compared to traditional reporting. Yet at first glance, the figures in this study suggest otherwise. However, looking at the mean values tells a different story, as it becomes apparent that the integrated reporting companies do provide a higher level of IC disclosures.

Still, one must take into account that this study only examined 30 companies from which 6 are using integrated reporting principles. This small sample of integrated reporting companies can have an effect on the results of IC disclosures and it should not be understood that there is a significant increase in the amount of IC disclosures. However, integrated reporting is a fairly new concept in Sweden. The <IR> Framework does not provide clear guidance on how to use and implement this new reporting concept, as an integrated report should be more than just combining the annual report with the sustainability report.

Nevertheless, the results indicate that there are differences in IC reporting between companies that applied integrated reporting and traditional annual report companies, which is consistent with the aim of integrated reporting declared by the IIRC (2015). It can be concluded that integrated reporting companies have a higher level of additional information, which give a deeper explanation of the IC disclosures.

As a final point, it may be too early to draw the conclusion that integrated reporting has led to a revival of IC reporting. This chapter only investigated how much and what type of IC information is disclosed in corporate reports. Still, this study illustrates the fact that IC reporting is common among every company in this study. Regardless of whether companies apply integrated reporting principles or rely on traditional annual reports companies, IC is reported. It seems that integrated reporting can contribute to a more formalized and accepted IC reporting framework. Maybe this might be a new stage in IC research.

References

Adrem, A. H. (1999), *Essays on Disclosure Practices in Sweden: Causes and Effects*, Lund University Press, Sweden.

Atkins, J. F. and Maroun, W. (2014), *South African Institutional Investors' Perceptions of Integrated Reporting*, ACCA Research Report.

Atkins, J. F. and Maroun, W. (2015), "Integrated reporting in South Africa in 2012", *Meditari Accountancy Research*, Vol. 23, No. 2, pp. 197–221.

Baboukardos, D. and Rimmel, G. (2016), "Relevance of accounting information under an integrated reporting approach: A research note", *Journal of Accounting and Public Policy*, Vol. 35, No. 4, pp. 437–452.

Beattie, V. and Thomson, S. (2007), "Lifting the lid on the use of content analysis to investigate intellectual capital disclosures in corporate annual reports", *Accounting Forum*, Vol. 31, No. 2, pp. 29–163.

Beattie, V., McInnes, B., and Fearnley, S. (2004), "A methodology for analysing and evaluating narratives in annual reports: A comprehensive descriptive profile and metrics for disclosure quality attributes", *Accounting Forum*, Vol. 28, No. 3, pp. 205–236.

Bukh, P. N., Nielsen, C., Mouritsen, J., and Gormsen, P. (2005), "Disclosure of information on intellectual capital indicators in Danish IPO prospectuses", *Accounting, Auditing & Accountability Journal*, Vol. 18, No. 6, pp. 713–732.

Cheng, M., Green, W., Conradie, P., Konishi, N., and Romi, A. (2014), "The International Integrated Reporting Framework: Key issues and future research opportunities", *Journal of International Financial Management & Accounting*, Vol. 25, No. 1, pp. 90–119.

Choong, K. K. (2008),"Intellectual capital: Definitions, categorization and reporting models", *Journal of Intellectual Capital*, Vol. 9, No. 4, pp. 609–638.

Cooke, T. E. (1989), "Voluntary corporate disclosure by Swedish companies", *Journal of International Financial Management & Accounting*, Vol. 1, No. 2, pp. 171–195.

Cordazzo, M. (2007), "Intangibles and Italian IPO prospectuses: A disclosure analysis", *Journal of Intellectual Capital*, Vol. 8, No. 2, pp. 288–305.

De Villiers, C., Rinaldi, L., and Unerman, J. (2014), "Integrated reporting: Insights, gaps and an agenda for future research", *Accounting, Auditing & Accountability Journal*, Vol. 27, No. 7, pp. 1042–1067.

Dumay, J. (2013), "The third stage of IC: Towards a new IC future and beyond", *Journal of Intellectual Capital*, Vol. 14, No. 1, pp. 5–9.

Dumay, J. (2014), "15 years of the *Journal of Intellectual Capital* and counting: A manifesto for transformational IC research", *Journal of Intellectual Capital*, Vol. 15, No. 1, pp. 2–37.

Dumay, J., Guthrie, J., and Puntilla, P. (2015), "IC and the public sector: A structured literature review", *Journal of Intellectual Capital*, Vol. 16, No. 2, pp. 267–284.

Eccles, R. G. and Krzus, M. P. (2014), *The Integrated Reporting Movement*, John Wiley & Sons, Inc., New Jersey.

Eccles, R. G. and Serafeim, G. (2011), *Accelerating the Adoption of Integrated Reporting*, available at: http://papers.ssrn.com/sol3/papers.cfm?abstract_id=1910965 (accessed 27 September 2016).

Edvinsson, L. and Malone, M. S. (1997), *Intellectual Capital: Realizing Your Company's True Value by Finding its Hidden Brainpower*, HarperBusiness, New York.

Elkington, J. (1997), *Cannibals with Forks: The Triple Bottom Line of 21st Century Business*, Capstone Publishing, Oxford, UK.

Gray, R. and Milne, M. J. (2002), "Sustainability reporting: Who's kidding whom?" *Chartered Accountants Journal of New Zealand*, Vol. 81, No. 6, pp. 66–70.

GRI (2010), *Carrots and Sticks: Promoting Transparency and Sustainability: An update on Trends in Voluntary and Mandatory Approaches to Sustainability Reporting*, available at: www.globalreporting.org (accessed 12 September 2016).

Guthrie, J., Ricceri, F., and Dumay, J. (2012), "Reflections and projections: A decade of intellectual capital accounting research", *The British Accounting Review*, Vol. 44, No. 2, pp. 68–92.

Higgins, C., Stubbs, W., and Love, T. (2014), "Walking the talk(s): Organisational narratives of integrated reporting", *Accounting, Auditing & Accountability Journal*, Vol. 27, No. 7, pp. 1090–1119.

Holthausen, R. W. and Watts, R. (2001), "The relevance of the value-relevance literature for financial accounting standard setting", *Journal of Accounting and Economics*, Vol. 31, Nos 1–3, pp. 3–75.

Institute of Directors in Southern Africa (IODSA) (2009), *The King Code of Governance for South Africa (2009) and King Report on Governance for South Africa (2009) (King-III)*, Lexis Nexus South Africa, Johannesburg.

Integrated Reporting Committee of South Africa (IRCSA) (2011), *Framework for Integrated Reporting and the Integrated Report*, available at: www.sustainabilitysa.org (accessed 12 September 2016).

International Integrated Reporting Council (IIRC) (2011), *Towards Integrated Reporting: Communicating Value in the 21st Century*, available at: www.integratedreporting.org/wp- content/uploads/2011/09/IR-Discussion-Paper-2011_spreads.pdf (accessed 12 September 2016).

International Integrated Reporting Council (IIRC) (2013), *The International <IR> Framework*, available at: www.integratedreporting.org/wp-content/uploads/2015/03/13–12–08-THE- INTERNATIONAL-IR-FRAMEWORK-2–1.pdf (accessed 12 September 2016).

International Integrated Reporting Council (IIRC) (2015), *Creating Value, Integrated Reporting <IR> and Investor Benefits*, available at: www.integratedreporting.org/wpcontent/uploads/2016/01/1323_CreatingValue_No3_8a-1.pdf (accessed 12 September 2016).

Kaplan, R. S. and Norton, D. P. (1992), "The balanced scorecard: Measures that drive performance", *Harvard Business Review*, Vol. 70, No. 1, pp. 71–79.

KONRAD (1988), D*en Nya Årsredovisningen: Att redovisa, analysera och värdera kunskapsföretag (The New Accounting: To Account, Analyse and Valuate Knowledge Companies)*, Affärsvärldens Förlag, Stockholm, Sweden.

KPMG (2013a), *The KPMG Survey of Corporate Responsibility Reporting 2013*, available at: www.kpmg.com/Global/en/IssuesAndInsights/ArticlesPublications/corp orate-responsibility/Documents/corporate-responsibility-reporting-survey-2013- exec-summary.pdf. (accessed 12 September 2016).

KPMG (2013b), *Integrated Reporting: Addressing the Reporting Gap*, available at: https://home.kpmg.com/content/dam/kpmg/pdf/2013/04/addressing-the- reporting-gap.pdf (accessed 12 September 2016).

KPMG (2015), *The KPMG Survey of Corporate Responsibility Reporting 2015*, available at: www.kpmg.com/CN/en/IssuesAndInsights/ArticlesPublications/Documents/kpmg-survey-of-corporate-responsibility-reporting-2015-O-201511.pdf (accessed 12 September 2016).

Meek, G. K., Roberts, C. B., and Gray, S. J. (1995), "Factors influencing voluntary annual report disclosures by U.S., U.K. and Continental European multinational corporations", *Journal of International Business Studies*, Vol. 26, No. 3, pp. 555–574.

Melloni, G., Stacchezzini, R., and Lai, A. (2016), "The tone of business model disclosure: An impression management analysis of the integrated reports", *Journal of Management & Governance*, Vol. 20, No. 2, pp. 295–320.

Meritum (2002), "Guidelines for managing and reporting on intangibles", *Meritum*, European Commission, Madrid.

Moneva, J. M., Archel, P., and Correa, C. (2006), "GRI and the camouflaging of corporate unsustainability", *Accounting Forum*, Vol. 30, No. 2, pp. 121–137.

Monterio, B. J. (2015), "Integrated reporting: A chat with the experts", *Strategic Finance*, Vol. 96, No. 8, pp. 35–39.

Mouritsen, J., Larsen, H. T., and Bukh, P. N. (2001), "Intellectual capital and the 'capable firm': Narrating, visualising and numbering for managing knowledge", *Accounting, Organizations and Society*, Vol. 26, No. 7, pp. 735–762.

Nielsen, C., Rimmel, G., and Yosano, T. (2015), "Outperforming markets: IC and the long-term performance of Japanese IPOs", *Accounting Forum*, Vol. 39, No. 2, pp. 83–96.

Petty, R. and Cuganesan, S. (2005), "Voluntary disclosure of intellectual capital by Hong Kong companies: Examining size, industry and growth effects over time", *Australian Accounting Review*, Vol. 36, pp. 32–48.

Rimmel, G. (2003), *Human Resource Disclosures: A Comparative Study of Annual Reporting Practice about Information, Providers and Users in Two Corporations*, BAS Publishing House, Sweden.

Rimmel, G., Dergård, J., and Jonäll, K. (2012), "Human resource disclosures in Danish Intellectual Capital Statements: Enhancing comparability of business models a decade ago?" *Journal of Human Resource Costing & Accounting*, Vol. 16, No. 2, pp. 112–141.

Rimmel, G., Nielsen, C., and Yosano, T. (2009), "Intellectual capital disclosures in Japanese IPO prospectuses", *Journal of Human Resource Costing & Accounting*, Vol. 13, No. 4, pp. 316–337.

Rowbottom, N. and Locke, J. (2016), "The emergence of <IR>", *Accounting and Business Research*, Vol. 46, No. 1, pp. 83–115.

Setia, N., Abhayawansa, S., Joshi, M., and Huynh, A. (2015), "Integrated reporting in South Africa: Some initial evidence", *Sustainability Accounting, Management and Policy Journal*, Vol. 6, No. 3, pp. 397–424.

Singh, I., and Van der Zahn, J. L. W. M. (2007), "Does intellectual capital disclosure reduce an IPOs cost of capital? The case of underpricing", *Journal of Intellectual Capital*, Vol. 8, No. 3, pp. 494–516.

Skandia (1994), *Visualising Intellectual Capital at Skandia: Supplement to Skandia's 1994 Annual Report*, Skandia Insurance Company Ltd, Stockholm.

Solomon, J. F. and Maroun, W. (2012), *Integrated Reporting: The Influence of King III on Social, Ethical and Environmental Reporting*, ACCA Research Report, ACCA, London.

South African Institute of Chartered Accountants (SAICA) (2010), *Competency Framework Detailed Guidance for Academic Programmes*, South African Institute of Chartered Accountants, Johannesburg, South Africa.

Stewart, T. A. (1997), *Intellectual Capital: The New Wealth of Organizations*, Nicholas Beardly Publishing Limited, London, UK.

Sveiby, K.-E. (1997), *The New Organizational Wealth: Managing and Measuring Knowledge-based Assets*, Barrett-Kohler Publishers, San Francisco, CA.

World Commission on Environment and Development, (1987), *Our Common Future*, available: www.un-documents.net/our-common-future.pdf (accessed 12 September 2016).

23

EMERGING INTEGRATED REPORTING PRACTICES IN THE UNITED STATES

Mary Adams

Introduction

The integrated reporting movement is a good example of the third stage of development of intellectual capital (IC) thinking: from raising awareness to theory building and frameworks, and now to IC in practice. While it is still in its infancy across the world and even less common in the United States (US), there are already some compelling examples of integrated reporting practice in the US. This chapter endeavours to examine the key characteristics of ten publicly-available US integrated reports to get a sense of this emerging practice.

The US context

Many of the issuers of integrated reports (including the majority of those studied here) are public companies that are already subject to an extensive and well-established reporting environment. Any examination of integrated reporting in the US has to take into account this existing regulatory context for reporting of financial and business results by public companies and/or those with large numbers of shareholders. The requirement most relevant to this discussion is the submission of an annual 10-K report that must include a structured analysis of the company's operations, risks, and financial performance. The structure is mandated to include four specific sections accompanied by 15 specific schedules.

For many companies, the 10-K functions as an annual report to shareholders, either on its own or with a short overview letter. Many companies also issue a separate, stand-alone annual report that uses graphics and thematic summaries that help the company tell its story to shareholders and, sometimes, to other stakeholders as well. These reports are not constrained in their content in the same way as a 10-K.

Integrated reporting

Integrated reporting is primarily associated with the International Integrated Reporting Council (IIRC). In December 2013, the IIRC issued the <IR> framework.[1] The <IR> framework consists of seven guiding principles: 1) strategic focus and future orientation; 2) connectivity of information; 3) stakeholder relationships; 4) materiality; 5) conciseness; 6) reliability and completeness; and 7) consistency and comparability. The <IR> framework also requires that integrated reports include eight content elements: 1) organizational overview and external environment; 2) governance; 3) business model; 4) risks and opportunities; 5) strategy and resource allocation; 6) performance; 7) outlook; and 8) basis of presentation.

Underlying the <IR> framework are three core concepts that are not required but are recommended as tools to achieve the principles. The first concept is value creation, how a company creates value for stakeholders and shareholders over the short, medium, and long term. The second is the need to explain the links between value creation for shareholders, stakeholders, and society at large. The third is 'the capitals' including financial, manufactured, intellectual, human, social and relationship, and natural capital. The <IR> framework's use of the phrase "intellectual capital" differs from common practice in the IC community. The common definitions of IC usually include human, relationship, and structural or organizational capital. Under this definition, the IC field studies three of the six IIRC capitals. The <IR> framework, however, uses the term IC to mean just structural capital.

Most, but far from all, of the Principles and Content Elements mirror the requirements and market practices for a 10-K. So for the purposes of this analysis, they are not a particularly fruitful avenue for understanding new or emerging practices and were not addressed in this analysis. However, the three core concepts do represent departures from mainstream practices and are the basis of this analysis.

Analytical approach

Since integrated reporting is emerging in the US market, I was curious about some of the fundamental starting decisions that an issuing company might ask itself such as: What do we call this report? Will it replace our annual report? Is this something we want to share with our investors? Should it be a document, a website, or both? What standards will we use to guide us?

Based on the analysis of the current <IR> framework, a company may also consider questions about the content of its report: How will we communicate our value creation model? Which capitals will we examine and how? Should we present an integrated scorecard to support our presentation? With these questions as a guideline, I identified 20 separate indicators that were used to examine each of the reports.

In choosing these indicators, I had three goals. The first was to answer basic questions about the positioning of the report. The second was to highlight different approaches to value creation, capitals, and measurement. The third was to use an analytical approach that was as objective and as repeatable as possible. Each of the 20 indicators is discussed in detail below. An Appendix summarizes the reports.

Companies selected

To be included on the list, a company had to either call its report an "integrated report" in either the title or the description of the report or issue a report that included metrics or discussion of all of the capitals. Using these criteria, ten companies were included in this analysis (see Table 23.1). These companies include a variety of businesses with different stories to tell; they all took different approaches to telling their story in an integrated way.

Table 23.1 Companies analyzed

Company	Industry
ArcelorMittal US	Steel
AEP	Energy
Clorox	Consumer
Coca-Cola Company	Food
Entergy	Energy
GE	Industrial
JLL	Real estate
Pfizer	Pharmaceuticals
Smithfield Foods	Food
Southwest	Airlines

Corporate status

Integrated reporting is not just for public companies. Internationally, there are also not-for-profit and other types of entities that are issuing integrated reports. This sample is no different. While most of the companies are public, one is private (Smithfield Foods) and the other is the US operation of a large multinational (ArcelorMittal). The remaining eight are public companies.

Report year

This study was completed in July 2016. By this point, most of the companies had already issued their reports for 2015. Two, however, had not yet released their 2015 reports. In one case, JLL had yet to release its integrated or sustainability reports. Smithfield is issuing its report in stages on line over the course of several months with some significant sections yet to come at the time of the study. So it made sense to use the full 2014 report for this analysis.

Report functional title

All the reports had essentially two titles. The first was a functional title that indicated the nature of the report. There was significant diversity in this category. Four of the companies used the word "integrated" in their title. Entergy[2] and ArcelorMittal[3] called theirs an "Integrated Report". Clorox used the name "Integrated Annual Report".[4] GE called theirs an "Integrated Summary Report".[5] There is no identifiable pattern here and it is safe to say that this pattern will continue into the future.

Southwest[6] used the name "One Report™" which references the reporting approach suggested in the book by the same name authored by Robert Eccles and Michael Krzus. AEP[7] issued an "Accountability Report", and Jones Lang Lasalle (JLL)[8, 9] and Smithfield used "Sustainability" as their functional title.[10]

Report theme

The second element of the title was a thematic one, which is how the company set the stage for the message of the report. There is no pattern in these results either, but they were included because they are a simple way of summarizing the company's overall intent for the report. For example, GE's theme was "Digital Industrial" and used its Integrated Summary Report to emphasize this core strategy for the company. Southwest's theme was "Without a heart, it's just a machine". Clorox used "Good Growth" and AEP, "The Power of Diversity". Finally, JLL used "Our cities. Our future".

Report purpose

An interesting choice in the integrated approach is whether a company decides to issue a report that is in addition to its existing reports or to replace these. In this sample, six of the companies offered a separate report that was supplemental to their annual reports.

Two of the public companies did present the report as their annual report. Clorox titled theirs as an "Integrated Annual Report" while Entergy used the title "Integrated Report". Southwest offered its Annual Report in the form of a 10-K with a three-page introductory letter. But its "One Report™" is available right next to the download for the Annual Report.

Both of the companies with non-public status, Smithfield and ArcelorMittal, used the report as their sole reporting platform. In all the other cases, the integrated report studied here was one of a number of reports issued by the company, so was classified as a "supplement".

In all cases but one, this analysis focuses on a single report from each company. The exception is JLL, which published a 22-page cover letter to its 10-K that included a 7-page discussion called the "Technology Imperative" focusing primarily on its IC. As IC is a particularly challenging capital for many companies to address, this presentation is included in this analysis for learning purposes.

Location of report on website

A further distinction between the reports is the location where they are offered on the corporate website. Here, it is encouraging that most companies provided a link to their report on their investor relations web pages. In the case of Clorox and Entergy, the report was the primary link. But five other companies provided a supplemental link to the integrated report alongside the annual report on their investor relations website. The exceptions included the two companies that do not have US investor relations (ArcelorMittal and Smithfield). The only public company that did not offer its report through investor relations was JLL.

Report media

In all but one case, the report was available as a downloadable document. The exception was AEP, which has a web-only presentation. Half of the companies went beyond the document and also built a stand-alone, interactive website that makes it easy to digest the content dynamically.

Number of report pages

The size of a document was an indicator of the extent of the information supplied. The range in size of the reports studied was significant. On the low end were JLL – 27, Clorox – 28, and Coca-Cola – 36.[11] On the high end were Pfizer – 137,[12] ArcelorMittal – 150, and Smithfield – 202. The average length of all the reports was 89 pages.

Identification of stakeholders

Every company studied used the word "stakeholder" or "stakeholders" at least once in the narrative of their reports. Three (Pfizer, AEP, and ArcelorMittal) used graphics or lists that

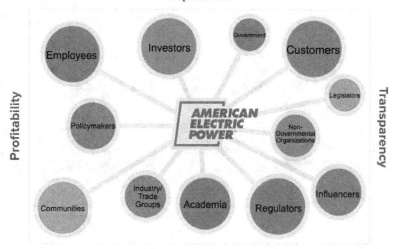

STAKEHOLDER ENGAGEMENT

Figure 23.1 AEP stakeholder graphic

specifically identified their non-shareholder stakeholder groups. These all displayed the stakeholders as nodes in an abstract network. The graphic developed by AEP to highlight its stakeholders can be found in Figure 23.1.

Citation of standards

Companies generally identified standards used as guidance in the preparation of the report. Others mentioned multiple standards (GAAP, GHG, SASB, UN Global Goals) with the most frequent standard being the GRI, cited by seven companies. Only one company (Coca-Cola) was silent on this issue. Three of the companies actually cited the <IR> framework in their reports. Two of these are the companies with international homes (Arcelor Mittal and Smithfield). The other is Entergy.

Assurance provider

There was an even split between companies on assurance. Six were silent on the subject. Three mentioned assurance for at least part of the report (such as financials). One (AEP) stated that assurance was provided by the company's internal auditors.

Value creation

Every company explained in its external reporting about how it "creates value" as part of its business model and operations, even if they do not specifically use the "value creation" phrase. In this sample, four of the companies relied on narrative only to explain their value creation.

It can be difficult to just use narrative to explain how all the elements of a business are combined in a value creation system. Although the <IR> framework does not specifically

369

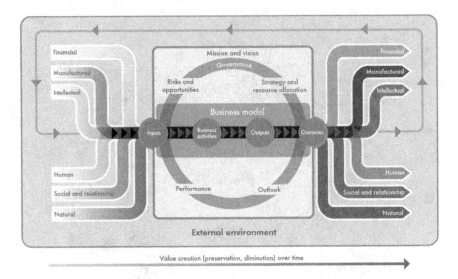

Figure 23.2　IIRC value creation graphic

recommend this, a visual graphic can be the simplest and most powerful way of explaining the workings of this complex system. In fact, the <IR> framework offers its own graphic, seen in Figure 23.2, to explain the overall concept.

Six of the companies also included a value creation graphic. Almost all the reports studied here included multiple graphics. So some judgment was required as to whether one of the graphics illustrated the overall value creation system of the company. There is no pattern to the approaches taken by the companies except that most included a lot of circles and connecting lines and arrows. Few specifically identified a flow or creation of value. Rather, they function as a visual inventory of key strategic goals and resources. To be classified as providing graphics in the count above, there had to be at least one graphic that tried to provide a big-picture illustration of the company's strategy and/or how the company creates value.

AEP's graphic is in a section of the report website called "Business Model Evolution". In it, the company identified four elements that it calls its "Foundation for the Future". Above a graphical representation of this foundation, AEP uses the graphic in Figure 23.3 to illustrate its strategic goals and opportunities. It explained this graphic as follows:

> We have significant opportunities to continue enhancing customer and shareholder value as we make strategic investments to deploy new technologies, generate reliable, cleaner energy and deliver solutions to meet customers' needs.

The graphic illustrates three spheres where it will build this value including: infrastructure development, sustainable electricity, and customer experience. These investment areas touched on many of the six capitals with human capital being notably absent.

ArcelorMittal's graphic, seen in Figure 23.4, endeavours to connect strategy and sustainability. An outside circle of words identifying resources is circulating around a number of strategic financial and business goals such as "optimize assets", "gain market share", and "achieve positive cash flow". The arrow simply flows around each of the two circles.

Figure 23.3   AEP value creation graphic

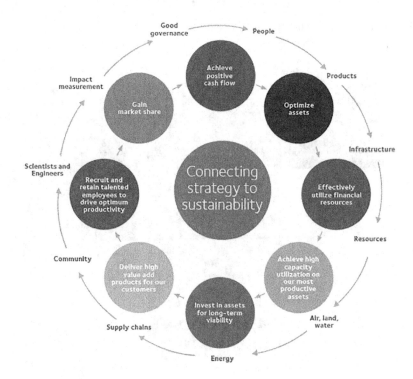

Figure 23.4   ArcelorMittal value creation graphic

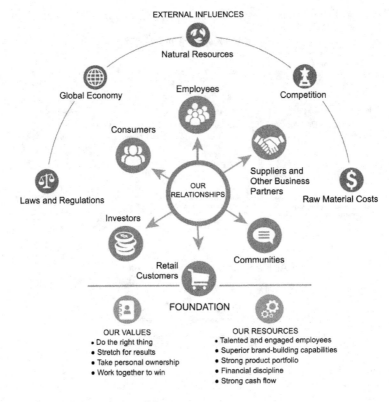

Figure 23.5 Clorex value creation graphic

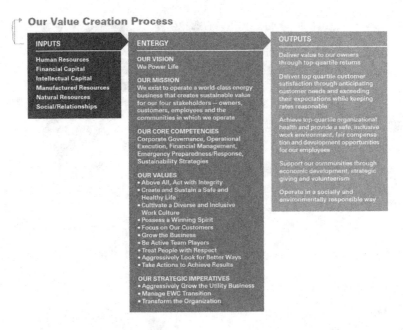

Figure 23.6 Entergy value creation graphic

Clorox organizes its graphic, seen in Figure 23.5, with relationships in the centre, values and resources as a foundation, and external influences as a dome over it all.

Entergy is one of the few in the sample that uses the IIRC inputs and outputs vocabulary. In fact, the graphic in Figure 23.6 is set up to show six kinds of capital inputs to the company's vision, mission, core competencies, values, and strategic imperatives. Out of this flow outputs that include big-picture financial, customer, workplace, community, and environmental outcomes such as "operate in a socially and environmentally sustainable way".

GE uses a simple graphic that shows how it creates value from horizontal capabilities and vertical expertise.

It expands on this concept with a full-page graphic that is too large to include here. The graphic has three levels: the first highlights what it terms the "value of scale and diversity", including leveraging scale, spreading ideas, and creating solutions. The second level illustrates the GE Store, which can be seen in the excerpt in Figure 23.7 with resource types surrounded by the key business units. The graphic is explained as follows:

> The GE Store is the transfer of technology, talent, expertise and connections through GE's massive, diverse network of businesses and markets. GE's businesses give and take from the Store, and in 2015, the Company made great progress.

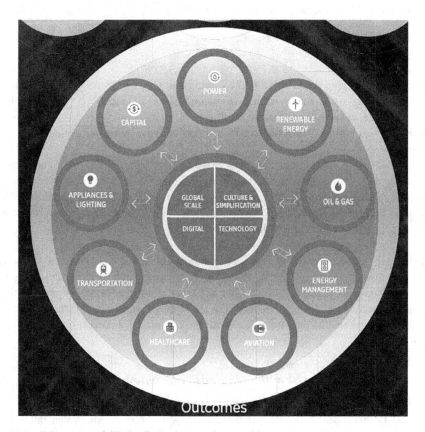

Figure 23.7   GE excerpt of GE detailed value creation graphic

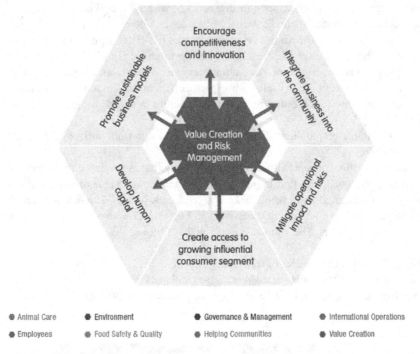

Figure 23.8 Smithfield value creation graphic

The third level highlights outcomes from the value creation (faster growth, expanding margins, developing leaders). Arrows show each business unit giving and receiving value from the core resources of scale, culture, digital and technology.

Smithfield uses Figure 23.8 at the end of its report with the following explanation:

> This table illustrates some of the ways in which our sustainability programs create value for a wide range of stakeholders while simultaneously improving Smithfield's own financial performance. We use the term "value creation" broadly and think of it in ways that go beyond just our own company's value. Our sustainability programs create substantial value for Smithfield Foods.

The core goals of value creation and risk management are at the centre of six strategic activities. Below the strategic circle, there are eight areas such as communities, governance, and animal care, each identified with a different coloured dot. In the pages following this graphic, there is a section for each of the six strategic activities. For each, there are a handful of strategic results that are tagged with the coloured dot corresponding to the eight result areas.

Use of the "capitals" vocabulary

In addition to value creation, one of the key ideas behind integrated reporting is the multi-capital model. This model highlights six types of value creation resources that fall into three categories. First is tangible resources, including financial and manufactured capitals. Second is

Strategic focus	IIRC's Six Capitals					
	Financial	Manufactured	Intellectual	Social and relationship	Human	Natural
Optimize assets	●	●	●		●	●
Effectively utilize financial resources	●	●				
Achieve high capacity utilization on our most productive assets	●	●			●	●
Invest in assets for long-term viability	●	●			●	
Deliver high value add products for our customers	●			●		
Recruit and retain talented employees to drive optimum productivity	●		●	●	●	
Gain market share	●			●		
Achieve positive cash flow	●					

Figure 23.9   ArcelorMittal capitals graphic

intangible resources, including human, intellectual, and relationship capitals. Third is environmental resources, including natural capital.

The underlying challenge of integrated reporting is to explain in a holistic way how a company uses these resources to support today's value creation commitments in ways that also ensure the continued strength of the resources in the future. As discussed in the previous section, companies are taking many different paths to explain their value creation systems. In US practice, this is not being accomplished by explicitly using the IIRC capitals vocabulary. This was confirmed by a word search in each of the reports for the use of the word "capitals".

Only two of the companies in the sample used the term. And these two each used it in a single graphic. The first is the Entergy value creation graphic in Figure 23.6 already discussed above, which shows the six capitals as inputs. The only other company in the sample that explicitly talked about its capitals is ArcelorMittal, which uses the table shown in Figure 23.9.

The table in this Figure identifies which capitals are important to eight key areas of strategic focus such as optimizing assets and delivering high value-add products for its customers.

Metrics for the capitals

Although the companies made scant use of the IIRC vocabulary, they all apply the concept, uniting discussions of tangible, intangible, and natural resources in a single report. To explore how the companies did this, I classified the types of resources included in the presentation according to the <IR> framework definition of each of capitals. The research method was a simple checklist that was applied to record whether the capital element was only addressed in the narrative or whether there were single- or multi-year metrics provided.

All the companies mentioned aspects of each of the capitals in the narrative. However, many also included specific metrics in tables and graphics. One report included just a single year of metrics across the board: JLL. AEP provided single-year for all but natural capital. The approach to reporting on each of the capitals is now examined.

Financial capital

The IIRC defines financial capital as "The pool of funds that is: available to an organization for use in the production of goods or the provision of services; or obtained through financing, such as debt, equity or grants; or generated through operations or investments".

Measures of financial capital are readily available through financial statements. All the reports included some financial metrics, with JLL and AEP limiting their focus to a single year. The type of metrics included revenues, margins, and profits in varying degrees of detail. Some included cash levels that would speak to financial assets as longer-term capital. A couple also referenced external debt ratings and stock trends.

Manufactured capital

The IIRC defines manufactured capital as:

> [m]anufactured physical objects (as distinct from natural physical objects) that are available to an organization for use in the production of goods or the provision of services, including: buildings; equipment; and infrastructure (such as roads, ports, bridges, and waste and water treatment plants). Manufactured capital is often created by other organizations, but includes assets manufactured by the reporting organization for sale or when they are retained for its own use.

Like financial capital, manufactured capital is tangible, easy to count, and often has accounting information associated with it, so it is easy to report on. Besides AEP and JLL (which used single-year metrics throughout), the only other company that reported single-year metrics for this category was Clorox. The rest of the sample reported multi-year metrics.

The kind of metrics generally included in the reports were plant numbers and capacity, as well as demographic and performance data on specific kinds of equipment and infrastructure.

Intellectual capital (IC)

The IIRC defines IC as "organizational, knowledge-based intangibles, including: intellectual property, such as patents, copyrights, software, rights and licenses; and 'organizational capital' such as tacit knowledge, systems, procedures and protocols".

IC is a new reporting category for most companies so it is the one with the least specific reporting. Half of the companies in the analysis addressed IC with narrative only. One of these five was GE. IC is actually at the heart of GE's new "digital industrial" strategy. Key to this strategy is the "GE Store", which is a name for the collective knowledge of the many diverse GE businesses. Despite its clear importance, the company did not attempt to measure the Store in any way. Several others addressed IC by discussing efficiency efforts, including Coca-Cola which featured a number of management accomplishments in generating efficiencies and streamlining its operations (although the effect of these changes on the other capitals was not assessed).

Three companies did include single-year metrics for the current year related to IC. AEP included data on customer calls, transactions processed, service levels, technology investment, and innovation efforts. Pfizer's IC data consisted mostly of new patents issued inside and outside the US. As explained earlier, I also gave JLL credit for the powerful review of its technology with single-year metrics that is actually in its Annual Report (separate from the Global Sustainability Report reviewed here) because it is a great example of an examination of IC.

The two companies providing multi-year IC data included Entergy and Smithfield. In Entergy's case, the data consisted of service level reporting and capability ratings. Smithfield included extensive discussions and metrics of food safety and quality (which speak to the company's processes and controls). There is also a detailed presentation of governance and management of a number of key business functions such as animal care, plant management, and quality control.

Human capital

The IIRC defines human capital as:

> People's competencies, capabilities and experience, and their motivations to inno-vate, including their: alignment with and support for an organization's governance framework, risk management approach, and ethical values; ability to understand, develop and implement an organization's strategy; and loyalties and motivations for improving processes, goods and services, including their ability to lead, manage and collaborate.

Compared with IC, there was much more use of human capital metrics. Coca-Cola mentioned the number of its "system associates" and used narrative to describe them. AEP, JLL, and Clorox all included data for a single year. The rest (six companies) included multi-year data. Common metrics included head count, diversity by gender and ethnicity, injuries, training hours/investment, engagement metrics, savings/retirement participation, and management makeup.

The Pfizer report also included 24 separate videos that feature individual employees talk-ing about what he or she is "working on". And the report section about the GE board included extensive metrics about the experience, diversity, tenure, and background of the company's board members.

Social and relationship capital

The IIRC defines social and relationship capital as:

> The institutions and the relationships within and between communities, groups of stakeholders and other networks, and the ability to share information to enhance individual and collective well-being. Social and relationship capital includes: shared norms, and common values and behaviors; key stakeholder relationships, and the trust and willingness to engage that an organization has developed and strives to build and protect with external stakeholders; and intangibles associated with the brand and reputation that an organization has developed; and an organization's social license to operate.

Every company is dependent on many kinds of relationships. Many elements of relationship capital are familiar in traditional annual reports, including customers, suppliers, and brands. Interestingly, Clorox joins Coca-Cola in the category of dealing with its relationships through the report narrative. GE joins JLL and AEP in providing a single year of data. The final five in the study all provide multi-year data.

Common metrics used included counts of customers (sometimes by industry segments) and suppliers. The consumer companies like Clorox and Coca-Cola all highlighted their brands. Pfizer had extensive narrative and metrics about patient groups served and helped. Smithfield included data about the production processes of its contract growers. Coca-Cola enumerated its bottling partners and consumer outlets. Entergy and AEP both addressed their relationships with regulators and their communities. JLL described socio-economic effects of its buildings. Many of the companies also included information on social outreach programs in their communities.

Natural capital

The IIRC defines natural capital as: "All renewable and nonrenewable environmental resources and processes that provide goods or services that support the past, current or future prosperity of an organization. It includes: air, water, land, minerals and forests; and biodiversity and eco-system health".

Reporting on natural capital is one of the hallmarks of integrated as opposed to traditional reporting. The breakdown included some variation from the other capitals. Coca-Cola was consistent in using narrative only. However, AEP used multi-year metrics in this category after using just single-year metrics in the other categories. In fact, it presented 15 years of data on carbon dioxide emissions and 7 years of data on water usage. GE swung the other way, including one page of selected singe-year metrics. Clorox and JLL were the others using single-year metrics. The most extensive information about natural capital can be found in the Smithfield report.

Multi-capital scorecard

To qualify in the prior sections as reporting on a specific capital, the information just had to be included somewhere in the report. However, seven of the companies also took the extra step of creating one or more scorecards to pull together data on multiple capitals. The most comprehensive scorecard was by Southwest. It provided two pages with five years of data at the beginning of each of three sections: performance, people, and planet. AEP had a stand-alone Performance Summary webpage with a graphical display of a single year of data tied together as a value creation story. Pfizer included a multi-page summary of selected key performance indicators with up to four years of data for a variety of capital elements. Although GE did not provide a single scorecard for the entire company (and is listed as a "No" here), its report did provide quite detailed snapshots/scorecards of each of its nine core lines of business.

Conclusion

If reference to the <IR> framework is a requirement for being considered an integrated report, then practice in the US is limited to just two US-based companies in our sample (JLL and EAP). But if a broader definition of integrated reporting is applied, as providing information about the full set of capitals and how they relate to value creation, then the full list of ten companies here qualify.

These examples show that the practice of integrated reporting is still in an emergent form. Each of these companies is taking steps in its own way to tell its stories to shareholders and stakeholders in a more holistic, integrated way. These examples are advanced enough to serve as inspiration for other companies to begin their own integrated journeys. And the companies issuing them bear watching as they continue to adapt and improve their reports in future years.

Other possible metrics

As explained in the introduction to this analysis, I endeavoured to find objective factors that could be replicated by other analysts with similar results. As the practice of integrated reporting grows, I believe that it will be important and helpful to develop databases of reporting practices. A more advanced analysis beyond the 20 elements analysed here could examine the specific names used for individual capital elements, how many metrics are used for each element, how many years of data are supplied, and how many years the company has been doing this kind of report. It would also be helpful to find more objective ways of analysing and/or classifying companies' approaches to communication of their value creation models.

Notes

1 http://integratedreporting.org/resource/international-ir-framework/.
2 http://integratedreport.entergy.com/.
3 www.usa.arcelormittal.com/sustainability/2015-integrated-report.
4 http://annualreport.thecloroxcompany.com/.
5 www.ge.com/ar2015/10k/.
6 www.southwestonereport.com/2015.
7 www.aepsustainability.com/.
8 www.jll.com/sustainability/sustainability-report.
9 www.jll.com/InvestorPDFs/JLL-2015-Annual-Report.pdf.
10 www.smithfieldfoods.com/integrated-report/2014/introduction.
11 www.coca-colacompany.com/2015-year-in-review.
12 www.pfizer.com/files/investors/financial_reports/annual_reports/2015/index.htm.

24

CAPITAL REPORTING IN SWEDEN

Insights about inclusiveness and integrativeness

Peter Beusch and Axel Nilsson

Introduction

Non-financial reporting has increased considerably among stock exchange listed companies over the past 30 years (Eccles and Krzus, 2010). However, until the latter stage of the last century, most social and environmental reporting was found in annual reports. Since then, companies have started to produce separate sustainability or corporate social responsibility (CSR) reports (De Villiers *et al.*, 2014). Over time, there has been significant growth in these stand-alone reports (Eccles and Krzus, 2010; Hahn and Kühnen, 2013) as information in the annual report is tailored mostly for shareholders and creditors only (Eccles and Krzus, 2010; De Villiers *et al.*, 2014).

Regulation in this area is changing with the EU recently adopting a directive on non-financial reporting that will force all large entities to provide information on non-financial matters (European Commission, 2016). In Sweden, all large organizations will be affected by the law that came into effect on 1 December 2016. The companies affected will have to either report on non-financial matters or explain why reporting is not relevant (EY, 2015).

During the last decade, the amount of information in separate reports has increased and there is a risk of information overload, which makes understanding the important linkages between the different parts of the reports more difficult for readers (De Villiers *et al.*, 2014). It has therefore been argued that for these reports to be meaningful, they must be better integrated (Eccles and Krzus, 2010). Thus, there have been various attempts and initiatives to combine both financial and non-financial performance management and its reporting (De Villiers *et al.*, 2014).

The Integrated Reporting <IR> framework of the International Integrated Reporting Council (IIRC) is one such framework. In 2011, it issued a discussion paper regarding its proposal for a new way of reporting and at the end of 2013 a first version of it was published (IIRC, 2016). The IIRC's vision is to use IR to bring capital allocation and corporate behaviour together with the overall goal of financial stability and sustainable development. Its mission is to bring IR and thinking into mainstream business practice as the norm in both the private and public sectors (IIRC, 2016). Originally, the intention was to replace annual reports with integrated reports (IIRC, 2011; De Villiers *et al.*, 2014), but this idea has been dropped (Flower, 2015).

The IIRC states that it wants to reduce silo reporting, reduce duplication, and improve the quality of information to capital providers with the intention of bringing about a more efficient and productive capital allocation (IIRC, 2016). Other potential benefits of IR include a longer-term focus than financial reporting, increased understanding of the importance of sustainability information and better integration within organizations (Roth, 2014).

The IIRC's <IR> framework has six capitals that are used to shape the discussion of 'value creation'. These are: financial capital, manufactured capital, intellectual capital, human capital, social and relationship capital, and natural capital (IIRC, 2013). Companies issuing integrated reports do not have to adopt these particular capitals or explicitly report on them. Their main purpose is to serve in the value creation discussion as well as acting as guidelines to help companies think about all forms of capital they use or affect (IIRC, 2016).

The IIRC is neither a standard setter nor a regulator in Sweden, which means that adopting IR is voluntary (PwC, 2013a). Integrated reporters with more inclusive capital models might well face lower cost of capital or reduced information asymmetry (EY, 2015). Alternatively, even though IR is relatively new, companies might choose to adopt it for the purposes of legitimacy or institutionalization (De Villiers *et al.*, 2014; Van Bommel, 2014).

IR and intellectual capital (IC) have many similarities as they share common objectives, that is, to use corporate reporting to communicate value creation (Mouritsen *et al.*, 2001; IIRC, 2013). Dumay *et al.* (2016, p. 168) therefore believe that one can draw "on how IC research has developed over time, to investigate how IR research is developing now and in the future". Although IR research has increased strongly in number of publications since the release of the first official <IR> guideline in December 2013, Dumay *et al.* (2016) argue that most of this research belongs to the first stage of development and thus focuses "on raising awareness of a specific research field's potential" (Petty and Guthrie, 2000, p. 155). Dumay *et al.* (2016, p. 178) recommend moving beyond this first stage of mostly normative research to test the IIRC's rhetoric by gathering "robust evidence in support of its further development" since empirical findings so far are "fragmented and inconclusive about <IR>'s benefits".

This chapter is an attempt to follow this call as it provides an account of disclosure of capital overall and IC more specifically in annual reports of large Swedish companies and in relation to the IIRC's six capitals concept. In doing so, the chapter explores and discusses the real achievements of a possible shift from a "financial capital market system" to an "inclusive capital market system" (Coulson *et al.*, 2015, p. 290) that recognizes the interconnection between, for example, finance, knowledge and other resources, the systems of governance that enable this, and extends accountability beyond financial transactions (Mio, 2016, p. ix). The research question is: what do large Swedish companies disclose in terms of the IIRC's six capitals concepts, how has this developed over time, and what patterns have emerged?

Literature review

The purpose of the following literature review is to outline the key elements of the IIRC's <IR> framework connected to the six capitals concept and illustrate the claimed benefits of this way of communicating with stakeholders. Critique of doing so is provided as well as the findings of the few studies that have investigated the six capital concepts.

The <IR> framework and the six capitals

The major vision of the IIRC (2013) is a world where *integrated thinking* is part of contemporary business practice in both the public and private sectors. Integrated thinking is defined "as the active consideration by an organization of the relationships between its various operating and functional units and the capitals that the organization uses or affects" (IIRC, 2013, p. 2). Integrated thinking is supposed to consider all factors that affect the ability to create value and the connections between them. The IIRC (2013) claims that these factors include, among others, inputs in terms of the six capitals, a company's business model and how it fits with the environment, activities, performance, output, and outcomes.

The <IR> framework states that the primary recipients of integrated reports are creditors and lenders, or "providers of financial capital" (IIRC, 2013, p. 4), but that an integrated report benefits all stakeholders with an interest in the value creation capabilities of an organization. The IIRC takes this definition to include a range of stakeholders such as employees, customers, suppliers, policymakers, regulators, and local communities (IIRC, 2013). The <IR> framework is further described as a principles-based framework by the IIRC (2013), aimed at achieving a balance between flexibility, prescription, and comparability. Consistent with this aim, the framework does not prescribe any specific performance indicators or measurement methods. It is up to the supplier of information to decide what is material to include, how to measure it, and how to disclose it. However, the IIRC (2013) believes that a combination of quantitative and qualitative information is required to best report on the value creation capabilities of an organization. The purpose of an integrated report is not to monetize the value of an organization at a certain point in time, the value of what is created, or the effects on the capitals (IIRC, 2013).

Chapter 2 in the <IR> framework describes the fundamental concepts that form the basis for the requirements and guidance found in the rest of the framework. It explains that value is not created by an organization alone. It is influenced by the external environment, created through relationships with stakeholders and dependent on various resources. It is the resources and relationships that are used or affected by an organization that are referred to by the IIRC (2013) as the six capitals. The capitals can also be considered as 'stocks of value' that an organization uses, creates, or affects when undertaking business. The overall value of the capitals is not fixed over time, in other words the IIRC does not see the capitals as a zero-sum game. The capitals are affected through business activities and there are activities that cause decreases to some capitals and increases to others (IIRC, 2013).

The claimed benefits of IR

IR is supposed to contribute to reporting improvements as increased integrated thinking and the integration of various sources of data will help companies adopt a more long-term view of the impact of their decisions on various capitals (Roth, 2014; Tweedie, 2014). However, the full value of IR can only be reached when it succeeds in articulating the links that exist between financial and non-financial performance and outcomes (Eccles and Serafeim, 2014). Short-term investors are the group with the least incentive to consider the effects of their companies' actions on other stakeholders, thus IR is least likely to be of interest to them (Tweedie, 2014). To really promote long-term investment, more regulatory incentives are needed as IR might be used to legitimize short-term actions as being part of a longer-term agenda (Tweedie, 2014).

Roth (2014) goes down the same regulatory path as Tweedie (2014) to put corporate sustainability information in front of analysts and highlights its importance for financial decisions. He argues that many analysts simply ignore separate corporate sustainability reports. This is supported by Ferns et al. (2008) who evaluated the ability of sustainability reports to reach and persuade their audience. They found that few people actually referred to the sustainability reports. Low credibility is stated as a possible reason for this outcome. The authors also claim that companies might have lost sight of the positive aspects of sustainability disclosures. Instead of using them as a way to build trust, they are issued as responses to the corporate pressures of not being worse than rivals.

It is claimed that switching from separate reporting to IR helps advance senior managers' understanding of sustainability performance because it is no longer the domain of a separate CSR department (Roth, 2014). Trying to figure out how to integrate a range of information is also beneficial for the overall organization (Eccles and Serafeim, 2014) and brings communication benefits because a better alignment between reported information and investor needs is expected. For that to happen, however, investors will require a better understanding of how financial and non-financial performance is managed by organizations, which separate reporting fails to provide (Eccles and Serafeim, 2014).

Therefore IR has the potential to become a catalyst in developing a common language for reporting and for improving risk management since organizations have to assess the connections between the capitals (Roth, 2014). When reaching its full potential, the IIRC's six capitals concept could aid a shift from 'financial capital markets' to 'inclusive capital markets' (Coulson *et al.*, 2015, p. 290), where the word *inclusive* should be taken to signal that resources other than those covered by traditional accounting are instrumental to long-term financial performance. Coulson *et al.* (2015) believe that encouraging companies to consider all forms of capitals they use, and the interconnectedness between them, helps to advocate for a shift from short-term to long-term thinking and from silo reporting to IR. Even if companies are not required to adopt the same definitions of capital as those presented in the <IR> framework, the IIRC hopes that the definitions will help companies think about what capitals they use (IIRC, 2013).

Critique of IIRC's <IR> approach

Monetization and more quantitative measures could be useful tools, alongside qualitative information, to gain a better understanding of the capitals (Coulson *et al.*, 2015). However, being too focused on assigning the capitals a monetary value means that there is a risk of cementing the economic understanding of capitals, possibly contradicting a broader understanding of what value is and the purpose of integrated thinking (Coulson *et al.*, 2015).

Brown and Dillard (2014) believe that the IIRC is mistaken in pushing for a 'business case' understanding of sustainability, an approach that has been common in the past to appeal to powerful business people. By highlighting a win–win situation, this approach has been somewhat successful in achieving incremental changes, but has failed to achieve more fundamental changes to established assumptions, processes, and techniques. One such example is the dominance of the capital market perspective in accounting standard setting. Brown and Dillard (2014) believe that fundamental changes need to be accomplished if we are to transit to a more sustainable society.

Both Cheng *et al.* (2014) and Flower (2015) make similar criticisms of the IIRC's framework as they see a focus on investors and creditors at the expense of other stakeholders. Flower (2015), in addition, stresses that while the IIRC recognizes both private costs and social costs and externalities, firms will only have to report on these if they have an impact on the value creating capabilities of the firms themselves. He further criticizes the lack of obligations in the framework. When comparing the framework to the IIRC's press release and discussion paper, he notes that the IIRC has retreated from imposing obligations on the firms reporting under IR and questions the ability of IR to have much of an impact on the financial reporting of companies today.

A prerequisite for achieving sustainability is that the overall stock of capital should not decrease as a result of business activities (Flower, 2015). Since a company is not obliged to adopt the same classification as the IIRC, the definitions of some of the capitals exclude certain components of the total capital base. For instance, regarding manufactured capital and natural capital, Flower (2015, p. 7) argues that only objects that are important for the firm's production process would be included, potentially excluding the negative effects of a range of objects otherwise included in the total capital.

In the <IR> framework, it is stated that while companies aim to create value overall, there might be cases where value creation in one area causes value destruction in another and whether the total effect on the overall stock of capital will be positive or negative depends on the perspective taken by the preparer (IIRC, 2013). The IIRC's framework (2013) accepts trade-offs between the capitals, but Flower (2015) argues that trade-offs are problematic because of the measurement of the capitals. He also believes that trade-offs involving a decrease of natural capital will almost never be in the interest of society as a whole.

Cheng *et al.* (2014) also discuss the trade-offs between the capitals and they conclude that there is a risk of great subjectivity when assessing the overall impact of a company's actions on the capitals. They believe that it might be difficult for organizations to explain some of their capitals in ways other than through "insubstantial narratives" (Cheng *et al.*, 2014, p. 98). When assessing the trade-offs that can happen between the capitals, how should one explain the choices made without "turning the disclosure into thinly veiled, self-promoting justification" (Cheng *et al.*, 2014, p. 98)? A final point of concern in Cheng *et al.*'s (2014) reasoning is that natural capital needs not necessarily to belong to a company, which means that decreases in natural capital do not have to be borne by the owners. Rather, stakeholders will bear the costs of decreases in natural capital. The authors therefore question the relevance of this information to the primary users, the investors and creditors, if they are not affected by decreases in natural capital.

When assigned a monetary value on the capitals, there is a danger that this is placing resources into the economic system that is partially responsible for destroying them. On this topic, Barter (2015) argues that natural capital is not to be seen as just one of the six capitals, rather it should be seen as a master set of which the other capitals are subsets. The reasoning behind this argument is that there is not a perfect substitutability between natural capital and the other, human made, capitals. Barter (2015) believes that when natural capital enters into the boardrooms, there is a risk of the concept hindering more radical solutions to environmental challenges. The author fears that when applying economic logic to nature, life forms with low economic value may be lost. Besides, assigning value to complex ecosystems is not an easy task; it might be that we are likely to trade 'sense for cents' but the problem is that "what makes economic sense is not always right and what is right is not always economic" (Barter, 2015, p. 372).

Studies on the IIRC's capital concept

There have been few empirical studies of the <IR>framework and the capital concept. In a content analysis of 22 annual and sustainability reports from UK companies and semi-structured interviews with senior managers, Robertson and Samy (2015) investigated the potential adoption of IR in the UK. The authors found that there is limited linking between financial and non-financial reports, hampering their usefulness. The authors believe that IR, therefore, might have a relative advantage over existing reporting practices, which would be beneficial for the diffusion of IR. They also reveal that several companies are positive about IR and that they are starting to integrate their reporting consistent with the <IR> framework. The authors point to UK specific legislation requiring companies to produce strategic reports that have some similarities with IR. They believe that legislation might benefit the diffusion of IR, at least in the UK. The authors also point to the complexity in IR regarding the measurement of the capitals as there is a lack of guidance from the IIRC but also a lack of studies in the area of value creation under a multiple capital models (Robertson and Samy, 2015).

A study that investigated capitals disclosure in South Africa was undertaken by Setia *et al.* (2015). They compared annual reports of 2009/2010 with the integrated reports of 2011/2012 for 25 companies listed on the Johannesburg Stock Exchange (JSE). In 2010, a regulation change that included IR as a listing requirement on the JSE came into effect, forcing listed companies to present integrated reports on a comply or explain basis. Setia *et al.* (2015) use the timing of this regulation change for comparison purposes. Capitals included in the study were human capital, natural capital, IC, and social and relationship capital. They found a significant increase in the disclosures of information on social and relationship capital in integrated reports compared to annual reports. For the rest of the capitals, however, there were no statistically significant increases. The authors believe that this could indicate that companies employ symbolic management in search of legitimacy and they question whether corporate behaviour has improved because of IR or whether it is empty rhetoric.

Setia *et al.* (2015) also found that companies that disclosed relatively little information prior to the regulation were those that improved the most, which indicated that the regulation had lowered the dispersion of the extent of disclosures. The results of the study suggested that the regulation had been successful in causing companies to disclose more non-financial information, which should be of interest for policymakers considering mandating IR (Setia *et al.*, 2015).

Eccles and Serafeim (2014), on the other hand, used a sample of 124 integrated reports produced by companies that took part in the IIRC's pilot programme or that are listed on the JSE to provide an overview of the disclosure of information related to the capitals. A content analysis using a four-point scoring system was applied. The authors found that manufactured and IC were the two capitals for which the least amount of information was disclosed. However, roughly 70 per cent of the reports were given a score of 2 or 3 for those capitals, meaning that the information was considered moderately detailed or detailed.

The most reported capital was financial capital, where roughly 85 per cent scored a 2 or a 3, followed by natural capital. The authors considered the relatively weak results for manufactured capital to be attributable to the relative decline in the importance of manufactured assets in the modern, knowledge-based economy. However, they did not present an explanation for the results regarding IC. The strong reporting of financial capital is attributed to its longstanding regulation, while the state of natural capital reporting could be explained by the rising pressure on companies to disclose environmental performance. The authors finish by stating that "a significant number of companies are still providing little capital-specific information even though these companies are considered leaders in integrated reporting" (Eccles and Serafeim, 2014, p. 11).

In a Swedish setting, PwC (2013b) studied large Swedish companies' current reporting compared to the IIRC's draft of the <IR> framework. PwC assessed the compliance for eight different areas derived from the content elements (e.g. business model, strategy, risks and opportunities, and outlook) of the framework. The results were mixed. For instance, most companies reported well on strategy and (financial) performance, while for governance the results were generally poor. Larson and Ringholm (2014) examined the compliance with the <IR> framework of Swedish listed firms, focusing on the content element governance. Their findings are similar to those of PwC (2013b), suggesting that there is still a long way to go with regards to governance disclosures. Most governance aspects were mentioned by a majority of the companies, but the descriptions were too short and too generic to meet information needs. They further found a highly significant positive relationship between size and level of compliance as larger companies tended to comply better with the <IR> framework. This finding is consistent with previous results that have shown that the amount of disclosure tends to increase with company size (Hahn and Kühnen, 2013; Frias-Aceituno *et al.*, 2014). As larger firms tend to have greater need for external financing, increased disclosure can thus be used as a way to enhance the relationships between companies and capital markets (Frias-Aceituno *et al.*, 2014).

Research methodology

The method chosen for this study was a content analysis of annual reports as they are seen as the primary source of information (Eccles and Krzus, 2010). In addition, one of the IIRC's initial aims was that IR would come to replace annual reporting (IIRC, 2011). Using annual reports also means that there is a possibility to backtrack and verify the data in case of uncertainty (Bowen, 2009). This study focuses on the capitals concept of the IIRC's <IR> framework although there are other interpretations of IR, such as the King III report in South Africa (De Villiers *et al.*, 2014). Should Swedish companies choose to produce integrated reports, for instance for reasons of legitimacy or through institutionalism, it is most likely that they would base them on the IIRC's version. Furthermore, the capitals concept is chosen because it is a foundation for IR (IIRC, 2013) and because it is an issue not previously studied in a Swedish context.

In addition, this study focused on large, listed Swedish companies since size has been found to be a factor that influences the likelihood of voluntary disclosures (Hahn and Kühnen, 2013; Frias-Aceituno *et al.*, 2014; Larson and Ringholm, 2014). Therefore, only companies listed on the OMX Stockholm 30 index were included. The OMXS30 contains the 30 most traded shares on the Stockholm Stock Exchange. However, financial institutions were excluded (four banks and two investment companies) from this study as their business models differ significantly from the remainder of companies in the sample. Additionally, since this study aimed to include the 2015 fiscal year, only companies that had published their annual reports prior to the data collection deadline (7 April 2016) were included (three more companies were excluded on this basis). Since Atlas Copco is listed twice (A and B shares), the final sample consisted of 20 companies (see Figure 24.1).

Given that IIRC's <IR> framework and the capitals concept were published in late 2013, annual reports for each company for the years 2011 and 2015 have been chosen in order to make comparisons over time. A difference of four years – two years before, even before the IIRC draft was available, and two years after the introduction of the new <IR> framework – is assumed to fit well for that purpose. Thus, the total sample used in this study consisted of 40 annual reports. The method follows procedures as described by Miles and Huberman (1994) and Collis and Hussey (2014) and involves three steps: data collection, data reduction, and data analysis. Thus, this study employed a content analysis where the information disclosed in the annual reports was classified according to pre-set categories of items (Setia *et al.*, 2015).

First, the 40 annual reports were collected from the companies' websites. The next step was to determine how the data would be coded (Collis and Hussey, 2014). Since the aim of this study was to gain an understanding of the 'what and how' Swedish companies report in relation to the six capitals, these – and their definitions – were used as the basis for the coding. The <IR> framework and insights from the methods employed by Setia *et al.* (2015) were used for that purpose, which resulted in 25 items to be studied. The six capitals are not distributed equally. For instance, manufactured capital is only represented by two items (4 and 5) while social and relationship capital is represented by six items (16 to 21). This is because the <IR> framework includes different amounts of examples for different capitals. The level of aggregation in the definitions differs between the capitals so there is not an even distribution of items across the capitals.[1]

A systematic procedure for finding, selecting, and evaluating the text found in the annual reports was then applied in order to answer the 'what and how'. This started with skimming the reports (first with help of the electronic word search function on the web and then with the help of a visual search/fast read through all pages in the annual reports) in order to find data that fitted the items determined. This data was then copied into a separate document, ordered by company, year, what capital it belonged to, and with a reference to the page number in the annual report where it was found. The definitions of the capitals formed the basis for the data selection. Moreover, during the classification, a scoring system was used to determine to what extent (how) the items were reported. This scoring system applied a three-point scale, similar to one in a previous study that used content analysis with a comparable purpose (Wang *et al.*, 2013), namely zero points when an item is not mentioned at all, one point when an item is mentioned but not explained, described or further elaborated on, and two points when an item is described, explained, or elaborated on (for instance, it is linked to other capitals, its role in the value creation or its use is explained).[1]

To illustrate the coding a sentence from Assa Abloy (2015, p. 9)[2] can be used: "Continuing professional development, skills and values are the basis for the Group's success". This relates to two capitals and three different items: item 11 'employee competence and capabilities', item 14 'human resource development', and item 21 'shared norms and common values'. Items 11 and 14 are classified as human capital, while item 21 is classified as social and relationship capital. It was decided that this short sentence would award Assa Abloy two points in each of the three items. The reason is that Assa Abloy, on pages 64 and 65, explains in more detail how and why 'development, skills and values' contribute to the success of the group. Moreover, as success can be interpreted as financial success, there is a link between financial capital on the one hand and human and social and relational capital on the other.

Descriptive results and analysis

The purpose of this section is to present the total scores for IR disclosure on capital of all companies. As can be seen in Figure 24.1, 14 out of 20 received a higher, 4 a lower, and 2 companies received the same total score in 2015 compared to 2011. Overall, the score increased by 11 per cent over the years (from 30.7 to 34.2, both out of 50), a change that is statistically not significant due to the small number of cases. The results show that there are large differences between the companies' disclosures and between the different capitals reported on. The range in 2011 is between 15 and 38 points and in 2015 it is between 21 and 43 points.

When discussing the overall results per company, it is worth noting that six companies (Boliden, SCA, SKF, SSAB, TeliaSonera, and Volvo) reported on their 'value creation models' using all or some of the capitals. However, the degree of specification in the reporting differs strongly. For instance, SCA merely lists the capitals but does not define them or give examples of what is included. Boliden,[3] on the other hand, provides more detailed information on what they consider to be part of their capitals. For instance, Boliden's IC is comprised of patents, exploration rights, environmental permits, reclamation expertise, the new Boliden way philosophy, and R&D partnerships with universities, colleges of further education, and suppliers (Boliden, 2015, p. 6). For some of the capitals, such as financial

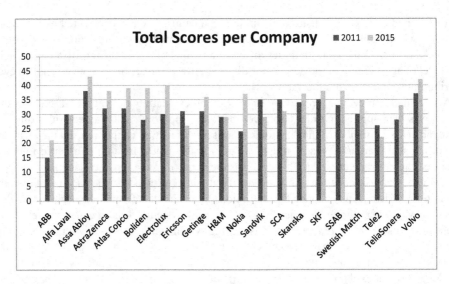

Figure 24.1   Total scores per company

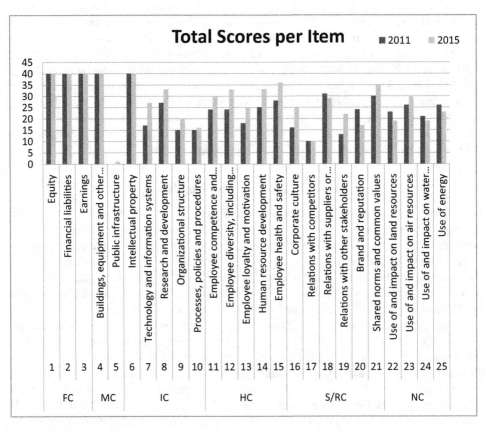

Figure 24.2   Total scores per item

and natural, Boliden also provides numbers such as 5.6 TWh of energy use. Boliden also provides a list of production outputs, economic and social effects, and environmental impact, in some cases described with numbers.

The rest of the companies are somewhere in-between SCA's and Boliden's reporting. SKF does not list all of the capitals and Volvo does not list them in the same way as the <IR> framework. Volvo splits its inputs and outcomes into economic, social, and environmental, with the capitals mentioned in the descriptions of each category.

The following more detailed observations have been made regarding disclosure across the six capitals in the annual reports, illustrated in Figure 24.2, which clarifies the total scores per item in relation to total annual reports studied. The following discussion also includes data calculated with help of the scoring system (0, 1, and 2 points) applied.

Financial capital and manufactured capital

All companies score the maximum six points for financial capital ('equity, financial liabilities, earnings') during both years, which is reasonable given the strong regulation of financial reporting. A similar, stable state of disclosure is also visible for manufactured capital, where 39 out of 40 annual reports received two points for both years on item 4 ('buildings, equipment, and other tangible property'). However, Boliden's 2015 annual report was the only exception here as it also scores on the rather 'new' item 5 ('public infrastructure'), that apparently has not yet gained momentum in a Swedish context.

In terms of relating the capitals to each other, this must be done with caution. Manufactured capital, for example, suffers from the fact that item four is fairly aggregated. Had 'buildings, equipment and other tangible property' been three separate items, it is likely that all three would have scored the maximum points. In that case manufactured capital would also enjoy a higher total average score during both years. No clear development patterns, however, are identifiable over time (2011 versus 2015).

Intellectual capital

Regarding IC, the results show that there are quite large changes between the years. In 2011, the average score was 5.7 out of 10. Compared with the other capitals, this is slightly below average. However, in 2015 the average score had increased to 6.8 out of 10, which is an average score when compared with the rest of the capitals. Thirteen (13) companies received a higher, five a lower, and two the same score in 2015 compared with 2011. The 19 per cent increase is the second highest of all capitals disclosed.

In contrast to financial and manufactured capital, one of the five items listed under IC was readily available in the financial statements, namely item 6 ('intellectual property'). Item 7 ('technology and information systems') was reasonably reported during 2011 with a score of 17 of 40. The increase of the disclosure of item 7 was the highest increase for any single item included in the study (59 per cent). Similar but weaker trends are visible for the rest of the items. Item 8 ('research and development') was already widely reported in 2011 but there was still an increase to 2015 (22 per cent). In fact, excluding the items that were found in the financial statements, item 8 ('research and development') was one of the most reported items during both 2011 and 2015. Item 9 ('organizational structure') and item 10 ('processes, policies, and procedures') were less well reported with scores that were among the bottom five during 2011 and still low in 2015.

Human capital

The capital that showed the highest increase between the years was human capital, with an average 32 per cent increase. Fourteen (14) companies received a higher score in 2015 than in 2011 (four the same and two a decrease). The average score of 7.9 out of 10 in 2015 is the second highest after (the mandatory) financial capital. The items listed under human capital were in general well reported, especially during 2015, and increasing patterns over the years were about equal. Items 12, 14, and 15 all score reasonably high during 2011 and exhibit a fairly substantial increase during 2015. All three are among the best disclosed items of those not included in the financial statements. Item 13 ('loyalty and motivation') is somewhat less reported during both years but shows, similar to the other human capital items, a fairly large increase between the years.

Social/relationship capital

The average score for social and relationship capital in 2011 was 6.2 out of 12, which is below the average score overall. In 2015 the average score had increased to 6.9, hence somewhat below the average of 2015 score across all capitals. No trend is visible as eight companies increased, six decreased, and six had unchanged scores over the years. There is a large variety not only in the six different items listed under social and relationship capital but also in the trend. Items 16 ('corporate culture') and item 19 ('relations with other stakeholders', such as customers, universities, and governments), reported similar low numbers with 16 and 13 respectively in 2011, however, with big increases to 25 and 22 in 2015. This increase (56 per cent and 69 per cent) is the highest increase over the four years when measured in percentage terms. Item 21 ('shared norms and common values') was widely reported during 2011 but still with a slight increase in 2015.

On the other hand, item 17 ('relations with competitors') was and still is, unsurprisingly, one of the least reported items during both years. Among the companies that reported on the item, such as Nokia or Tele2, issues such as common infrastructure or licensing between competitors seemed to be common topics. The remaining two items, item 18 ('relations with suppliers or distributors') and item 20 ('brand and reputation') were well reported in 2011 but experienced a drop in score for 2015. The drop of seven points for 'brand and reputation' was the largest drop found in the study for any single item.

Natural capital

Finally, the average score for natural capital was 4.8 out of 8 in 2011 and 4.6 out of 8 in 2015. In 2011, this was considered an average score across all capitals but the decrease in 2015 results in a below average score. Natural capital was the only capital to show a decrease between the years; all others show increases or are stable. In terms of the number of increases and decreases, natural capital shows a different pattern from the other capitals. Six companies received better scores in 2015, nine companies received the same score, and five companies received a lower score during the second year included in the study. Item 22 ('use of and impact on land resources'), item 24 ('water resources'), and item 25 ('energy usage') were all fairly well reported in 2011 but decreased by 2–4 points in 2015, resulting in below average scores.

On the other hand, item 23 ('use of and impact on air resources') showed a slight increase in 2015 and was fairly well reported during both years, usually in the form of reporting on emissions of CO_2. It is worth noting that regardless of whether the companies disclosed this information in the annual reports, some of them made references to their sustainability reports where these items were disclosed or further elaborated on. This indicates that information for these items might be available, even if that was not reflected in this study.

Overall patterns and comparison with similar studies

Overall, from 2011 to 2015, there has been a 20 per cent increase in disclosure of non-financial and non-material (intangible) capital, which is broadly the former domain of what was called IC (e.g. Dumay *et al.*, 2016). This is in line with earlier studies that report on an ever-growing importance of these capitals compared to, for example, manufactured capital (Eccles and Serafeim, 2014). The data from this Swedish study, however, does not support Eccles and Serafeim's (2014) finding that manufactured capital has declined in importance as this has remained the same in this study. Rather, in Sweden, it is the disclosure of natural capital that has decreased somewhat, which is also the only easily discernible change in the ranking table (Table 24.1) between the two years studied. This decrease is surprising when thinking of the efforts of the IIRC (2013) and other important norm setters (e.g. the Natural Capital Coalition, 2017)[4] in disseminating ideas regarding the disclosure of just natural capital.

When comparing the results for 2015 of this study with earlier findings, it is important to note the following. Setia *et al.* (2015) did not investigate financial or manufactured capital in their study of IR in South Africa, thus a comparison cannot be made for those two capitals. Eccles and Serafeim (2014) did investigate all capitals but looked only at 'integrated reports', which should be better aligned with the <IR> framework than annual reports investigated in this study. Setia *et al.* (2015) and Eccles and Serafeim (2014) also investigated other time frames/years and another country (South Africa).

This study mostly confirms the PwC (2013b) study that found that the areas investigated were reasonably well reported by large Swedish companies. Further, all companies in this study received the maximum points for their reporting on financial capital, whereas only 35 per cent of the reports received the maximum score in Eccles and Serafeim's (2014) study. One possible explanation is that the methodology used in this study does not differentiate enough between what Eccles and Serafeim (2014) would call 'moderate and detailed reporting'

Table 24.1 A ranking comparison

Rank	*This study (Sweden, 2011)*	*This study (Sweden, 2015)*	*Setia et al. (2015) (South Africa, 2011/12)*	*Eccles and Serafeim (2014) (South Africa, most likely 2012)*
1	Financial capital	Financial capital	Intellectual capital	Financial capital
2	Human capital	Human capital	Human capital	Natural capital
3	Natural capital	Intellectual capital	Natural capital	Human capital
4	Intellectual capital	Social/rel. capital	Social/rel. capital	Social/rel. capital
5	Social/rel. capital	Natural capital	—	Intellectual capital
6	Manuf. capital	Manuf. capital	—	Manuf. capital

as they used four scales. Another explanation is that Swedish annual reports are better aligned with the capitals concept of the <IR> framework than integrated reports, which seems unlikely.

Regarding the other capitals, the results of this study show some similarities and some differences with the results of Setia *et al.*'s (2015) study. Both studies find that the average disclosure of capital items has increased. However, Setia *et al.* (2015) found increases for all capitals they tested, while this study finds a small decrease (5 per cent) for natural capital.

Table 24.1 shows a somewhat shattered picture when comparing how the capital disclosure was ranked in the three rather similar studies (two columns for this study, one for 2011, and one for 2015). Clearly, financial capital was ranked on top and manufactured capital appears on the bottom of the ranking in the studies and the years where they are included. Regarding the other capitals (not tangible or financial), it seems that human capital disclosure ranks higher than the other capitals, and social and relationship capital ranks lower than the other capitals. Both, natural capital and IC do rank high and low in the different studies, thus no clear picture can be derived here.

Conclusions

The purpose of this chapter was to provide evidence of what Swedish companies disclose in their annual accounts in relation to the IIRC's six capitals concepts, how this has developed over time, and what patterns that can be observed. The results show that the average score for all capitals disclosures combined increased by 11 per cent from 2011 to 2015. Moreover, of the six capitals, only natural capital decreased slightly. Therefore, the small change over the years and the small change in patterns of disclosure can only be interpreted in one way. So far, the IR discourse, in academia and in practice, following the introduction of the IIRC's <IR> framework, has had very little impact on the actual disclosures made in Swedish OMX large cap listed companies.

The vague similarity of six of the companies' value creation models with the <IR> framework, however, suggests that there is some association. The fact that the IIRC's definitions of the capitals are vague and that the framework overall lacks obligations (Flower, 2015), therefore seems to be of little help in its adoption, at least in Sweden. It is therefore questionable whether it has already resulted in some sort of integrated thinking, which is IIRC's long-term vision (IIRC, 2013, p. 2).

However, this study suggests that what was feared about the new <IR> concept on capital (e.g. Flower, 2015) has taken place – that externalities would not be sufficiently disclosed, or only in positive terms. The exception to this seems to be CO_2 emissions, which is an area most likely influenced by other reporting frameworks, such as the GRI (references to the GRI are made in 26 annual reports and 7 of them contain GRI indicators). In addition, only in very few of the annual reports is some explanation provided as to links or relationships between the capitals (see Eccles and Serafeim, 2014) and none of the reports illustrated natural capital as a master set (see Barter, 2015).

Although not really the focus of this study, no references were found in the annual reports to the overall stock of capital, as discussed in Flower (2015). Similarly, nothing was found during the course of this study to assume that Swedish companies have answers to how to trade-off capitals as highlighted by Cheng *et al.* (2014) and Flower (2015). The disclosures provided in the annual accounts further indicates that Milne and Gray (2013) have a point in their criticism of the lack of focus on what sustainability really is and means when companies report on these matters as such information is missing in both years studied.

All in all, there seems to have been small improvements only, thus no fundamental changes took place during the four-year period covered in this study in terms of multiple capital reporting – and most of these are attributable to an increase of disclosure (20 per cent) of non-financial and non-material/intangible capitals. The IIRC's six capitals framework has, most likely, contributed somewhat to that development, but overall, voluntary report-ing frameworks appear to have a limited impact on the 'what and how' of capital disclosures in annual reports in Sweden. This supports the 'pessimistic' view of Dumay *et al.* (2016) regarding IR as a concept, as the study suggests it has been difficult to translate into prac-tice. The new EU-directives on non-financial reporting (European Commission, 2016), together with updated frameworks or templates of how to achieve 'integrated reporting' in organizations could mark a significant step towards more inclusive and integrated disclosure practices overall.

In terms of input, output, or even outcome of different capitals, but also specific items within each capital, little is shown and known today. In future research, it seems imperative to investigate if and how legislation helps to push forward changes in practice and what that means in terms of 'inclusiveness and integrativeness' (Coulson *et al.*, 2015) and in terms of real value creation (Dumay *et al.*, 2016) and, last but not least, the creation of real meaning. Such research may help solve the lack of knowledge regarding the fourth stage of IC research and practice as identified by Guthrie *et al.* (2012) and Dumay and Garanina (2013) but also the second stage of IR research (Dumay *et al.*, 2016).

At this point in time it is obvious that 'integrated thinking' has only just started to penetrate the organizational culture of the investigated companies in Sweden, which supports the find-ings of Dumay and Dai (2014, p. 19) that changing entrenched cultures is difficult and time consuming. It seems there is still a long way to go until a systematic shift from a 'financial capital market system' to an 'inclusive capital market system' takes place in Sweden.

Notes

1 Detailed information on data collection, coding instructions, and analysis is available from the authors.
2 www.assaabloy.com/Global/Investors/Annual-Report/2015/Annual%20Report%202015.pdf (accessed 5 May 2016).
3 http://ir.boliden.com/afw/files/press/boliden/201603091670-1.pdf (accessed 5 May 2016).
4 http://naturalcapitalcoalition.org/ (accessed 28 January 2017).

References

Barter, N. (2015), "Natural capital: Dollars and cents/dollars and sense", *Sustainability Accounting, Management and Policy Journal*, Vol. 6, No. 3, pp. 366–373.
Bowen, G. A. (2009), "Document analysis as a qualitative research method", *Qualitative Research Journal*, Vol. 9, No. 2, pp. 27–40.
Brown, J. and Dillard, J. (2014), "Integrated reporting: On the need for broadening out and opening up", *Accounting, Auditing & Accountability Journal*, Vol. 27, No. 7, pp. 1120–1156.
Cheng, M., Green, W., Conradie, P., Konishi, N., and Romi, A. (2014), "The international integrated reporting framework: Key issues and future research opportunities", *Journal of International Financial Management & Accounting*, Vol. 25, No. 1, pp. 90–119.
Collis, J and Hussey, R. (2014), *Business Research: A Practical Guide for Undergraduate and Postgraduate Students*, Palgrave Macmillan, New York.
Coulson, A. B., Adams, C. A., Nugent, M. N., and Haynes, K. (2015), "Exploring metaphors of capi-tals and the framing of multiple capitals: Challenges and opportunities for <IR>", *Sustainability Accounting, Management and Policy Journal*, Vol. 6, No. 3, pp. 290–314.

De Villiers, C., Rinaldi, L., and Unerman, J. (2014), "Integrated Reporting: Insights, gaps and an agenda for future research", *Accounting, Auditing & Accountability Journal*, Vol. 27, No. 7, pp. 1042–1067.

Dumay, J. and Dai, T. M. X. (2014), "Integrated thinking as an organizational cultural control?", in Critical perspectives on accounting conference, Toronto, Canada, 7–9 July.

Dumay, J. and Garanina, T. (2013), "Intellectual capital research: A critical examination of the third stage", *Journal of Intellectual Capital*, Vol. 14, No. 1, pp 10–25.

Dumay, J., Bernardi, C., Guthrie, J. and Demartini, P. (2016), "Integrated reporting: A structured litera-ture review", *Accounting Forum*, Vol. 40, No. 3, pp 166–185.

Eccles, R. G. and Krzus, M. P. (2010). *One Report: Integrated Reporting for a Sustainable Strategy*, John Wiley & Sons, Hoboken, New Jersey.

Eccles, R. G. and Serafeim, G. (2014), "Corporate and integrated reporting: A functional perspective", pp. 156–172, in Lawler, E., Mohrman, S., and O'Toole J. (Eds), *Stewardship of the Future*, Greenleaf, Sheffield, UK.

European Commission (2016), "Non-financial reporting", available at http://ec.europa.eu/finance/ company-reporting/non-financial_reporting/index_en.htm#news (accessed 5 May 2016).

EY (2015), "Hur påverkas svenska bolag av det nya EU-direktivet om icke-finansiell och mångfaldsinfor-mation?", available at www.ey.com/Publication/vwLUAssets/EY-CCASS-manfaldsinformation/$FILE/ EY-CCaSS-Lagforslaget-om-rapportering-om-hallbarhet-och-mangfaldspolicy.pdf (accessed 6 May 2016).

Ferns, B., Emelianova, O., and Sethi, S. P. (2008), "In his own words: The effectiveness of CEO as spokesperson on CSR-sustainability issues – Analysis of data from the Sethi CSR Monitor©", *Corporate Reputation Review*, Vol. 11, No. 2, pp. 116–129.

Flower, J. (2015), "The international integrated reporting council: A story of failure", *Critical Perspectives on Accounting*, Vol. 27, pp. 1–17.

Frias-Aceituno, J. V., Rodríguez-Ariza, L., and Garcia-Sánchez, I. M. (2014), "Explanatory factors of integrated sustainability and financial reporting", *Business Strategy and the Environment*, Vol. 23, No. 1, pp, 56–72.

Guthrie, J., Ricceri, F., and Dumay, J. (2012), "Reflections and projections: A decade of intellectual capi-tal accounting research", *The British Accounting Review*, Vol. 44, No. 2, pp. 68–82.

Hahn, R. and Kühnen, M. (2013), "Determinants of sustainability reporting: A review of results, trends, theory, and opportunities in an expanding field of research", *Journal of Cleaner Production*, Vol. 59, pp. 5–21.

IIRC (2011), "Towards integrated reporting: Communicating value in the 21st century", Discussion paper, available at www.theiirc.org/wp-content/uploads/ 2011/09/IR-Discussion-Paper-2011_single. pdf, accessed 18 May 2016.

IIRC (2013), "The International <IR> Framework", available at http://integratedreporting.org/wp-content/uploads/2013/12/13–12–08-THE-INTERNATIONAL-IR-FRAMEWORK-2–1.pdf (accessed 19 May 2016).

IIRC (2016), "The IIRC", available at http://integratedreporting.org/the-iirc-2/ (accessed 19 May 2016).

Larson, J. and Ringholm, L. (2014), *Governance Disclosures According to IIRC's Integrated Reporting Framework: Are Annual Reports of Swedish Listed Companies in Line with the Framework?* Master's thesis, University of Gothenburg, Gothenburg.

Miles, M. B. and Huberman, A. M. (1994), *Qualitative Data Analysis: A Methods Sourcebook*, Sage Publications, Thousand Oaks, CA.

Milne, M. J. and Gray, R. (2013), "W(h)ither ecology? The triple bottom line, the Global Reporting Initiative, and Corporate Sustainability Reporting", *Journal of Business Ethics*, Vol. 118, No. 1, pp. 13–29.

Mio, C. (Ed.) (2016), *Integrated Reporting: A New Accounting Disclosure*, Springer Nature, Macmillan, London.

Mouritsen, J., Larsen, H. T., and Bukh, P. N. D. (2001), "Intellectual capital and the 'capable firm': Narrating, visualising and numbering for managing knowledge", *Accounting, Organizations and Society*, Vol. 26, No. 7, pp. 735–762.

Petty, R. and Guthrie, J. (2000), "Intellectual capital literature review: Measurement, reporting and man-agement", *Journal of Intellectual Capital*, Vol. 1, No. 2, pp. 155–176.

PwC (2013a), "Point of view: Integrated reporting", available at www.pwc.com/us/en/cfodirect/assets/ pdf/point-of-view-integrated-reporting.pdf (accessed 19 May 2016).

PwC (2013b), "A benchmark study of Swedish large cap companies' reporting 2012", available at www.pwc.se/sv/bolagsstyrning/assets/a-benchmark-study-of-swedish-large-cap-companies-reporting-2013.pdf (accessed 19 May 2016).

Robertson, F. A. and Samy, M. (2015), "Factors affecting the diffusion of integrated reporting: A UK FTSE 100 perspective", *Sustainability Accounting, Management and Policy Journal*, Vol. 6, No. 2, pp. 190–223.

Roth, H. P. (2014), "Is integrated reporting in the future?", *The CPA Journal*, Vol. 84, No. 3, pp. 62–67.

Setia, N., Abhayawansa, S., Joshi, M., and Huynh, A. V. (2015), "Integrated reporting in South Africa: Some initial evidence", *Sustainability Accounting, Management and Policy Journal*, Vol. 6, No. 3, pp. 397–424.

Tweedie, D. (2014), "Integrated reporting: Symptom or cure of new capitalism's ills?" in Proceedings of the Critical Perspectives on Accounting Conference in Toronto, Canada, 7–9 July.

Van Bommel, K. (2014), "Towards a legitimate compromise? An exploration of integrated reporting in the Netherlands", *Accounting, Auditing & Accountability Journal*, Vol. 27, No. 7, pp. 1157–1189.

Wang, J., Song, L., and Yao, S. (2013), "The determinants of corporate social responsibility disclosure: Evidence from China", *Journal of Applied Business Research*, Vol. 29, No. 6, pp. 1833–1848.

PART IV

Stage 2
IC guidelines

25

KEY CONTRIBUTIONS TO THE INTELLECTUAL CAPITAL FIELD OF STUDY

Göran Roos

Introduction

Since the late 1990s, together with my colleagues, I have contributed to the field of intellectual capital (IC), and we have arrived at many insights, most of which we have published. This chapter is structured by key contribution domain and is presented in order of criticality of contribution and the associated publications are listed in the references.

The key contributions can be summarized as follows. First, the development of a proper measurement system – the conjoint value hierarchy measurement system or CVH for short – for capturing the value of real business systems including or involving IC. Second, the distinction between stocks (the balance sheet view) and flows or transformations (the profit and loss statement view). Third, the resource taxonomy grounded in economic behaviour of resources. Fourth, clarification of the distinction between intangibles and IC resources. Fifth, the IC Navigator as a strategic tool addressing the weaknesses in the resource-based view of the firm (RBV) toolbox. Sixth, recommendations for how to regulate around IC reporting and a methodological approach for the disclosure of IC. Seventh, a theoretically grounded and empirically verified relationship between epistemological paradigm held, resource and resource transformation managed, strategic logic and potential for competitive advantage. Eighth, the positioning and empirical verification of the IC lens as an important component in business model innovation. And finally, ninth, the application of the IC lens to the meso-economic level to inform policy decisions.

Measurement and evaluation

The key contributions in this area fall into two domains: the distinguishing between measurement systems (with all the associated requirements), and the performance evaluation tools.

Conjoint value hierarchy measurement system

The work undertaken with Dr Stephen Pike over a 15-year period has resulted in the CVH, which is a proper measurement system. Below is the summary of the key issues and main contributions (extracted from the key publications: Pike and Roos, 2004, 2007; Pike *et al.*, 2005; with some modifications).

Measurement is the process of assigning numbers to things in such a way that the relationships of the numbers reflect the relationships of the attributes of the things being measured. This definition of measurement applies not just to simple and familiar measurements, such as distance and mass, but also to the measurement of complex things, such as the value of businesses that need diverse sets of attributes to describe them. The construction of a measurement system requires the application of measurement theory, a branch of applied mathematics. The fundamental idea of measurement theory is that a measurement is not the same as the object being measured but is, instead, a representation of it. This means that if conclusions are to be drawn about the object, it is necessary to consider the nature of the correspondence between the attribute and the measurement. Proper use of measurement theory greatly reduces the possibility of making meaningless statements; for example, although 30 is twice 15, a temperature of 30°C is not twice a temperature of 15°C, since there is no simple correspondence between the numerical measure and the object. The formalization of measurement theory is a surprisingly recent development. The ideas of the modern theory of measurement date only from the 19th-century work of Helmholtz (1887), which laid the basis for one-dimensional extensive relational measurement theory. The formalization of measurement theory was motivated by the need to understand what it means to measure things in the social sciences. The catalyst for the formalization of measurement theory is generally accepted to be the psychologist S. S. Stevens (1946), with later interest from scientists in the field of quantum physics, although it was not until the 1970s that measurement was fully axiomatized (Scott and Suppes, 1958; Suppes and Zines, 1963; Krantz *et al.*, 1971; Narens, 1985; Suppes *et al.*, 1989; Luce *et al.*, 1990). It was shown that numerical representations of values and laws are only numerical codes of algebraic structures representing the real properties of these values and laws. Thus, hierarchical structures are primary representations of values and laws. When applying proper measurement systems for the measurement of the value of something, four important outcomes from the independence of value definition must be considered:

1   the object to be measured or valued and the context in which the object subsists must be precisely defined;
2   the definition is inclusive in its detail of all opinions and requirements from all stakeholders;
3   all participants (stakeholders) have equal dignity or importance, at least to begin with;
4   every participant is accountable for the veracity of his/her position.

When dealing with complex objects, the principles of axiology must be extended and the easiest way of doing this requires the use of multi-attribute value theory (MAVT). Note that MAVT is often considered to be similar to multi-attribute utility theory (MAUT) but with no uncertainties about the consequences of the alternatives, whereas MAUT explicitly recognizes uncertainties (Keeney and Raiffa, 1976).

MAVT allows the representation of complex entities using a hierarchical structure in which the elements of value are contained in a complete set of mutually independent attributes. Such value measurement structures can be made operational in conjoint structures by the incorporation of algorithms to represent the subjective judgements made by stakeholders. For reliable use, it requires the algorithms to be compliant with measurement theory in all places. The basic idea in conjoint measurement is to measure one attribute against another. Clearly, this must involve common scales, and one in which the scale ends have a defined meaning. In practice, making scales commensurable requires normalization onto a 0 to 1 scale and that input data are expressed on a ratio scale. If other scaling systems are used, such as interval and ordinal,

Tversky *et al.* (1988) have shown that they are incompatible with the axioms of measurement theory and commensurable scales cannot be constructed with them.

Using the above, we developed the CVH as a proper value measurement system. The development of a CVH measurement system to measure the value of a given object follows the following process. In the first step, the object in its context is defined by the stakeholders, taking into strict account the legitimacy of the stakeholder and the implied comparison that the context will provide. A hierarchical measurements system is an ordered triple, a non-empty set $\mathbb{A}$, containing all the attributes (a_i) of the entity, the relationships (r_i) between them, and the operations (o_i) upon them. These are usually expressed as:

$$\mathbb{A}_{i=1}^n = \{a_i, r_i, o_i\}$$

This means that for a set containing n elements:

$$\sum_{i=1}^n a_i = \mathbb{A} \text{ and } a_i \bigcap_{\substack{i=1 \\ j=1 \\ i \neq j}}^n a_j = 0$$

The only test that can be applied to demonstrate compliance with these conditions is proof by exhaustion. The hierarchical structure constructed along these lines simply describes the object to be measured but nothing more. It shows what 'ought' to be measured.

The second step is to build an operational isomorph. The practical problem that is almost always encountered is that some of the attributes that 'ought' to be measured cannot be easily measured in practice, and thus the stronger condition of homeomorphy cannot be invoked.

Thus, our description of the entity to be measured ($\mathbb{A}_{i=1}^n = \{a_i, r_i, o_i\}$) appears as an isomorphic measurement structure in which the attributes a_i are replaced in part or in whole by proxies b_i. As the measurement structure is an isomorph, r_i and o_i are preserved and the measurement structure is represented by another ordered triple, $\mathbb{B}$, where:

$$\mathbb{B}_{i=1}^n = \{a_i, r_i, o_i\}$$

It is necessary to ensure that the proxies (which can be measured reliably and reproducibly) are acceptable. Since these are not exactly the same as the defined attributes that 'ought' to be measured, it is necessary to test them to ensure that the conditions of completeness and distinctness have not been violated, but most of all that the aggregated meaning of $\mathbb{B}$ approximates to $\mathbb{A}$ in a way that is acceptable to the stakeholders. The method to test this is, again, proof by exhaustion, and the tests are as follows:

Assuming true isomorphism and $a_i \cong b_i$, that is, $b \neq \{bb_k\}$ b 6¼ $\{bb_k\}$, then $b_i \approx a_i$ and

$$b_i \bigcap_{\substack{i=1 \\ j=1 \\ i \neq j}}^n b_j = 0$$

It is easy to show and quantify the difference that sloppy mathematics makes to the results generated by a measurement system, but it is much harder to quantify the difference made by ill-chosen proxy measures. Given an acceptable isomorphic measurement system $\mathbb{B}$, the measurable attributes are b_i with relationships r_i. All that is now needed is to consider the nature of the binary operations o_i.

The simplest of aggregation algorithms is weighted addition, with aggregated value V of n attributes defined as:

$$V = \sum_{i=1}^{n} W_i V_i \text{ where } \sum_{i=1}^{n} w_i = 1$$

The simplicity of the weighted addition algorithm is often problematic, as it does not have the ability to show complex combination behaviours. This is especially important when the loss of performance of one combining attribute should lead to a complete loss of value in the combined higher-level attribute and this cannot be compensated for by a contribution from the other combining attribute. Marichal (1998) gives an excellent account of aggregation functions and their properties.

When a measurement system is used, the results are dependent to a large degree on the nature of the combination algorithm, which must be selected with care and conform to certain conditions of propositional logic. Failure to do this often introduces catastrophically large and variable errors into calculations. The key propositions that an algorithm must satisfy are those of commutativity and associativity, and they can be proved by algebraic means:

$$(f \circ g) \circ h = f \circ (g \circ h) = f \circ g \circ h \qquad \text{(associativity)}$$

$$f \circ g = g \circ f \qquad \text{(commutativity)}$$

where $\circ$ is the generalized binary operation of the aggregation function.

The penultimate step in constructing a measurement system is to customize copies of it so that it represents the behaviours of the individual stakeholders. This step ensures compliance with axiological requirements, in that the individual's views are maintained without interference or the averaging of those results from consensus processes. In practice, this means asking for opinions on the relative importance of the attributes, the natures of the attribute combinations, and the limits of performance.

In complex value measurement systems like the CVH, native performance scales are collapsed onto a non-dimensional value scale, which is normalized, between 0 and 1. The task is to define what 0 and 1 mean. It is usual to set 0 as that performance level that just becomes useful – in other words, 'the threshold of uselessness'. The meaning of 1 has two common alternatives: either that it means the 'best in class' or that it is some internally set strategic target. The choice between them is decided by the user of the CVH, but it is important that the basis be known.

The final step in producing a measurement system concerns the performance data to be used to operate the measurement system. All performance measures have two parts, the amount and the scale, but it is important to realize that there are many types of scale. If reliable results are to be obtained, then it is important that data are collected on an appropriate scale. For the purposes of proper measurement, only ratio or absolute scales are acceptable.

Bearing in mind the multiplicity of units that may arise and the fact that a measurement system requires a meaningful 0 to 1 scale, all data inputs must be commensurable, which, in practice, means normalizable. Some other conditions are also required of performance data to ensure that the measurement system functions properly. These are that:

$$(X \geq Y) \text{ if and only if } (X + Z) \geq (Y + Z) \qquad \text{(monotonicity)}$$

$$(X + Y) > X \qquad \text{(positivity)}$$

There exists a natural number n such that:

$(nX \geq Y)$ where $(1X = X)$ and $(n + 1)X = (nX + X)$ (Archimedean condition)

This is an example of a third part use of CVH in a situation where a proper measurement system is required (see, for example, Millar *et al.*, 2010).

Taxonomy, stocks and flows, and the IC Navigator

Given that IC as a lens can be seen as an extension of the resource-based theory of the firm, some key contributions come from aligning the IC lens with the resource-based view (RVB) of the firm as well as extending the IC lens to address weaknesses identified in the RBV of the firm.

The RBV of the firm originates implicitly with Barnard (1938), Selznick (1957), Chandler (1962), Sloan (1963), Rumelt (1974), Chandler (1977), and notably Penrose (1959), with articulation and further developments by Rumelt (1984), Wernerfelt (1984), Barney (1986), Dierickx and Cool (1989), and Barney (1991). Although, as identified by Seoudi (2009), the RBV is actually one of three distinct "strategic views" of the firm (the others being the dynamic capability view (exemplified by the writings of Nelson and Winter, 1982; Teece *et al.*, 1997) and the competence-based view (exemplified by Hamel and Heene, 1994; Sanchez and Heene, 1997)), for our purposes they can all be addressed in the same way since in the end, they all result in the same issues that require addressing.

Examples of the first is the initial contribution based on a set of firm cases that identified the importance of distinguishing between stocks and flows of IC (which complements and enhances the discussion in Dierickx and Cool, 1989) which was published in the heavily cited Roos and Roos (1997).

An example of the second is the issue that follows from Rumelt's (1984, p. 557) statement that "a firm's competitive position is defined by a bundle of unique resources and relationships and that the task of general management is to adjust and renew these resources and relationships as time, competition, and change erode their value". This requires management to have access to a tool that would allow it to evaluate the effectiveness by which it deploys the different resources in its resource bundle. It also requires a taxonomy for resources since the resources that a firm may have at its disposal have different characteristics. They may be non-appropriable (Meade, 1952; Bator, 1958; Arrow, 1974; Dierickx and Cool, 1989), firm-specific or co-specialized (Williamson, 1979, 1985; Teece, 1986; Dierickx and Cool, 1989), exhibit time compression diseconomies (Scherer, 1967; Mansfield, 1968; Reinganum, 1982), asset mass efficiencies or economies in the accumulation of resources or increasing returns (Wilson and Hlavacek, 1984; Dierickx and Cool, 1989; Cool *et al.*, 2016), interconnectedness of asset stocks (Dierickx and Cool, 1989; Garud and Nayyar, 1994), asset erosion (Dierickx and Cool, 1989), causal ambiguity (Lippman and Rumelt, 1982; Dierickx and Cool, 1989), learning-curve economies (Sanchez and Heene, 2004), capture of the value of positive externalities (Sanchez, 1999, 2002), and/or committed and motivated resources (Sanchez, 2008).

This raises the question of how to characterize and group resources based on attributes. The IC literature has synthesized the insights relating to resources from both the strategic and the economic literature and based on this produced a resource distinction tree (Roos *et al.*, 2005). The contribution made here was a joint effort that commenced as joint work with Leif Edvinsson whilst at Skandia in the form of contributions to the supplements to Skandia's Annual Report for the years 1996 and 1997 including IC Index simulations (Skandia, 1996a, 1996b, 1997), and was further developed in the two consecutive books, Roos *et al.* (1997, 2005), where the 2005 book is a substantial refinement of the taxonomy and framework put forward in the first book. The result is a framework that allows all resources to be grouped under one of five headings based on their characteristics: monetary, physical, relational, organizational, and human. Under each of these headings it is possible to find both tangible and intangible resources, and a clear understanding of this distinction was developed and published in Ballow *et al.* (2004).

Following Rumelt's 1984 statement, Barney (1986) points out that once relevant resources have been acquired they can be combined and recombined in a variety of ways to implement different strategies. From this follows that the way these resources are combined will determine the success by which the strategy is implemented. In other words, a firm's competitive position fundamentally relates to the uniqueness of a bundle of resources (Dierickx and Cool, 1989). The way the firm chooses to combine and deploy resources may be more or less effective, and high effectiveness requires an understanding of the cause and effect relations between deployment decisions and economic returns (Lippman and Rumelt, 1982). This view is echoed in Martín-de-Castro *et al.* (2006) who state (grounded in Grant, 1991; Amit and Schoemaker, 1993; Prahalad and Hamel, 1990; Teece *et al.*, 1997) that capabilities arise from the coordination of different resources and hence are dynamic and more complex than resources.

Based on this, Barney (1986, p. 1238) poses the question: "How can firms become consistently better informed about the value of strategies they are implementing than any other firms?" The answer provided by Barney is that in principle there are two different approaches. The first approach being to analyse the external environment in which the firm operates, but it is unlikely that this will generate the insights needed for the firm to achieve supra-normal returns since both the tools and the information required as well as the skill needed to put the tools into use for this type of analysis are available in the public domain and hence most firms pursuing this route will arrive at approximately the same conclusions. Thus Barney (1986, p. 1238) concludes, "Analysing a firm's competitive environment cannot, on average, be expected to generate the expectational advantages that can lead to expected above normal returns in strategic factor markets". The second approach is to analyse the resources that the firm has at its disposal. This information does not exist in the public domain, which would, given the access to tools and the skill to use such tools, provide the basis for supra-normal returns. At the time of Barney's (1986) writing, neither the tools nor the skills to use them existed but this problem articulation formed the impetus for the development of the IC Navigator as the tool to satisfy this need.

The IC Navigator work has taken around two decades to come to fruition in the form of a workable, well-grounded, and practical approach that allows management to identify the effectiveness by which it deploys its resource portfolio as well as raising questions, the answers to which will provide for the improvement of this effectiveness. This work aimed to do what Sanchez (2008) later articulates as the failure of the RBV to provide an adequate conceptual basis for identifying which entities can be considered resources that are "strategically valuable" to a firm in its current competitive context or which entities will be resources that will become strategically valuable in future competitive contexts. To address this failure, the RBV would have to offer conceptually clear, consistent, and delimited characterizations of the functional or behavioural properties of resources that would enable the unambiguous identification of resources, the distinguishing of different kinds of resources, and the drawing of logical inferences about the different ways in which different kinds of resources contribute to strategic value creation. The RBV provides no consistent, generally applicable conceptual basis for systematically identifying and evaluating resources in ways that would distinguish firm attributes that are "strategically valuable" resources from those firm attributes that are not. Hence, RBV researchers attempting to test the RBV's core proposition empirically have had no recourse but to revert to such arguments based on ad hoc and ex post characterizations of resources that directly result in resources identified ex post as being strategically valuable (by invoking some ad hoc environmental model or SWOT framework) were by that very fact the ex ante strategically valuable resources responsible for a firm's or firms' future success. This poses a tautological problem that limits the empirical value of the RBV framework. To address this failure, the RBV must develop a rigorous definition of resources that provides a consistent and coherent conceptual basis for distinguishing the different ways in which different kinds of firm attributes can contribute to creating strategic value and thus qualify as resources.

Further, the RBV fails to propose a credible chain of causality explaining how firms can actually use resources to create strategic value. Given this fundamental omission, the RBV fails to offer an adequate conceptual basis for systematically deriving hypotheses about how different kinds of resources and organizational processes for using resources may result in effective or ineffective realization of the strategic value of a firm's resources. The practical consequence of this fundamental omission is that the RBV has no theoretical basis for providing consistent counsel to managers about how they might improve their skills in defining and implementing organizational processes for using their firm's resources. To address this failure, the RBV must develop a clear understanding of how resource deployments create value and how changes in this resource deployment structure will impact the value creation.

Early iterations of the IC Navigator can already be seen in Roos *et al.* (1997) with consecutive insights, applications, and progression shown in Dragonetti and Roos (1998a, 1998b, 1998c), Roos and Lövingsson (1999), Roos and Jacobsen (1999), Rylander *et al.* (2000), Peppard and Rylander (2001a, 2001b), Gupta and Roos (2001), Roos *et al.* (2001, 2005), Chatzkel (2002), Fernström and Roos (2004), Fernström *et al.* (2004), Pike *et al.* (2005), Peng *et al.* (2007), Uchida and Roos (2008), Roos and Pike (2008), Chung *et al.* (2010), Pike and Roos (2011), Roos (2011c, 2014a), Burton *et al.* (2013), and De Zubielqui *et al.* (2015). The most complete description can be found in Roos (2014a). The IC Navigator is now a well-grounded, proven (applied in more than 1,000 firms), practical, and useful strategic tool that addresses all the weaknesses identified by Sanchez (2008) and also later by El Shafeey and Trott (2014).

Reporting and disclosure of IC

Reporting and disclosure of intangibles have been a feature of the IC landscape since its inception. Initial contributions to this field were made together with Leif Edvinsson for the supplements to Skandia's Annual Report for the years 1996 and 1997 including IC Index simulations, and was further developed in the book Roos *et al.* (1997) and the paper Rylander *et al.* (2000).

In Gupta *et al.* (2003), the first step towards a broader understanding of the corporate governance issues was taken by discussing corporate governance from the viewpoints of agency theory, stewardship theory, stakeholder theory, organizational theory, resource dependence theory, resource-based theory, and the IC perspective. Gupta *et al.* (2003) outline the complexities and propose a first version of a governance model in descriptive terms that can be linked to financial performance; establishes the value drivers of corporate control that are dynamically linked to financial performance measures such as share price; will provide a prescription of the performance measures (and expectations related thereto) that will necessarily be included in any corporate governance systems; provides the strategic management intervention points that are fundamental to managing the system (the short list of what should be managed where in the system); and identifies the trade-offs that inevitably need to be, and are, made.

This discussion was further refined in Burgman and Roos (2005) by identifying 12 influences that promote the need for operational and IC disclosure and reporting. To this discussion is then added the three necessary conditions for an IC reporting framework: a business enterprise classification scheme; the legal test for negligence and the requirement to report on operations; and a standard set of measures that fulfil the criteria for good information as relates to financial reporting and disclosure (validity; reliability; credibility of issuer; completeness; consistency; comprehensiveness; coverage or scope; objectivity relating to the bias or opinion expressed when the issuer interprets or analyses facts; accuracy, that is, the factually irrefutability, error rate, restatement rate, etc.; timeliness, that is, the modernity of the information; utility or usefulness; accessibility, that is, ease of use).

In Burgman and Roos (2006a, 2006b, 2007) and Burgman *et al.* (2007), the previous discussions are concluded by presenting a set of recommendations for companies that realize the value of reporting on IC and are about to embark on the journey of finding a suitable model for doing this. These recommendations include, first, finding a suitable model for disclosing IC information, which is a challenging task since it is about changing both internal and external stakeholders' way of thinking and view of the company. It is also about turning something that is today complex and dynamic in nature into something simple and practical. Therefore, it is of utmost importance that IC is demystified and laid bare in order to gain support within and outside of the company on its identification, quantification, and management. Second, finding a suitable model to use in its demystification, the organization first must assess and define its own management needs and how to go about addressing them. This is about predicting changes and their consequences, making sure that the management team fully supports the idea, and making sure that the model is aligned with the strategy of the company. Moreover, the company should take its own and others' experiences and insights into account and establish the factors critical to achieving as well as barriers to success. It is not recommended to launch into establishing a measurement system without having a sound understanding of the grounding principles of measurement. Sound and clear mental models are needed to be able to develop effective management systems. Third, the implementation is best done step by step. That way, feedback from internal and external stakeholders can be integrated along the way. In deciding which approach to take and which content to choose, the strategy of the company must be considered and used as a basis for the decision. Finally, the key performance indicators are defined and existing data is mapped. This is the stage where stakeholders get to comment on a draft reporting model. A methodology for arriving at what is to be reported is also proposed:

1 Identify drivers of enterprise value:

    a   establish value drivers and impacted financial accounts from standard balance sheet, profit and loss, cash flow statements and notes to the accounts;

    b   identify any 'missing' value drivers (generally investments in IC being expensed) and nominate these for management accounting balance sheet inclusion;

    c   capitalize 'investments' in IC resources and establish amortization schedules.

2 Identify primary value creating business processes:

    a   establish the company's value creating mega-business processes and sub-processes;

    b   identify the key value determining resources and activities (transformations) within each mega process;

    c   identify the key resource state (stock) and activity (transformation) performance metrics that give a comprehensive insight into how the company manages for value.

3   Functional resource utilization:

    a   identify the key functional resources being consumed in the administration of the value creation mega processes and sub-processes;
    b   establish the functional allocation of resources to the various mega- and sub-processes (e.g. from sales and marketing, accounting and finance, procurement, etc.);
    c   establish the revenue and cost implications of the functional allocation;
    d   establish the mark-to-market value of all the management accounting balance sheet resources (including all relevant IC resources).

4   Reporting and disclosure:

    a   establish the content and timing of operational and IC reporting and disclosure based on

        i   the value of such information to users
        ii   the legal concept of neglect.

Finally, accepting that no international rules exist for the reporting of IC, Burgman and Roos (2006a, 2006b, 2007) and Burgman *et al.* (2007) state that when the time for regulating comes, the following conditions should hold for IC reporting if rules and regulations are devised. First, operational reporting should be required as a complement to financial reporting in each and all reporting environments for publicly listed enterprises, the content and extent of which should be left to the company to decide. Second, the content of IC reporting should be established within the context of principles-based reporting and to draw its legal force from the test of neglect (of duty to information users). Third, IC reporting should be an embedded part of operational reporting and not proposed as a voluntary adjunct to either financial reporting or operational reporting. Fourth, there should be a regulatory sanctioned 'home' for operational reporting within the context of the reporting and disclosure legislative requirements within each legislative jurisdiction – whether at the country or supra-country (e.g. European Community) level. Examples of existing 'homes' that are being used to some extent for this purpose are the Management Discussion and Analysis (MDandA) in the US and Canada, and Management Commentary 'proposal' being discussed by the IASB. Fifth, the content of IC reporting should then be determined by reference to the enterprise's relevant business model/s – value chain, value shop, or value network – and an understanding of the specific drivers of enterprise value   resource states and resource creating and depleting activities, and capabilities – that are causally linked to value and its creation. Business model articulation may occur at the industry GICS (6-digit) or sub-industry GICS (8-digit) levels, with business models being identified according to the degree of homogeneity of business conduct among competitive peers. Sixth, independently, standards for resource measurement and activity performance measurement should be developed by standard setters (like the IASB) or professional bodies (like the Association of Certified Chartered Accountants) since there will need to be a consistent set of expectations in relation to the comprehensiveness and quality of data preparation as well as its interpretability. Seventh, finally, the mapping of capitalized IC resources for management purposes back to the financial accounts should be standardized. The credibility of IC recognition will only occur when managerially accounted for on an historical cost basis. This does not mean that we propose that IC should be reported on in the financial accounts, rather that when IC is reported on in the relevant disclosure section of an annual report and a value is to be attributed to an IC item, then it would be on the net historical cost of the investment made in it. What will be important to information users will be the identification of the IC resource as being causally connected to enterprise value in the eyes of management. What that contributes to overall enterprise value is up to the investors to decide. No attempt should be made by the company to mark-to-market except in the limited circumstances of self-generating and regenerating asset equivalents such as may exist with human capital.

Epistemology, knowledge management, strategic logics, IC, and competitive advantage

Epistemology as a concept within IC was first introduced in Pike and Roos (2002) and in Gupta *et al.* (2002) based on an epistemology classification tool developed. This tool was further deployed to create the analysed data for the paper by Marr *et al.* (2003). This paper allowed the identification of suitability of different knowledge management practices for different epistemological paradigms (see Table 25.1). The epistemological paradigms were extracted from Von Krogh and Roos (1995) and operationalized by Pike and Roos (2002). The three paradigms used are cognitivist, connectivist, and autopoietic. Cognitivists consider the identification, collection, and central dissemination of information as the main knowledge development activity. Organizations are considered as open organizations that develop increasingly accurate pictures of their pre-defined worlds through the assimilation of new information. Knowledge is developed according to universal rules; hence the context of the incoming information is important. Connectivists have many similarities to the cognitivist viewpoint but a difference being that there are no universal rules. As rules are team-based and vary locally, organizations are seen as groups of self-organized networks dependent on communication. The connectivists believe that knowledge resides in the connections and hence focus on the self-organized dispersed information flow. Autopoietics consider the context of information inputs as unimportant and it is seen as data only. The organization is a system that is simultaneously open (to data) and closed (to information and knowledge). Information and knowledge cannot be transmitted easily since they require internal interpretation within the system according to the individual's rules. Thus, autopoietics develop individual knowledge, and respect that process in others.

These insights were further refined as relates to the knowledge aspects of IC resources in Roos (2005a, 2005b). This work substantiated the claim that the epistemological outlook of people in organizations has a substantial impact on the effectiveness of the firm's value creation and needs to be aligned with both the type of IC resources that form the basis for the firm's competitive advantage and the type of strategic logics that dominate in the firm. The findings are that the higher the alignment is between the pairs of strategic logics (using the terminology of Stabell and Fjeldstad, 1998) and epistemological paradigms (Value Chain ↔ Cognitivist; Value Network ↔ Connectivist; Value Shop ↔ Autopoietic) the more effective the value creation of the firm. A further insight is that with the epistemological paradigms held by the individuals involved in executing and managing resource transformations with the taxonomy of these transformations a clearer picture emerges of how to maximize effectiveness using people holding appropriate epistemological paradigms to achieve this maximization (Table 25.2).

Figure 25.1 shows the insight as it relates to suitable combinations of epistemological paradigm held, strategic logic, resource managed, that can form the basis for a competitive advantage.

Table 25.1 Knowledge management practices and epistemological paradigms (extracted from Marr *et al.*, 2003)

	Knowledge creation	Knowledge acquisition	Knowledge sharing	Knowledge mapping	Knowledge storing	Knowledge codification
Cognitivists	Can be directed and managed	Is a process that can be executed by digital systems, codified both as a process and as an outcome and stored	Through digital or physical tools and intermediaries including codified instruction manuals or repositories	Mapping of knowledge (= information)	Digitally of physically stored (databases or documents)	Universal knowledge codification is a key concept
Connectivist	Unregulated within context specific rules	Captured through external relationships and converted into internal context specific knowledge	Through meetings, forums or groups, both structured and unstructured and both regulated and unregulated. These can be digitally assisted (e.g. groupware)	Mapping of information, rules and structures	Storage of information, information on rules and information on structures	Limited codification since not all knowledge can be codified in a context-free way
Autopoietic	Openness, freedom and, apparent chaos	Open bi-directional relationships and networks	Through unregulated (structured or unstructured) meetings and free-form discussions	Mapping of individuals and mapping of capabilities/knowledge of individuals	n/a	n/a

Table 25.2 Resources, resource transformations, and epistemologies (extracted from Roos, 2005a)

Transforming from	Transforming into	Appropriate epistemologies
Monetary resources	Monetary resources	Cognitivist epistemology
	Physical resources	Cognitivist epistemology
	Relational resources	Balanced cognitivist/connectivist epistemology
	Organizational resources	Balanced cognitivist/connectivist epistemology
	Human resources	Balanced cognitivist/autopoietic epistemology
Physical resources	Monetary resources	Cognitivist epistemology
	Physical resources	Cognitivist epistemology
	Relational resources	Balanced cognitivist/connectivist epistemology
	Organizational resources	Balanced cognitivist/connectivist epistemology
	Human resources	Balanced cognitivist/autopoietic epistemology
Relational resources	Monetary resources	Balanced cognitivist/connectivist epistemology
	Physical resources	Balanced cognitivist/connectivist epistemology
	Relational resources	Connectivist epistemology
	Organizational resources	Connectivist epistemology
	Human resources	Balanced connectivist/autopoietic epistemology
Organizational resources	Monetary resources	Balanced cognitivist/connectivist epistemology
	Physical resources	Balanced cognitivist/connectivist epistemology
	Relational resources	Connectivist epistemology
	Organizational resources	Connectivist epistemology
	Human resources	Balanced connectivist/autopoietic epistemology
Human resources	Monetary resources	Balanced cognitivist/autopoietic epistemology
	Physical resources	Balanced cognitivist/autopoietic epistemology
	Relational resources	Balanced connectivist/autopoietic epistemology
	Organizational resources	Balanced connectivist/autopoietic epistemology
	Human resources	Autopoietic epistemology

The role of IC in business model innovation

As the concept of business models became widely popularized and adapted, with a major contribution by Osterwalder (2004), it became clear that the relationships between the IC lens and the business model lens needed to be clarified. The focus that was chosen was that of business model innovation. In a series of publications this problem was addressed from both a theoretical and an empirical point of view (Roos and Pike, 2008; Peng *et al.*, 2011; Roos, 2011a, 2011b, 2012a, 2013, 2014b, 2016; Roos and Fusco, 2014; Roos and O'Connor, 2014; Dissanayake *et al.*, 2015; O'Connor and Roos, 2016). Based on this research it was found that the existing business model dimensions as provided by the literature are not aligned with a modern manufacturing operating environment. Instead the 21 relevant business model dimensions for this environment were identified and are shown in Table 25.3 in the order in which they will be addressed in a business model innovation process. The top three in terms of criticality for creating the new business model, as identified empirically, are marked in bold italics.

Roos (2014b) also contains a thorough literature review of the dimensions of a business model as articulated by 80 publications during the period 1993–2010 (excluding those publications that use already published dimensions).

As can be seen from Table 25.3, it is clear that not only does the IC lens fill a void in the business model innovation dimensions but it is empirically considered to be one of the three most important dimensions.

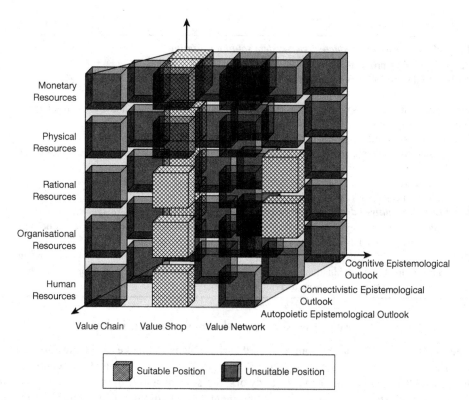

Monetary Resources
Physical Resources
Rational Resources
Organisational Resources
Human Resources

Value Chain   Value Shop   Value Network

Cognitive Epistemological Outlook
Connectivistic Epistemological Outlook
Autopoietic Epistemological Outlook

Suitable Position   Unsuitable Position

Figure 25.1   Key contribution to the relationship between epistemological paradigm held, resource and resource transformation managed, strategic logic, and potential for competitive advantage (Roos, 2005a)

Table 25.3 Empirically and theoretically derived and verified business model dimensions for manufacturing firms (Roos, 2014b)

Positioning of THIS business within the company's strategy

Description of the product-service-system/solutions offering

Identification of target customer segments, target consumer segments, and other definitive stakeholders

Value proposition for each of the target customer segments, target consumer segments, and other definitive stakeholders

Description how the target customer segments, target consumer segments, and other definitive stakeholders capture value from the offering

What competitive advantage does the offering enable or contribute to within the target customer segments, target consumer segments, and other definitive stakeholders

Value attribute, attribute preference and attribute performance for each of the target customer segments, target consumer segments, and other definitive stakeholders

What requirements must be fulfilled by the target customer segments, target consumer segments, and other definitive stakeholders in order to be able to benefit from the offering

Description of how the product-service-system/solutions offering should be implemented at the target customer segments, target consumer segments, and other definitive stakeholders to ensure the targeted benefits (value)

Place, role and strategy of THIS business in the business ecosystem of which it is part

---

(continued)

Table 25.3 (continued)

Technology base of the product-service-system/solutions offering

Design base of the product-service-system/solutions offering

Art base of the product-service-system/solutions offering

Reverse hermeneutic base for the product-service-system/solutions offering

Outgoing logistics and distribution channel choice for each of the target customer segments, target consumer segments, and other definitive stakeholders

Incoming logistics and supply chain choice

Relationship width, depth, and frequency for each of the target customer segments and other definitive stakeholders

Value configuration (value chain, value shop, value network) and associated transaction and coordination cost issues

Resources, competitive advantage, and resource deployment structure (IC Navigator)

Cost structure due to strategic choices and identification, and management objectives for associated economic value added drivers as well as bankruptcy predicting indicators

Revenue models with focus on accessing multiple profit pools and maximizing the number of revenue streams/pricing logic combinations aimed at achieving an economic value added for the business exceeding the revenue stream from its primary offering

---

The use of the IC lens on the meso-economic scale

The interest in looking at the contribution that the IC lens can make on the meso-economic level was first shown in Roos and Gupta (2005), Peng *et al.* (2012), and the sector review by Roos (2012b). This laid the groundwork for several applications of the IC lens to sectors and clusters, normally as a complement to technology roadmapping. Examples of these applications can be found in Ahlqvist *et al.* (2013), Dufva *et al.* (2013), Kraatz *et al.* (2014), Roos *et al.* (2014), Roos (2014c), Roos and O'Connor (2015), and O'Connor *et al.* (2015).

It is clear that this is a very useful complement that substantially enriches the basis for policy decisions relating to the meso-economic level and the use of an IC lens. At present, we are applying the IC lens as a complement to economic complexity theory and the first publication is Reynolds *et al.* (2017).

Conclusion

Since the late 1990s, my colleagues and I have made some key contributions to the field of IC. In the author's personal view, the greatest contributions can be found in the development of the IC Navigator to address the missing tool for the RBV of the firm and also as a complement in business model innovation and in the management of IC in general.

This is followed by the contribution to the ability to apply measurement to the field of IC (as well as other more complex objects with difficult or multi-dimensional attributes of value that must be captured) in the form of the CVH.

Neither of these contributions nor the contributions to the field of reporting and disclosure would have been possible without the contributions to the taxonomy of the field, and addressing confusions as to what stocks and flows of resources exist as well as addressing the confusion around the distinction between intangibles and IC.

It is clear from the work that is presently ongoing on the meso-economic scale that the IC lens is useful and able to contribute to insights around value creation on multiple scales.

References

Ahlqvist, T., Dufva, M., Kettle, J., Vanderhoek, N., Valovirta, V., Loikkanen, T., Roos, G., Hytönen, E., Niemelä, K., and Kivimaa, A. (2013), "Strategic roadmapping, industry renewal, and cluster creation: The case Green Triangle", Paper presented at 6th ISPIM: Innovation Symposium – Innovation in the Asian Century, 8–11 December, Melbourne, Australia.

Amit, R. and Schoemaker, P. J. (1993), "Strategic assets and organizational rent", *Strategic Management Journal*, Vol. 14, No. 1, pp. 33–46.

Arrow, K. E. (1974), *The Limits of Organization*, W. W. Norton and Company, New York

Ballow, J. J., Thomas, R. J., and Roos, G. (2004), "Future value: The $7 trillion challenge", *Journal of Applied Corporate Finance*, Vol. 16, No. 1, pp. 71–76

Barnard, C. (1938), *The Functions of the Executive*, Harvard University Press, Cambridge, MA.

Barney, J. B. (1986), "Strategic factor markets: Expectations, luck, and business strategy", *Management Science*, Vol. 32, No. 10, pp. 1231–1241.

Barney, J. B. (1991), "Firm resources and sustained competitive advantage", *Journal of Management*, Vol. 17, No. 1, pp. 99–120.

Bator, F. M. (1958), "The anatomy of market failure", *The Quarterly Journal of Economics*, pp. 351–379.

Burgman, R. and Roos, G. (2005), "Empirical and structural evidence for the increasing importance of intellectual capital reporting: Implications for European companies", paper presented at 1st EIASM Workshop on Visualising, Measuring, and Managing Intangibles and Intellectual Capital, 18–20 October, Ferrara, Italy.

Burgman, R. and Roos, G. (2006a), "Operational and intellectual capital reporting: A top-down risk-based approach to identifying, quantifying and reporting on enterprise value drivers", paper presented at 2nd EIASM Workshop on Visualising, Measuring, and Managing Intangibles and Intellectual Capital, 25–27 October, Maastricht, The Netherlands.

Burgman, R. and Roos, G. (2006b), "The information needs of internal and external stakeholders and how to respond: Reporting on operations and intellectual capital", paper presented at 2nd EIASM Workshop on Visualising, Measuring, and Managing Intangibles and Intellectual Capital, 25–27 October, Maastricht, The Netherlands.

Burgman, R. and Roos, G. (2007), "The importance of intellectual capital reporting: Evidence and implications", *Journal of Intellectual Capital*, Vol. 8, No. 1, pp. 7–51.

Burgman, R., Roos, G., Boldt-Christmas, L., and Pike, S. (2007), "Information needs of internal and external stakeholders and how to respond: Reporting on operations and intellectual capital", *International Journal of Accounting, Auditing and Performance Evaluation*, Vol. 4, No. 4, pp. 529–546.

Burton, K., O'Connor, A., and Roos, G. (2013), "An empirical analysis of the IC Navigator approach in practice: A case study of five manufacturing firms", *Knowledge Management Research and Practice*, Vol. 11, No. 2, pp. 162–174.

Chandler Jr., A. D. (1962), *Strategy and Structure*, The MIT Press, Cambridge, MA.

Chandler Jr., A. D. (1977), *The Visible Hand*, Harvard University Press, Cambridge, MA.

Chatzkel, J. (2002), "A conversation with Göran Roos", *Journal of Intellectual Capital*, Vol. 3, No. 2, pp. 96–117

Chung, S. Y., Peng, T. J. A., Roos, G., and Pike, S. (2010), "Intellectual capital resource transformation and inertia in inter-firm partnership", paper presented at the SMS Special Conference: Intersections of Strategy Processes and Strategy Practices, Track: Networks and Alliances for Competitive Advantage, 17–20 March, Kittilä, Finland.

Cool, K., Dierickx, I., and Almeida, L. (2016), "Asset mass efficiencies", *The Palgrave Encyclopedia of Strategic Management*, pp. 1–8.

De Zubielqui, G. C., O'Connor, A., and Seet, P. S. (2015), "Intellectual capital system perspective: A case study of government intervention in digital media industries" in Roos, G. and O'Connor, A. (Eds), *Integrating Innovation: South Australian Entrepreneurship Systems and Strategies*, University of Adelaide Press, Adelaide, Australia, pp. 277–302.

Dierickx, I. and Cool, K. (1989), "Asset stock accumulation and sustainability of competitive advantage", *Management Science*, Vol. 35, No. 12, pp. 1504–1511.

Dissanayake, M., O'Connor, A, and Roos, G. (2015), "How does a government business support program influence business growth? The case of a business model innovation program in Australia", 2015 Australian Centre for Entrepreneurship Research Exchange (ACERE) Conference, 3–6 February, Adelaide, Australia.

Dragonetti, N. C. and Roos, G. (1998a), "Assessing the performance of government programmes: An intellectual capital perspective", paper presented at the 18th Strategic Management Society Conference, 1–4 November, Orlando, Florida.

Dragonetti, N. C. and Roos, G. (1998b), "La evaluación de Ausindustry y el business network programme: Una perpectiva desde el capital intelectual", *Boletín de estudios económicos*, Vol. 53, No. 164, pp. 265–280.

Dragonetti, N. C. and Roos, G. (1998c), "Efficacy and effectiveness of government-sponsored programmes: An intellectual capital perspective" paper presented at the 2nd World Congress on Intellectual Capital, 21–26 January, Hamilton, ON.

Dufva, M., Ahlqvist, T., Kettle, J., Vanderhoek, N., Valovirta, V., Loikkanen, T., and Roos, G. (2013), "Future pathways for radical transformation of an industry sector", paper presented at the 6th ISPIM Innovation Symposium: Innovation in the Asian Century, 8–11 December, Melbourne, Australia.

El Shafeey, T. and Trott, P. (2014), "Resource-based competition: Three schools of thought and thirteen criticisms", *European Business Review*, Vol. 26, No. 2, pp. 122–148.

Fernström, L. and Roos, G. (2004). "Differences in value creating logics and their managerial consequences: The case of authors, publishers and printers", *International Journal of the Book*, Vol. 1, 493–506.

Fernström, L., Pike, S., and Roos, G. (2004), "Understanding the truly value creating resources: The case of a pharmaceutical company", *International Journal of Learning and Intellectual Capital*, Vol. 1, No. 1, pp. 105–120.

Garud, R. and Nayyar, P. R. (1994), "Transformative capacity: Continual structuring by intertemporal technology transfer", *Strategic Management Journal*, Vol. 15, No. 5, pp. 365–385.

Grant, R. M. (1991), "The resource-based theory of competitive advantage: Implications for strategy formulation", *California Management Review*, Vol. 33, No. 3, pp. 114–135.

Gupta, O. and Roos, G. (2001), "Mergers and acquisitions through an intellectual capital perspective", *Journal of Intellectual Capital*, Vol. 2, No. 3, pp. 297–309.

Gupta, O., Pike, S., and Roos, G. (2002), "Evaluating intellectual capital and measuring knowledge management effectiveness", in Performance Measurement and Management: Research and Action, Papers from the Third International Conference on Performance Measurement and Management, PMA Centre for Business Performance, Cranfield, UK.

Gupta, O., Pike, S., Roos, G., and Burgman, R. (2003, January), "Intellectual capital and improved corporate governance", paper presented at the 6th World Congress on the Management of Intellectual Capital and Innovation, 15–17 January, Hamilton, ON.

Hamel, G. and Heene, A. (Eds), (1994), *Competence-Based Competition*, John Wiley & Sons, Inc., New York.

Helmholtz, H. (1887), "Zahlen und Messen erkenntnistheoretisch betrachtet", in *Philosophische Aufsatze*, Fues's Verlag, Leipzig, pp. 17–52. (Trans. Bryan, C. L. (1930). *Counting and Measuring*, Van Nostrand, New York).

Keeney, R. and Raiffa, H. (1976). *Decisions with Multiple Objectives: Preferences and Value Tradeoffs*, John Wiley & Sons, Inc., New York.

Kraatz, J. A., Hampson, K. D., Parker, R. L., and Roos, G. (2014), "What next? Future directions for R&D investment", in Hampson, K. D., Kraatz, J. A., and Sanchez, A. X. (Eds) *R&D Investment and Impact in the Global Construction Industry*, Routledge, Abingdon, UK, pp. 284–309.

Krantz, D., Luce, R. D., Suppes, P., and Tversky, A. (1971), *Foundations of Measurement, Vol. I, Additive and Polynomial Representations*, Academic Press, London.

Lippman, S. A. and Rumelt, R. P. (1982), "Uncertain imitability: An analysis of interfirm differences in efficiency under competition", *The Bell Journal of Economics*, pp. 418–438.

Luce, D., Krantz, D., Suppes, P., and Tversky, A. (1990), *Foundations of Measurement, Vol. III, Representation, Axiomatization and Invariance*, Academic Press, London.

Mansfield, E. (1968), *The Economics of Technological Change*, W.W. Norton and Company Inc., New York.

Marichal, J. L. (1998), *Aggregation Operations for Multicriteria Decision Aid*, PhD thesis, University of Liège, Belgium.

Marr, B., Gupta, O., Pike, S., and Roos, G. (2003), "Intellectual capital and knowledge management effectiveness", *Management Decision*, Vol. 41, No. 8, pp. 771–781.

Martín-de-Castro, G., Emilio Navas-López, J., López-Sáez, P., and Alama-Salazar, E. (2006), "Organizational capital as competitive advantage of the firm", *Journal of Intellectual Capital*, Vol. 7, No. 3, pp. 324–337.

Meade, J. E. (1952), "External economies and diseconomies in a competitive situation", *The Economic Journal*, Vol. 62, No. 245, pp. 54–67.

Millar, L. A., McCallum, J., and Burston, L. M. (2010), "Use of the conjoint value hierarchy approach to measure the value of the national continence management strategy", *Australian and New Zealand Continence Journal*, Vol. 16, No. 3, pp. 81–88.

Narens, L. (1985), *Abstract Measurement Theory*, MIT Press, Cambridge, MA.

Nelson, R. R. and Winter, S. G. (1982), *An Evolutionary Theory of Economic Change*, Belknap Press, London.

O'Connor, A. and Roos, G. (2016), "Visualising intellectual capital transformations for strategic design of entrepreneurial business models", in Griffith, S., Carruthers, K., and Biemel, M. (Eds), *Visual Tools for Developing Student Capacity for Cross-Disciplinary Collaboration, Innovation and Entrepreneurship, Transformative Pedagogies in the Visual Domain Series*, Common Ground Publishing. Champaign, IL.

O'Connor, A., Du, K., and Roos, G. (2015), "The intellectual capital needs of a transitioning economy: A case study exploration of Australian sectoral changes", *Journal of Intellectual Capital*, Vol. 16, No. 3, pp. 466–489.

Osterwalder, A. (2004), *The Business Model Ontology: A Proposition in a Design Science Approach*, PhD Thesis, University of Lausanne, Switzerland.

Peng, T. J. A., Pike, S., and Roos, G. (2007), "Intellectual capital and performance indicators: Taiwanese healthcare sector", *Journal of Intellectual Capital*, Vol. 8, No. 3, pp. 538–556.

Peng, T. J. A., Pike, S., Yang, J. C. H., and Roos, G. (2012), "Is cooperation with competitors a good idea? An example in practice", *British Journal of Management*, Vol. 23, No. 4, pp. 532–560.

Peng, T. J. A., Yang, J. C. H., Pike, S., and Roos, G. (2011), "Intellectual capitals, business models and performance measurements in forming strategic network", *International Journal of Learning and Intellectual Capital*, Vol. 8, No. 3, pp. 328–347.

Penrose, E. T. (1959), *The Theory of the Growth of the Firm*, John Wiley & Sons, Inc., New York.

Peppard, J. and Rylander, A. (2001a), "Using an intellectual capital perspective to design and implement a growth strategy: The case of APiON", *European Management Journal*, Vol. 19, No. 5, pp. 510–525.

Peppard, J. and Rylander, A. (2001b), "Leveraging intellectual capital at APiON", *Journal of Intellectual Capital*, Vol. 2, No. 3, pp. 225–235.

Pike, S. and Roos, G. (2002), "Measuring the impact of knowledge management in companies", paper presented at the 5th World Congress on Intellectual Capital, Hamilton, 16–18 January, Ontario, Canada.

Pike, S. and Roos, G. (2004), "Mathematics and modern business management", *Journal of Intellectual Capital*, Vol. 5, No. 2, pp. 243–256.

Pike, S. and Roos, G. (2007), "The validity of measurement frameworks: Measurement theory", in Neely, A. (Ed.), *Business Performance Measurement: Unifying Theory and Integrating Practice*, Cambridge University Press, Cambridge, UK, pp. 218–236.

Pike, S. and Roos, G. (2011), "Measuring and valuing knowledge-based intangible assets: Real business uses", in Alonso, B. V., Castellanos, A. R., and Arregui-Ayastuy, G. (Eds), *Identifying, Measuring, and Valuing Knowledge-based Intangible Assets: New Perspectives*, IGI Global, Hershey, PA, pp. 268–293.

Pike, S., Fernström, L., and Roos, G. (2005), "Intellectual capital: Management approach in ICS Ltd.", *Journal of Intellectual Capital*, Vol. 6, No. 4, pp. 489–509.

Prahalad, C. and Hamel, G. (1990), "The core competence of the corporation", *Harvard Business Review*, Vol. 90, pp. 79–91.

Reinganum, J. F. (1982), "A dynamic game of R&D: Patent protection and competitive behaviour", *Econometrica: Journal of the Econometric Society*, pp. 671–688.

Reynolds, C., Agrawal, M., Lee, I., Zhan, C., Li, J., Taylor, P., Mares, T., Abedin, F., Morison, J., Angelakis, N., and Roos, G. (2017), "A sub-national economic complexity analysis of Australia's states and territories", *Regional Studies*. Vol. 51, pp. 1–12.

Roos, G. (2005a), "An epistemology perspective on intellectual capital", in Marr, B. (Ed.), *Perspectives on Intellectual Capital: Multidisciplinary Insights into Management, Measurement and Reporting*, Routledge, Abingdon, UK, pp. 196–209.

Roos, G. (2005b), "Epistemological cultures and knowledge transfer within and between organisations", in Bukh, P. N., Christensen, K., and Mouritsen, J. (Eds) *Knowledge Management and Intellectual Capital: Establishing a Field of Practice*, Palgrave Macmillan, London, pp. 149–172.

Roos, G. (2011a), "How to get paid twice for everything you do: Integrated innovation management", *Ericsson Business Review*, Vol. 2, pp. 55–57.

Roos, G. (2011b), "How to get paid twice for everything you do: Value appropriating innovations", *Ericsson Business Review*, Vol. 3, pp. 56–61.

Roos, G. (2011c), "Интегрированное управление инновациями – путь к удвоению отдачи от любой деятельности [Integrated management of innovation is the way to double the impact of any activity]", *Стратегический менеджмент* [*Strategic Management*], Vol. 4, pp. 270–290.

Roos, G. (2012a), "How to get paid twice for everything you do: Innovation management", *Ericsson Business Review*, Vol. 1, pp. 45–51.

Roos, G. (2012b), *Manufacturing into the Future*, Adelaide Thinkers in Residence, Government of South Australia, Adelaide.

Roos, G. (2013), "The role of intellectual capital in business model innovation: An empirical study", in Ordóñez de Pablos, P., Tennyson, R. D., and Zhao, J. (Eds), *Intellectual Capital Strategy Management for Knowledge-Based Organizations*, IGI Global, Hershey, PA, pp. 76–121.

Roos, G. (2014a), "The Intellectual Capital Navigator as a strategic tool", in Ordóñez de Pablos, P. (Ed.) *International Business Strategy and Entrepreneurship: An Information Technology Perspective*, IGI Global, Hershey, PA, pp. 1–22.

Roos, G. (2014b), "Business model innovation to create and capture resource value in future circular material chains", *Resources*, Vol. 3, No. 1, pp. 248–274.

Roos, G. (2014c), "Regional economic renewal through structured intellectual capital development", paper presented at the 11th International Conference on Intellectual Capital, Knowledge Management and Organisational Learning, 6–7 November, Sydney, Australia.

Roos, G. (2016), "Design-based innovation for manufacturing firm success in high-cost operating environments", *She Ji The Journal of Design, Economics and Innovation*, Vol. 2, No. 1, pp. 5–28.

Roos, G. and Fusco, M. (2014), "Strategic implications of additive manufacturing (AM) on traditional industry business models", paper presented at the Additive Manufacturing with Powder Metallurgy Conference, 18–20 May, Orlando, Florida.

Roos, G. and Gupta, O. (2005), "Strategy and intellectual capital management for dynamic industries", paper presented at World Congress, 19–21 January, Hamilton, ON.

Roos, G. and Jacobsen, K. (1999), "Management in a complex stakeholder organisation", *Monash Mt Eliza Business Review*, Vol. 2, pp. 82–93.

Roos, G. and Lövingsson, F. (1999), "El Proceso CI en el Nuevo Mondo de las Telecomunicacione", in Güell, A. M. (Ed.) *Homo faber, homo sapiens – La gestión del capital intelectual*, Ediciones del Bronce, Barcelona, pp. 141–169.

Roos, G. and O'Connor, A. (2014), "The contribution of intellectual capital to servitization of manufacturing firms: An empirical study", paper presented at the 11th International Conference on Intellectual Capital, Knowledge Management and Organisational Learning, 6–7 November, Sydney, Australia.

Roos, G. and O'Connor, A. (2015), "Government policy implications of intellectual capital: An Australian manufacturing case study", *Journal of Intellectual Capital*, Vol. 16, No. 2. pp. 364–389.

Roos, G. and Pike, S. (2008), "An intellectual capital view of business model innovation", in Bounfour, A. (Ed.). (2008), *Organizational Capital: Modelling, Measuring and Contextualising*, Taylor and Francis, UK, pp. 40–62.

Roos, G. and Roos, J. (1997), "Measuring your company's intellectual performance", *Long Range Planning*, Vol. 30, No. 3, pp. 413–426.

Roos, G., Ahlqvist, T., Dufva, M., Kettle, J., Vanderhoek, N., Hytönen, E., Niemelä, K., Kivimaa, A., Valovirta, V., and Loikkanen, T. (2014), "Regional economic renewal through structured knowledge development within an agglomeration economic framework: The case of the cellulose fibre value chain in the Mt. Gambier region of South Australia", paper presented at the 9th International Forum on Knowledge Asset Dynamics (IFKAD 2014), 11–13 June. Matera, Italy.

Roos, G., Bainbridge, A., and Jacobsen, K. (2001), "Intellectual capital analysis as a strategic tool", *Strategy and Leadership*, Vol. 29, No. 4, pp. 21–26.

Roos, G., Pike, S., and Fernström, L. (2005), *Managing Intellectual Capital in Practice*, Butterworth-Heinemann, New York.

Roos, J., Roos, G., Edvinsson, L., and Dragonetti, N. (1997), *Intellectual Capital: Navigating in the New Business Landscape*, Palgrave Macmillan, London.

Rumelt, R. P. (1974), *Strategy Structure and Economic Performance*, Harvard University Press, Cambridge, MA.

Rumelt, R. P. (1984), "Towards a strategic theory of the firm", in Lamb, B. (Ed.), *Competitive Strategic Management*, Prentice Hall, Englewood Cliffs, NJ, pp. 556–570.

Rylander, A., Jacobsen, K., and Roos, G. (2000), "Towards improved information disclosure on intellectual capital", *International Journal of Technology Management*, Vol. 20, No. 5, pp. 715–741.

Sanchez, R. (1999), "Modular architectures in the marketing process", *Journal of Marketing*, Vol. 63, pp. 92–111.

Sanchez, R. (2002), "Industry standards, modular architectures, and common components: Strategic incentives for technological cooperation", in Contractor, F. and Lorange, P. (Eds) *Cooperative Strategies and Alliances*, Elsevier Science, Oxford, UK, pp. 659–687.

Sanchez, R. (2008), "A scientific critique of the resource-base view (RBV) in strategy theory, with competence-based remedies for the RBV's conceptual deficiencies and logic problems", *Research in Competence-based Management*, Vol. 4, pp. 3–78.

Sanchez, R. and Heene, A. (1997), "Reinventing strategic management: New theory and practice for competence-based competition", *European Management Journal*, Vol. 15, No. 3, pp. 303–317.

Sanchez, R. and Heene, A. (2004), *The New Strategic Management: Organization, Competition, and Competence*, John Wiley & Sons, Inc., New York and Chichester, UK.

Scherer, F. M. (1967), "Research and development resource allocation under rivalry", *The Quarterly Journal of Economics*, pp. 359–394.

Scott, D. and Suppes, P. (1958), "Foundation aspects of theories of measurement", *Journal of Symbolic Logic*, Vol. 23, pp. 113–128.

Selznick, P. (1957), *Leadership in Administration*, Harper and Row, New York.

Seoudi, I. (2009), *The Resource-capability-competence Perspective in Strategic Management: A Reappraisal of the Epistemological and Theoretical Foundations*, PhD Thesis, Department of Economics, School of Graduate Studies. Case Western Reserve University, Cleveland, OH.

Skandia (1996a), *Customer Value. Intellectual Capital Supplement to Skandia's 1996 Annual Report*, Skandia, Stockholm.

Skandia (1996b), *Skandia and the Intellectual Capital Development*, CD-ROM, Skandia, Stockholm.

Skandia (1997), *Intelligent Enterprising. Intellectual Capital Supplement to Skandia's 6-Month Interim Report*, Skandia, Stockholm.

Sloan Jr., A. E. (1963), *My years with General Motors*, Doubleday, Garden City, NY.

Stabell, C. B. and Fjeldstad, Ø. D. (1998), "Configuring value for competitive advantage: On chains, shops and networks", *Strategic Management Journal*, Vol. 19, pp. 413–437.

Stevens, S. S. (1946), "On the theory of scales of measurement", *Science*, Vol. 103, pp. 677–680.

Suppes, P. and Zines, J. (1963), "Basic measurement theory", in Luce, R., Bush, R., and Galanter, E. (Eds), *Handbook of Mathematical Psychology Vol. 1*, John Wiley & Sons, Inc., New York, pp. 1–76.

Suppes, P., Krantz, D., Luce, D., and Tversky, A. (1989), *Foundations of Measurement, Vol. II, Geometrical, Threshold and Probabilistic Representations*, Academic Press, London.

Teece, D. J. (1986), "Firm boundaries, technological innovation, and strategic management", *The Economics of Strategic Planning*, pp. 187–199.

Teece, D. J., Pisano, G., and Shuen, A. (1997), "Dynamic capabilities and strategic management", *Strategic Management Journal*, Vol. 18, pp. 509–533.

Tversky, A., Slovic, P., and Sattath, S. (1988), "Contingent weighting in judgment and choice", *Psychological Review*, Vol. 95, pp. 371–384.

Uchida, Y. and Roos, G. (内田 and ルース, ヨ) (2008), 日本企業の知的資本マネジメント [*Intellectual Capital Management for Japanese Firms*], Chuokeizai-Sha Publishing, Chiyoda-ku, Tokyo, Japan.

Von Krogh, G. and Roos, J. (1995), *Organizational Epistemology*, St. Martin's Press, New York.

Wernerfelt, B. (1984), "A resource-based view of the firm", *Strategic Management Journal*, Vol. 5, No. 2, pp. 171–180.

Williamson, O. E. (1979), "Transaction-cost economics: The governance of contractual relations", *The Journal of Law and Economics*, Vol. 22, No. 2, pp. 233–261.

Williamson, O. E. (1985), *The Economic Institutions of Capitalism*, Free Press, New York.

Wilson, T. L. and Hlavacek, J. D. (1984), "Don't let good ideas sit on the shelf", *Research Management*, Vol. 27, No. 3, pp. 27–34.

26

VALUE CREATION IN BUSINESS MODELS IS BASED IN INTELLECTUAL CAPITAL

And only intellectual capital!

Henrik Dane-Nielsen and Christian Nielsen

Introduction

This chapter offers a novel perspective on how intellectual capital (IC) can be applied to the notion of business models. Our understanding of business models is that IC is present in different forms at all levels of the organization as described by Nielsen and Dane-Nielsen (2010), and is the only real value driver of any type of business model. A business model is thereby a description of how IC is used in the organization to create value. Nielsen (2011, p. 26) asserts that:

> A business model driven by intellectual capital may in some ways differ from business models driven primarily by other factors, such as financial capital or natural resources. When intellectual capital drives the business model of a company then competitive advantage may be particularly high, margins high and corporate flexibility good.

Knowledge and IC are important for the creation of value in the knowledge-based organization. However, in this chapter we argue that any type of technological development through the ages has had IC at its core, right from the invention of the plough, gunpowder, and steam engines to computers. In fact, any type of business or service is driven by the knowledge of how to do things. This is essentially because economic activities are driven by IC, and thereby we disagree with the arguments posed by Nielsen (2011) above.

One of the reasons for this is that business models are concerned with delivering a value proposition to users and/or customers, but the value proposition and the resources that support it never stand alone because they need to be supported by other activities. The problem with contemporary frameworks for visualizing companies' business models is that they often take the form of generic organization diagrams illustrating the process of transforming inputs to outputs in a chain-like fashion. A good example of this is found in the Integrated Reporting framework (IIRC, 2013) as well as in more management-oriented models such as the Business Model Canvas (Osterwalder and Pigneur, 2010). The core of the business model description should be focused on the connections between the different activities being performed in the company, in a reporting context often found as separated elements in the companies' reports. Companies often report a lot of non-financial information (e.g. customer relations, distribution channels, employee competencies, knowledge sharing, innovation, and risks) but this information may seem unimportant if the company fails to show how the various elements of the value creation collaborate and change.

This is where the IC perspective becomes imperative. Current perceptions of relationships and linkages often reflect only tangible transactions (i.e. the flow of products, services, or money). However, in analysing the value transactions inside organizations (intra-organizational) and between an organization and its partners (inter-organizational), there is a tendency to forget the often-parallel intangible transactions and interrelations that are taking place (Montemari and Nielsen, 2013). Our hypothesis is therefore that no organization, regardless of the type of business model being leveraged, can function without the appropriate IC to make use of machinery, increase financial capital, conduct processes, management actions, and so on. An organization's value drivers are always its IC.

Business models and configuring value

The concept of the business model offers a novel perspective from which to understand how companies become profitable, efficient, competitive, and sustainable: the latter being interpreted as the ability to survive in the long term. Much current focus in the field of business models concerns definitions, delimitations, and constructing frameworks for analysing business models (Wirtz *et al.*, 2016a) or innovating them (Wirtz *et al.*, 2016b; Foss and Saebi, 2017). Despite lacking unified theoretical groundings, at least according to Zott *et al.* (2011), many of these frameworks, ontologies, or models have proven to be successful in business and entrepreneurship practices. The most notable example of this is the Business Model Canvas published in Osterwalder and Pigneur's 2010 book, *Business Model Generation*, which has sold over 1,200,000 copies to date and been translated into over 30 languages. In its wake, several other tools and frameworks have been developed that perform additional and complementary analyses to that of the Business Model Canvas, for example, the Value Proposition Canvas (Osterwalder *et al.*, 2014) and the Kickass Company concept (Brøndum *et al.*, 2015; Nielsen *et al.*, 2016).

For a given company, it is important to be aware of the business model being applied for two reasons. First, the business model is the platform for executing corporate strategy. Therefore, if the business model is poorly configured or implemented, then the company will have difficulties in carrying through the strategy and ultimately then also meeting its non-financial and financial targets. Second, the business model affects the managerial processes of the organization because it directs the focus of how the firm does business. If the business model of a given firm relies on close ties with customers and the continuous involvement of strategic partners, then the managerial focus is expected to differ drastically from a situation where all customer interaction is web-based and all functions are in-house. In a similar manner, Mintzberg and Van Der Heyden (1999) argue that different forms of organization, or value configurations, carry different managerial foci, because the basis of value creation is different.

Positioning the business model

Baden-Fuller and Morgan (2010) argue that business models are distinct ways of doing business that can be distinguished from alternative modes of doing business and furthermore can be classified by the nature of how they are configured. Baden-Fuller and Morgan (2010) argue that a business model may be described as a model of how the firm does business. Sometimes the naming of the specific business model is done through the example of a well-known company. Five good examples of this are the business models of eBay, Dell, Ryanair, Gillette, and Skype. However, as Baden-Fuller and Morgan (2010, p. 157) note, behind most specific business model examples, the role models, there are scale models that "offer representations or short-hand descriptions of things that are in the world, while role models offer ideal cases to be admired". For the above examples, these would be the e-auction business model configuration (eBay), the disintermediation business model configuration (Dell), the no-frills business model configuration (Ryanair), the razors and blades business model configuration (Gillette), and the freemium business model configuration (Skype). A commonly applied business model definition that captures these notions of configuring a business is Osterwalder and Pigneur's (2010, p. 14): "A business model describes the rationale of how an organization creates, delivers, and captures value". Later in this chapter we apply these five cases to illustrate that IC is the key value driver of the value creation of a business model.

Notions of value

The notion of value is important, because value creation is at the heart of understanding business models and this concept seems to introduce a new level of analysis, different from, but related to, strategy, organization, and management. Akin to tribalism, there are many opposing views on what the term 'value' signifies. In accounting, the debate between cash-based and accruals-based accounting exists and in strategy there is the debate between Porter's (1985) market-based view and Barney's (1991) resource-based view. Another problem is that 'value' is used as a catch-all term focused on value for the consumer and wealth for the organization, which might be problematic. Typically, value is treated as an outcome of business activity (Conner, 1991) and, furthermore, Sirmon *et al.* (2007) argue that there is minimal theory explaining 'how' managers/firms transform resources to create value. Hence value is not only poorly defined but also poorly theorized.

A way of resolving this confusion is to distinguish between 'use value' and 'exchange value'. Use value is the benefit received from resources and capabilities and exchange value is the money that changes hands when resources, products, or services are traded (Bowman and Ambrosini, 2000). Figure 26.1 conceptualizes the relationships between concepts of value according to whether they are related to strategy, activities, or the stakeholders affected by the organization. Central to the business model literature is the term 'value proposition', which expresses the characteristics of the offering that the customer favours; hence it has close

STRATEGY	Value proposition			
	(The business model)			
STREAM	Value creation	Value delivery	Value realization	Value outputs
	(Business activities)	(The packaging)	(The transaction)	(Economic effects)
STAKEHOLDERS	Value outcomes			
	(Relationships with society and capital providers)			

Figure 26.1   Conceptualizations of value

resemblance to the term 'use value' applied in resource-based theory. The value proposition is an expression of uniqueness and differentiation of a product or service.

Another important value concept in the field of business models is that of 'value creation'. From a business model perspective, value creation expresses the business activities being performed and is closely related to 'value-added' (i.e. what extra value does the product/service have when it appears from the production process). An alternative way of understanding value creation is as cash flows, which are the ultimate liquidity (cash-based) effects of activities performed. Cash flows may differ despite identical activities due to the company's position and strength in the value chain. However, it can be argued that higher cash flows are a proxy of the strength and resilience of the business model. Beyond value creation comes the actual physical interaction between the company and its customers in the form of the delivery of value. Here the packaging of the product is the subject of analysis. This relates not only to the delivery channel but also to the combination of product, service, knowledge, and financing included in the delivery.

The notion of 'value realization' refers to the effects of physical and monetary transactions between the company and its customers. Through transactions, the company's activities are transformed into cash and from this converted into profits or losses depending on the company's ability to manage its activities and finances. From the business model perspective, value realization is merely an element of the mode of competition. As such, value realization leads to value outputs, which are the effects on the total value of the company, in terms of the balance sheet and market value. There is an important distinction between shareholder value and value to the customer. The IIRC (2013) introduced the idea of 'value outcomes' to represent a broader notion of corporate effects, for example on the total set of stakeholders and also the way the company affects users, customers, partners, and networks and vice versa. From this categorization of value, we can distinguish between different types of value drivers and thereby also gain a better understanding of different types of value drivers in relation to the business model.

The value drivers of business models

An important question to ask is: how do companies create value? In this chapter, we argue that in both for-profit and not-for-profit organizations it is only IC, for example in the form of knowledge of how to use resources, that drives value creation. The resources themselves create nothing. The notion of value drivers has been applied in a series of related fields to that of IC (e.g. Marr *et al.*, 2004; Cuganesan, 2005; Carlucci and Schiuma, 2007), such as R&D (Pike *et al.*, 2005), and customer relationship management (Richards and Jones, 2008). A business model is a description of an organization's value drivers as a whole.

Here, a value driver refers to any factor that enhances the total value created by an organization (Montemari and Nielsen, 2013), which is, in turn, the value that can be delivered to the actors involved in the business model (Amit and Zott, 2001). Value has different characteristics and can be split into several sub-dimensions (Amit and Zott, 2001; Ulaga, 2003; Cuganesan, 2005). One way of categorizing different perceptions of value and linking this to value drivers is provided by Nielsen *et al.* (2017). Their study identifies 251 different value drivers and categorizes them according to Taran *et al.*'s (2016) five-dimensional framework: value proposition, value segment, value configuration, value network, and value capture.

Table 26.1 illustrates how IC can be related to the different types of value drivers of business models according to Taran *et al.*'s (2016) five-dimensional framework. According to Nielsen *et al.* (2017), business models are representations of internal value drivers, the IC in the organization, and external value drivers, including relations to external partners. These are

Table 26.1 Value dimensions, value drivers, and intellectual capital

Value dimension	Examples of value drivers	Examples of underlying IC
Value proposition	Ease of use Quality Accessibility	Knowledge of competitors' products (HC and CC) Knowledge of customer needs (HC) Logistics planning and distribution network (SC)
Value segment	Packaging Distribution Communication Customer loyalty Lock-in	Knowledge of market behaviour, consumer needs and wants (CC) Knowledge of sales-triggers and buyer behaviour (HC and CC)
Value configuration	Material assets Immaterial assets Branding Processes IT-systems	Human resources / recruiting staff (HC) Purchasing / the quality of raw materials (HC) Manufacturing / building design, machinery, equipment, instruments (SC) Logistics / the economy of storage (SC) Technical solutions / technology (SC)
Value network	Partnerships Contracts	Stakeholders / surrounding society (SC)
Value capture	Financial capital Revenue models	Finance / shareholders (SC)

often interlinked, for example, the handling of external relationships, which is an important internal activity for many companies. IC can be in the form of relevant knowledge held by individuals employed in the organization or knowledge acquired from outside the organization for a specific functional purpose. For example, the value dimension 'value proposition' in Table 26.1, where 'accessibility' is a value driver. Behind the value driver 'accessibility' is knowledge about the customer's preferred mechanisms of buying and receiving the company's products, as well as logistics planning, but in addition to this, externally acquired knowledge relating to setting up the distribution platform. In many cases, companies have strategic partners running their distribution networks, and hence IC relating coordination with distribution partners also becomes relevant.

IC and value creation measures

The typical break-down of IC follows Edvinsson and Malone's (1997) IC-tree that divides IC into human capital, structural capital, and relational capital. Together with Edvinsson's (1997) Skandia Navigator, this proposed disaggregation of IC can be perceived as a standard method of categorizing IC (Stewart, 1997; Sveiby, 1997; Meritum, 2002). Human capital is viewed as everything the company cannot own, and structural capital is defined as "everything left at the office when the employees go home . . . Unlike human capital, structural capital can be owned and thereby traded" (Edvinsson and Malone, 1997, p. 11). Ultimately the creation of value comes from activities being performed by the company. All activities in an organization and all activities outside the organization involving inputs and outputs to and from the organization can be characterized as being economic activities, and all of these activities are controlled by structural IC in one form or another. Last, is the category of relational capital, which concerns the value embedded in supplier relations, customer relations, and strategic partnerships. Figure 26.2 illustrates the three subclasses of IC most commonly applied.

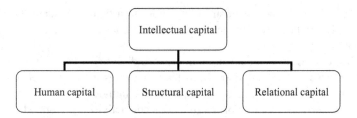

Figure 26.2   The three generic classes of intellectual capital (adapted from Edvinsson and Malone, 1997)

Nielsen and Dane-Nielsen (2010) critique this type of disaggregation, arguing that the summing up between subclasses in an accounting-like fashion completely ignores the fact that IC has different characteristics according to the levels of organization at which they are present. In similar fashion, Mouritsen and Larsen (2005) argue that it is the entanglement of the depicted subclasses of IC that creates value and not the subclasses by themselves. The mechanism by which IC is enacted is through the organization of activities, in a business model, in which the knowledge of the individual is utilized. This leads to the proposition that the value drivers in an organization are always IC, and nothing else, because all economic activities are controlled by people who, ideally, have the necessary knowledge in order to manage or perform the activities.

IC properties at different levels of the organization

We use the notion of 'emergentism' (Emmeche *et al.*, 1999) in the description of IC at the different levels of organization. Emergentism conceptualizes IC as represented throughout the organization by 'emergent entities' as 'emergent properties' (Nielsen and Dane-Nielsen, 2010) at different levels in the organization. Here, emergent entities are the carriers of the properties that create value and the properties of IC differ across levels of organization (Nielsen and Dane-Nielsen, 2010), both when a property has relations to a higher or a lower level of organization. In moving between different levels of the organization, completely different sets of properties emerge; in turn also affecting the units these are measured in (Wilson, 2015).

All activities relevant for the organization are performed in 'functions' with relations to other activities organized by the specific organizational structure, with emergent levels (Seibt, 2009). The propensity to form an emergent structure is, metaphorically speaking, the DNA of the organization. Within the notion of 'mereology', which is concerned with the study of parts and wholes, we find the notion of 'emergentism' (Stephan, 1999; Seibt, 2009), which originates from sociology (Sawyer, 2010) and biology (Kim, 1999; Potochnik, 2010), where scholars describe how natural phenomena and social communities result from a dominating hierarchical structure in nature (Rueger and McGivern, 2010).

It is important to emphasize that new emergent phenomena result in new entities (Emmeche *et al.*, 1999), which are carriers of new emergent properties on a different form. For example, knowledge of the individual employees in different functional departments can work together to form structural capital in the form of processes and technologies containing data about products, customers, or markets. This notion of IC having different properties at different levels of the organization (Nielsen and Dane-Nielsen, 2010) is equivalent to the relationship between the role of organ systems in an organism, as described within the field of medicine

(Potochnik, 2010). Hence, emergentism brings order to a field of random disorder (Rueger and McGivern, 2010), because disconnected components are ordered in a hierarchical system with functional levels.

We identify four levels of organization in order to discuss the value of IC. The first level is the individual level, where individual knowledge is expressed. In the second level, namely the group level, also known as functional departments, individuals are employed to perform tasks and here knowledge is a part of the functions and activities performed. The third level is the organizational level, which consists of a number of functional departments. The output from the organization is products or services. IC at the organizational level is embedded in the products and services. The fourth level is the market level and there are two markets. There is the market for products and services and then there is the market for companies, for example, the share market (the share value of the organization includes the value of IC within the company).

Activities create value for the organization, and activities at all different levels in the organization are driven by the knowledge of how to do things. It is not the stock of raw materials that creates value. It is not the machinery that creates value in the organization. It is the knowledge of how to use the machinery and sophisticated equipment and how to make use of the raw materials that is creating value. The stock of raw materials has no value in the warehouse as long as it just sits there. Only when used in the production of items, raw materials, or components, does the stock of materials become a means of value creation. The same goes for buildings, financing, machinery, equipment, and prepared marketing materials, and so on. These capitals are worth nothing without the knowledge of how to utilize them. IC used in activities is the driving force behind value creation, and knowledge of the organization's products and service is necessary for this value creation.

Customers do not create organizational value per se. Rather, it is the knowledge of the customers, their wishes and requirements, and the knowledge of how to sell, which ultimately create value. Long-term contracts with customers also carry value. However, behind the contracts lies knowledge of the market, knowledge of laws and regulations, and so on. Thus, IC creates value when applied in activities in the organization itself and in the transactions with other organizations. In this sense, value drivers can be seen as effects of the application of IC in concrete activities. These activities can take place at different levels of the organization in accordance with the specific relevant functional departments and they will result in emergent effects.

Next step performance measures

Mouritsen *et al.* (2003b) propose a model to analyse the interrelations of IC across two dimensions. The first is the type of IC and the second is whether the IC concerns resources, activities, or effects. Together with an understanding of the organization's strategy and the key management challenges facing the executive management, this model makes it possible to mobilize a series of questions to identify key IC indicators. Evaluating the effects of IC can therefore be done in a series of steps.

The first step is evaluating the identified indicators in a scorecard-like fashion in relation to a set of expected targets for each indicator. In a second step, the indicators can be evaluated in the analysis model (Mouritsen *et al.* 2003b) presented in Figure 26.3, by asking which indicators affect each other. Third, the analysis can be completed by asking whether some of the 12 boxes have missing indicators. Finally, with the indicators at hand, management should ask themselves how they fit into the story of what the company does and how it is unique.

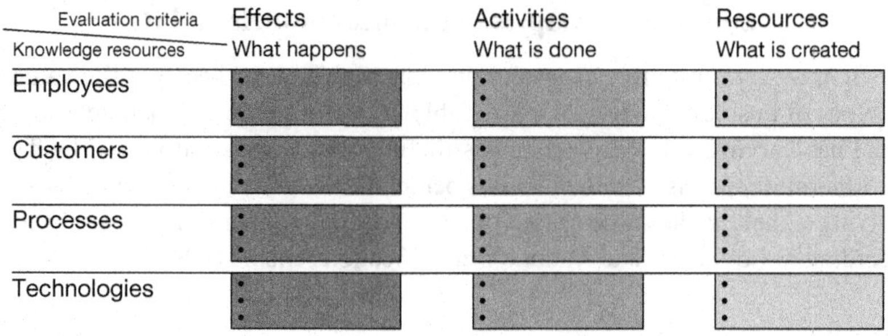

Evaluation criteria Knowledge resources	Effects What happens	Activities What is done	Resources What is created
Employees			
Customers			
Processes			
Technologies			

Figure 26.3 The analytical model

Source: www.vtu.dk/icaccounts

In this manner, management is gradually moving closer to understanding the effects of IC on the value creation of the organization. In order to assess if the composition, structure, and use of the company resources are appropriate, it is necessary to consider the development of the indicators over time, and finally the company may pursue relative and absolute measures for benchmarking across time and across competitors.

Unlike an accounting system, the analysis model is *not* an input/output model. There is no perception that any causal links between actions exist to develop employees and the effect in that area (e.g. increased employee satisfaction). The effect of such an action may appear as a customer effect. The employee becomes more qualified and capable of serving the customers better. The task of the analysis is thus to explain these 'many-to-many relations' in the model. The classification itself does not explain the relations, just as increased expenses for R&D alone do not lead to increased turnover in the financial accounting system.

It is essential to support a company's business model story with performance measures. While it may be acceptable for some companies merely to state that one's business model is based on mobilizing customer feedback in the innovation process, excellence would be achieved by explaining how this will be done, and even more demanding is proving the effort by indicating how many resources the company devotes to this effort, how active the company is in this matter, and whether it stays as focused on the matter as initially announced, and whether the effort has had any effect, for example, on customer satisfaction, innovation output, and so on. According to Bray (2010, p. 6):

> [r]elevant KPIs measure progress towards the desired strategic outcomes and the performance of the business model. They comprise a balance of financial and non-financial measures across the whole business model. Accordingly, business reporting integrates strategic, financial and non-financial information, is future-performance focused, delivered in real time, and is fit for purpose.

From an accounting perspective, the question of how to capture value creation and value trans-actions when value creation to a large extent goes on in a network of organizations and not inside an organization, as traditionally perceived, is problematic. Also, from a management perspective, the question of how to produce decision-relevant information is seriously chal-lenged by business model innovations and the advance of new types of business ecosystems, for example, based on crowd funding, social communities, virtual collaboration networks, and a competitive landscape based on business model 'innovation-ability'.

Empirical examples of business models and IC

In this section, we introduce five examples that illustrate how IC becomes the value driver of different types of business models. We use Table 26.1 as a frame to illustrate how each business model has varying value drivers across the five dimensions introduced by Taran *et al.* (2016). Furthermore, precisely which IC lies behind those value drivers. In the articulation of the underlying IC behind the value drivers of each of the five dimensions, we note the sub-class of IC according to Edvinsson and Malone's classification scheme (1997).

Example 1: eBay

eBay applies a business model configuration called 'The Mall', or 'e-Mall' configuration. It was initially coined by Timmers (1998) as a collection of shops or e-shops, usually enhanced by a common umbrella. The e-Mall is similar to a physical mall in that it consists of a collection of several shops – in this case web-shops. A closely related example to this way of doing business is the merchant model (Rappa, 2001), one-stop low-price shopping (Linder and Cantrell, 2000), and the shop in shop (Gassmann *et al.*, 2014). Revenues are generated from membership fees to the platform, transaction fees, and advertising. The typical value proposition of this business model configuration is that the web-shops benefit from professional hosting facilities and thereby are able to lower their costs and the complexity of being on the Internet. Furthermore, suppliers and buyers enjoy the benefits of efficiency/time-savings, no need for physical transport until the deal has been established, and global sourcing.

Table 26.2 illustrates that this business model configuration requires IC across a broad array of the sub-dimensions. The success of eBay is in part driven by its ability to create critical mass and global presence. Therefore, the human capital relating to international contract law and the value proposition of convenience offered through the customer capital perspective might be the prime IC of this business model configuration.

Table 26.2 Analysis of the e-Mall business model configuration

Value dimension	Examples of value drivers	Examples of underlying IC
Value proposition	One-stop convenient shopping Broad selection for consumers Larger potential customer base A platform for marketing	Market knowledge (HC) Marketing activities and databases (SC and CC)
Value segment	Automated Internet-based platform Customer/consumer segment Vendors	Technical knowledge (HC and SC) Customer behaviour intelligence (CC) Retail function (SC) Relationships to vendors (CC and SC)
Value configuration	Platform maintenance Web-platform	Technical knowledge (HC) Web supplier relations (CC) Processes structures and ICT (SC)
Value network	Supplier to platform activities Link with courier services	Customer behaviour intelligence (CC) Competitor intelligence (HC)
Value capture	Commission on vendor sales	International contract law (HC)

Example 2: Dell

The business model configuration used by Dell is called disintermediation. It cuts out the middlemen by delivering the offering directly to the customer through its own retail outlets, sales force or Internet-based sales rather than through intermediary channels, such as distributors, wholesalers, retailers, agents, or brokers. Related ways of doing business are the direct manufacturing model (Rappa, 2001), direct to consumer model (Weill and Vitale, 2001), and direct selling (Gassmann *et al.*, 2014). Dell has been successful by delivering directly to the customer a product or a service that had traditionally gone through an intermediary. By modularizing their product Dell allowed customers to choose varying configurations of the computers they ordered, thus creating a feeling of custom-made despite the prices generally beating the market. This was possible because of the cost savings from avoiding traditional intermediaries and because customers were prepared to buy at the website and wait for delivery instead of taking the computer home straight from the shop.

Table 26.3 illustrates that the success of this business model configuration revolves around minimizing the challenges created by the lack of physical store. Therefore, the IC behind the customer service, CRM, and the logistics becomes of vital importance. While the ability to minimize the challenges is based on customer capital, logistics and modular manufacturing are related mainly to structural capital.

Example 3: Ryanair

A typical low-cost airline, the Irish aviation company Ryanair applies the no-frills business model configuration (Gassmann *et al.*, 2014; Taran *et al.*, 2016). In this way of doing business,

Table 26.3 Analysis of the disintermediation business model configuration

Value dimension	*Examples of value drivers*	*Examples of underlying IC*
Value proposition	Same product at lower prices Customized products Superior customer service Fast delivery	Modular design and manufacturing (HC and SC) Technical knowledge (HC) IC for service departments and CRM solutions (CC) Consumer behaviour and needs (CC)
Value segment	Online channels Segmented market Mass market reach	Customer intelligence (CC) Marketing activities (SC)
Value configuration	Modularization Supply chain management Logistics Infrastructure management	Business economics and planning (SC)
Value network	Companies further back in the value chain	Market knowledge (CC) Supplier relationships (CC)
Value capture	Not specified, but creating customer loyalty and next purchase	Marketing activities (SC)

organizations offer a low-price, low service/product version of a traditionally high-end offering, in this case commercial aviation, consistent with Christensen and Overdorf's (2000) characterization of disruption (see also Markides, 2006). Similar labels for this way of doing business have been termed 'low touch' (Johnson, 2010), 'add-on' (Gassmann *et al.*, 2014), 'low-price reliable commodity' (Linder and Cantrell, 2002), and 'standardization' (Johnson, 2010). The key value driver, low prices for low service is the value proposition put forth by Ryanair. Hence, customers buy the basic offering cheap, and pay for add-ons in the product/service offering, for example, choice of seats, priority boarding, and baggage. A more in-depth account of Ryanair's business model and partnering with hotels, car rental services, airport transportation, and bargaining power towards the, typically smaller, airports is offered by Casadesus-Masanell and Ricart (2010). In reality we might question who Ryanair's most important customers are: the consumers or the airports? Ryanair achieves low costs at the smaller airports because it brings in high customer volumes and uses this as a bargaining tool.

Table 26.4 illustrates the IC of the no-frills business model applied by Ryanair. For Ryanair, efficiency is important, therefore structural capital related to operating procedures becomes the prime IC behind the value drivers. However, in addition to this, the human capital related to negotiating with airports and other types of strategic partners, which ensures the conversion of critical mass in terms of customer numbers to lower costs, is imperative to the survival of this particular company.

Example 4: Gillette

Gillette is renowned for its use of the 'bait and hook' business model configuration (Osterwalder and Pigneur, 2010). In this configuration companies seek to provide customers with an attractive, inexpensive, or free initial offer that encourages continuing future purchases of related

Table 26.4 Analysis of the no-frills business model configuration

Value dimension	Examples of value drivers	Examples of underlying IC
Value proposition	Traditional high-end offering at low price	Knowledge about competitors (SC) Market knowledge (CC)
Value segment	Self service Automated service Web platform Low and large base of the customer period Customers with low purchasing power	Customer behaviour (CC)
Value configuration	HR Low-cost infrastructure Standardized operating procedures (e.g. fast turnaround on the ground) Marketing Cost-control	Recruiting staff (SC)
Value network	Cost-effective supplier network Suppliers of related services that gain from access to large customer base	Bargaining power (HC)
Value capture	Low cost of suppliers from scale of operations Revenues based on add-on products and services	Supplier relations (CC) Customer needs (CC)

Table 26.5 Analysis of the bait and hook business model configuration

Value dimension	Examples of value drivers	Examples of underlying IC
Value proposition	Low price or free initial offer Quality System	Market understanding (CC) Marketing a consumer product (SC)
Value segment	Customers sensitive to initial offer	World wide market (CC) The brand (SC)
Value configuration	Brand Patents Developing follow-up products and accessories	Quality control (SC)
Value network	Marketing Production Logistics Retailing	Understanding retailers' needs for brands (CC)
Value capture	One-time low-margin sale followed by frequent high- margin sales	Consumer behaviour (CC) Consumer loyalty (CC) Consumer needs (CC)

products or services. This is also a much-used tactic in the printer business, for example the HP inkjet. This business model configuration is also known as razors and blades (Linder and Cantrell, 2000; Johnson, 2010; Gassmann *et al.*, 2014) or lock-in (Gassmann *et al.*, 2014). The key of this configuration is the close link between the inexpensive or free initial offer and the follow-up items on which the company earns a high margin as well as related product/service accessories. The key value driver is the achievement of lock-in and thereby also continued revenue streams.

Table 26.5 illustrates that this particular way of doing business relies heavily on customer capital and structural capital. The key to success for Gillette is the global presence of consistent and high-quality products, and the ability to protect the brand and the intellectual property. Procter & Gamble, which owns the Gillette series, is able to accomplish this because of its sheer size. Global presence, coupled with the lock-in mechanism of the business model, ensures that customers can turn their purchase of shaving equipment into a habit, regardless of where they are in the world.

Example 5: Skype

Skype applies a freemium business model configuration. The term freemium was first coined by Anderson (2009) and is in essence a business model that utilizes two types of customer segments. One segment is interested in a basic service for free, while the second, premium segment, is willing to pay for a more advanced product partly because the freemium segment provides critical mass to the business model. This way of doing business has similarities with the inside-out and no-frills business model configurations. The inside-out business model configuration (Osterwalder and Pigneur, 2010) is used by companies that sell their own developed R&D (i.e. intellectual properties or technologies that are under-used inside the company).

Table 26.6 shows that the structural capital of Skype is important to the functioning of the platform service and that the human capital that came up with the idea was central. However, it also illustrates that the notion of the double-sided platform of free and premium customer segments in the form of customer capital is vital for the success of Skype. This is because the

Table 26.6 Analysis of the freemium business model configuration

Value dimension	Examples of value drivers	Examples of underlying IC
Value proposition	Market coverage/market reach of the web-platform (structural capital)	Market understanding (CC)
		Find uncovered needs (HC)
	Free Internet-based call-service	Go-to-market strategy
	Cheap additional services	(HC)
Value segment	Knowledge about premium user service requirements (human capital)	Technical knowledge (SC)
		Market knowledge (CC)
	Conversion rate of free customers to paying customers (customer capital)	User needs and behaviour (CC)
	Degree of self-service for customer enquiries (customer capital)	
	Connects friends on a common communication platform	
Value configuration	Platform management (structural capital)	HR (HC)
	Software development	Technical knowledge (SC
	Automated services	and HC)
Value network	Distribution partners	Technical knowledge (SC
	Online payment service partners	and HC)
	Phone companies	Infrastructure (SC)
	Handset/headset partners	
Value capture	Subscription fees from premium customers (customer capital)	Customer behaviour (CC)
		Marketing activities (SC)
	Revenues from advertising to free customers (customer capital)	

most important aspect of the success is the ability to create the critical mass that allows the freemium model to flourish. It was clearly the human capital that formulated the go-to-market strategy that turned Skype into the company it is today. The market traction created by the founders ensured that Skype became synonymous with making phone calls over the Internet, best exemplified by the expression: "Let's Skype!"

Discussion and conclusions

This chapter argues that IC is the platform of any business model and its value creation, and that without IC there is no value creation. The examples applied above illustrate the relationship between each of these distinct business model configurations, their respective value drivers, and the IC elements that drive them.

These examples from five distinct business model configurations also illustrate that the value drivers of business models are IC entities at different levels of the organization. Individuals have relevant knowledge and work with other staff members in functional departments. An organization is made up of a number of interacting functional groups and departments, which together form the whole organization. Organizations, suppliers, and buyers act in a market and the price and volume of products are ultimately determined by so-called market forces. All of these are the results of an emergent process. Through the organization, right from the individual employee to the market level novel properties emerge at each level with new dimensions of IC. Hence, this chapter provides case study evidence to support the arguments of Nielsen and Dane-Nielsen (2010). Interaction and communication between individuals creates the output of the work done in the functional departments. Further, cooperation between the necessary functional departments and groups will create the final output of the organization that is valued by customers because it does a job for which they are willing to pay (Osterwalder *et al.*, 2014). However, the final monetary value of the output from an organization is determined by the market in which the organization is operating.

This 'emergentist' perspective is a research perspective that can be applied to many fields of research. For example, the notion of emergentism is used as a research perspective within biology and medicine (Kim, 1999) and also within philosophy (Potochnik, 2010). Emergentism is a discipline within mereology, the study of parts and wholes (Seibt, 2009). Emergent phenomena within the social space have been studied within sociology since the 1920s (Sawyer, 2010). This perspective argues that people, for example employees, act collectively to create new phenomena as collective knowledge and collective action that individuals do not hold by themselves. This is the foundation for claiming that IC at higher levels in a hierarchical structure, for example an organization, is different from the knowledge held by individual staff members in the organization. In doing so, this chapter offers a theoretically grounded lens for analysing and understanding business models by combining the perspectives of IC and emergentism from Nielsen and Dane-Nielsen (2010).

Also our analyses uncover several relevant action points for future studies that should be undertaken in order to further our understanding of IC in action, as well as of business models. This raises the question of the relationship between business models and different levels of the organization. Certainly, in our examples, we see that these business model configurations combine IC on several levels of the organization. But is this always the case? And can we talk of business models as organizational models or business models on an industry level? Furthermore, we find relevant connections between the prevailing understanding of business models based on certain value propositions to customers and the market level of our emergentist perspective. Here there is a fruitful avenue to follow in combining business models and market perspectives, for example, by viewing suppliers and buyers as non-managed organizations and markets as informal institutions.

A practical contribution of this chapter, besides the inspiration for managers of how to relate IC to the value drivers of specific business model configurations (Nielsen *et al.*, 2017), is that business models as managerial concepts might serve different purposes. Once the management team of a company has determined which is the business model configuration with which they are competing, this information can be used for multiple purposes. One such purpose is a managerial agenda. It entails managing, leading, and controlling the organization and establishing relationships with key strategic partners. Another purpose is communication. Here a wide array of potential stakeholders comes into play, including investors, employees, municipalities, customers, and strategic partners, and the notions of business models have proven themselves successful for aligning the views among such stakeholder groups on how the company works. Finally, there is also the business development purpose, also denoted as business model innovation. This perspective has received much attention from entrepreneurs in recent years, but has also entered into the established business sector and the academic curriculum.

The responsibility for managing, communicating, and innovating firms and their business models ultimately lies with the management team and the board of directors, while the use of the resulting analyses should be applicable to the whole organization. The application of business models may have implications on multiple time-horizons. In the short term, the notions of business models can help to evaluate the efficiency with which a company engages with customers. In the medium term, business models help companies to decipher whether customers are willing to pay for delivered value and how well the company utilizes strategic partners. On a more long-term basis, business models can help companies understand how to improve their overall concept for making money. Finally, it is evident that business models can serve a number of different managerial agendas. As seen above, business models might be concerned with managing, controlling, and making the organization efficient. However, business models might also serve purposes of managerial sensemaking in an innovation perspective (Michea, 2016), or open up new entrepreneurial possibilities (Lund and Nielsen, 2014).

References

Amit, R. and Zott, C. (2001), "Value creation in e-business", *Strategic Management Journal*, Vol. 22, Nos 6–7, pp. 493–520.

Anderson, C. (2009), *Free: The Future of a Radical Price*, Random House, New York.

Baden-Fuller, C. and Morgan, M. (2010), "Business models as models", *Long Range Planning*, Vol. 43, Nos 2–3, pp. 156–171.

Barney, J. B. (1991), "Firm resources and sustained competitive advantage", *Journal of Management*, Vol. 17, No. 1, pp. 99–121.

Bowman, C. and Ambrosini, V. (2000), "Value creation versus value capture: Towards a coherent definition of value in strategy", *British Journal of Management*, Vol. 11, No. 1, pp. 1–16.

Bray, M. (2010), *The Journey to Better Business Reporting: Moving beyond Financial Reporting to Improve Investment Decision Making*, KPMG, Sydney, Australia.

Brøndum, K., Nielsen, C., Tange, K., Laursen, F., and Oehlenschläger, J. (2015), "Kickass companies: Leveraging business models with great leadership", *Journal of Business Models*, Vol. 3, No. 1, pp. 22–28.

Carlucci, D. and Schiuma, G. (2007), "Knowledge assets value creation map: Assessing knowledge assets value drivers using AHP", *Expert Systems with Applications*, Vol. 7, pp. 814–822.

Casadesus-Masanell, R. and Ricart, J. E. (2010), "From strategy to business models and onto tactics", *Long Range Planning*, Vol. 43, No. 2, pp. 195–215.

Christensen, C. M. and Overdorf, M. (2000), "Meeting the challenge of disruptive change", *Harvard Business Review*, Vol. 78, No. 2, pp. 66–77.

Conner, K. R. (1991), "A historical comparison of resource-based theory and five schools of thought within industrial organization economics: Do we have a new theory of the firm?" *Journal of Management*, Vol. 17, No. 1, pp. 121–155.

Cuganesan, S. (2005), "Intellectual capital-in-action and value creation: A case study of knowledge transformation in an innovation process", *Journal of Intellectual Capital*, Vol. 6, No. 3, pp. 357–373.

Edvinsson, L. (1997), "Developing intellectual capital at Skandia", *Long Range Planning*, Vol. 30, No. 3, pp. 366–373.

Edvinsson, L. and Malone, M. S. (1997), *Intellectual Capital*, Piatkus, London.

Emmeche, C., Køppe S., and Stjernfelt F. (1999), "Explaining emergence", *Journal for General Philosophy of Science*, Vol. 28, pp. 83–119.

Foss, N. J. and Saebi, T. (2017), "Fifteen years of research on business model innovation: How far have we come, and where should we go?" *Journal of Management*, Vol. 43, No. 1, pp. 200–227.

Gassmann, H., Frankenberger, K., and Csik, M. (2014), *The Business Model Navigator*, Pearson Education Limited, Harlow, UK.

IIRC (2013), *The International <IR> Framework*, International Integrated Reporting Council, London, available at: www.theiirc.org.

Johnson, M. W. (2010), *Seizing the White Space: Business Model Innovation for Growth and Renewal*, Harvard Business Press, Brighton, MA.

Kim, J. (1999), "Making sense of emergence", *Philosophical Studies*, Vol. 95, pp. 3–36.

Linder, J. and Cantrell, S. (2000), *Changing Business Models: Surfing the Landscape*, Accenture Institute for Strategic Change, Cambridge, MA.

Linder, J. and Cantrell, S. (2002), "What makes a good business model anyway? Can yours stand the test of change?", *Outlook*, available at: www.accenture.com.

Lund, M. and Nielsen, C. (2014), "The evolution of network-based business models illustrated through the case study of an entrepreneurship project", *The Journal of Business Models*, Vol. 2, No. 1, pp. 105–121.

Markides, C. (2006), "Disruptive innovation: In need of better theory", *Journal of Product Innovation Management*, Vol. 23, No. 1, pp. 19–25.

Marr, B., Schiuma, G., and Neely, A. (2004), "The dynamics of value creation: Mapping your intellectual performance drivers", *Journal of Intellectual Capital*, Vol. 5, No. 2, pp. 312–325.

Meritum (2002), *Measuring Intangibles to Understand and Improve Innovation Management*, European Commission, Brussels.

Michea, A. (2016), *Enacting Business Models*, PhD dissertation, Copenhagen Business School.

Mintzberg, H. and Van der Heyden, L. (1999), "Organigraphs: Drawing how companies really work", *Harvard Business Review*, September-October, pp. 87–94.

Montemari, M. and Nielsen, C. (2013), "The role of causal maps in intellectual capital measurement and management", *Journal of Intellectual Capital*, Vol. 14, No. 4, pp. 522–546.

Mouritsen, J. and Larsen, H. T. (2005), "The 2nd wave of knowledge management: The management control of knowledge resources through intellectual capital information", *Management Accounting Research*, Vol. 16, No. 3, pp. 371–394.

Mouritsen, J., Bukh, P. N., Johansen, M. R., Larsen, H. T., Nielsen, C., Haisler, J., and Stakemann, B. (2003b), *Analysing Intellectual Capital Statements*, Danish Ministry of Science, Technology and Innovation, Copenhagen, available at: www.vtu.dk/icaccounts.

Nielsen, C. (2011), "When intellectual capital drives the business model, then", in Lloyd, A. and Reddy, M. (Eds), *Human Capital Handbook*, Hubcap-Digital, Hockliffe, UK, pp. 26–31.

Nielsen, C. and Dane-Nielsen, H. (2010), "The emergent properties of intellectual capital: A conceptual offering", *Journal of Human Resource Costing & Accounting*, Vol. 14, No. 1, pp. 6–27.

Nielsen, C., Lund, M., and Thomsen, P. (2017), "Killing the balanced scorecard to improve internal disclosure", *Journal of Intellectual Capital*, Vol. 18, No. 1, pp. 45–62.

Nielsen, C., Roslender, R., and Schaper, S. (2016), "Continuities in the use of the intellectual capital statement approach: Elements of an institutional theory analysis", *Accounting Forum*, Vol. 40, No. 1, pp. 16–28.

Osterwalder, A. and Pigneur, Y. (2010), *Business Model Generation: A Handbook for Visionaries, Game Changers, and Challengers*, John Wiley & Sons, Hoboken, NJ.

Osterwalder, A., Pigneur, Y., Bernarda, G., and Smith, A. (2014), *Value Proposition Design: How to Create Products and Services Customers Want*, John Wiley & Sons, Hoboken, NJ.

Pike, S., Roos, G., and Marr, B. (2005), "Strategic management of intangible assets and value drivers in R&D organizations", *R&D Management*, Vol. 35, No. 2, pp. 111–124.

Porter, M. E. (1985), *Competitive Advantage*, The Free Press, New York.

Potochnik, A. (2010), "Levels of explanation reconceived", *Philosophy of Science*, Vol. 77, No. 1, pp. 59–72.

Rappa, M. (2001), *Managing the Digital Enterprise: Business Models on the Web*, North Carolina State University, available at: http://digitalenterprise.org/models/models.html (accessed September 2015).

Richards, K. A. and Jones, E. (2008), "Customer relationship management: Finding value drivers", *Industrial Marketing Management*, Vol. 37, No. 2, pp. 120–130.

Rueger, A. and McGivern, P. (2010), "Hierarchies and levels of reality", *Synthese*, Vol. 176, pp. 379–397.

Sawyer, R. K. (2010), "Emergence in sociology: Contemporary philosophy of mind and some implications for sociological theory", *American Journal of Sociology*, Vol. 107, No. 3, pp. 551–585.

Seibt, J. (2009), "Forms of emergent interaction in general process theory", *Synthese*, February, pp. 166–479.

Sirmon, D., Hitt, M., and Ireland, R. D. (2007), "Managing firm resources in dynamic environments to create value: Looking inside the black box", *Academy of Management Review*, Vol. 32, No. 1, pp. 273–292.

Stephan, A. (1999), "Varieties of emergentism", *Evolution and Cognition*, Vol. 5, No. 1, pp. 49–59.

Stewart, T. A. (1997), *Intellectual Capital*, Nicolas Brealey Publishing, London.

Sveiby K. E. (1997), *The New Organizational Wealth: Managing and Measuring Knowledge-Based Assets*, Berrett-Koehler, San Francisco, CA.

Taran, Y., Nielsen, C., Thomsen, P., Montemari, M., and Paolone, F. (2016), "Business model configurations: A five-V framework to map out potential innovation routes", *European Journal of Innovation Management*, Vol. 19, No. 4, pp. 492–527.

Timmers, P. (1998), "Business models for electronic markets", *Journal on Electronic Markets*, Vol. 8, No. 2, pp. 3–8.

Ulaga, W. (2003), "Capturing value creation in business relationships: A customer perspective", *Industrial Marketing Management*, Vol. 32, No. 8, pp. 677–693.

Weill, P. and Vitale, M. R. (2001), *Place to Space*, Harvard Business School Press, Boston, MA.

Wilson, J. (2015), "Metaphysical emergence: Weak and strong", in Bigaj, T. and Wüthrich, C. (Eds), *Metaphysics in Contemporary Physics*, Brill, Leiden, Netherlands.

Wirtz, B. W., Göttel, V., and Daiser, P. (2016b), "Business model innovation: Development, concept and future research directions", *Journal of Business Models*, Vol. 4, No. 2, pp. 1–28.

Wirtz, B. W., Pistoia, A., Ullrich, S., and Göttel, V. (2016a), "Business models: Origin, development and future research perspectives", *Long Range Planning*, Vol. 49, No. 1, pp. 36–54.

Zott, C., Amit, R., and Massa, L. (2011), "The business model: Recent developments and future research", *Journal of Management*, Vol. 37, No. 4, pp. 1019–1042.

27

MAKING INTELLECTUAL CAPITAL MATTER TO THE INVESTMENT COMMUNITY

Morten Lund and Christian Nielsen

Introduction

Critics of intellectual capital (IC) argue that information of this sort is irrelevant to the investment community. This could be because the IC information is brought to the market in formats that are not timely (Dumay, 2016), or because the stakeholders in the investment community do not understand IC information (Holland and Johanson, 2003). On the other hand, studies have shown that the investment community in certain instances, such as Initial Public Offerings, actually does apply IC information (Bukh *et al.*, 2005; Nielsen *et al.*, 2006), but that during recurring valuations this information is contained elsewhere in the market for information than in official documents such as analyst reports (Nielsen, 2008). One avenue for improving the relevance of IC information is to create a stronger link to the future value creation scenarios of the given company through the concept of business models, which will illustrate the explicit interconnectedness of the value creating activities of the company. In another chapter in this companion, Dane-Nielsen and Nielsen (2017) argue that IC constitutes the only true value drivers of any business model.

Since the late 1990s, standard-setting bodies and academics have been discussing how to improve the informativeness of IC reporting and narrative reporting (e.g. in the form of management commentary, and lately this is reflected in the debate around Integrated Reporting). Over this period, which types of users such reporting is to be aimed at, and in turn, the perceptions of its possible content, have been the focus of a range of studies. Since the turn of the millennium, such new types of reporting have been addressing the needs of a much broader set of stakeholders than has financial reporting traditionally.

Lately, integrated reporting (<IR>) has become a dominant discourse in the business reporting debate, and has attracted significant attention within the academic research literature (De Villiers *et al.*, 2014), the global accountancy profession, and practitioner communities (Dumay *et al.*, 2016). <IR> places the concept of business models at the heart of organizing information and key performance indicators, and highlights investors as the main stakeholders (Roslender and Nielsen, 2017). This is consistent with the normative view of an organization's purpose, namely to generate profits, but is in conflict with the social and environmental discourse, despite its notable presence in the <IR> framework (Dumay, 2016).

The social and environmental discourse, like that of IC, is much more aligned with March and Olsen's (1989) logic of the appropriateness perspective, where corporate actions are concerned with communicating core values, mission statements, the business concept, political ideology, and social responsibility (Söderbaum, 2002, p. 191). Historically, the consequence of this is that the specific needs of professional users, such as private and institutional investors and financial analysts, have been downplayed somewhat in the business reporting debate. Some would go so far as to say that the investment community is rarely heard in these respects (PWC, 2007, p. 3). However, in 2009, the IASB released its *IFRS Practice Statement on Management Commentary* (IASB, 2009), specifically emphasizing existing and potential capital providers as the primary users of financial reporting and thereby also management commentary (IASB, 2009, p. 8). This emphasis is echoed by Bray (2010), who states that the social and environmental reporting movement is taking steps in the direction of attaining relevance towards the capital markets and that early adopters of such disclosures potentially could help build impetus for later regulation. The <IR> framework is a first serious attempt at providing a distinct business reporting focus to the investment community.

Since the Jenkins Report (AICPA, 1994), there has been extensive discussions about which information companies ought to disclose and whether financial reporting as we know it today conveys sufficient relevant information to the capital markets. Research relating to the agenda of management commentary has focused on which types of information companies are disclosing voluntarily in their annual reports (Beattie and Pratt, 2002; Vanstraelen *et al.*, 2003) or via their corporate websites (Fisher *et al.*, 2004), and which firm characteristics are influential on the extent of voluntary disclosure (Cooke, 1989; Adrem, 1999).

However, information flows from companies to the financial markets and other stakeholder groups are much more complex than those conveyed through historical financial statements (Dumay, 2016). Among the information channels that companies apply as disclosure channels are press and stock market releases, corporate newsletters, profiles and brochures, corporate websites, conference calls, the press, face-to-face meetings with stakeholders and investors, and social media. This leads to several challenges for companies as well as external stakeholders. First, from the company perspective, it is a question of ensuring connectivity between the various media and that the message is aligned across these. Second, from the stakeholder perspective, it is a question of always being up to date on what is happening in the company, which may entail following a number of different information channels.

Third, information flows from companies have become much more accessible to both private and professional stakeholders in the last decade through the rise of the internet and ubiquitous access to it through wi-fi connections and smartphones. At the same time, the complexity and amount of information have risen to unprecedented levels, making it more and more difficult for the 'ordinary' investor to calculate the consequences of such information and thereby also the actions of the companies in which they wish to invest.

Fourth, another challenge is approaches of communicating strategy and the business model (Bray, 2010). <IR> specifically uses the terminology of business models as an organizing element in its framework. However, this is done in a value chain-like fashion, as noted by Tweedie *et al.* (forthcoming). Contemporary companies are competitive due to their extremely complex structures and their ingenious ways of retracting value from networks of resources. Contemporary companies are not organized in the silos described in basic textbooks of organization (i.e. in simple value chains). However, when one reads the narrative sections of the same companies' financial reports, this could well be the impression one gets. The narrative sections of the financial annual report are therefore typically not aligned with the actual value creation setup of the company (Mintzberg and Van Der Heyden, 1999) and this might help to explain why professional users of financial reporting need to have additional information channels.

Therefore, we argue that management commentary needs to a much greater extent to illustrate the explicit interconnectedness between the value creating activities of the company. In other words, the narrative sections need to be aligned with the logic of the business model, thereby describing the specific structures and strategies of value creation, which are not always in the form of a value chain.

It has been suggested that a potential step in this direction could be to introduce the notion of industry specific value creating interrelations. In relation to this, the World Intellectual Capital Initiative (WICI, 2010, 2016) has been working on creating a set of industry-based KPI sets for its business reporting framework. Such industry taxonomies may be a good starting point as they can induce companies to start thinking in terms of what are their key value creating processes, activities, and partnerships. However, Nielsen *et al.* (2017a) argue that companies in the same industry can be immensely different (i.e. have different business models, and organizational and legal structures), and therefore it does not make sense to develop standards for either length or content of the management commentary. Therefore, such industry taxonomies might only be expected to be a part of the initialization of these developments where using the structure of business models is a fruitful avenue to pursue.

Conforming to users' needs, but which users?

Since the late 1990s, a myriad of reports and guidelines have addressed the value of IC reporting, business reporting, and management commentary narratives. Critics have questioned the ability of the more traditional reporting vehicles, such as annual reporting (Lev, 2001), but also voluntary and standalone IC reports (Dumay, 2016) and the contemporary <IR> (Dumay *et al.*, 2016) in presenting meaningful disclosures regarding IC and value creation. This section explores how business reporting may conform to users' needs by asking the critical question: Who are the users of business reporting?

It is important to consider who are the target stakeholders of a report. For example, Bray (2010) states that the most important user of business reporting is the investor. Similarly, Beattie and Pratt (2002) argue that the type of disclosures contained in the narrative sections of the financial report are important to investors and to analysts as these users base their earnings and cash flow expectations on both financial and non-financial information. This is because earnings and cash flow expectations are considered cornerstones in company valuation and non-financial information contributes to the accuracy of the valuation (Lang and Lundholm, 1993; Christensen and Demski, 2003). More informative disclosures and more explanation will thus reduce the information asymmetry between the company and the capital markets, thereby diminishing uncertainty regarding the company's future prospects (Botosan, 1997) and lead to more accurate forecasts on which investors can base their investment decisions (Lang and Lundholm, 1996).

In addition, Vanstraelen *et al.* (2003) find that higher levels of non-financial disclosures are associated with lower dispersion and higher accuracy of financial analysts' earnings forecasts. These arguments therefore illustrate that providing voluntary information (e.g. through IC reports) is a way of satisfying users' needs (McEwen and Hunton, 1999). The question then prevails whether the reporting vehicles of today, like IC reports and <IR> can fulfil these needs. Holman (2002) states that comprehensive business reporting should convey a broader representation of the company and its value creation logic than that communicated through financial reporting as it is practised today.

However, this notion of considering and researching the usefulness of annual reporting from a user perspective is not new. Lee and Tweedie's studies (1977, 1981) examined first the private investors' and second the institutional investors' perceptions of the usefulness of the corporate report. Arnold and Moizer (1984) and Pike *et al.* (1993) subsequently studied user requirements from the analyst's perspective. Bartlett and Chandler (1997) conducted a follow-up study of Lee and Tweedie's 1977 study, concluding that little had changed in those 20 years despite the efforts of the accounting profession and the business community to improve communication between management and shareholders.

Figure 27.1 is an illustration of the fact that the stakeholder focus in business reporting has not followed that of the surrounding business environment. For many years there was a much broader perception of relevant stakeholders in the business reporting literature than applied in practice. Starting out, the Jenkins Report (AICPA, 1994) had a rather narrow conception of relevant stakeholders, stating that the target users of business reporting were investors and financial analysts. Around the turn of the millennium, a much broader perception of relevant stakeholders was communicated in the literature. This was mirrored in the then flourishing IC reporting practices (Nielsen *et al.*, 2017b), but also in the Global Reporting Initiative (GRI, 2002) and the work by the World Business Council for Sustainable Development (Heemskerk *et al.*, 2003). However, recent developments have seen a contention of the broader stakeholder focus in the literature (IASB, 2009; Bray, 2010; IIRC, 2013a).

In the same timeframe, the stakeholder focus in businesses' actual business reporting practices have continually broadened, but without the late contraction as seen in the literature. The early 1990s saw the emergence of several management models, such as the Balanced Scorecard and Business Excellence, these having broader foci on customers and employees and not just investors. Around the turn of the millennium, with the advent of the concepts of the knowledge society and the new economy, this stakeholder perspective had broadened somewhat, and this has been driven further by the social and environmental accounting practices and focus on corporate governance in the wake of the financial crisis.

Although there is a great deal of agreement concerning the need for developments in corporate reporting practices, there is some ambivalence as to how this should be carried out. While some contributions argue that standard setters should be responsible for developing

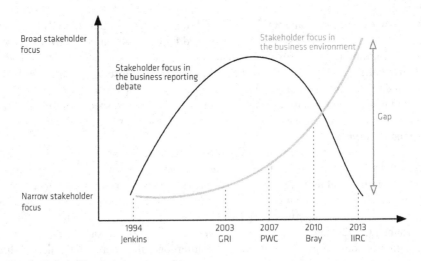

Figure 27.1 Stakeholder foci change over time

comprehensive models for business reporting (AICPA, 1994), others reason that changes must come from the business community (Bray, 2002, p. 3). The problem is that non-financial information is inherently idiosyncratic to particular industries (Upton, 2001) and also to individual firms because it varies with the applied business models (Nielsen *et al.*, 2017a). Therefore, it is not necessarily new accounting standards that are needed, rather standards for form, presentation, and disclosure of underlying assumptions, as suggested by DiPiazza and Eccles (2002).

The reasons advocated for improving companies' business reporting efforts relate to both external and internal objectives. Externally, relevance to the capital market is perceived as a main driver of business reporting, as the underlying premise that improving disclosure makes the capital allocation process more efficient and reduces the average cost of capital. FASB (2001) provides a number of concrete examples with helpful ideas to companies on how to describe and explain their investment potential to investors. Also, it is argued that a new generation of analytical tools is needed to enable company boards, shareholders, and investors to judge management performance and differentiate good, bad, and delinquent corporate stewardship (Eustace, 2001, p. 7). Moreover, Blair and Wallman (2001, p. 45) accentuate that more reliable and useful information to financial markets must be obtained by improving internal measurement, which creates a better understanding of the company's key value drivers.

Therefore, internal and external objectives become closely interrelated. Blair and Wallman (2001, p. 58) argue that:

> [t]he lack of good information about the most important value drivers in individual firms, and in the economy as a whole, makes it more difficult for managers within firms and individual investors in the capital markets to make sensible resource allocation decisions.

Also of internal relevance is the ability to communicate strategy, vision, and corporate objectives to employees throughout the firm. According to Bray (2002), enabling management and employees to understand the reporting and communication strategy of the company can be achieved by synchronizing the company's performance reporting with management's decision-making models.

Critics of management narratives, business reporting, and voluntary disclosures (Lev, 2001; Gu and Li, 2007) argue that the reliability of the information is questionable and that even if reliability was to be obtained through regulation or consistency of disclosures, there would still be the problems of the subjectivity of management and the shelf-life of the narratives. Creating confidence in non-financial information can be achieved through consistent practices (PWC, 2007), thereby generating user experience in understanding such performance measures, rather than creating prescriptive standards for these types of information. An underlying notion within the business reporting debate is that mandatory requirements are not satisfactory in order to meet users' needs and that the future of corporate reporting includes aspects currently perceived as voluntary (DiPiazza and Eccles, 2002). Eccles *et al.* (2001) argue that the implications of this will be moving companies' practices from a performance measurement agenda to a performance reporting agenda. In summary, if non-financial information is important for the management of the company, then it is also relevant for the investment community because it provides context for the financial numbers.

Creating comparable non-financial information is argued to be a means of increasing the reliability of key performance indicators (Nielsen *et al.*, 2006), like those that are presented in management commentary sections of annual reports (Blair and Wallman, 2001) or <IR>. Comparability can be thought of in two ways. First, it can relate to the ability to track non-financial information from period to period (FASB, 2001; Upton, 2001). Second, it can relate to the ability of benchmarking such information across companies (Bray, 2002). The industry-based KPI-taxonomies of WICI (2010) are an attempt at creating such benchmarking possibilities. However, a recent contribution by Nielsen *et al.* (2017a) revokes this, arguing that comparability should be sought towards similar business models and not merely in accordance with the industry.

Sandberg (2002, p. 3) argues that this is because recent changes in the competitive landscape have given rise to a variety of new value creation models within industries where previously the "name of the industry served as shortcut for the prevailing business model's approach to market structure". Examples of this are the recent disruptions of the taxi industry by Uber, the hotel industry being disrupted by Airbnb, and Netflix disrupting the business model of Blockbuster. As Hamel (2000) states, competition now increasingly stands between competing business concepts. Therefore, context needs to be capable of providing enough information for users to understand exactly how it is a given company has chosen to compete in its industry.

Business reporting themes

The previous section highlighted shifts in the conception of relevant stakeholders, but also that information relevant to management is also relevant to the investor community. This section establishes the types of information recommended by standard-setting bodies and other institutions since the late 1990s that companies disclose in order to meet demands for 'full information' from the investment community and other stakeholders. For the purpose of this discussion, eight different business reporting frameworks have been selected for review. The reports considered are: *Improving Business Reporting: A Customer Focus – Meeting the Information Needs of Investors and Creditors*, also referred to as the Jenkin's Report (AICPA, 1994), coded A; *Improving Business Reporting: Insights into Enhancing Voluntary Disclosures* (FASB, 2001), coded F; *Business and Financial Reporting: Challenges from the New Economy* (Upton, 2001), coded U; *Unseen Wealth* (Blair and Wallman, 2001), coded BW; *New Directions in Business: Performance Reporting, Communication and Assurance* (Bray, 2002), coded B; *Sustainable Development Reporting: Striking the Balance* (Heemskerk *et al.*, 2003), coded H; *Management Commentary Exposure Draft* (IASB, 2009), coded I; and *The Corporate Reporting Framework* (originally published in Eccles *et al.*, 2001, now used by WICI and PwC), coded P/W.

An overview of the types of information recommended by these frameworks is provided in Table 27.1. A wide spectrum of information, ranging from the more traditional financial and operating data, to management's analysis of data, to more forward-oriented information such as critical success factors, strategy, and IC are covered in these frameworks. Together, these types of information might be said to constitute the content of what a so-called flag-ship performance report should contain (Bray, 2010).

The model for business reporting proposed by Jenkins (AICPA, 1994, p. 44) initially identified ten components to be included in a corporate report and thereby also constitute the backbone of management commentary. Table 27.1 illustrates that there is broad agreement among the reports reviewed regarding the inclusion of elements such as management's operating data, management's analysis of financial and operating data, information on risks and opportunities, critical success factors, value drivers, objectives, strategy, and vision.

A much-applied critique of the 'usefulness' of narrative reporting has been the question of objectivity and timeliness of management commentary (Dumay and Guthrie, 2017). This becomes especially problematic in relation to the macro environment and the competitive landscape, where the situation can change even between the writing and publishing of the

Table 27.1 Business reporting recommendation themes

	Proposed business-reporting theme	A	F	U	BW	B	H	I	P/W
1	Financial data	X			X	X		X	X
2	Management's operating data	X	X	X	X	X		X	X
3	Management's analysis	X	X		X	X		X	
4	Risks and opportunities	X	X	X	X	X	X	X	X
5	Critical success factors	X	X	X	X	X	X	X	X
6	Objectives, strategy, vision	X	X		X	X	X	X	X
7	Comparable non-financial measures	X		X	X	X	X	X	
8	Background information	X	X			X		X	
9	Value drivers	X		X	X	X	X	X	X
10	Segment information	X		X	X			X	X
11	Intellectual capital			X	X	X		H	X
12	Effects of voluntary disclosure	X	X		X				
13	Corporate governance	X					X		X
14	Social, environmental, and sustainability disclosures					X	X		X
15	Macro environment, including regulation							X	X

narrative report. The investment community states in relation to this problem that the application of other information channels is a necessity for their decision making (Nielsen, 2005b; Bukh and Nielsen, 2010). Professional users apply a wide array of information sources and channels in addition to the annual report in order to enhance their contextual understanding (Holland, 2004). Such types of information may include competitors' data, market research reports, trade magazines, and face-to-face management briefings.

Other areas emphasized by these eight reports include segment information such as the break-up of information by line of business and type of expenditure (FASB, 2001), and generally the use of key performance indicators along multiple dimensions (Bray, 2002). Likewise, the significance of intangibles for value creation, as argued by Lev (2001), invokes that additional data about IC, including human resources, customer relationships, and innovation, is recommended in a majority of the reports. This category of information depicts the processes and infrastructure put in place to achieve organizational objectives (Bray, 2002, p. 13) and is thus important for understanding business models (Dane-Nielsen and Nielsen, 2017).

IC has been a major discourse within business reporting since the late 1990s (Beattie and Smith, 2013), but this particular theme seems to recently have been encapsulated by the <IR> discourse as an input-capital (Nielsen *et al.*, 2016). Early on in the debate, Bukh (2003) suggested the business model as a potential organizer of voluntary information such as that of IC, a message that Beattie and Smith (2013) later reinforced. The recent <IR> framework does, in fact, make use of the term business model as a central frame of reference; however, the IIRC's understanding of business models seems to be distanced from the mainstream, implying a focus on value propositions and customer value creation and delivery (Nielsen and Roslender, 2015). In the next section, we examine how companies can apply the ideas of the business model as a platform for strategy and thereby also as a platform for structuring the narrative sections of business reporting.

Business models as platforms for structuring narratives

The previous section highlighted which types of voluntary information were considered relevant for users of business reporting. Users were primarily understood as the representatives of the investment community. Despite the distinct investor focus of the eight reports reviewed in the previous section it is, however, worth noting that three of the reports studied argue for the mobilization of multiple stakeholders as recipients of information (Eccles *et al.*, 2001; Bray 2002; Heemskerk *et al.* 2003) and the importance of linking social and environmental measures to business objectives (Heemskerk *et al.* 2003). <IR> (IIRC, 2013a) takes an investor focus on business reporting, but argues for the importance of reporting about the effects of the corporation towards a broad stakeholder base. Hence it takes a perspective focused on report-ing *about* stakeholders, rather than reporting *for* stakeholders.

Dumay *et al.* (2017) argue that there is a reporting resurgence in IC. However, this resur-gence, they suggest, may be short lived if it only focuses on investors and managers, as it is no longer considered responsible for companies to prioritize profits before people and the environment. Therefore, there needs to be more research to understand how IC helps develop value beyond organizational boundaries, and this can be supported from a business model perspective. This is because business models naturally lend themselves to describing firms and firm boundaries by distinguishing between (i) internal value creation mechanisms of the firm, (ii) focal firm value creation that includes the immediate stakeholders such as suppliers and partners, and (iii) the broader societal effects of firm activities. Nielsen (2005a) provides the following definition of a business model:

> A business model describes the coherence in the strategic choices which makes possible the handling of the processes and relations which create value on both the operational, tactical and strategic levels in the organization. The business model is therefore the platform which connects resources, processes and the supply of a ser-vice which results in the fact that the company is profitable in the long term.

According to Nielsen's (2005a) definition, the business model bears closest resemblance to understanding the focal firm's value creation that includes the immediate stakeholders. The business model is concerned with delivering the value proposition of the company, but it is not the value proposition alone that makes a business model. It is, in itself, supported by a number of parameters and mechanisms relating to how the value proposition of the company is implemented. Conceptualizing the business model is therefore concerned with identifying the platform that connects resources and processes to value delivery. Analysing the business model, on the other hand, is concerned with gaining an understanding of precisely which levers of control are apt to deliver the value proposition of the company, while communicating the business model is concerned with identifying the most important performance measures, both absolute and relative measures, and relating them to the overall value creation story.

In line with Baden-Fuller and Morgan's (2010) terminology of business models as role models of ways to do business, and Lund and Nielsen's (2014) examples of business models as narratives capable of visualizing a set of complex future business options, Beattie and Smith (2013, p. 253) state that the business model concept offers a powerful overarching con-cept within which to refocus the IC debate, because business model narratives hold promise for linking value creation and value delivery with the value realization (capture) trajectory of the financial reporting profession (Nielsen and Roslender, 2015). However, if firms only disclose key performance indicators without disclosing the business model that explains the interconnectedness of the indicators (Bukh, 2003) and why precisely this bundle of indicators is relevant for understanding the firms' value creation (Nielsen *et al.*, 2017a), then chances are external users of the information are going to have a hard time making sense, let alone make judgements.

According to Montemari and Chiucci (2017), there exists little current research-based insight into how such an analysis and interpretation might be conducted. However, Nielsen *et al.* (2017a) and Dane-Nielsen and Nielsen (2017) illustrate that it is possible to analyse IC from a business model perspective and from this perspective to identify performance measures based on the specific business model configuration employed by a given company (Taran *et al.*, 2016).

Although <IR> (IIRC, 2013b) places the business model at the centre of its framework, the IIRC's particular interpretation of business models leaves out some very central notions of contemporary understandings, including the critical notion of the value proposition (Osterwalder and Pigneur, 2010), and this is problematic if it is to connect to how companies work with business model design and business model innovation internally. For Nielsen and Roslender (2015), a business model provides a framework for visualizing the relationship that exists between the three components of a generic value creation focus: 1) value creation; 2) value delivery; and 3) value capture. This should then also be visualized in management commentary.

The point of departure for some suggestions in relation to voluntary reporting and management commentary is to illustrate the flows of value creation by linking it to performance measures (Nielsen *et al.*, 2009), thus in turn connecting performance measures with management commentary. Mouritsen and Larsen (2005) label this a process of "entangling" the indicators, arguing that individual pieces of information and measurements by themselves can be difficult to relate to any conception of value creation. The problem with trying to visualize the company's business model is that it often ends up becoming a generic organization diagram illustrating the process of transforming inputs to outputs in a chain-like fashion like that depicted by the IIRC itself in Figure 27.2. As such, potential readers must be left wondering what is the core of the organization, because key differentiating aspects of the business model are drowned in attempts to illustrate the whole business. This is why the communicative aspects of focusing the information are so important (Nielsen and Madsen 2009).

Instead, the illustration of the business model should be focused on the connections between the different elements into which we traditionally divide the management review. This is illustrated in Figure 27.3, which shows the value drivers of Skype's business model in a Business

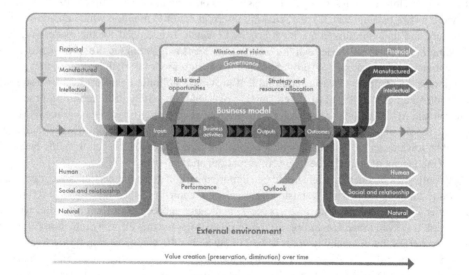

Figure 27.2   IIRC's business model

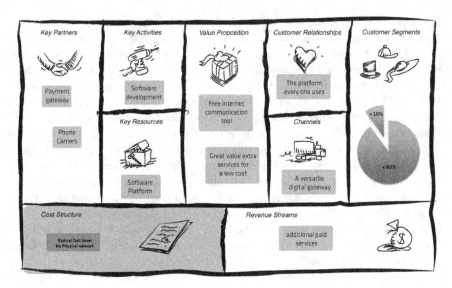

Figure 27.3   A business model canvas of Skype (adapted from Osterwalder and Pigneur, 2010)

Model Canvas and the key connections between these. Skype applies a Freemium[1] business model where approximately 90 per cent of the customers use a free service, while the remaining 10 per cent pay for a premium service. It is the critical mass provided by the free customer segment that creates the willingness of the premium customers to pay. The software platform that connects people globally is a crucial element of the business, and the key differentiator between Skype and traditional phone companies is that Skype does not carry the costs of land or GSM network installations. This is the company's cost advantage.

Companies typically report excessive amounts of information about customer relations, employee competences, knowledge sharing, product innovation, market developments, and risks, but this information set may be useless if the company at the same time fails to illustrate how these various elements of value creation interrelate; not to mention which changes in the company and its environment are most crucial to watch. It is crucial for the readers' understanding of the business model that the company presents a coherent picture of the company's value creation, for example by providing an insight into the interrelations that induce value creation in the company. Bearing in mind that providing unlimited datasets to users too may be problematic as it will lead to an information overload. In a study of IC reporting practices, Nielsen and Madsen (2009) discuss how such business reporting practices have moved from generic reporting practices stressing the disclosure of as much information to stakeholders as possible, towards a new discourse, which emphasizes reporting what is seen from the perspective of management, namely the 'right' information, and only that.

A company's business model should be supported by non-financial performance measures. It is one thing to state that the business model of a company relies heavily on mobilizing customer feedback in the innovation process, and quite another to explain how this will be achieved. It is even more demanding for the company to prove this effort by indicating: 1) how many resources the company devotes to it; 2) how active the company is in trying to achieve it, and whether it stays as focused as initially announced; and 3) whether the effort has had any effect, for example, on customer satisfaction, innovation output, and so on. According to Bray (2010, p. 6):

[r]elevant KPIs measure progress towards the desired strategic outcomes and the performance of the business model. They comprise a balance of financial and non-financial measures across the whole business model. Accordingly, business reporting integrates strategic, financial and non-financial information, is future-performance focused, delivered in real time, and is fit for purpose.

One of the keys to making management commentary matter to the investment community is therefore to emphasize the interconnectedness between parts of the narrative sections according to the logic of the business model. The adoption of <IR> has not yet stimulated new innovations in disclosures and disclosure mechanisms, which might be due to the fact that the disclosure guidance seems to be poor (Nielsen, 2006; Dumay *et al.*, 2017; Nielsen *et al.*, 2017b) and that the IIRC seems dismissive of the current rapid transformation in technologies and forces of mass communication (Dumay and Guthrie, 2017).

A final word of caution relates to how to compare business model information. The investment community loves to compare and to benchmark. However, they will need to change their mindset, because in today's business environment, the industry is not a proxy for a certain type of business model (Lev and Gu, 2016). If firms within the same industry operate on the basis of different business models, then different sets of competencies and knowledge resources will be key parts of value creation. Instead, in order to create meaningful comparisons, these must be conducted between identical business models (Nielsen *et al.*, 2017a). Montemari and Chiucci (2017) point out that the advantage of the business model is that it clarifies which IC elements are of the greatest importance and also what role they play in the company's value creation process. Thereby, the business model may prove itself an organizing element for companies wishing to compare and benchmark their IC information.

Conclusions

A business model description goes beyond an identification of the company's immediate cash flows to describe the company's value creating activities, the way it delivers and connects to customers, and the way it captures value from those transactions. In capital market language, one would say it is a statement on how the company will survive beyond the end of the budget period.

This chapter discussed the usefulness of IC in relation to the investment community and other stakeholders using voluntary corporate information. While many early contributions in the fields of management commentary and business reporting aspired towards creating higher volumes of information from companies, some of the later contributions are more concerned with focusing on the information set. Some information is better than none, but we all know that there is a limit to the amount of information users can screen and apply, even for expert users like institutional investors and analysts (Plumlee, 2003). Passing a certain threshold will move the general understanding of the company away from transparency rather than towards it (Nielsen and Madsen, 2009). It will therefore have to be contended whether a "flag-ship business report", as Bray (2010) describes, should entail real-time insight on financial and non-financial performance measures to the capital market that potentially could feed into analyst models.

A solution that would make IC reporting matter (more) to the investment community is one that emphasizes the interconnectedness between parts of the narrative sections according to the logic of contemporary business model understandings. These are built on value propositions (Osterwalder and Pigneur, 2010) and not value chains as applied in <IR> (IIRC, 2013b).

This chapter identified a series of inconsistencies due to a mismatch between business reporting orientation and the general stakeholder orientation in the business community. While Eccles and Krzus (2010) illustrate the possibility of integrating financial reporting with social and environmental reporting, Bray (2010) suggests that the social and environmental reporting movement is moving towards the capital markets and furthermore that early adopters potentially could build impetus for later regulation. However, such a movement will give rise to conflicts of interest as such professional stakeholders will be more apt to pursue a normative perspective on disclosure streams. Hence, this chapter concludes that propositions of aligning management commentary with business models may lead to challenges for both companies and external stakeholders, and that regulation should be concerned with creating guidance on how to structure management commentary and strengthen such narrative statements through relevant performance measures.

We have argued that management commentary sections need to be aligned with the logic of the business model applied by the specific company, thereby describing the specific structures and strategies of value creation. This would enable the identification of performance measures that could enhance the credibility of the reporting. One of the keys to making IC matter to the investment community is therefore to emphasize the interconnectedness between parts of the narrative sections according to the logic of the business model; but a logic that, according to Tweedie *et al.* (forthcoming), is different from the misunderstood conception applied by the IIRC (2013b). From a regulation perspective, this chapter therefore concludes that guidance should be concerned with helping companies structure and strengthen their narrative statements by helping them in defining possible relevant performance measures and explaining these.

Note

1 The term Freemium was coined by Anderson (2009).

References

Adrem, A. (1999), *Essays on Disclosure Practices in Sweden: Causes and Effects*, Doctoral dissertation, Institute of Economic Research, University of Lund, Sweden.

AICPA (1994), *Improving Business Reporting: A Customer Focus: Meeting the Information Needs of Investors and Creditors; and Comprehensive Report of the Special Committee on Financial Reporting*, American Institute of Certified Public Accountants, New York.

Anderson, C. (2009), *Free: The Future of a Radical Price*, Random House, London.

Arnold, J. and Moizer, P. (1984), "A survey of the methods used by UK investment analysts to appraise investments in ordinary shares", *Accounting and Business Research*, Vol. 14, No. 55, pp. 195–207.

Baden-Fuller, C. and Morgan, M. (2010), "Business models as models", *Long Range Planning*, Vol. 43, Nos 2–3, pp. 156–171.

Bartlett, S. A. and Chandler, R. A. (1997), "The corporate report and the private shareholder: Lee and Tweedie twenty years on", *British Accounting Review*, Vol. 29, pp. 245–261.

Beattie, V. and Pratt, K. (2002), *Voluntary Annual Report Disclosures: What Users Want*, Institute of Chartered Accountants, Scotland.

Beattie, V. and Smith, S. J. (2013), "Value creation and business models: Refocusing the intellectual capital debate", *British Accounting Review*, Vol. 45, No. 4, pp. 243–254.

Blair, M. and Wallman, S. (2001), *Unseen Wealth*, Brookings Institution, Washington, DC.

Botosan, C. A. (1997), "Disclosure level and the cost of equity capital", *The Accounting Review*, Vol. 72, No. 3, pp. 323–349.

Bray, M. (2002), *New Directions in Business: Performance Reporting, Communication and Assurance*, The Institute of Chartered Accountants in Australia.

Bray, M. (2010), *The Journey to Better Business Reporting: Moving Beyond Financial Reporting to Improve Investment Decision-making*, KPMG, Sydney, Australia.

Bukh, P. N. (2003), "The relevance of intellectual capital disclosure: A paradox?" *Accounting, Auditing & Accountability Journal*, Vol. 16, No. 1, pp. 49–56.

Bukh, P. N. and Nielsen, C. (2010), "Understanding the health care business model: The financial analyst's point of view", *Journal of Health Care Finance*, Vol. 37, No. 2, pp. 8–25.

Bukh, P. N., Nielsen, C., Gormsen, P., and Mouritsen, J. (2005), "Disclosure of information on intellectual capital in Danish IPO prospectuses", *Accounting, Auditing & Accountability Journal*, Vol. 18, No. 6, pp. 713–732.

Christensen, J. A. and Demski, J. S. (2003), *Accounting Theory: An Information Content Perspective*, McGraw-Hill, Boston, MA.

Cooke, T. E. (1989), "Voluntary corporate disclosure by Swedish companies", *Journal of International Financial Management and Accounting*, Vol. 1, pp. 171–195.

Dane-Nielsen, H. and Nielsen, C. (2017), "Value creation in business models is based on intellectual capital: And only intellectual capital!" in Guthrie, J., Dumay, J., Ricceri, F., and Nielsen, C. (Eds), *The Routledge Companion to Intellectual Capital*, Routledge, London, pp. 418–434.

De Villiers, C., Rinaldi, L., and Unerman, J. (2014), "Integrated reporting: Insights, gaps and an agenda for future research", *Accounting, Auditing & Accountability Journal*, Vol. 27, No. 7, pp. 1042–1067.

DiPiazza, S. A. Jr. and Eccles, R. G. (2002), *Building Public Trust: The Future of Corporate Reporting*, John Wiley & Sons, Inc., New York.

Dumay J. (2016), "A critical reflection on the future of intellectual capital: From reporting to disclosure", *Journal of Intellectual Capital*, Vol. 17, No. 1, pp. 168–184.

Dumay, J. and Guthrie, J. (2017), "Involuntary disclosure of intellectual capital: Is it relevant?" *Journal of Intellectual Capital*, Vol. 18, No. 1, pp. 29–44.

Dumay, J., Bernardi, C., Guthrie, J., and Demartini, P. (2016), "Integrated reporting: A structured literature review", *Accounting Forum*, Vol. 40, No. 3, pp. 166–185.

Dumay, J., Guthrie, J., and Rooney, J. (2017), "The critical path of intellectual capital", in Guthrie, J., Dumay, J., Ricceri, F., and Nielsen, C. (Eds), *The Routledge Companion to Intellectual Capital*, Routledge, London, pp. 21–39.

Eccles, R. G. and Krzus, M. (2010), *One Report: Integrated Reporting for a Sustainable Strategy*, John Wiley & Sons, Inc., Hoboken, NJ.

Eccles, R. G., Herz, R. H., Keegan, E. M., and Phillips, D. M. (2001), *The Value Reporting Revolution: Moving Beyond the Earnings Game*, John Wiley and Sons, Inc., New York.

Eustace, C. (2001), *The Intangible Economy: Impact and Policy Issues*, Report of the High Level Expert Group on the Intangible Economy, EU Commission, Brussels.

FASB (2001), *Improving Business Reporting: Insights into Enhancing Voluntary Disclosures*, Steering Committee Business, Reporting Research Project, Financial Accounting Standard Board, London.

Fisher, R., Oyelere, P., and Laswad, F. (2004), "Corporate reporting on the internet: Audit issues and content analysis of practices", *Managerial Auditing Journal*, Vol. 19, No. 3, pp. 412–439.

GRI (2002), *Sustainability Reporting Guidelines*, Global Reporting Initiative, Boston, MA.

Gu, F. and Li, J. Q. (2007), "The credibility of voluntary disclosure and insider stock transactions", *Journal of Accounting Research*, Vol. 45, No. 4, pp. 771–810.

Hamel, G. (2000), *Leading the Revolution*, Harvard Business School Press, Boston, MA.

Heemskerk, B., Pistorio, P., and Scicluna, M. (2003), *Sustainable Development Reporting: Striking the Balance*, World Business Counsel for Sustainable Development (WBCSD), Geneva.

Holland, J. (2004), *Corporate Intangibles, Value, Relevance and Disclosure Content*, Institute of Chartered Accountants of Scotland, Edinburgh, UK.

Holland, J. B. and Johanson, U. (2003), "Value relevant information on corporate intangibles: Creation, use, and barriers in capital markets – Between a rock and a hard place", *Journal of Intellectual Capital*, Vol. 4, No. 4, pp. 465–486.

Holman, R. (2002), "The annual report of the future", *CrossCurrents*, No. 3, pp. 4–9.

IASB (2009), *Management Commentary*, Exposure Draft ED/2009/6, IASC Foundation Publications Department, London.

IIRC (2013a). *The International IR Framework*, International Integrated Reporting Council. Available at: www.iirc.org.

IIRC (2013b), *Business Model: Background Paper for Integrated Reporting*, International Integrated Reporting Council, London. Available at: www.theiirc.org.

Lang, M. H. and Lundholm, R. J. (1993), "Cross-sectional determinants of analyst ratings of corporate disclosures", *Journal of Accounting Research*, Vol. 31, No. 2, pp. 246–271.

Lang, M. H. and Lundholm, R. J. (1996), "Corporate disclosure policy and analyst behaviour", *The Accounting Review*, Vol. 71, No. 4, pp. 467–492.

Lee, T. A. and Tweedie, D. P. (1977), *The Private Shareholder and the Corporate Report*, Institute of Chartered Accountants in England and Wales, London.

Lee, T. A. and Tweedie, D. P. (1981), *The Institutional Investor and Financial Information*, Institute of Chartered Accountants in England and Wales, London.

Lev, B. (2001), *Intangibles: Measurement, Management and Reporting*, Brookings Institution Press, Washington, DC.

Lev, B. and Gu, F. (2016), *The End of Accounting and the Path Forward for Investors and Managers*, John Wiley & Sons, Inc., Hoboken, NJ.

Lund, M. and Nielsen, C. (2014), "The evolution of network-based business models illustrated through the case study of an entrepreneurship project", *Journal of Business Models*, Vol. 2, No. 1, pp. 105–121.

March, J. G. and Olsen, J. P. (1989), *Rediscovering Institutions: The Organizational Basis of Politics*, The Free Press, New York.

McEwen, R. A. and Hunton, J. E. (1999), "Is analyst forecast accuracy associated with accounting information use?" *Accounting Horizons*, Vol. 13, No. 1, pp. 1–16.

Mintzberg, H. and Van der Heyden, L. (1999), "Organigraphs: Drawing how companies really work", *Harvard Business Review*, September-October, pp. 87–94.

Montemari, M. and Chiucci, M. S. (2017), "Enabling intellectual capital measurement through business model mapping: The Nexus case", in Guthrie, J., Dumay, J., Ricceri, F., and Nielsen, C. (Eds), *The Routledge Companion to Intellectual Capital*, Routledge, London, pp. 266–283.

Mouritsen, J. and Larsen, H. T. (2005), "The 2nd wave of knowledge management: The management control of knowledge resources through intellectual capital information", *Management Accounting Research*, Vol. 16, No. 4, pp. 371–394.

Nielsen, C. (2005a), "Comments on the IASB discussion paper concerning Management Commentary", Available at: www.iasb.org/current/comment_letters.asp.

Nielsen, C. (2005b), *Essays on Business Reporting: Production and Consumption of Strategic Information in the Market for Information* PhD Dissertation, Copenhagen Business School.

Nielsen, C. (2006), "Comments on the IASB discussion paper concerning Management Commentary", Available at: www.ifrs.org/Current-Projects/IASB-Projects/Management-Commentary/DP05/Comment-Letters/Documents/16_230_CL2.pdf (accessed 27 September 2016).

Nielsen, C. (2008), "A content analysis of analyst research: Health care through the eyes of analysts", *Journal of Health Care Finance*, Vol. 34, No. 3, pp. 66–90.

Nielsen, C. and Madsen, M. T. (2009), "Discourses of transparency in the intellectual capital reporting debate: Moving from generic reporting models to management defined information", *Critical Perspectives on Accounting*, Vol. 20, No. 7, pp. 847–854.

Nielsen, C. and Roslender, R. (2015), "Enhancing financial reporting: The contribution of business models", *British Accounting Review*, Vol. 47, No. 3, pp. 262–274.

Nielsen, C., Bukh, P. N., Mouritsen, J., Johansen, M. R., and Gormsen, P. (2006), "Intellectual capital statements on their way to the Stock Exchange: Analyzing new reporting systems", *Journal of Intellectual Capital*, Vol. 7, No. 2, pp. 221–240.

Nielsen, C., Lund, M., and Thomsen, P. (2017a), "Killing the balanced scorecard to improve internal disclosure", *Journal of Intellectual Capital*, Vol. 18, No. 1, pp. 45–62.

Nielsen, C., Roslender, R., and Bukh, P. N (2009), "Intellectual capital reporting: Can a strategy perspective solve accounting problems?" in Lytras, M. D. and Ordóñez de Pablos, P. (Eds), *Knowledge Ecology in Global Business*, IGI Global, Hershey, PA, pp. 174–191.

Nielsen, C., Roslender, R., and Schaper, S. (2016), "Continuities in the use of the intellectual capital statement approach: Elements of an institutional theory analysis", *Accounting Forum*, Vol. 40, No. 1, pp. 16–28.

Nielsen, C., Roslender, R., and Schaper, S. (2017b), "Explaining the demise of the intellectual capital statement in Denmark", *Accounting, Auditing & Accountability Journal*, Vol. 30, No. 1, pp. 38–64.

Osterwalder, A. and Pigneur, Y. (2010), *Business Model Generation: A Handbook for Visionaries, Game Changers, and Challengers*", John Wiley & Sons, Inc., Hoboken, NJ.

Pike, R. H., Meerjanssen, J., and Chadwick, L. (1993), "The appraisal of ordinary shares by investment analysts in the UK and Germany", *Accounting and Business Research*, Vol. 23, No. 92, pp. 489–499.

Plumlee, M. A. (2003), "The effect of information complexity on analysts' use of that information", *The Accounting Review*, Vol. 78, No. 1, pp. 275–296.

PWC (2007), *"Corporate Reporting: Is It What Investment Professionals Expect?* Pricewaterhouse Coopers International Limited, London.

Roslender, R. and Nielsen, C. (2017), "Lessons for progressing narrative reporting: Learning from the experience of disseminating the Danish Intellectual Capital Statement approach", unpublished working paper.

Sandberg, K. D. (2002), "Is it time to trade in your business model?", *Harvard Management Update*, January, pp. 3–5.

Söderbaum, P. (2002), "Business corporations, markets and the globalisation of environmental problems", in Havila, V., Forsgren, M., and Håkansson, H. (Eds), *Critical Perspectives on Internationalisation*, Pergamon, Amsterdam, pp. 179–200.

Taran, Y., Nielsen, C., Thomsen, P., Montemari, M., and Paolone, F. (2016), "Business model configurations: A five-V framework to map out potential innovation routes", *European Journal of Innovation Management*, Vol. 19, No. 4, pp. 492–527.

Tweedie, D., Nielsen, C., and Martinov-Bennie, N. (forthcoming), "Evolution or abandonment? Contextualising the business model in integrated reporting", *Australian Accounting Review*.

Upton, W. S. (2001), *Business and Financial Reporting: Challenges from the New Economy*, Special Report, Financial Accounting Standard Board.

Vanstraelen, A., Zarzeski, M. T., and Robb, S. W. G. (2003), "Corporate nonfinancial disclosure practices and financial analyst forecast ability across three European countries", *Journal of International Financial Management and Accounting*, Vol. 14, No. 3, pp. 249–278.

WICI (2010), *Concept Paper on WICI KPI in Business Reporting*, World Intellectual Capital/Assets Initiative. Available at: www.wici.org.

WICI (2016), *WICI Intangible Reporting Framework, Version 1, September 2016*, World Intellectual Capital/Assets Initiative. Available at www.wici.org.

28

INTELLECTUAL CAPITAL PROFILES AND FINANCIAL PERFORMANCE OF THE FIRM

Henri Hussinksi, Paavo Ritala, Mika Vanhala,
and Aino Kianto

Introduction

Several authors have suggested that firm performance and value creation accrue mainly from intangible resources (e.g. Grant, 1996; Makadok, 2001; Hamilton, 2006; Ferreira and Hamilton, 2010). The intellectual capital (IC) literature is especially interested in the contents and value of such resources. IC can be defined as the sum of the intangible and knowledge-related resources that an organization can utilize in its productive processes in the pursuit of value creation. IC tends to be further divided into several constituent elements or dimensions, representing the various sources and locations where the firm's intangible assets reside. Previous studies have provided ample evidence on the positive relationship between IC and different firm performance outcomes (e.g. Edvinsson and Malone, 1997; Sveiby, 1997; Bontis, 1998; Chen *et al.*, 2004; Subramanian and Youndt, 2005; Yang and Kang, 2008; Cabello-Medina *et al.*, 2011; Bornay-Barrachina *et al.*, 2012; Hsu and Sabherwal, 2012; Hsu and Wang, 2012; Leitner, 2011).[1] As IC research has passed from general awareness raising to theory building and then practice-based stages (Guthrie *et al.*, 2012; Dumay, 2013), much novel knowledge has been created concerning the role of intangibles in companies.

However, questions remain: are all IC elements equally important for firm performance? In the almost inevitable situation of resource scarcity, are there some IC elements which are 'must have' and some which are simply 'nice to have'? What about the optimal combination of IC elements – are there some configurations that are likely to produce the best results? In this study, we build on the argument that different types of IC have different types of performance implications, and that notable firm-specific differences exist in the configurations of IC. This kind of a configurational approach to the IC–performance relationship supported by time-lagged objective data[2] has so far been missing in the literature.

In this chapter, we discuss our recently introduced conceptual categorization of different IC dimensions (Inkinen *et al.*, 2014), and continue with an empirical study that first clusters different configurations of IC dimensions to specific profiles and then examines the effect of these profiles on time-lagged financial performance variables. Conceptually, we begin by elaborating the standard tripartite division of IC and suggest that from the financial perspective of the firm, the relevant IC categories include other dimensions in addition to the traditional human, structural, and relational capital. In particular, our framework includes the firm's renewal capital (e.g. Kianto *et al.*, 2010), entrepreneurial capital (e.g. Erikson, 2002) and trust capital (Mayer *et al.*, 1995). We also suggest that the knowledge residing in organizational relationships should be divided into internal relational capital and external relational capital, as they refer to different stakeholders (Inkinen *et al.*, 2014). We therefore specifically address the configurations of seven types of IC dimensions in groups of firms and examine how these IC profiles impact financial performance in terms of the firm's return on assets (ROA).

Our study contributes to the IC literature by providing a finer-grained understanding on the underlying configuration of firms' intangible resources and their effect on financial performance, measured with time-lagged, objective, and publicly available data. Our findings also offer practical application, as by better understanding the typical IC profiles of firms and their relationship with financial performance, managers can make more informed decisions on which aspects of their companies they should develop.

Theoretical and conceptual background

IC can be defined as the sum of all the knowledge and competences within an organization, which can be used in its pursuit of competitive advantage (Roos and Roos, 1997; Stewart, 1997; Sullivan, 1998). IC consists of information, intellectual property, intellectual material, knowledge, core techniques, customer relationships, and experience (Stewart, 1997). In the following, we first discuss different dimensions of IC and then the implications for firm performance.

Dimensions of IC

The literature has been established broadly around a three-dimensional division of IC into human, structural/organizational, and relational/social capital (e.g. Edvinsson and Malone, 1997; Roos and Roos, 1997; Stewart, 1997; Sveiby, 1997; Bontis, 1998; Nahapiet and Ghoshal, 1998; Sullivan, 1998; Lu and Hung, 2011). Human capital refers to the organization's only resource that is capable of thinking (Stewart, 1997) and includes the skills, knowledge, experience, and motivation of organizational members (e.g. Freel, 2005). Structural (or organizational) capital includes "all the non-human storehouses" of knowledge within a firm (Bontis *et al.*, 2000), ranging from databases and information systems to culture-carrying facilities and artefacts, as well as organizational processes. Finally, relational (or social) capital consists of relationships and the value and knowledge embedded in and available through them (Edvinsson and Malone, 1997; Roos and Roos, 1997; Nahapiet and Ghoshal, 1998). It foremost includes relationships with customers, but other important stakeholders may also be considered.

The three-dimensional categorization of IC is established, clear, and explicit. However, from the configurational point of view, we believe that a finer-grained approach is also warranted. In particular, we suggest that an additional four elements could be seen as aspects of IC, which may significantly contribute to financial performance of the firm. These include renewal capital in terms of an organization's capacity to renew its knowledge through learning, acquiring new skills, and creatively changing its operations (e.g. Kianto *et al.*, 2010); trust capital, referring to the trust embedded in its internal and external relationships (e.g. Mayer *et al.*, 1995); and entrepreneurial capital, or the competence and commitment related to entrepreneurial activities in the organization (e.g. Erikson, 2002). Moreover, relational capital could further be split into internal and external categories because the two categories relate to relationships with different stakeholders, and are therefore likely to have different performance implications (Inkinen *et al.*, 2014).

Overall, we suggest that the inclusion of the additional dimensions adds to the comprehensive and holistic understanding of IC as a phenomenon, and therefore presents opportunities for a better understanding of financial performance implications of different configurations of IC. Such a broad view relies on a wide understanding of knowledge and intangible assets, including not only the explicit outcomes or structures but also the potential embedded in the organization.

IC and firm performance

Among the key IC research areas is its association with performance and value creation (e.g. Ricceri, 2008; Guthrie *et al.*, 2012; Inkinen, 2015). Overall, the empirical literature has produced significant evidence on the positive relationship between IC and firm performance. In particular, previous studies have pointed out that firm performance is not reliant on one but several types of specialized knowledge (Kamukama *et al.*, 2010; Maditinos *et al.*, 2010; Sharabati *et al.*, 2010; Cabello-Medina *et al.*, 2011; Leitner, 2011; Hsu and Sabherwal, 2012; Jardon and Martos, 2012; Kim *et al.*, 2012; see also Kogut and Zander, 1992; Grant, 1996; Grant and Baden-Fuller, 2004). Researchers have also identified a significant correlation between the firm's overall level of IC and its performance outcomes, such as financial performance (Youndt *et al.*, 2004), new product development (Chen *et al.*, 2006), and innovation performance (Wu *et al.*, 2008).

The question of which IC dimensions have the most substantial impact on firm performance has inspired a lively debate among academics. A multitude of empirical studies has addressed the relative impact of different IC dimensions. Some studies have found particular merits for human capital (e.g. Bontis *et al.*, 2007; Tovstiga and Tulugurova, 2007; Cabello-Medina *et al.*, 2011; Hormiga *et al.*, 2011), while other articles have highlighted the effect of structural capital (Yang and Lin, 2009; Aramburu and Sáenz, 2011; Delgado-Verde *et al.*, 2011) or relational capital (Bozbura, 2004; Huang and Hsueh, 2007; Čater and Čater, 2009). Moreover, some studies have gone beyond the traditional tripartite categorization of IC and revealed that renewal capital (alternatively labelled as innovation capital) is closely linked with the firm's ability to utilize existing knowledge and create new knowledge (Maditinos *et al.*, 2010) and continuous development of new products, services, and innovations (Tseng and Goo, 2005). In addition, organizational trust has been found to support collaboration and cooperation (Mayer *et al.*, 1995) and innovation performance (Ellonen *et al.*, 2008). Furthermore, many scholars have argued for the effect of entrepreneurially oriented activities on firm performance. These relate to the self-directed activities within the firm, including risk-taking, better recognition of new business opportunities, and the willingness and ability to make courageous decisions (see e.g. Hughes and Morgan, 2007).

Given the broad variety of findings in terms of distinct elements of IC or their combinations for firm performance, we believe that it is worthwhile to proceed towards a more detailed, configurational view of the different bundles or profiles of overall IC dimensions of the firm. In fact, surprisingly little is known about whether and how distinct bundles or profiles of IC dimensions affect a firm's financial performance. To tackle this issue, we apply a configurational approach to examine the impact of IC on financial performance. Following Youndt *et al.* (2004), we define a configurational approach to IC as a perspective where we identify internally consistent groups of organizations exhibiting distinct levels of IC dimensions, which are called IC profiles. For example, some organizations may focus more on human capital and other organizations on relational capital, while a third group of organizations might take a broader approach and focus on developing human, structural, and relational capital. While Youndt *et al.* (2004) have already examined the impact of IC profiles on financial performance, we go further in providing a more overarching and detailed configurational view using a seven-dimensional model of IC, as well as examining the causal implications with time-lagged financial performance indicators.

In this study, we do not formulate explicit hypotheses for which dimension of IC – or which type of configuration among those – would be more beneficial than others. Rather, we adopt a deliberately exploratory and empirical approach to examine first the patterns of how IC dimensions are configured in firms, and whether different profiles emerge. We then use those profiles to examine whether the firms representing different profiles exhibit different levels of financial performance output. We believe that this approach is feasible in the current state of the literature, which is very scant regarding the evidence between IC configurations and financial performance of the firm.

Methods

Sample and data collection

We collected the data for this study in autumn 2013 through a survey instrument adminis- tered in all Finnish firms with at least 100 employees, using the key-informant technique. The initial population of companies was identified through the Intellia database. A total of 1,523 companies was considered suitable for the initial sample. A professional research com- pany contacted all the eligible firms by telephone and asked the person in charge of human resources to respond to the questionnaire. While the approach of using a single respondent to assess the IC of the firm has its limitations, our rationale was that a person responsible for human resources would be the most suitable respondent because the questions on IC were mostly personnel or knowledge-based. We emphasized confidentiality of the company's infor- mation, and promised a summary of the results as a compensation to the respondents. Of the 1,523 companies contacted, 259 responded, representing a response rate of 17.0 per cent. The largest industries in the sample were manufacturing (37.8 per cent), and wholesale and retail trade (16.2 per cent). Other notable industries were services (9.7 per cent) and transportation and storage (8.1 per cent). Most of the respondents held a position such as the HR director or manager (77.9 per cent), other director or manager (8.8 per cent), or managing director (6.9 per cent), which indicates their expertise in assessing IC issues.

Measures

We adapted the measures for IC categories from the previous literature where applicable and developed new measures otherwise. To develop suitable measures, we first conducted a thor- ough review of the literature. In order to confirm the operational validity and psychometric robustness of the scales, we pre-tested the initial scales by means of statistical analyses with a sample of Finnish managers ($N = 151$). To determine the content validity of the scales, we used an international panel of experts to assess the scales and give their insights. We incorporated the suggestions of these experts and the pre-test participants in the development of the final scales.

Independent variables

We adapted the basic themes for the scale for internal relational capital from Kianto (2008) with inspiration from Yang and Lin (2009). We likewise adapted the external relational capital scale (Kianto, 2008) and the scale for structural capital from Kianto and colleagues (Kianto,

2008; Kianto *et al.*, 2010). The insights of Bontis (1998) and Yang and Lin (2009) formed the basis for the human capital scale. We built upon work by Hughes and Morgan (2007), Kianto *et al.* (2010), and García-Morales *et al.* (2006) to develop the scale for renewal capital. In developing the scale for trust capital, we utilized the conceptual inspiration from Mayer *et al.* (1995) and Vanhala *et al.* (2011). Finally, we employed the key ideas from Hughes and Morgan (2007) to measure entrepreneurial capital. All of the measures were based on a five-point Likert scale (1 = strongly disagree, 5 = strongly agree). Appendix 1 lists the measures and the wording of the items, as well as the reliability indications and factor loadings. We discuss the measurement model validation in detail in the results section.

Dependent variables

To measure the financial performance of the firm, we used ROA. ROA is defined as net income divided by total assets, and researchers have adopted it widely as a measure of firm performance in the literature (see, e.g. Barnett and Salomon, 2012). We utilized ROA from the fiscal year 2014 in order to establish a one-year time lag between measuring the IC dimensions and objective financial performance of the firms. The data was obtained from the publicly available Amadeus database. To allow for the analysis of variance tests across financial performance groups, we composed a new measure for ROA by classifying it in seven categories: 1) lower than −10 per cent; 2) from −10 per cent to −5 per cent; 3) from −5 per cent to 0 per cent; 4) from 0 per cent to 5 per cent; 5) from 5 per cent to 10 per cent; 6) from 10 per cent to 15 per cent; and 7) over 15 per cent.

Results

In terms of the analysis, the first step was to assess the reliability and validity of the measurement models. We then used a cluster analysis to identify the different kinds of combinations of IC dimensions (i.e. IC profiles) among the companies. Finally, we tested the differences of levels in financial performance with a one-way analysis of variance (ANOVA) comparison of means. We deemed ANOVA testing suitable for our particular approach since it enables unambiguous testing of mean differences between categorical populations in the data (here, different IC profiles and different levels of ROA).

Measurement models

We tested the measurement model for IC by means of confirmatory factor analysis (CFA) with LISREL 8.50, and we used PRELIS 2.50 to compute the covariance matrix using the maximum likelihood estimation method.

The proposed seven-factor solution (seven-dimensional model of IC) was supported. First, the measurement model produced a good fit. According to researchers such as Hair *et al.* (2006), the root mean square error of approximation (RMSEA) should be around 0.06 while the goodness-of-fit index (GFI), the comparative fit index (CFI), the non-normed fit index (NNFI), and the incremental fit index (IFI) should reach 0.90. Our model meets these limits (see Appendix 1).

Second, the CFA found that the loadings of all the items were high and statistically significant (see Appendix 1). In other words, they were all related to their specified constructs, verifying the posited relationships between the indicators and constructs. Furthermore, all constructs exceeded the threshold levels for construct reliability (> 0.60) and Cronbach's alpha (> 0.70). Thus, the model provides reliable measurement of IC.

Finally, we evaluated the discriminant validity with two methods. We first assessed whether the average variance extracted was greater than the variance shared between a given construct and the other constructs in the model (i.e. the squared correlation between two constructs; Fornell and Larcker, 1981). The constructs of our study fulfilled this condition. In addition, we evaluated discriminant validity with the method recommended by Anderson and Gerbing (1988) by comparing two models (constructs correlating freely vs. correlations fixed as equal to one) for each possible pair of constructs. All chi-square difference tests were significant, which indicates that all pairs of constructs correlated at less than one. In sum, these two tests provided evidence of a sufficient level of discriminant validity.

Overall, the model assessments gave good evidence of validity and reliability for the operationalization of the concepts. The final model consists of 22 items that cover 7 dimensions of IC: internal (three items) and external (three items) relational capital; structural capital (three items); human capital (three items); renewal capital (three items); trust capital (four items); and entrepreneurial capital (three items).

Cluster analysis

We used cluster analysis to identify the most distinct combinations of the abovementioned seven IC dimensions possessed by the studied companies. We applied a hierarchical cluster analysis using Ward's method (Hair *et al.*, 2006). Then we tested the possible cluster structure of three to six clusters and selected the solution of four clusters representing the four distinctive combinations of IC dimensions.

Cluster 1, labelled as 'generalist IC firms', represents the companies with an average level of overall IC and low levels of renewal (3.14) and entrepreneurial capital (2.91). These companies thus emphasize the firm's current knowledge assets, and might encounter difficulties in taking risks and proactively renewing and creating IC. Cluster 2, 'specialist IC firms', includes companies with an average level of overall IC, while showing high levels of human (4.05) and trust (4.16) capital. Cluster 3 includes companies that could be described as 'IC superstars', that is, companies that possess high levels of overall IC across all dimensions: the lowest being entrepreneurial (3.96) and the highest human capital (4.56). Finally, cluster 4 represents the companies that could be described as the polar opposite of cluster 3; in other words, these companies have low levels of overall IC varying from 2.25 in entrepreneurial capital to 3.23 in trust capital and are therefore labelled 'IC laggards'.

How then are the different IC profiles distributed between industry sectors in Finland and do these reflect the underlying industry context? Beginning from the IC superstar profile, our results suggest that all-around IC-rich firms are present especially in the knowledge-intensive industry categories, such as administrative and support services, information and communication, and services, while being under-represented in construction, manufacturing, and wholesale and retail trade. Conversely, IC laggards are slightly over-represented in manufacturing and wholesale and retail trade, while less represented in information and communication services. Moreover, generalist IC firms are slightly over-represented in transportation and storage, manufacturing, and wholesale and retail trade, whereas they appear less often in information and communication, services, and construction. Specialist IC firms are the most over-represented IC profile in the professional, scientific, and technical activities as well as being slightly over-represented in construction; in contrast, only a few specialist IC firms are found in administrative and support services and services in general.

ANOVA

Next we tested the differences of levels in ROA between different IC profiles. We used a one-way ANOVA comparison of means, with the Tamhane *post hoc* test for the comparisons. First, the results indicate that among all IC profiles, the specialist IC firms had the highest ROA (4.81) compared to generalist IC firms (4.22), IC superstars (4.51), and IC laggards (3.41). In addition, we found statistically significant differences between some of the IC profiles in ROA. The difference between specialist IC firms and IC laggards had a significance level of 0.003, while the difference between IC superstars and IC laggards can be interpreted by using a more liberal interpretation (significance level of 0.112).

Discussion and implications

In this study, we utilized a survey research strategy to collect data from Finnish companies and identified different IC profiles and their associations with financial performance of the firm. Based on the cluster analysis, we identified four distinct IC profiles: generalist IC firms, specialist IC firms, IC superstars, and IC laggards. In terms of their association with financial performance, we found that specialist IC firms (i.e. firms with average overall IC but particularly high human and trust capital) had the highest ROA output. We also identified statistically significant differences between IC profiles, as specialist IC firms and IC superstars outperformed IC laggards in terms of ROA.

Our study introduces a multi-dimensional framework with seven different categories of IC, and adopts a configurational approach to empirically identify IC profiles of firms. These profiles offer useful implications for financial performance. The adopted approach and the results provide implications for both research and practice of IC management, which are discussed in the following sections.

Implications for research

Overall, our results show strong empirical support for the key argument in IC literature that IC substantially impacts a firm's performance. This finding is significant because only very few previous studies have been able to address the IC–firm performance link. To bridge this gap, we provide evidence using a time-lagged dataset combining intra-firm survey data and objective public financial data. Therefore, our study significantly extends the performance management discussion related to IC. It especially contributes to the literature by revealing that a combination of a high amount of human capital and trust capital is of particular importance for the financial performance of the firm. That is, investments in skilled and motivated experts and establishing a trait of trust in internal and external relationships are likely to increase financial performance.

The results also underline the importance of a relatively novel and little discussed dimension of IC: trust capital. While there exists an abundance of evidence that trust is an essential facilitator of knowledge processes and organizational phenomena in general (e.g. Politis, 2003; Levin and Cross, 2004; Blomqvist *et al.*, 2005; Chowdhury, 2005; Ellonen *et al.*, 2008; Holste and Fields, 2010; Vanhala and Ritala, 2016), its role has so far been largely neglected in the IC literature.

In addition, according to our results, the overall level of IC is indeed a solid predictor of financial performance, but a high level of IC does not guarantee a superior level of firm performance. Instead, companies may be better off specializing in a few IC dimensions, such as human and trust capital. As such, investments in IC development may not be beneficial in a linear fashion, but the implications from such investments might be more non-linear and *configurational*. In other words, one size does not fit all, and more is not always better. From this perspective, our results partially deviate from the findings of Youndt *et al.* (2004), which indicated that the overall amount of IC is a decisive factor for financial performance of the firm. However, based on the poor performance of IC laggards, which possess a low overall level of IC, it seems that missing IC dimensions are nevertheless holding firms back from performing well.

Implications for practice

As for managerial implications, this study suggests that IC management is an impactful approach for supporting firm performance. More specifically, a firm's profitability is partly based on elements of IC such as employees' skills and knowledge, organizational structures, systems, ICT tools, relationship networks, organizational trust, learning ability, and entrepreneurial behaviours. Therefore, well-designed development programs to address these issues can result in a significant payoff.

Overall, ensuring a requisite average level of all of these elements ensures stable knowledge-based value creation, demonstrated also as high financial performance. In contrast, a low level of intangibles is likely to impair an organization's capabilities to operate, and is likely to lead to decreased profitability. Therefore, it is important that value creation through intangibles is supported by conscious and systematic management activities (e.g. Foss and Michailova, 2009; Foss and Minbaeva, 2009; Andreeva and Kianto, 2012).

Furthermore, it seems that the most beneficial combination is that of human capital and a high level of organizational trust. Personnel skills, motivation, and expertise coupled with well-functioning relationships 'smoothed' by trust enable the efficient and effective utilization of organizational resources, and thereby can lead to performance increases. Human capital and trust can be built through measures such as well-designed, transparent, and consistent human resource management practices (e.g. López-Cabrales *et al.*, 2009; Minbaeva, 2013; Inkinen *et al.*, 2015).

We also suggest that, in addition to looking at individual IC dimensions, it is important to assess and manage the overall *configuration* of IC within the firm in order to reap the best possible financial performance outcomes. Interestingly, and in part counter to previous research evidence, our study demonstrates that firms are able to achieve superior financial performance through a focused IC strategy wherein they specialize in only some aspects of IC. Based on our results, while all types of IC are potentially beneficial, investments in the development of human capital and establishing a trait of trust within relationships is particularly useful.

In terms of industrial differences, there are several interesting findings. We noted that IC superstars were over-represented within industries in which daily work is quite knowledge-intensive, such as information and communication, whereas industry categories where daily work is characterized by routines, for example, wholesale and retail trade, were over-populated with IC laggards. Interestingly, we also noticed that the profile of specialist IC firms was strongly related to professional, scientific, and technical activities related industries.[3] This suggests that highly specialized skills, knowledge, and expertise, as well as a high level of trust, are valued assets in activities such as research, architecture, and legal services, which require active collaboration and intra- and inter-organizational trust. Moreover, generalist IC firms (i.e. those low in renewal and entrepreneurial capital) were slightly more closely linked with traditional industries such as transportation and storage, manufacturing, and wholesale and retail trade, than with professional, scientific, and technical activities, or information and communication.

This finding could indicate that the large companies within traditional industries struggle with the pace of business these days, as they may be reluctant to introduce and implement new ideas and hesitate in making brave decisions. Overall, these findings are supported by researchers such as Axtle-Ortiz (2012), who stated that attributes such as geographical location, industry sector, and organization size are factors that shape a firm's IC.

Our study also has implications for public policy. Governments should invest in education and allow free mobility of labour, in order to facilitate a sufficient supply of diverse and skilled human capital for their companies. In addition, governments should act transparently and responsibly in order to increase the trait of trust within the society. Finland offers a great example and benchmark in terms of both perspectives. Finland has one of the best educational systems globally (OECD, 2016) and as a European Union (EU) member state, allows free movement for workers within the EU. These two factors support a highly competent supply of human capital to companies, and our results show that it is important to the performance of firms. Also, Finland is one of the least corrupt countries in the world (Transparency International, 2017) where people trust the government, organizations, and most importantly – each other. Indeed, in this study the results imply that trust is not just a virtue, but it also yields economic benefits.

Future research directions

Our focus on IC profiles and financial performance of firms could inspire various future research directions. First of all, our study could be replicated in other countries with different economic and socio-political backgrounds in order to elaborate the role of IC as a key firm performance driver in different country contexts. Future studies could also focus on a single industry or compare two or more industries, which would allow us to better distinguish the salience and magnitude of IC in, for example, the knowledge-intensive business services sector and traditional manufacturing industry. Furthermore, while we identified four different IC profiles in Finnish firms, further studies with data from other kinds of organizations and from other countries could examine whether the profiles we identified are sufficiently general, or mostly country- or industry-specific. Future studies could also investigate the antecedents and activities for building a competitive IC profile for a company, as well as contingency factors affecting which types of IC profiles are suitable for certain types of outcomes. We believe that our study provides feasible starting points for these and other research directions.

Appendix 1. Measurement items

Concept	Item	Factor loading	CR	Alpha
Intellectual capital	*To what extent do the following statements apply to your company (1 = completely disagree, 5 = completely agree)*			
Internal relational capital	Different units and functions within our company – such as R&D, marketing and production – understand each other well	.616[a]	.75	.74
	Our employees frequently collaborate to solve problems	.771***		
	Internal cooperation in our company runs smoothly	.721***		

External relational capital	Our company and its external stakeholders – such as customers, suppliers and partners – understand each other well	.620[a]	.77	.77
	Our company and its external stakeholders frequently collaborate to solve problems	.776***		
	Cooperation between our company and its external stakeholders runs smoothly	.776***		
Structural capital	Our company has efficient and relevant information systems to support business operations	.518[a]	.63	.73
	Our company has tools and facilities to support cooperation between employees	.602***		
	Our company has a great deal of useful information in documents and databases	.679***		
Human capital	Our employees are highly skilled at their jobs	.736[a]	.78	.76
	Our employees are highly motivated in their work	.626***		
	Our employees have a high level of expertise	.827***		
Renewal capital	Our company has acquired a great deal of new and important knowledge	.613[a]	.76	.75
	Our company can be described as a learning organization	.748***		
	The operations in our company can be described as creative and inventive	.773***		
Trust capital	The way our company operates is characterized by an atmosphere of trust	.730[a]	.75	.75
	We keep our promises and agreements	.677***		
	Our company seeks to take the interests of its stakeholders into account in its operations	.603***		
	The expertise of our company inspires trust in stakeholders	.613***		
Entrepreneurial capital	Our employees are excellent at identifying new business opportunities	.746[a]	.79	.79
	Our employees show initiative	.745***		
	Our employees have the courage to make bold and difficult decisions	.752***		

a Significance level is not available because the coefficient is fixed at 1. *** Statistically significant at 0.01 significance level.
Measurement model: Chi-square = 326.97, df = 188, p = 0.00, RMSEA = 0.054, GFI = 0.897, CFI = 0.978, NNFI = 0.973, IFI = 0.978.

Notes

1 See also Inkinen (2015) for a systematic review of empirical research on IC and firm performance.
2 In this case, time-lagged measurement means that data for the independent variable (IC) was collected before the dependent variable (financial performance), which fulfils the time-order condition of causality (Hair *et al.*, 2006).
3 Based on standard industrial classification TOL 2008, professional, scientific, and technical activities include the following industry sub-categories: legal and accounting activities, activities of head offices, management consultancy activities, architectural and engineering activities, technical testing and analysis, scientific research and development, advertising and market research, other professional, scientific and technical activities, and veterinary activities.

References

Anderson, J. C. and Gerbing, D. W. (1988), "Structural equation modeling in practice: A review and recommended two-step approach", *Psychological Bulletin*, Vol. 103, No. 3, pp. 411–423.

Andreeva, T. and Kianto, A. (2012), "Does knowledge management really matter? Linking KM practices, competitiveness and economic performance", *Journal of Knowledge Management*, Vol. 16, No. 4, pp. 617–636.

Aramburu, N. and Sáenz, J. (2011), "Structural capital, innovation capability, and size effect: An empirical study", *Journal of Management and Organization*, Vol. 17, No. 3, pp. 307–325.

Axtle-Ortiz, M. A. (2012), "Perceiving the value of intangible assets in context", *Journal of Business Research*, Vol. 66, No. 3, pp. 417–424.

Barnett, M. L. and Salomon, R. M. (2012), "Does it pay to be *really* good? Addressing the shape of the relationship between social and financial performance", *Strategic Management Journal*, Vol. 33, No. 11, pp. 1304–1320.

Blomqvist, K., Hurmelinna, P., and Seppänen, R. (2005), "Playing the collaboration game right— Balancing trust and contracting", *Technovation*, Vol. 25, No. 5, pp. 497–504.

Bontis, N. (1998), "Intellectual capital: An exploratory study that develops measures and models", *Management Decision*, Vol. 36, No. 2, pp. 63–76.

Bontis, N., Keow, W. C. C., and Richardson, S. (2000), "Intellectual capital and business performance in Malaysian industries", *Journal of Intellectual Capital*, Vol. 1, No. 1, pp. 85–100.

Bontis, N., Seleim, A., and Ashour, A. (2007), "Human capital and organizational performance: A study of Egyptian software companies", *Management Decision*, Vol. 45, No. 4, pp. 789–801.

Bornay-Barrachina, M., De la Rosa-Navarro, D., López-Cabrales, A., and Valle-Cabrera, R. (2012), "Employment relationships and firm innovation: The double role of human capital", *British Journal of Management*, Vol. 23, No. 2, pp. 223–240.

Bozbura, F. T. (2004), "Measurement and application of intellectual capital in Turkey", *The Learning Organization*, Vol. 11, No. 4, pp. 357–367.

Cabello-Medina, C., López-Cabrales, A., and Valle-Cabrera, R. (2011), "Leveraging the innovative performance of human capital through HRM and social capital in Spanish firms", *International Journal of Human Resource Management*, Vol. 22, No. 4, pp. 807–828.

Čater, T. and Čater, B. (2009), "(in)Tangible resources as antecedents of a company's competitive advantage and performance", *Journal for East European Management Studies*, Vol. 14, No. 2, pp. 186–209.

Chen, Y.-S., Lin, M.-J. J., and Chang, C.-H. (2006), "The influence of intellectual capital on new product development performance: The manufacturing companies of Taiwan as an example", *Total Quality Management and Business Excellence*, Vol. 17, No. 10, pp. 1323–1339.

Chen, J., Zhu, Z., and Hong, Y. X. (2004), "Measuring intellectual capital: A new model and empirical study", *Journal of Intellectual Capital*, Vol. 5, No. 1, pp. 195–212.

Chowdhury, S. (2005), "The role of affect-and cognition-based trust in complex knowledge sharing", *Journal of Managerial Issues*, Vol. 17, No. 3, pp. 310–326.

Delgado-Verde, M., Castro, G. M., and Navas-López, J. E. (2011), "Organizational knowledge assets and innovation capability: Evidence from Spanish manufacturing firms", *Journal of Intellectual Capital*, Vol. 12, No. 1, pp. 5–19.

Dumay, J. (2013), "The third stage of IC: Towards a new IC future and beyond", *Journal of Intellectual Capital*, Vol. 14, No. 1, pp. 5–9.

Edvinsson, L. and Malone, M. (1997), *Intellectual Capital: Realising Your Company's True Value by Finding Its Hidden Brainpower*, Harper Collins, New York.

Ellonen, R., Blomqvist, K., and Puumalainen, K. (2008), "The role of trust in organisational innovativeness", *European Journal of Innovation Management*, Vol. 11, No. 2, pp. 160–181.

Erikson, T. (2002), "Entrepreneurial capital: The emerging venture's most important asset and competitive advantage", *Journal of Business Venturing*, Vol. 17, No. 3, pp. 275–290.

Ferreira, S. and Hamilton, K. (2010), *Comprehensive Wealth, Intangible Capital, and Development*, World Bank Policy Research Working Paper No. 5452.

Fornell, C. and Larcker, D. F. (1981), "Evaluating structural equation models with unobservable variables and measurement error", *Journal of Marketing Research*, Vol. 18, No. 1, pp. 39–50.

Foss, N. and Michailova, S. (Eds). (2009), *Knowledge Governance: Processes and Perspectives*, Oxford University Press, Oxford, UK.

Foss, N. and Minbaeva, D. (2009), *Governing Knowledge: The Strategic Human Resource Management Dimension*, SWG Working Papers, 3/2009. Copenhagen Business School.

Freel, M. S. (2005), "Patterns of innovation and skills in small firms", *Technovation*, Vol. 25, No. 2, pp. 123–134.

García-Morales, V. J., Llorens-Montes, F. J., and Verdú-Jover, A. J. (2006), "Antecedents and consequences of organizational innovation and organizational learning in entrepreneurship", *Industrial Management & Data Systems*, Vol. 106, No. 1, pp. 21–42.

Grant, R. M. (1996), "Toward a knowledge-based theory of the firm", *Strategic Management Journal*, Vol. 17, No. S2, pp. 109–122.

Grant, R. M. and Baden-Fuller, C. (2004), "A knowledge accessing theory of strategic alliances", *Journal of Management Studies*, Vol. 41, No. 1, pp. 61–84.

Guthrie, J., Ricceri, F., and Dumay, J. (2012), "Reflections and projections: A decade of intellectual capital accounting research", *The British Accounting Review*, Vol. 44, No. 2, pp. 68–82.

Hair, J. F., Black, W. C., Rabin, B. J., Anderson, R. E., and Tatham, R. L. (2006), *Multivariate Data Analysis*, Pearson Education, Upper Saddle River, NJ.

Hamilton, K. (2006), *Where Is the Wealth of Nations? Measuring Capital for the 21st Century*, World Bank Publications, Washington, DC.

Holste, J. S. and Fields, D. (2010), "Trust and tacit knowledge sharing and use", *Journal of Knowledge Management*, Vol. 14, No. 1, pp. 128–140.

Hormiga, E., Batista-Canino, R. M., and Sánchez-Medina, A. (2011), "The role of intellectual capital in the success of new ventures", *International Entrepreneurship and Management Journal*, Vol. 7, No. 1, pp. 71–92.

Hsu, I.-C. and Sabherwal, R. (2012), "Relationship between intellectual capital and knowledge management: An empirical investigation", *Decision Sciences*, Vol. 43, No. 3, pp. 489–524.

Hsu, L.-C. and Wang, C.-H. (2012), "Clarifying the effect of intellectual capital on performance: The mediating role of dynamic capability", *British Journal of Management*, Vol. 23, No. 2, pp. 179–205.

Huang, C.-F. and Hsueh, S.-L. (2007), "A study on the relationship between intellectual capital and business performance in the engineering consulting industry: A path analysis", *Journal of Civil Engineering and Management*, Vol. 13, No. 4, pp. 265–271.

Hughes, M. and Morgan, R. E. (2007), "Deconstructing the relationship between entrepreneurial orientation and business performance at the embryonic stage of firm growth", *Industrial Marketing Management*, Vol. 36, No. 5, pp. 651–661.

Inkinen, H. (2015), "Review of empirical research on intellectual capital and firm performance", *Journal of Intellectual Capital*, Vol. 16, No. 3, pp. 518–565.

Inkinen, H., Kianto, A., and Vanhala, M. (2015), "Knowledge management practices and innovation performance in Finland", *Baltic Journal of Management*, Vol. 10, No. 4, pp. 432–455.

Inkinen, H., Kianto, A., Vanhala, M., and Ritala, P. (2014), "Intellectual capital and performance: Empirical findings from Finnish firms", in Carlucci, D., Spender, J. C., and Schiuma, G. (Eds), *Proceedings of the 9th International Forum on Knowledge Asset Dynamics*, University of Basilicata, Matera, Italy, pp. 2918–2933.

Jardon, C. M. and Martos, M. S. (2012), "Intellectual capital as competitive advantage in emerging clusters in Latin America", *Journal of Intellectual Capital*, Vol. 13, No. 4, pp. 462–481.

Kamukama, N., Ahiauzu, A., and Ntayi, J. M. (2010), "Intellectual capital and performance: Testing interaction effects", *Journal of Intellectual Capital*, Vol. 11, No. 4, pp. 554–574.

Kianto, A. (2008), "Development and validation of a survey instrument for measuring organizational renewal capability", *International Journal of Technology Management*, Vol. 42, No. 1–2, pp. 69–88.

Kianto, A., Hurmelinna-Laukkanen, P., and Ritala, P. (2010), "Intellectual capital in service- and product-oriented companies", *Journal of Intellectual Capital*, Vol. 11, No. 3, pp. 305–325.

Kim, T. T., Kim, W. G., Park, S. S. S., Lee, G., and Jee, B. (2012), "Intellectual capital and business performance: What structural relationships do they have in upper-upscale hotels?", *International Journal of Tourism Research*, Vol. 14, No. 4, pp. 391–408.

Kogut, B. and Zander, U. (1992), "Knowledge of the firm, combinative capabilities, and the replication of technology", *Organization Science*, Vol. 3, No. 3, pp. 383–397.

Leitner, K.-H. (2011), "The effect of intellectual capital on product innovativeness in SMEs", *International Journal of Technology Management*, Vol. 53, No. 1, pp. 1–18.

Levin, D. Z. and Cross, R. (2004), "The strength of weak ties you can trust: The mediating role of trust in effective knowledge transfer", *Management Science*, Vol. 50, No. 11, pp. 1477–1490.

López-Cabrales, A., Pérez-Luño, A., and Cabrera, R. V. (2009), "Knowledge as a mediator between HRM Practices and innovation activity", *Human Resource Management*, Vol. 48, No. 4, pp. 485–503.

Lu, W.-M. and Hung, S.-H. (2011), "Exploring the operating efficiency of technology development programs by an intellectual capital perspective: A case study of Taiwan", *Technovation*, Vol. 31, No. 8, pp. 374–383.

Maditinos, D., Šević, Z., and Tsairidis, C. (2010), "Intellectual capital and business performance: An empirical study for the Greek listed companies", *European Research Studies Journal*, Vol. 13, No. 3, pp. 145–167.

Makadok, R., (2001) "Toward a synthesis of the resource-based and dynamic-capability views of rent", *Strategic Management Journal*, Vol. 22, No. 5, pp. 387–401.

Mayer, R. C., Davis, J. H., and Schoorman, F. D. (1995), "An integrative model of organizational trust", *Academy of Management Review*, Vol. 20, No. 3, pp. 709–734.

Minbaeva, D. (2013), "Strategic HRM in building micro-foundations of organizational knowledge-based performance", *Human Resource Management Review*, Vol. 23, No. 4, pp. 378–390.

Nahapiet, J. and Ghoshal, S. (1998), "Social capital, intellectual capital and the organizational advantage", *The Academy of Management Review*, Vol. 23, No. 2, pp. 242–266.

OECD (2016), *PISA 2015 Results (Volume I): Excellence and Equity in Education*, OECD Publishing, Paris.

Politis, J. D. (2003), "The connection between trust and knowledge management: What are its implications for team performance", *Journal of Knowledge Management*, Vol. 7, No. 5, pp. 55–66.

Ricceri, F. (2008), *Intellectual Capital and Knowledge Management: Strategic Management of Knowledge Resources*, Routledge, London.

Roos, G. and Roos, J. (1997), "Measuring your company's intellectual performance", *Long Range Planning*, Vol. 30, No. 3, pp. 413–426.

Sharabati, A.-A. A., Jawad, S. N., and Bontis, N. (2010), "Intellectual capital and business performance in the pharmaceutical sector of Jordan", *Management Decision*, Vol. 48, No. 1, pp. 105–131.

Stewart, T. (1997), *Intellectual Capital: The New Wealth of Organizations*, Doubleday, New York.

Subramanian, M. and Youndt, M. A. (2005), "The influence of intellectual capital on the types of innovative capabilities", *Academy of Management Journal*, Vol. 48, No. 3, pp. 450–463.

Sullivan, P. (1998), *Profiting from Intellectual Capital: Extracting Value from Innovation*, John Wiley & Sons, Inc., New York.

Sveiby, K. E. (1997), *The New Organizational Wealth: Managing and Measuring Knowledge-Based Assets*, Berrett-Koehlen, New York.

Tovstiga, G. and Tulugurova, E. (2007), "Intellectual capital practices and performance in Russian enterprises", *Journal of Intellectual Capital*, Vol. 8, No. 4, pp. 695–707.

Transparency International (2017), *Corruption Perceptions Index 2016*, Transparency International, Berlin.

Tseng, C.-Y. and Goo, Y.-J. J. (2005), "Intellectual capital and corporate value in an emerging economy: Empirical study of Taiwanese manufacturers", *R&D Management*, Vol. 35, No. 2, pp. 187–201.

Vanhala, M. and Ritala, P. (2016), "HRM practices, impersonal trust and organizational innovativeness", *Journal of Managerial Psychology*, Vol. 31, No. 1, pp. 95–109.

Vanhala, M., Puumalainen, K., and Blomqvist, K. (2011), "Impersonal trust: The development of the construct and the scale", *Personnel Review*, Vol. 40, No. 4, pp. 485–513.

Wu, W.-Y., Chang, M.-L., and Chen, C.-W. (2008), "Promoting innovation through the accumulation of intellectual capital, social capital, and entrepreneurial orientation", *R&D Management*, Vol. 38, No. 3, pp. 265–277.

Yang, S. and Kang, H.-H. (2008), "Is synergy always good? Clarifying the effect of innovation capital and customer capital on firm performance in two contexts", *Technovation*, Vol. 28, No. 10, pp. 667–678.

Yang, C. and Lin, C. (2009), "Does intellectual capital mediate the relationship between HRM and organizational performance? Perspective of a healthcare industry in Taiwan", *International Journal of Human Resource Management*, Vol. 20, No. 9, pp. 1965–1984.

Youndt, M. A., Subramanian, M., and Snell, S. A. (2004), "Intellectual capital profiles: An examination of investments and returns", *Journal of Management Studies*, Vol. 41, No. 2, pp. 335–361.

29

DOES INTELLECTUAL CAPITAL MATTER FOR ORGANIZATIONAL PERFORMANCE IN EMERGING MARKETS?

Evidence from Chinese and Russian contexts

Aino Kianto, Tatiana Garanina, and Tatiana Andreeva

Introduction

In understanding the foundations of organizational performance, the knowledge-based approach has emerged as a key perspective in which a firm's intellectual capital (IC) is seen as a major driver of organizational success and a source of competitive advantage (Edvinsson and Malone, 1997; Sveiby, 1997; Nahapiet and Ghoshal, 1998; Petty and Guthrie, 2000; Ricceri, 2008; Dumay and Guthrie, 2012). There is widespread agreement that IC significantly impacts organizational performance, and extensive empirical research in developed countries confirms this relationship (e.g. Edvinsson, 1997; Johnson and Soenen, 2003; Tseng and Goo, 2005; Wu and Tsai, 2005; Puntillo, 2009).

But is this the same for emerging markets? Does IC matter in this context? In many emerging countries, the economy depends heavily on natural or other tangible resources – indeed, resource extraction in emerging economies more than doubled between 1985 and 2005 (Dittrich *et al.*, 2011). The quality of available human capital in these labour markets may also differ, and executives frequently complain about the gap between the needs of industry and the skills and knowledge acquired in domestic universities.[1] Additionally, emerging countries suffer from a 'brain drain', as the most skilled and experienced candidates leave for developed countries, whose search for talent extends worldwide (PricewaterhouseCoopers, 2014).

It seems likely, then, that the relevance of IC and its contribution to the performance of firms in emerging markets may differ from the findings in the mainstream IC literature. IC research in general thus far has progressed through three main stages (Guthrie *et al.*, 2012; Dumay and Garanina, 2013; Dumay, 2013):

1   creation of awareness of the phenomenon and importance of IC;
2   building and testing normative IC frameworks; and
3   critical and performative approach to IC and its management.

Along with its call for idiosyncratic and practice-based understandings of IC, the third stage, if somewhat implicitly, invites a more contextual and localized approach to IC. However, such an approach has been little applied in the extant IC research. In line with recent calls for the deeper contextualization of theories developed in the West (Michailova, 2011; May and Stewart, 2013), we suggest that a better understanding of the role of IC in emerging markets can enrich and advance IC theory, as well as helping managers of both multinational companies and local businesses to achieve greater efficiencies by understanding cross-cultural differences.

The research question examined in this chapter is: how does IC impact the performance of companies in China and Russia? These major emerging economies are of particular interest to IC research for several reasons. First, both have joined the World Trade Organization (WTO) relatively recently (China in 2002 and Russia in 2012). As they become more integrated into the global economy, the competitive pressures on Chinese and Russian companies have intensified substantially, forcing them to develop and exploit IC to survive and succeed (Kianto *et al.*, 2013; Wang *et al.*, 2014). In this environment, IC management can be an important means of enhancing financial efficiency, and as both countries have also emphasized innovation in their plans for national development, IC management is likely to be of particular importance (Kianto *et al.*, 2013).

It has been argued that there are fundamental differences between Western and Eastern countries in terms of knowledge and IC management practices (Jansson *et al.*, 2007; Zhao, 2008; Kianto *et al.*, 2013; May and Stewart, 2013). As China is a leading representative of Eastern management philosophy and Russia lies somewhere between Western and Eastern approaches, a comparison of the two systems should be especially interesting, both for further research and for its application to business.

Managing IC in China and Russia: putting the story in context

The dominant approach to IC, utilized by most researchers in the field, distinguishes it into three main elements: human, relational, and structural capital (Edvinsson and Malone, 1997; Stewart, 1997; Sveiby, 1997; Bontis, 1998; Molodchik *et al.*, 2014). The following sections consider the peculiarities of the context in the two focal countries (China and Russia) that may potentially impact the quality and availability of intellectual resources, as well as how organizations manage those resources. These are presented by the three main elements of IC.

The Chinese Government has recently begun to pay more attention to education as the most direct means of improving the value of human capital. For example, in 1998, China's Ministry of Education announced its "211 Project", selecting some 60 universities for a national programme to improve teaching systems and enhance human capital (Zhao, 2008). In line with such government policies to intensify the development of human capital, Chinese corporations now invest increasingly in internal training systems to enhance the generation of new ideas and knowledge sharing among employees (Zhao, 2008). Now, leading companies abroad employ many Chinese people who are "elite in science and technology" (Chen *et al.*, 2004, p. 198).

At the same time, there is some evidence of a lack of talented employees, particularly among managers and professionals (Farrell and Grant, 2005; Tung, 2007; Zhu *et al.*, 2008). Because industrial enterprises in China have paid insufficient attention to developing IC – and especially human capital – for a long time (Liu and White, 2001), most human capital is concentrated within research institutes, universities, and subsidiaries of foreign companies (Chen *et al.*, 2015), and there is considerable scope for improvement in this regard.

Chinese culture has a positive influence on knowledge sharing, enhancing a company's human capital through *Guanxi*-principles of collectivism and Confucian dynamism that influence the specifics of knowledge management in China (Yeh *et al.*, 2006; Chang and Lee, 2007; Lin and Dalkir, 2010). *Guanxi* is a very important element in trust-based relations and is considered to increase the efficiency of knowledge sharing (Hutchings and Michailova, 2006; Hutchings and Weir, 2006). As a shared value, collectivism may help to increase the intensity of knowledge exchange between employees, so enhancing human capital. With its focus on harmony, Confucian dynamism also positively supports knowledge sharing (Huang *et al.*, 2008). For example, Chinese employees strive for more harmony and compromise in group work, which leads to a higher level of knowledge sharing than in groups consisting of US nationals (Jiacheng *et al.*, 2010).

In the context of human capital, Russia has traditionally been characterized by a strong legacy of scientific and technological excellence, and many of its companies have their roots in research establishments, reflecting a focus on processes of renewal and development (Tovstiga and Tulugurova, 2009). Employees in these kinds of Russian enterprises show a high level of competence, reflecting scientific and technical expertise, and professionalism. At the same time, it is important to mention a Grant Thornton survey of 34 countries indicating that the main problem faced by Russian companies is a lack of qualified personnel (Domcheva, 2014). Employee outflow from Russia is very high, and the country is currently experiencing the largest brain drain in 20 years. According to Russia's state statistical agency, 350,000 people emigrated from Russia in 2015 – ten times more than five years ago (Bershidsky, 2016).

The intensity and efficiency of a company's human capital depend on knowledge management practices. The barriers to effective implementation of knowledge management systems created by the complexity of Russian business culture are analysed in Michailova and Husted (2003), Michailova and Hutchings (2006), and May and Stewart (2013). First, although Russian culture is usually said to be characterized by collectivism, it is very common for Russian people to split into their own small group versus "the others" (Michailova and Hutchings, 2006), precluding efficient knowledge sharing outside this group (Michailova and Husted, 2003). Michailova and Hutchings (2006) go on to say that Russian employees are very sensitive to distance setting, and they identify three levels of division: the company as a whole, all employees, and colleagues. This leads to a lack of knowledge sharing intensity between groups and hinders implementation of knowledge sharing systems, which may in turn obstruct enhancement of human capital.

Second, it is a norm of Russian culture that knowledge is correlated with personal status and power. As a consequence, employees do not tend to share knowledge unnecessarily or without gaining some material benefit (Michailova and Husted, 2003; Michailova and Hutchings, 2006). This is a legacy of the Soviet era, when all information flows were strictly controlled and people were afraid to share information (May and Stewart, 2013). This characteristic again blocks knowledge sharing, making enhancement of a company's human capital less efficient.

In summary, then, China and Russia differ in their capacity to develop human capital. In combination with the particularities of Chinese culture, government support to improve the national educational system and investment by Chinese companies in internal training systems can be expected to create a friendly environment for the enhancement of human capital, positively influencing company financial performance. At the same, however, it should be noted that this strong focus on human capital has emerged only relatively recently (Liu and White, 2001), and that much of that human capital is concentrated in research institutes, universities, and subsidiaries of foreign companies (Chen *et al.*, 2015). In contrast, the Russian situation is characterized by several factors that weaken the development of human capital, including a poor knowledge sharing environment, a poor economic situation, and high levels of brain drain.

In terms of China, the second element of IC, relational capital, is impacted by peculiarities of local relational systems. Chinese business networks are characterized by family business systems that have been widespread in Southeast Asia for a long time (Jansson et al., 2007) and are considered the organizing principle of economic activity (Hamilton, 1996). Membership is a matter not just of gaining admission to the network but of becoming a trusted member in a networked market (Ramström, 2005). Personal relations in China are very strong, and these form the base for firm-specific relations. As relations are highly personified, and the principle of collectivism also predominates, these networks have a deterministic rather than a supporting role in business relationships (Jansson et al., 2007). Chinese business networks are socially strong, last for many years and "represent a continuity of collective common interests (families, communities, and sets of friends and relatives)" (Jansson et al. 2007, p. 960). In this environment, it is not uncommon to contact someone you know to resume business relations even after a long break.

In general, formal and written control and regulations are much less important in Chinese business than informal relations. This preference for personal relations over formal contracts is a matter of flexibility (Michailova and Worm, 2003). In Chinese business culture, it is much worse to be blacklisted than to be sued in court, as all the members of that business network will terminate relations (Jansson et al., 2007).

In the context of relational capital, the characteristics of Russian culture are reflected in how personal relations often precede or even become a prerequisite for business relationships (Salmi, 1996; Michailova and Worm, 2003). Networking is now a key element of doing business in Russia, and Russian companies appear to be skilled in this regard (Puffer and McCarthy, 2011). For that reason, one might expect relational capital to be of particular importance for Russian companies. Hutchings and Michailova (2004) confirmed that what is sometimes considered a negative aspect of Russian culture in fact creates new opportunities for knowledge sharing and enrichment of relational capital. The importance of personal relations in business can be explained by the weak legitimacy of formal institutions (Puffer and McCarthy, 2011; McCarthy et al., 2012).

Russian business networks are based more on autonomous individuals and voluntary individual actions (Jansson and Ramström, 2005). Additionally, the unstable economic situation and generally volatile environment means that Russian networks are oriented to the short term and are characterized by an absence of trust and reputation (Gurkov, 1996). Russian businessmen tend not to adapt their relations to deal with new environmental conditions, but rather terminate them and seek new partners (Hallén and Johanson, 2004). According to Huber and Wörgötter (1998), the closed and hierarchical survivalist networks that now predominate in Russia emerged from 'grey' markets and are based on ties created during the socialist era. However, with entry to the WTO and integration into the global environment, the role of these networks should diminish, as they stand in sharp contrast to the international business networks found in most Western countries.

While China and Russia differ in some respects, such as who is included in the relationship network and how exactly these relationships are built and maintained (Wong and Tam, 2000; Jansson et al., 2007), the present analysis confirms that relationships play a very important role in business in both countries. It seems reasonable to assume, then, that organizations in such contexts would typically exhibit strongly developed relational capital.

In the Chinese context, the third IC element, structural capital, is impacted by the tendency of Chinese companies to put a strong focus on competitiveness and performance indicators as they are going global. To achieve their ambitious goals, Chinese companies must improve internal business processes that are also balanced against social issues of high importance in society (Jansson *et al.*, 2007). Chinese companies tend to be serious about the quality of internal business processes. For many companies, the implementation and certification of quality, environmental, and occupational health and safety management systems have been prioritized to increase market competitiveness (Zeng *et al.*, 2007).

According to some observers, it is not always clear how Chinese companies work, as they seem to do little planning or budgeting (Ramström, 2005). This can be explained in terms of the flexibility of Chinese firms in volatile situations (Backman, 2001), which is closely linked to internal innovation. Chinese corporations are characterized by relatively high levels of R&D expenditure and patents. From their inception in 1985, patent applications have grown rapidly (Sun, 2000; Frietsch and Wang, 2007), securing the rights to new ideas developed in-house. There are two forms of innovation specific to Chinese companies: new products developed in China and introduced to the market, and products that quickly imitate foreign products (Li and Atuahene-Gima, 2001). The latter strategy also involves significant changes to existing products that improve consumer benefits and choice. According to Wang (2004), China has made great efforts to revise and upgrade its intellectual property-related legislation to meet the requirements of WTO membership. Nevertheless, there remains scope to improve the implementation and enforcement of intellectual property protection in terms of its efficiency (Wang, 2004).

In the context of structural capital, Russian companies face many environmental barriers (Andreeva and Garanina, 2016), one of which is that the level of protection of property rights is very low. Because the registration process is very time consuming, Russian organizations tend not to register intellectual property rights (Molodchik and Nursubina, 2012). Additionally, Russian companies often lack management competences and tend to rely too heavily on informal management mechanisms (Puffer and McCarthy, 2011), all of which lead to deficiencies in internal management processes (e.g. Gurkov *et al.*, 2012), especially those for managing and retaining knowledge within an organization (Andreeva and Ikhilchik, 2011).

For Russian companies, it is usual to plan the development of internal processes. The autocratic leadership approach to company management means that the typical Russian manager thinks in terms of how to gain control over internal business processes and to maintain power over business operations within existing networks (Holt *et al.*, 1994). Many researchers and businessmen have concluded that some of Russia's economic problems relate to management inefficiency (Elenkov, 2002).

In summary, for both countries, entry to the WTO and the challenges presented by the economic environment have created the need for business process efficiency. At the same time, it can be said that the internal business processes of Chinese companies are much more flexible, increasing their potential competitiveness (Backman, 2001). Although Russian managers are used for planning, managerial efficiency in the country remains quite low (Elenkov, 2002), and certain bureaucratic difficulties (such as registration of intellectual property rights) weaken the development of structural capital, indicating that structural capital is better developed in Chinese companies.

Do IC elements matter for organizational performance in emerging markets?

The above discussion shows how characteristics of the Chinese and Russian contexts influence the quality and availability of IC to organizations, and how it is managed. However, more advanced development of a given element of IC need not have any significant effect on organizational performance. For example, on the basis of the above discussion, one might hypothesize that relational capital strongly influences business performance in China and Russia. However, this may not hold if the level is generally high in all of the companies; according to the logic of the resource-based view, in such a situation relational capital is no longer a unique and rare resource, meaning that it will not generate advantage over competitors (Dierickx and Cool, 1989; Barney, 1991). In such a circumstance, high relational capital would be needed just to enter the game (that is, doing business), but it would make little difference in terms of playing the game better than others.

We have analysed the existing studies devoted to the relationship between IC elements and different performance indicators in Chinese and Russian companies. The Appendix presents an overview of empirical studies of the impact of IC on firm performance in China and Russia. It should be noted that these studies do not present a homogenous group of studies, but differ in several important respects. The studies have utilized various conceptualizations of the consistency of IC, different methods to measure IC, as well as various operationalizations for company performance, and different kinds of study samples. Of 16 papers, 9 only address human and structural capital as elements of IC, and leave relational capital unexamined. The methods applied for evaluating IC can be categorized in three types: questionnaires (Chen *et al.*, 2004; Tovstiga and Tulugurova, 2009; Wang *et al.*, 2014; Chen *et al.*, 2015; Andreeva and Garanina, 2016), proxy indicators (Bayburina and Golovko, 2008; Garanina, 2011; Molodchik and Nursubina, 2012), and secondary data analysed with the Value Added Intangible Coefficient (VAIC) method by Pulic (2000) (Chan, 2009; Bykova and Molodchik, 2011; Chu *et al.*, 2011; Tomchuk *et al.*, 2013; Xiao, 2013; Lu *et al.*, 2014). It should be noted that one of the disadvantages of the VAIC method is that it only addresses two elements of IC (human and structural capitals), and relational capital is out of its scope, meaning that all studies applying this method also adhere to the reduced conceptualization of IC. In terms of evaluation of organizational performance, some authors (e.g. Chan, 2009; Bykova and Molodchik, 2011; Tomchuk *et al.*, 2013; Xiao, 2013; Lu *et al.*, 2014) have focused on financial data that represent accounting (ROA, ROE, or ROS) and market performance indicators (market capitalization or Tobin's Q), while others have concentrated not on financial but rather operational performance by analysing the innovative effectiveness of companies (Molodchik and Nursubina, 2012; Wang and Chen, 2013; Chen *et al.*, 2015).

It was possible to identify eight previous studies that have empirically examined the impact of IC on company performance in the Chinese market. Chan (2009) examined 33 public companies traded on the Hong Kong Stock Exchange and found that structural capital positively impacted their financial performance, measured by market valuation, ROE, and ATO. Surprisingly, this study found that human capital had a negative effect on the performance metrics. With the help of the same evaluation approach to measure IC elements – VAIC – Chu *et al.* (2011) got almost the same results. These authors found that structural capital has a positive impact on financial performance while the results for human capital are mixed as it had either a positive or negative relationship with financial performance, depending on the indicators analysed. In their research, Lu *et al.* (2014) collected data from 34 Chinese life insurance companies. These authors came to the conclusion that both structural and human capitals had a positive relationship with the performance metrics measured with the help of the DEA method, with human capital prevailing. Xiao (2013) analysed 198 listed companies in China. With the help of the VAIC method, the author defined that both human and structural capitals are positively related to general growth indicators of total assets, net profit, revenue, and owners' equity, with structural capital having a higher positive impact on financial performance. In the paper by Chen *et al.* (2004), the authors analyse the relationship between the performance index indicator and IC elements based on the data of 31 innovative companies in China. They came to the conclusion that human, structural, and relational capitals are positively related to financial performance.

There are also some papers where the authors analysed the impact of IC elements not only on financial performance (as for example in Chen *et al.*, 2015), but also on innovative performance and innovative capabilities (Wang and Chen, 2013; Wang *et al.*, 2014). The main differences in these papers are reflected in the power of the relationship between IC elements and performance indicators – some authors defined that the highest influence has the structural element (Chen *et al.*, 2004; Wang and Chen, 2013) while the others came to the conclusion that relational capital is mostly related to financial and innovative indicators (Chen *et al.*, 2015).

Seven empirical studies addressing the impact of IC on firm performance in Russia were identified. As in the case of studies examining Chinese firms, several authors have applied the VAIC methodology to the Russian context. Bykova and Molodchik (2011) analysed 115 companies from the Perm region and Tomchuk *et al.* (2013) considered 15 companies from the same region and found a positive relationship between human and structural capital and such financial performance indicators as ROE and ROS.

Tovstiga and Tulugurova (2007, 2009) used questionnaires to define the impact of IC elements on external (socio-political, technological, and economic) and internal performance indicators. Based on a sample of 42 small technology-intensive enterprises, the authors came to the conclusion that structural and human capital are positively related to companies' performance indicators. Almost the same result was obtained by Andreeva and Garanina (2016) who surveyed 240 top managers of Russian manufacturing companies. They found that structural capital had a stronger influence on performance than human capital, while relational capital did not have a significant impact.

Several authors have used the method of proxy to analyse the IC elements on the Russian market with the help of open sources of information. The results of these studies have been very mixed. For example, Bayburina and Golovko (2008) chose 19 companies from various industry sectors and came to the conclusion that human and structural capital positively influence intellectual enterprise value. Garanina (2011) found a positive relationship between all three elements of IC and a price per share of 43 Russian companies from the extractive industry, power engineering, and communication services. Even though some industry differences were found, the general conclusion is that human capital has the strongest impact on the dependent variable. At the same time, Molodchik and Nursubina (2012) found a negative influence of human capital on a share of new products in the product line while relational and structural capital are positively related to this innovation performance indicator of 60 Russian companies.

As we can see, different studies have reported disparate results concerning the IC-performance relationship, from negative (e.g. Chan, 2009), through non-significant (Wang and Chen, 2013), to positive (e.g. Tovstiga and Tulugurova, 2009). Furthermore, in various studies, different IC elements have emerged as the strongest performance drivers. The inconsistency of these findings confirms that there is as yet no clarity about how IC elements impact company performance indicators in these two countries. The conflicting results can be explained in terms of differences in sample settings, regional development levels, and methods employed (Cabrita and Bontis, 2008; F-Jardón and Martos, 2009; Sydler *et al.*, 2014). These differences in methodology make direct comparison of existing findings problematic. Moreover, most of these studies used the VAIC method (Pulic, 2000), which has recently been much criticized for its inaccuracy in measuring IC (Ståhle *et al.*, 2011). To empirically test potential contextual differences in the IC-performance relationship, the same methodology would need to be applied to both countries to enable a valid comparison, as well as more accurate measurement of IC. The present study addresses this need.

Research methods

Sampling and data collection

The study employed a survey research strategy. Data were collected during 2014, using a survey instrument that was targeted at firms in Russia and China with at least 100 employees. In China, data were collected from 139 firms, using both telephone interviews and an online survey. Most of those companies (81.1 per cent) were involved in manufacturing. They were located mostly in the province of Ningbo (66 per cent), followed by Shenzen (14 per cent). In Russia, data were collected from 86 companies, again using telephone interviews and an online survey. Most of the companies were located in St Petersburg (55 per cent) and Moscow (28 per cent). The sample included both manufacturing and service companies.

The key informant technique was utilized, meaning that one respondent per company provided responses to the survey. In China, the largest group of respondents (37 per cent), although familiar with their company's knowledge-related issues, did not want to reveal their specific job title. The next largest groups of key informants were experts (29 per cent) and non-HR managers and directors (28 per cent). In Russia, most respondents (31 per cent) were experts, followed by HR managers and directors (24 per cent) and managing directors (21 per cent). Key descriptors of the surveyed companies are presented in Table 29.1.

Measures

The research instrument was a structured questionnaire, translated to Chinese and Russian from the original English version developed by Kianto, Inkinen, Ritala, and Vanhala under the auspices of Lappeenranta University of Technology, Finland, and previously reported in Inkinen, Kianto, *et al.* (2014) and Inkinen, Vanhala, *et al.* (2014), and Kianto, Gang, and Lee (2015) and Kianto, Saenz, and Arambaru (2015). Development of the scale was based on a thorough review of the literature and two pre-tests with Finnish datasets ($N = 151$ and $N = 259$). Research questionnaires were carefully translated to Mandarin Chinese and Russian languages by experts who were knowledgeable about the topic and fluent in both languages. This means that, content-wise, the research instrument was identical for all data collection locations.

Table 29.1 Descriptive statistics

	China	*Russia*
Total sample	139	86
Age (mean; sd (*N*))	25.02; 16.56 (43)	19.2; 12.215 (81)
Personnel (mean; sd (*N*))	7,192.45; 36,840.79 (83)	7,073.23; 23,329.29 (84)
Industry	(%)	(%)
Largest	Manufacturing (81.1)	Wholesale and retail trade (22.4)
2nd largest	Information and communication (3.3)	Manufacturing (20)
3rd largest	Construction (3.3)	Information and communication (15.3)
4th largest	Transport and storage (3.3)	Services (14.1)

The research instrument included statements to which the respondents reacted by means of a five-point Likert scale, anchored by *I strongly agree/disagree*. All key study variables were measured with composites comprising several items. For the independent variables, human capital items (3) were adapted from Bontis (1998) and Yang and Lin (2009). Structural capital items (3) were based on Kianto (2008a, 2008b) and Kianto *et al.* (2010), and the three relational capital items were taken from Kianto (2008a, 2008b). The dependent variable (company market performance) was taken from Delaney and Huselid (1996). Logarithms of company age and size were utilized as control variables. Survey instruments are available from the authors.

Findings

The first step of the analysis was to assess the functionality of the adopted measurement scales in the samples. As the scales had already been validated with larger samples, Cronbach's α was utilized to assess the internal consistency of the scales. All scales returned alpha values above 0.7, indicating good internal consistency and validity. The means of all IC elements were assessed to be higher in Russian than in Chinese firms.

Next, correlations between study variables were calculated for each country sample. For both Russian and Chinese samples, all three IC elements were significantly correlated with market performance. As IC elements showed high inter-correlations with each other, variance inflation factor (VIF) scores were inspected for multicollinearity problems. As VIF scores were well below the cutoff point of 2.5, multicollinearity was not detected, and it was possible to proceed with the regression analyses. Full data tables of the scale reliabilities, descriptives, and correlations are available from the authors.

Finally, regression analyses were performed to test the impact of the different IC elements on organizational performance. Table 29.2 displays the results of the regression models for the two countries, indicating that in China, none of the three IC elements has a statistically significant impact on performance. However, structural capital comes very close to the threshold of significance at $p = 0.055$ and β-coefficient of 0.410. In China, 14 per cent of the variance in performance is explained. In Russia, only human capital has an impact on market performance, with a β-coefficient of 0.510. Structural capital and relational capital do not influence performance. Overall, the model explains 32 per cent of variation in organizational performance.

Table 29.2 Effect of elements of intellectual capital on company market performance

Element	China		Russia	
	Standardized coefficients	Sig.	Standardized coefficients	Sig.
Human capital	0.089	0.649	0.510	0.000
Structural capital	0.410	0.055	−0.096	0.445
Relational capital	0.079	0.699	0.181	0.129
Control variables				
Age of organization	0.082	0.654	0.041	0.674
Size of organization	−0.119	0.500	0.176	0.070
Adjusted R^2	0.14		0.32	

Discussion and conclusions

In this analysis of the impact of IC on organizational performance in Russia and China, it was found that in Russia, only human capital exerts a significant impact on firm performance. In China, only structural capital comes statistically close to impacting performance, but even here, the impact is very slight.

Only one of the several earlier studies of the Russian market (Garanina, 2011) identified human capital as the key IC element influencing company financial performance, assessing its impact as much higher than that of other elements of IC. At the same time, almost all the papers applying a VAIC approach found a positive relationship between human capital and financial performance indicators (Tovstiga and Tulugurova, 2007; Bayburina and Golovko, 2008; Bykova and Molodchik, 2011; Tomchuk *et al.*, 2013), but the impact of HC on financial performance indicators differed little from that of other elements.

For Chinese companies, only structural capital was found to relate positively to performance indicators. This result echoes Chan (2009), whose studies of a sample of companies from the Hong Kong Hang Seng Index found that of all IC elements, only structural capital was positively related to ROA and ROE. Rather than national characteristics, a possible alternative explanation of structural capital's role as the only near-significant predictor of performance in China is the large proportion (81 per cent) of manufacturing companies in the sample. This begs the question of whether industry-specific influences rather than national-level factors mainly determine IC's impact on performance (Andreeva and Garanina, 2016).

Based on these findings, it seems that intangibles may indeed be of less relevance for the performance of firms in emerging economies, contrary to their importance for value creation in developed countries. Some of the available evidence suggests that the impact of IC on national economic wealth is higher in more developed countries (Ståhle *et al.*, 2015); based on our findings, it seems that a similar contingency may also exist at firm level.

To our knowledge, this chapter is the first comparative analysis of IC management in emerging markets. The finding that IC impacts performance in different ways in Russia and China suggests that although emerging economies are sometimes grouped together, they should not be. The likelihood of fundamental institutional differences among emerging economies means that they should be examined individually rather than simplistically grouped together, with a view to identifying their idiosyncratic characteristics. The study contributes to the IC literature by furthering the emergent cross-cultural approach.

The literature review confirms the significant disparities among previous findings. At the same time, some similarities can be identified where the sample includes companies from the same industry, suggesting that the key elements of IC for financial performance vary by industry. For application to business, we propose that the focus on a particular element of IC should be based on the industry to which a company belongs.

For Russian managers, the general core implication is that human capital is a valuable resource that can improve financial performance indicators. According to Andreeva and Garanina (2016), this element was also important in improving financial performance indicators in manufacturing companies, although the significance of structural capital was higher. In summary, the results suggest that in Russian companies, human capital is a valuable resource for value creation that positively influences financial results, but in particular industries, other elements may prove more significant.

For the Chinese sample, the conclusions are less clear, as the obtained results align only with Chan (2009). Nevertheless, the Appendix invites the conclusion that structural capital is always a significant factor in value creation for Chinese companies. This means that Chinese managers should pay particular attention to internal structure, culture, business processes, and knowledge documentation and sharing systems to make their companies more competitive in the global economic environment.

As is commonly the case, this study has several limitations. First, only a limited number of companies were surveyed (86 in Russia and 139 in China). As both are vast countries with a sizeable population of firms, our results cannot be said to provide an overview of Russian or Chinese firms in general, but represent only a limited perspective on a group of firms in each country.

Second, the current study involved a subjective assessment of organization performance by the respondents rather than an evaluation based on some objective or external information. However, in Russia and China, it is difficult to acquire information about companies' financial performance. Not all companies in these countries provide information about their performance to publicly accessible databases, and even if they do, the figures have to be regarded with caution. Additionally, the cross-sector nature of our research samples would have made it difficult to find more specific and targeted performance metrics that would at the same time be relevant for so wide a range of firms. For that reason, we had to be content with subjective assessments of firms' generic market performance.

The limitations of this study suggest some fruitful avenues for future research. Several of these limitations relate to the nature of the data collected, involving subjective measures of performance, collected at the same time as the data on IC elements. Some prior research found that IC has a delayed effect on organizational performance (e.g. Väisänen *et al.*, 2007). In combination with the long-term nature of relational capital, this finding suggests that this component of IC may still affect the performance of Russian and Chinese companies when studied over a longer time. This hypothesis can be tested in future studies, using time-lagged performance data. Further studies might also use objective performance measures, or a combination of subjective and objective, to investigate more comprehensively the link between IC and performance.

Extending the discussion about various measurement methods for IC (e.g. financial proxies versus surveys), future studies might incorporate both types of measures to compare their accuracy in measuring IC components, as well as their value as predictors of organizational performance.

One further interesting direction would be to explore the specifics of the different sectors or industries in greater detail – for example, the nature of the link between IC elements and performance in service firms. One can hypothesize that human capital might be expected to have the strongest impact in this sector (e.g. Kianto *et al.*, 2010). Or again, how would IC elements link to performance in telecom companies? In this sector, we can hypothesize that relational capital may have the strongest impact (e.g. Garanina, 2011). Extending such arguments to other sectors can contribute to a more nuanced understanding of the role of IC, so increasing efficiency of management. In conclusion, aligning with May and Stewart (2013), we believe that extending the inquiry to other emerging economies as diverse institutional and cultural contexts will contribute to further development of IC theories.

Appendix 1. Empirical studies of the relationship between IC elements and firm performance in Russian and Chinese companies

Author	Country /Industry /Sample	Research method for evaluation of IC elements	Company performance indicators	Findings concerning the relationship*		
				HC	RC	SC
Chinese companies						
Chen *et al.*, 2004	31 innovative companies in China	Questionnaire	Performance index defined as the arithmetical mean of rate of returns of net assets and enterprise growth	+	+	++
Chan, 2009	33 companies trading on the Hong Kong Stock Exchange	VAIC	Market valuation, ROE, asset turnover (ATO)	–	N/A	+
Chu *et al.*, 2011	167 companies trading on the Hong Kong Stock Exchange	VAIC	Market capitalization, return on assets, return on equity, asset turnover	+/–	N/A	+
Lu *et al.*, 2013	34 Chinese life insurance companies	VAIC	Performance index calculated using DEA method	++	N/A	+
Wang and Chen, 2013	164 companies from high-technology and non-high-technology industries	Questionnaire	Innovative capabilities	no	+	++
Xiao, 2013	198 listed companies in China	VAIC	General growth indicator of total assets, net profit, revenue and owner equity	+	N/A	++
Wang *et al.*, 2014	228 high-technology companies in China	Questionnaire	Operational and financial performance indicators	+	+	+
Chen *et al.*, 2015	149 trading companies in China	Questionnaire	Innovation performance, financial performance, technical competencies	+	++	+
Russian companies						
Tovstiga and Tulugurova, 2007	20 innovative enterprises from St. Petersburg	Questionnaire	Internal factors (revenue growth, operations improvement, and customer satisfaction) and external factors (comparative competitiveness, measured on a ten-point scale)	+	N/A	+

Bayburina and Golovko, 2008	19 companies; various industry sectors	Method of proxy indicators	Intellectual enterprise value	+	N/A	+
Tovstiga and Tulugurova, 2009	42 small technology-intensive enterprises founded post-Perestroika (1990 and onwards), mostly in the scientific devices/equipment manufacturing sectors and IT-related industry	Questionnaire	Internal and external factors	+	N/A	++
Garanina, 2011	43 companies from extractive, power engineering, communication services, and metallurgy sectors	Method of proxy indicators	Price per share	++	+ / no	+
Bykova and Molodchik, 2011	115 companies from Perm region; no information on industry sector	VAIC	ROE, revenue growth rate	+	N/A	+
Molodchik and Nursubina, 2012	Russia (60 companies) and USA (143 companies); no information on industry sector	Method of proxy indicators	Share of new products in product line (innovation performance indicator)	–	+	+
Tomchuk et al., 2013	15 companies from Perm region; no information on industry sector	VAIC	Return on sales	+	N/A	+

Notes:

HC = human capital
RC = relational capital
SC = structural capital
++ = a strong positive relationship was found, identified as having higher coefficients in the model compared to other variables
+ = a positive relationship was found
– = a negative relationship was found
no = no relationship was found
n/a = data not available as this element was not included in the model

Note

1 *The Economist* (2008), "People for growth: The talent challenge in emerging markets. A report from the Economist Intelligence Unit", available from: http://graphics.eiu.com/upload/People_for_growth. pdf (accessed 15 October 2015).

References

Andreeva, T. and Garanina, T. (2016), "Do all elements of intellectual capital matter for organizational performance? Evidence from Russian context", *Journal of Intellectual Capital*, Vol. 17, No. 2, pp. 397–412.

Andreeva, T. and Ikhilchik, I. (2011), "Applicability of the SECI Model of Knowledge Creation in Russian cultural context: Theoretical analysis", *Knowledge and Process Management*, Vol. 18, No. 1, pp. 56–66.

Backman, M. (2001), *Asian Eclipse, Exposing the Dark Side of Business in Asia*, John Wiley, Singapore.

Barney, J. (1991), "Firm resources and sustained competitive advantage", *Journal of Management*, Vol. 17, No. 1, pp. 99–120.

Bayburina, E. R. and Golovko, T. V. (2008), "The empirical research of the intellectual value of the large Russian companies and the factors of its growth", *Journal of Corporate Finance Research*, Vol. 2, No. 6, pp. 5–19.

Bershidsky, L. (2016), "Russia is not dying from a brain drain", *Bloomberg*, available at: www.bloomberg.com/view/articles/2016-07-06/russia-is-not-dying-from-a-brain-drain (accessed 1 July 2016).

Bontis, N. (1998), "Intellectual capital: An exploratory study that develops measures and models", *Management Decision*, Vol. 36, No. 2, pp. 63–76.

Bykova, A. A. and Molodchik, M. A. (2011), "The influence of intellectual capital on companies' performance indicators" *vestnik SPbGU, Serija Menedzhment*, Vol. 1, pp. 27–55.

Cabrita, M. D. R. and Bontis, N. (2008), "Intellectual capital and business performance in the Portuguese banking industry", *International Journal of Technology Management*, Vol. 43, Nos 1–3, pp. 212–237.

Chan, K. H. (2009), "Impact of intellectual capital on organisational performance", *The Learning Organization*, Vol. 16, No. 1, pp. 22–39.

Chang, S. C. and Lee, M. S. (2007), "The effects of organizational culture and knowledge management mechanisms on organizational innovation: An empirical study in Taiwan", *The Business Review, Cambridge*, Vol. 7, No. 1, pp. 295–301.

Chen, J., Zhao, X., and Wang, Y. (2015), "A new measurement of intellectual capital and its impact on innovation performance in an open innovation paradigm", *International Journal of Technology Management*, Vol. 67, No. 1, pp. 1–25.

Chen, J., Zhu, Z., and Xie, H. Y. (2004), "Measuring intellectual capital: A new model and empirical study", *Journal of Intellectual Capital*, Vol. 5, No. 1, pp. 195–212.

Chu, S. K. W., Chan, K. H., and Wu, W. W. Y. (2011), "Charting intellectual capital performance of the gateway to China", *Journal of Intellectual Capital*, Vol. 12, No. 2, pp. 249–276.

Delaney, J. and Huselid, M. A. (1996), "The impact of human resource management practices on perceptions of organizational performance", *Academy of Management Journal*, Vol. 39, No. 4, pp. 949–969.

Dierickx, I. and Cool, K. (1989), "Asset stock accumulation and sustainability of competitive advantage", *Management Science*, Vol. 35, No. 12, pp. 1504–1511.

Dittrich, M., Giljum, S., Polzin, C., Lutter, S., and Bringezu, S. (2011), "Resource use and resource efficiency in emerging economies: Trends over the past 20 years", available from: http://seri.at/wpcontent/uploads/2011/03/SERI_WorkingPaper12.pdf (accessed 20 October 2015).

Domcheva, E. (2014), "Not the right people [online]", *Rossijskaja gazeta – Federal'nyj vypusk*, 6422 (150). Available from https://rg.ru/2014/07/08/kadri.html (accessed 1 July 2016).

Dumay, J. (2013), "The third stage of IC: Towards a new IC future and beyond", *Journal of Intellectual Capital*, Vol. 14, No. 1, pp. 5–9.

Dumay, J. and Garanina, T. (2013), "Intellectual capital research: A critical examination of the third stage", *Journal of Intellectual Capital*, Vol. 14, No. 1, pp. 10–25.

Dumay, J. and Guthrie, J. (2012), "IC and strategy as practice: A critical examination", *International Journal of Knowledge and Systems Science*, Vol. 3, No. 4, pp. 28–37.

Edvinsson, L. (1997), "Developing intellectual capital at Skandia", *Long Range Planning*, Vol. 30, No. 3, pp. 366–373.

Edvinsson, L. and Malone, M. (1997), *Intellectual Capital: Realising Your Company's True Value by Finding Its Hidden Brainpower*, Harper Collins, New York.

Elenkov, D. S. (2002), "Effects of leadership on organizational performance in Russian companies", *Journal of Business Research*, Vol. 55, No. 6, pp. 467–480.

Farrell, D. and Grant, A. J. (2005), "China's looming talent shortage", *McKinsey Quarterly*, available at: www.mckinsey.com/mgi/overview/in-the-news/looming-talent-shortage-in-china (accessed 1 July 2016).

F-Jardón, C. M. and Martos, M. S. (2009), "Intellectual capital and performance in wood industries of Argentina", *Journal of Intellectual Capital*, Vol. 10, No. 4, pp. 600–616.

Frietsch R. and Wang, J. (2007), "Intellectual property rights and innovation activities in China: Evidence from patents and publications", available from: www.isi.fraunhofer.de/isi-wAssets/docs/p/de/diskpap_innosysteme_policyanalyse/discussionpaper_13_2007.pdf (accessed 1 July 2016).

Garanina, T. (2011), "Intellectual capital structure and value creation of a company: Evidence from Russian companies", *Open Journal of Economic Research*, Vol. 1, No. 2, pp. 22–34.

Gurkov, I. (1996), "Changes of control and business reengineering in Russian privatized companies", *International Executive*, Vol. 38, Vol. 3, pp. 359–388.

Gurkov, I., Zelenova, O., and Saidov, Z. (2012), "Mutation of HRM practices in Russia: An application of CRANET methodology, *International Journal of Human Resource Management*, Vol. 23, No. 7, pp. 1289–1302.

Guthrie, J., Ricceri, F., and Dumay, J. (2012), "Reflections and projections: A decade of intellectual capital accounting research", *The British Accounting Review*, Vol. 44, No. 2, pp. 68–92.

Hallén, L. and Johanson, M. (2004), "Integration of relationships and business network development in the Russian transition economy", *International Marketing Review*, Vol. 21, No. 2, pp. 158–171.

Hamilton, G. G. (1996), *Asian Business Networks*, Walter de Gruyter, Hong Kong.

Holt, D. H., Ralston, D. A., and Terpstra, R. H. (1994), "Constraints on capitalism in Russia: The managerial psyche, social infrastructure, and ideology", *California Management Review*, Vol. 36, No. 3, pp. 124–141.

Huang, Q., Davison, R. M., and Gu, J. (2008), "Impact of personal and cultural factors on knowledge sharing in China", *Asia Pacific Journal of Management*, Vol. 25, No. 3, pp. 451–471.

Huber, P. and Wörgötter, A. (1998), *Political Survival or Entrepreneurial Development? Observations on Russian Business Networks Location: Global, Area, and International Archive*, available from: http://escholarship.org/uc/item/5z5633ts (accessed 1 July 2016).

Hutchings, K. and Michailova, S. (2004), "Facilitating knowledge sharing in Russian and Chinese subsidiaries: The role of personal networks and group membership", *Journal of Knowledge Management*, Vol. 8, No. 2, pp. 84–94.

Hutchings, K. and Michailova, S., (2006), "The impact of group membership on knowledge sharing in Russia and China", *International Journal of Emerging Markets*, Vol. 1, No. 1, pp. 21–34.

Hutchings, K. and Weir, D. (2006), "Guanxi and Wasta: A comparison", *Thunderbird International Business Review*, Vol. 48, No. 3, pp. 141–156.

Inkinen, H., Kianto, A., Vanhala, M., and Ritala, P. (2014), "Intellectual capital and performance–Empirical findings from Finnish firms", paper presented to the International Forum on Knowledge Asset Dynamics (IFKAD), 11–13 June, Matera, Italy.

Inkinen, H., Vanhala, M., Ritala, P., and Kianto, A. (2014), "Assessing measurement invariance of intellectual capital", paper presented to the 10th EIASM Interdisciplinary Workshop on Intangibles, Intellectual Capital and Extra-Financial Information, 18–19 September, Ferrara, Italy.

Jansson, H. and Ramström, J. (2005), "Facing the Chinese business network in Southeast Asian markets: Overcoming the duality between Nordic and Chinese business networks", paper presented to the 21st Annual IMP Conference, Erasmus University, Rotterdam. Available from: www.impgroup.org/uploads/papers/4705.pdf.

Jansson, H., Johanson, M., and Ramström, J. (2007), "Institutions and business networks: A comparative analysis of the Chinese, Russian, and West European markets", *Industrial Marketing Management*, Vol. 36, pp. 955–967.

Jiacheng, W., Lu, L., and Francesco, C. A. (2010), "A cognitive model of intra-organizational knowledge-sharing motivations in the view of cross-culture", *International Journal of Information Management*, Vol. 30, No. 3, pp. 220–230.

Johnson, R. and Soenen, L. (2003), "Indicators of successful companies", *European Management Journal*, Vol. 21, No. 3, pp. 364–369.

Kianto A. (2008a), "Assessing organisational renewal capability", *International Journal of Innovation and Regional Development*, Vol. 1, No. 2, pp. 115–129.

Kianto, A. (2008b), "Development and validation of a survey instrument for measuring organizational renewal capability", *International Journal of Technology Management*, Vol. 42, Nos 1–2, pp. 69–88.

Kianto, A., Andreeva, T., and Pavlov, Y. (2013), "The impact of intellectual capital management on company competitiveness and financial performance", *Knowledge Management Research and Practice*, Vol. 11, No. 2, pp. 112–122.

Kianto, A., Gang, L., and Lee, R. (2015), "Knowledge management practices, intellectual capital and firm performance: Empirical evidence from Chinese companies", paper presented to the European Conference on Knowledge Management (ECKM), 3–4 September, Udine, Italy.

Kianto, A., Hurmelinna-Laukkanen, P., and Ritala, P. (2010), "Intellectual capital in service and product-oriented companies", *Journal of Intellectual Capital*, Vol. 11, No. 3, pp. 305–325.

Kianto, A., Saenz, J., and Aramburu, N. (2015), "Knowledge-based human resource practices, intellectual capital and innovation", paper presented to the EIASM 30th Workshop on Strategic Human Resource Management, 8–10 April. Brussels, Belgium.

Li, H. and Atuahene-Gima, K. (2001), "Product innovation strategy and the performance of new technology ventures in China", *Academy of Management Journal*, Vol. 44, No. 6, pp. 1123–1134.

Lin, Y. and Dalkir, K. (2010), "Factors affecting KM implementation in the Chinese community", *International Journal of Knowledge Management*, Vol. 6, No. 1, pp. 1–22.

Liu, X. L. and White, S. (2001), "Comparing innovation systems: A framework and application to China's transitional context", *Research Policy*, Vol. 30, No. 7, pp. 1091–1114.

Lu, W. M., Wang, W. K., and Kweh, Q. L. (2014), "Intellectual capital and performance in the Chinese life insurance industry", *Omega*, Vol. 42, pp. 65–74.

May, R. C. and Stewart, W. H. (2013), "Building theory with BRICs: Russia's contribution to knowledge sharing theory", *Critical Perspectives on International Business*, Vol. 9, Nos 1–2, pp. 147–172.

McCarthy, D., Puffer, S. M., Dunlap-Hinkler, D., and Jaeger, A. (2012), "A stakeholder approach to the ethicality of BRIC: Firm managers' use of favors", *Journal of Business Ethics*, Vol. 109, pp. 27–38.

Michailova, S. (2011), "Contextualizing in international business research: Why do we need more of it and how can we be better at it?" *Scandinavian Journal of Management*, Vol. 27, No. 1, pp. 129–139.

Michailova, S. and Husted, K. (2003), "Knowledge-sharing hostility in Russian firms", *California Management Review*, Vol. 45, No. 3, pp. 59–77.

Michailova, S. and Hutchings, K. (2006), "National cultural influences on knowledge sharing: A comparison of China and Russia", *Journal of Management Studies*, Vol. 43, No. 3, pp. 383–405.

Michailova, S. and Worm, V. (2003), "Personal networking in Russia and China: Blat and Guanxi", *European Management Journal*, Vol. 21, No. 4, pp. 509–519.

Molodchik M. and Nursubina J. S. (2012) "Innovations and intellectual capital of a company: The analysis of panel data", V sbornike: Sovremennye strategii innovacionnogo razvitija. Trinadcatye Drukerovskie chtenija, Pod redakciej R.M. Nizhegorodceva, Novocherkassk, Russia, pp. 231–237.

Molodchik, M., Shakina, E., and Barajas, A. (2014), "Metrics for the elements of intellectual capital in an economy driven by knowledge", *Journal of Intellectual Capital*, Vol. 15, No. 2, pp. 206–226.

Nahapiet, J. and Ghoshal, S. (1998), "Social capital, intellectual capital and the organizational advantage", *Academy of Management Review*, Vol. 23, No. 2, pp. 242–266.

Petty, R. and Guthrie, J. (2000), "Intellectual capital literature review: Measurement, reporting and management", *Journal of Intellectual Capital*, Vol. 1, No. 2, pp. 155–176.

PricewaterhouseCoopers (2014), "A new vision for growth: Key trends in human capital", available from: www.pwc.com/gx/en/hr-management-services/pdf/pwc-key-trends-in-human-capital-2014.pdf (accessed 15 October 2015).

Puffer, S. M. and McCarthy, D. J. (2011), "Two decades of Russian business and management research: An institutional theory perspective", *Academy of Management Perspectives*, Vol. 25, No. 2, pp. 21–36.

Pulic, A. (2000), VAIC: An accounting tool for IC management", *International Journal of Technology Management*, Vol. 20, Nos 5–8, pp. 702–714.

Puntillo, P. (2009), "Intellectual capital and business performance: Evidence from Italian banking industry", *Journal of Corporate Finance Research*, Vol. 4, No. 12, pp. 96–115.

Ramström, J. (2005), *West Meets East. Managing Cross-institutional Business Relationships with Overseas Chinese*, Doctoral dissertation, Åbo Akademi University Press, Åbo, Finland.

Ricceri, F. (2008), *Intellectual Capital and Knowledge Management: Strategic Management of Knowledge Resources*, Routledge, London.

Salmi, A. (1996), "Russian networks in transition: Implications for managers", *Industrial Marketing Management*, Vol. 25, No. 1, pp. 37–45.

Ståhle, P., Ståhle, S., and Aho, S. (2011), "Value added intellectual coefficient (VAIC): A critical analysis", *Journal of Intellectual Capital*, Vol. 12, No. 4, pp. 531–551.

Ståhle, P., Ståhle, S., and Lin, C. (2015), "Intangibles and national economic wealth – A new perspective on how they are linked", *Journal of Intellectual Capital*, Vol. 16, No. 1, pp. 20–57.

Stewart, T. (1997), *Intellectual Capital: The New Wealth of Organizations*, Doubleday, New York.

Sun, Y. (2000), "Spatial distribution of patents in China", *Regional Studies*, Vol. 34, No. 5, pp. 441–454.

Sveiby, K. E., (1997), *The New Organizational Wealth: Managing and Measuring Knowledge Based Assets*, Berrett Koehler, San Francisco, CA.

Sydler, R., Haefliger, S., and Pruksa, R. (2014), "Measuring intellectual capital with financial figures: Can we predict firm profitability?" *European Management Journal*, Vol. 32, No. 2, pp. 244–259.

Tomchuk, D., Perskij, Ju., and Sevodina, V. (2013), "Intellectual capital and return: Characteristics and evaluation", *Resursy, informacija, snabzhenie, konkurencija*, Vol. 2, pp. 330–334.

Tovstiga, G. and Tulugurova, E. (2007), "Intellectual capital practices and performance in Russian enterprises", *Journal of Intellectual Capital*, Vol. 8, No. 4, pp. 695–707.

Tovstiga, G. and Tulugurova, E. (2009), "Intellectual capital practices: A four-region comparative study", *Journal of Intellectual Capital*, Vol. 10, No. 1, pp. 70–80.

Tseng, C. Y. and Goo, Y. J. (2005), "Intellectual capital and corporate value in an emerging economy: Empirical study of Taiwanese manufacturers", *R&D Management*, Vol. 35, No. 2, pp. 187–201.

Tung, R. L., (2007), "The human resource challenge to outward foreign direct investment aspirations from emerging economies: The case of China", *International Journal of Human Resource Management*, Vol. 18, No. 5, pp. 868–889.

Väisänen, J., Kujansivu, P., and Lönnqvist, A. (2007), "Effects of intellectual capital investments on productivity and profitability", *International Journal of Learning and Intellectual Capital*, Vol. 4, No. 4, pp. 377–391.

Wang, D. and Chen, S. (2013), "Does intellectual capital matter? High-performance work systems and bilateral innovative capabilities", *China International Journal of Manpower*, Vol. 34, No. 8, pp. 861–879.

Wang, L. (2004), "Intellectual property protection in China", *International Information and Library Review*, Vol. 36, No. 3, pp. 251–263.

Wang, Z., Wang, N., and Liang, H. (2014), "Knowledge sharing, intellectual capital and firm performance", *Management Decision*, Vol. 52, No. 2, pp. 230–258.

Wong, Y. H. and Tam, J. L. M. (2000), "Mapping relationships in China: Guanxi dynamic approach", *Journal of Business and Industrial Marketing*, Vol. 15, No. 1, pp. 57–70.

Wu, W. Y., and Tsai, H. J. (2005), "Impact of social capital and business operation mode on intellectual capital and knowledge management", *International Journal of Technology Management*, Vol. 3, Nos 1–2, pp. 147–171.

Xiao, Y. (2013), "Research of the effectiveness of the growth of SMEs under intellectual capital driven-based on the empirical analysis of SMEs in China listed companies", *Information Technology Journal*, Vol. 12, No. 20, pp. 5669–5672.

Yang, C. and Lin, C. (2009), "Does intellectual capital mediate the relationship between HRM and organizational performance? Perspective of a healthcare industry in Taiwan", *International Journal of Human Resource Management*, Vol. 20, No. 9, pp. 1965–1984.

Yeh, Y. J., Lai, S. Q., and Ho, C. T. (2006), "Knowledge management enablers: A case study", *Industrial Management and Data Systems*, Vol. 106, No. 6, pp. 793–810.

Zeng, S. X., Shi, J. J., and Lou, G. X. (2007), "A synergetic model for implementing an integrated management system: An empirical study in China", *Journal of Cleaner Production*, Vol. 15, No. 18, pp. 1760–1767.

Zhao, S. (2008), "Application of human capital theory in China in the context of the knowledge economy", *International Journal of Human Resource Management*, Vol. 19, No. 5, pp. 802–817.

Zhu, C. J., Cooper, B., De Cieri, H., Thomson, S. B., and Zhao, S. (2008), "Devolvement of HR practices in transitional economies: Evidence from China", *International Journal of Human Resource Management*, Vol. 19, No. 5, pp. 840–855.

PART V

Stage 1

IC importance

30

INTEGRATED REPORTING AND THE CONNECTIONS BETWEEN INTEGRATED REPORTING AND INTELLECTUAL CAPITAL

Charl de Villiers and Pei-Chi Kelly Hsiao

Introduction

Integrated reporting (IR) is a form of disclosure that focuses on communicating the interactions between financial and non-financial information. There is a particular emphasis on telling the future value creation story of the reporting organization with reference to the organization's strategy, business plan, and the six capitals: financial, manufactured, intellectual, human, social and relationship, and natural capital (IIRC, 2013). Others in this book have recognized the close relationship of IR with intellectual capital (IC) (Dumay *et al.*, 2017). IC's structural capital resembles IR's intellectual capital, human capital remains human capital, and IC's relational capital maps to IR's social and relationship capital.

This chapter provides details on the origins and developments of IR, and the connections between IR and IC. It discusses prior literature and points to research opportunities at the intersection between IR and IC. Conclusions are presented on the advantages for proponents of IC to collaborate with and benefit from the efforts of the IR movement.

Origins, promoters, and supporters of IR

The International Integrated Reporting Council (IIRC) was established in 2010 based on the initiative of the Prince of Wales' Accounting for Sustainability Project and the Global Reporting Initiative (GRI) (IIRC, 2010). As such IR was founded on the concept of sustainability. The timing of IIRC's foundation in the aftermath of the global financial crisis also points to the dissatisfaction of players in the capital markets, and perhaps society as a whole, with existing forms of corporate reporting. Accounting and reporting were seen as deficient in terms of their focus on the past instead of future value creation plans, and on financial information as opposed to a balanced disclosure of both financial and non-financial information. There has been growing acknowledgement that future oriented and non-financial information may be more meaningful in explaining current corporate valuations.

The IIRC engaged in a wide-ranging consultation process in an effort to finalize the International Integrated Reporting Framework (IIR framework), which was achieved in December 2013. The framework emphasizes future value creation and the need to integrate financial and non-financial information in a single report, instead of providing information as separate sections/reports. The IIRC encourages the IR process to be driven by integrated thinking, which is meant to promote a long-term outlook, countering the short-termism of both managers and investors, which some commentators see as the cause of the global financial crisis.

The IIRC promotes IR by visiting and presenting at conferences and universities, and engaging with regulators and corporates. The IIRC has various boards and activities that involve the CEOs of multinationals, representatives of the large audit firms, and regulators and other influential individuals. For example, IIRC participates in the Corporate Reporting Dialogue, an initiative aimed at improving corporate disclosure, working alongside the United Kingdom's Carbon Disclosure Project, the Climate Disclosure Standards Board, the Financial Accounting Standards Board, the GRI, the International Accounting Standards Board, the International Organization for Standardization, and the US Sustainability Accounting Standards Board (SASB) (Corporate Reporting Dialogue, 2015).

Apart from regulators, corporate preparers, the accounting profession, and investors have taken note of the IR movement. For example, Business 20 (2014), consisting of business leaders from the G20 countries, subscribe to IR. While IR is a listing requirement in South Africa, on an apply or explain basis, Australian funds (Kitney, 2014), the Securities and Exchange Board of India (Business Standard Reporters, 2014), and the accountancy profession in Singapore (Kee *et al.* 2014) have expressed intentions to support IR. In addition, more than 100 multinationals participate in the IIRC's pilot programme and many others, for example General Electric, are now issuing integrated reports (Fairfield, 2016).

Interplay between IIRC, GRI, SASB, and WICI

The IIR framework is a voluntary principles-based framework that guides the preparation of an integrated report. An integrated report prepared according to the IIR framework focuses on connecting financial with non-financial information to communicate the organization's future value creation plans to capital providers, specifically referring to strategy and the business model (IIRC, 2013). The framework includes seven guiding principles, eight content elements, and introduces the concepts of integrated thinking and the six capitals. Although the IIR framework provides report preparers with a direction for implementing the IR process, it does not prescribe specific or technical instructions. The IIRC does not suggest any key performance indicators or metrics for managers to consider and therefore the IIR framework needs to be supplemented by other reporting guidance.

As one of the IIRC's co-founders, the GRI is an international organization that champions sustainability reporting by continuously developing and promoting its own sustainability reporting standards. The GRI's voluntary disclosure standards are meant to help report preparers understand and communicate their impacts on sustainability issues. Sustainability reporting is "an intrinsic element of integrated reporting" (GRI, 2013, p. 85); hence, one of the main objectives during the development of the GRI G4 Sustainability Reporting Guidelines (G4) was to offer guidance on linking the sustainability reporting process to the preparation of an integrated report (GRI, 2015). GRI G4 provides specific economic, environmental, and social indicators for reporters to consider.

Similar to GRI guidelines, the sustainability accounting standards developed by the SASB offers guidance on sustainability indicators. The SASB signed a memorandum of understanding with the IIRC, agreeing to work in unison to strengthen corporate sustainability reporting and disclosure practices (IIRC, 2014). The SASB standards provide publicly traded US corporations with industry-specific guidance for the disclosure of environmental, social, and governance information to be used in statutory filings.

Specifically focused on IC, the World Intellectual Capital/Assets Initiative (WICI) is an international organization focused on improving the reporting of intangible assets. The WICI has been working in collaboration with the IIRC, focusing its efforts on providing industry-specific guidance on the disclosure of intellectual, relational, and human capitals. The WICI (2016) developed the WICI Intangibles Reporting Framework (WIRF), which shares several characteristics with the IIR framework. The purposes of both frameworks are to guide reporting practices in communicating how organizations generate value and achieve business sustainability, and to encourage more efficient allocation of resources. WIRF is a voluntary principles-based framework that defines and classifies intangibles. WIRF identifies five principles for intangibles reporting, provides examples of indicators, and suggests a structure for intangibles reporting.

The efforts of the IIRC, the GRI, the SASB, and the WICI contribute to a common goal: the alignment of organizational operations with sustainable value creation, and the enhancement of the efficiency of the resource allocation decisions of both internal and external stakeholders. While the IIR framework provides an overarching direction, reporters may find it useful to use it in combination with other guidelines, such as those provided by the GRI, the SASB, and the WICI, to take steps towards IR.

Links between the IIR framework and IC

Corporations do not typically disclose separate IC reports (Dumay, 2016). This is attributed to the prominence of other forms of disclosure, such as sustainability reporting and IR, which also communicates IC and value creation (Dumay, 2016). As IC management and reporting falls under the broad scope of IR, management's focus on the communication of specific IC information may experience a resurgence. IC is reflected in three of the IIR framework's six capitals, and both IC and the IIR framework emphasize value creation and the business model.

Six capitals

The IIR framework encourages the assessment and disclosure of resources and relationships related to organizational operations in six capitals, namely: financial, manufactured, intellectual, human, social and relationship, and natural capitals. The capitals represent stocks of values that change or are transformed by the activities and outputs of the organization. Three intangible capitals defined in the IIR framework as intellectual, human, and social and relationship broadly align with the three components of IC, respectively, structural capital, human capital, and relational capital (WICI, 2016).

Value creation

The notion of corporate value has departed from the traditional short-term focus on shareholder returns to incorporate impacts on long-term sustainability and societal wellbeing. A core focus of IR is on understanding and communicating "the ability of an organization to create value in the short, medium and long term" (IIRC, 2013, p. 2). This focus correlates with the function of IC, which reflects organizational knowledge, intellectual property, and experience that contributes to value creation (Dumay, 2016). The IIRC (2013) emphasizes that the focus of integrated reports is to explain how value is created for capital providers; however, focusing attention on one capital, such as financial capital, at the expense of others is unlikely to maximize value creation in the long term. An organization's external environment affects its ability to create value and therefore managers need to attain an optimal balance of the six capitals. Knowledge-based resources are a critical component of value creation in modern economies (Bini *et al.*, 2016), suggesting that the measurement and management of IC lies at the core of understanding and communicating value creation.

Business models and strategy

Business models explain how strategy is implemented and are a representation of an organization's value creation processes. The business model shows how resources are transformed into value and highlights the interrelationships between various elements in the value creation process (Beattie and Smith, 2013; Bini *et al.*, 2016). The business model is one of the IIR framework's content elements. The IIR framework suggests disclosing key inputs, business activities, outputs, and outcomes, and connecting such information with other framework elements such as strategy and performance. Similarly, the IC concept is concerned with the transformation of resources into value and is often related to the concepts of strategy, competences, and activities (Beattie and Smith, 2013). IC is therefore embodied in an overarching business model, and the business model is a way to make sense of IC complexity (Bini *et al.*, 2016).

IC and IR literature

While the body of academic literature on IR is growing, it is currently limited due to the novelty of the framework and the lack of long-term practical experience with IR as many organizations are still grappling with implementation issues. This section reviews selected works in the IR literature that are relevant to IC management and reporting. For a broader insight of available studies, De Villiers *et al.* (2014) discuss the development of IR in greater detail, De Villiers *et al.* (2016) provide a thematic discussion of the IR literature, and Dumay *et al.* (2016) provide a structured literature review.

There are few IR studies that relate to IC as it is common for researchers to focus on the environmental and social aspect of IR, rather than the IC related components (e.g. Knauer and Serafeim, 2014; Stubbs and Higgins, 2014; Atkins *et al.*, 2015; Bernardi and Stark, 2016). Studies such as García-Sánchez *et al.* (2013) and Frías-Aceituno *et al.* (2013) have, in turn, interpreted their results based on a sustainability focus. Focused on identifying the determinants of IR, those two studies examined the impacts culture and institutional systems have on the preparation of integrated reports. García-Sánchez *et al.* (2013) found corporations operating in countries with stronger collectivist and feminist values are leaders in information integration. The findings are attributed to stakeholders in these cultures having greater demand for sustainability-related performance information as they place greater emphasis on improving the quality of life for broader society. Frías-Aceituno *et al.* (2013) found companies in code law systems are more likely to issue integrated reports, attributing the results to code law societies (e.g. France) being more communitarian and thus more accepting of broader stakeholder rights, compared to common law systems where shareholder interests take precedence (e.g. the US).

Organizational change

Evidence from Australia by Higgins *et al.* (2014) and Stubbs and Higgins (2014) suggests IR does not stimulate radical changes to reporting processes in the early stages of adoption. IR is seen as an extension to sustainability reporting, therefore leading to incremental changes rather than stimulating innovation in reporting processes (Stubbs and Higgins, 2014). Higgins *et al.* (2014) found managers consider IR to be about story-telling and meeting stakeholder expectations, resembling a means of communicating that a company's strategy is sustainable and aligns with corporate responsibility. The findings of these two studies largely concentrate on the external reporting process and corporate social responsibility. While this may be affected by the interview prompts the researchers used, managers appear to lack consideration in terms of the internal effects IR has on IC.

A case study by Parrot and Tierney (2012) found IR and stakeholder engagement to be fundamental contributors to a corporation's success. Although it is challenging for managers to achieve a balance between multiple stakeholder interests and financial, environmental, and social aspects, addressing ethical and relational considerations is seen as necessary for long-term value creation. Parrot and Tierney (2012) highlight the importance of stakeholder engagement and management, which can be seen as relational capital in IC terms.

Corporate disclosures

Emerging evidence suggests that IR may have a positive effect on the amount of IC disclosed. Terblanche and De Villiers (2015) analysed locally listed and cross-listed South African companies and found companies that prepared an integrated report disclose more IC information. Moreover, regardless of whether the company was cross-listed on another bourse there was no significant difference to the level of IC disclosures. Setia *et al.* (2015) also investigated the context of South Africa and found that the introduction of IR has resulted in significant increases in the disclosure on intellectual, human, and social and relational capital. The extent of the increase in disclosure on social and relational capital has been greater than the disclosure on other capitals. Through an analysis of international corporations engaging in IR, Eccles *et al.* (2015) found corporations are emphasizing IC in their strategic focuses as there is a tendency for manufacturing corporations to link strategy to product innovation and non-manufacturing corporations linking strategy to developments in human capital and relational capital. However, Melloni (2015) found corporations focus on relational capital over human and structural capital in integrated reports. Furthermore, the tone of IC disclosure resembles opportunism, suggesting managers use it to manipulate corporate image.

Content analysis has been commonly used by researchers to assess the quality of integrated reports, often using the IIR framework as a basis for analysis. Eccles *et al.* (2015) suggests there needs to be clearer explanations on how managers determined stakeholder priority and to link risks to corporate goals. Moreover, more disclosure in terms of the projection of environmental, social, and governance performance and forward-looking information in general. Similarly, Stent and Dowler (2015) consider the best practice disclosures in New Zealand to be close to the requirements of the IIR framework; however, improvement should be made regarding the connectivity of information, reporting against industrial or regional benchmarks, and reporting on uncertainties and outlook. Melloni (2015) notes a lack of quantitative and forward-looking information, specifically in relation to IC disclosure. This finding is supported by Wild and Van Staden (2013), who found that although most companies in their sample of 58 addressed financial, human, natural, and social and relationship capitals in their reports, manufactured and IC were not widely addressed, being disclosed in only 40 per cent of the reports.

Information environment

Studies based on investors' use of integrated reports have suggested that IC and sustainability-related information affects capital allocation decisions. A case study by Knauer and Serafeim (2014) found integrated thinking and reporting attracts long-term investors. It is suggested that long-term investors are attracted to increases in the transparency of policies and practices, and communication of human capital, leadership and governance, and environment performance information. Atkins and Maroun (2015) found South African investors view the connectivity between social, ethical, environmental, and governance issues with financial materiality as a core element to IR. Although investors view integrated reports as an improvement on traditional annual reports, reports have been criticized for being too lengthy, containing excessive repetition, and following a box-ticking approach to compliance.

Through examining the quality of IR disclosures, with IC disclosure being an integral part of the quality assessment, Barth *et al.* (2016) found a positive association between high quality integrated reports and stock liquidity and firm value, with the change in firm value mainly driven by changed future cash flow expectations, rather than changed risk assessments. Zhou *et al.* (2017) found a decrease in analyst forecast error when IR quality was higher, while no clear association was found between disclosure quality and analyst forecast dispersion.

The role of IC in IR

While the IIR framework guides the preparation of an external report, IR is a process that concerns the restructuring of internal measurement systems as well as the provision of an integrated report (Rowbottom and Locke, 2016). As evident from the previous section, it is common for early IR research to focus on the external reporting component of IR. The long-term thinking encouraged by IR may need to be further emphasized, however complex it may be to think of value creation as broadly as that promoted by the IIRC. Van Bommel (2014) documents conflicting perspectives held by various stakeholder groups regarding the expected role of IR in society. The emphasis on value for capital providers ultimately means a focus on financial capital, which generates bias rather than legitimate compromise and diverts efforts from enhancing societal wellbeing and long-term sustainability (Van Bommel, 2014; Flower, 2015). The concerns expressed by Flower (2015), Brown and Dillard (2014), and Van Bommel (2014) over the IIR framework's focus on value creation for capital providers and its promotion of IR as a business case could be welcomed by the proponents of IC. That is, IC has arguably always had a value creation and business case focus. In terms of the IR literature, IC does not appear to be a main focus despite IC disclosures potentially benefiting from the IR movement.

Adams (2015) views the IIR framework as a means to encourage managers to think about profit maximization and corporate success differently. There needs to be further developments in accounting regarding the measurement and reporting of non-financial capitals for integrated reports to bring about a meaningful change to corporate disclosures. Abhayawansa (2014) reviewed 20 guidelines and frameworks related to the external reporting of IC. The paper identifies that most of the IC guidelines and frameworks propose the disclosure of a separate IC document that elaborates on a company's value creation process without integrating

IC information with other non-financial information. Abhayawansa (2014) views the IIR framework as an opportunity for IC reporting to reinvent itself. As there is limited guidance provided in the IIR framework for the integration of IC information, the available IC frameworks could be useful in framing IC information within an integrated report.

Conclusions and where research opportunities for IC and IR meet

The IR movement involves important players at all levels in society and the capital markets. Early evidence suggests that IR is being implemented and adopted at a more rapid rate than previous reporting initiatives. As such, and given the similarities between several of the characteristics and components between IC and IR, it is worth paying attention to IR and to consider the implications for the IC movement.

The three components of IC, structural, human, and relational capital, are three of the six capitals promoted by IR, albeit called by slightly different names. In addition, both the IR and the IC movements emphasize value creation and the business case for reporting. Therefore, any headway made by the IR movement in promoting IR can only benefit IC disclosure. Proponents of IC should consider ways to collaborate with the IR movement, as well as ways to leverage off the activities of the IIRC.

Given the small number of studies to date that address the intersection(s) between IC and IR, several research opportunities present themselves. For example, the following questions could be answered with the help of empirical data:

1   How does the advent of IR influence the IC movement?

    a   in individual reporters:

        i   assessed on the basis of disclosures;
        ii   assessed on the basis of activities and agenda within reporters;

    b   in the activities and agenda of regulators;
    c   in research.

2   How are these answers influenced by whether IR is adopted voluntarily, as is the case in much of the world, or whether IR is mandatory, as is the case in South Africa?

Several other research opportunities are bound to become evident with the passage of time.

References

Abhayawansa, S. A. (2014), "A review of guidelines and frameworks on external reporting of intellectual capital", *Journal of Intellectual Capital*, Vol. 15, No. 1, pp. 100–141.

Adams, C. A. (2015), "The International Integrated Reporting Council: A call to action", *Critical Perspectives on Accounting*, Vol. 27, pp. 23–28.

Atkins, J. and Maroun, W. (2015), "Integrated reporting in South Africa in 2012: Perspectives from South African institutional investors", *Meditari Accountancy Research*, Vol. 23, No. 2, pp. 197–221.

Atkins, J. F., Solomon, A., Norton, S., and Joseph, N. L. (2015), "The emergence of integrated private reporting", *Meditari Accountancy Research*, Vol. 23, No. 1, pp. 28–61.

Barth, M. E., Cahan, S. F., Chen, L. and Venter, E. R. (2016), "The economic consequences associated with integrated report quality: Early evidence from a mandatory setting", available from: https://ssrn.com/abstract=2699409.

Beattie, V. and Smith, S. J. (2013), "Value creation and business models: Refocusing the intellectual capital debate", *The British Accounting Review*, Vol. 45, No. 4, pp. 243–254.

Bernardi, C. and Stark, A. W. (2016), "Environmental, social and governance disclosure, integrated reporting, and the accuracy of analyst forecasts", *The British Accounting Review*. doi: http://dx.doi.org/10.1016/j.bar.2016.10.001.

Bini, L., Dainelli, F., and Giunta, F. (2016), "Business model disclosure in the strategic report: Entangling intellectual capital in value creation process", *Journal of Intellectual Capital*, Vol. 17, No. 1, pp. 83–102.

Brown, J. and Dillard, J. (2014), "Integrated reporting: On the need for broadening out and opening up", *Accounting, Auditing & Accountability Journal*, Vol. 27, No. 7, pp. 1120–1156.

Business 20 (2014), *Unlocking Investment in Infrastructure: Is Current Accounting and Reporting a Barrier?* available from: http://integratedreporting.org/wp-content/uploads/2014/06/unlocking-investment-in-infrastructure.pdf (accessed 24 January 2017).

Business Standard Reporters (2014), "Sebi wants yearly tell-all accounts", *Business Standard*, available from: www.business-standard.com/article/markets/sebi-wants-yearly-tell-all-accounts-114091701199_1.html (accessed 24 January 2017).

Corporate Reporting Dialogue (2015), *Navigating the Corporate Reporting Landscape*, available from: http://corporatereportingdialogue.com/wp-content/uploads/2015/05/CRD-Mapping-Document_website_070515.pdf (accessed 24 January 2017).

De Villiers, C., Rinaldi, L., and Unerman, J. (2014), "Integrated reporting: Insights, gaps and an agenda for future research", *Accounting, Auditing & Accountability Journal*, Vol. 27, No. 7, pp. 1042–1067.

De Villiers, C., Venter, E. R., and Hsiao, P.-C. K. (2016), "Integrated reporting: Background, measurement issues, approaches and an agenda for future research", *Accounting & Finance*. doi: 10.1111/acfi.12246.

Dumay, J. (2016), "A critical reflection on the future of intellectual capital: From reporting to disclosure", *Journal of Intellectual Capital*, Vol. 17, No. 1, pp. 168–184.

Dumay, J., Bernardi, C., Guthrie, J., and Demartini, P. (2016), "Integrated reporting: A structured literature review", *Accounting Forum*, Vol. 40, No. 3, pp. 166–185.

Dumay, J., Guthrie, J., and Rooney, J. (2017), "The critical path of intellectual capital", in Dumay, J., Guthrie, J., Ricceri, F., and Nielsen, C. (Eds) *The Routledge Companion to Intellectual Capital*, Routledge, London, pp. 21–39.

Eccles, R. G., Krzus, M. P., and Ribot, S. (2015), "Models of best practice in integrated reporting 2015", *Journal of Applied Corporate Finance*, Vol. 27, No. 2, pp. 103–115.

Fairfield, C. (2016), "GE launches integrated summary report", *BusinessWire*, available from: www.businesswire.com/news/home/20160314006354/en/GELaunches-Integrated-Summary-Report (accessed 24 January 2017).

Flower, J. (2015), "The International Integrated Reporting Council: A story of failure", *Critical Perspectives on Accounting*, Vol. 27, pp. 1–17.

Frías-Aceituno, J. V., Rodríguez-Ariza, L., and García-Sánchez, I. M. (2013), "Is integrated reporting determined by a country's legal system? An exploratory study", *Journal of Cleaner Production*, Vol. 44, pp. 45–55.

García-Sánchez, I.-M., Rodríguez-Ariza, L., and Frías-Aceituno, J.-V. (2013), "The cultural system and integrated reporting", *International Business Review*, Vol. 22, No. 5, pp. 828–838.

GRI (2013), *G4 Sustainability Reporting Guidelines: Reporting Principles and Standard Disclosures*. Available from: www.globalreporting.org/resourcelibrary/GRIG4-Part1-Reporting-Principles-and-Standard-Disclosures.pdf (accessed 7 December 2016).

GRI (2015), *G4 Sustainability Reporting Guidelines: Frequently Asked Questions*. Available from: www.globalreporting.org/resourcelibrary/G4-FAQ.pdf (accessed 7 December 2016).

Higgins, C., Stubbs, W., and Love, T. (2014), "Walking the talk(s): Organisational narratives of integrated reporting", *Accounting, Auditing & Accountability Journal*, Vol. 27, No. 7, pp. 1090–1119.

IIRC (2010), Formation of the International Integrated Reporting Committee (IIRC). Available from: http://integratedreporting.org/wp-content/uploads/2011/03/Press-Release1.pdf (accessed 7 December 2016).

IIRC (2013), *The International <IR> Framework*. Available from: http://integratedreporting.org/wp-content/uploads/2013/12/13-12-08-THE-INTERNATIONAL-IR-FRAMEWORK-2-1.pdf (accessed 7 December 2016).

IIRC (2014), *SASB and IIRC Announce Memorandum of Understanding*, available from: http://integratedreporting.org/news/sasb-and-iirc-announce-memorandum-of-understanding (accessed 7 December 2016).

Kee, H. Y., Larsen, M., and Seng, T. B. (2014), "Should S'pore firms adopt integrated reporting?" *The Business Times*, p. 22.

Kitney, D. (2014), *Super Funds Enthusiastic about Reporting Regime* [online]. Available from: www. theaustralian.com.au/business/wealth/super-funds-enthusiastic-about-reporting-regime/news-story/ d208ffd12380b9a84ef040c22a03e31c (accessed 24 January 2017).

Knauer, A. and Serafeim, G. (2014), "Attracting long-term investors through integrated thinking and reporting: A clinical study of a biopharmaceutical company", *Journal of Applied Corporate Finance*, Vol. 26, No. 2, pp. 57–64.

Melloni, G. (2015), "Intellectual capital disclosure in integrated reporting: An impression management analysis", *Journal of Intellectual Capital*, Vol. 16, No. 3, pp. 661–680.

Parrot, K. W. and Tierney, B. X. (2012), "Integrated reporting, stakeholder engagement, and balanced investing at American Electric Power", *Journal of Applied Corporate Finance*, Vol. 24, No. 2, pp. 27–37.

Rowbottom, N. and Locke, J. (2016), "The emergence of <IR>", *Accounting and Business Research*, Vol. 46, No. 1, pp. 83–115.

Setia, N., Abhayawansa, S., Joshi, M., and Huynh, A. V. (2015), "Integrated reporting in South Africa: Some initial evidence", *Sustainability Accounting, Management and Policy Journal*, Vol. 6, No. 3, pp. 397–424.

Stent, W. and Dowler, T. (2015), "Early assessments of the gap between integrated reporting and current corporate reporting", *Meditari Accountancy Research*, Vol. 23, No. 1, pp. 92–117.

Stubbs, W. and Higgins, C. (2014), "Integrated reporting and internal mechanisms of change", *Accounting, Auditing & Accountability Journal*, Vol. 27, No. 7, pp. 1068–1089.

Terblanche, W. and De Villiers, C. (2015), "The influence of integrated reporting and internationalisation on intellectual capital disclosures", *South African Accounting Association Conference 2015*, pp. 1–34.

Van Bommel, K. (2014), "Towards a legitimate compromise?: An exploration of Integrated Reporting in the Netherlands", *Accounting, Auditing & Accountability Journal*, Vol. 27, No. 7, pp. 1157–1189.

WICI (2016), *WICI Intangibles Reporting Framework: Version 1.0*. Available from: www.wici-global. com/wirf/WICI_Intangibles_Reporting_Framework_v1.0.pdf (accessed 7 December 2016).

Wild, S. and van Staden, C. (2013), "Integrated reporting: Initial analysis of early reporters – an institutional theory approach", *7th Asia Pacific Interdisciplinary Accounting Research Conference*, pp. 1–39.

Zhou, S., Simnett, R., and Green, W. (2017), "Does integrated reporting matter to the capital market?" *Abacus*, Vol. 53, No. 1, pp. 94–132.

31

THE RELEVANCE OF
IC INDICATORS

Bino Catasús

Introduction

In which ways do numbers matter? This question is central to the discussion of the relevance of intellectual capital (IC) indicators. Although our fascination for numbers stretches back over the centuries, it was not until the 13th century that we entered into an age of measurement (Crosby, 1997). Crosby shows that then as now, the first challenge of any measurement activity is to develop a method to capture the world in numbers. Such methods were developed to capture time, space, mathematics, and music, but also to keep track of organizational activity through keeping books. Bookkeeping has over the years had a particular role in society and the practice of bookkeeping has developed into something more than the mere systematic organizing of receipts.

One of the strengths of bookkeeping is that the practice has retained and developed its scientific approach (Porter, 1996) and adding to its aim to represent truth, the ideal of accounting also has an explicit ambition to be fair. Numbers emanating from an accounting system are, however, not only approached as a true and fair representation, they are also boundary objects (Qu and Cooper, 2011) that can move and become important in other contexts. This highlights that technologies, such as accounting, can move between practices. These characteristics, that is, trustworthiness, fairness, and mobility, make the measurements emanating from an accounting system into a technology *für alles*.

It is, thus, not surprising that the practice as well as the study of accounting has become a more central activity in society in general, but in the IC discourse in particular. The IC discourse builds on the proposition that attaining, managing, and (dis)investing IC is central to the success of the organization. If this proposition is correct, then it makes sense to measure IC to support not only management but also other stakeholders, such as the providers of financial and other resources. And, since "every society keeps the records most relevant for its major values" (Haire *et al.*, 1959, p. 108), it is not surprising that IC researchers have focused on studying and developing measurements of knowledge, development, and relationships (Meritum, 2002). This, in turn, may lead to a focus on measurements, accounts, reports, and key performance indicators (KPIs) for a plethora of aspects of the organization, begging the question: do we need all these numbers?

Power (1992, p. 477) suggested that "accounting theorists have much to contribute to the project of determining the proper limits of technologies of quantification". This chapter elaborates on the ways in which IC indicators can (not) work. That is, the argument in this chapter is that we can look beyond an unsophisticated model where we approach IC indicators as the start of a successful firm. Instead we can approach IC indicators as a technology mobilized for many reasons that may (or may not) answer the questions we are asking. This chapter emphasizes the idea of relevance of numerical representation of an organization's IC. It does so by first discussing how indicators differ from other types of measurement and then asks why we produce or demand IC indicators. Here I suggest that there are a number of possible reasons for the production of indicators and that, perhaps somewhat guilelessly, the arguments are (nearly) always clothed in a functional dress. That is to say, it is presumed that IC indicators exist only because organizations want to create value. The chapter then considers Power's proposition about the limits of indicators by discussing the production, transmission, and consumption of IC indicators.

From measurements to indicators: towards the relevance of IC representations

Although it may be considered a naïve approach to IC measurement, one could argue that it is possible to map *all* the IC of an organization. However, doing so misses the fact that IC measurement, like any measurement, can only be simplified representations of particular aspects of the organization for a particular time period for a particular reader of the accounts. In fact, a measurement is always a simplification. Even though this 'limitation' exists, the universe of possible measurements is a vast one and the potential to measure 'more' has probably never been as large. One of the reasons is that the cost for the organization to construct, gather, and store measurements has become lower because of changes in technology and business models. This potential has also increased the demand for more measurement of IC. The 'accountingization' of IC (Dumay, 2009) is an example of how members of organizations demand numbers to make sense of their activities.

At the same time, psychologists (Miller, 1956) and others (Nielsen and Madsen, 2009) suggest that the processing of measurements and information is heavily affected by the amount of information, and this leads us to sometimes simplify complex situations by developing anchors as cognitive shortcuts (Tversky and Kahneman, 1975). Thus, the paradox in play is that (i) organizations measure more, (ii) organizations want even more measurements, and (iii) organizations use the same limited amount of information to make sense of operations and strategies (Figure 31.1). Thus, the demand for measurement is larger than the supply, which in turn is larger than the consumption. The paradox suggests that we can move from the idea to develop all possible measurements to a development of measurements that matter.

Different from, but still a part of, all measurements, indicators can be seen as quantitative representations that are of *importance* to the organization. From the 1990s onwards, indicators have often been labelled KPIs, pointing to the fact that the organizations (as well as consultants) deemed it important to separate indicators from KPIs. Catasús *et al.* (2001) argued that indicators can be understood as (i) quantitative representations that are (ii) produced by

---

The demand for measurements > the supply of measurements > the consumption of measurements

---

Figure 31.1   The measurement paradox

measuring in a systematic way and (iii) that these measurements are considered interesting for the users of the number. Thus, IC indicators are relevant quantitative representations that are produced in a systematic way.

The objective of measurements in financial reports is, according to the International Accounting Standards Board (IASB), for the measurement to be decision useful. The main argument for this is that the IASB develops standards to support investors and other suppliers of financial resources. The users are seen as rational, self-interested actors (Young, 2006) that use the financial report to make decisions. The main qualitative characteristics, that is, the qualities that are needed to achieve decision usefulness, are that they are relevant and that they give a faithful representation. IC indicators may be approached differently because the quantitative measurements are not only for decision making; for example, they may be useful for learning. If relevance is the main objective, then IC indicators need not, at the outset, have the ambition to give a fair representation (i.e. completeness, neutrality, and free from error) because indicators can be relevant without these characteristics. Thus, by drawing from the conceptual framework of financial reporting, but refuting the overall objective of decision usefulness, there is a possibility to change the perspective of qualitative characteristics, in which two core concepts are key: material and relevant.

If relevance is the main objective, the designer of indicators needs to pose a number of questions (Catasús *et al.*, 2016). For example, is it relevant to know how many patent applications the organization has submitted to the patent office? The question that follows this question is whether this information matters or not. Matter, here, is not an issue of merely decision usefulness as is the case in financial reporting because it can be of value in terms of understanding organizational performance. We can imagine a quantitative representation that no one cares about and that would, by definition, be a measurement but not an indicator. We can also imagine a quantitative representation that we do not care about if it does not have a particular value. An example could be accidents at a production site. A value of 0 of this measurement would be relevant but of no concern, but a value of 1 could be relevant and material. To be an indicator, the quantitative representation has to be *relevant*, that is, someone cares about the representation, and *material*, in other words, someone cares about the value. This, however, begs the question: for whom are indicators relevant?

For whom are indicators relevant?

There are, arguably, three main approaches to answering this question. One way of considering the question is to view relevance from an agency theory perspective. In their influential paper, Jensen and Meckling (1976) hypothesized that people are self-interested utility maximizers and that if such a hypothesis were true, then one party needs to incorporate control mechanisms in order to lower the risk of "deviant behavior" (p. 308):

> If both parties to the relationship are utility maximizers, there is good reason to believe that the agent will not always act in the best interests of the principal. *The principal can limit divergences from his interest by establishing appropriate incentives for the agent and by incurring monitoring costs designed to limit the aberrant activities of the agent.*

Importantly, as "if" in the first statement suggests, agency theory rests on the hypothesis that behaviour can be (but does not have to be) explained by self-interest. Nevertheless, this approach has been used to explain the relationship between shareholders and management. The main argument is that there is a need to align managers' interests with shareholders' interests. Further, this position suggests that the principal defines which quantitative representation can be called an indicator since it is the principal's perspective that is relevant. This might explain why there is a discourse in IC research that holds that more IC information could be included in reports since it may be relevant for the value of the firm (Bozzolan *et al.*, 2003; Too and Wan Yusoff, 2015). Consistent with this, and mirroring the argument of Lev and his colleagues (Lev and Sougiannis, 1996; Aboody and Lev, 1998), the efficiency of the capital market (Fama, 1970) may be harmed if the firm does not report relevant information to capital providers.

An alternative approach to IC indicators is to define relevance from a managerial or even strategic perspective (Nahapiet and Ghoshal, 1998). The managerial approach dominates control literature in general, and the balanced scorecard in particular, and the literature emphasizes that measurements should be connected to what (the management thinks) is important in the organization. This can change with both time and space and is also heavily affected by the management's approach to what is important. The managerial approach may indeed be fully aligned with the agency theory approach, like the balanced scorecard. However, it is also possible, and maybe even likely, that the managerial approach to IC differs from the ways in which shareholders view resources. The reason for this may indeed be time preferences, norms, and the fact that management is part of the IC of the firm. Or, as some authors would argue, fashions in management thinking (Abrahamson, 1996; Fincham and Roslender, 2003).

A third approach is to view IC indicators as being relevant to many stakeholders (Riahi-Belkaoui, 2003; Guthrie *et al.*, 2004). This approach suggests that the organization is a part of a network of competing interests and that the firm needs to handle these to create legitimacy and a social licence to operate in relation to the surrounding society. Typically, this approach suggests that IC indicators are not mainly for the shareholders or for management, but rather for the stakeholders that are influential in the context in which the organization operates. One of the challenges of this approach is that different stakeholders may have different interpretations of the same number. As an example, a trade union may look differently at a salary cut compared to the owners. Another drawback is that the number of IC indicators may 'explode' since all stakeholders by definition have their own 'stake' and their own interests.

Even though we find three main groups to which IC indicators are relevant (i.e. shareholders, managers, and stakeholders) this only partly helps us understand how measurements become relevant. The next question we need to consider is why we measure. This question opens up a possibility that not all IC indicators are produced to achieve a particular end.

Why do we produce or demand IC indicators?

The question of why people do what they do is, arguably, the most investigated question in science. The answers, generally speaking, contradict each other. Even so, the issue of the objectives of indicators needs to draw from some theories of why people act and why they think that IC indicators are important. In the following section I will present a model with ideal types, which according to George and James (1994, p. 636) are:

> [s]implified descriptions that emphasize certain distinguishing features of a construct to such an extent that, whereas the ideal type rarely is found empirically, it serves the useful purpose of being a standard by which to evaluate real-world observations.

Thus, an ideal model is not primarily an empirical mode, but a mirror in which we may reflect on which arguments prevail and which are ignored.

One possible way to enter the development of a typology is to think of the tension between intrinsic and extrinsic motivation. Intrinsic motivation is what is believed to be the desire that comes from within oneself, that is, motivations that are more difficult to change. Some argue that it is reasonable to approach motivation as mainly intrinsic and that there is a 'natural' intrinsic motivation. It may thus be argued, as agency theory purports, that people intrinsically seek utility maximization. If this is the case, the objectives of IC indicators should be developed so that there is a fit between the motivation of the actor and the indicator.

On the other end of the continuum we find the idea of extrinsic motivation. Extrinsic motivation emanates from outside the individual (or organization) and can, typically, be understood as what people do to please others. It can be characterized as formal or informal pressure. Formalized external pressure can be anything from an incentive scheme to regulation. Implicit external pressure is typically norms. For example, organizational culture may affect the ways the members of the organization approach their work and statements like: "This is how we do it around here", pinpoints that there is an extrinsic motivation in play.

It is also useful to discuss underlying logic, which may be used to deem an act as appropriate. By juxtaposing deontology and utilitarism we are given a possibility to create another perspective on why we do what we do. Although there is a much more nuanced discussion in philosophy, we can approach deontology as the action being guided by a rule or a principle. That is, if we embrace a deontological approach, we recognize the adequacy of an action by judging to what degree the action adheres to a set rule or principles. Utilitarism, instead, makes the case that the appropriate action is the one that maximizes utility. So, different from rule-following which is an ex ante proposition, it is the consequence of action that is evaluated in utilitarism. Certainly, we can imagine that the two perspectives coincide but we can also imagine situations in which they are conflicting. By combining these two distinctions (extrinsic and intrinsic; deontology and utilitarism) we can construct a model of ideal types to help us discern different reasons how people and organizations find it relevant to produce, transmit, and consume IC indicators (Figure 31.2).

The two-by-two model in Figure 31.2 suggests there are four different ways to understand why we do what we do and, in particular, why accounting efforts are carried out. To be sure, this ideal model cannot predict or present a full picture of the workings of IC indicators. Nevertheless, a model like this one highlights that relevance may indeed be developed from a

Figure 31.2   Why we do what we do

plethora of positions. Importantly, in the functional stream of research, it is primarily 'utility', that is how IC indicators are relevant for value creation, which is in focus. Now all four aspects will be discussed: satisfaction, legitimacy, regulation, and utility.

IC indicators and satisfaction

The ongoing debate about intrinsic and extrinsic motivation has also been discussed in the IC discourse (Chang and Birkett, 2004). Here, as in other places, the idea of intrinsic motivation as a driver for work behaviours has been seen as an ideal motivation, since it is said to affect creativity and performance. This is, however, only true if the intrinsic motivation is coupled with the goals of the organization. That is, goal internalization is central if learning becomes something that the organization can use (Dumay *et al.*, 2013). However, it is possible to approach the relevance of IC indicators as something that is purely personal and that is not linked to any organizational ambition.

To argue that an IC indicator is relevant because the indicator communicates something that is 'nice-to-know', may depict the organization as nothing but a network of individual preferences. At the extreme, taking this position downplays the raison d'être of the organization and anything may or may not be relevant. On the other hand, organizations may indeed benefit from the playfulness that may come out of a broader approach to relevance (Catasús and Kristensson Uggla, 2007). That is, accepting that a manager believes, for example, that it is relevant to construct a human resource indicator presenting how many after-work beers have been consumed in the group, can be seen as an indicator that has little to do with decision usefulness. There are several things being done in workplaces that take place because people like to do them. Is it not playfulness rather than gravity that fosters innovation (March, 1981)?

Interestingly, however, the argument that "I just think it is interesting to know" does not have a particularly high currency in the organization (Catasús, 2000). In fact, the arguments for IC in general are positioned on the right side of Figure 31.2. Researchers have, however, suggested that organizations produce accounts to mitigate demands from the external environment (see, for example, DiMaggio and Powell, 1983). In the following section, we will discuss how IC indicators can be developed to achieve such an objective.

IC indicators for creating legitimacy

A vast amount of research has advocated that it is central to include the external pressures of the organization in the analysis if we aim to understand why and how organizations act. In particular, in institutional theory, the overarching argument is that we should not neglect that organizations are affected by the surrounding society and that society develops norms (or institutionalized myths) of what constitutes adequate behaviour (Nielsen *et al.*, 2016). If organizations adjust to the norms of the surrounding society, the organization will be able to keep/achieve the legitimacy. According to DiMaggio and Powell (1983), there are three types of external pressures that affect the organization: coercive pressure (such as laws and regulation), normative pressure (such as the general discourse in management), and mimetic pressure (such as organizational heroes that the organization want to follow). These pressures affect the organization to produce IC indicators. The question is whether they are relevant.

The answer from an institutional theory perspective is yes. Organizations need to "become a legitimate player" in the organizational community. Although the search for legitimacy probably is not the explicit objective for the IC indicator, researchers like Nielsen *et al.* (2016) show that organizations react to external pressure when they produce (or stop producing)

IC indicators. That is, even though the content of the indicators may be irrelevant, the mere activity of measuring and reporting is relevant for others. Legitimacy, however, may be temporary. Nielsen and colleagues (2016) found that many companies that were reporting according to the Danish guidelines for IC statements abandoned their work after some time. In another analysis of the reasons why this happened, Schaper (2016) concluded that it was the low perceived value of IC reports both internally for managerial purposes as well as externally for disclosure practices.

IC indicators for regulation

Whereas the primacy of shareholders and other creditors is explicit in regulations concerning financial reporting, the European Union's directive 2014/95/EU is an effort to shift the focus. By making the organization the centre of the analysis, the directive suggests a move to a broader set of actors. Article two in the directive states that "the disclosure of non-financial information . . . is of importance for the interests . . . [of] shareholders and other stakeholders alike".

The directive, that is, what is transformed into laws in the member states, explicitly states that organizations should supply "information to the extent necessary for an understanding of the undertaking's development, performance, position and impact of its activity, relating to, as a minimum, environmental, social and employee matters, respect for human rights, anti-corruption and bribery matters". Although these suggestions emanate from the sustainability agenda, issues such as employee and social matters can be seen as important for the approach to human capital (employees) and relational capital (social matters) (Meritum, 2002).

Moreover, the directive suggests that the firm should report "non-financial key performance indicators relevant to the particular business" (Article 19a). That is, there is a demand for (large) firms to report relevant information for all relevant stakeholders (including management). The coercive pressure to produce relevant indicators might, however, be problematic if all stake-holders are invited. The stakeholder approach has been criticized for being merely a mapping activity in which *more* information is better than *relevant* information; that stakeholder theory emphasizes what is relevant for stakeholders and that is nonsensical for management; and that organizations may operate under particular circumstances in which stakeholders are poorly equipped to ask relevant questions (Key, 1999). Moreover, the definition of stakeholder as someone having a stake in the firm indicates that there are different views of what is relevant. Therefore, from a reporting perspective, a stakeholder approach to indicators risks some indicators being relevant for some stakeholders and many numerical representations being irrelevant for other stakeholders.

The distinction between measuring IC and reporting IC indicators may be a fruitful divide to increase the nuances of IC. To make this distinction we may look at measuring as some-thing that is concerned with *something* to measure and is an activity that precedes reporting. Measuring is a technical activity in which the 'mapmaker' tries to capture the world in a reasonable way and the success is affected by the methods and equipment he or she has. Reporting, on the other hand, is an activity concerned with *someone* and includes some idea of communication. Reporting involves an idea of a receiver (listener, reader, analyst), and the success of the report relies not merely on the quality of the measurement but also on the ways the measurements are communicated and received. Thus, one of the central questions for the actor involved in reporting practices is: to whom am I reporting?

Legitimacy is not the only form of efficiency that the organization seeks. In fact, when Meyer and Rowan (1977) popularized the idea of how organizations have to adjust to external demands, they did so from the conviction that functional rationality only explains part of the ways in which the organization acts. From this position, one may forward the proposition that organizations are not merely a bundle of legitimacy-seeking actions. Instead, it is also possible to see efforts relating to 'technical performance, that is, a situation where the aim and the methods of seeking to achieve this aim are functional'. It is probably fair to conclude that in organizations as well as in normative managerial literature, the dominant idea is that organizations should work with a means to achieve a functional end.

When IC reporting is for the (potential) supplier of financial resources, we may think of reporting as a means to disclose information about which controls are being used and how the incentive systems are designed (compare agency theory). The challenges for such reporting practice are to report the indicators that are decision useful and can help the reader of the report to answer the question: should I continue, discontinue, increase, or lower my supply of financial resources to the firm? The report, consequently, can be set up as a narrative of how net cash flows are affected by the variation of the IC indicators.

IC indicators for utility: value creation

A dominant theme in the management discourse is the emphasis of means and ends. In fact, it is fair to say that management studies can be thought of as the development of (ideas of) linkages between action and outcome. Although these linkages may be implicit and never discussed, they may also be a part of the explicit idea of how to develop and harvest from the IC. As an example, some organizations believe that it is important to have customer service open 24/7. Behind such a position we may find an idea of a link between the access to the firm and the perceived value for the customer. The next link in this narrative might be that an increased value for the customer links to increased sales that in turn, the argument might be, leads to more profitability. Other examples can be that the education level of new employees is central to the value being delivered and another perceived link could be that gender balance is a successful indicator for R&D. That is, to find relevance we need to look for the ways that the links between IC indicators and financial indicators are constructed.

Certainly, the links between action and profit are invariably more complex than the proposed correlations above. Nevertheless, the IC indicators (such as education, opening hours, and gender balance) open up the possibility to hypothesize and investigate linkages. Again, although the linkages between, for example, the gender balance among R&D engineers and profitability might be weak, the production and investigation of the IC indicator may open up discussions about which IC is the most important or which IC has the most explanatory power. Thus, approaching the linkages from a functional perspective, the indicators of the inputs and outputs of links offer a possibility to know something about the ways in which the organization can improve.

IC indicators can, thus, be used as a technology for learning. And even the ideas of linkages, as already discussed by Kaplan and Norton (1992) (and criticized by, for example, Nørreklit, 2000), suggest that indicators are relevant if we can learn more about how the organization produces value. Learning can be to search for new links, to test old links, and maybe even to reject old ideas about links. In one sense, again addressing Myer and Rowan's ideas, learning activities can be a way for the organization to problematize the rationalized myths that organizations tend to accept without questioning.

If IC indicators are numbers that are of core importance to the organization, then it is reasonable that the organization keeps track of particular maximums and minimums. As an example: one question that many HR managers are faced with is how large an employee turnover is acceptable? To answer this question, the organization, from a functional perspective, would have collected information in the form of indicators and by learning from those indicators the organization would have decided on an optimum level that would have been the target. In practice, however, the level of, for example, employee turnover depends on many things outside the control of the organization and it might be impossible to come up with an optimum level of employee turnover. At the same time, the organization might have years of experience and they might have developed an idea of a balance between getting new ideas (too low employee turnover) and having experienced employees (too high employee turnover).

As a consequence, another aim for indicators is to work as a set of alarms that could act as triggers for action, as triggers for management to re-prioritize or as reflection points. Such an aim, however, demands an explicit idea of when to trigger the alarm, which in turn demands a firm belief (or knowledge) about tipping points in the organization. Here, the organization needs to discuss materiality, that is, which value of the indicator, or trend of indicators is alarming.

It is not difficult to see financial indicators that can work as alarms (such as cash available), but is there the equivalent in IC management? While it is possible that some organizations may say yes, most organizations would instead have alarms that have to do with how the indicators are changing. For example, a reasonable indicator for an education firm is the number of applications to the courses supplied by the organization. If the number of applications to a (still fully-booked) course has been going down dramatically over the last three years, then the trend of this indicator may indeed sound an alarm for the organization.

What IC indicators can (not) do

IC indicators do not, by themselves, do anything. The adage that holds that 'what gets measured gets managed' obfuscates the fact that there is someone doing the managing after the measurement has been communicated (Catasús *et al.*, 2007). Thus, one proposition is that indicators have many functions. Again, it might be relevant to start with agency since the theory suggests that there are two ways in which "aberrant activities" (Jensen and Meckling, 1976) can be mitigated: incentives and control. Here, control relates to a form of accountability and the hypothesis is that if there is pressure to account for one's behaviour through IC indicators, the actor will act in line with the control instruments imposed by the principal. Incentives, on the other hand, are hypothesized to have the same end result, but the underlying argument is that actors will strive to act according to what is beneficial to their own self-interest.

Still, this argument is counterintuitive to the IC agenda where knowledge is the main issue at stake. That is, one of the hypotheses in the IC discourse is that knowledge is the most important resource and that knowledge of how to manage this knowledge is at the centre of IC management. Thus, it is not control and incentives that should be at the core of the development of IC indicators but learning about how the organization should organize resources (human, structural, and relational) to be able to offer value. Employees play a major part in the IC of the firm (Dumay, 2016) and there is reason to believe that IC indicators need to be helpful for them to make good decisions. That is, according to the agency model, the IC discourse holds that employees may, in fact, produce and use IC indicators in such a way that value is increased more than if the shareholders control or incentivize action through IC indicators.

Incentives

Albeit heavily criticized as a management tool (Kohn, 1993; Edvinsson and Camp, 2005), incentives are a part of many organizations. Incentives, it is argued, align the interests of the employee with the owner/manager by directing the attention to what *should* be relevant.

Incentives, like any management control technology, however, need to be designed in such a way that they are considered as fair (Libby, 1999). If they are not, Libby notes, people "will become demotivated and destructive actions may be taken" (p. 127). Consequently, if IC indicators are used as a means for incentivizing employees, the issue of fairness is at the heart of the concern.

Fairness, however, poses a challenge since it often demands simple proxies such as 'sales', 'calls to customers', or 'allocation of the competence development budget'. Developing IC indicators for incentives demands a measurement system that resembles the qualitative criteria that are imposed on financial accounting through, for example, the conceptual framework. This, in turn, may lead to IC indicators being a part of the numbers game, in which case incentives may lead to a focus on managing the numbers (Hope and Fraser, 2013).

A more general problem with incentivizing IC indicators is that the narrative of links between actions needs to be 'long' in order to fit with the idea of shareholder wealth. As an example:

IF we train our employees (IC indicator 1)
THEN
the employees will create better processes (IC indicator 2)
THEN
customers will be more satisfied (IC indicator 3)
THEN
they will be willing to pay more (financial indicator 1)
THEN
the organization will be more profitable (financial indicator 2)
THEN
the firm will be more worth (share price)

Such a narrative is weak (at best) not only because it is problematic in so far as how all indicators should be measured, but mainly because the links are fragile. And if these ideas of correlation are weak then the question arises, in which of these lines should IC indicators work as the basis for incentives?

Learning

The IC research field has its roots in the proposition that knowledge matters and that if the firm can manage knowledge of different sorts (individual, organizational, and relational), then it stands a better chance to deliver value. Consequently, there is potential for IC indicators as empirical observations that may be linked to other IC indicators and to learn about correlations. That is, IC indicators may work as learning devices. In practice, this means that indicators may be used to find correlations. The balanced scorecard was premised on this idea of measuring performance drivers. Although it is reasonable that all organizations have ideas of performance drivers, they are, however, difficult to discern. How much training should the employees get? How much marketing is enough? What is an acceptable level of customer retention?

Still, there is an argument that it is possible to use the covariance of IC indicators as a means to reflect on how links can be unpacked. For example, in Sweden, the discourse about health activities (such as memberships to gyms) should be sponsored by the organization. The most prevailing argument is that there is a negative correlation between health activities and the level of sick leave. However, a study found that there was no correlation between the number of people that were sponsored by the organization and the level of sick leave. Notably, learning activities are as important (if not more important) when the hypotheses are refuted as when they show a significant correlation.

Attention

March and Olsen once suggested that attention is a scarce resource in the organization. In 1956, Miller (1956) suggested that, as individuals, we cannot attend to more than five to nine sources of information if we want the information to be relevant. This argument, often labelled information overload in the IC discourse (Stewart and Ruckdeschel, 1998; Nielsen and Madsen, 2009), addresses the fact that the user of information is severely limited in terms of the amount of information he or she can receive and process. Regardless, attention is also a matter of priorities and one argument is that IC indicators may affect emotions and, therefore, priorities.

Imagine that you have an organization (maybe a nursery) that reports that 80 per cent of all employees and 50 per cent of all managers are women. These indicators may (or may not) create attention. If the firm instead goes on to create a new indicator that combines these two indicators we find that in this organization the possibility for a woman to become a manager is 1 in 16 and for men it is 1 in 4. Imagine another firm that has an employee turnover of 20 per cent (maybe a telemarketing firm). This number may be translated into the fact that – on average – the employees work for five years. Imagine also that this indicator is benchmarked across the industry, where the median turnover is 30 per cent. These indicators may (or may not) seem dramatic and relevant, but one of the findings from earlier research is that when IC information is translated into something that connects the information to everyday life, or that the indicators are dramatic in relation to, for example, competitors, then the numbers are more likely to be attended to (Catasús and Gröjer, 2003).

It is fair to conclude that not all IC indicators are attended to and that, as a consequence, relevance is 'not there' but can be created through the ways in which the IC indicator is constructed and communicated (Catasús *et al.*, 2016). Research shows that the fate of the IC indicator is in the hands of the consumer of the indicator (Chiucchi *et al.*, 2016; Chiucchi and Montemari, 2016) and relevance is not created by 'merely' reporting on IC.

Conclusion

The argument in this chapter has been that relevance as a concept is dependent on who the indicators are for, why we are measuring, and what is the goal of having an IC indicator. Over 60 years ago, Ridgway (1956, p. 247) concluded that "Quantitative performance measurements – whether single, multiple, or composite – are seen to have undesirable consequences for over-all organizational performance".

The important lesson from this chapter is that although we live in an age where measurements are omnipresent and where the measurement paradox drives measurement activities, we cannot expect all measurements to achieve what we want. Instead we might want to approach a subset of measurement as IC indicators and use them as a means to (i) mobilize interest about (ii) reflecting and learning about the ways IC affects practice because the conundrum of organizing will never be resolved – it is a continuous mystery. But, one key is the indicator. Is that why it is called a key indicator?

References

Aboody, D. and Lev, B. (1998), "The value relevance of intangibles: The case of software capitalization", *Journal of Accounting Research*, Vol. 36, pp. 161–191.

Abrahamson, E. (1996), "Management fashion", *Academy of Management Review*, Vol. 21, No. 11, pp. 254–285.

Bozzolan, S., Favotto, F., and Ricceri, F. (2003), "Italian annual intellectual capital disclosure: An empirical analysis", *Journal of Intellectual Capital*, Vol. 4, No. 4, pp. 543–558.

Catasús, B. (2000), "Silent nature becomes normal: A study of environmental reporting", *International Studies of Management & Organization*, Vol. 30, No. 3, pp. 59–82.

Catasús, B. and Gröjer, J.-E. (2003), "Intangibles and credit decisions: Results from an experiment", *European Accounting Review*, Vol. 12, No. 2, pp. 327–355.

Catasús, B. and Kristensson Uggla, B. (2007), "Reinventing the university as driving force of intellectual capital", in Chaminade, C. and Catasús, B. (Eds), *Intellectual Capital Revisited. Paradoxes in the Knowledge Intensive Organization*, Edward Elgar, Cheltenham, UK, pp. 61–77.

Catasús, B., Ersson, S., Gröjer, J.-E., and Yang Wallentin, F. (2007), "What gets measured gets... on indicating, mobilizing and acting", *Accounting, Auditing & Accountability Journal*, Vol. 20, No. 4, pp. 505–521.

Catasús, B., Ferri, P., and Von Laskowski, S. (2016), "Accounting and the hope of action", *European Accounting Review*, Vol. 25, No. 2, pp. 403–419.

Catasús, B., Gröjer, J.-E., Högberg, O., and Johrén, A. (2001), *Boken om nyckeltal*, Liber, Lund, Sweden.

Chang, L. and Birkett, B. (2004), "Managing intellectual capital in a professional service firm: Exploring the creativity–productivity paradox", *Management Accounting Research*, Vol. 15, No. 1, pp. 7–31.

Chiucchi, M. S. and Montemari, M. (2016), "Investigating the 'fate' of intellectual capital indicators: A case study", *Journal of Intellectual Capital*, Vol. 17, No. 2, pp. 238–254.

Chiucchi, M. S., Giuliani, M., and Marasca, S. (2016), "The rise and fall of IC reporting in Italy: Evidence from the field", *ECIC2016-Proceedings of the 8th European Conference on Intellectual Capital: ECIC2016*, Academic Conferences and Publishing Ltd.

Crosby, A. W. (1997), *The Measure of Reality: Quantification in Western Europe, 1250–1600*, Cambridge University Press, Cambridge, UK.

DiMaggio, P. J. and Powell, W. W. (1983), "The iron cage revisited: Institutional isomorphism and collective rationality in organizational fields", *American Sociological Review*, Vol. 48, No. 2, pp. 147–160.

Dumay, J. (2009), "Intellectual capital measurement: A critical approach", *Journal of Intellectual Capital*, Vol. 10, No. 2, pp. 190–210.

Dumay, J. (2016), "A critical reflection on the future of intellectual capital: From reporting to disclosure", *Journal of Intellectual Capital*, Vol. 17, No. 1, pp. 168–184.

Dumay, J., Yu, A. and Humphreys, P. (2013), "From measuring to learning? Probing the evolutionary path of IC research and practice", *Journal of Intellectual Capital*, Vol. 14, No. 1, pp. 26–47.

Edvinsson, L. and Camp, J. (2005), "Intelligent remuneration in the knowledge economy for growth of intellectual capital", *Journal of Human Resource Costing & Accounting*, Vol. 9, No. 2, pp. 112–122.

Fama, E. F. (1970), "Efficient capital markets: A review of theory and empirical work", *The Journal of Finance*, Vol. 25, No. 2, pp. 383–417.

Fincham, R. and Roslender, R. (2003), "Intellectual capital accounting as management fashion: A review and critique", *European Accounting Review*, Vol. 12, No. 4, pp. 781–795.

George, J. M. and James, L. R. (1994), *Levels Issues in Theory Development*, JSTOR [online, registration required].

Guthrie, J., Petty, R., Yongvanich, K., and Ricceri, F. (2004), "Using content analysis as a research method to inquire into intellectual capital reporting", *Journal of Intellectual Capital*, Vol. 5, No. 2, pp. 282–293.

Haire, M., Dahl, R. and Lazarsfeld, P. (1959), *Social Science Research on Business: Product Potential*, Columbia University Press, New York.

Hope, J. and Fraser, R. (2013), *Beyond Budgeting: How Managers Can Break Free from the Annual Performance Trap*, Harvard Business Press, Boston, MA.

Jensen, M. C. and Meckling, W. H. (1976), "Theory of the firm: Managerial behavior, agency costs and ownership structure", *Journal of Financial Economics*, Vol. 3, No. 4, pp. 305–360.

Kaplan, R. S. and Norton, D. P. (1992), "The balanced scorecard: Measures that drive performance", *Harvard Business Review*, Vol. 70, No. 1, pp. 71–79.

Key, S. (1999), "Toward a new theory of the firm: A critique of stakeholder 'theory'", *Management Decision*, Vol. 37, No. 4, pp. 317–328.

Kohn, A. (1993), "Why incentive plans cannot work", *Harvard Business Review*, Vol. 71, No. 5, pp. 54–63.

Lev, B. and Sougiannis, T. (1996), "The capitalization, amortization, and value-relevance of R&D", *Journal of Accounting and Economics*, Vol. 21, No. 1, pp. 107–138.

Libby, T. (1999), "The influence of voice and explanation on performance in a participative budgeting setting", *Accounting, Organizations and Society*, Vol. 24, No. 2, pp. 125–137.

March, J. G. (1981), "Footnotes to organizational change", *Administrative Science Quarterly*, pp. 563–577.

Meritum (2002), *Guidelines for Managing and Reporting on Intangibles*. European Commission, Brussels.

Meyer, J. W. and Rowan, B. (1977), "Institutionalized organizations: Formal structure as myth and ceremony", *American Journal of Sociology*, Vol. 83, No. 2, pp. 340–363.

Miller, G. A. (1956), "The magical number seven, plus or minus two: Some limits on our capacity for processing information", *Psychological Review*, Vol. 63, No. 2, pp. 81.

Nahapiet, J. and Ghoshal, S. (1998), "Social capital, intellectual capital, and the organizational advantage", *Academy of Management Review*, Vol. 23, No. 2, pp. 242–266.

Nielsen, C. and Madsen, M. T. (2009), "Discourses of transparency in the intellectual capital reporting debate: Moving from generic reporting models to management defined information", *Critical Perspectives on Accounting*, Vol. 20, No. 7, pp. 847–854.

Nielsen, C., Roslender, R, and Schaper, S. (2016), "Continuities in the use of the intellectual capital statement approach: Elements of an institutional theory analysis", *Accounting Forum*, Vol. 40, No. 1, pp. 16–28.

Nørreklit, H. (2000), "The balance on the balanced scorecard: A critical analysis of some of its assumptions", *Management Accounting Research*, Vol. 11, No. 1, pp. 65–88.

Porter, T. M. (1996), *Trust in Numbers: The Pursuit of Objectivity in Science and Public Life*, Princeton University Press, Princeton, NJ.

Power, M. (1992), "After calculation? Reflection on critique of economic reason by André Gorz", *Accounting, Organizations and Society*, Vol. 17, No. 5, pp. 477–499.

Qu, S. Q. and Cooper, D. J. (2011), "The role of inscriptions in producing a balanced scorecard", *Accounting, Organizations and Society*, Vol. 36, No. 6, pp. 344–362.

Riahi-Belkaoui, A. (2003), "Intellectual capital and firm performance of US multinational firms: A study of the resource-based and stakeholder views", *Journal of Intellectual Capital*, Vol. 4, No. 2, pp. 215–226.

Ridgway, V. F. (1956), "Dysfunctional consequences of performance measurements", *Administrative Science Quarterly*, Vol. 1, No. 2, pp. 240–247.

Schaper, S. (2016), "Contemplating the usefulness of intellectual capital reporting", *Journal of Intellectual Capital*, Vol. 17, No. 1, pp. 52–82.

Stewart, T. and Ruckdeschel, C. (1998), *Intellectual Capital: The New Wealth of Organizations*, Wiley Online Library.

Too, S. W. and Wan Yusoff, W. F. (2015), "Exploring intellectual capital disclosure as a mediator for the relationship between IPO firm-specific characteristics and underpricing", *Journal of Intellectual Capital*, Vol. 16, No. 3, pp. 639–660.

Tversky, A. and Kahneman, D. (1975), *Judgment Under Uncertainty: Heuristics and Biases. Utility, Probability, and Human Decision Making*, Springer, Dordrecht, The Netherlands.

Young, J. J. (2006), "Making up users", *Accounting, Organizations and Society*, Vol. 31, No. 6, pp. 579–600.

INDEX

Printed in the United States
by Baker & Taylor Publisher Services